ACCESS
CHICAGO

P9-DNV-323

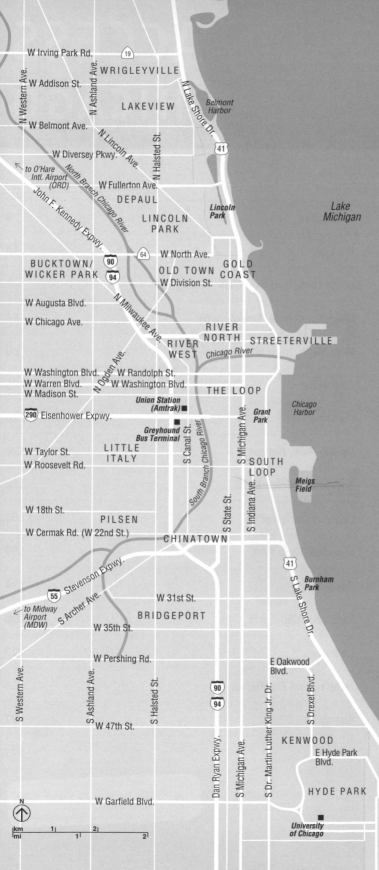

ORIENTATION

Rising up brazen and brilliant from the plains of America's heartland, Chicago astonishes. The nation's third-largest city covers 229 square miles and stretches 29 miles along the shores of **Lake Michigan**, a Great Lake that looks more like an infinite sea. Suburbs in six counties expand the metropolitan area to 3,721 square miles, collectively known as "Chicagoland." European explorers first came upon this part of the world in 1680 and were followed a century later by fur trappers and soldiers. The settlement of 340 people was incorporated as a town in 1833, and its name was derived from the Illini word *che-cau-gou*, meaning either "wild onion" or "strong and great." Today more than three million people reside here in a colorful mosaic, from the old guard to recent émigrés from Korea, Poland, India, and Iran.

The city's complex character and raucous history are legendary. Chicago is the city that rebuilt itself from the ground up in no time flat after the devastating Great Fire of 1871. And this is the city where Al Capone celebrated St. Valentine's Day in 1929 with a machine-gun massacre of rival gangsters. From the formation of labor unions to antiwar marches during the 1968 Democratic National Convention, great social events have unfolded here too.

Chicago is a virtual textbook of architectural styles. The spectacular skyline stretches from the Gothic **Tribune Tower** to the Art Deco **333 North Michigan Avenue** to the sleek Modernism of **Mies van der Rohe**'s steel-and-glass skyscrapers, then reaches up to America's tallest building—the **Sears Tower**. Closer to ground level, the city boasts elegant turn-of-the-19th-century mansions in the **Gold Coast**, which is studded with literally hundreds of historic buildings, and **Frank Lloyd Wright**'s groundbreaking Prairie School designs, which live on throughout **Oak Park** and at his masterful **Robie House** on the **University of Chicago** campus.

Visitors are dazzled by the array of stores and glitzy shopping malls preening along the **Magnificent Mile**, fascinating **Shedd Aquarium**, and the treasures of the **Art Institute of Chicago**, including one of the country's most extensive collections of Impressionist paintings. Baseball fans won't want to miss a pilgrimage to historic **Wrigley Field**, home of the **Cubs**. **Lake Shore Drive** is another must-see, a stunningly scenic route skirting the city and lake.

In 1893, during the World's Columbian Exposition, a visiting reporter dubbed Chicago the "Windy City" because of all the bragging residents did about the place. Boastfulness can still be discerned here. Even an insult—as when New York essayist A.J. Liebling called Chicago the "Second City"—is proudly flaunted like a scar from a hard-won battle. Chicago is, after all, birthplace of the Chicago blues as well as home to an internationally acclaimed symphony orchestra, a renowned theater scene, a bustling financial district, miles of public beaches, acres of parks, world-class cuisine, and the ever-popular deep-dish pizza—a diversity of riches that begs exploration and enjoyment

Getting to Chicago

Chicago and vicinity now have five telephone area codes: 312, 773, 847, 708, 630. Generally speaking, locations in downtown and near downtown are 312. Locations within the city but away from downtown are 773. The other three area codes are for the suburbs. Check at the beginning of each chapter to see the area code for attractions listed in that section.

Airports

O'Hare International Airport (ORD)

O'Hare International Airport (ORD) is 17 miles northwest of the **Loop** on the **John F. Kennedy Expressway** (**Interstate 90**). The nation's busiest airport, it covers a vast area (the distance between two concourses can be over a mile); the terminals are connected by pedestrian

3

passageways, moving sidewalks, and a free "people mover" shuttle that circulates every 7.5 minutes among the three domestic terminals, the international terminal (terminal 5), and the long-term parking facility. To make connections, allow at least 30–50 minutes between flights and 1.5 hours for international flights. The airport is fully accessible to people with disabilities. www.ohare.com

AIRPORT SERVICES

Airport Emergencies	773/894.9111
Currency Exchange	773/462.9973
Customs and Immigration	773/894.2900
First Aid	773/686.2288/9
Ground Transportation	773/686.2200
Information	773/686.2200
Lost and Found	773/686.2201
Main Number	773/686.2200
Paging	773/686.2200
Parking	773/686.7530
Police	773/686.2230, 773/894.9111
Traveler's Aid	773/894.2427
Airport Service Hotline	800/832.6352

AIRLINES

Air Canada	Term 2	800/247.2262
America West	Term 2	800/235.9292
American	Term 3	800/433.7300
American Eagle	Term 3	800/433.7300
British Airways	Term 5	800/247.9297
Continental	Term 2	800/525.0280
Delta	Term 3	800/221.1212
Northwest	Term 2	800/225.2525
Ted	Term 1	800/241.6522
United		800/241.6522
United Express		800/241.6522
US Airways		800/428.4322

Getting to and from O'Hare International Airport

By Bus

Continental Airport Express (312/454.7800, 888/2 THE VAN) offers door-to-door bus service to about 50 downtown and suburban hotels. Service is offered daily, at 10-minute intervals, between 6AM and 11:30PM. Departures are from the lower level of each terminal. www.airportexpress.com

The **Regional Transit Authority** (312/836.7000) provides public bus service to several suburbs. Buses depart from the lower levels of **terminals 1, 2**, and **3**. www.rtachicago.com

By Car

From the airport to the Loop, head east on the Kennedy Expressway and follow the signs. Exit at either **Ohio**

Street (north downtown area) or **Congress Parkway** (South Loop). The trip takes 30 to 90 minutes, depending on traffic.

From the Loop to the airport, follow signs on the Kennedy Expressway (Interstate 90) west to O'Hare. A free, elevated people mover runs every 7.5 minutes from the remote long-term parking lot to all terminals.

RENTAL CARS

The following car-rental agencies staff 24-hour counters in the baggage-claim areas of **terminals 1, 2**, and **3**; in **terminal 5**, consult the information board in the main lobby. All provide courtesy buses between the terminals and their lots.

Alamo	773/694.4640, 800/327.9633
Avis	773/825.4600, 800/831.2847
Budget	800/527.0700
Dollar	800/800.4000
Enterprise	847/929.3320, 800/325.8007
Hertz	773/686.7272, 800/654.3131
National	773/694.4640, 800/328.4567

By Limousine

Car service to the city, suburbs, and far-flung towns is offered by several companies. Counters are located in the baggage claim areas; call 773/686.2200 for information.

By Taxi

Taxis line up at the lower level of each terminal. Share-a-Ride drivers take several passengers to separate downtown locations for a per-person fare. **American United** (773/248.7600), **Checker** (312/243.2537), **Flash** (773/561.1444), and **Yellow** (312/829.4222) have 24-hour service. A cab ride to the Loop costs about $35.

By Train

The **Chicago Transit Authority** (**CTA**; 312/836.7000) operates 24-hour train service to and from the airport on the **Blue Line**. This mode is frequently the fastest and is convenient if you're traveling light. (Getting to the station requires some walking and stair climbing.) Trains depart every 10 minutes from the lower level under the main parking lot; the trip to the Loop takes 40 minutes. The fare is $1.75.

Midway Airport (MDW)

Smaller (and often saner) than O'Hare, **Midway Airport** serves nine domestic airlines. It is located 10 miles southwest of the Loop off the **Adlai E. Stevenson Expressway** (**Interstate 55**) at 5600 South Cicero Avenue. www.flychicago.com

AIRPORT SERVICES

Airport Emergencies	773/838.0600
First Aid	773/838.0600

How to Read This Guide

Access® Chicago is arranged by neighborhood so you can see at a glance where you are and what is around you. The numbers next to the entries in the following chapters correspond to the numbers on the maps. The type is color-coded according to the kind of place described:

Restaurants/Clubs: Red

Hotels: Purple | **Shops: Orange**

🏕 **Outdoors: Green** | **Sights/Culture: Blue**

♿ **Wheelchair accessible**

WHEELCHAIR ACCESSIBILITY

An establishment (except a restaurant) is considered wheelchair accessible when a person in a wheelchair can easily enter a building (i.e., no steps, a ramp, a wide-enough door) without assistance. Restaurants are deemed wheelchair accessible *only* if the above applies *and* if the rest rooms are on the same floor as the dining area and their entrances and stalls are wide enough to accommodate a wheelchair.

RATING THE RESTAURANTS AND HOTELS

The restaurant ratings take into account the quality, service, atmosphere, and uniqueness of the restaurant. An expensive restaurant doesn't necessarily ensure an enjoyable evening; however, a small, relatively unknown spot could have good food, professional service, and a lovely atmosphere. Therefore, on a purely subjective basis, stars are used to judge the overall dining value (see the star ratings at right). Keep in mind that chefs and owners often change, which sometimes drastically affects the quality of a restaurant. The ratings in this guidebook are based on information available at press time.

The price ratings, as categorized at right, apply to restaurants and hotels. These figures describe general price-range relationships among other restaurants and hotels in the area. The restaurant price ratings are based on the average cost of an entrée for one person, excluding tax and tip. Hotel price ratings reflect the base price of a standard room for two people for one night during the peak season.

RESTAURANTS

★	Good
★★	Very Good
★★★	Excellent
★★★★	An Extraordinary Experience
$	The Price Is Right (less than $15)
$$	Reasonable ($16–$24)
$$$	Expensive ($25–$40)
$$$$	Big Bucks ($40 and up)

HOTELS

$	The Price Is Right (less than $130)
$$	Reasonable ($130–$200)
$$$	Expensive ($200–$300)
$$$$	Big Bucks ($300 and up)

MAP KEY

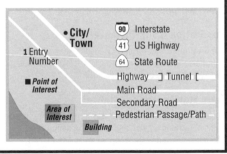

90	Interstate
41	US Highway
64	State Route
	Highway ⌐ Tunnel ⌐
	Main Road
	Secondary Road
	Pedestrian Passage/Path

• City/Town
1 Entry Number
■ Point of Interest
Area of Interest
Building

Ground Transportation	773/838.0600
Information	773/838.0600
Lost and Found	Call individual airline
Paging	Call individual airline
Parking	773/838.0600
Police	773/838.3003
Traveler's Aid	773/894.2427

AIRLINES

Air Trans	800/825.8538
American	800/433.7300
American Trans Air	800/225.2995
Com Air	800/927.0927
Continental	800/525.0280
Frontier	800/432.1359

Northwest	800/225.2525
Southwest	800/435.9792

Getting to and from Midway Airport

BY BUS

Continental Air Transport (312/454.7800) provides door-to-door bus service between the airport and a dozen downtown hotels. Buses run daily, with departures every 30 minutes between 6AM and 10PM.

BY CAR

Driving from the Loop, take Lake Shore Drive or the **Dan Ryan Expressway** (**Interstates 90** and **94**) south to the Stevenson Expressway, exit at **Cicero Avenue**, and continue 2 miles south. The trip can take anywhere between 30 and 60 minutes, depending on traffic.

RENTAL CARS

The following car-rental agencies, which have service counters in the baggage-claim areas, provide 24-hour service.

Alamo	773/581.4531, 800/327.9633
Avis	800/831.2847
Budget	800/527.0700
Dollar	800/800.4000
Enterprise	773/735.8860, 800/325.8007
Hertz	773/735.7272, 800/654.3131
National	773/581.4531, 800/328.4567

BY LIMOUSINE

Information on limousine service between **Midway Airport** and Chicago and its suburbs is available at the main terminal information booth or by calling 773/838.0600.

BY TAXI

Taxis line up outside the main terminal. A trip to the Loop usually takes between 30 minutes and 1 hour, depending on traffic.

BY TRAIN

The CTA's (312/836.7000) **Orange Line** runs between Midway and the Loop daily every 10 minutes between 5AM and 11PM. The trip takes 25 minutes, and the view (it's all aboveground) is striking.

Bus Station (Long-Distance)

The **Greyhound Bus Terminal** is located in the Loop (630 W Harrison St, at S Des Plaines St). For local information, call 312/408.5930; for national, 800/231.2222.

Train Station (Long-Distance)

Chicago is a major hub for **Amtrak** service, with approximately 50 trains arriving and departing daily. **Union Station** is located in the Loop, at **West Adams** and **South Canal Streets**. For information, call 800/USA.RAIL.

Getting Around Chicago

BICYCLES

Although cycling is not a practical means of transportation around the city, cyclists enjoy mile after mile of paths meandering along Lake Michigan and through Chicago's many parks. **Lincoln Park** is particularly pretty for cycling and has bikes available for rent.

BOATS

Chicago's position at the junction of lake and river makes it an ideal city to tour by water. For details see "Tours," page 7.

BUSES

The CTA's (312/836.7000; 312/917.0713 for the hearing impaired) comprehensive system of buses

provides a convenient way to get around the city—or to the suburbs via **PACE** buses. Buses run daily; schedules vary, but exact times and routes are given at bus stops and on CTA maps. Use your judgment in taking a bus after dark.

All fares on CTA buses require exact change and are paid into a vending machine on the bus, which issues a transit card. One-way fare is $1.50; transfers, which allow you to switch to two other connecting routes (bus or train) within 2 hours, cost an additional 30 cents. If you expect to be using the CTA with some frequency, you may insert more money into the machine to increase the ride credit on your transit card. Children under age 7 ride free; children between ages 7 and 11, seniors, and people with disabilities pay discounted fares. Other discounted fares take effect at different times.

DRIVING

Although gridlock doesn't paralyze Chicago's busiest streets, driving in the Loop, Magnificent Mile, or **River North** areas on weekdays can be slow and confusing. Most Loop streets run one way in alternate directions. A cavernous underpass—**Lower Michigan Avenue** and **Lower Wacker Drive**—runs from **Congress Parkway** to **Grand Avenue**, bypassing heavy traffic. Access to this underground route is on Grand Avenue west of Michigan Avenue, on Congress Parkway at Lower Wacker Drive, and at several points along **North Wacker Drive**.

Chicago's expressways are good routes for long hauls, though they're no fun during rush hour. Major expressways include the **Stevenson** (**Interstate 55**) to the **Southwest Side** and beyond; the Dan Ryan (I-94), running south of the Loop; the Kennedy (I-90), running north and northwest of the Loop and breaking off into the **Edens Expressway** (I-94) to the northern suburbs; and the **Eisenhower Expressway** (**Interstate-290**), which heads due west of the Loop.

Finding a parking spot in or even near the Loop takes time, money, or both. Most curbside spots have meters, usually with 30-minute limits. Watch out for signs that prohibit parking or designate a tow zone, as the cops are dead serious about handing out tickets. If your car gets towed, the ransom will be at least $100 cash. Parking is available in the **Grant Park Garage** (312/742.7530) off Michigan Avenue. Access is off **Randolph**, **Monroe**, and **Van Buren Streets**. Next best are **Self-Park** garages; one always seems to be right around the corner. Avoid leaving valuables in your car, even in the trunk, wherever you park.

SUBWAYS AND ELEVATED TRAINS

What's collectively known as the El includes subways as well as elevated trains and crisscrosses the entire city (see the **CTA/Metra map** on the inside back cover). Continual but inconsistent upgrading has left some parts of the system looking seedy and others sleek. For the most part, it's clean and dependable, with routes that take you directly to or within a few blocks of your destination.

The CTA is a good choice in lieu of driving in the jam-packed Loop, Magnificent Mile, or River North areas, though the system gets crowded during weekday rush hours. Most trains run 24 hours; for safety's sake, don't take them after the evening rush hour. The CTA recently went to an automated pay system without fare-takers, so finding a human being to answer questions is virtually impossible. All fares on CTA trains require exact change and are paid into a vending machine in the station, which issues a transit card. One-way fare is $1.75; transfers, which allow you to switch to two other connecting routes (bus or train) within 2 hours, cost an additional 25 cents. If you expect to be using the CTA with some frequency, you may insert more money into the machine to increase the ride credit on your transit card. Children under age 7 ride free; children between ages 7 and 11, seniors, and people with disabilities pay discounted fares. Other discounted fares take effect at different times.

Taxis

Cabs may be hailed in the street; they are unoccupied if the top light is on. In some downtown areas—around the **Fulton Street** dance clubs, for instance—you'll need to call one for a pickup. Companies include

American United 773/248.7600
AMM's Limos...773/792.1126
Checker...312/243.2537
Flash 773/561.1444
Yellow 312/829.4222

Tours

By Boat

The city of Chicago exists because it is here that Lake Michigan meets the **Chicago River,** forming a link between the Great Lakes and the Mississippi River, or, by extension, between the Atlantic Ocean and the Gulf of Mexico. Native Americans used this link for hundreds of years. One of the best ways to see Chicago is still from the water, and there are several sightseeing boats from which to choose. The **Chicago Architecture Foundation** (312/922.3432, 312/751.1380) conducts tours along the Chicago River that focus on the city's remarkable architectural wealth. **Wendella** (312/337.1446) and **Mercury Cruises** (312/332.1353) have tour boats that go out onto the lake, leaving from the **Michigan Avenue Bridge** by the **Wrigley Building. Chicago from the Lake** (312/527.2002) offers architecture and history tours leaving from River East Plaza (435 E Illinois St, at N McClurg Ct), as well as mealtime cruises. *Spirit of Chicago* (866/211.3804) and *Odyssey* (888/741.0281) have mealtime cruises that depart from **Navy Pier** (700 E Grand Ave, at N Streeter Dr). *Chicago's First Lady* (847/358.1330) departs from the Michigan Ave bridge. Most boat tours are available from May through October, and the *Spirit of Chicago* offers cruises throughout the year.

By Bus

Bus tours are offered by **American Sightseeing** (312/251.3100), **Gray Line of Chicago** (312/251.3107), and **Chicago Trolley** (312/663.0260). **Untouchable Tours** (881.1195) does a lighthearted tour of gangster sites. Occasionally the Chicago Architecture Foundation (312/922.3432) conducts bus tours; its guides are well informed.

By Foot

Chicago is a great city for walkers (it's flat, like most of the Midwest). For information about walking tours, ask at your hotel desk or call any of the following organizations:

Chicago Architecture Foundation 312/922.3432
Chicago Historical Society 312/642.4600
Friends of the Chicago River 312/939.0490

However you tour the city, the **Chicago Tour Guides Institute** (733/276.6683) can provide guides (between March and October) to conduct your tour in almost any language, from A to V (Arabic to Vietnamese).

Trains

There are 12 commuter lines offering daily service to the suburbs and **Southeast Side**, departing from four different stations in the Loop. For information on services of all lines, call 312/836.7000.

Walking

Chicago is easily—perhaps best—explored on foot. For self-guided walking tours, a number of titles are available at local bookstores. A particularly good one is *Walking with Women Through Chicago History*, available at the bookstores of the Chicago Architecture Foundation (224 S Michigan Ave, at E Jackson Blvd, 312/922.3432) or the **Chicago Historical Society** (1601 N Clark St, at W North Blvd, 312/642.4600).

FYI

Accommodations

As in most big cities, it's best to make hotel reservations as far in advance as possible before a visit. In Chicago, reservations are essential during the Fourth of July holiday and the prime convention months of May, June, September, and October. In addition to hotels, the area has a variety of bed-and-breakfast establishments; for information: bed and breakfast.com; chicago-bed-breakfast.com

CityPass

CityPass is a national program of discount ticket books for six major entertainment and cultural attractions in different cities. Tickets cost 50% less than box office prices if you were to visit each individually. **Chicago CityPass** attractions are the Art Institute of Chicago, the Field Museum, the Museum of Science and Industry, Adler Planetarium and Astronomy Museum, Shedd Aquarium, and the John Hancock Observatory. The booklet also includes a savings certificate from Marshall Field's. CityPass booklets may be purchased at the main entrance to any of the six CityPass attractions, city visitor center ticket offices, or online at www.citypass.com. Adults, $49; seniors, $25; and youth 3–11, $39. 888/330.5008.

Climate

Chicago is notorious for its unseasonable climate, especially in the winter months when subzero temperatures, icy winds, and snow challenge even the hardiest travelers. In spring, you can expect a combination of lingering winter and balmy summer previews—often in the same day. Summer is for the most part very pleasant, although the thermometer can top 100 degrees at times. The prolonged autumn season, when it's generally sunny yet cool, is the ideal time for a visit. But whenever you visit, be prepared for rapid changes in temperature.

Months Temperature Range (°F)

Month	
January	15–31
February	18–34
March	27–45
April	38–59
May	47–70
June	57–79
July	61–83
August	60–82
September	52–75
October	42–66
November	30–48
December	19–35

Drinking

The drinking age is 21. No store may sell liquor on Sunday before noon.

Hours

Opening and closing times for shops, attractions, coffeehouses, and so on are listed only by day(s) if normal hours apply (opening between 8 and 11AM and closing between 4 and 7PM). In unusual cases, specific hours are given.

Money

At O'Hare International Airport, international currencies can be converted at the **Foreign Currency Exchange** (773/462.9973), in the international terminal (terminal 5). In town, there is Travelex (19 S LaSalle St, at W Madison St, 312/807.4941). Banks, many stores, and restaurants accept traveler's checks, generally requiring a photo ID. You can purchase them at **American Express**

Weather Facts:

· Average wind speed in the Windy City: 10.2 miles per hour

· Number of days a year the temperature is 32 degrees F or below: 121

· Number of days a year the temperature is above 90 degrees F: 21

· Percentage of clear days during a typical year: 23%

The four stars in the flag of Chicago represent the Fort Dearborn Massacre (1812), the Great Fire (1871), the World's Columbian Exposition (1893), and the Century of Progress Fair (1933).

(605 N Michigan Ave, at E Ohio St, 312/943.7840), Travelex (see above), and most major banks. Banks are generally open Monday through Friday between 8:30AM and 5:30PM.

Personal Safety

As in any city, use common sense: If an area looks questionable, stay out of it. Much of the **South Side** and **West Side** are anything but hospitable. Exceptions are **Little Italy**, **Chinatown**, **Hyde Park**, and **Pullman**, which are reachable by cab or car. On the **North Side**, even the nicest areas can be next to trouble spots, so stay within the neighborhood boundaries as defined in this book. Sometimes safety is a matter of day and night. The lakefront, public parks, the Loop, and the **South Loop** are active during the day but are often deserted after dark; take a cab or car directly to nighttime destinations in these areas. On the other hand, the Magnificent Mile, **Oak Street**, and **Rush** and **Division Streets** in the Gold Coast are active well into the night. Just stay within well-lighted areas and watch out for seedy characters who might have an eye on your wallet or purse. Pickpockets are especially active in downtown shopping crowds during the winter holidays.

Publications

The city's largest daily newspaper, the *Chicago Tribune*, concentrates on national news and features as well as local news. The tabloid *Chicago Sun-Times* has a smaller staff and is regarded as a lesser publication. In fall 2002, the *Tribune* launched an afternoon weekday paper, the *Red Eye*, and the *Sun-Times* launched a competitor, the *Red Streak*. If you can't find a copy, they've probably folded from hemorrhaging red ink. The *Chicago Daily Defender* serves the city's African-American population. The *Reader* is a highly regarded free weekly with reviews and extensive entertainment listings; look for it around downtown and in Lincoln Park and Wicker Park. *New City*, another weekly freebie, has helpful listings, especially for art galleries. *Chicago* magazine is a glossy monthly aimed at an upscale audience, with numerous event and restaurant listings. *Chicago Social* is a new freebie monthly targeted to the upper crust, with an angle on the singles scene, available in high-end shops. Another monthly, *North Shore*, has listings for north of the city. The weekly *Crain's Chicago Business* provides in-depth coverage of local business, and the free weeklies *Windy City Times* and *Chicago Free Press* cater to the gay and lesbian community. The city's ethnic population is served by various publications, most notably the *Chicago Jewish Star*, the largest and oldest independent Jewish newspaper in the Chicago area, available downtown in stores and news boxes. There are several foreign-language newspapers, including a Polish daily, *Zgoda*; a Spanish weekly, *La Raza*; and *Hankook Ilbo* (*Korea Times*), which is published Monday through Saturday.

Radio Stations

AM:

670	WSCR	Sports
720	WGN	Talk/sports

780	WBBM	News radio
890	WLS	Talk/news

FM:

88.7	WLUW	Loyola University public radio
91.5	WBEZ	National public radio
93.7	WXRT	Alternative rock
97.9	WLUP	Rock
98.7	WFMT	Fine arts
107.5	WGCI	Rap, R&B, Black affairs

RESTAURANTS

Reservations are essential at most trendy or expensive restaurants, and it's best to book far in advance at such dining spots as **Tru, Charlie Trotter's, Everest Room, Ambria,** or **Le Français**. If you want to avoid crowds, ask about late seatings. In general, jackets and ties are not required, except at the posh and popular places, and most establishments accept credit cards.

SHOPPING

North Michigan Avenue has become one of the leading shopping streets in the world; from **Armani** to **Escada, Tiffany** to **Barneys**, branches of international retailers are located here and on adjacent Oak Street. **State Street,** long the nation's leading retail street, has lost its former glamour. However, it's reviving as a center for off-price retailing, with stores like **Filene's, T. J. Maxx,** and **Toys "R" Us**. For funkier, offbeat items,

visit the numerous stores along **Halsted Street,** particularly near **Armitage Avenue** (2000 N). To see how city-dwelling Chicagoans shop for basic necessities, visit the sprawling shopping area just west of the intersection of **West North** and **North Clybourn Avenues**.

SMOKING

City laws require all restaurants to have nonsmoking sections and prohibit smoking in theaters and public buildings and on public transportation.

STREET PLAN

One 19th-century visitor described Chicago as "the most right-angle town" he'd ever seen—a characteristic that proves helpful in finding your way around. Except for the rare diagonal, streets are arranged on a grid, with the zero point for addresses at the intersection of **State** and **Madison Streets** in the Loop. The city's North Side is north of Madison Street, and the South Side is south of it. The West Side is west of State Street. In the Loop and north of it, most of the **East Side** stretches along Lake Michigan; as far south as Hyde Park, though, the lake is over 3 miles east of State Street. Street numbers generally run in increments of 100 per block, with six blocks to a mile. Streets on the North Side and north-south streets on the South Side generally have names, whereas east-west streets on the South Side for the most part go by numbers. Chicagoans, by the way, will say "thirty hundred," not "three thousand."

Phone Book

EMERGENCIES

Ambulance/Fire/Police	911
AAA Emergency Service	866/968.7222
Dental Referral	312/836.7300

Hospitals

Children's Memorial Hospital, Lincoln Park	773/880.4000
Northwestern Memorial Hospital, Streeterville	312/926.2000
Rush–Presbyterian–St. Luke's Medical Center, West Side	312/942.5000
Medical Referral (nonemergency)	312/670.3670
Pediatric Referral	800/KIDSDOC
Poison Control	800/942.5969
Rape Crisis Hotline	888/293.2080
24-Hour Pharmacy	312/664.8686

SPORTS AND RECREATION

Chicago Bears	847/615.2327
Chicago Blackhawks	312/455.7000
Chicago Bulls	312/455.4000
Chicago Cubs	773/404.2827

Chicago Fine Arts Hotline	312/346.3278
Chicago Music Alliance	312/987.9296
Chicago White Sox	312/674.1000
Chicago Wolves	800/THE.WOLV
Illinois Lottery Winning Numbers	312/976.6060 ($1.95 service charge)
Movies	312/444.FILM
Special Events Hotline	312/744.3370

VISITORS' INFORMATION

American Youth Hostels	312/360.0300
Amtrak	800/USA.RAIL
Chicago Transit Authority/Regional Transit Authority	312/836.7000
Greyhound/Trailways Bus Lines	800/231.2222
Handicapped Services Information	312/744.4016, 312/744.7050
Legal Assistance Foundation	312/341.1070
Passport Information	800/375.5283
Time and Weather	312/976.8367 ($1.95 service charge)
Western Union	800/325.6000

CHICAGO CELEBRATIONS

From Latin music concerts and funny film festivals to Venetian boat parties and the annual singing of Christmas carols to the inhabitants of the **Lincoln Park Zoo**, Chicago offers festivities for folks of all ages every month of the year. For more information on the following activities, call the Chicago Office of Tourism (312/744.2400).

January

The boat show at McCormick Place makes summer seem closer.

The Cubs convention and Sox Fest brings dreams of summer.

February

Black History Month celebrates the cultural heritage of African-Americans through various events and displays at Navy Pier.

Chicago Chinese New Year Parade (mid-February) kicks off the new year in Chinatown.

March

St. Patrick's Day Parade unleashes Irish pride and carousing. The politicians are out in full force and the river is dyed green.

Newberry Library Mystery Book Fair celebrates the mystery novel with readings and signings by mystery writers.

April

Lincoln Park Conservatory and Garfield Park Conservatory Spring and Easter Flower Shows (throughout April) display a stunning array of springtime flora.

Earth Day (22 April) teaches families about the earth's natural resources around the city.

Ikenobo Ikebana Japanese Flower Arranging Show (first weekend of April) highlights traditional and unique Japanese flower arrangements and illustrates the fundamentals of Japanese flower arranging at the **Chicago Botanic Garden**.

May

Art Chicago in Millennium Park (early May) features the work of both emerging and well-known artists represented by local, regional, national, and international galleries.

June

Chicago Blues Festival (first weekend in June) is the largest free blues festival in the world, with 3 days of great blues performed by top blues artists at **Grant Park**.

57th Street Art Fair (first weekend in June), near the University of Chicago campus, attracts artists from throughout North America.

Chicago Gospel Festival (early June), held at Grant Park, is a joyous and free celebration of gospel music.

Old Town Art Fair (second weekend in June) features more than 225 invited artists at the oldest juried art fair in the US.

Printer's Row Book Fair means thousands of new, used, rare, and antiquarian books for sale, as well as events like author signings and readings.

Taste of Chicago (last week in June and first week in July) serves up culinary delights from more than 70 restaurants, peppering the festivities with terrific live music.

TAXES

The local sales tax is 8.75%.

TICKETS

The main ticket sources are **Ticketmaster** (312/559.1212) and **Hot Tix** (312/977.1755). Hot Tix booths are located at 78 W Randolph, between N Clark and N Dearborn; and at the **WaterWorks Visitor Center**, 163 E Pearson St, at N Michigan Ave. The two Chicago booths are open Tuesday through Friday between 8:30AM and 6PM, Saturday between 10AM and 6PM, and Sunday between noon and 5PM. Hot Tix tickets are also available at **Tower Records**, but purchases there are cash only.

TIPPING

Leave a 15-20% gratuity in restaurants and for personal services. Taxi drivers expect a 15% tip.

TIME ZONE

Chicago is on Central Standard Time, 1 hour behind New York and 2 hours ahead of California.

July

Independence Day Concert and Fireworks (3 July) provides one of the summer's most spectacular events as the **Grant Park Symphony Orchestra**'s rousing rendition of the *1812 Overture* accompanies a huge fireworks display.

Chinatown Summer Fair (late July) features a sidewalk sale, farmers' market, art fair, stage show, and children's activities.

Chicago's Venetian Night (late July) is an evening aquatic parade along the downtown shoreline of Lake Michigan.

Bughouse Square Debates in Washington Park, across from Newberry Library, revives an old tradition.

August

Gold Coast Art Fair (second weekend in August) is an outdoor art show exhibiting the works of artists from over 25 states and countries.

Chicago Air and Water Show (third weekend in August) provides demonstrations of skill by teams of international aviation and aquatics experts.

Viva! Chicago Latin Music Festival (last weekend in August) brings international performers from Mexico, Central America, South America, and the Caribbean, as well as national and local groups.

Chicago International Concours d'Elegance (late August) is a showcase for vintage automobiles just south of **Buckingham Fountain** in Grant Park.

September

Chicago Jazz Festival (Labor Day weekend) brings together top international and local jazz musicians and millions of fans for this free concert in Grant Park.

Berghoff Oktoberfest (mid-September) lures about 100,000 revelers for a 4-day street party. Hosted by the **Berghoff Restaurant**, the party takes over West Adams Street (between South State and South Dearborn Streets) for a celebration of bratwurst, beer, and German music.

October

Chicago International Children's Film Festival is the nation's oldest and largest competitive festival for children's films.

Chicago International Film Festival (mid-October) screens films from around the world at various theaters throughout the city.

November

Chicago Humanities Festival hosts speeches, concerts, dramatic readings, and panel discussions at various cultural institutions.

Magnificent Mile Lights Festival (mid-November) kicks off the holiday season with a festive weekend as the stores unveil their Christmas windows, and 150 trees along **Michigan Avenue** are lit with 600,000 lights.

December

In the Spirit is a monthlong celebration of the different holiday traditions of Christmas, Hanukkah, and Kwanzaa. Events throughout the city include storytelling, films, music, dance, and theater.

Carol to the Animals gives humans the gift of singing Christmas carols to their four-legged friends at the Lincoln Park Zoo.

VISITORS' INFORMATION OFFICES

Chicago Office of Tourism information centers are located in the **WaterWorks Visitor's Center** (163 E Pearson St, at N Michigan Ave; open daily, 7:30AM-7PM), and the **Chicago Cultural Center** (77 E Randolph St, at N Michigan Ave; open M-F 10AM-6PM, Sa 10AM-5PM, and Su 11AM-5PM). The general information number is 312/744.2400. The web site is www.cityofchicago.org/tourism.

Commerce, culture, and City Hall politics coalesce and collide downtown in the Loop, where movers and shakers make the world of Chicago go 'round. All roads lead here: the expressways, **Lake Shore Drive** and other main thoroughfares, commuter and freight trains, boats, buses, subways, the El–and, in decades past, cable cars that converged in an embracing loop, giving the area its name. Since the 1970s, **State Street** has lost much of its retail cachet to the famous shopping strip known as the **Magnificent Mile**. But it is still home to **Marshall Field's**, located in a stately building designed a century ago by **Daniel Burnham**, and **Louis Sullivan**'s cast-iron–adorned **Carson Pirie Scott & Company**; stores abound one block east on **Wabash Avenue**. Only one block farther east, the **Art Institute of Chicago** and **Orchestra Hall** mark **Michigan Avenue**. Across this thoroughfare stretches **Grant Park**, which is the site of the annual jazz, blues, and gospel festivals, as well as the **Taste of Chicago** fair. West of State Street, concrete canyons exude money and might, from bank headquarters and stock exchanges to Holabird & Roche's turn-of-the-20th-century **City Hall** and **Skidmore, Owings & Merrill**'s **Sears Tower**, America's tallest

building (eclipsed as the *world's* tallest in 1997 by the higher spires on the Petronas Towers in Kuala Lumpur, Malaysia). Enclosing it all in a quiet curve is **Wacker Drive** on the banks of the **Chicago River**, where it all began.

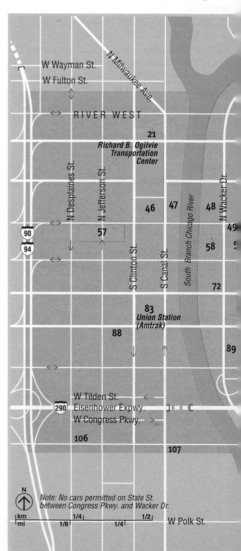

In 1837 the town, filled with log cabins and 4,170 people, was incorporated as a city. Its first marketplace was already developing along a street called **South Water Market** (now Wacker Drive) on the south bank of the Chicago River. By 1840 the population had mushroomed to 30,000. Wealthy citizens built homes in the Loop, especially south of **Van Buren Street** in what is now the **South Loop**, an easy commute from their business offices. Many working-class immigrants lived in shantytowns near the river or in slums hidden in alleys behind the business district. In the 1850s the city's first architect, **John Mills Van Osdel**, and his colleagues began designing buildings as tall as five stories along nearby **Lake Street**.

Meanwhile, entrepreneur Potter Palmer bought three-quarters of a mile of land along State Street. He knocked down a sorry strip of shanties, paved the street, and persuaded the **Field, Leiter, and Company** department store to rent a building he constructed, thus inspiring the birth of a new center of commerce. In 1870 Palmer opened his first **Palmer House Hotel.** (Today it's in its third building at Wabash Avenue and **Monroe Street.**) A year later, everything went up in smoke when the Great Fire—believed to have started in a barn just to the southwest—reduced most of Chicago to rubble in 3 days. In a show of amazing resilience, the city quickly rebuilt itself, this time in accordance with a new law that permitted only brick or stone buildings in and near the Loop. Downtown became strictly business, as workers moved on to cheaper neighborhoods and the wealthy built mansions farther south on Prairie Avenue.

The 1880s marked the start of the Loop's heyday, which lasted for more than half a century. Train stations and shipping piers connected the city to the rest of the world. Corporations built their national headquarters here. The Chicago School of Architecture emerged, with such eminent names as **Adler & Sullivan** and **Burnham & Root.** The Loop became a center of culture, entertainment, and hospitality, with world-class theaters and hotels. But the 1940s brought the flight of business and industry to the suburbs, and it wasn't until the **Prudential Building** was constructed in 1955 that growth again seemed possible. In 1978 State Street was closed to vehicular traffic in an attempt to revive ailing

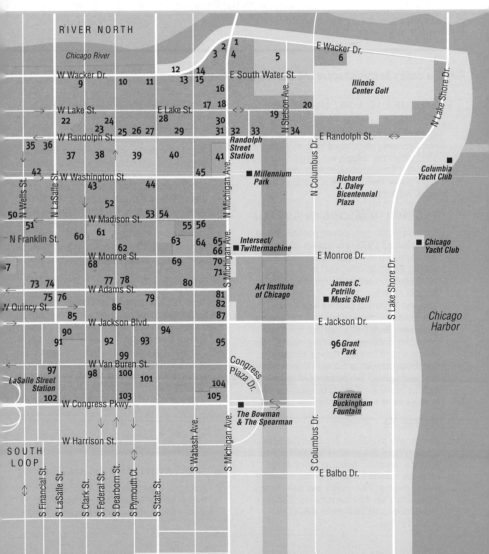

businesses, but many failed anyway. Now it has been reopened to traffic, as part of yet another city initiative to revitalize the Loop. Modeled in part on the makeover of Times Square in New York, this effort, using tax-increment financing, federal funding, and corporate sponsorship, seems to be working so far. One part of the effort involves creating a "theater district," by adding the remodeled **Oriental** and **Cadillac Theaters** on Randolph Street, as well as a new **Goodman Theatre** on Dearborn Street, to the revival started with the rehabilitation of the Chicago Theater on State Street in the early 1990s. Three noteworthy hotels—the **Allegro**, the **Monaco**, and the **Burnham**—have opened in recent years, and Sears has returned to the Loop with a State Street store. After long delays and cost overruns, the spectacular **Millennium Park** has opened at the north end of **Grant Park**.

A stroll through the Loop is a must, whether to shop, immerse yourself in the culture, or simply gape at the tall buildings. Activity of every sort is at its frenzied height Monday through Friday between 8AM and 6PM. On evenings and weekends, the area is far quieter, but not nearly as deserted as it was in the early 1990s. Stores on State Street are now open on Sunday, and people stroll along Michigan Avenue until late at night, particularly in the summer. For a perfect introduction to the Loop, start your visit with one of several guided tours offered by bus or boat; see the "Orientation" chapter for suggestions.

All area codes in this chapter are 312 unless otherwise noted.

1 SITE OF OLD FORT DEARBORN

Bronze bricks embedded in the sidewalks just south of the Chicago River mark the outline of Fort Dearborn, which stood here from 1803 to 1812, when the outpost was abandoned and its fleeing inhabitants were massacred by angry Native Americans. ♦ N Michigan Ave and E Wacker Dr

2 360 NORTH MICHIGAN AVENUE

Crowned by an open, domed pavilion, **Alfred S. Alschuler**'s 1923 neoclassical skyscraper was angled on its irregular site to face the **Wrigley Building**, completed in 1922, and the 1920 Michigan Avenue Bridge. The griffins and coats of arms from the city of London that grace the lobby and concave exterior are reminders that this was originally the **London Guarantee Building** (it was later the **Stone Container Building**). Once truly majestic, the central arched entrance flanked by four Corinthian columns is not what it once was— the building itself has deteriorated somewhat, and the newer surrounding buildings outdo it in elegance. ♦ At E Wacker Dr

3 HOTEL 71

$$ Formerly the Clarion Executive Plaza, this 39-story hotel reopened in fall 2002 after getting a complete makeover aimed at the business traveler. It's billed as "the hotel that works," playing off Chicago's own self-invoked motto. There are 422 guest rooms, 32 suites, and 8 "dedicated boardroom suites," all unusually spacious. Rooms overlooking the river have spectacular views. Amenities include high-speed Internet access, cable TV, and a 24-hour fitness room. All rooms have ergonomic leather chairs, large work desks, and individually controlled air conditioning for recovering from long, hot meetings. Conference equipment and office tech gear are right on hand. A restaurant in the hotel serves breakfast, lunch, and dinner, but there are other options nearby that deserve your attention. ♦ 71 E Wacker Dr (between N Wabash and N Michigan Aves). 346.7100; fax 346.1721 & www.hotel71.com

3 MATHER TOWER

Built in 1928, **Herbert H. Riddle**'s 41-story pencil-like tower was once the tallest building in Chicago. It now carries the distinction of having the smallest floor space per floor of any building downtown. On November 24, 2002, visitors to Chicago were treated to a surprise engineering spectacle: An 11-ton steel framework, the last piece in the steel skeleton of a new four-story cupola, was airlifted to the roof of the building by helicopter and set in place after some wild spinning. ♦ 75 E Wacker Dr (between N Wabash and N Michigan Aves)

4 333 NORTH MICHIGAN AVENUE

Based on **Eliel Saarinen**'s second-prize design for the **Tribune Tower, Holabird & Root**'s 1928 structure was Chicago's first Art

Deco skyscraper and the last of four buildings forming a gateway between the Loop and North Michigan Avenue. Its strong vertical tower, capped with clifflike setbacks, rises from a smooth, polished marble base. At the fifth floor, Fred Torrey's 7-foot-high limestone panels carved in low relief depict episodes of early Chicago history, including those involving Father Jacques Marquette and the Fort Dearborn Massacre. ♦ Between E South Water St and E Wacker Dr

5 ILLINOIS CENTER

The world's largest mixed-use project is built on more than 80 acres of obsolete rail yards once operated by the **Illinois Central Railroad**. **Mies van der Rohe** conceived the original design, which was begun in 1967; various architects have been involved since. **One Illinois Center** was the first building completed in this vast, rather sterile complex, and the addition of **Two** and **Three Illinois Center** and **Boulevard Towers** did nothing to humanize the scale. *Splash*, a colorful sculpture by Jerry Peart, was installed on the plaza in 1986 and brought a spot of warmth to these dark, looming canyons. The underground level has a variety of shops that seem to go out of business and change owners frequently.

Within Illinois Center:

LAKESHORE ATHLETIC CLUB

Kisho Kurokawa designed this building in 1990. Six floors of white walls and glass, topped with Japanese wind sculptures, enclose luxury health facilities for people who don't mind taking out a second mortgage to pay the dues. The club boasts a 100-foot-high indoor rock-climbing wall, tons of fitness equipment, basketball and handball courts, a rooftop terrace with a sundeck, a pool, an alfresco restaurant, and a full-service European spa for massages and skin treatments. Open to members, as well as guests of any downtown hotel, for $20, it's worth a look-see just for fun. ♦ Daily. 211 N Stetson Ave (between E Lake and E South Water Sts). 616.9000

HYATT REGENCY CHICAGO

$$$ Conventioneers favor the 2,019 modestly furnished guest rooms in this hotel that occupies two towers of the center. The main public space is a multilevel glass-enclosed lobby complete with a pool and waterfall surrounded by lush greenery. Amenities include the **Networks Bar & Grill**, **Stetson's Chop House**, and the glassed-in **Big Bar**, whose view alone might intoxicate. Slightly more expensive, the **Regency Club** section of the west tower has its own concierge and private lounge with complimentary continental breakfast. VIP suites have fireplaces and saunas. Weekend rates are available. ♦ 151 E Wacker Dr (at N Stetson Ave). 565.1234, 800/233.1234; fax 565.2966 ♿ www.chicagoregency.hyatt.com

6 SWISSÔTEL CHICAGO

$$$ A dramatic glass triangle at the eastern edge of **Illinois Center** (see above), this luxury high-rise hotel with 630 rooms offers a quiet European ambiance and fantastic views. Large guest rooms, writing desks, seating areas, and two-line phones are standard. Complimentary valet services include pressing and mending, and newspapers are delivered every morning. The **Penthouse Health Spa**, which overlooks the lake, has a heated pool, exercise equipment, whirlpool, sauna, and steam room and offers Swedish massage. The executive business center provides secretarial services, computers, telex, and fax. ♦ 323 E Wacker Dr (between N Lake Shore and N Columbus Drs). 565.0565, 800/637.9477; fax 565.0540 ♿ www.chicago.swissotel.com

Within the Swissôtel Chicago:

THE PALM

★★★$$$ This is the second location for Chicago's branch of the world-famous New York steak house, with its wall-to-wall wood trim, caricatures on the walls, and high-backed booths. Jumbo steaks and giant lobsters are the specialties, but the veal parmigiana and steamed clams serve as faithful reminders of the restaurant's Italian roots. Save room for the Key lime pie. ♦ Daily, lunch and dinner. 616.1000. Also in Northbrook, 847/239.7256

7 333 WEST WACKER DRIVE

In 1983 this building put **Kohn Pedersen Fox** on the Chicago map with a three-story marble-and-granite base relating to the street, and a sheer, green glass wall bowed to follow and reflect the Chicago River's curve. ♦ Between N Franklin and W Lake Sts

8 225 WEST WACKER DRIVE

The architectural firm of **Kohn Pedersen Fox** designed this well-proportioned office building in 1989. The structure has four corner towers linked in pairs like bedposts. These links are metal bridges, architecturally reminiscent of the many beautiful and graceful bridges spanning the Chicago River. ♦ At N Franklin St

---

Restaurants/Clubs: Red | Hotels: Purple | Shops: Orange | Outdoors/Parks: Green | Sights/Culture: Blue

9 WATERVIEW TOWER

They're paving a parking lot and putting up paradise. At least that's what the future residents who are forking over big, big dough for one of the 48 penthouse homes in this 89-story commercial and residential tower are thinking. Designed and developed by Teng and Associates, it's being trumped on advance publicity by the taller tower going up across the river. The building is scheduled for completion in 2007. ◆ 111 W Wacker Dr (at N Clark St)

10 LEO BURNETT BUILDING

Roche/Dinkeloo Associates' 1989 design is related to **Robert A. M. Stern**'s 1975 late entry to the Chicago Tribune Tower Competition, which in turn translated **Adolf Loos**'s famous Ionic column entry of 1922 into a Postmodern form. Here a freestanding monumental column sheathed in a checkerboard pattern of granite has a giant order of abstract columns forming the base, a device that repeats at setback and crown. ◆ 35 W Wacker Dr (at N Dearborn St)

11 RENAISSANCE CHICAGO HOTEL

$$$ This upscale entry in the Marriott hotel empire is a 27-story modern facility, facing north and overlooking the Chicago River. Riverview rooms cost a bit more, but they're worth it. There are 555 rooms in all, including 40 suites, with a mauve-and-gray color scheme and dark wood décor. Amenities include a swimming pool and fitness club, in-room fax, modem, and data ports. Designed with the business traveler in mind, there are four executive floors, 15 meeting rooms, and a conference center that can fit up to 1,000 people. But families (and pets) are welcome, with weekend packages available. The Great Street restaurant serves formal meals and casual fare. ◆ 1 W Wacker Dr (at N State St). 372.7200; fax 372.0093, 800.468.3571 ♿ www.renaissancehotels.com

12 HEALD SQUARE

The square was named for Captain Nathan Heald, ill-fated commandant of Fort Dearborn when in 1812, the fort was evacuated and its fleeing occupants massacred. In 1941 a bronze statue by sculptor Lorado Taft with Leonard Crunelle was dedicated here; it depicts George Washington flanked by two entrepreneurs: English-born Robert Morris and Polish-born Haym Salomon. These American businessmen were the principal financiers of the Revolutionary War, and the monument is intended, as inscribed, to be a "symbol of American tolerance and unity and of the cooperation of people of all races and creeds in the upbuilding of the United States." ◆ E Wacker Dr (between N Wabash Ave and N State St)

13 35 EAST WACKER DRIVE

Thielbar & Fugard and **Giavar & Dinkelberg** designed this building, which was completed in 1926. The letters *JB*, worked into the neo-Baroque ornament throughout, are reminders that this was originally the **Jewelers Building**. The 17-story tower is crowned by a domed, column-encircled pavilion that contains the office of architect **Helmut Jahn**. Until 1940, tenants could drive into the building from Lower Wacker Drive, go straight into an elevator, exit, and park on their floor. ◆ At N Wabash Ave

14 SEVENTEENTH CHURCH OF CHRIST, SCIENTIST, CHICAGO

Designed in 1968 by **Harry Weese & Associates**, this travertine marble church was curved to fit the site, with a bronze-and-glass lobby recessed behind a sunken platform to shield it from the street. Notice the domed lantern centered over the reader's platform in the semicircular auditorium space. ◆ 55 E Wacker Dr (at N Wabash Ave). 236.4671

15 HOTEL MONACO

$$ Formerly the Oxford House, a hotel that had been on the decline for years, this 14-story facility has undergone a most welcome and delightful face-lift, courtesy of the San Francisco–based Kimpton Hotel Group, which also has remodeled and opened the new **Burnham** and **Allegro** hotels in the Loop. The lobby, with a stunning marble floor, is a vibrant two-story Art Deco "living room," giving a hint of what's to come. The rooms are soft and warm, wonderfully decorated in pastels, with comfortable, plush furniture designed to make you feel right at home. Standard amenities in the 170 rooms and 22 suites are two-line phones, voice mail, data ports, fax machines, and complimentary 800 and credit card access calls. The suites include two-person Fuji tubs, and there are 30 rooms specially designed for tall guests—high ceilings and long beds. The overall atmosphere is one of luxurious whimsy, helped along by complimentary evening wine receptions in the lobby with chair massages and tarot card readers, and the availability of a complimentary goldfish to keep you company! For serious folks, there is a fitness room. In addition to being a different and pleasurable experience, given the rates at some of the upscale cookie-cutter franchises, the Monaco also is something of a bargain.

THE REBUILDING OF WACKER DRIVE

On November 29, 2002, Chicago capped off a colossal public-works project: the rebuilding of Wacker Drive, the curvaceous double-decker Beaux Arts boulevard that cuts a swath between the Loop and the Chicago River. The 21-month, $200 million reconstruction effort was alternately a cause for consternation and awe for those who come to the city on a daily basis. It was an inconvenience for commuters and pedestrians during rush hour, but a remarkable architectural and engineering show to marvel at during lunch hour. Completed in 2003, the project added a new monumental plaza at the river's edge between State Street and Wabash Avenue and a river walk that runs from Michigan Avenue to Lake Street.

Created as a result of Daniel Burnham and Edward Bennett's 1909 Plan of Chicago, the street was constructed in 1926 and named for civic booster Charles Wacker, who campaigned hard for the plan to be put into place. The upper level was intended for vehicular traffic, and the lower level was meant to serve boat traffic seeking access to the fish and vegetable markets along the river. Boat shipping gave way to trucking, and between 1949 and 1958, the road was extended south to Congress Parkway. In the postwar suburbanization of the city, resourceful commuters found Lower Wacker to be a convenient artery to bypass Loop traffic.

The roadway deteriorated so badly over the years that by the 1990s, it was clear that it would need to be rebuilt or closed. Lower Wacker had become a dark, crumbling cavern that served as a refuge for the homeless. (To spare embarrassment during the 1996 Democratic convention, the city rounded people up beforehand and took them to shelters.) In its renovated state, Lower Wacker is now a bright and wider thoroughfare.

Architects for the reconstruction project were DLK Architecture, Johnson Lasky Architects, Muller & Muller Architects, and Janet Attarian of the city's Bureau of Bridges. The road was moved 50 feet southward to carve out room for the new riverside plaza. Preservationists and architecture critics have applauded the restoration of many of the aesthetic touches from the road's original design—such as limestone ballustrades and obelisks, as well as the addition of planters and benches to give the busy street a more relaxed and inviting feeling.

At the ribbon-cutting ceremony to mark the reopening of Wacker, the city staged a reenactment of the famous Lower Wacker police chase scene from the movie *Blues Brothers*. But like city traffic, it moved at low speed.

There are several packages available. Within the hotel, **South Water Kitchen** does a good job serving grilled and roasted meats. ♦ 225 N Wabash Ave (at E South Water St). 960.8500, 800/397.7661; fax 960.8538. www.monaco-chicago.com

16 HARD ROCK HOTEL

$$$ The historic **Carbide and Carbon Building**, originally designed in 1929 by Daniel and Hubert Burnham, sons of Daniel Burnham, has undergone a welcome rehab. From its black polished-granite base to its green terra-cotta-clad tower to its Art Deco lobby, the building is a masterpiece. The new hotel features hi-tech amenities, including CD/DVD entertainment systems, Nintendo game stations, high-speed Internet and Wi-Fi in all 381 guest rooms, which include 13 suites. There's a lounge that features live music (naturally), and an attached gift shop that sells Hard Rock souvenirs (obviously). Room service is available 24 hours. Within the hotel, the dining option is the **China Grill**, a glitzy link to a hip New York chain. ♦ 230 N Michigan Ave (at E South Water St) よ

17 JOFFREY BALLET OF CHICAGO

The legendary dance company moved to Chicago in 1995. It was a fitting move, considering that the company's first performance, in 1956, took place here, and that the Joffrey has performed more times in Chicago than in any other US city. Since its move to Chicago, local performances have taken place in the **Auditorium Theatre** (50 E Congress Pkwy, at S Wabash Ave). Summer performances have been scheduled as part of the annual Ravinia Festival in **Highland Park** on the North Shore. A state-of-the-art rehearsal space at the corner of State and Lake opened in 2005. ♦ 70 E Lake St (between N Michigan and N Wabash Aves), suite 1300. 739.0120, fax 739.0119. www.joffrey.com

17 SELF-PARK GARAGE

In 1986 **Tigerman, Fugman, McCurry** created the ultimate expression of building as billboard. The façade of this 10-level parking garage is painted to look like the front end of an antique car, complete with hood ornament, tire-tread awnings, and a vanity plate that

Restaurants/Clubs: Red | Hotels: Purple | Shops: Orange | Outdoors/Parks: Green | Sights/Culture: Blue

reads SELF PARK. ◆ 60 E Lake St (between N Michigan and N Wabash Aves)

18 THAT'S OUR BAG, INC.

A huge inventory of handbags, carryalls, briefcases, and luggage is sold at discount prices. ◆ Daily. 200 N Michigan Ave (at E Lake St). 984.3510. Also at several other Loop locations

19 TWO PRUDENTIAL PLAZA

Since 1990, **Loebl Schlossman & Hackl**'s set-back granite tower has punctuated the skyline at the north end of **Grant Park**. The various shades of gray granite and tinted glass were chosen to harmonize with the adjacent limestone-and-aluminum **Prudential Building**. The best feature of "Two Pru," as it is commonly known, is the one-acre **Beaubien Plaza** (named for the city's first innkeeper) on the northwest corner of the block, graced with waterfalls and terraces and shielded from the summer sun by the original **Prudential Building**. ◆ N Stetson Ave and E Lake St

20 FAIRMONT HOTEL

$$$ This copper-roofed, pink granite neoclassical building stands in contrast to the giant glass boxes that make up most of the nearby **Illinois Center** (see page 15). Each of the 700 rooms is individually decorated in contemporary to period furniture, and all have wonderful views of Millennium Park, **Grant Park**, and **Lake Michigan**. The hotel is popular with business travelers, who can take advantage of secretarial services, closed-circuit TV, telex, fax, and meeting facilities. Other perks include guest membership in a nearby health club and valet and concierge service. Within the hotel, **Aria** restaurant merits ($$$★★) at least one meal during your stay. Weekend packages are available. Frequent corporate travelers receive special discounts. ◆ 200 N Columbus Dr (at E Lake St). 565.8000, 800/527.4727; fax 856.1032 ♿ www.fairmont.com/chicago

21 NINE

★★$$$ When it opened in 2000, Nine was a very hot and very cool place to see and be

seen. It's still a fine place to dine. It's named for the age at which owners Michael Morton and Scott DeGraff first met. Childhood friend Michael Kornick (chef/owner of **mk**) designed the menu, so it was a sure bet that the food would be good. The interior is funky but chic, with pillars covered with mirrored tiles and a high domed ceiling painted in silver. There's a circular bar just for champagne and caviar, and an upstairs Ghost Lounge where the drink of choice is a glow-in-the-dark Midori martini. Prime steaks, chops, and seafood are the dominant fare, expertly prepared under the direction of Michael Shrader. Simplicity is the guiding principle, but the basic is somehow transformed into the exotic. Sea bass wrapped in pancetta is a catch of the year. Caviar comes six different ways, but the best is in a cone! Top it all off with a root beer float, served with warm chocolate-chip cookies for dessert. ◆ American. ◆ Reservations recommended. M-F, lunch and dinner; Sa, dinner. 440 W Randolph St (between N Canal and N Clinton Sts). 575.9900 ♿

22 JAMES R. THOMPSON CENTER

No one is indifferent to **Murphy/Jahn**'s 1985 structure, named for the governor who commissioned it. Outside, gray- and salmon-colored piers rise like a modern Stonehenge along Randolph and Clark Streets, and Jean Dubuffet's black-and-white sculpture, *Monument with Standing Beast*, anchors the corner. Although the red-and-blue-paneled exterior is not wearing well, the interior is spectacular, with offices ringing the skylit rotunda. Two glass elevator shafts rise through the space, and the top-floor view down into the classically patterned marble and granite floor is awesome—and dizzying. Chicagoans visit the offices to get help with their taxes, renew their driver's licenses, and obtain postal service. Those with a more leisurely agenda can enjoy a lunchtime concert played in a resounding acoustical space or have a snack at the **Great State Fare** food court downstairs. ◆ W Randolph and N Clark Sts

Within the James R. Thompson Center:

ILLINOIS ARTISANS SHOP

Works by some of the state's finest craftspeople are for sale here. ◆ M-F. Second floor. 814.5321

ILLINOIS ART GALLERY

Frequently changing exhibitions here showcase Illinois artists' work in such media as painting, sculpture, quilting, and performance art. ◆ M-F. Second floor. 814.5322

23 HOT TIX BOOTH

Run by the Chicago League of Theatres, this kiosk sells full-price, advance-sale tickets as well as half-price and discounted day-of-performance tickets for shows throughout the city. Half-price tickets for Sunday are available on Saturday. Be prepared to wait in line. ♦ Tu-F, 8:30AM-6PM; Sa 10AM-6PM; Su, noon-5PM. 78 W Randolph St (between N Dearborn and N Clark Sts). Also at WaterWorks Visitor Center, 163 E Pearson St (at N Michigan Ave), Tower Records stores, and 950 Skokie Blvd, Skokie. www.hottix.org

24 GOODMAN THEATRE

Named for Kenneth Sawyer Goodman, a dramatist-poet who died in World War I and whose parents donated the money for construction, the Goodman Theatre was for many years located in the Art Institute of Chicago. In November 2000, it opened in this new location, a 170,000-square-foot state-of-the-art complex built with a combination of government and private funding. Widely regarded as one of Chicago's finest theater companies (along with Steppenwolf), the Goodman is regarded by the city as the anchor for its recently created "theater district." The Goodman complex houses two theaters: the 856-seat proscenium stage Albert Ivar Goodman Theatre and the 400-seat flexible Owen Bruner Goodman Theatre. The complex is an intriguing marriage of two older existing theaters and all-new construction. The Bruner, at the north end of the complex, is a reconstruction of the former Selwyn Theater; the larger Ivar, at the south end of the complex, is all-new construction. Between the two, the main lobby is a reconstruction of the former Harris Theater, with administrative offices and rehearsal space on the upper level and costume shop and dressing rooms on the lower level. Architectural services on the project were provided by a joint venture of Toronto-based Kuwabara Payne McKenna Blumberg (KPMB) and Chicago-based **Decker Legge Kemp** (DLK). Under artistic director Robert Falls, shows at the Goodman have ranged from innovative versions of Shakespeare to the latest from August Wilson, who delivered the dedication address and whose play, *King Hedley II* was the debut presentation in the Albert. Each season usually ends with a musical, such as Stephen Sondheim's *Gold!* Other noteworthy productions have included the American premiere of Alan Ayckbourn's *House* and *Garden*, a pair of linked plays performed simultaneously by the same cast in the Albert and the Owen; August Wilson's *Gem of the Ocean*; and *The Doll House*, Rebecca Gilman's adaptation of the Ibsen play. Through a program called Tix-at-Six, tickets are available at half price at 6PM, on the day of performances. ♦ 170 N Dearborn St (between W Randolph and W Lake Sts). 443.3800, fax 443.3821 & www.goodmantheatre.org

25 DELAWARE BUILDING

This High Victorian Italianate structure designed by **Wheelock & Thomas** was erected immediately following the Great Fire of 1871 and is the oldest building in the Loop. It was restored in 1988 by **Hasbrouck Peterson Associates**, and even the ground-floor **McDonald's** seems graceful here. ♦ 36 W Randolph St (at N Dearborn St)

26 FORD CENTER ORIENTAL THEATRE

Central to the city's plan to create a theater district featuring "Broadway in Chicago" is the restored Oriental Theatre. Originally opened in 1926 as a movie house that also featured live performances, the Oriental was designed by famed theater architects the **Rapp Brothers**, **George** and **Cornelius**, who also designed the **Chicago** (175 N State St) and **Palace** (151 W Randolph). The first show to grace the restored stage was *Ragtime*. Recent productions have included *Jesus Christ Superstar* and *Little Shop of Horrors*. ♦ 24 W Randolph St (between N State and N Dearborn Sts). 782.2004 & www.broadwayinchicago.com

27 SCHOOL OF THE ART INSTITUTE DORMITORY

If this modern building looks very similar to the magnificent **Reliance Building** one block to the south, it's okay to blink, but don't think you're going crazy. Architect **Laurence Booth** designed this dormitory for students who attend the **School of the Art Institute** with that very idea in mind. At the request of Tony Jones, the president of the School of the Art Institute, Booth agreed to engage in a bit of repartee with the terra-cotta-clad masterpiece designed by **Daniel Burnham and Company** more than a century earlier. Instead of terra-cotta, Booth used a material called glass fiber-reinforced concrete. And although the ornate details of the original are of course lacking, Booth did manage to effectively mimic the look by using the famous "Chicago windows": fixed central panes with operable windows on their flanks. The effect is that the two buildings stand as bookends to the empty expanse of block 37, which someday may be

---

Restaurants/Clubs: Red | Hotels: Purple | Shops: Orange | Outdoors/Parks: Green | Sights/Culture: Blue

developed. ♦ 162 N State St (at W Randolph) ⓖ www.artic.edu

27 SCHOOL OF THE ART INSTITUTE GENE SISKEL FILM CENTER

Named for the late *Chicago Tribune* film critic, this is the new location of the film center, which attracts serious film buffs to see a wide range of art, classic, and overlooked films, sometimes supplemented with personal appearances by the filmmakers. ♦ Daily. 164 N State St (at W Randolph St) 846.2600. www.siskelfilmcenter.org

28 CHICAGO THEATER

Celluloid illusion and architectural fantasy went hand in hand when this lavish movie palace designed by **Rapp & Rapp** first opened its doors in 1928. The grandeur of the interior's baroque forms was restored in 1986 by **Daniel P. Coffey & Associates** after a period of neglect, and now concerts, touring companies of Broadway musicals, dance performances, and variety shows take the stage. A white terra-cotta triumphal arch hides behind the huge marquee. ♦ 175 N State St (between E Randolph and E Lake Sts). 462.6300

29 BROADBAND CAFE

$ Don't have your laptop with you but need to check your e-mail? Then this would be a good place to visit. If your stomach starts to growl, there are pastries, sandwiches, and even a few lunch specials. ♦ Daily. 58 E Randolph St (between N Wabash Ave and N State St). 252.0060

30 GUILD FOR THE BLIND CONSUMER PRODUCT CENTER

Shopping for products for the 10 million Americans who have serious vision impairment can be very difficult for obvious reasons. The most convenient way is through the mail, but that means that merchandise cannot be inspected before it is purchased. This terrific little shop has an amazing array of items (about 250 in all) designed to make life more manageable and fulfilling for people who are blind. And because it is a not-for-profit, customers can expect reasonable prices. ♦ 17th floor—180 N Michigan Ave (between E Randolph and E Lake Sts). M-F: 8:30AM-4:30PM. 236.8569, fax 236.8128. www.guildfortheblind.org

30 PAULINE BOOK AND MEDIA CENTER

The Daughters of St. Paul perform their mission of preaching through communication by selling Roman Catholic and inspirational books, tapes, and videos in shops like this throughout the US. A peaceful chapel in the back of the shop is open during store hours. Mail order is available. ♦ M-Sa. 172 N Michigan Ave (between E Randolph and E Lake Sts). 346.4228. www.pauline.org

31 150 NORTH MICHIGAN AVENUE

Turned on a 45-degree angle and bisected into two triangular towers, this 1984 office building by **A. Epstein & Sons** has a sloping glass roof that slices diagonally through the top 10 floors. At night this slanted diamond is dramatically outlined in a string of white lights. Although its sail-like mirrored planes and distinctive top are generally admired by the public, architects and the press have criticized the prominently located building as being disruptive of Michigan Avenue's architectural continuity. ♦ At E Randolph St

32 RANDOLPH STREET STATION

The **South Shore** and **Metra Electric** trains going to Chicago's South Side are served by this station, which is entirely undistinguished except for one brief piece of gangster lore. Jake Dingle, a reporter who covered Al Capone and friends, was assassinated here; after his death, it was discovered that he'd been getting huge payoffs from the boys for letting them know what the police and FBI knew about them. ♦ E Randolph St and N Michigan Ave. 836.7000

33 PRUDENTIAL BUILDING

Built in 1955 from a design by **Naess & Murphy**, this gray limestone and aluminum structure was the tallest building in the city for more than a decade. Look for sculptor Alfonso Iannelli's exterior relief of the Rock of Gibraltar, which is the company's trademark. ♦ 130 E Randolph St (at N Beaubien Ct)

34 AON BUILDING

Holding the title of the tallest marble-clad structure in the world turned out to be more liability than asset for the owners of what was originally the **Standard Oil Building**. Designed by **Edward Durell Stone** with **Perkins & Will** and built in 1974, this monolith was clothed in white Carrara marble that proved unable to withstand Chicago's extreme temperatures and high winds. The gleaming white panels have been replaced with speckled granite. The reflecting pool in the lower level plaza contains *Sounding*, a 1975 sculpture designed by Harry Bertoia; its breeze-ruffled clusters of copper rods produce pleasant metallic sounds. ♦ 200 E Randolph Dr (at N Stetson Ave)

35 HOTEL ALLEGRO

$$ One of Chicago's newest, and arguably its hippest, hotels is the result of a smart, creative renovation of the sagging old **Bismarck**, once legendary for its smoke-filled, secretive back-room meetings of the city's politicos. The ghosts of pols past still haunt the halls, despite the warm, colorful makeover by celebrated interior designer Cheryl Rowley. This 18-story hotel has 483 guest rooms, including 31 luxury suites with Jacuzzis and VCRs. Services and amenities include CD players, fax machines, two-line speaker phones, honor bars, irons and ironing boards, and hair dryers in every room. Twelve meeting rooms, each of which can accommodate up to 300 people, theater style, are included in the more than 17,000 square feet of meeting space. Within the Allegro, **312 Chicago** offers a reason to eat in. Nonsmoking rooms and weekend packages are available. ♦ 171 W Randolph St (at N Wells St). 236.0123, 800/643.1500; fax 236.0917 ♿ www.allegrochicago.com

36 CADILLAC PALACE THEATRE

Designed by legendary theater architects **George** and **Cornelius W. Rapp**, the brothers also responsible for the design of the **Chicago** and **Oriental Theaters**, this theater first opened in 1926 and became known as the flagship of the Orpheum Circuit, a chain of 50 theaters presenting vaudeville throughout the US and Canada. With rose-marbled walls, crystal chandeliers, gold plaster ornamentation, and huge mirrors, the theater resembles a French palace, which was the intention. During the mid-1970s, the management of the **Bismarck** (now the **Allegro**) transformed the auditorium into a banquet hall. In 1999, the 2,300-seat theater underwent a $20

million renovation. Lobbies have been restored to their original grandeur, including restoration of the stonework and original plaster, reconstructed to blend with its historical context. After the Cadillac division of General Motors purchased naming rights, the **Cadillac Palace** opened in November 1999 with a production of *Aida*. As part of the city's "Broadway in Chicago" concept, productions have included shows such as *Sweet Chairty* and *The Lion King*. ♦ 151 W Randolph St (at N LaSalle St). 977.1700. www.cadillacpalace.com, www.broadwayinchicago.com

37 CITY HALL–COUNTY BUILDING

The mayor hangs his hat on the fifth floor of this massive neoclassical structure designed by **Holabird & Roche** and built in 1911. Ongoing melodramas and aldermanic turf battles are acted out in the **City Council Chamber** on the second floor. Council meetings are open to the public, and when certain issues are up for debate, it's great entertainment. There is no set day for meetings, which are held about every 2 weeks. ♦ Bounded by N Clark and N LaSalle Sts and W Washington and W Randolph Sts. 744.3081 ♿

38 RICHARD J. DALEY CENTER

Civil courts and city and county offices are contained within this building's triple bays of russet Cor-Ten steel, which requires no maintenance and becomes more handsome with the passing years. Designed by **C.F. Murphy Associates**, the center opened in 1965. An eternal flame flickers in the adjacent plaza in memoriam to the late Richard J. Daley, mayor of Chicago for 21 years. The site of many civic gatherings, both organized and spontaneous, the plaza is perhaps best known as home to the Cor-Ten steel *Chicago Picasso*. Installed in 1967, the 50-foot-high Cubist sculpture is an abstraction of a woman's head. During the holidays, Chicago's official Christmas tree is set up on the plaza. The tree is created by lashing together as many as a hundred smaller evergreens to form one giant tree, which is trimmed with tens of thousands of ornaments and colored lights. ♦ Bounded by N Dearborn and N Clark Sts and W Washington and W Randolph Sts

38 WEST EGG CAFE

$ Basically a greasy spoon with a touch of class, this is a convenient stop for a quick bite. For breakfast, which is served all day, there are homemade muffins and eggs prepared some 30 different ways. For later in the day, there are salads, sandwiches, and pasta. ♦ American. M-F, breakfast and lunch.

Restaurants/Clubs: **Red** | Hotels: **Purple** | Shops: **Orange** | Outdoors/Parks: **Green** | Sights/Culture: **Blue**

21

66 W Washington St (between N Dearborn and N Clark Sts). 236.3322. Also at 620 N Fairbanks Ct (between E Ohio and E Ontario Sts). 280.8366

39 BLOCK 37

One of the several edifices demolished at this site was the office building where **Louis Sullivan** reportedly met his future partner, **Dankmar Adler**. Another razed office building on the site housed Clarence Darrow's law office. A huge mural by Roger Brown decorates a Commonwealth Edison substation that couldn't be demolished. **Helmut Jahn** was to design a shopping galleria on the spot, but the bottom fell out of the building boom before anything went up. In the 1980s a group of visionaries led by Cultural Affairs Commissioner Lois Weisberg decided that the city-owned land ought to be dedicated to public use: It became a giant outdoor skating rink in winter (see below) and Gallery 37, an arts-based employment program for teens, in summer. As *Access* went to press, there were reports that a possible deal was in the works to begin redevelopment, but if that plan were to fall through, it would not be the first time. ♦ Bounded by N State and N Dearborn Sts and W Washington and W Randolph Sts

Within Block 37:

SKATE ON STATE

Not quite as elegant as New York City's Rockefeller Center, this outdoor rink isn't quite as cramped either. There's a warming room and skate-rental area. Skating is also available two blocks east at Millennium Park. ♦ Admission. Dec-Mar: daily, when weather permits. 744.2883

40 MARSHALL FIELD'S

With more than 450 departments and 73 acres of merchandise, this Chicago legend would take untold days to explore. The story goes that Marshall Field said, "Give the lady what she wants," and the store has been doing just that since it opened (in a different location) in 1853. **D.H. Burnham & Co.** designed the present store between 1893 and 1907. Everything you could ever want in fashion, housewares, and furniture is arranged in departments around two galleried atriums, one of which is topped with a glass-mosaic dome designed by Louis Comfort Tiffany and unveiled in 1907. Specialty shops within the store feature designer boutiques, exotic food-stuffs, rare books, estate jewelry, and more. Melt-in-your-mouth Frango mints are Chicago's most popular take-home gift. A $110 million renovation restored the gold leaf to main-floor columns, added a skylit escalator atrium, and expanded the men's department to fill an entire city block along Wabash Avenue.

Among the augmentations is **Down Under**, a city of small shops on the lower level offering a dizzying array of housewares, hosiery, and more. The gourmet wine and food shops are near a bright, inviting food court, with various offerings that may be enjoyed at nearby tables. The seventh floor also has several restaurants to choose from, including the **Walnut Room** (781.3125) and the **Frango Café** (781.3181), an ice-cream parlor. Personal shoppers are available to assist you, and the bridal registry is an excellent service. And be sure to see the intricately created Christmas windows. An annual tradition among Chicagoans is lunch at the **Walnut Room** overlooking the towering, sparkling Christmas tree. In February 2005, Federated Department Stores announced that it was buying Field's parent company, May, setting up the possibility that one of Chicago's most venerated names would be changed. ♦ Daily. 111 N State St (between E Washington and E Randolph Sts). 781.1000. Also at Water Tower Place, 835 N Michigan Ave (at E Pearson St). 335.7700 ♿

41 CHICAGO CULTURAL CENTER

Shepley, Rutan & Coolidge, the Boston firm commissioned to design the **Art Institute of Chicago**, designed this 1897 building in the neoclassical style. Along Michigan Avenue, an Ionic colonnade supports a frieze bearing the names of historic authors. The main entrance, on the Washington Street side, opens to a grand staircase made of white Carrara marble inlaid with marble-and-glass mosaics. Head up these magnificent stairs to **Preston Bradley Hall**, lush with more marble and mosaics and topped by a spectacular illuminated Tiffany stained-glass dome. The **Grand Army of the Republic Exhibition Hall** (third floor on the north side) was inspired by Italian Renaissance palaces. Once the main library, the building presents a wide variety of high-quality cultural offerings, from art exhibitions—historical and contemporary—to lectures, concerts (particularly every Wednesday at noon), films, and theatrical performances; all are free to the public. This building is a must-see. ♦ Daily. 78 E Washington St (at N Michigan Ave)

42 CROW'S NEST RECORDS

Friendly, knowledgeable salespeople and a huge inventory make this one of the best stores in the city to buy CDs and tapes. ♦ M-Sa. 175 W Washington (between N LaSalle and N Wells Sts). 346.3489

43 CHICAGO TEMPLE (FIRST UNITED METHODIST CHURCH OF CHICAGO)

The "Chapel in the Sky," built in 1923 to plans by **Holabird & Roche**, rises 400 feet above ground, and its spire can be viewed only from

MOLE'S-EYE VIEW OF CHICAGO

Neither rain nor sleet nor rush-hour pedestrian traffic jams can keep you from walking in relative ease in the **Pedway**. Chicago's still-growing underground walkway connects the major buildings listed here, offers entrances to **CTA** public transportation, and is lined with numerous shops, services, and cafés. Recent renovations of some sections have made it a very pleasant stroll. The walkway is open Monday through Friday between 6:30AM and 6PM.

1	203 North LaSalle Street	7	Chicago Cultural Center
2	State of Illinois Center	8	Prudential Building
3	Chicago Title & Trust Center	9	Randolph Street Station
4	Richard J. Daley Center	10	3 First National Plaza
5	City Hall/County Building	11	First National Bank of Chicago
6	Marshall Field's		

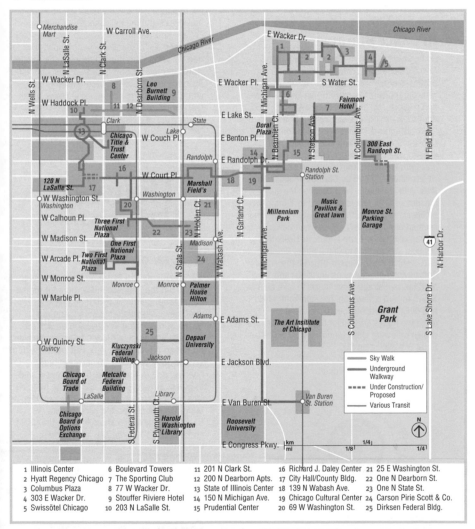

1 Illinois Center	6 Boulevard Towers	11 201 N Clark St.	16 Richard J. Daley Center	21 25 E Washington St.
2 Hyatt Regency Chicago	7 The Sporting Club	12 200 N Dearborn Apts.	17 City Hall/County Bldg.	22 One N Dearborn St.
3 Columbus Plaza	8 77 W Wacker Dr.	13 State of Illinois Center	18 139 N Wabash Ave.	23 One N State St.
4 303 E Wacker Dr.	9 Stouffer Riviere Hotel	14 150 N Michigan Ave.	19 Chicago Cultural Center	24 Carson Pirie Scott & Co.
5 Swissôtel Chicago	10 203 N LaSalle St.	15 Prudential Center	20 69 W Washington St.	25 Dirksen Federal Bldg.

Restaurants/Clubs: Red | Hotels: Purple | Shops: Orange | Outdoors/Parks: Green | Sights/Culture: Blue

a distance. At street level, a series of small stained-glass windows depicts the history of the church. Joan Miró's 93-foot-tall sculpture, *Miró's Chicago*, installed in 1981, sits in the adjacent narrow plaza. ♦ 77 W Washington St (at N Clark St)

45 INTERNATIONAL IMPORTING BEAD AND NOVELTY COMPANY

Baubles, bangles, and beads of every size, shape, color, and material pack this shop. So do theater people, clothing designers, and ordinary folks awed by all the goodies, from sequined patches to feathered Las Vegas–style headdresses. ♦ M-Sa. 111 N Wabash Ave (at E Washington St), seventh floor. 332.0061

44 RELIANCE BUILDING

Completed in 1895, this most elegant of the Chicago School skyscrapers, with large expanses of glass and delicate Gothic ornament wrought in creamy terra-cotta, fell into disrepair and neglect until the city of Chicago purchased it for $1.2 million in 1993, some 18 years after it was listed as a National Historic Landmark. Construction on the **Reliance Building**, an elegant structure designed by **Daniel Burnham** and **John Wellborn Root**, began in 1890 and was finished in 1895 by **Charles Atwood**, after Root died. Preceding by 3 decades the glass façades of skyscrapers designed by European architects in the 1920s, the 14-story structure seemed almost to defy gravity when viewed by Chicagoans in the early 1900s. In 1998, the city sold the building to Canal Street Hotel, L.L.C., which hired Chicago-based firms **Antunovich Associates** as architects and **McClier** as restoration architects to take on the $27.5 million restoration. The storefront, which had been altered, has been re-created to resemble Root's original bronze-and-granite design with wide glass windows. ♦ 32 N State St (at W Washington St)

Within the Reliance Building:

HOTEL BURNHAM

$$$ Appropriately, the hotel is named for **Daniel Burnham**, the legendary Chicago city planner to whom the advice "Make no small plans" is attributed and whose firm originally designed the historic building. The restoration of the building in the form of this

charming hotel is one of the most welcome improvements to downtown Chicago since the **Harold Washington Library** opened. It stands as proof, says *Chicago Tribune* architecture writer Blair Kamin, "that the city's old treasures can be put to modern uses." The lobby faithfully replicates the original building, including the mosaic floor, multi-colored marble ceiling, ornamental elevator grilles, and archways. The furnishings are leather and mahogany, giving the area a clubby atmosphere. Furnishings in the 103 guest rooms and 19 suites have deep blue and gold accenting, and beds have rich blue velvet headboards. Amenities include use of an in-house fitness facility, multiline phones, fax machines, and voice mail; 24-hour room service; complimentary morning paper and coffee; and evening wine reception. The hotel bills itself as "distinctively pet friendly"; call for details. Within the Burnham Hotel, the **Atwood Café** (named for Burnham's partner Charles Atwood) is a 75-seat restaurant serving contemporary American cuisine (daily, breakfast, lunch, and dinner). ♦ 1 W Washington St (at N State St). 782.1111, 877/294.9712; fax 782.0899. www.burnhamhotel.com

45 HEAVEN ON SEVEN

★$ Burgers and BLTs are on the coffee shop menu, but the cognoscenti come here for the Cajun food: gumbo, Cajun fried chicken, jambalaya, oyster-shrimp salad, and red beans and rice that will give you an itch for the Big Easy. Once a hidden treasure, **Heaven on Seven** has become very well known, with a second (and roomier) city location and a bustling one in Naperville. If you want a seat at lunch, arrive before 11:30AM; the obscure location doesn't deter enthusiastic regulars. Mardi Gras is celebrated here in style. ♦ Cajun/Creole/coffee shop ♦ M-Sa, breakfast and lunch. 111 N Wabash Ave (between E Washington and E Randolph Sts), seventh floor. 263.6443. Also at 600 N Michigan Ave (at E Ohio St), second floor. 280.7774

46 NORTHWESTERN ATRIUM CENTER

Architect **Helmut Jahn** successfully adapted the 1930s' streamlined forms to the building requirements of the 1980s in this impressive mixed-use building of green glass and aqua-tinted steel, constructed in 1987. Unlike many of his colleagues, who were inspired by older styles and buildings, Jahn is an unabashed modernist in his use of materials. The north and south façades step back in a series of curves to create a striking profile (undoubtedly inspired by the cascading walls and light fixtures in the **Board of Trade** lobby—both the original and Jahn's addition). An arched entrance on Madison Street leads to a dramatic multilevel lobby that serves the train station and office tower. The lobby's exposed-steel structure is inspired by the great 19th-century iron-skeleton train sheds. Here and at **O'Hare Airport**'s **United Airlines Terminal**, Jahn has created dynamic spaces that recapture the excitement of travel for even the most jaded commuter. ◆ 500 W Madison St (at N Canal St)

Within Northwestern Atrium Center:

RICHARD B. OGILVIE TRANSPORTATION CENTER (CHICAGO & NORTHWESTERN STATION)

This grand dame among railway stations was here long before the modern edifice that sits atop it. Entered from the north side of the building on the second level, it's one of four stations serving commuter railroads from the suburbs and beyond. ◆ 836.7000

47 RIVERSIDE PLAZA

In 1929 this **Holabird & Root** design was built right over train tracks leading into **Union Station** (the train smoke is vented through the roof). The riverfront plaza, which provides the best view of the building, shows its vertical piers and deep setbacks. The relief carving on the base depicts great people in the history of journalism, from an ancient scribe to a Lino-typist. The real treat is just inside the entrance: In the long tunnel-like concourse leading to the **Ogilvie Transportation Center** is a ceiling mural by John Warner Norton that uses jazzy, semiabstract forms to show the activities of the building's first owner, the *Chicago Daily News*. In the summer you can beat the traffic and reach Michigan Avenue by boat from the plaza. Vessels operated by the **Wendella** company dock here. ◆ 400 W Madison St (between N Wacker Dr and N Canal St)

48 CIVIC OPERA HOUSE

Above the grand colonnade along Wacker Drive rises this 1920s tower typical of archi-tects **Graham, Anderson, Probst & White**. The lavishly decorated Art Deco auditorium, home to the **Lyric Opera of Chicago** since the

1950s and used by ballet companies and other traveling troupes, has Egypt-inspired details. Jules Guerin selected rich vermilion and orange accented with gold leaf as the interior color scheme; he also designed the stage's lovely fire-curtain mural. The masks of comedy and tragedy and lyre, trumpet, palm leaf, and laurel wreath motifs appear in terra-cotta and bronze on the exterior and interior. Many Chicagoans consider it well worth making a cultural commitment to **Lyric** performances by buying season tickets. ◆ 20 N Wacker Dr (between W Madison and W Washington Sts). Lyric Opera box office: 332.2244 ᕲ www.lyricopera.org

49 ONE SOUTH WACKER DRIVE

Another of **Helmut Jahn**'s attempts to evoke 1930s skyscrapers with a glass box, this 1982 building's huge floor areas defy efforts at streamlining. ◆ At W Madison St

50 *DAWN SHADOWS*

This black-painted steel sculpture designed in 1983 by Louise Nevelson was inspired by the configuration of the elevated train tracks above Wells Street. One of the best views of the piece is from the station platform. ◆ Madison Plaza Bldg, 200 W Madison St (at N Wells St)

51 181 WEST MADISON STREET

Closely spaced columns of white granite with narrow mullions soar to nickel-plated finials at the parapets of this 1990 **Cesar Pelli & Associates** tower. The surface flattens on a gray day and shimmers when the sun shines. ◆ At S Wells St

52 TRATTORIA NO. 10

★★$$ Good basic and creative pasta dishes are the hallmarks of this attractive subterranean restaurant, which is warmly decorated with stucco walls, a terra-cotta floor, and a beamed ceiling. It's popular with the lunchtime business crowd, and because the menu and prices are the same at lunch and dinner, it's an especially good deal in the evening. The hot-appetizer buffet served at cocktail time, which includes all of the menu's appetizers plus pastas cooked and sauced before your eyes, is highly recommended. ◆ Italian ◆ M-F, lunch and dinner; Sa, dinner. Reservations recommended. Valet parking after 5:30PM. 10 N Dearborn St (between W Madison and W Washington Sts). 984.1718 ᕲ

52 SOPRAFFINA MARKETCAFFE

★$ Off-hours are likely best for a lunchtime visit to this popular cafeteria-style eatery—the line is long at noon, and all seats are filled

---

Restaurants/Clubs: Red | Hotels: Purple | Shops: Orange | Outdoors/Parks: Green | Sights/Culture: Blue

quickly. Run by the same people who operate **Trattoria No. 10** (see above), it offers lighter and less pricy fare—thin-crust pizza with spinach, asparagus, and goat cheese, along with a host of vegetable and pasta salads. Takeout is available, and Italian condiments, oils, and vinegars are sold in the market in the front of the restaurant. ♦ Italian ♦ M-F, 11AM-4PM. 10 N Dearborn St (between W Madison and W Washington Sts). 984.0044 & Also at 222 W Adams (between S Wells and S Franklin Sts), 726.4800; Aon Bldg, 200 E Randolph Dr (at N Stetson Ave), 729.9200; and other Loop locations

53 SEARS

One of the noteworthy changes that has taken place in the Loop in the 21st century is the return of Sears, which started here in the 19th century. After an 18-year hiatus in the suburbs, the company has opened its doors once again. Renovation of the exterior of the 17-story Boston Building, originally designed by **Holabird & Roche** in 1893, was done by **Daniel P. Coffey & Associates**. A pair of gray granite columns extend to the cornice on the second floor, in contrast with 19-foot-high windows framed in gold tones. The interior design was done by the Retail Group of Seattle along with Sears planners. Despite the decidedly un-Sears-like ambiance—the store feels spacious and uncluttered—it remains to be seen how successful the enterprise will be. Perhaps the company's recent acquisition of Lands' End will help. Meanwhile, you can still buy all the merchandise that the department store is known for—from washing machines to the jeans that go in them. ♦ Daily. 2 North State St (at W Madison St) 373.6000 & www.sears.com

54 ONE NORTH STATE

Though State Street hasn't yet fully regained its vitality as the nation's leading shopping street, some new stores indicate the direction a rejuvenation might take. Head up the escalator for **T. J. Maxx**'s often unruly collection of clothing, housewares, and decorative items, then down for **Filene's** extensive assortment of things to wear. At street level, **Garrett's** popcorn is a popular destination for commuters, and **Dunkin' Donuts** serves the anti-Starbucks crowd. ♦ Daily. 1 N State St (at E Madison St)

When a vacancy occurs on the city council—because of a death, resignation, or conviction for a criminal offense—the mayor has the authority to appoint a person to serve out the term. Of the 50 aldermen currently on the city council, almost half were first appointed to the council by Mayor Richard M. Daley.

55 SILVERSMITH BUILDING

Designed by **Peter J. Weber** of the celebrated firm **D. H. Burnham & Co.**, the **Silversmith** is an overlooked gem of the Arts and Crafts style, built in 1897. Like most buildings of the period, it also followed the Chicago Commercial style—over five stories tall, few façade projections, and a regular rhythm of same-size windows—prompted by the demands of commerce following the Great Fire of 1871. The upper floors have a warm monochromatic redbrick and unglazed terra-cotta, rounded-corner flat pilasters, and rough brick attached columns. The lower floors, clad in dark green terra-cotta, have a simple zigzag surround on the windows, typifying the geometrical designs that marked the Arts and Crafts movement. The Silversmith acquired its name because of its original use by jewelers and silversmiths, who found its generous natural light and ventilation an asset to their work. Over the years, it fell into disrepair, until it was purchased by developer David Friedman in 1994. It was listed on the National Register of Historic Places in 1997. ♦ 10 S Wabash Ave (at E Madison St)

Within the Silversmith Building:

CHICAGO
THE SILVERSMITH

THE CROWNE PLAZA CHICAGO— THE SILVERSMITH

$$$ Continuing the trend started in Lower Manhattan, this was the first Loop project in which a venerable (and practically vacant) office building was converted into a boutique hotel. Ronna Friedman, wife and partner of developer David Friedman, supervised the interior decoration to create a look that faithfully replicates the Arts and Crafts style of the original building. To this end, she has furnished the hotel with reproductions of Stickley furniture from the period. The overall result is an atmosphere of sophistication and efficiency. There are 143 guest rooms, including 63 suites. All have 12-foot ceilings, oversize bathrooms, and extra-large windows. (During the rehab, three layers of glass were installed behind the original windows to soundproof the rooms from the El train, which rolls by outside.) There are numerous conveniences, such as in-room video checkout, data ports, and dual phone lines, as well as a full-service health club facility. Within the hotel, **Ada's Famous Deli** offers casual dining. ♦ 372.7696 (37-CROWNE); fax 372.7320 & www.crownplaza.com

56 JEWELERS ROW

For more than 150 years, the heart of Chicago's jewelry business has been located in a series of buildings along Wabash Avenue. Hundreds of businesses, many of which are still small family operations, are packed into the one-block stretch between Madison and Washington Streets. Within the street-level **Wabash Jewelers Mall**, 60 jewelers, separated only by their glass display cases, deal in every sort of jewelry imaginable, from birthstone rings to out-of-this-world diamond-and-ruby necklaces. Some are wholesalers, some retailers, and some make and repair jewelry at workbenches right in front of you. ♦ M-Sa. Mallers Bldg, 5 S Wabash Ave; 29 E Madison St; 5 N Wabash Ave; Wabash Jewelers Mall, 21 N Wabash Ave. 263.1757; 55 E Washington St

Within the Mallers Building:

MALLERS COFFEE SHOP & DELI

★$ This gem of a coffee shop is tucked away on the third floor. Fast service and arguably the best Reuben sandwich in the city keep those in the know coming back day after day. ♦ Deli ♦ M-F, breakfast and lunch. 263.7696

57 PRESIDENTIAL TOWERS

Solomon Cordwell Buenz & Associates' complex of four 49-story apartment towers with a 40-foot skylit atrium and an 80,000-square-foot mall is notable for several reasons, none of them architectural. Heralded as the hope of the blighted West Loop, it has been a financial headache since completion in 1986. Construction was subsidized with federal funds from the Department of Housing and Urban Development (HUD) obtained with the help of former US Representative Dan Rostenkowski, who arranged an exemption from public funding requirements, before being convicted of financial hanky-panky. ♦ 555-625 W Madison St (between S Clinton and S Des Plaines Sts)

58 CHICAGO MERCANTILE EXCHANGE

This is the most boisterous of the city's many trading exchanges. Futures and options on agricultural commodities (think pork bellies), foreign currencies, interest rates, stock market indices, and gold are traded on two separate floors via the open outcry system, wherein crowds of grown men and women shout loudly, make frantic hand signals, and jump up and down to get the seller's attention. The fourth-floor viewing gallery has been closed to the public, but there is a visitors' center in the lobby. ♦ Free. M-F, 7AM-3:15PM. 30 S Wacker Dr (at W Monroe St). 930.8249 &

59 303 WEST MADISON STREET

Color and disciplined variety characterize **Skidmore, Owings & Merrill**'s finely detailed, modestly scaled 1988 office building, geared to the smaller tenant. Leaded colored glass in the spirit of **Frank Lloyd Wright** enlivens the Franklin Street entrance. ♦ At S Franklin St

60 CHICAGO LOOP SYNAGOGUE

Look for the *Hands of Peace* metal sculpture by Israeli artist Henri Azaz stretching out from the façade, and the stained-glass window by Abraham Rattner illuminating the spacious interior of this 1958 building, which was designed by **Loebl Schlossman & Bennett**. ♦ 16 S Clark St (between W Monroe and W Madison Sts). 346.7370 &

61 BANK ONE BUILDING

C.F. Murphy Associates with **Perkins & Will** designed this building, which was completed in 1969. Tapered and graceful, the sweeping curve of its north and south sides expresses its functional needs: The larger floor area is at the base, where commercial banking operations are located. The plaza is a popular summertime gathering place. Ledges offer comfortable perches for sun worshipping, chatting, munching, and enjoying summer lunchtime concerts, and Marc Chagall's massive five-sided architectural mosaic, *The Four Seasons* (1975), provides a focal point. The 70-foot-long piece depicts the artist's fantasy views of Chicago in all seasons. A mosaic bed of flowers "planted" on the top of the sculpture can be appreciated only from the windows of surrounding skyscrapers. ♦ 2 S Dearborn St (at W Madison St)

On the Bank One plaza:

NICK'S FISHMARKET

★$$$ Big, comfy booths, each with a phone jack and a dimmer switch, are conducive to privacy—whether for business or romance—at the new venue of this restaurant with an Art Deco décor. The fresh fish is fine, especially grilled, as are the hard-to-find seafood choices, such as Hawaiian *opakapaka* (pink snapper) and abalone. Service is attentive, even obsequious; prices are steep, and it's open late. In addition to the main dining room is the more casual **Nick's Bar and Grill**. There's valet parking after 6PM. ♦ Seafood ♦ M-F, lunch and dinner; Sa, dinner. Reservations required; jacket recommended. 621.0200. Also at 10275 W Higgins Rd (at Mannheim Rd), Rosemont. 847/298.8200 & www.nicksfishmarketchicago.com

Restaurants/Clubs: Red | Hotels: Purple | Shops: Orange | Outdoors/Parks: Green | Sights/Culture: Blue

62 INLAND STEEL BUILDING

In 1957 **Skidmore, Owings & Merrill** boldly turned this stainless-steel and glass-curtain–walled skyscraper design inside out. Supporting columns on the exterior allow for unbroken floor space inside; even the mechanical facilities (including elevators) are housed in a separate structure to the east. ♦ 30 W Monroe St (at S Dearborn St)

62 SHUBERT THEATER

Touring Broadway musicals often land in this 1904 theater, designed by **Edmund C. Krause**. Included in the new "Broadway in Chicago" program, the Shubert has undergone something of a rebirth, offering productions such as *Sweet Charity* and *Tallulah* with Kathleen Turner. ♦ 22 W Monroe St (between S State and S Dearborn Sts). 977.1700 ♿ www.broadwayinchicago.com

63 CARSON PIRIE SCOTT & COMPANY

This stunning building, **Louis Sullivan**'s last major commission in Chicago, was built between 1899 and 1904. Above the second story of what was originally the **Schlesinger & Meyer Company Store**, the steel frame is clad in terra-cotta. At street level, intricate cast-iron panels framing display windows are encrusted with **Sullivan**'s ornamentation that melds natural and geometric forms. His rounded corner entrance is spectacular. Additions by **D.H. Burnham & Co.** and **Holabird & Root** follow **Sullivan**'s design. In 1979 it was beautifully restored by **John Vinci**. As for the store, **Carson**'s doesn't carry the high-end merchandise you find at **Field's**, but the selection is wide and of good quality. **Level Six** is the spot for linens and housewares designed for the yuppie market. The **Corporate Level** caters to the needs of the stylish businesswoman, offering everything from beautiful suits to the shoes, belts, and scarves that complete an ensemble. ♦ Daily. 1 S State St (at E Madison St). 641.7000 ♿

64 IWAN RIES & CO.

Since 1857, this tobacco store has been purveying pipes (it stocks more than 25,000), cigars (a refrigerated walk-in humidor holds a fine selection that can be warmed immediately in the store's microwave), tobacco, and smoking accessories directly

Starting in the early 1900s and throughout most of this century, the intersection of State and Madison Streets was often called the world's busiest corner. The truth of the statement was never tested, but it did lure many tourists to the spot.

and by mail to a vast number of aficionados. Don't miss the **Pipe Museum** within the store; it has many rare and elaborately carved pieces. ♦ M-Sa. 19 S Wabash Ave (between E Monroe and E Madison Sts), second floor. 372.1306. www.iwanries.com

65 GAGE GROUP

In 1899 **Holabird & Roche** designed these three commercial buildings for the wholesale millinery trade. Then the tenant of the northernmost building commissioned **Louis Sullivan** to design a more elaborate façade. In 1902 four stories were added to the building, altering the original proportions, and in the early 1950s, the ground floor's cast-iron ornament was removed; a fragment of it is now on display across the street in the **Art Institute of Chicago** (see page 35). ♦ 18-30 S Michigan Ave (between E Monroe and E Madison Sts)

66 UNIVERSITY CLUB

In 1909 **Holabird & Roche** added Collegiate Gothic, appropriately enough, to the potpourri of building styles along the avenue. This is a private, members-only club, but visitors can wander into the lobby. ♦ 76 E Monroe St (at S Michigan Ave)

67 AT&T CORPORATE CENTER

Though built in 1989, this **Skidmore, Owings & Merrill** skyscraper has polished granite-curtain walls with strong vertical lines that recall the styles of the 1920s. Go into the luxuriant lobby of Italian marble, gold leaf, and rich wood trim, which also features a masterful trompe l'oeil mural by Richard Haas. Take the escalator to the second level for great views through a series of wood-trimmed cutouts. The "bustle" addition to the south is the **US Gypsum Building**, which was designed by the same architects in 1991. **Café Bon Appetit** (332.1075) offers light fare for breakfast and lunch Monday through Friday. ♦ 227 W Monroe St (between S Wells and S Franklin Sts)

68 ITALIAN VILLAGE

★$$ Three restaurants are housed in one building. **La Cantina** is a clublike café that serves both American and Italian specialties with seafood. **The Village** is decorated with murals of villages, twinkling star lights, and booths like individual houses. It serves good, traditional, reasonably priced Italian food and is popular with the young business crowd. **Vivere** has a dramatic Baroque décor courtesy of hotshot designer **Jordan Mozer** and features sophisticated regional Italian dishes along with an outstanding selection of about 1,500 wines. These restaurants are some of a handful in the Loop that keep late-night hours. ♦ Italian ♦ La Cantina: M-F, lunch and dinner; Sa, dinner. The Village: daily, lunch and dinner; Vivere: M-F, lunch and dinner; Sa, dinner. Valet parking for dinner only. 71 W Monroe St (between S Dearborn and S Clark Sts). La Cantina and The Village, 332.7005; Vivere, 332.4040

69 PALMER HOUSE HILTON

$$$ The Great Fire reduced Potter Palmer's original hotel to ashes only 13 days after it opened, but it was rebuilt in 1875. The French Empire-style lobby of **Holabird & Roche**'s elegant 1927 replacement, complete with 12 ceiling paintings by Louis Rigal, is located on the second floor; the first is given over to an arcade of shops and restaurants. The 1,639 rooms and 88 suites are warmly residential with rich hues and walnut furnishings. Two rooms per floor are designed for guests with disabilities. The two-story, top-level **Towers** is an exclusive section with its own lobby, lounge, and concierge. The fitness center has a pool, whirlpool, steam room, sauna, and exercise equipment and offers aerobics and massages. A business and conference center has computers and secretarial services. Restaurants include the once trendy **Trader Vic's**; the **French Quarter**, which serves American food; and **Big Downtown**, a sports bar and grill. Weekend packages are available. ♦ 17 E Monroe St (between S Wabash Ave and S State St). 726.7500, 800/445.8667; fax 917.1779 ♿

Within the Palmer House Hilton:

PENDLETON PRODUCTS STORE

An abundance of rich plaids fills this small arcade shop, which carries blankets, scarves, and apparel. It would be difficult to choose a favorite tartan. ♦ M-Sa. 119 S State St (between E Adams and E Monroe Sts). 372.1699 ♿

70 ARTS & ARTISANS, LTD.

Filled with handcrafted work by American designers, this shop is a good spot to find a souvenir for someone really special. Browse among the vases, lamps, paperweights, kaleidoscopes, and jewelry displayed. ♦ Daily. 108 S Michigan Ave (between E Adams and E Monroe Sts). 641.0088; fax 855.0994. www.artsandartisans.com

71 COSI

★$ Already a fixture on the East Coast, with 43 locations, this relative newcomer to Chicago is a welcome addition to the upscale fast-food dining scene started with the **Corner Bakery** a few years ago. Cosi is Italian for "things," and there are many things Italian on the menu and in the décor. It has three personalities, depending on the time of day. In

the morning it's a coffee and muffin bar, around lunchtime it's soup and sandwiches served cafeteria style, and after 5PM there's table service. The specialty is panini, sandwiches made with rectangular bread that has the texture of pizza crust and the taste of a home-baked biscuit. ♦ Italian café ♦ Daily, breakfast, lunch, and dinner. 116 S Michigan Ave (between E Adams and E Monroe Sts). 263.6595 ♿ Also at 57 E Grand Ave (between N Rush St and N Wabash Ave). 321.1990 ♿, and several other locations around the city

72 RAND MCNALLY MAP AND TRAVEL STORE

An excellent selection of travel guides and maps, historic, topographic, and the basic road variety, is offered. The great array of literature and video travelogues for the armchair traveler, geographic games and toys, and language guides may well give you wanderlust even if you aren't planning a journey. ♦ M-F. 150 S Wacker Dr (at W Adams St). 332.2009. Also at 444 N Michigan Ave (at E Illinois St). 321.1751

73 W CHICAGO CITY CENTER

$$$ Formerly the Midland Hotel, this 1920s hotel sits in the heart of the financial district. Following a recent renovation in which the facility was spiffed up to create a more hip look, the lobby has been remodeled to create the feel of a comfortable living room. If you've got teenagers in your house, the DJ spinning music from the surrounding balcony may indeed make you feel like you're at home. There are 390 guest rooms, 47 "mega-size" rooms, and 12 suites. All have oversize desks with new tech conveniences, including high-speed Internet access. Within the hotel the **WE Cafe** serves Northern Italian fare in a relaxed atmosphere, the **W Cafe** provides casual Mediterranean, and drinks flow freely in the **W Living Room** and **Whiskey Bar**. If you need a workout, there's a fitness center in the hotel. Weekend packages are available. ♦ 172 W Adams St (between S LaSalle and S Wells Sts). 332.1200; fax 917.5771 ♿ www.whotels.com

74 190 SOUTH LASALLE STREET

John Burgee and **Philip Johnson**'s first building in Chicago went up in 1987. The five-story red granite base is similar to the **Rookery Building** across the street (see page 30), and the copper-clad gabled top recalls architect **John Wellborn Root**'s now-demolished Masonic Temple. The pink granite tower is an elegant addition to the LaSalle Street canyon, and the cathedral-scale lobby is its showpiece. Rich marble spans floors and

---

Restaurants/Clubs: Red | Hotels: Purple | Shops: Orange | Outdoors/Parks: Green | Sights/Culture: Blue

walls, and the dazzling barrel-vaulted ceiling is covered in gold leaf. *Chicago Fugue*, a 28-foot-high welded bronze sculpture by Anthony Caro, fills a niche at the northern end; the south lobby is dominated by an iridescent weaving by Helena Hernmarck that pictures the Chicago Plan of 1909. ♦ At W Adams St

75 SYDEL & SYDEL LTD.

High-quality gems, beautifully designed jewelry, and outstanding service make this store a particular favorite of LaSalle Street businesspeople with a romantic mission. Husband and wife Jeff and Mary Lou Sydel are among those who will attend to your needs with patience and excellent advice. ♦ M-F; Sa by appointment only. 208 S LaSalle St (between W Quincy and W Adams Sts). 332.4653

76 ROOKERY BUILDING

This well-known Chicago gem, with its rusticated masonry base, Romanesque arches, and Moorish and Venetian details, has presided over South LaSalle Street since 1888, when it was built to plans by **Burnham & Root**. The building's name derives from the temporary **City Hall** that occupied the site after the 1871 fire; the dilapidated structure was a favorite pigeon roost. Two rooks at the LaSalle Street entrance playfully refer to these origins. In 1905 **Frank Lloyd Wright** was commissioned to remodel the lobby and light court, and this interior space retains his designed ornament. The building was restored in 1991 to its circa-1910 appearance by the **McClier Corporation** and **Hasbrouck Peterson Associates**. ♦ 209 S LaSalle St (between W Quincy and W Adams Sts)

77 MARQUETTE BUILDING

This 1895 building's restrained decoration and pattern of large windows that express the steel structure within make it the archetypal Chicago School office building. Although the monumental cornice that originally terminated the base-shaft-capital composition was removed in the 1950s, the rest of the façade, including the original storefronts, was carefully restored by **Holabird & Roche** in 1980. Notice the superb entrance and lobby on Dearborn Street. Entrance-door kickplates sport tomahawks, and pushplates are adorned with bronze panther heads designed by Edward Kemeys, a 19th-century animal sculptor whose best-loved beasts are the **Art Institute** lions (see page 37). Elaborate panels above the front door and in the lobby illustrate events in the life of Father Jacques Marquette, the French missionary who was one of the first Europeans to traverse the upper Mississippi in the 17th century. J.A. Holzer designed the lobby balcony's mosaic of Tiffany glass and mother-of-pearl; he later worked on the Tiffany mosaics at the **Chicago Cultural Center**. ♦ 140 S Dearborn St (at W Adams St)

78 BANK ONE CENTER

Designed by Ricardo Bofill, this 39-story tower is a welcome addition to the former site of Montgomery Ward's, which had been vacant for more than 15 years. Built like a classic column with a heavy base, the building's curved glass walls create brilliant reflections during sunrise and sunset. The gold sculpture in the lobby is a limited-edition cast of the *Winged Victory of Samothrace*. ♦ 131 S Dearborn St (at W Adams St)

79 BERGHOFF RESTAURANT

★★$$ The bustling beer-hall atmosphere in this oak-paneled landmark dates back to 1893, when the enterprise was founded as an outdoor beer garden at the World's Columbian Exposition. Particularly favored by tourists, the huge dining room is usually full, so expect a wait at lunch and before 7PM. German classics such as Wiener schnitzel and sauerbraten are recommended, and the creamed spinach is a nice side order. Wash down your meal with a mug of Berghoff light or dark beer, on tap. The **Berghoff Café**, a stand-up bar on the east end of the main floor offering freshly carved roast beef, turkey, and corned beef sandwiches on fresh Berghoff's bread, is a fun and inexpensive spot for a quick lunch. ♦ German/American ♦ M-Sa, lunch and dinner. Reservations recommended for five or more. 17 W Adams St (between S State and S Dearborn Sts). 427.3170 ♿

80 MILLER'S PUB

★$$ Since 1935 this bustling watering hole and chophouse has been a popular haunt, particularly for night owls. The walls are festooned with autographed publicity shots of celebrities who have visited through the years. Go for the ambiance, not the cuisine. ♦ American ♦ Daily, lunch and dinner until 2AM. 134 S Wabash Ave (at E Adams St). 645.5377 ♿

81 RUSSIAN TEA CAFE

★★$$ Not too long ago, Klara and Vadim Muchnik were in their native Uzbekistan, but Chicagoans are fortunate they found their way here to open this charming spot around the corner from **Symphony Center**. Ukrainian borscht is the house specialty; the marinated beets and Tashkent carrot salad are far better here than tourists in the Muchniks' homeland are likely to have; the gefilte fish and stuffed cabbage are also winners. Afternoon tea is served from 2:30 to 4:30PM. ♦ Russian ♦ Daily, lunch and dinner. Reservations recommended. 77 E Adams St (between S Michigan and S Wabash Aves). 360.0000

81 POSTER PLUS

Chicago's largest collection of vintage posters, including spectacular selections of London Transport Board, **South Shore** line, and French advertising posters, is sold here. Also offered are historic Chicago, fine art, and contemporary placards. ♦ Daily. 200 S Michigan Ave (at E Adams St). 461.9277 ♿ www.posterplus.com

82 ORCHESTRA HALL/ SYMPHONY CENTER

Daniel Burnham, an Orchestral Association trustee, donated his services to this project, a response to complaints about the vastness of the **Auditorium Theatre** lodged by Theodore Thomas, organizer and first conductor of the **Chicago Symphony Orchestra** (**CSO**). The redbrick Georgian Revival–style building with its more intimate hall was a significant addition to the prominent cultural institutions springing up along Michigan Avenue at the turn of the 19th century. In October 1997, a $110 million, 3-year renovation and expansion project headed by the firm of **Skidmore, Owings & Merrill** was completed. The renovated space includes a new artistic support wing, an education and administration wing, a six-story arcade that runs from South Wabash to South Michigan Avenues, and an atrium rotunda illuminated by a skylight that links the three buildings. New facilities include **Buntrock Hall**, a smaller rehearsal/performance space; practice rooms; a radio broadcast and recording studio; and the **Eloise W. Martin Center**, the CSO's interactive music-learning space. Within Orchestra Hall, the renovation included making acoustical improvements, enlarging the stage, raising the roof, and adding an acoustical canopy and new seating.

Daniel Barenboim is currently music director of this internationally renowned orchestra, now more than a century old. Tickets to single

performances can be difficult to come by, as subscribers tend to fill the house. But persevere—the concerts are well worth the effort. The hall is also home to **Chicago Symphony Chorus**, which presents, among other performances, the annual *Do-It-Yourself Messiah*. ♦ Box office M-Sa; Su varies according to concert schedule. 220 S Michigan Ave (between E Jackson Blvd and E Adams St). 294.3333 ♿ www.cso.org

Within Symphony Center:

RHAPSODY

★★★$$ This dazzling, glass-walled restaurant offers a view into the **Symphony Center** atrium. It also features exquisite cuisine. From the excellently presented dishes—including lobster salad, rack of baby lamb chops with herb oil, and turkey pot pie with sage cream sauce—the accent here is distinctly American. The desserts, especially the chocolate ice cream–vanilla custard bombe with raspberry sauce, rate a standing ovation. Service is efficient; the waiters really race around during the bustling preconcert rush. The back entrance to the hall will save you a few precious moments getting to your seat before the curtain, and you can also enter the restaurant on Adams Street. ♦ American ♦ M-F, lunch and dinner; Sa, Su, dinner. Reservations recommended. 65 E Adams St (between S Michigan and S Wabash Aves). 786.9911 ♿

CHICAGO SYMPHONY STORE

This gift shop sells recordings of the **Chicago Symphony Orchestra** and **Chorus**, as well as a variety of upscale, music-themed souvenirs, including music boxes and lamps. ♦ Daily; until 30 minutes after concert on performance nights. 294.3345 ♿ www.symphonystore.com

83 UNION STATION

The vast restored lobby here evokes the era when train travel was an experience in itself, not just a means of getting from one place to another. **Amtrak** trains as well as commuter lines from the suburbs use this station. ♦ W Adams and S Canal Sts. Amtrak, 800/USA.RAIL; Metra (suburban line), 836.7000

84 SEARS TOWER

Built in 1974, this is America's tallest building. **Skidmore, Owings & Merrill**'s innovative structural system consists of nine square tubes that together form a larger square. The tubes rise to different levels—only two of them continue all the way to the top—and create a dramatic staggered profile. The 1,454-foot-tall structure was the highest

---

Restaurants/Clubs: Red | **Hotels: Purple** | **Shops: Orange** | **Outdoors/Parks: Green** | **Sights/Culture: Blue**

allowed by the Federal Aeronautics Administration at the time it was built. More than 100 elevators transport the 12,000 people who visit the building each day. Take a ride to the **Skydeck Observatory** on the 103rd floor for a spectacular panoramic view. In 1985 the same architectural firm added a four-story vaulted atrium on Wacker Drive to enlarge the lobby and make the retail space more appealing. The *Chicago Experience* at the visitors' center is a multi-image slide show. Also featured is a 9-foot working model of the tower. ♦ Skydeck: fee. Daily until 10PM April-Oct, 8PM Nov-March. Last ticket sold 30 minutes before closing. 233 S Wacker Dr (between W Jackson Blvd and W Adams St). 875.9696 ♿ www.the-skydeck.com

Within the Sears Tower:

UNIVERSE

In 1974, sculptor Alexander Calder turned on the switch activating the motors that power the five colored elements of his dynamic piece. A sun, a black pendulum, and three flowers are among the moving parts of this 33-foot-high construction. ♦ Calder level

MRS. LEVY'S DELI

$ This huge New York–style deli does a land-office business. Lunchtime waits are long, whether you want a black leather booth or favor the pale green lunch counter. Signed photographs of celebrities who have eaten here line the walls, along with advertisements for Mrs. Levy's own brand of matzoh balls and other treats. Milk shakes are a specialty and worth the calories. ♦ Deli ♦ M-F, breakfast and lunch. S Franklin St (between W Jackson Blvd and W Adams St). 993.0530

THE CORNER BAKERY

★$ This branch of the local chain (one of which seems to be popping up on every corner in Chicago) is ideal for a light lunch or afternoon coffee break. Fresh salads, sandwiches, and a variety of rolls and breads are served up with a tasty selection of juices and a pleasing blend of coffees. ♦ Deli ♦ M-F, breakfast, lunch, and early dinner. Franklin St (between W Jackson Blvd and W Adams St). 466.0200. Also at numerous locations throughout the city

85 BANK OF AMERICA BUILDING

Formerly the **Continental Illinois National Bank and Trust Company**, this building may be due for another renaming, pending the results of bank-merger mania. Its classical exterior is relatively unadorned. This 1924 building's striking feature is the grand, block-long banking floor with majestic Ionic columns, painted friezes, and high coffered ceiling. **Graham, Anderson, Probst & White**

were the architects. The smell of coffee (courtesy of **Starbucks**) greets visitors to the handsome lobby. Walls once lined with tellers' booths are now home to a collection of stores, including **Ann Taylor**. ♦ 231 S LaSalle St (between W Jackson Blvd and W Quincy St)

Within the Bank of America Building:

86 FEDERAL CENTER

Shortly before his death, **Mies van der Rohe** (with **Schmidt, Garden & Erickson, C.F. Murphy Associates**, and **A. Epstein & Sons**) designed these buildings, completed in 1975. Light gray granite paves the plaza and building lobbies of the vast 4.5-acre site. The spare geometry and sleek sophistication of these three velvety black steel-and-glass structures—a single-story post office and two office buildings—are heightened by contrast to Alexander Calder's red *Flamingo* stabile (1974). Pedestrians can walk through the soaring curves of this 53-foot-tall sculpture, a favorite Chicago landmark. ♦ S Dearborn St (between W Jackson Blvd and W Adams St)

CAFFÉ BACI

★$ Garlic, dried peppers, and herbs decorate the entrance to this Italian deli—and accent the food as well. There are American sandwiches (prime rib, turkey breast) and Italian panini sandwiches (try the eggplant with mozzarella), plus a variety of salads. The café serves *dolci* (sweets) and *bibite* (drinks), for midmorning or afternoon snacks too. ♦ American/Italian ♦ M-F, breakfast and lunch. 629.1818. Also at 77 W Wacker Dr (at N Clark St). 629.2224; 2 N LaSalle St (at W Madison St) 629.2215. www.caffebaci.com

87 SANTA FE BUILDING

Originally the **Railway Exchange Building**, this was the location of **Daniel Burnham's** architectural office. Burnham designed it himself; it was completed in 1904. On the exterior, bright white-glazed terra-cotta is delicately molded in classical details. Elegantly restored in 1985 by **Frye, Gillan & Molinaro**, the skylit lobby with its grand central staircase must be visited. The stenciled Pompeiian decoration on the skylight rafters and the marble floor pattern with a five-color border were part of the original design but weren't added until the restoration. ♦ 224 S Michigan Ave (at E Jackson Blvd)

Within the Santa Fe Building:

Chicago Architecture Foundation (CAF) Shop and Tour Center

Visitors wishing to unravel the mysteries and histories of Chicago's buildings and neighborhoods should not pass up this shop. In addition to its huge selection of architecture books and periodicals, guidebooks and maps, children's books and toys, and unusual gifts with an architectural bent, the center has an exhibition gallery and offers lectures and more than 50 tours (by foot, bike, boat, and bus) that cover most of Chicago. ♦ Fee for tours. Daily. 922.3432; fax 922.0481. Also at John Hancock Michigan (875 N Michigan Ave). 751.1380 ♿ www.architecture.org

Sherry-Brener Ltd.

Here's a music publisher that also sells fine handmade musical instruments, mainly string, new and used (99% of good violins are over 300 years old, instructs the proprietor). The shop also repairs instruments and offers lessons for the serious student. ♦ Daily. 427.5611 ♿ www.guitarsofspain.com

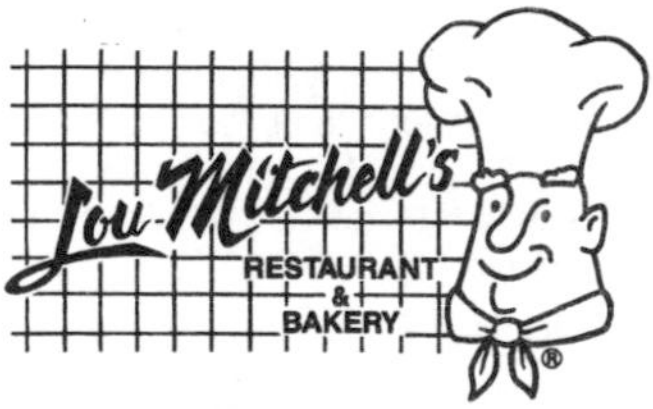

88 Lou Mitchell's

★$ This hole-in-the-wall has been popular for breakfast since it opened in 1935, thanks to really good coffee with fresh cream, double-yolk eggs, omelettes and hash browns served in skillets, and homemade jams. On Saturday expect a long wait for a seat at the cafeteria-style tables. ♦ American ♦ Daily, breakfast and lunch. 565 W Jackson Blvd (between S Clinton and S Jefferson Sts). 939.3111

89 311 South Wacker Drive

Kohn Pedersen Fox's largest—and least successful—Chicago endeavor was built in 1990. The 65-story structure is the tallest reinforced concrete building in the world, and its façade features a dizzying composition of granite and glass. The landscaping surrounding the building is impressive, and the barrel-vaulted winter garden is an attractive pass-through to the restaurant **Yvette Wintergarden**. ♦ Between W Van Buren St and W Jackson Blvd

90 Jack Schwartz

This little gem of a shop has peddled fine cigars since 1921. The original Mr. Schwartz has been blowing smoke rings in the great beyond for quite a while now, but the current owner, Bill O'Hara, can tell you everything you need to know about selecting just the right smoke for any occasion. And those smokes include a special exclusive house blend called Westminster. ♦ M-F 7:30AM-5PM. 141 W Jackson Blvd (at S LaSalle St). 782.7898, 888/SEE-JACK. www.jackschwartz.com

91 Chicago Board of Trade

This Art Deco monument to commerce (illustrated below) looks north up LaSalle Street, Chicago's equivalent to New York's Wall Street. The board was founded by 82 merchants in 1848 to stabilize grain prices and create a regulated marketplace. The world's oldest and largest futures and options-on-futures exchange was designed by **Holabird & Root** and built in 1930; **Murphy/Jahn** conceived the 1980 addition. The institution's agrarian focus is represented by relief sculptures

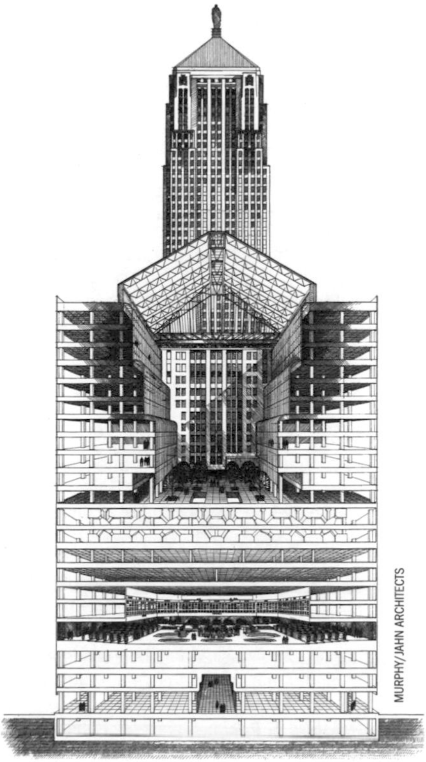

MURPHY/JAHN ARCHITECTS

flanking the huge clock over the entrance: A hooded figure holds a sheaf of wheat, and a Native American grasps a stalk of corn. The pyramidal roof is crowned by sculptor John Storrs's 30-foot statue of *Ceres*, the Roman goddess of grain. Cascading tiers of black-and-buff marble detail the striking three-story lobby. ♦ 141 W Jackson Blvd (between S LaSalle and S Financial Sts). 435.3590. www.cbot.com

92 MONADNOCK BUILDING

Boston developer Peter Brooks's demand that the exterior be without ornament was met by one of architect **John Wellborn Root**'s most powerful designs. No frills are needed, given the rhythm of gently projecting bays in this majestic structure (built in 1891) of deep purple-brown brick. The north half has load-bearing walls, 6 feet thick at street level (one of the tallest buildings ever constructed that way), whereas the south half (added 2 years later by **Holabird & Roche**) has a skeletal steel frame. This is a must-see. ♦ 53 W Jackson Blvd (between S Dearborn and S Federal Sts)

Within the Monadnock Building:

CAVANAUGH'S BAR AND RESTAURANT

$$ Standard fare, including burgers, chicken, and a variety of salads, is served in a pleasant wood-paneled room. Plenty of booths and tall, round bar tables are among the seating options. ♦ American ♦ M-F, lunch and dinner. 939.3125

93 CHICAGO BAR ASSOCIATION

This 16-story granite and precast-concrete melding of neo-Gothic and Miesian influences by **Tigerman, McCurry** went up in 1990. ♦ 321 S Plymouth Ct (between W Van Buren St and W Jackson Blvd)

94 DEPAUL UNIVERSITY LOOP CAMPUS

More than 10,000 students attend classes here at the colleges of law and business and the **School for New Learning** of this Catholic university (see the "Lincoln Park/DePaul" chapter for information on the main campus). Until 1989, the college's main building was the flagship store of the **Goldblatt Bros. Department Store**, and the *R* repeated throughout the exterior decoration is a reminder that this was originally built as a Rothschild store in 1912, designed by **Holabird & Roche**. A graceful, Prairie-style renovation created ground-floor retail space. While you're here, take a look at the nearby buildings on Jackson, which are vaguely medieval in style. ♦ 1 E Jackson Blvd (at S State St). 362.8000

95 THE SAVVY TRAVELLER

All manner of travel guides, maps, travel-oriented literature, and travel accessories are sold here. The shop also offers programs such as cooking demonstrations and lectures by travel authors. ♦ Daily. 310 S Michigan Ave (between E Van Buren St and E Jackson Blvd). 913.9800 ♿ www.thesavvytraveller.com

96 GRANT PARK

During the 1920s this park was built on landfill in accordance with **Daniel Burnham**'s Chicago Plan of 1909, a design blueprint that was influential in Chicago's development. The park occupies the northern edge of a strip of parks and beaches that stretches for miles on the South Side. Designed in French classical style, the park's 220 acres feature the country's largest remaining stand of elm trees, two symmetrical rose gardens, and vast grassy spaces that have invited promenades, picnics, and protests—the most famous occurred during the 1968 Democratic National Convention. The city's annual music galas, including jazz, blues, and gospel festivals, attract millions; an evening at any of these is a must. In the last week of June and the first week of July, the park becomes the site of the annual **Taste of Chicago**, a 10-day feeding frenzy featuring food from many of Chicago's leading restaurants. ♦ Concerts: W, F-Su nights June through August. Bounded by Lake Michigan, Michigan Ave, E Roosevelt Rd, E Randolph Dr, and E Randolph St. Concert information, 819.0614

Within Grant Park:

THE BOWMAN AND THE SPEARMAN

Two statues of Indians on horseback in heroic poses, bow and spear drawn, mark the entrance to the park at Congress Parkway. They were designed in 1928 by Ivan Meštrović.

INTERSECT/TWITTERMACHINE

These whimsical sculptures were unveiled in 1998. *Intersect*—the work of Chicago artist Carolyn Ottmers—is an arrangement of giant aluminum leaves engraved with maps of various Chicago neighborhoods. Above it and hidden in the trees, *Twittermachine*—created by German artists Stefan Micheel and Hans Winkler—features a box containing a solar-powered computer chip that emits birdlike chirps when sunlight hits it.

CLARENCE BUCKINGHAM FOUNTAIN

In 1927 Kate Buckingham presented this Beaux Arts fountain of Georgia pink marble to the city in honor of her brother Clarence, a trustee and benefactor of the **Art Institute**. Symbolizing Lake Michigan, **Bennett, Parsons & Frost**'s rococo fountain sits in a pool containing four bronze sea horses (cast by Marcel François Loyau) representing the four states that border the lake: Illinois, Wisconsin, Minnesota, and Michigan. Nearly 1.5 million gallons of water circulate through the fountain, and the colored lights that play off the water are a favorite attraction on warm nights. Nearly 8,000 rosebushes, planted in beds to resemble the gardens of Versailles, surround the fountain.

CHICAGO YACHT CLUB AND COLUMBIA YACHT CLUB

These private clubs (the **Columbia** is located in the formerly seafaring *Abegwiet* docked in the harbor) welcome members of yacht clubs from around the world. Even if you lack such status, you can still enjoy a warm-weather stroll nearby, taking in the pretty view of **Chicago Harbor** and, to the south, **Burnham Harbor**, where anyone is entitled to launch a boat. Every August, boat owners throughout the city decorate their vessels with colored lights and parade them against a black

backdrop of water and sky in the magical Venetian Night Boat Parade. ◆ Chicago: S Lake Shore and E Monroe Drs; 861.7777. Columbia: 111 N Lake Shore Dr (between E Monroe and E Randolph Drs); 938.3625

RICHARD J. DALEY BICENTENNIAL PLAZA

Several seasonal activities are offered at this public recreational facility. In winter an outdoor 80-by-135-foot ice-skating rink offers great views of the lake and the Loop; the same rink is used for roller skating in summer. Skates are available for rental. There are also 12 lighted tennis courts; call ahead to reserve time. Immediately south of the plaza is Chicago's largest garden of prairie wildflowers. ◆ Admission for skating and tennis. Tennis: daily, Apr-Oct. Skating: daily; Dec-Mar, when weather permits. 337 E Randolph Dr (between N Lake Shore Dr and N Michigan Ave). 747.2200. www.chicagoparkdistrict.com

ART INSTITUTE OF CHICAGO

Incorporated in 1879 for the purpose of maintaining a museum and a school of art, the institute grew steadily under the direction of

Restaurants/Clubs: Red | Hotels: Purple | Shops: Orange | Outdoors/Parks: Green | Sights/Culture: Blue

Charles L. Hutchinson, first president of the board of trustees and president of the Corn Exchange National Bank. Chicago's leading businessmen and philanthropists, all trustees of the museum (among them Potter Palmer, John J. Glessner, and Martin A. Ryerson),

agreed that the occasion of the 1893 World's Columbian Exposition was an excellent time to build a grand museum to both represent and accommodate the city's cultural expansion. Chicago architects **Burnham & Root** were invited to submit a design for the building,

POSTMODERNS ON PARADE: SCULPTURE IN THE LOOP

On 15 August 1967, Mayor Richard J. Daley pulled a cord and unveiled Pablo Picasso's sculpture in the Civic Center Plaza. Although onlookers expected to see a dazzling masterpiece, they were far from impressed. One alderman actually introduced a motion in the City Council that it be removed and replaced by a monument to Cubs baseball hero Ernie Banks. Yet since that time the sculpture has become an accepted, even beloved, part of the cityscape, visited as often as the Art Institute or the John Hancock Center. It also helped inspire architects to provide more space for public artwork around their new buildings, and as a result, many sculptures in a variety of media by internationally recognized artists have sprung up all over the Loop—and beyond. Here's a 12-stop tour of some of the best:

1 *Monument with Standing Beast* (1985, Jean Dubuffet): **James R. Thompson Center** (see page 18), W Randolph and N Clark Sts

2 *Untitled Picasso Sculpture* (1967, Pablo Picasso): **Richard J. Daley Center** (see page 21), W Washington St (between N Dearborn and N Clark Sts)

3 *Being Born* (1982, Virginia Ferrari): This stainless steel sculpture consists of two circular elements, one within the other, standing about 20 feet high and set within a marble reflecting pool. A gift of the Tool and Die Institute, it is a tribute to the precise skills of die making. N State and E Washington Sts

4 *Miró's Chicago* (1967, Joan Miró; installed 1981; see page 24): W Washington St (between N Dearborn and N Clark Sts)

5 *Batcolumn* (1977, Claes Oldenburg): To some, this 100-foot-tall statue is simply an oversize baseball bat; to still others, a breezy phallic symbol. You choose. Social Security Administration Bldg, W Madison and N Jefferson Sts

6 *Dawn Shadows* (1983, Louise Nevelson; see page 25): Madison Plaza, W Madison and N Wells Sts

7 *The Four Seasons* (1975, Marc Chagall): **First National Bank of Chicago** plaza (see page 27), W Monroe St (between S Dearborn and S Clark Sts)

8 *Radiant I* (1958, Richard Lippold): This delicate construction of gold, stainless steel, and copper set above a reflecting pool was one of the first pieces of sculpture by a contemporary American artist placed on public view in Chicago. **Inland Steel Building**, 30 W Monroe St (at S Dearborn St), lobby

9 *Untitled Light Sculpture* (1980, Chryssa Varda): Six identical translucent acrylic modules joined by slim polished aluminum rods are suspended in the eight-story atrium lobby. White neon tubing is electronically programmed for repeated patterns of lighting intensity. 33 W Monroe St (between S State and S Dearborn Sts), lobby

10 *Universe* (1974, Alexander Calder; see page 32): **Sears Tower**, 233 S Wacker Dr (between W Jackson Blvd and W Adams St), lobby

11 *Flamingo* (1974, Alexander Calder): **Federal Center** (see page 32), S Dearborn St (between W Jackson Blvd and W Adams St)

12 *Ceres* (1930, John Storrs): **Chicago Board of Trade** (see page 34), 141 W Jackson Blvd (between S LaSalle and S Financial Sts)

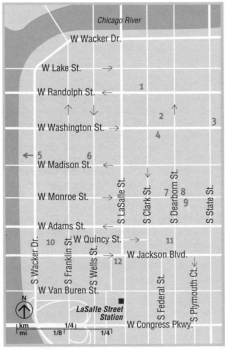

which was to be located in the park. **John Wellborn Root**'s premature death and **Daniel Burnham**'s preoccupation as chief of construction for the exposition led to the commission being given to the Boston firm of **Shepley, Rutan & Coolidge**, who completed this structure, designed in a traditional classical Renaissance style, in 1892. Architects who contributed to the building's interior include **Coolidge & Hodgdon (McKinlock Court**, 1924); **Holabird & Root (North Wing**, 1956); **Shaw, Metz & Associates (Morton Wing**, 1962); **Skidmore, Owings & Merrill (East Wing**, 1976), and **Hammond, Beeby & Babka (Rice Wing**, 1988). The **Departments of Prints and Drawings** and **Photography** have study centers here, where members and students can examine objects that are not on display in the galleries. The **Ryerson** and **Burnham Libraries** have a fantastic collection of art and architectural publications. Capped by a skylight in 1987, the **Grand Staircase** rises elegantly from the main entrance, where there is a circular information center to get you started. The second-floor galleries of European art are arranged chronologically (from Late Medieval to Postimpressionist), with paintings and sculpture in skylit chambers, and prints and drawings in the corridor galleries. This organization provides a rare opportunity to study the development of particular artists and their subjects in various media: In **Gallery 218** hangs Canaletto's *Portico with a Lantern* in oil; the etching is in the adjacent corridor. The Impressionist collection is renowned, and highlights include five of the paintings in Monet's *Haystack* series and Caillebotte's *Paris Street, Rainy Day*. Seurat's *Sunday Afternoon on the Island of La Grande Jatte—1884–1886*, which inspired Stephen Sondheim's Broadway musical *Sunday in the Park with George*, may be the museum's best-known painting.

Although it's impossible to recount the treasures of each department, a tour of the essentials would include the **Edward B. Butler Gallery**, an entire roomful of mesmerizing works by George Inness; the following 15 paintings: *Bathers by a River* by Matisse, *Nighthawks* by Edward Hopper, *Snowfield, Morning, Roxbury* by John La Farge, *Nocturne in Grey and Gold* by Whistler, *Croquet Scene* by Winslow Homer, *Mère Grégoire* by Courbet, *Still Life: Corner of a Table* by Henri Fantin-Latour, *House of Mère Bazot* by Daubigny, *The Millinery Shop* by Degas, *Bedroom at Arles* by Van Gogh, *Landscape: Window Overlooking the Woods* by Vuillard, *Mater Dolorosa* by Dieric Bouts, *The Nativity* by the Master of the Historia Friderici et Maximiliani, *American Gothic* by Grant Wood, and *The Adoration of*

the *Christ Child* by Jacob Cornelisz van Oostsanen; and the reconstructed **Trading Room** of the **Chicago Stock Exchange**. Designed by **Adler & Sullivan**, the stock exchange building was demolished in 1972. In 1976, **Vinci-Kenny Architects** began their intricate reassembly of the trading room that had been salvaged from the razing, resulting in this remarkable display.

The two bronze lions standing guard at the Michigan Avenue entrance were unveiled in 1894 and were immediately adopted by Chicagoans as the symbol of the museum. Designed by American sculptor Edward L. Kemeys, these majestic animals don wreaths at Christmas and have even on occasion sported giant **Bears** helmets and **Cubs** caps.

Several construction projects have been completed in recent years. The new **Kraft Education Center** was the **Children's Museum** until Kraft endowed the museum with funds to overhaul and expand its special galleries and programs for children. Also restored (and installed in new galleries) were the extremely popular **Miniature Thorne Rooms**, 68 dollhouse-scale re-creations of period interiors. The elegant new **Rice Building** is home to *American Arts* and *20th-Century American Painting and Sculpture* and has the vast **Regenstein Hall** for changing exhibitions.

The gardens are spectacular in spring, summer, and fall. Beautifully groomed, they are a favorite haven of museum employees and workers from nearby office buildings who come to read, relax, and people-watch. The museum publishes *The Art Institute of Chicago: The Essential Guide*, which includes discussion of 256 favorite and notable objects. Free guided tours are offered each day; for schedules inquire at the information desk. ◆ Admission; free on Tuesday. Children age 5 years and younger admitted free. Daily; Th until 8PM. 111 S Michigan Ave (between E Jackson and E Monroe Drs). Wheelchair-accessible entrance on S Columbus Dr. 443.3600 ⅙ www.artic.edu

Within the Art Institute of Chicago:

SCHOOL OF THE ART INSTITUTE

What began as the **Chicago Academy of Design** in 1866 became the **Chicago Academy of Fine Arts** in 1879, with academic and exhibiting functions. In 1882 the name was changed to the **Art Institute**. The first director of the school, William French, brother of sculptor Daniel Chester French, held the post until 1914. Georgia O'Keeffe, Thomas

THE BEST

Joanie Bayhack
Vice President, Corporate Communications
WTTW11 and 98.7WFMT

If you live in Chicago for many years, you can really rack up favorite places, which are really about unforgettable experiences. Some of mine are:

Southbound Lake Shore Drive in the summer—driving with the top down and blasting Stevie Wonder. The view of the former **Playboy Building** at night with the name blazing in neon lights. That's where I got my first job.

The lobby of the **Four Seasons Hotel** all dressed up for Christmas—an elegantly appointed tree, lavish flowers, and the scent of pine. Sitting by the fire in the bar with a robust glass of Cabernet and watching far wealthier people.

The soft golden glow of **Coco Pazzo Café** on St. Clair. For Mexican, Rick Bayless's **Frontera Grill** and **Topolobampo**. You'll never forget the incredible food and margaritas. (Although the margaritas could make you forget the incredible food.) Working at WTTW11 and 98.7WFMT has led me to some wonderful places on the Northwest Side: for takeout, **Ken's Mandarin** on McCormick Avenue. Fresh, healthy Chinese, immaculate, warm service, and consistently great food. And the new **Via Veneto** on Lincoln Avenue. Some of the best Italian in Chicago.

Hart Benton, Grant Wood, Claes Oldenburg, and Leon Golub are among the illustrious graduates. ♦ 280 S Columbus Dr. Public information, 899.5100; 800/232.7242

MUSEUM SHOP

Along with a good selection of exhibition catalogs and art books, this store also sells children's books, calendars, posters, postcards, lovely jewelry, and various gift items. Even if you don't go to the museum, come here for beautifully designed Christmas cards featuring pieces from the collection. ♦ First floor. 443.3583

GARDEN RESTAURANT

★$ This is a nice spot to enjoy a refreshing lunch of cold soup, a fresh fruit plate, or a salad. It's enclosed on all four sides by museum galleries. A jazz band plays on Tuesday evenings. ♦ American ♦ Daily lunch. 539.9675

THE CAFE

$ This is a cheerful and inexpensive place to eat; it uses the same kitchen as the **Garden Restaurant**. ♦ American ♦ Daily, lunch; Tu, early dinner. East side, lower level. 443.3600

MILLENNIUM PARK

So it cost a few hundred million more than its original price tag and it took 4 years longer than its original completion date. **Millennium Park**, a 24.5-acre addition to **Grant Park** that is built over railroad tracks, finally opened to the public in 2004. Despite the controversy surrounding its construction, most people agree it's a pretty swell place. ♦ Millennium Park is bounded by Michigan Ave to the west, Columbus Dr to the east, Randolph St to the north and Monroe St to the south. 861.9503. www.millenniumpark.org

Within Millennium Park:

WRIGLEY SQUARE PERISTYLE

The peristyle reprises the colonnades designed by Chicago architect Edward Bennett (designer of Buckingham Fountain) that once stood on the spot but were razed in 1953. Forty-foot granite columns overlook a reflecting pool and have a base with inscriptions of the names of the park's million-dollar donors.

CLOUD GATE

This 110-ton kidney-shaped sculpture is the first public sculpture in the US by Anish Kapoor. The mirrorlike surface creates stunning reflections of the city skyline, and visitors can walk underneath it.

CROWN FOUNTAIN

Probably the favorite spectacle in the park, the fountain features twin 50-foot towers at either end of a long granite expanse. The towers have video screens on which the faces of 1,000 different Chicagoans are displayed for 13 minutes at a time, and water cascades down the towers from openings in their mouths. It was designed by Spanish sculptor Jaume Plensa.

JAY PRITZKER PAVILION

Designed by Frank Gehry, the band shell and centerpiece of the park is crowned by 679 interlocking stainless steel panels that form a series of curving structures to make a trellis. The pavilion has seating for 4,000. A lawn the

Through 2004, Richard M. Daley has been mayor of Chicago for 16 years. His father, Richard J. Daley, was mayor for 22 years. Together they have served as mayor for 38 of the last 50 years.

Mayor Richard M. Daley has not debated a political opponent since 1989.

size of three football fields can accommodate 7,000 more.

Harris Theater for Music and Dance

This 1,492-seat theater provides a stage for 12 different performing arts groups. 334.7777

McCormick Tribune Ice Rink

During warmer months, this 16,000-square-foot oval serves as an activity center and outdoor exhibition space. In summer 2002, it featured the acclaimed photography exhibit "The Earth from Above." Free skating from November to early March. ♦ Daily, 9AM-10PM. Skate rental available. 742-PLAY. (55 N Michigan Ave)

BP Bridge

Also designed by Frank Gehry, the 925-foot-long pedestrian bridge connects Millennium Park to Daley Bicentennial Plaza.

Lurie Garden

Named for philanthropist Ann Lurie, this 3-acre garden features 240 different varieties of perennials.

97 LaSalle Street Station

This is one of four stations serving commuter railroads to the suburbs. Trains pull in right under the **Stock Exchange**. ♦ 414 S LaSalle St (between W Congress Pkwy and W Van Buren St). 836.7000

97 Chicago Board Options Exchange

The country's largest exchange for trading stock options is housed in a 1985 structure by **Skidmore, Owings & Merrill**. The pedestrian bridge that spans Van Buren Street is perhaps the only one to win an award from the American Institute of Architects. By linking the exchange to the **Board of Trade**, it creates the largest contiguous trading floor area in the US. The bridge has a raised floor that contains raceways for every conceivable electrical connection between exchanges. The steel-truss structure doesn't need any support where it joins the exchange, which was designed with the bridge in mind, but it requires a giant pier where it meets the Board of Trade addition. Visitors may watch the action from the fourth-floor viewing gallery. Groups of 10 or more (college age or older) can take a more extensive tour. ♦ Free. M-F, 8.30AM-3PM. 400 S LaSalle St (at W Van Buren St). 786.7492

98 Metropolitan Correctional Center

Few visitors to Chicago can gaze on this triangulated monolith from outside without asking, "What's *that?*" Heaven forbid you should end up posing the question from inside—it's a federal prison. Somewhat innovative in design, the top 16 stories have 5-inch-wide windows—the maximum width permitted in a federal corrections institution. The bottom 11 floors, which house administrative offices, have larger windows. ♦ S Clark and W Van Buren Sts

99 Fisher Building

A steel skeleton supports expanses of glass and pale salmon-colored terra-cotta, and flat and trapezoidal window bays alternate across the façade of this 1896 building by **D.H. Burnham & Co.** (with a 1907 north addition by **Peter J. Weber**). Elaborate Gothic arches share the upper level with carved eagles and salamanders; in a play on the building's name, lower stories are encrusted with fish (see the Dearborn Street entrance), crabs, shells, and other aquatic forms. ♦ 343 S Dearborn St (at W Van Buren St)

100 Old Colony Building

Holabird & Roche's projecting rounded-corner bays distinguish this office building, constructed in 1894 at a time when the south end of Dearborn Street was emerging as the center of the printing industry in the Midwest. Backing on Plymouth Court, the building is a tribute to the Plymouth Colony, whose seal is located at the doorways. ♦ 407 S Dearborn St (at W Van Buren St)

101 Harold Washington Library Center

The opening of the world's second-largest public library (only the British Library in London is bigger) in 1991 ended almost 2 decades of frustration for Chicago's library users. During that period, the collection was split up and housed in several satellite locations while the City Council pondered where to build a central library and how to pay for it.

That's now history, thanks to this state-of-the-art facility—named after the city's first African-American mayor, who was a notorious bookworm—housing more than two million volumes. Features include an 18,000-square-foot children's library; a 400-seat auditorium/theater; a TV studio and film/video center; special collections on Chicago theater, the Civil War, and Harold Washington himself; materials in 90 foreign

---

Restaurants/Clubs: Red | **Hotels: Purple** | **Shops: Orange** | **Outdoors/Parks: Green** | **Sights/Culture: Blue**

THE BEST

Tony Fitzpatrick

Artist

Favorite sights: The duck pond at **Lincoln Park Zoo**; the tunnels under the **Green Mill** lounge that gangsters used to use to escape during Prohibition.

Eating: **Wishbone** on Lincoln Avenue—double down on the brussels sprouts; **Le Meritage** on Damen—steep but worth every buck; for Mexican, **Mama Cita's** on Southport; **El Tapatio** at Ashland and Roscoe.

Best places to buy a gift for your wife when you're trying to get out of the doghouse: **Pink**, **Robin Richman**, **Saffron**.

Best music venues: **The Hideout**, **Old Town School of Folk Music** (be sure to check out the murals).

Best bookstores: **Fagin's** on Milwaukee Avenue: great for books on natural history and the sciences; **Sandmeyer's** in the South Loop; **Chicago Comix** on North Clark Street.

Best movie theater: The **Music Box**.

For kids: Buy them stuff at **Red Balloon**, entertain them at **Glazed Expressions**.

Best framing shop: **MCM** on Damen.

---

languages; and a language-learning center. Artworks punctuate the interior; an intriguing tribute to Washington can be viewed from the lobby rotunda; the ninth-floor gallery atrium is lush and sun drenched. This 10-story, neoclassical structure, designed by **Hammond, Beeby & Babka**, references numerous city landmarks: The red-granite base and brick walls are bows to the **Rookery** and **Monadnock Buildings**, both by **Burnham & Root**; the arched entrances recall **Adler & Sullivan**'s **Auditorium Building**; and the façade and roof pediments echo the style of the **Art Institute**. The steel-and-glass-curtain wall along the Plymouth Court side is a Modernist touch. Free tours and a video overview are available in the **Orientation Theater** on the third floor. ◆ M-Th, 9AM-7PM; F-Sa, 9AM-5PM; Su, 1-5PM. 400 S State St (at W Van Buren St). Public information, 747.4300 ᜱ www.chipublib.org

102 CHICAGO STOCK EXCHANGE

In this version of a marketplace, buyers and sellers—through their agents—gather to trade stocks of American and foreign businesses. Organized in 1882, it is the second-largest exchange in the US and ranks fifth in the

Beaubien Court (120 E Randolph St, between E Randolph and E Lake Sts) was named after "Jolly Mark" Beaubien (1800–1881), fur trader, ferryman, innkeeper, and fiddle player. Mark and his brother, Jean Baptiste, fathered a total of 43 children, more than the entire population of the city in 1829.

Balbo Drive in Grant Park was named after General Italo Balbo, an Italian aviator who visited the 1933 Century of Progress International Exposition with his flying armada.

world. ◆ 440 S LaSalle St (at W Congress Pkwy). 663.2222

Within the Chicago Stock Exchange building:

Everest

EVEREST ROOM

★★★★$$$$ This stunning safari-style restaurant, perched 40 stories above LaSalle Street and the financial heart of the Midwest, is a must-visit for dedicated foodies. Dishes, all innovative and many prepared in the classic French tradition with a contemporary touch, are spectacularly presented on oversize dinnerware. Among the outstanding seafood and game specialties is salmon soufflé. Desserts are delectable, and the wine list is very good, with a strong selection of white wines from chef Jean Joho's native Alsace. Service is impeccable, and even the waiters' trays are graced with fresh flowers. Although high-level wheeling and dealing certainly occurs here, it's a place for romance as well. For the best view, ask for a table on the lower level along the windows. An eight-course prix-fixe degustation menu is available for a minimum of two diners, and private business luncheons can be arranged for six or more. ◆ French ◆ Tu-Sa, dinner. Reservations required. Free valet parking. 40th floor. 663.8920. www.leye.com

103 MANHATTAN BUILDING

In 1890 this became the first tall office building to have a frame completely constructed of iron and steel. Also note **William Le Baron Jenney**'s terra-cotta

In 1991 the renowned Chicago Symphony Orchestra's centennial gala concert was interrupted when souvenir alarm clocks presented to patrons went off during the program.

ornament and variety of window treatments.
♦ 431 S Dearborn St (at W Congress Pkwy)

104 FINE ARTS BUILDING

Originally housing a showroom and factory for Studebaker carriages, the rosy Romanesque **Studebaker Building** (designed by **Solon Spencer Beman** and built in 1885) was converted in 1889 into two theaters on the first floor, and offices, artists' studios, and practice rooms on the upper floors. At that time, "All Passes—ART Alone Endures" was carved inside the entrance. Among the many whose creative endeavors found a haven in the "Carnegie Hall of Chicago," L. Frank Baum and illustrator William W. Denslow collaborated on *The Wonderful Wizard of Oz*; architect **Frank Lloyd Wright** and sculptor Lorado Taft had studios here; and drama teacher Ann Morgan staged the first American performances of plays by George Bernard Shaw and Henrik Ibsen. Current residents include **Performing Arts Chicago**, the **Jazz Institute of Chicago**, the **Boitsov Classical Ballet Company**, and the **Hungarian Opera Workshop**. Numerous music teachers have their studios here too. A walk through the hallways on many an evening is a stroll through a chorus of voices and instruments from behind closed doors. ♦ 410 S Michigan Ave (between E Congress Pkwy and E Van Buren St)

Within the Fine Arts Building:

ARTISTS RESTAURANT

$ This is your basic Greek restaurant, serving spinach pie, as well as cheeseburgers and various coffees. The sidewalk patio is an excellent place for people watching in sunny weather. ♦ Greek ♦ Daily, breakfast, lunch, and dinner. 939.7855 &

105 AUDITORIUM BUILDING

President Grover Cleveland laid the cornerstone in 1887, and 3 years later, this Romanesque Revival–style edifice designed by **Adler & Sullivan**, with its great rusticated granite arches, opened to rave reviews. Among other distinctions, it was the heaviest building in the world (110,000 tons). In its early days the now-defunct **Auditorium Hotel** was the

first choice of Chicago's distinguished visitors, and the architects were among those who established offices at this address. The acoustics and sightlines of the **Auditorium Theatre** are renowned, as is its lavish interior, designed by **Louis Sullivan**. Mosaic floors, sinuously curved balconies, stained-glass windows, murals on side walls and the proscenium arch, gold stenciling, and encrusted ornament throughout are a feast for the eyes, thanks to the loving restoration work of architect **Harry Weese**, completed in 1967. The building's fortunes have fluctuated over the years, and it has served many purposes: In 1891 an indoor baseball game took place in the theater; the stage was used as a bowling alley for servicemen during World War II. After decades of neglect, the building was acquired by **Roosevelt University** in the 1940s and offices and hotel rooms were converted into classrooms. (Its Michigan Ave lobby is very much worth a stop, and make sure you see the building model on display there.) Performances by Bob Dylan, Elvis Costello, the **Joffrey Ballet**, and Garrison Keillor have put the theater back in the limelight. Inquire about tours. ♦ Box office: Daily. 50 E Congress Pkwy (at S Wabash Ave). 922.4046 &

106 GREYHOUND BUS TERMINAL

The terminal handles **Greyhound** and **Trailways** long-distance bus services. ♦ 630 W Harrison St (at S Desplaines St). 800/231.2222

107 MAIN POST OFFICE

This massive structure is headquarters for what surveys have indicated is the country's worst local postal system in terms of customer satisfaction. A self-service facility on the Harrison St side is open 24 hours a day, 7 days a week. ♦ 433 W Harrison St (at S Canal St). 800/275.8777

When the play *The Wizard of Oz* ran in Chicago in 1900, it took in $160,000 in 14 weeks and played to an audience of 180,000. The author, L. Frank Baum, lived in Chicago for almost 20 years.

Chicago-based Sears, Roebuck and Co. introduced the benefit of profit sharing to its employees in 1916.

Restaurants/Clubs: Red | Hotels: Purple | Shops: Orange | Outdoors/Parks: Green | Sights/Culture: Blue

A morning of shopping, an afternoon excursion to the **Field Museum**, and an evening of fine dining at **Prairie** or **Printer's Row** are all in a day's walk in the South Loop. Chicago's founders put their soul into this part of town, as evidenced by the surviving elegant Old World hotels and the distinguished architecture. But with the area's continued development around the turn of the 19th century, these early developers lost heart and forsook the area for more pristine quarters to the north.

Today the South Loop, bordered by **Lake Michigan**, the **Chicago River**, **Cermak Road**,

and **Congress Parkway**, is springing back to life. The historic **Printing House Row District**, just south of Congress Parkway, has been transformed into apartments, offices, restaurants, and shops. New residential complexes such as **Dearborn Park** are home to a middle-class populace that enjoys a short commute to work and a rich choice of urban entertainment, from fine dining, live blues, and jazz at local clubs to Chicago **Bears** games at **Soldier Field.** The South Loop also boasts the handsome **Prairie Avenue Historic District** south of **18th Street**, and the **McCormick Place Convention Complex**, one of the busiest convention centers in the nation.

The history of the South Loop dates to the early 1800s. In 1836, when Chicago was still a settlement of log cabins clustered near the river, Henry and Caroline Clarke opened a general store here. With dreams of grandeur, they built a white frame Greek Revival house on what was then the shore of Lake Michigan. The **Clarke House**, still standing near its original location in the Prairie Avenue Historic District, is the city's oldest surviving building. Around the time of the city's incorporation in 1837, many wealthy merchants, wanting to live near their businesses in the Loop, settled south of **Van Buren Street**. Development here continued after the Great Fire of 1871 roared through the city's center. **Clarke House** and the surrounding environs were unscathed. Elaborate mansions along **Prairie Avenue** between **16th** and **22nd Streets** were built for prosperous merchants and captains of industry, including entrepreneurs Potter Palmer, Philip Armour, Marshall Field, and John Glessner. They were members of the congregation of the **Second Presbyterian Church**, which they supported in great style, lavishly decorating it with stained-glass windows designed by Louis Comfort Tiffany.

But the area did not remain a wealthy enclave when a decidedly inelegant bunch moved next door. Prostitutes, gamblers, and other denizens of Chicago's vice district relocated from downtown to **Dearborn Street** between **Polk** and **16th Streets,** just a few blocks from **Prairie Avenue.** This new **Levee District**, presided over by politicians "Hinky Dink" Kenna and "Bathhouse John" Coughlin, flourished until 1915. The area took on an industrial grittiness when four of Chicago's six major train depots, including **Dearborn Railroad Station**, were constructed nearby, complete with clamoring freight yards and warehouses. Around the turn of the 19th century, the proximity of such sleazy activities triggered the exodus of many families north to the Gold Coast.

In yet another example of Chicago's tumultuous history, this reversal didn't last either, although recovery was slow. **Daniel Burnham**'s Chicago Plan of 1909 paved the way for the development of the city's exceptional lakefront park system, including the South Loop's **Burnham Park**. Between World War I and World War II, more than $1 billion was spent on landfill for Lake Michigan's shoreline, which now supports an abundance of parks and recreational and cultural facilities.

Today the South Loop has been revitalized by new construction of apartment complexes and adaptive reuse projects that combine the commercial and the residential. A major renovation restored one of the city's grand old hotels, the **Chicago Hilton and Towers.** But by far the most notable change was the 1998 completion of a massive transportation project that involved extending **Roosevelt Road** and rerouting the northbound lanes of **Lake Shore Drive.** The city thus created a grassy lakefront museum campus that allows pedestrians to visit three jewels among Chicago's cultural institutions: the **Field Museum, Shedd Aquarium,** and **Adler Planetarium.**

All area codes in this chapter are 312 unless otherwise noted.

1 PRINTING HOUSE ROW DISTRICT

In the late 1880s Chicago's printing industry began locating in this area, which was convenient to the then new **Dearborn Railroad Station**. This district is now included on the National Register of Historic Places, and many of the subtly detailed brick loft buildings have been renovated for new uses. ♦ S Dearborn St (between W Polk St and W Congress Pkwy)

HOTEL BLAKE

$$$ In 1995, the architectural firm of **Booth/Hansen & Associates** joined the top floors of two 19th-century buildings to a new building, then standardized the rooms to create this hotel, which was the Hyatt until the end of 2004. The 1886 redbrick **Duplicator Building** (operator unknown) is less elaborate than the neoclassical light brick **Morton Building** (an 1896 design by **Jenney & Mundle**). The Kor Hotel Group took over the building in 2005, with plans to do some renovations to the 161 rooms, which had featured 12-foot ceilings and a second phone and color TV in each bathroom. ♦ 500 S Dearborn St (at W Congress Pkwy). 986.1234; fax 939.2468 ⅃ www.hotelblake.com

Within the Hotel Blake:

CUSTOM HOUSE

As ACCESS went to press, plans were underway to reopen the celebrated Prairie restaurant. Given that it will be operated by chef Shawn McClain (of Spring and Green Zebra), it is likely to shine as one of the city's best restaurants. Drop us a line and let us know what you think.

2 EDWARDO'S

★$ This eatery is one of Chicago's several branches of a national chain that serves up healthful pizzas made from natural ingredients. Basil is grown on the premises, and fresh tomatoes, spinach, mushrooms, and sweet peppers are among the many topping choices. The stuffed spinach pizza is delicious. The open, high-ceilinged loft space with wood floors is bright and attractive and can accommodate large groups. ♦ Pizza ♦ Daily, lunch and dinner. 521 S Dearborn St (between W Harrison St and W Congress Pkwy). 939.3366. Also at numerous locations throughout the city

3 PONTIAC BUILDING

This is **Holabird & Roche**'s oldest remaining skyscraper. Built in 1891, the 14-story building, clad in dark brown brick, does not express its steel frame as clearly as later buildings do, such as the Loop's **Marquette**, but the four-window bays on the Dearborn Street side are graceful, and there is lovely terra-cotta detailing at the cornice and just above the second floor. Listed on the National Register of Historic Landmarks, it was renovated in 1985 by **Booth/Hansen & Associates**. ♦ 542 S Dearborn St (between W Harrison St and W Congress Pkwy)

4 MERGENTHALER LINOTYPE BUILDING

Kenneth Schroeder's playful 1982 renovation is typical of his imaginative approach to adaptive reuse. Now an apartment building, the principal façade of the 1917 structure by **Schmidt, Garden & Martin** is left relatively unchanged, whereas the brick sidewall features bright red gridded window frames and full-story triangular pop-out bays. Part of an old building (**Tom's Grill**, a long-closed hamburger stand) remains on the corner, treated as an archaeological fragment. Residents drive into the parking lot through a freestanding roll-up door from an old loading dock. ♦ 531 S Plymouth Ct (between W Harrison St and W Congress Pkwy)

5 TASTE OF SIAM

$$ This airy dining spot is notable for serving a wide range of Thai food at reasonable prices. Its soups and salads are quite good. ♦ Thai ♦ Daily, lunch and dinner. 600 S Dearborn St (at W Harrison St). 939.1179 ⅃

6 MUSEUM OF CONTEMPORARY PHOTOGRAPHY

The first museum in the Midwest devoted exclusively to photography was founded in 1967 by **Columbia College**, a 4-year alternative arts college at the same address. Works on exhibit are by both eminent and emerging artists from around the world. The diverse roles photography plays—as a medium of artistic expression, a means of documenting life and the environment, a way to enhance technology, and a commercial tool—are

---

THE BEST

Buddy Guy

Musician

My club, **Buddy Guy's Legends**, where I can hear great blues seven nights a week, and meet and greet my friends and fans from around the world when I am not on tour.

Love the city skyline from the **Observatory** and the new **Navy Pier**; trying to catch a **White Sox** or **Bulls** game; picking up a **Maxwell Street**–style Polish sausage; driving through one of the many forest preserves; and, like almost everyone else, marveling at the politics of this great city.

presented. ♦ Free. M-Sa; closed Aug. 600 S Michigan Ave (at E Harrison St). 344.7104 ♿ www.mocp.org

7 SPERTUS MUSEUM OF JUDAICA

The largest Jewish museum in the Midwest boasts an excellent permanent collection of religious and decorative art objects representative of Jewish life and culture through the centuries. Special exhibitions range from works by Jewish artists to broad topics relevant to Judaism. The *Zell Holocaust Memorial* is unforgettable. The **Rosenbaum Artifact Center** is a unique, hands-on exhibition that enables children (and grown-ups) to play at being archaeologists in the ancient Near East. ♦ Admission. M-F, Su. 618 S Michigan Ave (between E Balbo Dr and E Harrison St). 922.9012 ♿ www.spertus.edu

8 MERLE RESKIN THEATRE

Originally named the **Blackstone Theater**, this facility has been owned and operated by **DePaul University** since 1988. Designed in 1910 by **Marshall & Fox** in French Renaissance style with interior finishes of walnut and gold, the theater resembles a European opera house. It stages a series of student productions, including presentations for children. The renovated 1,340-seat facility also hosts opera and dance companies. ♦ 60 E Balbo Dr (between S Michigan and S Wabash Aves). 922.1999. www.theatreschool.depaul.edu

9 BLACKSTONE HOTEL

If ever a building were ripe for a major restoration, this is it. Unfortunately it hasn't happened yet, so the building remains closed. Designed by **Marshall & Fox** and opened in 1910, the Blackstone has seen a lot of Chicago history. The phrase "smoke-filled room" was coined here during the 1920 Republican convention, when clouds of cigar smoke enveloped reporters waiting to learn the name of the party's presidential nominee (Warren G. Harding). The banquet scene in the 1987 movie *The Untouchables* was filmed here. With great views of the lake and **Grant Park**, hopefully someone will put the touches

on a major rehab and this registered National Historic Landmark building will open again. ♦ 636 S Michigan Ave (at E Balbo Dr)

10 GRACE PLACE

A 1915 three-story printer's building is now an ecumenical house of worship, thanks to an award-winning 1985 conversion by **Booth/Hansen & Associates**. There's a meeting space at street level, a sanctuary for concerts and services on the second floor, and a worship area enclosed by a circular wall and arched windows in the third-floor loft, whose huge timber structure was left in place. The only overtly religious symbol—a metal cross—doubles as a structural support. In an unusual arrangement, the church is shared by **Grace Episcopal Church**, **Christ the King Lutheran Church**, and **Makom Shalom Synagogue**. ♦ 637 S Dearborn St (between W Polk and W Harrison Sts). Grace Episcopal, 922.1426; Christ the King Lutheran, 939.3720; Makom Shalom, 913.9030

11 SANDMEYER'S BOOKSTORE

Owners Ulrich and Ellen Sandmeyer have assembled an excellent selection of books for the traveler—from practical guidebooks to good reads for those who never leave their living rooms. Books both by Chicagoans and about the city are well represented. The spacious and attractive shop also carries wonderful titles for children and high-quality fiction for adults. ♦ Daily; Th until 8PM. 714 S Dearborn St (between W Polk and W Harrison Sts). 922.2104; fax 922.2104

12 KASEY'S TAVERN

Located in an 1883 building that housed one of the first printers in the area, this has been a tavern since 1890. Until 1974, when the conversion of **Printer's Row** into a residential area began, the bar kept printers' hours of 8AM to 6PM. Now it's a neighborhood hangout, where patrons can watch sports, play pool, or listen to the jukebox. During the Printer's Row Book Fair each June, the Nelson Algren Society meets here to swap stories of the famed Chicago writer. No food, other than frozen pizza and the barkeep's fried eggs, but the beer's on tap and there's wine and espresso. ♦ Daily. 701 S Dearborn St (between W Polk and W Harrison Sts). 427.7992

Restaurants/Clubs: Red | Hotels: Purple | Shops: Orange | Outdoors/Parks: Green | Sights/Culture: Blue

13 FRANKLIN BUILDING

The highly decorated façade of **George C. Nimmons**'s 13-story brown-brick building comes as a bit of a surprise in this utilitarian neighborhood. Abstract multicolor terra-cotta designs enliven the upper stories, and panels between the first and second floors pay homage to the printing trade. The detailing is masterful throughout. ♦ 720-36 S Dearborn St (between W Polk and W Harrison Sts)

Within the Franklin Building:

GOURMAND COFFEEHOUSE

$ Before *Starbucks* was a household word, this place was pouring espresso for folks seeking a caffeine fix. The menu offers a variety of brewed gourmet coffees and baked goods, and the café also sells many types of coffee beans. Try the hot chocolate—rich Ghirardelli chocolate in steamed milk. ♦ Café ♦ Daily, 7AM-11PM. 728 S Dearborn St. 427.2610

14 LAKESIDE PRESS BUILDING

This eight-story brick building, on the National Register of Historic Places, was originally a printing factory owned by the R.R. Donnelley Company (note the company seal with Indian chiefs' heads on the façade). It was designed in 1897 by **Howard Van Doren Shaw**, an architect better known for luxurious residential commissions. The solidity of the masonry walls, with their strong corners and thick piers that visually support a massive top story, contrasts with the delicate metal-and-glass window areas of the middle stories. In 1986 a major rehabilitation was completed, and in 1992 it became a dormitory for nearby **Columbia College**. ♦ 731 S Plymouth Ct (at W Polk St)

15 HOTHOUSE

Hothouse is a not-for-profit center featuring a wide range of musical acts and performance art performed by a variety of nonmainstream local, national, and international talent, usually for less than $10. There are two separate performance spaces, each seating about 200. ♦ Club: M-Th, 6PM-1AM; F-Sa, 6PM-2AM; Su, 6PM-midnight. 31 E Balbo Ave (between S State St and S Wabash Ave). 362.9707; fax 362.9708

16 AMERICAN FLORAL ART SCHOOL

Everything a budding florist could want to know about opening a flower shop and more is taught here. Visitors are welcome. ♦ M-F. 634 S Wabash Ave (between E Balbo Ave and E 8th St), second floor. 922.9328

17 CHICAGO HILTON AND TOWERS

$$$ When designed in 1927 by **Holabird & Roche**, the former **Stevens Hotel** was billed as the largest in the world and offered such recreational extravagances as an 18-hole rooftop golf course. The hotel was renamed for owner Conrad Hilton in the 1950s and still reflects its $185 million renovations of 1985–1986. Public spaces and the 1,620 guest rooms and suites are grand and luxurious. The hallways drip with chandeliers, and the rooms are rich in cherrywood furnishings and plush fabrics. Amenities include a state-of-the-art health club complete with a heated skylit pool, spa, and saunas, as well as private offices for business travelers. The exclusive **Towers**, with a separate registration desk and concierge, has a European air and offers the comforts of a small hotel. The complex includes three restaurants: **Buckingham's** for steak and seafood (see below); the **Pavilion**, a coffee shop open between 5:30AM and 1AM; and **Kitty O'Shea's**, a cozy pub with authentic Irish food and live Irish folk music nightly. The weekend packages are a good deal. ♦ 720 S Michigan Ave (between E Eighth St and E Balbo Dr). 922.4400, 800/445.8667; fax 922.5240 ♿ www.hilton.com

Within the Chicago Hilton and Towers:

BUCKINGHAM'S

★★$$$$ Grilled steaks are served in anything but a steak-house setting. From the polished marble floors to the rich upholstery, this dining room exudes gentility. Entrées come with a fluffy baked potato or rice or fresh vegetables al dente. The dessert cart seems ready to sink beneath the weight of rich, chocolate confections, along with the most satisfying servings of ice cream and cheesecake. ♦ American ♦ Daily, dinner; Su, brunch. Reservations required. 294.6600 ♿

18 BUDDY GUY'S LEGENDS

Bluesman Buddy Guy plays here, as do other legendary blues musicians, and visitors such as Ron Wood and Bill Wyman often join in. An adjacent eatery that you can enter through the club features tasty barbecued meats and sandwiches. ♦ Cover. Daily until 2AM; Sa until 3AM. 754 S Wabash Ave (at E Eighth St). 427.0333. www.buddyguys.com

THE BEST

Anne Mollo-Christensen

Vice President, Business Development

Outside magazine

Independent bookstores are still the **best place to buy books**. And Chicago's best is **Unabridged Bookstore**, at 3251 N Broadway. The bookshelves are packed with handwritten reviews and recommendations from the staff. Great for book suggestions for kids and teens.

Best Thai: Joy's Noodles, 3257 N Broadway. Great food, kid friendly, reasonably priced.

Best place to see a movie: Music Box on Southport. This big old theater has clouds and stars painted on the ceiling and a real, old-time Wurlitzer organ player to introduce classic weekend movies. A must.

Best splurge breakfast: Toast at 746 W Webster. Not cheap, and long waits on weekends, but this small, hip breakfast spot seems worth it every time. Try the pepper eggs or the pancake specials.

Best place to buy wine: Sam's Wine and Spirits, just northwest of North and Clybourn. Great deals and knowledgeable staff in what may be the largest—and best—wine store in the country.

Best place to buy goodie-bag gifts for kids' parties: Uncle Fun on Belmont. Looking for that beloved Captain & Tennille action figure from your youth? This is where you'll find it. Tons of vintage toys, figures, postcards, and gag gifts all crammed into a small storefront.

Best gallery (where you can also take classes): Lillstreet Art Center at Montrose and Ravenswood. Lillstreet's gallery showcases some of the most amazing art pieces you can imagine, but the real draw is the classes in clay, glass, and textiles. Great kids' programs too.

Best cupcakes: Sweet Mandy B's at Webster and Racine. Stop in for coffee and a cupcake or take some home for dessert. For a change try the layer cakes, muffins, or brownies. An alternate is the Angel Food Bakery at 1636 West Montrose down the street from Lillstreet Art Center.

Best dinner out without breaking the bank: Tie between **Tournesol** (4343 N Lincoln) and **Le Bouchon** (1958 N Damen).

Best pasta: Pasta Bowl, 2434 N Clark. This cash-only restaurant is fast, good, and a great place to bring the kids.

19 RIVER CITY

These curvilinear poured-concrete buildings were designed in 1984 by **Bertrand Goldberg**, the architect who designed **Marina City** 25 years earlier. Apartments surround the courtyard atrium, which contains interior streets lined with shops. Complete with a 70-slip marina, restaurants, and other services, it's a little city within a city. ♦ 800 S Wells St (at W Polk St)

20 POWELL'S BOOKSTORE

Chicago's best used-book store, Powell's carries more than 300,000 scholarly, academic, general interest, and out-of-print titles. ♦ Daily. 828 S Wabash Ave (between E Ninth and E Eighth Sts). 341.0748. Also at 2850 N Lincoln Ave (between W Diversey Pkwy and N Lakewood Ave). 773/248.1444 ♿; 1501 E 57th St (at S Harper Ave). 773/955.7780 ♿

21 MUSEUM CAMPUS

Following an ambitious construction project that rerouted Lake Shore Drive, the city developed a sprawling lakefront area that enables visitors to travel on foot among three museums—the **Field**, **Shedd Aquarium**, and **Adler Planetarium**. A free trolley is available to carry leg-weary visitors. ♦ S Lake Shore and E William McFetridge Drs

Within the Museum Campus:

THE FIELD MUSEUM

More than 20 years passed before the natural history collection that originated at the 1893 World's Columbian Exposition secured a permanent home in this vast Georgia marble and terra-cotta building (see the floor plan page 48). Endowed by Marshall Field Sr., it was designed by **D.H. Burnham & Co.** and **Graham, Anderson, Probst & White** to resemble a Greek temple—the ultimate architectural form at the time. **Harry Weese & Associates** planned the 1975 renovation and the 1986–1987 restoration. Despite the acres of floor space, less than 1% of the museum's artifacts and specimens are on view. Besides creating a busy calendar of temporary exhibits on such topics as *Archaeopteryx*, *Butterflies*, and the *Sacred Arts of Haitian Voodoo*, the museum has taken great steps in recent years to improve and enliven its permanent exhibits and to add new ones, emphasizing hands-on displays and activities suited for children. Major new exhibits include *Messages from the Wilderness*, *Africa*, and *Life Over Time*, which traces 3.8 billion years of life on earth—from DNA to dinosaurs through to the origin of

Restaurants/Clubs: Red | Hotels: Purple | Shops: Orange | Outdoors/Parks: Green | Sights/Culture: Blue

The Field Museum

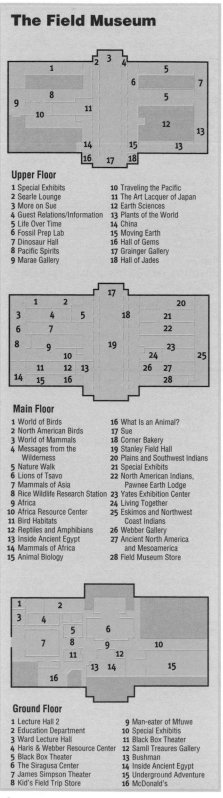

Upper Floor

1 Special Exhibits	10 Traveling the Pacific
2 Searle Lounge	11 The Art Lacquer of Japan
3 More on Sue	12 Earth Sciences
4 Guest Relations/Information	13 Plants of the World
5 Life Over Time	14 China
6 Fossil Prep Lab	15 Moving Earth
7 Dinosaur Hall	16 Hall of Gems
8 Pacific Spirits	17 Grainger Gallery
9 Marae Gallery	18 Hall of Jades

Main Floor

1 World of Birds	16 What Is an Animal?
2 North American Birds	17 Sue
3 World of Mammals	18 Corner Bakery
4 Messages from the Wilderness	19 Stanley Field Hall
5 Nature Walk	20 Plains and Southwest Indians
6 Lions of Tsavo	21 Special Exhibits
7 Mammals of Asia	22 North American Indians, Pawnee Earth Lodge
8 Rice Wildlife Research Station	23 Yates Exhibition Center
9 Africa	24 Living Together
10 Africa Resource Center	25 Eskimos and Northwest Coast Indians
11 Bird Habitats	26 Webber Gallery
12 Reptiles and Amphibians	27 Ancient North America and Mesoamerica
13 Inside Ancient Egypt	28 Field Museum Store
14 Mammals of Africa	
15 Animal Biology	

Ground Floor

1 Lecture Hall 2	9 Man-eater of Mfuwe
2 Education Department	10 Special Exhibits
3 Ward Lecture Hall	11 Black Box Theater
4 Haris & Webber Resource Center	12 Samll Treaures Gallery
5 Black Box Theater	13 Bushman
6 The Siragusa Center	14 Inside Ancient Egypt
7 James Simpson Theater	15 Underground Adventure
8 Kid's Field Trip Store	16 McDonald's

humans. More recently, the museum has developed *Living Together*, which presents a framework for understanding cultural diversity; *Underground Adventure*, an exhibit that takes visitors into the unexplored wilderness underfoot to learn about organisms in the soil and the importance of soil ecosystems to life on earth; and the celebrated reconstruction of Sue, the largest and most complete *Tyrannosaurus rex* discovered to date. The tomb of Pharaoh Unis-ankh, excavated and brought to Chicago in 1908, anchors the *Inside Ancient Egypt* exhibit. In the *Place for Wonder*, children can handle meteorites, shells, skeletons, and countless other objects to their hearts' content. *Traveling the Pacific* transports visitors from Chicago's mercurial weather to a re-created coral island, complete with the sounds of birdcalls and crashing waves, and a life-size, glowing lava flow that was cast from an active volcanic flow in Hawaii. The *Nature Walk* takes visitors on a long, winding trail through prairies, wetlands, woodlands, and ocean shores. Check the directories posted throughout the museum for news on special programs held daily. Thanks mostly to Sue the dinosaur, the Field has become the most popular tourist site in Chicago. A **McDonald's** is located on the ground floor, and there's a **Corner Bakery** on the main floor. ♦ Admission; free Wed. Daily. 922.9410 ᚷ www.fieldmuseum.org

JOHN G. SHEDD AQUARIUM

The world's largest indoor aquarium (see the floor plan page 49) was the gift of John G. Shedd, president and chairman of the board of **Marshall Field & Company**, in 1930. Inhabited by more than 6,000 aquatic animals of every shape and hue, the aquarium is endlessly fascinating. Don't miss the sea anemones, river otters, or the feedings in the *Coral Reef* exhibit (daily at 11AM, 2PM, 3PM; no 3PM feedings Monday through Friday, September through April). Divers enter this 90,000-gallon re-creation of a Caribbean coral reef and talk to visitors through a microphone while they feed sharks, sea turtles, eels, and hundreds of tropical fish. Tear yourself away long enough to take a look at the architectural details of this **Graham, Anderson, Probst & White** building. Wave and shell patterns border the central room, and colorful mosaics of crabs and lobsters march across the tops of majestic doorways framed by classical columns. Harmoniously appended to the aquarium's lake side, the vast **Oceanarium** is the world's largest indoor marine mammal facility. Designed by **Lohan Associates** and opened in 1990, it is home to Pacific black whales, beluga whales, sea otters, dolphins, and seals. Visitors can wander through the main exhibit, which re-creates the rocky coastlines of southeast Alaska and the Pacific Northwest, complete with nature trails,

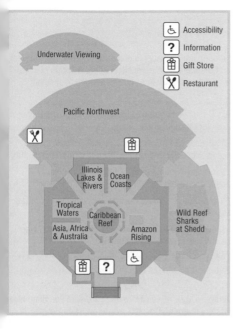

- ♿ Accessibility
- ? Information
- 🎁 Gift Store
- 🍴 Restaurant

Underwater Viewing

Pacific Northwest

Illinois Lakes & Rivers
Ocean Coasts
Tropical Waters
Caribbean Reef
Asia, Africa & Australia
Amazon Rising
Wild Reef Sharks at Shedd

merchandising: **Sears, Roebuck & Company** executive Max Adler financed the building and imported its Zeiss projector from Germany, where it had been designed in 1923. Antique astronomical instruments are displayed, and navigation, the history of exploration, and space travel are the subjects of exhibitions. Narrated *Sky Shows* in the domed theater change throughout the year and are always engrossing and informative. After the Friday-night show, visitors can tour the **Doane Observatory**, where a 20-inch telescope provides celestial views. Weekend *Sky Shows* for the 6-and-under crowd are popular. Spectacular views of the city skyline may be seen from the promontory leading to the planetarium, a perfect place for a warm-weather picnic or watching the sun set. The promontory is also home to three impressive pieces of sculpture. The *Thaddeus Kosciuszko Memorial* (1904, by Kasimir Chodzinski) is a bronze equestrian statue honoring the Polish hero who fought in the American Revolution and later for the freedom of his native country. *Nicolaus Copernicus* (1823, by Bertel Thorvaldsen) depicts the father of modern astronomy holding a compass and an armillary sphere, a model of the solar system. The bronze *Sundial* (1980, by Henry Moore) directly in front of the planetarium stands 13 feet high, marking the hour of the day. A new wing added in 1999 made space for several new exhibits and the new **Sky Pavilion**, which includes the world's first **StarRider Theater**, featuring state-of-the-art computer projection and a sophisticated audience participation system to create a 3-D, interactive virtual-reality experience. ♦ Admission; free Tu. Daily; F until 9PM. 922.STAR ♿ www.adlerplanetarium.org

streams, rocks, and forest vegetation. A 60,000-gallon penguin habitat is another great feature. ♦ Admission. Daily. Advance ticket purchase recommended for Oceanarium. 939.2438 ♿ www.sheddaquarium.org

ADLER PLANETARIUM

This pink granite dodecahedron (each of its 12 sides representing a sign of the zodiac), designed in 1930 by **Ernest A. Grunsfeld Jr.**, was the country's first planetarium. Like the **Field Museum** and the **Shedd Aquarium**, it was built with money made by

Adler Planetarium

TALES FROM THE WINDY CITY

Chicago is often depicted as a tough, hustler's town; the penetrating edge of city life makes it a perfect backdrop for mystery and crime novels. It is also one of the best examples of the immigrant experience, not to mention political chicanery. Here are a few of the books that evoke both the historical and modern atmosphere of this constantly changing metropolis:

A Beer at a Bawdy House, by David J. Walker (Minotaur, 2000). Detective Kirstin and her attorney husband Dugan help a bishop who is being blackmailed in the latest from a popular Chicago writer.

Black Metropolis: A Study of Negro Life in a Northern City (University of Chicago Press, revised edition 1993). This sociological study chronicles the life of Chicago's African-American community through the first half of the 20th century.

Boneyards, by Robert Campbell (Pocket Books, 1993). The Edgar Award–winning author of the Jimmy Flannery mystery series presents a powerful modern-day epic of a politically connected Irish Catholic family in Bridgeport.

Boss: The Life and Times of Richard J. Daley, by Mike Royko (NAL-Dutton, 1988). The late prizewinning newspaper columnist offers a scathing portrayal of the reign of the first Mayor Daley.

Chicago by Gaslight: A History of Chicago's Netherworld, 1880–1920, by Richard Lindbergh (Academy Chicago, 1996). A browsable, colorful collection of facts and anecdotes compiled by a local historian.

Chicago, City on the Make, by Nelson Algren (McGraw-Hill, 1951). In hard-boiled prose, Algren tells the story of the city through stories of its people—from the native Potawatomi, to the 1919 Black Sox, to gangster Al Capone, and, finally, to social worker and reformer Jane Addams.

Chicago Confidential, by Max Allan Collins (New American Library, 2002). The award-winning novelist and filmmaker pens another riveting and wonderfully researched historical mystery featuring Chicago private eye Nate Heller.

Collected Stories, by Harry Mark Petrakis (Lake View Press, 1987). The critically acclaimed novelist paints a vivid portrait of life in Chicago's Greek neighborhoods.

Good Cop, Bad Cop, by Barbara D'Amato (Forge, 1998). A pair of fictional brothers with the Chicago Police Department are pitted against each other because of a scandalous true incident that took place years ago.

Division Street: America, by Studs Terkel (New Press, 1993). A Chicago classic by a Chicago classic.

Homeland, by John Jakes (Doubleday, 1993). Jakes weaves an evocative portrait of the turn-of-the-19th-century immigrant experience through the rise of one German family.

Hospital, by Sidney Lewis (The New Press, 1994). One of the nation's last public hospitals comes alive in this riveting oral history.

Jaded, by Eugene Izzi (Simon & Schuster, 1996). Fictional detective Jake Philips investigates dirty Chicago cops.

The Jungle, by Upton Sinclair (NAL-Dutton, reissued 1989). Written as an indictment of the harsh treatment of immigrants who worked in the Chicago stockyards, this book resulted in the first regulation of the food industry and the passage of the Pure Food and Drug Act.

Killer on Argyle Street, by Michael Raleigh (St. Martin's Press, 1995). This murder mystery set in Uptown Chicago abounds with vivid descriptions of the neighborhood's diversity and its Vietnamese and Cambodian residents.

Left for Dead, by Paul Engleman (St. Martin's Press, 1997). This Shamus Award–winning author's mystery novel is based on the 1969 police raid in which Black Panther leader Fred Hampton was killed.

The Secret Lives of Citizens, by Thomas Geoghegan (Pantheon, 1998). Noted Chicago labor attorney and playwright offers trenchant insights into the political workings of the Windy City.

There Are No Children Here, by Alex Kotlowicz (Doubleday, 1991). An acclaimed reporter provides a remarkable account of life growing up in one of Chicago's housing projects.

Total Recall, by Sara Paretsky (Delacorte, 2001). A case of insurance fraud on Chicago's South Side leads investigator V.I. Warshawski to an international conspiracy reaching back to Nazi Europe.

Unspeakable Acts, Ordinary People, by John Conroy (Knopf, 2000). Portions of this brilliant journalistic effort concern one of the Chicago Police Department's worst scandals ever and were first published in the *Chicago Reader*.

Windy City Knights, by Michael Black (Five Star, 2004). Private eye Ron Shade prowls the city streets in the second thriller by a writer-cop who knows those streets well.

Writing Chicago: Modernism, Ethnography, and the Novel, by Carla Cappetti (Columbia University Press, 1993). A comparison and parallel study of the fiction of Chicago writers Nelson Algren, Richard Wright, and James Farrell.

22 DEARBORN PARK

This community sprang up from abandoned railroad yards in the late 1970s. The diverse dwellings include town houses, garden apartments, and high-rises landscaped to suggest a suburb in the city. ♦ Bounded by S State and S Clark Sts and W 18th and W Polk Sts

Within Dearborn Park:

DEARBORN STATION

The oldest surviving railroad passenger terminal in Chicago, this Romanesque Revival building of red sandstone and brick detailed in terra-cotta was designed by **Cyrus L.W. Eidlitz** in 1885 and restored by **Kaplan/McLaughlin/Diaz** in 1986. This landmark's façade is handsome, and the tower provides a wonderful terminus for Dearborn Street. The interior houses a small sandwich bar and a large medical office. Several events are based here during the Printer's Row Book Fair in mid-June. ♦ 47 W Polk St (between S Plymouth Ct and S Clark St)

23 GIOCO

★★★$$$ More than 10 years after artist Tony Fitzpatrick woke folks up to the funky possibilities of the far South Loop by opening an art gallery, **World Tattoo**, on this desolate stretch of South Wabash Avenue, someone has finally dared to open a restaurant. Not surprisingly, it's Jerry Kleiner who sparked the development of restaurant row on W Randolph St when he opened **Vivo**. Odds are good that Kleiner, who also owns **Marche** and **Red Light**, will make a successful go of it with **Gioco**, which can mean "gamble" in Italian. Chef Joe Rosetti's rustic Italian cooking is the perfect match for the location and the décor, which is distressed exposed brick with patches of plaster. Rumor has it that the location was a speakeasy during Prohibition, so there's a booth fashioned from an old safe and a private room in back with a hidden entrance. Rosetti perfected his chops at **Smith & Wollensky** and **Park Avenue Café**, and his approach to Italian is hearty and filling. One of the two steak entrées is topped with cheese, and the chicken Vesuvio is worth writing home about. For seafood, try scallops wrapped in prosciutto and served with Sardinian couscous or lobster gnocchi. Simple desserts include lemon tart with roasted pine nuts and ricotta cheesecake. ♦ Italian ♦ Reservations recommended. M-F, lunch and dinner; Sa-Su, dinner. 1312 S Wabash Ave (at E 13th St) 939.3870 &

24 OPERA

★★★$$$ Opened in December 2002, this dramatic space, located across the street from **Gioco**, may be the key piece in bringing fine-dining stability to the South Loop. Housed in a former Baptist church, the décor is wildly theatrical, with layered paint treatments giving way to flowing velvet curtains. Owners Jerry Kleiner and Howard Davis called on the imaginative Paul Wildermuth, who cut his chopsticks at **Ben Pao** and **Red Light**, to fuse his creative notions with Chinese standards. The results are delicious. A degustation menu is available for $60, less than what a real night at the opera would cost. ♦ Asian ♦ Daily, dinner. Reservations recommended. 1301 S Wabash Ave (at E 13th St). 461.0161 &

25 SOLDIER FIELD

A colonnade of hundred-foot concrete Doric columns rises majestically behind Chicago **Bears** fans braving icy winds to support their football team. In warmer weather, the stadium hosts such performers as Bruce Springsteen, Madonna, and the Rolling Stones. Originally constructed in 1926 by **Holabird & Roche** as a war memorial, the stadium has since been remodeled to accommodate the football team.

In 2001 a controversial proposal to modernize the facility was announced and hastily approved, not allowing time, critics say, for assessing the impact of the project on the city's lakefront. Barely had the last Bears fan stumbled out of the stadium following the final home game of the 2001 season before the demolition phase of the project began. The cost was a staggering $600 million, prompting other

critics to wonder why the city was subsidizing a project that mostly benefits a private enterprise. (The city maintained that nearby lakefront improvements are also part of the plan.) The design called for the placing of an oversize bowl within the exterior columns that brings to mind a UFO landing in a sci-fi film with something less than a budget of 600 million *lire*. Couple that with increased fees for season tickets and the displacement of season ticket holders, and you get a high level of high-volume public grumbling that persisted long after the stadium opened in September 2003. ♦ E William McFetridge Dr (just east of S Lake Shore Dr). Ticket information, 747.1285. www.soldierfield.net

26 THE COTTON CLUB

Behind an ordinary commercial storefront lies a sophisticated jazz club. Modeled after the New York City original, the interior is done in gold tones, chrome, and Art Deco mirrors. The staff serves in tuxes, and the talent, such as Cassandra Wilson and the Art Porter Quartet, is always tops. On Friday and Saturday night, jazz in the front room is supplemented by disco dancing in a dark room in back. ♦ Cover. Daily, 6PM-2AM; F, Sa until 4AM. 1710 S Michigan Ave (between E 18th and E 16th Sts). 341.9787 &

27 NATIONAL VIETNAM VETERANS ART MUSEUM

The war that America would like to forget (and, some would say, apparently did) is movingly depicted in a wide and free range of artistic forms by more than 100 Vietnam vets. Admission. M, 11AM-5PM; Tu-F, 11AM-6PM; Sa, 10AM-5PM; Su, noon-5PM. 1801 S Indiana Ave (at E 18th St). 326-0270. www.nvvam.org

28 BURNHAM HARBOR

From early May through late October, anyone is permitted to launch a boat from here and sailboats are available for rent (747.0737). During the summer, many Chicago yacht owners live here aboard their vessels. For a pleasant warm-weather stroll, walk along the harbor through **Burnham Park** from the **McCormick Place Convention Complex** up to the **Adler Planetarium**.

29 NORTHERLY ISLAND

Talk about your flight being canceled. Opened in 1947 as a small lakefront airport, Meigs

Field's single runway was suddenly demolished in the middle of the night on March 31, 2003, on orders from Mayor Daley. The airport, which had limited use from businesspeople and political operatives traveling between Chicago and the state capital, Springfield, had been the subject of a long-running territorial dispute between Daley and state officials. Daley's long-term plan is to turn the land into a nature park, but in the short term, the 78-acre peninsula will serve as a summer outdoor-entertainment venue operated by Clear Channel Communications.

30 SECOND PRESBYTERIAN CHURCH

In 1874 **James Renwick**, famous for the Smithsonian Institution building in Washington, DC, designed this neo-Gothic structure using mottled limestone from nearby quarries. The building burned in 1900, and **Howard Van Doren Shaw**, a member of the church, rebuilt the interior with muralist-decorator Frederic Clay Bartlett. Wealthy parishioners lavished artwork on their church, including spectacular stained-glass windows by Sir Edward Burne-Jones, Louis Comfort Tiffany, and John La Farge. ♦ 1936 S Michigan Ave (at E Cullerton St). 225.4951 &

31 PRAIRIE AVENUE HISTORIC DISTRICT

After the 1871 fire that ravaged the city's center, Chicago's leading entrepreneurs—including Potter Palmer, Philip Armour, Marshall Field, George Pullman, and John Glessner—built elegant mansions in every style in this area, which had escaped the blaze and was convenient to the business district. Around the turn of the 19th century, when the neighborhood became more industrial, the elite left Prairie Avenue and relocated to the city's North Side. Although only a few of the grand residences remain, this historic district—a veritable outdoor architectural museum—is well worth a visit. For tours, contact the **Glessner House** or **Clarke House** (see below). ♦ S Prairie Ave (between E Cermak Rd and E 18th St). 326.1480; fax 326.1397

Within the Prairie Avenue Historic District:

JOHN J. GLESSNER HOUSE

Designed in 1886 for industrialist John Glessner, this unique and elegant home of rusticated granite is Chicago's only surviving building by premier American architect **Henry Hobson Richardson**. Much of the interior has been restored in the English Arts and Crafts style favored by the Glessners. The Chicago Architecture Foundation maintains the house as a museum. ♦ Admission. Tours: W-Su, noon-4PM. House open only for tours. Reservations required for groups of 10 or more. Discounted tickets for combined tour of Glessner House and Clarke House (see below). 1800 S Prairie Ave (at E 18th St). 326.1480. www.glessnerhouse.org

HENRY B. CLARKE HOUSE

Also known as the **Widow Clarke House**, this Greek Revival–style home was built in 1836 by Henry B. Clarke when Chicago was still a small pioneer town, on a small part of 20 acres of land he had purchased the year before. It is the oldest surviving building in Chicago, and one of the only wood-frame structures to have escaped the Great Fire of 1871. Purchased by the city in 1977, the house—which has been moved twice in its history—now sits at a location within a few blocks of its original site. Meticulously restored and furnished, the house is a museum operated by the Chicago Architecture Foundation. Tours begin at the **Prairie Avenue Tour Center** in the **Glessner House** museum next door (see above). ◆ Admission. Tours: W-Su, noon-3PM. House open only for tours. Reservations required for groups of 10 or more. Discounted tickets for combined tour of Clarke House and Glessner House (see above). 1827 S Indiana Ave (at E 18th St). 326.1480 &

32 WILLIE DIXON'S BLUES HEAVEN FOUNDATION

On the site of the original Chess Records recording studio, where such notables as Muddy Waters, Howlin' Wolf, Chuck Berry, and Bo Diddley recorded the music that put the rhythm into rhythm 'n' blues, another blues legend, the late songwriter Willie Dixon, worked to create this tribute to the music for which Chicago is best known. The purpose of the foundation is to educate people about the history of the blues, to help older blues artists get royalties and health care, and to nurture young artists who are keeping the music alive. There's a gift store downstairs and a refurbished recording studio in the original space on the second floor. ◆ Admission. M-F, noon-3PM; Sa, noon-2PM. Tours of the museum and area blues clubs are available. 2120 S Michigan Ave (between E Cermak Rd and E 21st St). 808.1286. www.bluesheaven.com

33 MCCORMICK PLACE CONVENTION COMPLEX

This massive convention center was built in 1971 to replace one that burned down in 1969. Architect **Gene Summers** was clearly influenced by **Mies van der Rohe**. The roof cantilevers 75 feet over walls of painted steel that frame 7-by-8-foot plates of gray glass. The center, along with the newer north building that features over 700,000 square feet of exhibition space designed by **Skidmore, Owings & Merrill**, hosts some of the largest conventions in the country, attracting more than four million trade and public show visitors annually. The brainchild of Colonel Robert R. McCormick, the former owner of the *Chicago Tribune* who never lived to see his dream realized, the complex's ever-popular annual auto and boat shows, held in January and February, are open to the public; the National Restaurant Association show (open to the trade only) draws huge crowds in June. The Hyatt Regency McCormick Place, connected via the Grand Concourse pedestrian walkway, is a favorite of convention attendees. ◆ 2301 S Lake Shore Dr (at E 23rd St). 791.7000; fax 791.6543 & www.mccormickplace.com

Within McCormick Place Convention Complex:

ARIE CROWN THEATER

Named after a Lithuanian immigrant who became an American success story, this cavernous theater once seated 5,000 and played host to some of Chicago's most spectacular events. Unfortunately, when McCormick Place was struck by fire in 1969, the rebuilding of the main complex forced a partial reconstruction of the theater, which resulted in a venue that—despite seeing the likes of Carol Channing and Yul Brynner tread its boards—soon became notorious for its atrocious acoustics. Happily, following an extensive $6.5 million renovation, the Arie Crown is now architecturally and acoustically new and improved, boasting of state-of-the-art facilities and amenities, while still retaining its charm as a traditional venue in Chicago. This recipient of the 1999 Chicago AIA Interior Architecture Honor Award is a convenient place to catch performances. ◆ 791.6000 &

THE BEST

Max Allan Collins
Award-Winning Crime Novelist/Filmmaker

Best DVD /laser disc store: **QED Laser** on Ogden Avenue in Westmont. Great selection, great prices, knowledgeable staff; rental and incredible retail selection, always on sale.

Restaurants/Clubs: Red | Hotels: Purple | Shops: Orange | Outdoors/Parks: Green | Sights/Culture: Blue

MAGNIFICENT MILE/STREETERVILLE

Glitzy and ritzy, the Magnificent Mile is a shopper's dream come true. Saks Fifth Avenue, Neiman Marcus, Bloomingdale's, Water Tower Place, and scores of specialty shops, fine restaurants, and luxury hotels run a mile along Michigan Avenue from the Chicago River north to Oak Street, where consumerism gets even more serious in ultrachic designer boutiques. An architectural showplace, the avenue is anchored at its southern tip by the Gothic Tribune Tower and terra-cotta–clad Wrigley Building, and on the north by the palatial Drake Hotel and the polished pink granite office and shopping complex known as One Magnificent Mile. Some of the city's most exclusive residences—among them Benjamin Marshall's mansard-roofed 999 Lake Shore Drive and Mies van der Rohe's twin apartment buildings—hug Lake Michigan as Lake Shore Drive curves south into the neighborhood of Streeterville, where the colossal Ferris wheel towering over renovated Navy Pier comes suddenly into view.

Difficult though it may be to envision today, much of this part of town was under

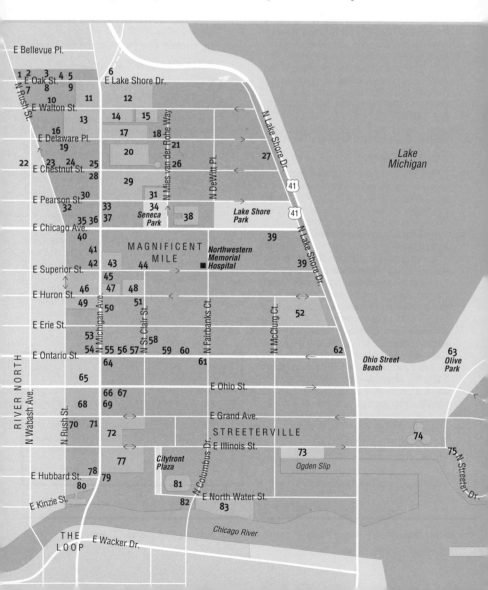

water until about 100 years ago when a seedy character who called himself Captain Streeter ran a boat aground off **Chicago Avenue**. When he could not free his boat, he began his own landfill project. The area along the Chicago River thrived until the 1950s, packed with factories, railheads, warehouses, and shipyards. Its growth has long been linked to that of the adjacent Near North Side, where wealthy citizens were settling in the late 19th century. Among the signs of prosperity was the **Fourth Presbyterian Church** at **Grand** and **Wabash Avenues**, which held its first service only hours before the 1871 Chicago Fire ravaged the community. Famous survivors of the fire were the **Water Tower** and its **Pumping Station**. Completed just two years before the blaze and still standing today, they are landmarks on the avenue.

The 1920 opening of the **Michigan Avenue Bridge** connecting the North and South Sides was a major spur to growth. In 1921 the **Wrigley Building**, home office of the chewing-gum manufacturer, rose beside the river at the bridge's northern end. **Raymond Hood** and **John Mead Howells's** winning entry in the international design competition for the **Tribune Tower** went up nearby in 1924. The grand **Drake Hotel**, by Benjamin Marshall, crowned the north end of the avenue in 1920. The nearby 14-story **Palmolive Building** (later to be called the **Playboy Building**, and today known as **919 North Michigan Avenue**) was a veritable skyscraper when it was built in 1929, topped by an airplane navigational beacon. That same year, Shriners flocked to their extravagant new **Medinah Athletic Club**. The Depression bankrupted the club only five years later, as the once-flourishing commerce on the block screeched to a halt. The building has since been restored as the luxurious **Hotel Inter-Continental Chicago**.

The Michigan Avenue/Streeterville area remained an affluent community after the Depression, and it wasn't until the late 1960s and early 1970s that it developed its current identity as a high-end retail district. The 1970 arrival of the quarter-mile-high **John Hancock Center**, a combination of apartments, offices, and commercial space, played an important part. But the real turning point was the 1976 construction of **Water Tower Place**. Anchored by a major branch of **Marshall Field's**, a downtown presence for more than a century, this seven-story vertical mall signaled the determined march of retail development northward from the Loop. This development has continued virtually nonstop, as new upscale malls have

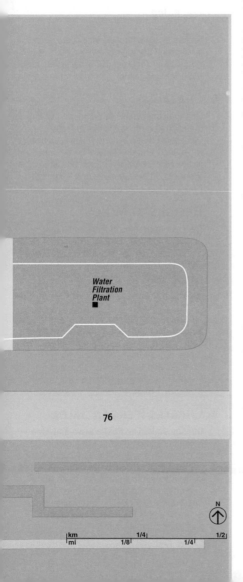

Water
Filtration
Plant

76

km   1/4   1/2
mi   1/8   1/4

appeared on every block of North Michigan Avenue, starting with the 1983 unveiling of One Magnificent Mile up through the 2000 opening of **The Shops at North Bridge**. A major project of special note has been the rehabilitation of Navy Pier as a suitable site for Chicago's famed annual international art exposition (now called **Art Chicago**) and other public events. Most of Navy Pier's shops and restaurants practically shout "tourist trap." Still, the area is a bustling lakefront carnival with an IMAX theater, Ferris wheel, **Chicago Children's Museum**, the **Chicago Shakespeare Theater**, and a variety of ongoing activities and events.

Eager for business to support the high rents, most stores along Michigan Avenue and Oak Street are open 7 days a week, though it's always wise to check before going. Crowds can get thick on weekends, so shop on weekdays to avoid the hordes. Make a day's excursion of the Magnificent Mile. Break for lunch or dinner at one of the many restaurants in the area, then take a relaxing stroll along the posh residential streets near the lake.

All area codes in this chapter are 312 unless otherwise noted.

1 GENEVA SEAL

Geneva Seal offers an array of fine timepieces and custom jewelry, with accessibility to loose diamonds and colored stones. ◆ Daily. 1003 N Rush St (at E Oak St). 377.0100 www.genevaseal.com

2 SUGAR MAGNOLIA

Women's and children's attire and accessories that are sure to delight and surprise are available here. Cozy flannel nightgowns, 1940s-style wool overcoats, and kids' leather jackets are equally smart. This is probably the most affordable clothing shop on Oak Street. ◆ Daily. 34 E Oak St (between N Lake Shore Dr and N Rush St). 944.0885

2 MALCOLM FRANKLIN ANTIQUES

Dan Sullivan upholds his grandfather's standard of carrying only the finest English antique furnishings here, as well as in the New York branch. Both are considered among the best antiques stores in the country. ◆ M-Sa. 34 E Oak St (between N Lake Shore Dr and N Rush St). 337.0202; fax 337.8002

3 ESQUIRE THEATRE

Designed in 1938 by **Hal** and **William L. Pereira**, this snazzy, bilevel Art Moderne theater borrowed its name from *Esquire* magazine (founded a few years earlier in Chicago) to project an image of sophistication. Unfortunately, the large space has been chopped up into six theaters showing first-run films. ◆ 58 E Oak St (between N Lake Shore Dr and N Rush St). 280.0101

3 JIL SANDER

The first **Jil Sander** boutique in the United States carries the entire collection of Jil Sander designs for men and women, ranging from casual day wear to evening attire. ◆ M-Sa. 48 E Oak St (between N Michigan Ave and N Rush St). 335.0006

4 CHASALLA

This shop specializes in European fashions for men and women, from suits to jeans. Designers carried include Dolce & Gabbana, Hugo Boss, Cinque Mode al Dente, and Gianfranco Ferre. ◆ Daily, 70 East Oak St (between N Lake Shore Dr and N Rush St). 640.1940

DESIGNS BY MING

The custom designs include bridalwear, pillows, evening bags, and accessories. ◆ M-Sa. 70 East Oak St (between N Lake Shore Dr and N Rush St). 649.1510. www.designsbyming.com

5 ALEX SEPKUS

A newcomer to the Oak Street scene, the **Alex Sepkus** boutique carries imaginative jewelry from Sepkus, along with Linda Anoraks, Pedro Braggart, Julie Baker, Michael Nobel, Steven Sketcher, and Leopoldville Polio. ◆ M-Sa. 106 E Oak St (between N Michigan Ave and N Rush St). 440.0044

5 CHARLES IFERGAN SALON

Offering everything from a wash-and-style before a night on the town to a major makeover, this is one of the most popular salons around. On Saturday mornings, especially in June, the shop is filled with brides and attendants getting pampered for the big day. ◆ Tu-Sa. 106 E Oak St (between N Lake Shore Dr and N Rush St). 642.4484. www.charlesifergan.com

The Best

Jack Hartman,
Executive Director
Illinois Tollway

Best party of the year: World's Largest Block Party at Old St. Patrick's Church.

Best bistro in the city: Bistro Margot on Wells.

Best bistro in the suburbs: Bistro Banlieue in Lombard.

Best alfresco dining in the summer: O'Brien's Restaurant on Wells south of North.

Best Italian food on the North Side: Zia's in Edison Park.

Best eclectic food: Mambo Grill on Clark.

Best winter break: Skating at Millennium Park.

Best places to take the kids: The fountains at Millennium Park; Navy Pier Winter Wonder Festival, Ferris wheel; Shedd Aquarium for beluga whales and dolphins; and the Botanic Garden in the summer.

Best collection of kitchen, bath, and building products: LuxeHome on the first floor of the Merchandise Mart.

Best way to go to a Sox or Cubs game: CTA Red Line.

Best wine shop: The House of Glunz on Wells at Division.

Best ice cream shop: Ice Cream Bar at Monroe and Clinton for drink-themed ice cream treats.

Best suburban bar: Sullivan's in Forest Park.

5 Hermès

From Paris, **Hermès** offers an array of fashion accessories for men and women, including luxurious silk scarves and ties. ♦ M-Sa. 110 E Oak St (between N Lake Shore Dr and N Rush St). 787.8175. www.hermes.com

5 Marilyn Miglin

Makeup designers in this tiny boutique sit across from their customers at lighted booths, demonstrating proper technique by applying cosmetics to half of the client's face and letting her do the other half. Founded by a former model and dancer, the boutique uses custom products made in a nearby lab and not tested on animals. ♦ M-Sa. 112 E Oak St (between N Lake Shore Dr and N Rush St). 943.1120; fax 943.1184. www.marilynmiglin.com

5 Oak Street

On days when the weather doesn't send you scurrying into a nearby vertical mall, this one-block stretch is a shopper's paradise. Elegant boutiques for men's and women's clothing, shoes, jewelry, linens, and stationery, plus wonderful salons that pamper with manicures or new hairstyles, will entertain browsers and buyers for hours. The stores' hours are as individualized as their selections: Some are open Sunday, others aren't; some close at 5PM, others at 6:30PM. Call first if there's a specific store you want to visit. ♦ Between N Michigan Ave and N Rush St

5 Ultimo

Ultimate is indeed the word for this fashion boutique frequented by both celebrities and the merely well dressed looking for the latest from Valentino, Armani, and Sonia Rykiel, among others. Don't expect the salespeople to fall all over themselves to assist you. ♦ M-Sa. 114 E Oak St (between N Lake Shore Dr and N Rush St). 787.0906

6 Lake Shore Drive Pedestrian Tunnel

Cross beneath the highway to the Gold Coast's Oak Street Beach and miles of paved paths perfect for a walk, run, or bike ride. Another underpass in this area is at East Superior Street.

7 Barneys

The Big Apple's legendary men's clothier has evolved into an upscale purveyor of fashions and accessories for both men and women. ♦ Daily. 25 E Oak St (at N Rush St). 587.1700 ♿

8 Pratesi

Shop here for the world's most luxurious bed linens, manufactured in Florence for generations. ♦ M-Sa. 67 E Oak St (between N Michigan Ave and N Rush St). 943.8422; fax 943.9377

Oak Street Shopping

LAKE SHORE DRIVE		MICHIGAN AVENUE
mens- and womenswear **Ultimo**		**Judith Ripka** *jewelry*
cosmetics **Marilyn Miglin**		**Optica** *optician*
leather goods **Hermès**		**Stephane Kelian** *shoes/accessories*
womenswear **Janis**		**Giorgio Armani** *mens- and womenswear/*
		leather goods/accessories
Ultimate Bride		**Trabert & Hoeffer** *jewelry*
Charles Ifergan Salon		**Billy Hork Gallery** *posters/original art*
gifts/accessories **Elements**		**Water Mark** *stationery*
jewelry/handicrafts **Alaska Shop**		**Arden B** *womenswear*
womenswear **Betsey Johnson**	OAK STREET	**Kate Spade** *leather boutique*
clothing **Chasalla**		**Pratesi** *linens*
shoes/accessories **Fenaroli**		**Nicole Miller** *womenswear/perfume*
legwear **Wolford Boutique**		**In Chicago** *men's sportswear*
linens **Private Lives**		**Luca Luca** *womenswear*
menswear **Tessuti**		**Lester Lampert** *jewelry*
womenswear **Jil Sander**		
day spa **Channings**		**Chacok** *womenswear*
cigars **Blue Havana**		**CP Shades** *womenswear*
maternitywear **A Pea in a Pod**		**George Greene** *menswear*
		Loro Piana *knitwear*
womens- and childrenswear **Sugar Magnolia**		**Marianne Strokirk** *hair and skin care salon*
Malcom Franklin Antiques		**Atlas Galleries**
shoes **Sansapelle**		**Barneys** *mens- and womenswear*
watches/jewelry **Geneva Seal**		

RUSH STREET

Nicole Miller

8 NICOLE MILLER

One of several scattered around the country, this individually owned shop features Miller's famed "conversation" prints (because they always get talked about) in scarves, ties, and tops, plus distinctive fragrances and bath products. ♦ Daily. 63 E Oak St (between N Michigan Ave and N Rush St). 664.3532; fax 664.3676. www.nicolemiller.com

8 LUCA LUCA

Very classy Italian fashions for women, many in strong pastels and distinctive fabrics, are on hand here. ♦ M-Sa. 59 E Oak St

Chicagoan David Mamet won the Pulitzer Prize for drama in 1984 for the play *Glengarry Glen Ross*.

William Wrigley Jr. became a successful soap and cleaning products salesman by giving away chewing gum as a premium. The gum was so popular that in 1893 he started manufacturing his own Wrigley's Spearmint and Juicy Fruit gum.

(between N Michigan Ave and N Rush St). 664.1512

LESTER**L**AMPERT

8 LESTER LAMPERT

Specializing in expertly refashioned antique jewelry, this store has been in the same family for four generations. Many pieces are produced on the premises. ♦ M-Sa. 57 E Oak St (between N Michigan Ave and N Rush St). 944.6888. www.lesterlampert.com

8 YVES SAINT LAURENT RIVE GAUCHE

One of the most historic and important houses of design, **Yves Saint Laurent** still holds its edge among the top fashion designers. New to Chicago, the famous boutique features avant-garde women's ready-to-wear, as well as handbags, accessories, and fragrances. ♦ M-Sa. 51 E Oak St (between N Lake Shore Dr and N Rush St). 751.8995. www.ysl.com

9 KATE SPADE

This superchic boutique carries an attractive and ever-expanding line of high-quality leather goods. The chain owes some of its popularity to references on the HBO TV series *Sex and the City*. ♦ Daily. 101 East Oak St (between N Lake Shore Dr and N Rush St). 654.8853

9 MARINA RINALDI

Sixty percent of American women wear sizes 12 and up. Italian retailer Marina Rinaldi saw a little wiggle room in that fact. With four stores already thriving elsewhere, the company's fifth opened in Chicago in December 2002. Aiming to bring Italian taste to plus-size women, the three-level, 4,500-square-foot shop serves women sizes 10 to 22, offering a wider selection than at its Saks boutique. From leather boots to alpaca coats, the goods are designed to present a look of sophistication and slim the figure. The company expects Chicago to be a top-selling market. (Just wait until they hit Milwaukee.) ♦ M-Sa. 113 E Oak St. 867.8700

9 WATER MARK

If none of a variety of packaged invitations suits your fancy, place a special order from a vast selection of Crane's and the like. You also can have whatever stationery you choose personalized. ♦ M-Sa. 109 E Oak St (between N Michigan Ave and N Rush St). 337.5353

10 PANE CALDO

★$ Regional Italian antipasti and pasta are featured at this charming café and bakery. There's a large take-out menu. ♦ Italian ♦ Daily, lunch and dinner. 72 E Walton St (between N Michigan Ave and N Rush St). 649.0055; fax 274.0540 ♿

11 ONE MAGNIFICENT MILE

Three hexagonal cubes of polished pink granite—variously 21, 49, and 58 stories high—brace one another vertically and are oriented to avoid casting summer shadows on Oak Street Beach. This 1983 **Skidmore, Owings & Merrill** design was the most striking addition to the North Michigan Avenue skyline until the arrival of the **900 North Michigan** building on the next block. The towers of the skyscraper are occupied by offices and condos; at the base, expensive shops and restaurants afford visitors browsing, buying, and dining options. In addition to the listings below, **Giacomo, Tod's,** and **Enrico Cashmere** are located here. ♦ 940-80 N Michigan Ave (between E Walton and E Oak Sts)

Within One Magnificent Mile:

SPIAGGIA

★★★$$$$ The prices may empty your pocketbook, but this handsome bilevel restaurant, with its dramatic floor-to-ceiling windows overlooking the lake, is a winner, thanks partly to the knowledgeable staff. Thin-crust boutique pizzas are among the best starters. Main courses range from succulent roasted chicken and other game birds to inventively garnished meats and fish. All dishes are beautifully presented, but in less than overwhelming quantities. The wine list is extensive, and its offerings are expensive. ♦ Northern Italian ♦ Daily, dinner; F-Su, lunch and dinner. Jacket required. Reservations required. 980 N Michigan Ave, second floor. 280.2750; fax 943.8560 ♿ www.levyrestaurants.com

CAFÉ SPIAGGIA

★★$$ **Spiaggia**'s casual little sister, done in the same décor on a reduced scale, proffers pizzas and pastas in two narrow rooms. Wines are available by the glass or bottle. The easygoing, friendly service and excellent coffee win praise. It's worth a stop, if only for an incomparable cup of espresso or cappuccino made from Italy's foremost brand of beans (Illy Caffè). ♦ Northern Italian ♦ Daily, lunch and dinner. 980 N Michigan Ave, second floor. 280.2755; fax 943.8560 ♿

𝕿𝖍𝖊 𝕯𝖗𝖆𝖐𝖊
—— HOTEL ——

12 DRAKE HOTEL

$$$ Modeled after Renaissance palaces by architect **Benjamin Marshall**, this hotel has played host to kings, queens, and presidents since 1920. The public areas are opulent, as are most of the 535 rooms and suites, with plush fabrics and period pieces. Some rooms, however, are surprisingly drab and cramped; check in advance that yours isn't. The Executive Business Women's Suites have foldaway beds, so the bedroom can be readily converted to a conference room. For the business traveler, secretarial service, fax and telex, and a notary public are available. Within the hotel are a number of adequate restaurants, plus the **Palm Court,** an exceptionally pretty, flowery refuge for afternoon tea or cocktails. In March 2005, the Drake announced plans for a $55 million renovation that will update rooms and beds. Weekend

Magnificent Mile Shopping

OAK STREET | LAKE SHORE DRIVE

One Magnificent Mile
shops within include:

furs **Revillon Paris**
salon **Giacomo**

Drake Hotel
shops within include:
Georg Jensen *jewelry/china/crystal/silver*

WALTON STREET

900 North Michigan Avenue
shops within include:
department store **Bloomingdale's**
mens- and womenswear **Mark Shale**
silver **Pavillon Christofle**
mens- and womenswear **Gucci**
leather goods **Coach Store**
Cashmere Cashmere
womenswear **Jessica McClintock**
jewelry/womenswear **Isis/My Sister's Circus**
handwear **Glove Me Tender**

MICHIGAN AVENUE

Louis Vuitton *womens accessories*

Elizabeth Arden *salon*
Bulgari *jewelry*

Westin Hotel

DELAWARE PLACE

Fourth Presbyterian Church

John Hancock Center
shops within include:
Richard Gray Gallery

CHESTNUT STREET

clothing **Plaza Escada**

clothing/housewares **Filene's Basement**

Borders Books

Water Tower Place
shops within include:
Marshall Field's *department store*
Lord & Taylor *department store*

Laura Ashley *womens- and childrenswear/ home furnishings*
Crabtree & Evelyn *perfume/gifts*

Accent Chicago *souvenirs*

PEARSON STREET

Water Tower   **Chicago Water Works**

CHICAGO AVENUE

mens- and womenswear **Ralph Lauren**
mens- and womenswear **Banana Republic**
jewelry **Tiffany & Co.**

Neiman Marcus *department store*
Peninsula Hotel

SUPERIOR STREET

Chicago Place
shops within include:
department store **Saks Fifth Avenue**
Talbots
womens- and childrenswear/accessories/shoes
womenswear **Ann Taylor**
Bockwinkel's Grocery
body care products **Body Shop**
gallery/gift shop **Chiaroscuro**
linens **Sassparella Ltd.**

Enzo Angiolini *shoes*
Brooks Brothers *clothing*

HURON STREET

men's shoes **Hanig's**

Gap Kids
Cole Haan *shoes/accessories*
Niketown *sportswear*

Map continues on next page

Magnificent Mile Shopping, continued

ERIE STREET

housewares/home furnishings **Crate & Barrel**

Ermenegildo Zegna *menswear*

jewelry **Cartier**

Burberry *mens- and womenswear*

ONTARIO STREET

600 North Michigan Avenue
shops within include:
Eddie Bauer
mens- and womenswear/accessories
clothing **Marshall's**
Linens 'n Things
videos **The Viacom Store**

MICHIGAN AVENUE

United Airlines
American Express Travel Service
Florsheim Shoes

OHIO STREET

books and music **Virgin Megastore**
Chicago Marriott
shoes **Kenneth Cole**
Circle Gallery

Wrigley Building

The Gap *sportswear*
Atlas Galleries
Timberland *outdoor clothing/shoes/accessories*
Hammacher Schlemmer *luxury housewares/gifts*
Hotel Inter-Continental Chicago
Tribune Tower

packages are available. ♦ 140 E Walton St (between N Lake Shore Dr and N Michigan Ave). 787.2200, 800/55.DRAKE; fax 397.1948 ♿

Within the Drake Hotel:

CAPE COD ROOM

★$$$ Once the city's premier seafood house, this cozy New England–style spot with red-checkered tablecloths and nautical decorations remains popular, though the food has lost its luster. The Bookbinder's soup (red snapper in a tomato-vegetable broth enhanced with sherry) is a signature item. ♦ Seafood ♦ Daily, lunch and dinner. Jacket and tie required. Reservations recommended. 787.2200 ♿

COQ D'OR

★$ Dimly lighted whatever the time of day, this clubby place pours countless cocktails (arguably the best martini in the city) and serves hearty food such as cheese omelettes, roast beef sandwiches, and strip steaks. On evenings, except Sunday and Monday, a live piano player sets a festive mood. ♦ American ♦ Daily, lunch and dinner. Music: Tu-Sa, 8:30PM-1:30AM. 787.2200 ♿

GEORG JENSEN

Jewelry and lines of fine china, crystal, and silver from the famed Danish company are sold here. Prices are high, and service can be haughty. A bridal registry is available. ♦ M-Sa. 642.9160

13 900 NORTH MICHIGAN AVENUE

In 1989 **Kohn Pedersen Fox** and **Perkins & Will** designed this king-size addition to the North Michigan Avenue skyline. The tower (pictured page 62) contains restaurants and high-end retail stores on the first eight floors, anchored by **Bloomingdale's** and the **Four Seasons Hotel**, with offices and condominiums rising above. The department store is nicer than its New York counterpart; the linens, housewares, and fine china departments are among the best in the city. More than a hundred shops ring the marble-clad atrium, among them the **Coach Store**, **Ballantyne Cashmere**, and **Gucci**. ♦ Daily. Reduced-rate parking is available, with tickets validated by the tenants. At E Delaware Pl

Within 900 North Michigan Avenue:

MARK SHALE

Catering primarily to a yuppie clientele, this appealing five-level store has a good selection of relatively conservative men's and women's attire and accessories. Semiannual sales at Christmas and in early summer offer great bargains. Alterations are gratis. ♦ Daily. 440.0720; fax 440.8690 ♿ www.markshale.com

PAVILLON CHRISTOFLE

The first Chicago location of France's premier silversmith carries a lovely assortment of silverplate, sterling, stainless, and gold-plated

---

Restaurants/Clubs: Red | Hotels: Purple | Shops: Orange | Outdoors/Parks: Green | Sights/Culture: Blue

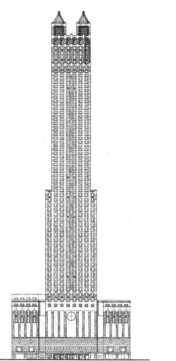

KOHN PEDERSEN FOX

flatware, fine French crystal and china, and select pieces of 18-karat gold and sterling silver jewelry. ◆ Daily. Street level. 664.9700 &
www.christofle.com

JESSICA MCCLINTOCK

Cinderella could have a ball in these dresses. Bolts of silk, satin, velvet, linen, and lace go into San Francisco–based McClintock's designs for old-fashioned, romantic dresses. Her exquisite bridal gowns are laden with beading and lace, and her pint-size party dresses are every little girl's fantasy. ◆ Daily. Fifth level. 944.2025 &

ISIS/MY SISTER'S CIRCUS

Specializing in fashionable and distinctive one-size-fits-most casual clothing, this imaginative shop also has a jewelry department that includes the work of talented Chicago designers. ◆ Daily. Third level. 664.7140. Also at 823 W Armitage Ave (between N Halsted and N Dayton Sts). 773/665.7290 &

GLOVE ME TENDER

One of the only stores in the country exclusively devoted to handwear carries more than 80 lines for men, women, and children,

Chicago attracts nearly 50 million visitors a year. About 30 million come here for leisure; about 20 million, on business.

from evening gloves to designer dishwashing gloves. ◆ Daily. Fifth level. 664.4022 &
www.glovemetender.com

TUCCI BENUCCH

★$$ This lighthearted, crowded, reasonably priced takeoff on an Italian villa serves fine pizzas, good roasted chicken, seafood, and pastas. A nice touch: Crusty bread comes with a puddle of lushly herbed olive oil. ◆ Italian ◆ Daily, lunch and dinner. Fifth level. 266.2500 &

FOUR SEASONS HOTEL

$$$$ From the street-level lobby, guests take an elevator to the seventh-floor reception desk, lounges, and restaurants. This vast floor is elegantly furnished, with plush seating areas everywhere. An inviting, darkly paneled bar is a great place for drinks. In the beautiful, airy **Conservatory**, lacy cloths cover the low tables for afternoon tea and scones, and a pianist plays in the late afternoon; it's also a perfect spot for a cocktail in the evening, when a mellow jazz combo plays. The **Seasons Café** offers the "express lunch" of your life—in 18 minutes for $19.50. The 344 rooms are opulent, with English furnishings, three two-line phones, a stocked bar, and bathrooms, complete with robes and cotton balls. Maid service is twice daily. For the business traveler, soundproofed boardrooms with audiovisual equipment and adjoining windowed dining salons are available. Other features include a swimming pool under a skylight, rooftop running track, aerobics room, and exercise equipment. Weekend rates are available. ◆ 120 E Delaware Pl (between N Michigan Ave and N Rush St). 280.8800, 800/332.3442; fax 280.1748 & www.fourseasons.com
Within the Four Seasons Hotel:

SEASONS

★★★$$$$ There's a hint of French Canadian in chef Robert Sulatycky's menu, which changes with the seasons (naturally) and features light preparations, among them delicious fish and fowl dishes and crisp fresh vegetables. The wine list is extensive, and the surroundings are elegant, with dark woodwork and warm, red-patterned carpets. Request a table overlooking the lake. A children's menu is available. ◆ American ◆ Daily, breakfast, lunch, and dinner. Jacket recommended. Reservations recommended. 649.2349 &

14 919 NORTH MICHIGAN AVENUE

Known to Chicagoans for years as the **Palmolive Building** and later the **Playboy Building**, **Holabird & Root**'s elegant 1930 limestone tower is one of the city's finest Art Deco skyscrapers. Both graceful and powerful, the building has finely balanced setbacks and a lighting scheme that emphasizes its dramatic

CAN WE TALK?

Chicago is home to the *Jerry Springer Show* and *Oprah*. If your life isn't colorful enough to be a panelist, you can at least be a member of the studio audience. Admission to the shows is free, but you must reserve well in advance. The more flexible your dates, the better your chances.

Jerry Springer

WMAQ-TV, 454 N Columbus Dr (NBC Tower), at E Illinois St, 321.5365. www.jerryspringertv.com

Oprah

Harpo Studios, 1050 W Washington Blvd, at N Aberdeen St, 591.9222. www.oprah.com

Make telephone reservations at least 2 months in advance; staffers will take your name and later confirm your seat reservation.

verticality. **Skidmore, Owings & Merrill** restored the storefronts to their original Art Deco elegance. The 150-foot-tall mast crowning the building was originally an airplane navigational beacon visible for 60 miles. It went dark after high-rises were constructed nearby and residents complained of the light. ♦ At E Walton St

ELIZABETH ARDEN
THE RED DOOR SALON

ELIZABETH ARDEN

Splurge on a Maine Chance Day (which includes a 1-hour body massage; facial; manicure and pedicure; lunch; a shampoo, haircut, and styling; and makeup application) or just take a Red Door Beauty Break (which includes a half-hour neck, shoulder, back massage; manicure; and makeup application). ♦ Daily. 988.9191 & www.reddoorsalons.com

15 MILLENNIUM KNICKERBOCKER CHICAGO

$$ Each room in this recently renovated, attractive hotel has a comfortable sitting area; some of the 305 rooms even have canopy beds. Rooms on the 14th floor offer a taste of 1920s Chicago: Secret doors leading to a central staircase are carved into the walls, enabling guests who used the rooms as Prohibition-era speakeasies to make quick getaways. One restaurant, **The Nix**, offers contemporary American cuisine and Asian fusion. Weekend packages are available. ♦ 163 E Walton Pl (between N Mies van der Rohe Way and N Michigan Ave). 751.8100, 800/621.8140; fax 751.9205 &

SIDNEY GARBER
FINE JEWELRY

16 SIDNEY GARBER

This well-established jeweler is known for his exceptional selection of fine gems in classic styles. ♦ M-Sa. 118 E Delaware Pl (between N Michigan Ave and N Rush St). 944.5225; fax 944.5326 &

17 WESTIN HOTEL

$$$ Though popular with conventioneers, this gray concrete slab houses 751 rooms of average comfort and negligible character. The Executive Level offers additional perks: a welcome gift, complimentary hors d'oeuvres, and continental breakfast. All guests enjoy concierge services, plus free health club, sauna, and reasonably priced laundry service. Weekend packages are available. There are three restaurants, including **Grill on the Alley**, a clone of a popular Beverly Hills eatery that serves excellent steaks and seafood, and one that sometimes features live jazz in the evening. ♦ 909 N Michigan Ave (at E Delaware Pl). 943.7200, 800/228.3000; fax 649.7456 &

18 DOUBLETREE GUEST SUITES

$$$ Each of the hotel's 345 spacious three-room suites is equipped with a minibar, two telephones, and two TVs with free cable. Amenities include a rooftop health club with pool, an exercise room, a sauna, a whirlpool, and panoramic views of the city and Lake Michigan. Meeting rooms and boardrooms can be reserved for business functions. Within the hotel are two highly regarded bistros, the **Park Avenue Café** and the more casual **Mrs.**

Restaurants/Clubs: Red | Hotels: Purple | Shops: Orange | Outdoors/Parks: Green | Sights/Culture: Blue

Park's Tavern. Packages for weekends and extended stays are available. ♦ 198 E Delaware Pl (at N Mies van der Rohe Way). 664.1100, 800/222.8733; fax 664.9881 ♿

19 THE WHITEHALL HOTEL

$$ This 70-year old luxury hotel is done in a European style, starting with the prints of hunting dogs and horses in the lobby that suggest an Old World club. But after a face-lift a few years back, all 221 rooms are stocked with modern amenities and comforts, such as two-line phones, a phone in the bathroom, voice mail, data ports, and video games. Within the hotel, **Molive** restaurant serves American cuisine with a hint of the Mediterranean. It's a sidewalk café when the weather permits. With other, more luxurious hotels opening up in the area, the **Whitehall** is marketing itself as a value. Weekend packages are available, and its web site announces online rates "starting at $129." ♦ 105 E Delaware Pl (between N Michigan Ave and N Rush St). 944.6300. www.hotelwhitehallchicago.com ♿

20 JOHN HANCOCK CENTER

The tapered profile of "Big John" has anchored North Michigan Avenue since it was built by **Skidmore, Owings & Merrill** in 1970. Layers of retail, parking, office, and residential spaces make up this multi-use giant. Its sunken plaza fronting the avenue underwent a badly needed overhaul in 1994. The dramatic cross-bracing is part of an ingenious framing system that creates a rigid, tubelike tower, structurally efficient and resistant to wind. Although the **Hancock** is 327 feet shorter than the **Sears Tower**, its observation deck offers views of the lake and the Loop that make it a favorite of Chicago natives. Ride a high-speed elevator to the **Skydeck Observatory** on the 94th floor or sit down to a meal in the **Signature Room** on the 95th floor (see below); both offer spectacular vistas in every direction, especially at night. A better bargain is a visit to the massive **Images Lounge** on the 96th floor, where you can sip a drink—kids can have a soda—and take in the view for about the same price you'd pay for entry to the **Observatory**. Everyone else has the same idea, though, so expect a long wait for a seat, and be prepared to settle for one without much of a view. ♦ Fee for Observatory. Daily, 9AM-12PM. 875 N Michigan Ave (between E Chestnut St and E Delaware Pl). 751.3681 ♿

Within the John Hancock Center:

SIGNATURE ROOM

★★$$$ Incredible views of the city and lake provide a backdrop for meals at this lofty, dramatic perch. The ambitious, au courant food is good, but not great; dishes sometimes taste

as experimental as their names sound. Those with hearty appetites may opt for roasted pork tenderloin with sausage and cornbread stuffing. For breathtaking vistas at a slightly gentler cost, try the luncheon buffet or Sunday brunch. ♦ American ♦ M-Sa, lunch and dinner; Su, brunch and dinner. No tennis shoes, jeans, or athletic wear allowed. Reservations required for dinner. 787.9596; fax 280.9462 ♿

RICHARD GRAY GALLERY

Paintings, drawings, sculpture, and prints from the earlier masters of the 20th century, as well as current avant-garde artists, are sold here. Works by Picasso, Matisse, Moore, and Susan Rothenberg, among others, are displayed. ♦ M-F, Sa by appointment. 25th floor. 642.8877 ♿

THE CHEESECAKE FACTORY

$ More than just cheesecake, but 40 varieties of that as well. With crowds and long lines, confusion reigns. The menu offers fusion foods such as Tex-Mex egg rolls and Cajun jambalaya pasta. ♦ Café ♦ Daily, lunch and dinner. Street level. 337.1101 ♿

21 RAPHAEL HOTEL

$$ This reasonably priced 172-room hotel is perfect for those looking for intimacy and tastefully furnished rooms. The two-story lobby boasts cathedral windows, and the quaintly decorated rooms have sitting areas, stucco walls, and beamed ceilings. Although it can't offer the features of a large, expensive hotel, it does have very attentive service. A very pleasant restaurant is open for breakfast only. Weekend packages are available. ♦ 201 E Delaware Pl (at N Mies van der Rohe Way). 943.5000, 800/983.7870; fax 943.9483 ♿

22 HOTEL SOFITEL (WATER TOWER PLACE)

$$$$ Opened in summer 2002, the **Sofitel** is aiming to give the **Peninsula** a run for your money. The stunning 32-story prism-shaped building was designed by French architect Jean-Paul Viguier. Owing to its corner position, the hotel has two prominent façades with east and southwest exposures. The result is a tremendous amount of natural light coming in and great views going out. There are 415 elegantly appointed rooms and 62 suites, all with French accents. Marble-floor bathrooms have separate tub and shower. Rooms have three two-line phones, data ports, high-speed Internet access and web TV. When you're done telecommunicating, you can work out in the fitness room and gym or head right to the intimate **Le Bar.** There are 12 meeting and banquet suites for 12 to 40 people and a 4,500-square-foot ballroom. The **Cafe des Architectes** serves breakfast, lunch, and

dinner (Sunday, brunch only), with a wide range of prices. ◆ 20 E Chestnut (at N Wabash Ave). 324.4000, 800/SOFITEL; fax 337.9797 ♿ www.sofitel.com

23 MATERIAL POSSESSIONS

Everything for your table is here, in every medium, including handwoven mats, highly stylized contemporary place settings, earthy pottery, and sparkling glass. Most pieces would not be found in a department store, and many are unique. ◆ Daily. 54 E Chestnut St (between N Michigan Ave and N Rush St). 280.4885

24 TREMONT HOTEL

$$$ This small, attractive hotel was renovated in 1985 in the style of an English manor. The brass-and-wood-detailed lobby has the aura of a comfortable men's club, and the 137 rooms and penthouse suites have period furnishings. There's a concierge, multilingual staff, and turndown service complete with cognac. The hotel's **Crickets** restaurant has been replaced by **Mike Ditka's**, owned by former **Bears** coach Mike Ditka and specializing in the two necessities of life—meat and beer. ◆ 100 E Chestnut St (between N Michigan Ave and N Rush St). 751.1900, 800/621.8133; fax 751.9253 ♿ www.tremontchicago.com

25 FOURTH PRESBYTERIAN CHURCH

The founding congregation worshipped in its new church at another location for the first time on 8 October 1871, just hours before the Chicago Fire began and burned it to the ground. All but 5 of the 321 members lost their homes in the flames. This impressive Gothic Revival church, the congregation's second, was built in 1914 by **Ralph Adams Cram**. **Howard Van Doren Shaw**, one of the church's many prominent members, designed the parish house and the fountain in the ivy-trimmed courtyard (the most romantic church courtyard in the city). The ceiling murals were designed by Frederic Clay Bartlett. (This duo also collaborated on the **Second Presbyterian Church** near Prairie Avenue.) Excellent concerts are offered periodically at lunchtime and on Sunday afternoon. Holiday services are standing room only. ◆ 126 E Chestnut St (at N Michigan Ave)

26 CHALFINS' DELI

★$ This compact New York–style deli is colorful, lively, and full of great smells and tastes. Scrambled eggs with Nova Scotia

Fourth Presbyterian Church

salmon, thick-cut challah French toast, and other breakfasts can be ordered all day. Real winners are the pastrami and corned beef sandwiches served with spicy mustard. Takeout and delivery are available. ◆ Deli ◆ M, breakfast and lunch; Tu-Su, breakfast, lunch, and early dinner. 200 E Chestnut St (at N Mies van der Rohe Way), lower level. 943.0034; fax 943.8207

26 THE SALOON

★★$$$ Vegetarians need not stop here. The meaty menu includes dishes like surf and turf and even huge surf and turf, a large lobster tail, and Kansas City bone-in strip steak. Other succulent dishes are a slow-smoked 1-pound pork chop, blackened prime rib, and

Restaurants/Clubs: Red | **Hotels: Purple** | **Shops: Orange** | **Outdoors/Parks: Green** | **Sights/Culture: Blue**

65

whole roasted chicken. Brunch features a Santa Fe–style menu with Southwest barbecue and Texas chili. ♦ American ♦ Daily, lunch and dinner. 200 E Chestnut St (at N Mies van der Rohe Way). 280.5454. www.saloonsteakhouse.com

27 860-80 NORTH LAKE SHORE DRIVE APARTMENTS

The detailing in this pair of sleek steel-and-glass apartment towers, built in 1952, is masterful and subtle, the trademark of their architect, **Mies van der Rohe**. He later designed the apartments at **900-10 Lake Shore Drive**, and both pairs of buildings are home to many practicing Chicago architects. ♦ Between E Chestnut St and E Delaware Pl

28 FREE TROLLEY STOP

The white-and-brown sign on this block, and at 10 other locations along North Michigan Avenue, signifies the stopping point for a free trolley that runs between the Magnificent Mile and Navy Pier. Wrapped in green vinyl and modeled after the famous San Francisco transport, the trolley began running on weekends but may also be available on weekdays. Ask for information at the **Water Works** tourist information center across the street. ♦ N Michigan Ave (at E Chestnut St)

28 PLAZA ESCADA

This German import's Eurochic décor, with bright lighting and lots of white marble, focuses attention on the designer's ready-to-wear fashions, all artfully displayed more by color than by style. Prices are high: Be prepared to mortgage the farm. ♦ Daily. 840 N Michigan Ave (at E Chestnut St). 915.0500 ℹ

29 WATER TOWER PLACE

Designed in 1976 by **Loebl Schlossman Dart & Hackl** with **C.F. Murphy Associates**, this marble-clad, reinforced-concrete building is one of the first and most successful vertical shopping malls in the country. **Lord & Taylor** and **Marshall Field**'s are the anchors, and shops and restaurants fill seven stories. Movie theaters on two levels, each with several screens, provide another entertainment alternative should you run out of steam riding the

The Great Chicago Fire burned at a rate of 65 acres per hour.

McClurg Court was named after a mild-mannered bookseller, Alexander C. McClurg, who led one of the bloodiest charges of the Union forces in Atlanta. After the Civil War he was offered a career in the military, but he returned to Chicago and resumed selling books.

escalators or glass-enclosed elevators between retail stops. Shops include **Brookstone**, **Crabtree & Evelyn**, **Gap**, **Papyrus**, **Eileen Fisher**, **Rogers & Hollands Jewelers**, **Sharper Image**, **Victoria's Secret**, **The Walking Company**, and **Whitehall Jewelers**. ♦ Most stores open daily. 835 N Michigan Ave (at E Pearson St) ℹ www.shopwatertower.com

Within Water Tower Place:

ACCENT CHICAGO

Get your Chicago souvenirs here: T-shirts, tote bags, **Cubs** baseball hats, the recipe and the pan for deep-dish pizza, and zillions of postcards. ♦ Daily, 9AM-10PM. Seventh level. 944.1354. Also at Sears Tower (233 S Wacker Dr between W Jackson Blvd and W Adams St, 993.0499) and numerous other locations throughout the city ℹ

30 BISTRO 110

★★$$ Garlic lovers will find paradise in this bustling spot the instant they sample a buttery roasted bulb spread on good French bread. Wood-oven–roasted meats, fish, and fowl are pungent with garlic and herbs. The décor is bright, with polished light wood floors and murals by Judith Rifka. ♦ French ♦ Daily, lunch and dinner; F, Sa, until midnight. Reservations recommended. 110 E Pearson St (between N Michigan Ave and N Rush St). 266.3110 ℹ www.levyrestaurants.com

31 RITZ-CARLTON HOTEL

$$$$ The 12th-floor lobby is grand, complete with a skylit fountain. All of the 435 spacious rooms have king-size beds, plush and polished furnishings, and two-line speaker phones. A health club with a swimming pool, exercise equipment, a whirlpool, steam rooms, a sauna, and massages are offered courtesy of the hotel. A concierge is very helpful, and attention to guests' personal needs is exceptional. You can have lunch or afternoon tea in the lobby **Greenhouse**. The **Café** offers good casual fare with a nice view of the lobby. The lobby is especially attractive at Christmas, when it is ablaze with poinsettias. Weekend rates are available. ♦ 160 E Pearson St (between N Mies van der Rohe Way and N Michigan Ave). 266.1000, 800/332.3442; fax 266.1194 ℹ

Within the Ritz-Carlton Hotel:

The Dining Room

★★★★$$$$ This beautiful room, laden with exquisite flowers and romantically lighted, is a perfect setting for a special occasion. The food is special too, beginning with the complimentary appetizers. Among the excellent entrées are crepes filled with spinach and lobster tail, and breast of guinea hen braised in foie gras essence. Provocative desserts include rich Cointreau mousse sprinkled with berries and candied orange peels. Dainty little post-dessert sweets perfectly cap the meal. A prix-fixe menu and good low-calorie spa selections are offered, and there's a very good wine list too. Presentations, table appointments, and service meet the same high standard. A fine pianist plays during dinner. ◆ French ◆ M-Sa, dinner; Su, brunch and dinner. Reservations recommended. 573.5223 ♿

32 St. James Chapel/ Quigley Seminary

Step through an arched entryway on busy Rush Street and enter into another world altogether. A complex of Gothic buildings designed in 1917 and 1925 by **Gustav Steinbeck** surrounds a paved courtyard. That it's filled with parked cars only heightens the rather eerie illusion that you have been magically transported to Paris. Gargoyles, statue-filled niches, and spiky copper-covered dormers and towers complete the overall effect. The exteriors are a jewel-box setting for the real treasure—the seminary's chapel. Modeled after Sainte-Chapelle in Paris, the chapel features a brilliant display of stained glass. The 14 windows, designed and executed by Robert Giles, contain more than a half-million pieces of handmade English glass. The seminary was named for Chicago's Archbishop James Quigley, who in 1905 established **Cathedral College** to prepare boys for the priesthood. He died 10 years later, and his successor, Archbishop George Mundelein, fulfilled his plans for a larger seminary. ◆ M-F, 8AM-4PM. Pick up a visitor's pass around the corner at 103 E Chestnut St. 831 N Rush St (at E Pearson St). 787.9343

33 Chicago Horse and Carriage Company

Top-hatted drivers with horse-drawn carriages are lined up and ready to take you for a romantic tour of the northern end of the Magnificent Mile, or elsewhere by request. ◆ E Pearson St and N Michigan Ave. 944.9192

34 Seneca Park/Eli M. Schulman Playground

Local apartment dwellers and visitors alike do well to bring their kids to this compact public playground—the only one in this part of town—to let them burn off pent-up energy on the swings and slides. Funds for the facilities were raised by the Schulman family (of the popular **Eli's** across the street), who personally donated a good part of them. Note sculptor Deborah Butterfield's *Horse* on the park's eastern side; rising behind it is the **Museum of Contemporary Art**. ◆ E Chicago Ave and N Mies van der Rohe Way

PARK HYATT CHICAGO

35 Park Hyatt Chicago

$$$$ After being closed for an extensive renovation, the 203-room Park Hyatt has been reborn as one of Chicago's most luxurious (and priciest) hotels. From the moment you enter the lobby and glimpse Gerhard Richter's masterful painting *Piazza del Duomo, Milan*, you know that you are stepping into a deluxe hotel. A list of the amenities and comforts would take a month to recite, but here are just a few: Eames chairs, Brno desk chairs designed by Mies van der Rohe, DVD and CD players with an assortment of movies and music selections, refrigerator, minibar, two-line phones with category-five data ports, and in-room safes with laptop computer rechargers. In the bathrooms, which are closed off by sliding cherry-wood doors, there are double sinks, oversize tubs, walk-in showers with two heads, and flat-screen LCD TVs. *Convenience, comfort,* and *cost* are the bywords here. ◆ 800 N Michigan Ave (at E Chicago Avenue). 335.1234; fax 239.4000, 800/233.1234 ♿ www.hyatt.com

Within the Park Hyatt:

NoMI

★★★$$$$ Great views of North Michigan Avenue (for which the restaurant is named) and the Lake are the main attraction at this elegant seventh-floor venue that also has a 50-seat outdoor terrace when the weather permits. Chef Sandro Gamba, a finalist in the James Beard Foundation's "Rising Star Chef" award in 2000, has created a thoughtful menu with an upscale French accent that includes a strong emphasis on sushi/sashimi. One of the signature dishes is Carnaroli risotto, which features wild mushrooms, prosciutto, and fresh parsley. Authentic French breakfast is a special treat, with hot chocolate, baguette, fruit-tart brioche, and apple compote. ◆ French ◆ Sushi ◆ Daily, breakfast, lunch, and dinner; Sa-Su, brunch. Reservations recommended. 239.4030 ₺

GIORGIO ARMANI

The renowned Italian designer's boutique is filled with men's and women's suits, eveningwear, leather goods, and accessories. ◆ M-Sa. 752.2244

36 WATER TOWER

In 1869 **W.W. Boyington**, one of Chicago's first architects, designed the **Water Tower**

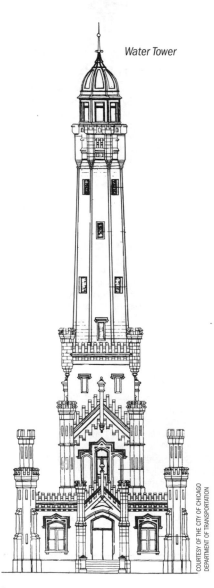

Water Tower

COURTESY OF THE CITY OF CHICAGO
DEPARTMENT OF TRANSPORTATION

(pictured left) in a naive imitation of the Gothic style. This is one of the few buildings to survive the Great Fire of 1871. In 1882 Oscar Wilde visited Chicago and described this structure as a "castellated monstrosity with pepper boxes stuck all over it." The city has plans to spice it up at the cost of $6.5 million and turn it into the home of the Lookingglass Theatre. (Actor David Schwimmer, a founding member of the company, donated $250,000 to the project, completed in 2003.) The surrounding park recently underwent a makeover courtesy of acclaimed fashion photographer and Chicago native Victor Skrebneski. Even before that, it was a popular spot for an alfresco lunch—and some people watching. ◆ 800 N Michigan Ave (at E Chicago Ave). 744.2400 ₺

37 CHICAGO WATER WORKS

The **Old Water Tower**'s **Pumping Station** now houses a **Chicago Office of Tourism Visitors' Information Center** and a **Hot Tix** booth. It's worth a stop to get your bearings and find out what special events are going on around the city. ◆ Daily. 163 E Pearson St (at N Michigan Ave between E Chicago Ave). 744.2400 ₺ www.cityofchicago.org/tourism

Within the Chicago Water Works:

LOOKINGGLASS THEATRE

In June 2003, with great fanfare, the city unveiled, within this landmark building, the new performance facility of **Lookingglass Theatre**, the company founded in 1988 by, among others, *Friends* star David Schwimmer, then a Northwestern grad. Designed by Morris Architects/Planners, Inc., the project entailed converting the existing space into two theaters, a main stage that can seat 270 and a rehearsal studio that also serves as space for classes and special events. Schwimmer, who still is active in the company, directed the first performance in the new theater, an adaptation of the Studs Terkel book *RACE: How Blacks and Whites Think and Feel About the American Obsession*. ◆ 337.0665. www.lookingglasstheatre.org ₺

Museum
of
Contemporary
Art

38 MUSEUM OF CONTEMPORARY ART (MCA)

Founded in 1967 to expand the Chicago art world beyond the bounds imposed by the conservative **Art Institute,** the **MCA** is dedicated to the avant-garde. Robert Fitzpatrick, the new head of MCA, has received credit for bringing new vitality to the museum's mission. Recent special exhibits of note have showcased the work of Ed Ruscha, Katarina Fritsch, and William Kentridge. In 2001, a program by Chicago artist Tony Fitzpatrick created especially for kids opened with Chicago schoolchildren participating in an interactive show. The $46 million building, opened in the summer of 1996, covers 220,000 square feet, almost seven times the space of its former incarnation. The building and sculpture garden were designed by Berlin architect **Josef Paul Kleihues.** It includes a museum shop, a 15,000-square-foot studio-classroom facility, a 15,000-volume art library, and a 300-seat theater for film screenings and lectures. Although the museum is completely wheelchair accessible, many visitors will climb the 32-step grand staircase that Kleihues likens to the propylaea of the Acropolis. After they're done, they can dine in the museum restaurant, **Puck's at the MCA,** a Wolfgang Puck effort that has a seasonal menu and an express menu (397.4034). ◆ Admission; free Tu evenings. Tu, 10AM-8PM; W-Su, 10AM-5PM. 220 E Chicago Ave (at N Mies van der Rohe Way). 280.2660 ᴕ www.mcachicago.org

39 NORTHWESTERN UNIVERSITY SCHOOL OF LAW/AMERICAN BAR ASSOCIATION (ABA)

At the eastern edge of the campus, along Lake Shore Drive, is the university's law school and the high-rise headquarters of the ABA. Completed in 1984, **Holabird & Root**'s complex is an exceptionally subtle and well-detailed modern addition to the neighboring Collegiate Gothic buildings of **James Gamble Rogers,** built from 1926 to 1927. Note the four-story atrium that joins old and new buildings on Chicago Avenue, and the granite buttresses that echo the earlier limestone forms. ◆ Northwestern University School of Law: 357 E Chicago Ave (between N Lake Shore Dr and N Fairbanks Ct). ABA: 750 N Lake Shore Dr (at E Superior St). www.nwu.edu

40 AMERICAN GIRL PLACE

The ultimate place for mother–daughter (and, what the heck, grandma too) bonding, this three-story shop is the retail section of the incredible doll phenomenon based in Wisconsin. There are pricey dolls galore, naturally, and all the accessories to go with them. Plus there's a café for tea and cookies and a 150-seat theater for special programs. ◆

Daily. 111 E Chicago Ave (between N Michigan Ave and N Rush St). 943.9400. www.americangirlplace.com

41 BANANA REPUBLIC

Of this contribution to Chicago architecture by New York's famed **Robert A.M. Stern,** one local critic commented, "Well, at least it's not any larger." Distinctly out of place in its surroundings, this branch of the national clothing chain looks like the Nairobi Airport hangar transported to North Michigan Avenue. Inside, hide stretches over the hanging lamps, leather and slate cover the floor, and a glass staircase somehow manages to look like a rope bridge. Architecture purists may scoff at this tribute to a land of pith helmets that never was, but shoppers who favor the chain's merchandise are likely to enjoy this store. ◆ Daily. 744 N Michigan Ave (between E Superior St and E Chicago Ave). 642.0020 ᴕ www.bananarepublic.com

41 RALPH LAUREN

Polo, anyone? The internationally known designer has designs on your wallet in this shop that features every conceivable product that bears his name or logo. An adjacent restaurant serves designer food. ◆ Daily. 750 N Michigan Ave (between E Superior St and E Chicago Ave). 280.1655. www.polo.com

41 TIFFANY & CO.

Whether dressing for a game of tennis or for an inaugural ball, those with dollars come here to spend them on dazzling jewels. The boutique carries special collections designed by Paloma Picasso and Elsa Peretti. ◆ Daily. 730 N Michigan Ave (between E Superior St and E Chicago Ave). 944.7500 ᴕ www.tiffany.com

42 THE PENINSULA HOTEL

$$$$ If you have any doubt that we've really reached the 21st century, a stay at the **Peninsula** will convince you. The web site provides virtual tours in two different computer platforms. With every room in the hotel wired with the latest technology, guests get to find out what it's like to be Bill Gates for a day. But it comes at a price that might make even Bill's eyes bulge. The moment you step into the soft, elegant peach-tinted lobby, you'll feel peachy, the hotel promises, experiencing "an immediate sense of belonging and comfort." Every indulgence of the discerning business and leisure traveler will be "attended to with gracious warmth." Each of the 339 luxuriously appointed guest rooms and suites has a state-of-the-art electronic control system. The marble bathroom has separate tub and shower. No mere fitness

room, the Peninsula has a 14,000-square-foot spa on the 19th and 20th floors, from which spectacular views of the Lake and North Michigan Avenue are always an option. On warm sunny days, you can lounge on the outdoor deck. A hydrotherapy Vichy shower can take the edge off a hard day of shopping. Or perhaps you'd prefer a Pilates class. Room service is available 24/7, naturally. Dining and drinking options are in abundance. **Shanghai Terrace** offers Asian delicacies. **The Lobby** offers all day dining and afternoon tea. **The Bar** is a cozy spot to unwind. **Pierrot Gourmet** is a street-level patisserie with a fine wine selection. If you can't afford to stay at the Peninsula, take the Internet tour. After a bad day, it's a virtual vacation in itself. ♦ 108 E Superior St (at N Michigan Ave). 337.2888; fax 751.2888 ♿

Within the Peninsula Hotel:

AVENUES

★★★★$$$$ When you settle into a world-class hotel with all the amenities you could want, you may not want to leave for dinner. At the **Peninsula**, you don't have to. **Avenues** is one of Chicago's finest eateries. In September 2004, Graham Elliot Bowles came in to serve as head chef. Bowles is a Food & Wine Magazine Best New Chef of 2004, and was garnering raves for his work at the Jackson House Inn in Woodstock, Vermont. Shortly thereafter, Brian Schoenbeck left **NoMI** to join him as pastry chef. In a warm, cushy dining room with an open kitchen and glass-encased wine cellar, you can luxuriate in leather armchairs while waiting for your meal. For starters, try the truffled frog's legs risotto. Entrées favor seafood selections such as chorizo-crusted Chatham cod, but the juniper-scented venison loin tempts one to stay on land. Desserts include lemon-thyme parfait, pineapple-carpaccio polenta cake, and terrine of heirloom beets with Roquefort ice cream, so remember to leave room. There's a three- or four-course degustation menu starting at $68. ♦ American contemporary ♦ Reservations recommended. Tu-Sa, dinner. 573.6754

43 NEIMAN MARCUS

Just the place to pick up that perfect little $1,000 christening gown—it simply wouldn't be **Neiman Marcus** at a lesser price. Designer salons on the second floor include Chanel and Ungaro. The fourth floor boasts the outstanding Epicure Department, a gourmet shop that carries caviar, exotic cheese, choco-lates from around the world, and foods freshly prepared in local restaurants. The store also has a full-service salon that offers customers hair care, makeup, and massages. The four-story building is actually part of the **Olympia Center** (built in 1984 by **Skidmore, Owings & Merrill**), a 63-story pink granite office and condominium tower that fronts Chicago Avenue. Note the glass keystone in the Michigan Avenue arch. ♦ Daily. 737 N Michigan Ave (at E Superior St). 642.5900 ♿ www.neimanmarcus.com

44 FITZPATRICK CHICAGO HOTEL

$$$ Formerly the **Summerfield Suites**, this facility has undergone a face-lift to elevate it to a luxurious boutique hotel with an Irish motif. There are 100 spacious rooms and 40 suites, all with data ports, Internet access, cable TV, and other electronic comforts. It's designed to serve the business traveler and pamper the vacationing tourist. Room service is available 24 hours a day. Within the hotel, **Fitzers Pub** serves Irish breakfast and, for lunch and dinner, Irish standards such as shepherd's pie. Check the web site for Internet deals. ♦ 166 E Superior St (between N Fairbanks Ct and N Michigan Ave). 787.6000; fax 787.4331. www.fiztpatrickhotels.com

45 BROOKS BROTHERS

Traditional styles for men, women, and boys fill the two floors of this classic haberdashery. ♦ Daily. 713 N Michigan Ave (between E Huron and E Superior Sts). 915.0060. Also at 209 S LaSalle St (between W Quincy and W Adams Sts). 263.0100 ♿ www.brooksbrothers.com

46 CHICAGO PLACE

Built in 1990, this 43-story multi-use complex consists of an eight-floor retail mall designed by **Skidmore, Owings & Merrill** and a 272-room apartment tower designed by **Solomon Cordwell Buenz & Associates**. The three-part clear, stained-glass, and colored windows on the exterior of the eight-story base are classic Chicago School references, and the curving corners evoke **Louis Sullivan's Carson Pirie Scott & Company** building. The first two stories are clad in various shades of pink and green granite, whereas the upper levels of the base and tower are painted concrete. Inside, the mall is decorated with Prairie School colors and motifs, with space for 80 specialty shops and restaurants. Note Mrs. O'Leary's cow and other local icons in the lobby mural. Anchors are the seven-story Midwest flagship store of **Saks Fifth Avenue**, **Ann Taylor**, **Talbots**, and **Bockwinkel's Grocery**, Michigan Avenue's only full-service grocery store. The top floor of the mall has a palm garden/food court with a flowing stream; covered by a barrel-vaulted glass roof, it evokes European winter gardens of the late 19th century. ◆ Daily. Free parking (with a validated ticket) is available in a small lot at the lower level. 700 N Michigan Ave (at E Huron St). www.chicagoplace.com

Within Chicago Place:

BODY SHOP

Based in Brighton, England, this boutique for lotions and potions now has branches in a number of US cities. Whether you prefer Grapefruit Shampoo or Peppermint Foot Lotion, you'll be happy to know that all the products are animal- and environment-friendly. ◆ First level. 482.8301 &

CHIAROSCURO

An art gallery that's also a gift shop, this is a browser's heaven full of wall art, statuary, whimsical folk sculpture, hand-painted furniture, handwoven apparel, an outstanding selection of jewelry, and handmade art cards. ◆ Fourth level. 988.9253 & www.chiaroart.com

47 ALLERTON CROWNE PLAZA HOTEL

$$$ This famous hotel, from which Don McNeil once broadcast the Breakfast Club radio show from the "make-believe ballroom" at the Tip Top Tap, has undergone a long-overdue face-lift courtesy of the Crowne Plaza chain. The 23rd floor is now a real ballroom overlooking Michigan Avenue, and many of the 445 rooms and 57 suites on the upper floors afford great city views as well. A sauna and fitness room have been added, as well as in-room amenities to suit the business traveler: modem and data ports, voice mail, dual phone lines, minibar and coffeemaker, in-room safe and individual temperature control, express video checkout, complimentary newspaper. Within the hotel, the **Taps** restaurant serves breakfast, lunch, and dinner and is open between 6:30AM and 11PM; room service is available 24 hours a day. Weekend rates are available. ◆ 701 N Michigan Ave (at E Huron St). 440.1500, 800/2CROWNE; fax 440.1819 & www.crowneplaza.com

48 RADISSON HOTEL & SUITES

$$$ Formerly the **Sheraton Plaza**, this facility recently underwent a $9 million renovation. It has 350 rooms with 90 suites appointed with comfortable contemporary furnishings. Definitely geared to the business traveler, the hotel has computer ports in every room; there's also a health club and an outdoor pool. **Becco d'Oro**, an upscale ristorante, serves breakfast, lunch, and dinner daily. ◆

160 E Huron St (at N St. Clair St). 787.2900, 800/333.3333; fax 787.5158 & www.radisson.com

49 CITY PLACE

Boisterously decorated with red granite and blue reflective and tinted glass and accented with medallions and chevrons, this 40-story mixed-use complex (pictured below) was built by **Loebl Schlossman & Hackl** in 1990. The **Omni Chicago Hotel** occupies floors 5 through 25, and there are 13 floors of offices above that. ◆ 676 N Michigan Ave (at E Huron St)

Within City Place:

OMNI CHICAGO HOTEL

$$$ All of the 367 suites here are luxuriously furnished with fine upholstery and polished woods and equipped with wet bars and two telephones; all offer incredible views. Guests are treated to nightly turndown service, complimentary newspaper, overnight laundry, and 24-hour room service. A fully equipped health club with an indoor pool sits beneath a skylight on the top floor. For $1,000 to

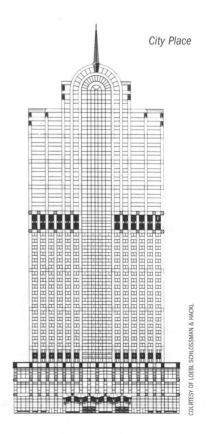

City Place

COURTESY OF LOEBL SCHLOSSMAN & HACKL

Restaurants/Clubs: Red | Hotels: Purple | Shops: Orange | Outdoors/Parks: Green | Sights/Culture: Blue

$1,500 a night, guests can select from a few suites designed in the signature styles of **Frank Lloyd Wright**, **Charles Rennie Mackintosh**, and **Mies van der Rohe**, among other darlings of Modernism. Business services and two deluxe boardrooms are available, as are weekend packages. ◆ 944.6664, 800/843.6664; fax 266.3017 ᷁ www.omni-hotels.com

Within the Omni Chicago Hotel:

Cielo

★$$$ The sky seems to be the limit here, with floor-to-ceiling windows overlooking Michigan Avenue and a trompe l'oeil mural of the sky on the domed ceiling (hence the name). A wood-burning oven and grill add an Italian accent to the menu, but the focus is on foods from the Adriatic, Mediterranean, and Atlantic coasts. Dinner entrées include roasted duckling basted with lavender honey and rabbit with muscat wine and figs. ◆ Mediterranean ◆ Daily, breakfast, lunch, and dinner. 944.7676 ᷁

50 Cole Haan

Fine footwear and leather fashion accessories, many hand-sewn, are sold here, as are Italian-made handbags, briefcases, and luggage. ◆ Daily. 673 N Michigan Ave (between E Erie and E Huron Sts). 642.8995 ᷁

50 NikeTown

In some years, this glossy, high-tech, three-level store has eclipsed the **Museum of Science and Industry** as the most popular tourist attraction in the city. Packed with sports memorabilia, innovative displays (the wall behind the swimming equipment is alive with tropical fish), and a basketball court for trying out your new high-tops, it's worth visiting just to take a look. ◆ Daily. 669 N Michigan Ave (between E Erie and E Huron Sts). 642.6363 ᷁ www.niketown.com

51 Tru

★★★★$$$$ Named one of *Chicago* magazine's best new restaurants of 2000, **Tru** epitomizes haute cuisine at its haughtiest. A partnership between Rich Melman and award-winning chefs Rick Tramonto and Gale Gand (she does the desserts; he does the rest), this is one of the most talked-about eateries to open in a long time. From the moment you step inside and glimpse the stylized cobalt sculpture of a woman's torso, art by Andy Warhol, and the Riedel glasses, you know that you are in for a peak dining experience. There is no arguing that Tramonto's French-influenced creations and Gand's imaginative

Of the 20 eateries named "best new restaurants" by *Chicago* magazine in 1998, 7 have closed.

treats raise food preparation to an expressive art. But it all can get just a bit precious: Caviar is served on a glass staircase, fish tartare is delivered on a mirror, salad comes packaged in a Japanese bento box. Be prepared for a special gustatory experience, expect to devote a whole evening to having it, and don't allow yourself to think about the fact that there are people living in housing projects just 20 blocks away. A three-course prix-fixe menu starts at $70; the kitchen table is available at $150 per person and likely will require a 2 month advance reservation. ◆ American contemporary ◆ M-Sa, dinner; lunch for parties of 10 or more by appointment. Jacket required. Reservations required. No smoking permitted. 676 N St. Clair St (at E Huron St). 202.0001 ᷁

52 680 North Lake Shore Place

In 1926 **Nimmons & Dunning** added a blue-and-brown Gothic Revival tower to their brick-and-terra-cotta building, which had been erected two years earlier as the American Furniture Mart. Renovated in 1984 by **Lohan Associates**, it now houses condominiums, a retail arcade, and offices, including those of the Playboy empire. Before Playboy moved in, the building's address had been 666 North Lake Shore Drive. It was changed because the original numerals led some to call it the "Sign-of-Satan Building." ◆ 680 N Lake Shore Dr (at E Huron St)

Within 680 North Lake Shore Place:

Treasure Island

This gourmet grocery store has a fantastic take-out deli that caters to every possible taste, from roasted chicken to bulging hand-carved sandwiches to bounteous salads. It makes for a perfect summertime picnic at the lakefront right across the street. ◆ Daily. 664.0400 ᷁

53 Crate & Barrel

Designed in 1990 as an elegant "machine for selling" by **Solomon Cordwell Buenz &**

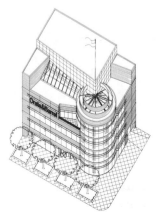

COURTESY OF SOLOMON CORDWELL BUENZ & ASSOCIATES

Associates, this five-story glass-and-white-aluminum building (pictured page 72) is the flagship store of the housewares and home furnishings chain. Chicagoan Gordon Segal started the business in 1962 in a small store in the Old Town neighborhood, using overturned crates and barrels as merchandise displays. (That location later became an outlet store and has been replaced by an even bigger outlet on West North Avenue, where bargain hunters can find last season's merchandise at rock-bottom prices.) This store, which has the sleek look of an ocean liner, stands out among the traditional masonry buildings of Michigan Avenue. A glassy corner rotunda is full of escalators that carry you past tempting displays of everything from culinary equipment to contemporary furniture. ◆ Daily. 646 N Michigan Ave (between E Ontario and E Erie Sts). 787.5900 ᕫ. Also at 850 W North Ave (at N Claybourn Ave). 573.9800 ᕫ Outlet at 800 W North Ave (at N Halsted St). 787.4775 ᕫ www.crateandbarrel.com

54 CARTIER

This is Chicago's preeminent jewelry store, carrying impeccably crafted gold rings, necklaces, and bracelets; extraordinary gemstones; handsome wristwatches; and china and stationery. ◆ M-Sa. 630 N Michigan Ave (between E Ontario and E Erie Sts). 266.7440 ᕫ www.cartier.com

55 BURBERRY

Expect quality and high prices at this two-floor emporium of fine British clothing for men and women. The specialties are outerwear and raincoats. ◆ Daily. 633 N Michigan Ave (at E Ontario St). 787.2500 ᕫ www.burberry.com

56 JOE O'NEIL'S BAR & GRILL

★$ For as long as most people can remember, this dark, cozy tavern was one of the few places along North Michigan Avenue where someone could get a basic beer and burger with no muss and fuss. It was owned by Howard Jones, a garrulous and occasionally grouchy barkeep. Now that Howard has gone off to that great tavern in the sky, his friend Joe O'Neil has taken the place over. It's still a gem and a bargain, a reminder of the days when this was still a neighborhood. A back terrace is open in summer. ◆ American ◆ Daily, lunch and dinner. 152 E Ontario St (between N St. Clair St and N Michigan Ave). 787.5269

57 BICE

★$$$ Although this branch of the Milan-based chain does not attract the trendsetters and beautiful people the way it used to, it is still a popular spot. The menu is extensive, with a good selection of pasta, risotto, veal, and chicken prepared in a variety of ways, sometimes with exotic or unexpected ingredients. The best people watching is in the bar and, in good weather, the sidewalk café. ◆ Italian ◆ Daily, lunch and dinner. Reservations recommended. 158 E Ontario St (between N St. Clair St and N Michigan Ave). 664.1474

57 RED ROOF INN

$ A great price and a prime location make this 195-room link in the motel chain one of the best deals in town. Standard, clean, and comfortable, the rooms are equipped with voice mail, cable TV (including HBO), and a service of free local phone calls. The **Coco Pazzo Café**, an offshoot of the excellent *ristorante* on West Hubbard Street, is one of the best outdoor cafés in the neighborhood for people watching—it also serves great Italian food. ◆ 162 E Ontario St (at N St. Clair St). 787.3580, 800/733.7663; fax 787.1299 ᕫ

58 CAPITAL GRILLE

★★★$$$$ A relative newcomer on the steakhouse scene, this is yet another clubby joint in which to have your steak and eat it too, and wash it down with a martini or three. Dry-aged choice is the cut, and if you're a steak lover, you'll leave sated. For starters try the steak tartar or the $40 cold shellfish platter. Choose from five styles of potatoes. And leave room for cheesecake and Key lime pie. ◆ Steakhouse ◆ 633 N St. Clair St (at E Ontario St).337.9400 ᕫ

58 WYNDHAM CHICAGO

$$$ Located one block east of Michigan Avenue, this sparkling new 17-story facility is designed for the comfort of the business traveler. There are 417 oversize guest rooms, 49 executive suites, and 45 "corner kings." In-

---

Restaurants/Clubs: Red | Hotels: Purple | Shops: Orange | Outdoors/Parks: Green | Sights/Culture: Blue

room amenities include voice mail and data ports, coffeemaker, hair dryer, minibar, and complimentary newspaper. There's a full exercise facility with indoor pool, whirlpool, sauna, and masseuse. Twelve meeting rooms with more than 20,000 square feet of flexible meeting space and a 4,500-square-foot grand ballroom make this a facility that corporate meeting planners may want to consider. Room service is available 24 hours a day. ♦ 633 N St. Clair St (at E Erie St). 573.0300, 877.999.3223 ♿ www.wyndham.com

Within the Wyndham Chicago:

CALITERRA
CAL ITAL BAR & GRILLE

CALITERRA

★★★$$$ On the second floor, Caliterra is a pleasant, comfortable restaurant with a menu that nicely merges Californian and Tuscan cuisine. The windowed space affords a nice view of the busy streets below, and the open kitchen affords an equally nice view of the goings-on in executive chef Rick Gresh's place of work. Gourmet brick-oven pizzas, though a bit on the pricey side, offer a nice start. A more adventurous opener is the Ahi tuna with ginger soy sauce, cucumbers, and wasabi. Pastas and main courses are done with simplicity and imagination—the angel hair tossed with fresh tomato and basil and the seared veal chop with crispy fried Portobello mushrooms are winners. For dessert, try the baked Alaska. ♦ Cal-Ital ♦ Daily, breakfast, lunch, and dinner. 274.4444 ♿

59 LES NOMADES

★★★$$$$ Subdued sandy colors, antique chandeliers, and hardwood floors give this establishment a distinctly French ambiance. Widely regarded as one of the best dining places in Chicago, this elegant salon features such fine cuisine as Jonah crab cake on Dijon beurre blanc crowned with frizzled sweet potato; roasted duck breast; and sautéed Arctic char with citrus sauce and lemon-scented couscous. Save room for at least one of the remarkable desserts—perhaps pineapple tarte tatin with lemongrass ice cream. The wine list is excellent and the martini is first-rate. ♦ French ♦ Tu-Sa, dinner. Reservations recommended. 222 E Ontario St (between N Fairbanks Ct and N St. Clair St). 649.9010 ♿

60 RON OF JAPAN

$$$ This branch of an Ōsaka-based chain of steak houses has a flair for the dramatic. Seating is at huge seashell-shaped red-vinyl booths, and many meals are prepared table-side at *teppanyaki* tables. Waitresses scurry about in kimonos, and the prime rib is presented on a samurai sword. Some seafood is available. ♦ Steak house ♦ Daily dinner. 230 E Ontario St (between N Fairbanks Ct and N St. Clair St). 644.6500

61 SCHATZ BUILDING

This place has a history: Once home to Chicago's famed **Chez Paree** nightclub and, briefly, the school that began as the **American Bauhaus** and became the **Institute of Design**, it's now owned by a sculptor named Lincoln Schatz; a few other artists have studios here too. Inside is a lively little restaurant, **Cucina Italiana**, offering quick and inexpensive meals, and a jazz and blues place called **Milt Trenier's**. Along the North Fairbanks Court side of the building is a massive mural inspired by Michelangelo's *Moses*. ♦ 247 E Ontario St (at N Fairbanks Ct)

Within the Schatz Building:

WEST EGG CAFE

$ Order breakfast all day at this noisy, friendly spot. Also available at table or counter are salads, sandwiches, and pasta. ♦ American ♦ Daily, breakfast and lunch. 620 N Fairbanks Ct (at E Ontario St). 280.8366

62 W CHICAGO LAKESHORE

$$$ Starwood recently did a major remodeling project that transformed a worn-out Holiday Inn into one of the hippest places in town. Situated along Lake Shore Drive near **Navy Pier**, it's the only hotel in Chicago directly overlooking Lake Michigan. There are down-stuffed beds in each of the 556 guest rooms and suites, along with oversize desks, high-speed Internet access, and other technological conveniences. There's also a "munchie box," which the hotel describes as a "snacker's utopia," and the hotel offers "whatever/ whenever" service to handle special requests. **Whiskey Sky** is a supercool rooftop lounge that offers jaw-dropping views of the Lake. It's a great place to unwind after a workout in the fitness center or a swim in the indoor heated pool. The **Lobby Bar** is a comfortable, smartly appointed room that serves light fare from 6AM to 10PM. The **Wave** restaurant serves well-prepared Mediterranean cuisine in a casual setting and is open until 11PM. ♦ 644 N Lake Shore Dr (at E Ontario St). 943-9200; fax 255-4411 ♿ www.whotels.com

63 OLIVE PARK

🅿 This public park, built to camouflage a water-filtration plant on the lake shore, boasts a wonderful view of the skyline. The grass and park benches are perfect for a picnic. During the summer, this is the site of several festivals. A small public beach sits immediately to the west. Access is by an underpass at East Grand

Avenue or from **Navy Pier** parking lots. ◆ N Lake Shore Dr and E Ohio St

64 SZECHWAN

★★$$ Opened by popular Chinese restaurateur George Kwan, this spot features dim sum and noodle dishes served alongside specials ranging from moo shu pork to sautéed swordfish. With well-executed regional cuisine in a casual atmosphere, this is a pleasant change of pace. ◆ Chinese ◆ Daily, lunch and dinner. 625 N Michigan Ave (at E Ontario St). 482.9898

65 600 NORTH MICHIGAN AVENUE

Many Chicagoans have become alarmed about the creeping of suburbia into the city, as Ohio and Ontario Streets continue their transformation into tourist strips conveniently connected to the Kennedy Expressway. This recently completed retail mall strengthens their case. Stores in this mall include branches of **Eddie Bauer**; **Marshalls**, a discount clothing store chain; and **Linens 'n Things**, a chain emporium of sheets and towels. There's a multiplex movie theater and **The Viacom Store**, a video palace for those with short attention spans. The eatery is **Heaven on Seven**, an offshoot of a popular lunchtime haunt in the Loop. ◆ Daily. At E Ohio St ♿

66 THE GAP

The Midwest flagship store of the casual-wear giant covers three levels and half a city block. The reason it's worth noting is that it is perhaps the most appealing new building to go up on North Michigan Avenue in a long time. Dominated by windows, it is one of the few structures in recent years that has preserved light in the darkening neighborhood. Credit goes to imaginative architect **Stanley Tigerman**. ◆ Daily. 555 N Michigan Ave (at E Ohio St). 494.8580, 800/GAPSTYLE ♿ Also at numerous locations throughout the city. www.gap.com

67 SAYAT-NOVA

★$$ The walls of this romantic room are adorned with Oriental tapestries and curve into semiprivate alcoves. A compact menu features mostly familiar Middle Eastern cuisine, from hummus to shish kebab. ◆ Middle Eastern ◆ M-Sa, lunch and dinner; Su,

dinner. 157 E Ohio St (between N St. Clair St and N Michigan Ave). 644.9159

68 CHICAGO MARRIOTT

$$ Huge yet comfortable, this bustling hotel is one of the city's most popular convention venues. Long registration lines snake through the marble-floored lobby, which is just a step away from an extravagant atrium bar and lounge. Both lobby and lounge are encircled by retail shops. The more than 1,100 rooms are fairly standard, with modern furnishings and anonymous artwork on the walls. A health club and indoor swimming pool are available to all guests. Restaurants within the hotel are **J.W.'s Steakhouse** and **Allie's Grill**. ◆ 540 N Michigan Ave (between E Grand Ave and E Ohio St). 836.0100, 800/228.0265; fax 836.6139 ♿

Within the Chicago Marriott:

VIRGIN MEGASTORE

The retail outgrowth of the Virgin Records label, this corner music and book emporium features an astonishing selection of CDs, tapes, videos, DVDs, and books. Browse till you drop, then revive yourself with a cup of Italian roast in the second-floor café. ◆ Daily, until 11PM. 645.9300

KENNETH COLE NEW YORK

For the woman who's feeling footloose and fancy free, this chic shoe boutique is a very fine place to be. ◆ Daily. 644.1163. www.kennethcole.com

69 TIMBERLAND

This shop is part of a chain specializing in rugged outdoor clothing, boots and shoes, and accessories. ◆ Daily. 545 N Michigan Ave (between E Grand Ave and E Ohio St). 494.0171 ♿

70 LE MERIDIEN HOTEL

$$$ This 13-story, international hotel has a French-inspired décor. The 311 large guest rooms include 33 suites, and all have high-speed Internet access. There is a spa with steam room, Jacuzzi, and fitness equipment. Dining options in the hotel include **Cerise**, an upscale bistro, and **Le Rendez-Vous Bar**,

---

Restaurants/Clubs: Red | Hotels: Purple | Shops: Orange | Outdoors/Parks: Green | Sights/Culture: Blue

which offers a light menu of appetizers, sandwiches, and salads. The multilingual staff and concierge may make **Le Meridien** an attractive choice for foreign visitors. ♦ 521 N Rush St (between W Illinois St and W Grand Ave). 645.1500, 800.543.4300 &

71 THE SHOPS AT NORTH BRIDGE

The malling of North Michigan Avenue seems to have reached critical mass with the completion of yet another shopper's paradise. This complex, which "bridges" to its anchor store, **Nordstrom**, in the River North area to the west, has four levels and includes mostly national stores with franchises featuring merchandise ranging from toys and clothes for kids to clothes and toys for moms. Among the shops are **Ann Taylor**, **The Lego Store**, **Benetton**, **Optica**, **Swatch**, **Sephora**, and **H2O+**. The fourth-floor eatery is dubbed Chicago's Magnificent Meal and includes local casual-dining favorites such as **Fluky's** hot dogs, **Pot Belly Sandwich Works**, and **Tuscany Café**. ♦ Daily. 520 N Michigan Ave (at E Grand Ave) 327.2300 & www.northbridgechicago.com

Within The Shops at North Bridge:

HILLIGOSS GALLERIES

HILLIGOSS GALLERIES

This is the city entry of a gallery that has been in historic Long Grove, Illinois, for 10 years. Tom Hilligoss handles a wide variety of contemporary works, as well as prints by such high-profile masters as Rembrandt, Renoir, Monet, Chagall, and Picasso. ♦ Fourth floor. 755.0300

HANIG'S MEPHISTO

This is another prominent foot in the door for a local family shoe store known for high quality and reasonable prices. In addition to selling shoes, civic-minded merchant Peter Hanig was responsible for getting the city interested in "Cows on Parade," the celebrated outdoor art program that decorated city streets in the summer of 1999 and has since been copied by other cities. ♦ Second floor. Daily. 494.9808. www.hanigs.com

72 HOTEL INTER- CONTINENTAL CHICAGO

$$$ Designed by **Walter W. Ahlschlager**, the hotel opened in 1929 as the **Medinah Athletic Club**, an opulent leisure site for members of the Shriners and their families. When the Depression hit, the place went bankrupt. In ensuing years, the property operated as a succession of hotels, collecting more layers of paint and plaster with each new identity. Multimillion-dollar renovations undertaken by **Harry Weese & Associates** in the late 1980s uncovered long-forgotten terra-cotta frescoes, murals, marble walls and floors, and bronze and brass trim, all of which have been painstakingly restored under the direction of Lido Lippi, who was involved in preliminary research for the restoration of Rome's Sistine Chapel. The 41-story Indiana limestone façade was cleaned and the original gold leaf and gold-plate highlighting were renewed. The building is crowned with a mosquelike dome that was gilded and illuminated to shimmer at night. Ask to tour the hotel's meeting room and ballroom areas, which are a mélange of fantastic styles from many cultures, including Egyptian, Roman, Greek, Spanish, and Asian—from the Assyrian hall of lions to the massive French Renaissance ballroom.

Renovated in 2002, the hotel has 807 rooms and 72 suites, all with the amenities expected of a high-end business hotel. All hotel guests may use the health club, which boasts a mosaic-tile indoor swimming pool that was once the training site for Olympic gold medalist and future Tarzan Johnny Weissmuller. ♦ 505 N Michigan Ave (between E Illinois St and E Grand Ave). 944.4100, 800/327.0200; fax 944.1320 & www.intercontinental.com

73 RIVER EAST PLAZA

This former commercial shipping terminal was restored in 1989 and turned into a sprawling mall, **North Pier**, which soon became one of the most popular spots in town with the younger set, especially suburbanites and out-of-towners. But success was fleeting—before it could even fill all of its retail space, the regulars stopped showing up as much. Soon many of the retailers jumped ship as well. The result: a virtual brick ghost town that's trying to recapture its short-lived splendor, with shops that include a framing store, hair salon, and gourmet grocery. There's a wonderful view of the city from the back dock, behind which boat tours depart. ♦ 435 E Illinois St (between N Streeter Dr and N McClurg Ct). 836.4300

Within River East Plaza:

DICK'S LAST RESORT

$$ Large groups can have a good time at this boisterous restaurant with long rows of tables,

a warm-weather patio on the pier, and a Dixieland band contributing to the atmosphere. The burgers are big and juicy, and tin buckets keep your french fries hot or your beer cold. The huge beer list includes a 25-ounce African Mamba, something of a house specialty. ◆ American ◆ Daily, lunch and dinner; M-Th, Su, until 2AM; F, Sa, until 3AM; during winter: daily until 12:30AM. 836.7870

74 LAKE POINT TOWER

In 1968 **Schipporeit-Heinrich** and **Graham, Anderson, Probst & White**, whose architects had been students of **Mies van der Rohe** at the **Illinois Institute of Technology**, based the design of this curving three-lobed tower on a visionary skyscraper Mies had proposed for Berlin almost 50 years earlier. Located near the foot of **Navy Pier** and rising to a height of 645 feet, this condominium building affords its residents extraordinary views. Its two-story base features a private landscaped park with a lagoon and a swimming pool. ◆ 505 N Lake Shore Dr (at E Illinois St)

75 STREETER DRIVE

This short curve of a street at the head of **Navy Pier** is named for Captain George Wellington Streeter, who, with his wife, Maria, was beached near here in the late 19th century when their excursion boat accidentally ran aground on a sandbar. When they couldn't free their boat, they decided to fill up the lake around it with dirt from nearby construction sites. Streeter was aided by other squatters, who built shanties on the new land. The Chicago police tried many times to remove the Streeters and other residents of what had grown to a 180-acre shantytown. (Streeter was briefly imprisoned after someone was killed during an attempted ouster.) He officially lost his battle in 1918, when a court ordered his removal and the burning of the shanties. ◆ Between E Grand Ave and E Illinois St

76 NAVY PIER

Built in 1916 as the **Municipal Pier**, this 3,000-foot-long structure was intended to serve both commercial and excursion boats, but commercial shipping moved to South Side's Lake Calumet and the automobile came into general use, knocking the wind out of the sails of the excursion-boat business. That left Chicago with a magnificent prome-nade that extends over a half mile out into the lake. For decades the city tried to figure out what to do with it. The US Navy occupied it during World War II (hence its name), and it was later the first Chicago campus for the **University of Illinois**. The spacious domed auditorium at the eastern end was modestly

renovated by the city in 1976; the annual International Art Expo started using it at about the same time. After that, the pier drew various ethnic festivals, food fairs, and other art shows. In 1991, the city finally embarked on a multimillion-dollar renovation, which included shoring its pilings and tearing down all but the two main buildings at the western end of the pier and the auditorium.

Today the pier is one of Chicago's major tourist attractions, with over 40,000 square feet of restaurants and retail shops. A six-story glass atrium houses the **Crystal Gardens**, a year-round, 1-acre indoor botanical park featuring lush gardens and palm trees and evergreens surrounding fountains and public seating. The **Ferris wheel** rises to 150 feet and is modeled after the very first Ferris wheel (built for Chicago's 1893 World's Columbian Exposition). Illuminated by thousands of lights at night, the wheel accommodates 240 passengers for each 7.5-minute ride.

The **Musical Carousel** documents the history of the pier with hand-painted scenes on the rounding boards, and the 38 hand-painted animals were designed to represent the different styles used throughout the history of the carousel. During the summer, there are concerts at the Skyline Stage, a 1,500-seat outdoor theater. ◆ Daily; Ferris wheel and carousel operate seasonally. 700 E Grand Ave (at N Streeter Dr). 595.7437 ♿ www.navypier.com

Within Navy Pier:

CHICAGO CHILDREN'S MUSEUM

CHICAGO CHILDREN'S MUSEUM

Known for its interactive and creative exhibits, the 57,000-square-foot facility offers exhibits like the *Inventing Lab*, where children are given the raw materials to create their own computer software programs, musical instru-ments, and flying machines. Other exhibits include *Waterways*, where children don rain-coats to experiment with water, and the

---

Restaurants/Clubs: Red | Hotels: Purple | Shops: Orange | Outdoors/Parks: Green | Sights/Culture: Blue

Climbing Schooner, which allows youngsters to climb the riggings 35 feet to the crow's nest and then slide down a ladder to the lower deck. ◆ Admission. Daily, until 8 PM. Family Pavilion. 527.1000 ♿ www.chichildrensmuseum.org

NAVY PIER IMAX THEATER

This 440-seat theater has a five-story, 80-foot-wide screen with a film format 10 times that shown in conventional theaters. The 1-ton movie projector magnifies the image 300 times. Recent shows included *Sharks* and *Robots*. ◆ Admission. M-Th, 10AM-9PM; F, Sa, 10AM-1AM; Su, 11AM-7PM. Family Pavilion. 595.5MAX ♿ www.imax.com/chicago

CHICAGO SHAKESPEARE THEATER

Chicago Shakespeare Theater is Chicago's professional theater dedicated to the works of William Shakespeare. Founded as Shakespeare Repertory in 1986 by artistic director Barbara Gaines, the company changed its name when it moved to **Navy Pier** in October 1999. Productions take place in a state-of-the art 510-seat courtyard-style theater. The Main Floor, Dress Circle, and Gallery wrap gracefully around the thrust stage, making it an intimate and dynamic space. Only nine rows separate the most distant seat from the actors on stage. Gaines and the company have received 26 Jefferson Awards, including Best Production and Best Director. The theater also features a flexible 180-seat studio theater, a teacher resource center, an English-style pub, a Shakespearean bookstall, and a special events room with breathtaking views of Chicago's skyline. ◆ 595.5600 ♿ www.chicagoshakes.com

In its November 2004 issue, *Chicago* magazine named the following as "the 20 very finest restaurants" in and around the city: Tru, Charlie Trotter's, Everest, Topolobampo/Frontera Grill, Spiaggia, Seasons, Pluton, NoMI, Naha, Arun's, Blackbird, Carlos', LeFrancais, Les Nomades, Ambria, Moto, Gabriel's, Spring, Crofton on Wells, MK.

77 TRIBUNE TOWER

An international design competition held by the *Chicago Tribune* in 1922 yielded numerous famous designs in addition to **Hood & Howells**'s prizewinning Gothic tower, which many considered retro in an era of emerging modern style. Today it is the grand old gentleman of North Michigan Avenue, and Chicagoans wouldn't trade its buttressed tower for anything. At street level, the walls have embedded stones—each of them labeled—that were pirated from famous and ancient monuments worldwide by the newspaper's foreign correspondents. These include pieces of the Parthenon, Notre Dame, and the Pyramids. Set into the north wall of the lobby is a stone from the Cave of the Nativity in Bethlehem, where Christ is said to have been born.

Also at street level is a fully equipped **WGN Radio** studio. (**WGN** is owned by the *Chicago Tribune*, and the station's call letters derive from the newspaper's old boast of being the "world's greatest newspaper.") Here you can watch through a glass window as traffic, sports, and business reports are given by local radio personalities, with whom you can converse through a microphone when they are off the air. The newspaper is printed at the **Freedom Center**; free 45-minute tours are given during business hours Monday through Friday. ◆ Daily. Tours offered every hour, by reservation. 435 N Michigan Ave (between the Chicago River and E Illinois St); Freedom Center: 777 W Chicago Ave (between the Chicago River and N Halsted St). Tour reservations, 222.2116

78 BILLY GOAT TAVERN

$ This journalists' hangout was the inspiration for the late John Belushi's "cheebugga, cheebugga" short-order routines on *Saturday Night Live*. Otherwise, it's an underground greasy spoon serving merely adequate hamburgers. It's located on Lower Michigan Avenue; access is down the stairs from North Michigan Avenue. In recent years, the owners have opened other locations in an attempt to cash in on the cachet. Because atmosphere is the only thing going for it, stick with the original. ◆ Burgers ◆ Daily, 7AM-2AM. 430 N Michigan Ave (at E Hubbard St), lower level. 222.1525. Also at numerous locations around the city.

79 PIONEER COURT

This well-kept plaza is a handsome addition to the cityscape. Tall prairie grasses and fir trees predominate in a graceful series of plantings interspersed with fountains. Walk through here to reach the **NBC Tower**. ◆ N Michigan Ave (between the Chicago River and E Illinois St)

80 WRIGLEY BUILDING

Graham, Anderson, Probst & White built this white terra-cotta–clad building in 1922. The clock tower has been a distinctive landmark at the gateway to the Magnificent Mile since the Michigan Avenue Bridge crossed the Chicago River. It has always been dazzlingly floodlit from the opposite bank. The chewing-gum company's corporate offices are situated here (its factory is on the city's South Side). ♦ 400 N Michigan Ave (at the Chicago River)

Within the Wrigley Building:

KENYON OPPENHEIMER, INC.

Open since 1969, this gallery is devoted to original prints by 19th-century naturalist John James Audubon at prices that range from two to five figures. By all means visit the fairy-tale courtyard garden in back. Hidden away in a coach house behind the garden is a laboratory where experts conserve and restore artwork on paper. ♦ M-Sa. 642.5300 ᕝ www.audubonart.com

81 NBC TOWER

Harking back to the streamlined Deco skyscrapers of the 1920s and 1930s, this building's strong vertical lines rise to a spire emblazoned with the corporate peacock emblem. Built by **Skidmore, Owings & Merrill** in 1989, this is an elegant addition to the Chicago skyline. In the lobby, note Chicago artist Roger Brown's *City of the Big Shoulders*: barns and trucks and skyscrapers in Day-Glo browns and greens. On the North Columbus Drive side of the building, visit the **NBC Tower Gift Shop**, which sells hats and bags and jogging clothes with insignias from shows like *Saturday Night Live* and the gone-but-not-forgotten *Seinfeld*. ♦ Daily. 455 N Cityfront Plaza (between E North Water and E Illinois Sts); NBC Tower Gift Shop: 454 N Columbus Dr (between E North Water and E Illinois Sts). 832.0484 ᕝ

82 *CHICAGO RISING FROM THE LAKE*

This three-ton bronze sculpture by the late artist Milton Horn—commissioned by the city and completed in 1954—originally adorned a parking garage on West Wacker Drive. In

1983, when the garage was demolished, the city somehow lost track of the sculpture. It was ditched in a dry, tarpaulin-covered swimming pool on the South Side and later moved to a weedy salvage yard on the West Side. Following its rediscovery, it was restored and moved to its current location on the wall of the Columbus Drive Bridge in April 1998. Horn's staggering piece depicts a buxom woman holding sheaves of grain in her left hand while embracing a bull with her right arm, symbolizing Chicago's past as a leader in commodities, transportation, and the stockyards. ♦ E North Water St and N Columbus Dr

83 SHERATON HOTEL AND TOWERS

$$ Bordering the Chicago River, the city's largest convention and business hotel boasts the Midwest's largest ballroom (nearly 40,000 square feet) as well as 1,200 guest rooms. The **Towers** section, which has enjoyed the presidential and senatorial company of Bill and Hillary Clinton on occasion, offers upgraded accommodations and services on four private floors. Guests can use the private health club or take advantage of easy access to bike and jogging trails. **Shula's**, a steakhouse named for a football coach from another section of the country, serves dinner daily; the **Riverside Café** is convenient for breakfast, lunch, or dinner. A lobby bar, **Waves**, offers nightly entertainment and a view of the river; **Spectators** is a sports bar. In the summer, the riverside **Esplanade** is a lovely place for a drink or light meal. ♦ 301 E North Water St (at N Columbus Dr). 464.1000, 800/233.4100; fax 329.6929 ᕝ

At the Sheraton Hotel and Towers:

CLOCK SCULPTURE

If you've ever wanted to see a time machine, visit the plaza in front of the hotel. There, sculptor Vito Acconci's *Floor Clock* goes round in a circle twice daily; the minute hand is about 20 feet long.

River North/
River West

North Branch Canal

N Dayton St.

N Halsted St.

N Clybourn Ave.

Stanton Park

W Eastman St.

W Evergreen Ave.

W Division St.

N Elston Ave.

N Throop St.

N Crosby St.

N Howe St.

N Larrabee St.

W Thomas St.

**BUCK-
TOWN**

N Willard Ct.

N Racine Ave.

N North Branch St.

N Cherry Ave.

N Hickory Ave.

N Hooker St.

N Kingsbury St.

W Hobbie St

W Bliss St.

W Haines St.

North Branch Chicago River

W Chestnut St.

N May St.

W Fry St.

N Carpenter St.

N Lessing St.

W Chestnut St.

Eckhart Park

W Chicago Ave.

N Ogden Ave.

10

N Morgan St.

N Sangamon St.

W Superior St.

North Branch Cicago River

N Noble St.

N Elizabeth St.

N Willard Ct.

W Huron St.

W Huron St.

W Ancona St.

N Green St.

N Larrabee St.

W Erie St.

90 94

John F. Kennedy Expwy.

N Peoria St.

W Erie St.

W Ohio St.

W Ohio St.

N Milwaukee Ave.

N Union Ave.

66

W Grand Ave.

65

W Hubbard St.

RIVER WEST

W Kinzie St.

W Carroll Ave.

N Union St.

N Ada St.

N Elizabeth St.

N Racine Ave.

N May St.

W Wayman St.

W Fulton St.

N Desplaines St.

N Jefferson St.

W Lake St.

W Randolph St.

N Aberdeen St.

N Carpenter St.

N Morgan St.

N Sangamon St.

N Peoria St.

N Green St.

N Halsted St.

90 94

W Washington Blvd.

W Madison St.

RIVER NORTH/RIVER WEST

Although the Magnificent Mile is synonymous with upscale shopping and dining, in recent years, River North has exploded with restaurants, shops, and activity, ranging from attractions tailored for tourists to preferred destinations for locals. Perched confidently behind **Michigan Avenue** are turn-of-the-19th-century brownstones, the Roman Catholic **Holy Name Cathedral**, and the **Episcopal Cathedral of St. James**, as well as the national headquarters of the American Medical and American Library Associations and the PTA. With the recent construction of the **Shops at North Bridge** mall on Michigan Avenue, which is linked to **Nordstrom** on **Rush Street** by glassed-in pedestrian overpasses, Mag Mile and River North have finally merged. A nine-block area bounded by **Michigan Avenue** on the east, **State Street** on the west, **Ontario Street** on the north, and **Illinois Street** on the south has been designated "North Bridge" by the city, in effect creating a visitors' zone that includes **Disney Quest, ESPN Zone, Joe's Stone Crab** restaurant, **Homewood Suites** hotel, and plenty of parking. Notably lacking in open public space, the area feels cramped and tends to be very congested with cars. Despite the self-conscious planned commercialization in this area and along **Ohio** and **Ontario Streets** leading to the **Kennedy Expressway** (Interstates 90 and 94), farther to the west, River North still boasts galleries and studios that rival New York City's SoHo in number and variety and a wide range of fine-dining options, such as **Crofton on Wells, Coco Pazzo,** and **Frontera Grill.** Farther west again, just beyond the **Chicago River,** is the lower-rent district of River West, home to lesser art galleries, converted lofts, and an ever-changing array of fringe dance clubs and restaurants that just cannot seem to draw enough business to stay open. Combined, the two neighborhoods are bounded more or less by **Rush Street, Milwaukee Avenue,** the Chicago River, and **Chicago Avenue.**

The Irish were the first European immigrants to arrive in the area, settling near the river and north to **Erie Street.** In the 1840s they provided labor for the iron foundries, mills, and shipyards along the east bank. In 1849 they built their own simple church, **Holy Name Chapel.** Today the massive **Holy Name Cathedral** stands on the same site, on **State Street** at **Superior Street.** In 1856 industrial growth was hastened by the construction of a bridge (which no longer exists) at **Rush Street** that linked the city's **North** and **South Sides,** and German and Swedish settlers joined the area's Irish. After the Great Fire of 1871, wealthy Anglo-Saxons were able to rebuild rapidly and remained in the area, but the first wave of immigrants moved on. (They were eventually replaced by Italians.)

In 1920 the **Michigan Avenue Bridge** went up, and **LaSalle Street** was widened for automobiles, giving River North residents improved access to the Loop. Manufacturing continued to thrive along the river, but in the decade following World War I, industry faltered and many factories were converted into warehouses for downtown businesses. In 1930, **Marshall Field & Company** opened a gigantic warehouse beside the river; now known as the **Merchandise Mart;** this wholesale showroom is still the largest commercial building in the world.

The 1950s brought a decline in status to parts of River North, and its huge mansions became seedy rooming houses or ticky-tacky apartments. Subsequent renovation helped remedy this situation, and except for the infamous Cabrini-Green housing project along the river just north of Chicago Avenue, it's all rather high rent today. The area has seen dramatic change since the 1970s: First, economic downturns led to the widespread shuttering of factories and warehouses; then these deserted buildings were snatched up by artists, photographers, and other creative souls in need of large, cheap spaces. Next came a handful of art galleries, their owners fed up with cramped quarters and sky-high rents on the other side of Michigan Avenue. Even a disastrous fire in 1989, which destroyed millions of dollars in artwork when nine galleries burned to the ground, did not deter growth. Today at least 50 galleries are situated within a six-block-square area along **Superior** and **Huron Streets**. In the mid-1980s additional galleries began appearing in the River West area. The 1990s saw the conversion of abandoned warehouses into late-night dance clubs along **Fulton Street**, where other warehouses still serve as a major meat-and-produce wholesale market during the day.

River North is especially fun to visit during festive Friday-night openings, when any number of galleries introduce new shows and the crowds can be as offbeat as the artwork. The biggest blasts take place on the Friday after Labor Day and the first or second Friday in January, when all the galleries have openings at once. Many stay open Sundays during the month of May, when an international art exposition is in town.

All area codes in this chapter are 312 unless otherwise noted.

1 KIKI'S BISTRO

★★$$$ A dining room resembling a rustic country cottage provides a charming setting in which to enjoy typical French bistro fare. Start with purée of salted cod with white truffle oil or with sausage wrapped in pastry. Good main courses include the grilled sea bass in onion vinaigrette and the sautéed calf's liver with pearl onions and wine vinegar sauce. Don't pass up the rich chocolate-laced crème brûlée for dessert. ♦ French ♦ M-F, lunch and dinner; Sa, dinner. Reservations recommended. 900 N Franklin St (at W Locust St). 335.5454 & www.kikisbistro.com

2 MK THE RESTAURANT

★★★$$$ Chef Michael Kornick worked at the **Pump Room** and **Gordon** and served as executive chef at **Marche**, so when **mk** opened in late 1998, no one was surprised to find that it was a very fine place to dine. Kornick's spin on contemporary American cuisine shows a sense of restrained originality, falling mercifully short of the exhibitionism that one encounters at a place such as **Tru**. The eclectic menu includes appetizers ranging from fettuccine with shaved black truffles and Parmigiano-Reggiano, to sautéed sweetbreads with caramelized endive

and a sherry-shallot sauce to a simple tuna tartare and entrées ranging from venison with Zinfandel-braised onions and apple-endive salad to a delightful monkfish-lobster combination plate. Pastry chef Mindy Segal finishes things off with magical treatments of apples, bananas, and pineapples and demonstrates a seemingly perfect understanding of the possibilities of chocolate. The space is dramatic, a two-level open loft with exposed brick, charcoal, and tan colors and shiny railings on the upper level. All of this makes for one wonderful place. A six-course degustation menu ($72 without wine) is a wise choice. The lunchtime menu includes a lobster sandwich and a grilled-to-perfection hamburger. ♦ American contemporary ♦ Daily, dinner. Reservations recommended. 868 N Franklin St (at W Locust St). 482.9179 & Also at 350 S Happ Rd in Northfield. 847/716.6500. www.mkchicago.com

3 PLUTON

★★★$$$ After winning acclaim with Jacky's Bistro in Evanston, chef-proprietor Jacky Pluton has brought his welcome skills to the city in a warm, intimate dining room that seats 50. The contemporary menu is strong on American ingredients, including farm-raised, organic, regional, and artisanal products, accented with European and Asian influences. The changing degustation menu (starting at $99) ranges from 5 to 10 plates, with several options for each course. The international wine list has more than 500 bottles. ♦ Contemporary/French ♦ Tu-Sa, dinner. Reservations recommended. 873 N

Orleans St (at W Chestnut St). 266.1440; fax 266.8925

4 750 NORTH ORLEANS STREET

The lobby of this converted warehouse, now filled with art galleries, boasts six murals that attract crowds who try to identify the local personalities portrayed. Chicagoan Robbie Boijeson painted the primitive-style series while she attended medical school. The mural facing the entryway depicts Chicago's late mayor Harold Washington and syndicated newspaper columnists Ann Landers and the late Mike Royko, among others. The last mural features the **Bears'** former coach, Mike Ditka, and fellow sports celebs. ◆ At W Chicago Ave

Within 750 North Orleans Street:

CAROL EHLERS GALLERY LTD.

The work of such contemporary photographers as Tom Bamberger, Steven Foster, Irving Penn, and Sandy Skoglund is featured in this gallery, along with vintage photographs. ◆ Tu-Sa; closed weekends in July and Aug. 642.8611; fax 642-9151 ♿

ABRAHAM LINCOLN BOOKSHOP

Civil War and Lincoln history buffs from around the country are attracted to this warm and inviting store, which is more like a museum. Floor-to-ceiling glass-doored bookcases display art, books, and documents from the era. Proprietor Daniel Weinberg is frequently called on to authenticate Lincoln memorabilia. He's glad to share his knowledge, even with browsers. ◆ M-Sa. 357 W Chicago Ave (between N Orleans and N Sedgwick Sts). 944.3085

5 MERITAGE INTERNATIONAL IMPORTS

This gallery carries Asian contemporary fine art along with exotic antiques and artifacts from China, Korea, Thailand, and Africa. ◆ Tu-Sa, or by appointment. 740 N Franklin St (between W Superior St and W Chicago Ave). 573.1700; fax 573.1960. www.meritageimports.com

6 PAPER SOURCE

A paper fetishist's nirvana, this shop carries a fascinating variety of papers made by hand, machine, and mold. The stationery and artists' supplies are imported from around the world. Fans of rubber-stamp art will enjoy the array of designs, from the novel to the normal. ◆ Daily. 232 W Chicago Ave (at N Franklin St). 337.0798 ♿ www.paper-source.com

7 ALAN KOPPEL GALLERY

This large double-storefront space with open windows affords a wonderful glimpse of modern masters and leading contemporary artists to people who are just strolling along Chicago Avenue. Make a point of stopping in to see work by such modern and contemporary artists as Diane Arbus, Walker Evans, Edward Lipski, and Andy Warhol. ◆ M-Sa. 210 W Chicago Ave (between N Franklin and N Wells Sts). 640.0730; fax 640.0202. www.alankoppel.com

8 CARL HAMMER GALLERY

Nontraditional, self-taught, and outsider artists are the primary focus here, most notably Chicago's own Mr. Imagination, who produces carved works in sandstone. ◆ Tu-Sa. 740 N Wells St (between W Superior St and W Chicago Ave). 266.8512; fax 266.8510. www.hammergallery.com

8 PORTALS LTD.

A fantastic arrangement of naive paintings by international artists is juxtaposed with fine 18th- and 19th-century furniture and decorative objects—for example, Karen Halt's *When a Man Loves a Woman* is displayed beside a handsome Gillows & Company writing desk. The spacious seventh-floor gallery was the inspiration of interior designer Nancy McIlvaine and her art-collector husband, and it is indeed beautiful, with wide arched windows providing great views of the neighborhood. ◆ Tu-Sa. 742 N Wells St (between W Superior St and W Chicago Ave). 642.1066; fax 642.2991. www.portalsgallery.com

9 HOTEL ST. BENEDICT FLATS

This lively 1883 Victorian Gothic composition of brick and stone designed by **James J. Egan** is a charming part of the 19th-century streetscape, with apartments above small shops. Note the variety of bay treatments and the incised lintels and art glass transoms above the windows. The owner repeatedly threatened to tear the building down to make way for something more lucrative, but much community protest saved it, and the building acquired landmark status in 1990. ◆ 50 E Chicago Ave and 801 N Wabash Ave

Within the Hotel St. Benedict Flats:

STREETER'S TAVERN

Named after the raucous boatman who built up Streeterville, the community east of Michigan Avenue, this is your basic popcorn-and-beer spot, popular with college students. ◆ Daily. 944.5206

10 THE SILVER PALM

★ $$ If you've traveled on Amtrak lately, you know that dining in the dining car has lost much of the charm that it once had. David Gevercer, who owns the **Matchbox** bar next door, is trying to bring it back. The **Silver Palm** is a rehabbed 1947 railroad dining car that takes its name from the ACL Railroad's Chicago-to-Florida run. The menu features dishes with train-inspired names: Southern Pacific Railways double ginger duck (braised duck with fresh and candied ginger) and the Seaboard Airline Railroad's shrimp and scallop po' boy (deep-fried with pickled green tomatoes and Cajun remoulade). Desserts include an eclair with praline pastry cream and tasty apple pie. Unlike on a train, the Silver Palm offers a carry-out option. The bar is well stocked with bourbon and scotch. If you're in the drinking mood, you may want to move next door to the Matchbox, which bills itself as the city's most intimate bar. That's because it's as narrow as the aisle on a train car. ♦ American contemporary. ♦ Tu-Sa, dinner, late kitchen. 768 N Milwaukee Ave (at N Ogden Ave). 666.9322 &

11 ZEALOUS

★★★$$$$ Chef-owner Michael Taus established a reputation for a suburban restaurant by the same name. In 2000, he closed that one and moved to this former River North warehouse, quickly proving that many people in the city had been missing the opportunity to try something very special. With knowledgeable servers in Donna Karan suits, a glass-enclosed wine cellar, and a chef's table where guests dine amid a grove of bamboo trees, Taus has clearly thought through the atmosphere and look. But the real attraction here is the food, which is simply superb, a delightful blending of unusual flavors. Be sure to try the lobster gazpacho and veal sweetbreads with black pepper beignet.♦ American contemporary ♦ Jackets required. Reservations recommended. Tu-Sa, lunch and dinner. 419 W Superior St. 475.9112 & www.zealousrestaurant.com

12 CLUB LAGO

★$ A neighborhood restaurant and bar, this has been a River North fixture since the 1950s, before the area became chic. The large lunch crowd jams the bar and packs the tables. Old-fashioned Italian standards include decent chicken Vesuvio (roasted chicken, potatoes, and peppers) and fried calamari. ♦ Italian ♦ M-F, lunch and dinner until 8PM; Sa, lunch. 331 W Superior St (between N Franklin and N Orleans Sts). 337.9444

13 ANDREW BAE GALLERY

This gallery carries an extensive collection of contemporary Asian art, including the work of Kwang Jean Park. ♦ Tu-Sa. 300 W Superior St (at N Franklin St). 335.8601; fax 335.8602. www.andrewbaegallery.com

13 ARCHITECH

As the name suggests, this is Chicago's leading gallery of architectural art, featuring, among other fascinating material, the Hedrich Blessing photography collection. A recent exhibit included drawings and prints by Frank Lloyd Wright and his cabinetmaker George Mann Niedecken. ♦ Th-Sa, noon-6PM. 730 N Franklin, second floor (at W Superior St). 475.1290. www.architechgallery.com

14 STEPHEN DAITER GALLERY

On the fourth floor, you'll find rare photography from the 1920s to the 1960s, mostly documentary and experimental. ♦ Tu-Th, by appt.; F-Sa. 311 W Superior St (between N Franklin and N Orleans Sts). 787.3350; fax 787.3354. www.stephendaitergallery.com

14 RUSSELL BOWMAN ART ADVISORY

Works by Warhol, Mapplethorpe, and Chicagoans Roger Brown and Ed Paschke are among the modern and contemporary art exhibited here. ♦ Tu-Th, by appt.; F-Sa. 311 W Superior St (between N Franklin and N Orleans Sts). 751.9500; fax 751.9572. www.bowmanart.com

14 PRINTWORKS GALLERY

Works on paper, including limited-edition prints, drawings, and photographs, are on display here. Artists' books are a specialty; such artists as Audrey Niffenegger write the text, hand-set the type, wood-cut the images, and bind the books to create these one-of-a-kind volumes. The gallery represents emerging and major artists whose prints do not generally appear elsewhere, among them Leon Golub, Richard Hunt, Ellen Lanyon, Seymour Rosofsky, and Hollis Sigler. Amicable gallery directors Sidney Block and Bob Hiebert enthusiastically pore over their collection for visitors and explain aspects of the printmaking process. ♦ Tu-Sa, and by appointment. 311 W Superior St (between N Franklin and N Orleans Sts). 664.9407; fax 664.8823

Animation genius Walt Disney was born in Chicago. Disney received 39 Oscars in his lifetime, the most ever received by one person.

14 MICHAEL FITZSIMMONS DECORATIVE ARTS

Concentrating on 20th-century US architectural and decorative art, this gallery is also the
world's largest dealer of original **Frank Lloyd
Wright** furniture, leaded glass, and drawings.
♦ Tu-Sa. 311 W Superior St (between N
Franklin and N Orleans Sts). 787.0496; fax
787.6343. www.fitzdecarts.com

14 SCHWEBEL COMPANY

Exceptional 19th- and 20th-century American
antique furnishings and accessories are the
stock in trade at this gallery. ♦ M-F and by
appointment. 311 W Superior St (between N
Franklin and N Orleans Sts). 280.1998

15 HABATAT GALLERIES

Contemporary sculpture is the theme here,
featuring the work of, among others, Dale
Chihuly, Howard Ben Tre, Daniel Clayman, and
Toots Zynsky. ♦ Tu-Sa. 222 W Superior St
(between N Wells and N Franklin Sts).
440.0288; fax 440.0207.
www.habatatchicago.com

15 MARX-SAUNDERS GALLERY

This small gallery features contemporary glass
art, including Michael Rogers's delicate cast
crystal, John Wolfe's cast laminated glass, and
blown-glass sculpture by Vernon Brejcha. ♦ Tu-
Sa. 230 W Superior St (between N Wells and
N Franklin Sts). 573.1400; fax 573.0575.
www.marxsaunders.com

15 SCHNEIDER GALLERY

Contemporary photography by American and
international artists is the focus here. ♦ Tu-Sa.
230 W Superior St (between N Wells and N
Franklin Sts). 988.4033; fax 440.9256.
www.schneidergallerychicago.com

15 GRUEN GALLERIES

A strange but wonderful juxtaposition of
African artifacts and Old World–style forged
iron objects is found here. Among the African
works are towering carved-wood funerary
figures from Zaire and intricately beaded
chairs from Cameroon. Ironwork table bases,
chairs, bedframes, chandeliers, candelabra,
and more are produced by Erwin Gruen, a
Berlin-born blacksmith. Ask to see his gigantic
shop of whirring machinery in the basement.
♦ M-Sa. 226 W Superior St (between N Wells
and N Franklin Sts). 337.6262; fax
337.7855. www.gruengalleries.com

15 ANN NATHAN GALLERY

The emphasis is on three-dimensional
objects, whether functional or fantastic.
Notable pieces have included Brian Sauve's
4-foot-diameter globe of 1950s floral TV trays
riveted together patchwork style; Lynn
Zetzman's *Portrait of a Contemporary*, a male
figure fashioned almost entirely from men's
ties; and hand-painted cabinets and mosaic
tile figures by Leslie Hawk. ♦ Tu-Sa. 212 W
Superior (between N Wells and N Franklin
Sts). 664.6622; fax 664.9392.
www.annnathangallery.com

16 ROBERT HENRY ADAMS FINE ART

This pleasant space features Modern
American Art and Modernist and Regionalist
paintings, drawings, sculpture, and
photographs, including work by Chicago artists
Marin, Calder, Moholy-Nagy, Schwartz, Bohrod,
Martinelli, and others. ♦ Tu-F, 10AM-5PM; Sa,
noon-5PM. 715 N Franklin (between W Huron
and W Superior Sts). 642.8700; fax
642.8785. www.adamsfineart.com

17 NORTHERN ILLINOIS UNIVERSITY GALLERY

Students, alumni, and guest artists display
their work at this nonprofit gallery. Exhibits
have included Mary Jo Bang's *An Ever Rolling
Stream*, a series of timeless, surrealistic
black-and-white photos of France. ♦ Tu-Sa;
closed in Aug. 215 W Superior St (between N
Wells and N Franklin Sts). 642.6010; fax
642.9635

17 MAYA POLSKY GALLERY

A tribute to the fall of the Iron Curtain, this
place is an eye-opener. The Russian art world
has been observing pre- and post-Perestroika
society and transforming those visions into
searing images, usually very realistic and
rarely complimentary. There's also art from
Poland and elsewhere in Eastern Europe. A
Russian herself, Ms. Polsky generously
describes the work and the artists for visitors.
♦ Tu-Sa. 215 W Superior St (between N Wells
and N Franklin Sts). 440.0055; fax
440.0501. www.mayapolskygallery.com

17 JEAN ALBANO GALLERY

Contemporary American painting, sculpture,
and constructions by both established and
emerging artists are the trade at this gallery,
which emphasizes West Coast artists. ♦ Tu-Sa.
215 W Superior St (between N Wells and N
Franklin Sts). 440.0770; fax 440.3103.
www.jeanalbanogallery.com

18 MONGERSON GALLERIES

Featuring works by Thomas Hart Benton, Colin
Campbell Cooper, Frederic Remington, and
Charles Marion Russell, this is a place to find
19th- and 20th-century American and

Western art. ♦ Tu-Sa. 704 N Wells (at W Superior St). 943.2354; fax 943.9560. www.mongersongalleries.com

18 GWENDA JAY ADDINGTON GALLERY

Paintings and sculpture by American and European artists are featured. Shows have included steel-and-pine furniture by Los Angeles architect **Thom Mayne**. ♦ Tu-Sa. 704 N Wells St (at W Superior St). 664.3406; fax 664.3388. www.gwendajay.com

19 MANIFESTO

The ultimate source for architect-designed furniture, lighting, and accessories, this gallery focuses on licensed reproductions of European and American pieces designed between 1890 and 1940, with some contemporary designs. The high-end wares include dining tables by Italian architect **Carlo Scarpa** and carpets, furniture, and tableware by Josef Hoffmann. ♦ Tu-Sa. 755 N Wells St (between W Superior St and W Chicago Ave). 664.0733; fax 664.5472. www.manifestofurniture.com

19 ROY BOYD GALLERY

Roy and Ann Boyd represent contemporary abstractionists, most of them from Chicago. The gallery also has a collection of photography from Russia, Lithuania, and Estonia. Ask to see the lovely sculpture garden in back. ♦ Tu-Sa. 739 N Wells St (between W Superior St and W Chicago Ave). 642.1606; fax 642.2143. www.royboydgallery.com

20 BLUE CHICAGO

Relocated from its original spot on North State Street, this club has established itself as one of the main stops on the city's blues music circuit, with local and national acts strutting their stuff. A single cover charge will get you into its sister club, **Blue Chicago at Ohio** (536 N Clark St). ♦ Cover. Tu-Sa, 8PM-2AM. 736 N Clark St (between W Superior St and W Chicago Ave). 642.6261

21 LE LAN

★★★$$$ The name means "the orchid" in Vietnamese, and business has been blooming since it opened its doors in 2004. The concept is casual dining, though the prices are not. A collaborative effort by all-star chefs Ronald Liccioni (Les Nomades) and Arun Sampanthavivat (Arun's), Le Lan has a menu with surprise twists on some classic dishes and, as one would expect, some delightful flavors and aromas. Roast bass with lemon-

grass is a real crowd pleaser, as is the glazed ribeye. The brown-and-green color scheme is a nod to the colors of Vietnam. There's an international wine list and a specialty drinks menu that includes a tamarind martini. ♦ French/Vietnamese. ♦ Reservations recommended. M-Sa, dinner. 749 N Clark St (between W Superior St and W Chicago Ave). 280.9100 ♿

22 HOLY NAME CATHEDRAL

Designed by **Patrick C. Keely**, this has been the cathedral of the Catholic Archdiocese of Chicago since 1874, when its dedication drew a crowd of more than 5,000 and featured a parade of 18 bands and a 25-priest choir. The 1979 visit of Pope John Paul II attracted a huge audience, as have performances by Luciano Pavarotti and the **Chicago Symphony Orchestra**. The interior of the Victorian Gothic church is warm and welcoming, with an ornate wooden ceiling and elaborate stone carving. Of particular note are the impressive organ loft at the back of the church and the three wide-brimmed hats hanging above the main altar. Tradition decrees that a departed cardinal's official hat, or *galeros*, be suspended from the ceiling of his cathedral. (These belonged to the late cardinals Mundelein, Stritch, and Meyer.) The cathedral has been renovated twice: in 1914, by **Henry J. Schlacks**, and in 1968, by **C.F. Murphy Associates**. ♦ 735 N State St (at E Superior St). 787.8040

22 MELANEE COOPER GALLERY

This is a showcase for contemporary art with a focus on surface and texture. ♦ Tu-Sa. 740 N Franklin St (between W Superior St and W Chicago Ave). 202.9305; fax 202.9307. www.melaneecoopergallery.com

23 BARTLOW GALLERY

Looking to take home a little something by Chagall or Miró or Picasso or Matisse? You can take a peek at this gallery of modern and contemporary painting and sculpture. ♦ Tu-Sa. 44 E Superior St (between N Wabash Ave and N Rush St). 337.1782; fax 337.2516. www.bartlowgallery.com

23 SPENCER WEISZ GALLERIES

Featuring one of the largest antique poster collections in the country, this gallery is also a custom framing and paper restoration facility. ♦ M-Sa. 46 E Superior St (between N Wabash Ave and N Rush St). 527.9420; fax 923.0910. www.antiqueposters.com

24 GIORDANO'S

★$$ Stop here for a slice or a whole tasty stuffed pan pizza, but insist on sitting at a table near the window, so that you can watch the action on Rush Street. ♦ Pizza ♦ Daily, lunch and dinner. 730 N Rush St (at E Superior St). 951.0747. Also at 236 S Wabash Ave (between E Jackson Blvd and E Adams St), basement level. 939.4646. Also at numerous other locations in the city and suburbs &

25 SCOOZI!

★★$$ At the front of yet another restaurant from Lettuce Entertain You Enterprises, a big red tomato beckons. Inside, the noisy crowd at the bar is packed three deep; the bustling 320-seat dining room has a decadent European feel, with distressed walls, dark woods, and old-fashioned embellishments; and Italian talk radio blares in the bathrooms. Despite the scene, the chef turns out some serious Italian fare, including a wonderful pizza *boscaiola* (with roasted Portobello mushrooms, fontina cheese, prosciutto, walnuts, and truffle oil). Desserts include a super ricotta cheesecake. ♦ Italian

♦ Daily, dinner. 410 W Huron St (between N Sedgwick St and N Hudson Ave). 943.5900 & www.leye.com

26 GREEN DOOR TAVERN

★$ This cozy spot has been a bar since 1921. Set in one of the first buildings to go up after the Chicago Fire, it boasts many of its original fixtures and has antiques hanging from the walls and ceiling. Crowds show up for the basic home cooking: hamburgers with baked beans and coleslaw, good meat loaf, mashed potatoes, and gravy. There's a wide assortment of imported and domestic beers. ♦ American ♦ Daily, lunch and dinner; closed Su in July and Aug. 678 N Orleans St (between W Erie and W Huron Sts). 664.5496

27 ZOLLA/LIEBERMAN GALLERY INC.

In 1976, dealer Roberta Lieberman pioneered in the development of this area by moving into a nearly abandoned warehouse one block east of her current location, spurring an

---

NOT THE BEST

David Murray

Writer

A few bad things about Chicago—after all, no place is perfect.

Chicago buses: Like most American cities, Chicago once had a functional and convenient streetcar system. Or so the fable goes. Why do we accept as true the unlikely idea that crowded streetcars barreling down the middle of the street were better than buses? Because if you've ever been on a crowded, hot, lurching bus in Chicago—or if you've ever waited a half hour in winter for one to come along, only to be swamped by an entire squadron of six packed buses in a row—you'd endorse a plan to release 50,000 saddled donkeys into the city for commuters' convenience.

Chicago-style pizza: Look—the pizza is good in Chicago. But it's also good in New York. And it's not bad in Knoxville, Tennessee. If you ask 10 Chicagoans what makes their pizza special, you'll get many different answers, most of which will bake down to

"deep dish." But as anyone but a Chicagoan knows, Chicago doesn't do deep-dish pizza any better than they do it in Cincinnati. If you're looking for an earthy Chicago eating experience, better to go for some good Polish or Ukrainian chow.

Ed Debevic's: This is the faux '50s-style burger place on Wells Street where the waiters and waitresses proactively treat you badly, as they do in the national chain Dick's Last Resort. As far as I can tell, there are only four reasons to go to Ed Debevic's: (1) You love Dick's and go there every Friday night, but you worry that the aspiring actors and actresses who wait tables there are getting "corporatized." (2) You think Don Rickles is absolutely hilarious. (3) You're so bored by your dining companions that you welcome any interruption, however rude, in the conversation at the table. (4) All of the above.

The following types of Chicagoans: Those who would bother to tell you the *real* reason it's called the Windy City; those who never take the El—and worse, those who brag about taking the El exclusively; and, of course, those who would presume to tell you what you should and shouldn't do in the city.

exodus of other galleries from Michigan Avenue and stimulating the rapid growth of Chicago's art community here. Her artists tend to be rather avant-garde, although she also represents Deborah Butterfield, whose graceful iron *Horse* adorns **Seneca Park** east of the **Water Tower**. This street-level gallery has windows all around, so you can look at current offerings before going in. ◆ Tu-Sa. 325 W Huron St (between N Franklin and N Orleans Sts). 944.1990; fax 944.8967

27 NACIONAL 27

★$$ Lettuce Entertain You Enterprises has done one of its successful retooling acts, putting a new hat on the busy, noisy, fun Mexican restaurant **Hat Dance** and replacing it with a busy, noisy, fun restaurant with dancing whose name represents the 27 Latin American nations. The black-and-white shades of the old room have given way to blond wood. The cuisine pretty much covers all the countries, with items such as *boniato* (a Cuban sweet potato), *pupusas* (stuffed homemade tortillas), and snapper Brasileno, cooked with coconut and—you guessed it—Brazil nuts. On weekends, late at night, the dining room turns into a dance floor, with a live DJ dishing out the sounds of salsa. In warm weather, there's an outdoor dining area in back. ◆ Latin ◆ Daily, dinner. Reservations recommended. 325 W Huron St (between N Franklin and N Orleans Sts). 664.2727; fax 649.0256 & www.leye.com

27 KASS/MERIDIAN GALLERY

Prints by contemporary and modern masters include Alexander Calder lithographs from the 1960s and works by Roy Lichtenstein, Joan Miró, Robert Motherwell, Andy Warhol, and Pablo Picasso. ◆ Tu-Sa. 325 W Huron St (between N Franklin and N Orleans Sts). 266.5999; fax 266.5931. www.kassmeridian.com

28 NICOLE GALLERY

Along with Haitian art and Shona sculpture from Zimbabwe (including works by Henry Munyaradzi), **Nicole** features Chicago collagist Allen Stringfellow. ◆ Tu-Sa. 230 W Huron St (at N Franklin St). 787.7716; fax 787.7798. www.nicolegallery.com

29 ALDO CASTILLO GALLERY

International fine art is featured here, with special emphasis on the art of Latin America. Exhibits are sometimes held in cooperation with the Latino Cultural Center of Chicago. ◆ Tu-Sa, or by appointment. 233 W Huron (at N

Franklin St) 337.2536; fax 337.3627. www.artaldo.com

30 ALLEN'S

★★$$ Named for its chef-proprietor, Allen Sternweiler, formerly at Printer's Row, this is a casual American café with an international flavor. Floor-to-ceiling glass doors separate the bar and dining area, which helps to ease the noise. Boozehounds will like the bar, with its extensive offering of cognacs, single-malt scotch, and small-batch bourbons. The seasonal menu favors farm-raised game and fresh fish, with such entrées as Iowa prime beef, rabbit loin, and venison. Lunch options include sandwiches, salads, soups, and small portions of dinner entrées. ◆ Contemporary ◆ M-F, lunch and dinner; Sa, dinner. 217 W Huron St (between N Wells and N Franklin Sts). 587.9600; fax 587.9617

31 STUDIO V

Eye-catching items fill this Art Deco studio: graphics, telephones, perfume bottles, funny flamingos, fine clothing, funky earrings, and neon wall clocks reminiscent of old diners. ◆ M-Sa, noon-6PM. 672 N Dearborn St (between W Erie and W Huron Sts). 440.1937 & www.studiovchicago.com

32 CITY SOURCE/CITY STITCHER

Since moving from its location in an old mansion, this shop has lost some of its charm. But it still carries a nice selection of gifts, home accessories, and needlework, and it stocks a mind-boggling inventory of all-natural threads. Hundreds of needlepoint and cross-stitch canvases cover the walls, and the stock of all-natural threads is like a rainbow that fills an entire room. ◆ M-Sa. 1 E Huron St (at N State St). 664.5499. www.citystitcher-needlepoint.com

33 EPISCOPAL CATHEDRAL OF ST. JAMES

Designed by **Edward Burling** in 1857 and then reconstructed by **Burling & Adler** in 1875, the cathedral's English Gothic exterior conceals the city's most unusual and beautiful ecclesiastical interior. The walls are covered with Arts and Crafts stencil patterns in 25 colors, designed in 1888 by New York architect **E.J. Neville Stemt** and carefully restored in 1985. Most US church interiors are copies of Old World designs, but the decoration here is pure 19th-century Americana, done at the peak of the stenciling craze, and the effect is highly original. The **Chapel of St. Andrew** was built by **Ralph Adams Cram** and **Bertram G. Goodhue** in 1913. In 1985 **Holabird & Root** completed a restoration. ◆ 65 E Huron St (between N Rush St and N Wabash Ave). 787.7360

34 ERIE CAFÉ

★★★$$$ Somewhat off the beaten track, this Italian-style steak house near the North Branch of the Chicago River is owned by Ron Lenzi, the son-in-law of Gene Michelotti, who founded the fabled establishment **Club Gene & Georgetti, Ltd.** Exposed brick, blond wood, and leather chairs spread through a large open room convey the correct impression that this is a solid place built for serious eating. Aged prime steaks and chops and a predictable selection of seafood and fish populate the menu, along with traditional specialties such as chicken Vesuvio. Key lime pie and cheesecake fill out the meal. There's no new ground here, just old familiar terrain. Those who like the terrain will find it quite satisfying. ◆ Steak house/Italian ◆ M-Sa, lunch and dinner; Su, dinner. 536 W Erie St (between Kingsbury and the Chicago River). 266.2300. www.eriecafe.com

35 BARNARD, LTD.

Talk about eclectic. June Barnard bought out the former Bregstone Associates shop at Wabash and Congress in 1996 and moved it here. Filled with plastic and ceramic pieces and figures, the cluttered but pristine shop features artificial food, decorations, and props for holidays, parties, and special events. The stuff doesn't come cheap. At Thanksgiving time, the plastic turkey with all the trimmings is a big hit but will set you back $130. For the happy hour that lasts forever, an acrylic martini costs $37.50. ◆ 375 W Erie St (between N Orleans and N Sedgwick Sts). 475.0210; fax 475.0215. www.barnardltd.com

36 MR. BEEF

★$ Don't leave Chicago without sampling one of the city's sloppiest and most delectable indigenous gastronomical delights: an Italian beef sandwich smothered in hot and sweet peppers. This River North restaurant does one of the best. ◆ Italian ◆ M-F, breakfast, lunch, and early dinner; Sa, lunch. 660 N Orleans St (between W Erie and W Huron Sts). 337.8500 &

37 303 WEST ERIE STREET

Talk about clawing your way to the top! Scaling the brick wall of this renovated factory is artist Jim Stone's *Climbing Yuppies*, a life-size pair of male and female executives making their way up on ropes, briefcases at their sides. The artist dressed department-store mannequins in suits, pumps, and wingtips, then sprayed them with fiberglass to make them rock hard and weather resistant. Building co-owner Burt Lewis, who commissioned the project, originally envisioned burglars scaling the walls, but his partners suggested a sculpture that would reflect the target market that they are trying to interest in their renovated loft rentals. ◆ At N Franklin St

38 FOGO DE CHAO

★$$$ An empty stomach and a full wallet are needed to make the most of this Brazilian eatery. Choose from 16 different grilled meats served at your table by guys in gaucho get-ups. You'll have to get up if you want any greens—a salad bar fills the vegetable option. It's all you can eat, so the idea is to **Chao** down. But you'll have to cough up $24.50 for lunch or $38.50 for dinner. ◆ Brazilian. ◆ M-F, lunch and dinner; Sa, Su, dinner. Reservations recommended. 661 N LaSalle St (at W Erie St). 932.9330

39 SAMUEL M. NICKERSON HOUSE

One of the few surviving mansions from Chicago's Gilded Age, the building was designed in 1883 by **Burling & Whitehouse** for Samuel Nickerson, a transplanted New Englander who made a fortune in distilleries before founding the First National Bank of Chicago. The sober façade belies an interior so lavish it is known as the "marble palace." When the house went up for sale after World War I and prospective single-family buyers for a 30-room mansion were scarce, Charles Osborne spearheaded a campaign to buy the house and donate it to the **American College of Surgeons**, from which Love acquired it for his gallery. ♦ M-Sa. 40 E Erie St (at N Wabash Ave)

40 REZA'S

★★$$ This sprawling space has seen several restaurants come and go; even **Berghoff's**, the tourists' favorite in the Loop, didn't make it here. Now a branch of a popular budget-priced uptown restaurant, it seems to have the magic touch. Start with the hummus and eggplant dips, but save room for an ample portion of kabob, stew, lamb shanks, or game hen. The price of an entrée includes lentil soup, lots of raw veggies, fluffy rice, plus pita. The wine list is small but adequate. This is a great spot for a crowd after gallery hopping. And you can usually find a parking place on the street, particularly in the evenings. ♦ Middle Eastern ♦ Daily, lunch and dinner. 432 W Ontario St (between N Orleans and N Kingsbury Sts). 664.4500 ᕒ www.rezasrestaurant.com

41 CHILPANCINGO

★★★$$$ Generoso Bahena worked under celebrated chef Rick Bayless, cooking at **Frontera Grill** and **Topolobampo** for 12 years. The restaurant is named for the capital of Guerrero on Mexico's Pacific coast, a town where the menu says "everything goes." Anything goes with the restaurant, starting with the babbling fountain and curving staircase that meet you as you step through a massive revolving door into the spacious room with piñatas hanging from the high ceiling. The cuisine, as done so well by such other chefs as Bayless and Patrick Concannon of **Don Juan's**, is gourmet Mexican, and Geno, as he is known, also does it quite well. There are some traditional Mexican dishes such as enchiladas, but what makes the place noteworthy is the imaginative treatment of game dishes and roasts such as pork and lamb. Adjacent to **Chilpancingo** is a bar and grill, a more casual space for those in a hurry, with some of the

selections from the restaurant. ♦ Gourmet Mexican ♦ M-Sa, lunch and dinner; Su, dinner. 358 W Ontario St (at North Orleans St). 266.9525 ᕒ www.chilpancingorestaurant.com

42 SPY BAR

Around a corner, down a flight of stairs, you'll discover a long, dark, smoke-filled room. Lounge at the bar that runs almost the whole length of the club or dance to disco tunes provided by live DJs. ♦ Club cover charge. Tu, Th-Sa nights. 646 N Franklin St (between W Erie and W Ontario Sts). 587.8779. www.spybarchicago.com

43 ED DEBEVIC'S

$ Quite possibly the only diner in the world that has valet parking, this 1950s-style spot was opened by Lettuce Entertain You Enterprises in the mid-1980s. The atmosphere is frenetic and noisy. Food runs along the lines of burgers, mashed potatoes, and meat loaf, all washed down with Green River soda pop. The ever-friendly waitpersons will urge coconut cream pie on you for dessert—go for it. It's a fun place to bring kids, but expect a wait and a fairly large check, considering the offerings. ♦ Diner ♦ Daily, lunch and dinner. 640 N Wells St (between W Ontario and W Erie Sts). 664.1707

44 CARSON'S—THE PLACE FOR RIBS

★$$ Big, meaty, moist, tangy-sweet ribs are presented on huge platters. Ditto for the steaks and barbecued chicken. All entrées are served with a choice of potato—choose au gratin—plus salad or coleslaw and fresh rolls. Desserts include giant chocolate sundaes. Heavy advertising makes this a major tourist trap, albeit one you might actually *want* to be trapped in. ♦ Ribs ♦ Daily, lunch and dinner. 612 N Wells St (between W Ohio and W Ontario Sts). 280.9200 ᕒ www.ribs.com

45 SPORTS AUTHORITY

For decades, this was **Morrie Mages**, the world's largest sporting goods store. Its eight floors were stocked with everything for golf, tennis, hunting, skiing, camping, aerobics, scuba diving, safari hunts—you name it—most at a good discount. Since the store's purchase by **Sports Authority**, the selection has remained extensive. On the outside of the building, a wall of fame displays concrete handprints of Chicago sports celebrities past and present, among them, **Bears** running back Walter Payton, **Blackhawks** hockey star Bobby Hull, and **DePaul University Demons** basketball coach Ray Meyer. ♦ M-Sa, 9:30AM-9:30PM; Su, until 7PM. 620 N LaSalle St (between W Ohio and W Ontario Sts). 337.6151. www.sportsauthority.com

---

Restaurants/Clubs: Red | Hotels: Purple | Shops: Orange | Outdoors/Parks: Green | Sights/Culture: Blue

46 HARD ROCK CAFE

★$$ From the outside this building, designed by **Tigerman, McCurry** in 1985, resembles a mammoth 18th-century orangerie. Inside, the collection of rock 'n' roll memorabilia dazzles, the ear-splitting music pounds, and the tourists—from teenagers to grandparents—keep coming. The burgers are good. ♦ American ♦ Daily, lunch and dinner. 63 W Ontario St (between N Dearborn and N Clark Sts). 943.2252 ♿ www.hardrock.com

47 CHICAGO CHOP HOUSE

★★$$$ Served in a cozy two-story town house, the meat-and-potatoes meals here start with a whole loaf of fresh bread and a house salad, then get down to business with expertly cooked steak that can weigh up to 64 ounces. Chicken and seafood are also available. There's piano music every evening. ♦ Steak house ♦ M-F, lunch and dinner; Sa, Su, dinner. 60 W Ontario St (between N Dearborn and N Clark Sts). 787.7100

47 EXCALIBUR

Now a nightclub, this 1892 building by **Henry Ives Cobb** was known as "The Castle" in the 19th century, when it was built as headquarters for the Chicago Historical Society. The granite-faced fortress has dramatic arched windows and sharply pitched roofs and

BAD BOYS IN GANGLAND

Though the Mayors Daley and many civic boosters don't like to admit it, the mere name of Chicago conjures up scenes of Al Capone and his fellow gangsters shooting up the city, *Godfather* style. And little wonder: Between 1920 and 1933, battles by the Mob (or Mafia) over control of bootlegging operations, gambling, prostitution, and other lucrative, illegal activities resulted in some 700 gangland murders. More than half a century has passed since then, but Chicago can't seem to shake its notorious reputation. Blame it on guys like these:

Big Jim Colosimo started out as a precinct captain and whorehouse owner at the beginning of the 20th century. Ultimately he controlled the **South Side**'s liquor and gambling operations, pulling in a personal income of about $50,000 a month. The flamboyant gang leader also owned a restaurant where he regularly dished out spaghetti to Enrico Caruso and other opera stars he adored. In 1920 rivals shot him in the head outside the restaurant. His funeral was attended by 5,000 people, many of them judges and politicians. Al Capone, Colosimo's bodyguard, boasted that he pulled the trigger, but no one seems to know for sure.

Johnny Torio, Colosimo's successor, oversaw an army of about 800 gunmen and grossed about $70 million a year. He paid generous bribes to keep the law off his back: One police chief drew $1,000 a day. After barely surviving an assassination attempt in 1924, Torio relocated to New York, and his operation was taken over by Al Capone.

Dion O'Banion, a florist and safecracker, had delivered newspapers as a kid and carried a press card throughout his life; once, when caught robbing a safe, he used the card to convince police that he was actually doing a news story. He controlled the **North Side**'s bootleg supply and liked to hijack trucks carrying other gangs' liquor. One day in 1924, while making bouquets in the floral shop he operated across the street from **Holy Name Cathedral**, he was shot dead by three of Capone's boys.

Hymie Weiss, whose real last name was Polish and six syllables long, was an accomplished liquor hijacker, safecracker, jewel thief, and murderer. He is said to have coined the phrase "take him for a ride," in which a rival was driven to a secluded part of town and bumped off. He and rival Al Capone tried to kill each other several times. In 1926 Weiss was machine-gunned to death on the steps of **Holy Name Cathedral**. (The cornerstone of the church was damaged by bullets and later replaced.)

Alphonse "Al" Capone was one of the most violent gangsters Chicago has ever known. Nicknamed "Scarface" because of the scar on his left cheek from a dance-hall fight, he oversaw hundreds of gang killings and personally mangled many a foe with a baseball bat. In 1925 Bugs Moran's gang riddled his car with bullets, but Capone turned out not to be in it. The following year, a cavalcade of 10 cars sent by Hymie Weiss drove past a restaurant where Capone was eating and let loose with a reported 10,000 machine-gun rounds in less than 10 seconds; Capone survived by diving to the floor. In 1929 his boys lined up six of Bugs Moran's gang in a **Lincoln Park** garage (no longer there) and machine-gunned them to death in the infamous St. Valentine's Day Massacre. Capone finally found his match in the Internal Revenue Service. Indicted for tax evasion in 1931, he was found guilty and sentenced to 10 years in prison. Shortly after his release, he died of syphilis.

Though in Chicago and elsewhere the Mob is hardly a thing of the past, teenage drug dealers have been stealing the headlines in recent times, particularly in the city. Moblike activities have shifted to suburban areas and are said to maintain a hold on some workers at exposition centers and airports.

For a taste of gangster-era Chicago, take the **Untouchable Tour** (773/881.1195), which departs from the northwest corner of North Clark and West Ohio Streets, in front of the **Rock 'n' Roll McDonald's**.

gables. Each of its four floors—three stories plus basement—spans 11,000 square feet. Following the society's move to larger quarters in the 1930s, the building saw a succession of tenants. It served as everything from a Moose lodge to offices for the Federal Music Projects of the Works Progress Administration to the **Institute of Design**, founded by Bauhaus guru László Moholy-Nagy. In the late 1960s, a group of investors bought it to create a nightclub, a plan that finally materialized when attorney F. Lee Bailey purchased it from them and opened **The Gallery**. It went through two more incarnations before becoming **Excalibur** in the late 1980s. A gigantic entertainment complex popular among a mainstream crowd, the club offers billiards and video games in the basement, a main-floor cabaret with dance music from the 1950s to 1970s, and a gigantic multilevel dance club with current tunes. ♦ Cover. M-F, Su, 5PM-4AM; Sa, until 5AM. 632 N Dearborn St (at W Ontario St). 266.1944. www.acesplaces.com

48 COMMONWEALTH EDISON SUBSTATION

This 1989 building shares a lineage with the neighboring **Hard Rock Cafe** and is an unusual case of an architect being contextual with his own recent work. Both were designed by **Stanley Tigerman**, whose handling of the restaurant's scale and window treatments was inspired by the 1929 Georgian Revival power station that was on this site. The substation was slated for demolition, but Tigerman's replacement repeats its basic motifs and even reuses some fragments. The building looks like an English country pavilion—except for the large mechanical louvers that fill the limestone window surrounds. ♦ N Dearborn and W Ontario Sts

49 RED HEAD

In its previous incarnations (first **Outtakes**, then **The Fish Head**) this club aimed to be supercool, with bouncers admitting only the hip. Changing times and an aging clientele have turned it into another kind of chic bar, this one with live music on weekends. The owners have kept the amazing 900-gallon, 50-foot-long aquarium that was the former club's trademark. ♦ Daily, 7PM-4AM; Sa; until 5AM. 16 W Ontario St (between N State and N Dearborn Sts). 640.1000. www.redheadpianobar.com

50 OSTERIA VIA STATO

$$$ Many things have been said about Richard Melman's skill at operating restaurants. Here's another: He knows when to fold them. As ACCESS went to press, the Lettuce Entertainment chain had closed the Greek taverna **Pa'Pagus** and was about to open its successor, **Osteria via Stato**. The name translates as "Tavern on State," and the concept is a multicourse fixed-price ($35.95) traditional Italian meal. Send us *una carta* and let us know what you think of the latest from Lettuce. ♦ Daily, *pranzo e cena*. 620 N State St. 642.8450 ᴋ www.leye.com

51 LENOX SUITES

$$ This all-suites hotel in an older renovated building is just one block from the expensive digs on Michigan Avenue. Though the décor is plain, each of the 324 suites is furnished with a fully equipped kitchen and wet bar. Amenities include a daily newspaper, in-room movies, and access to a local health club. Special rates for weekends and extended stays are available. ♦ 616 N Rush St (between E Ohio and E Ontario Sts). 337.1000, 800/44.LENOX; fax 337.7217 ᴋ www.lenoxsuites.com

Within Lenox Suites:

HOUSTON'S

★$$ The diverse menu at this dark, clubby restaurant—big with the business lunch and after-work crowd—includes delicious spinach-artichoke dip for chips, cobb salads, homemade soups, fresh fish filleted in-house daily, and hickory-grilled steaks. ♦ American ♦ Daily, lunch and dinner. 649.1121. www.houstons.com

52 LAWRY'S—THE PRIME RIB

★$$$ A former McCormick mansion (so many relatives of reaper manufacturer Cyrus McCormick lived in this neighborhood at one time that it was known as McCormickville) provides a suitably ornate setting for prime rib, the only entrée on the dinner menu. It's served in the English tradition from a silver-domed platter, accompanied by salad, mashed potatoes, and Yorkshire pudding. The lunch menu has more variety. ♦ American ♦ M-F, lunch and dinner; Sa, Su, dinner. Reservations recommended. 100 E Ontario St (at N Rush St). 787.5000

53 TIFFANY STAINED GLASS

Stained-glass pieces in the Tiffany style, from windows to wisteria lamps, are this store's specialty, and they are made on-site. Former mayor Jane Byrne came here for the city's official gift to Pope John Paul II during his 1979 visit and left with a small made-to-order window depicting the pontiff on one side and

---

Restaurants/Clubs: **Red** | Hotels: **Purple** | Shops: **Orange** | Outdoors/Parks: **Green** | Sights/Culture: **Blue**

the Chicago skyline on the other. ◆ M-F, noon-5PM; Sa, 10AM-3PM. 216 W Ohio St (between N Wells and N Franklin Sts). 642.0680. www.tiffanystainedglass.com

54 MODERNICA

A visually captivating furniture showroom, **Modernica** is run by folks who say they are dedicated to producing furnishings that reflect the design innovations associated with Modernism: solid pieces with a futuristic bent, but warm and suited to everyday use.◆ M-Sa, 11AM-6PM; Su, noon-5PM. 555 N Franklin (at W Ohio St). 222.1808; fax 222.1815. www.modernica.com

55 MIG AND TIG

This attractive showroom of high-end traditional furniture, specializing in dining-room chairs and tables, is a venture that began in the North Shore town of Winnetka and has made its way down to the city. ◆ M-Sa. 549 N Wells St (at W Ohio St). 644.8277; fax 644.2477. www.migandtig.com

56 SAWBRIDGE STUDIOS

Selling "furniture with a story," this place will entice even the most casual visitor to learn more. The handcrafted pieces range from bird-houses and CD racks to dining-room sets and sleigh beds, with magnificently smooth wooden cutting boards, quilts, pillows, and Arts and Crafts–style pottery. Among the craftspeople featured are Chicagoan Jeff Miller (contemporary) and Vermonters Charles Shackleton (Scottish and Irish styles) and the McGuire family (Shaker). Many of the larger pieces are pictured and described on sepia-toned cards that shoppers can take home. ◆ M-Sa. 153 W Ohio St (between N Wells and N LaSalle Sts). 828.0055; fax 828.0066. Also in Winnetka, 847/441.2441 & www.sawbridge.com

57 BEST WESTERN RIVER NORTH HOTEL

$$ One of the best bargains in the area, this hotel offers 150 modern rooms and suites, a rooftop sundeck, an enclosed swimming pool, and exercise equipment. There's a restaurant on-site and free valet parking, and special weekend packages are available. ◆125 W Ohio St (between N Clark and N LaSalle Sts). 467.0800, 800/727.0800; fax 467.1665 & www.bestwestern.com

58 ROCK 'N' ROLL MCDONALD'S

$ The busiest and most visually stimulating "Micky D's" in the city, this neon-flickering place is packed with 1950s memorabilia, from a flame-red 1963 Corvette to Archie and Veronica dolls and working arcade games. Customers in line tap their feet to the sounds of Buddy Holly, Connie Francis, and Elvis. Too bad the food's no better than at any other **McDonald's**. There's free parking in a big lot, but don't leave your car here while you visit another Ontario Street spot, or you'll help make a towing company rich. ◆ Fast food ◆ Daily, 24 hours. 600 N Clark St (at W Ohio St). 664.7940 &

59 EMBASSY SUITES HOTEL

$$ Part of a national chain, this attractive hotel located three blocks from Michigan Avenue offers a lot for your money, including complimentary breakfast and cocktails. Each of the 358 suites has a kitchen with a wet bar and a well-lighted dining/work table. ◆ 600 N State St (at W Ohio St). 943.3800, 800/EMBASSY; fax 943.7629 &

60 TREE STUDIOS BUILDING

Lawyer and philanthropist Lambert Tree had this three-story building constructed by the **Parfitt Brothers** in 1894 to offer Chicago artists a place to work instead of the garrets and basements they could typically afford. Arranged around a courtyard behind Tree's home, the studios provided charming if spartan workspace for 17 artists. Natural light streamed through the large windows on State

Street, and huge doors between the studios could be opened for parties and exhibitions. The ground floor was divided into small shops housing galleries and art-supply stores. In 1912 and 1913, additions on Ontario and Ohio Streets were designed by **Hill & Woltersdorf**. Among the first to work here were popular painters Wellington Reynolds, Pauline Palmer, and Frederick Freer. At one time or another in the mid-1900s, most of Chicago's better-known artists have lived here, including painters Macena Barton, Rowena Fry, and Natalie Henry; muralist Louis Grell; sculptor John Breyn; and James Alan St. John, who first drew Edgar Rice Burroughs's *Tarzan*. In the 1940s, actor-artist Burgess Meredith and other movie stars were tenants, but they threw such wild parties that they were kicked out. In 2002, a major renovation carried out by Friedman Properties and architect Daniel P. Coffey was done in connection with the construction of **Bloomingdale's** on the site of the former **Medinah Temple**. Stroll through the courtyard and let us know what you think of their work. ♦ 4 E Ohio St (at N State St)

61 BLOOMINGDALE'S HOME & FURNITURE

New Yorkers tend to look on **Bloomingdale's** as a temple among department stores. It's fitting, then, that in its Chicago incarnation, this four-story complex is housed in the old auditorium of what was originally the **Medinah Temple**, built in 1911 by **Huehl & Schmid**. After several years of sometimes heated planning and redevelopment proposals, the bid to renovate the ersatz Middle Eastern temple and the neighboring **Tree Studios** went to the king of River North redevelopment, Albert Friedman. Although some preservationists are unhappy with the results, the redesign by **Daniel P. Coffey & Associates** is considered far superior to a plan presented in 1999 by developer Steven Fifield, which would have built a 49-story structure on the block, adding to the concrete jungle created by developer John Buck in the adjacent North Bridge section. The store opened in February 2003 with great fanfare that included a concert in the auditorium space. ♦ M-Sa, 10AM-9:30PM; Su, 11AM-7PM. 600 N Wabash Ave (at E Ohio St). 324.7500 & www.bloomingdales.com

61 PIZZERIA UNO

$ This is where Chicago deep-dish pizza began. The late Ike Sewell introduced the taste treat to the city in 1943. With only 18 small tables and five booths, there's almost always a traffic jam (the pizza takes 45 minutes to cook). Many people opt for the larger **Pizzeria Due** up the block (619 N Wabash St, between E Ohio and E Ontario Sts). Both places offer an "express lunch" for $4.95 from 11:30AM to 3PM. ♦ Pizza ♦ Daily, lunch and dinner, late kitchen. 29 E Ohio St (at N Wabash Ave). 321.1000; fax 321.1665. www.unos.com

62 CALIFORNIA PIZZA KITCHEN

$ Is it possible for California superthin crust pizza with imaginative (some might say "ridiculous") toppings to survive in the land of deep-dish Chicago-style pizza? Apparently the answer is yes. This brightly lit café is a popular casual dining spot for weary shoppers and tourists. It's also open for a light late-night snack. ♦ Pizza ♦ Daily, lunch and dinner. 52 E Ohio St (at N Wabash Ave). 787.6075. Also at Water Tower Place, 835 N Michigan Ave (at E Pearson St). 787.7300 &

63 ESPN ZONE

For those who want to know what it feels like to be "in the zone," as athletes say, this is the place to find out. A multilevel sports entertainment emporium featuring electronic games, video sports highlights, sports-related products, and casual dining, ESPN zone caters to jocks of all ages and both genders. Admission is free, but you'll get clipped for each amusement chosen. ♦ Daily. 43 E Ohio St (at N Wabash Ave). 644.ESPN & www.espnzone.com

64 BIG BOWL ASIAN KITCHEN

★$ This sidewalk café serves complete meals in bowls, featuring soups and salads. A popular item is three chix on stix (three skewers of chicken and a variety of vegetables served with chicken broth and a crispy noodle cake). ♦ M-Sa, lunch and dinner. 60 E Ohio St (at N Rush St). 951.1888. Also at 6 E Cedar St (at N State St). 640.8888 & www.bigbowl.com

64 CHICAGO HARLEY-DAVIDSON

The Milwaukee motorcycle has traveled a long, long way toward respectability from its one-time association with outlaw bikers. For those who want people to think they ride hogs, even if they're frightened to drive family vans, this store offers a dizzying selection of merchandise with the Harley logo festooned on it. But there are no motorcycles for sale. ♦ Daily. 66 E Ohio St (at N Rush St). 274.9666. www.chicagoharley.com

---

Restaurants/Clubs: Red | **Hotels: Purple** | **Shops: Orange** | **Outdoors/Parks: Green** | **Sights/Culture: Blue**

65 THYME

★★★$$$ Under the direction of chef-owner John Bubala (previously at **Marche** and **Four Seasons Boston**), the old **Danilo's** restaurant was transformed into a dramatic space marked with statues, mirrors, custom furniture, and blue-bottle-accented chandeliers. The menu is long on spit-roasted game, with French and Italian accents, prepared in a display kitchen. Among entrées, try the tenderloin tail with horseradish potatoes and pesto. Vegetarians will find much to cheer about in the appetizers, which include cheese spinach and corn sauce ravioli among a selection favoring fish and seafood. An extensive wine list leans toward white wines. An adjacent bar is a comfortable spot to listen to the Brazilian jazz and other live music that plays on some weeknights. In warm weather, ask to be seated in the outdoor dining garden. ♦ Contemporary ♦ Reservations recommended. Daily, dinner. 464 N Halsted St (at W Grand Ave). 226.4300, fax 226.0311 &

66 FUNKY BUDDHA LOUNGE

Hip-hop, house, and Latin sounds provided by DJs and sometimes by live bands propel the feet at this supercool lounge that caters to well-heeled youngsters between 21 and 50. From the Buddha sculpture at the door, done by local artist Suhail, to the long black-leather and fake leopard-skin benches across from the wooden bar to a collection of Victorian lounge chairs, the décor is interesting to say the least. ♦ Club cover. Tu-Sa nights. 728 W Grand Ave (between N Halsted and N Union Sts). 666.1695; fax 666.1895. www.funkybuddha.com

67 CYRANO'S BISTROT & WINE BAR

★★$ Serving well-prepared, high-quality food at lower prices than most restaurants in the area, **Cyrano's** ranks as perhaps River North's greatest dining value. The restaurant is simple and charming in décor and presentation. There are some very nice personal touches from chef Didier Durand and his wife, Jamie, starting with the curry-flavored butter that accompanies the bread. A three-course daily prix-fixe for $25 might include lobster salad, lamb chops, and crème anglaise. If you're game, try ostrich pâté to start, an excellent bouillabaisse, and rotisserie duck. The wine list is eccentric and includes selections from Bergerac. ♦ French bistro. ♦ Tu-F, lunch and dinner; Sa, dinner. Reservations recommended. 546 N Wells St (between W Grand Ave and W Ohio St). 467.0546 &

68 CROFTON ON WELLS

★★★$$$ Named by *Chicago* magazine as one of the city's 10 best new restaurants in 1998, this wonderful little room was drawing raves from diners even before it received that notice. Chef and owner Suzy Crofton, who earned critical acclaim at **Montparnasse**, offers an inventive approach to contemporary cuisine, whether it's an appetizer such as barbecued quail on braised beet greens or a main dish such as the pork loin with smoked apple chutney. A four-course prix-fixe menu is available for $45. The wine list is thoughtful, and the atmosphere is tranquil, with soft jazz music playing in the background. ♦ American ♦ M-Sa, dinner. Reservations recommended. 535 N Wells St (between W Grand Ave and W Ohio St). 755.1790

69 ANTI-CRUELTY SOCIETY ADDITION

Constructed in 1978 by **Stanley Tigerman & Associates**, this is another of their billboard buildings (like the **Self-Park Garage** in the Loop). In this case, the whimsical design resembles a dog-food can, with a framed upright on the roof forming a pull tab. The two-story windows are curved to resemble the cheeks of a basset hound. ♦157 W Grand Ave (between N LaSalle and N Wells Sts)

70 FADÓ IRISH PUB

$ Well, actually, it's a little fancier than most neighborhood pubs you'll find in Ireland, but in a neighborhood mostly populated with formal dining options, this stands out as a welcome casual spot for a leisurely beer and a good bite. Words of wisdom from James Joyce and Brendan Behan are on the place mats, and there's live Irish music on Tuesday and Saturday nights and Sunday afternoons, as well as European sports broadcasts via satellite. ♦ Irish pub ♦ Daily, lunch and dinner. 100 W Grand Ave (at N Clark St). 836.0066. www.fadoirishpub.com

70 BLUE CHICAGO AT OHIO

During the 1950s, this part of Chicago was quite "blue"—full of pornographic bookstores and bars that ripped off unsuspecting tourists. Now it's a chic restaurant row, with some delightful shops nestled between eateries. Fitting, then, that this successful spin-off of the original **Blue Chicago** (a little farther north on Clark Street) should have settled here too. Both clubs feature performances by top local and national blues acts, such as Johnny B. Moore and Willy Cat and the Japs. A single, inexpensive cover charge is good for both venues. ♦ Cover. M-Sa, 8PM-2AM; shows start 9PM. 536 N Clark St (at W Ohio St). 661.0100

71 JAZZ SHOWCASE

Owned by a legend himself, Joe Segal, this is one of Chicago's consistently best clubs for quality jazz performed by noted local and national musicians. On Sunday afternoons, kids get in free, so turn them on to some jazz. ♦ Cover. Tu-Sa, 8PM-2AM; Su, 4PM-midnight. 59 W Grand Ave (between N Dearborn and N Clark Sts). 670.2473

72 ROCK BOTTOM BREWERY

★$ This huge bar and restaurant offers sampler-size portions of their house-brewed beers and all ales. Along with the brewmaster's suggestions is a hearty American grill menu featuring good burgers, ribs, chicken, fish, salads, and more. Other attractions include seven billiard tables and children's and late-night menus. But perhaps the biggest draw of all is the **Mug Club**, in which members can bring their own mugs and order brews at reduced prices; not surprisingly, there is a waiting list. ♦ American ♦ Daily, lunch and dinner. 1 W Grand Ave (at N State St). 755.9339 ⟨ www.rockbottom.com

73 HILTON GARDEN INN

$$ Opened in November 1999, the 357-room **Hilton Garden Inn** is a stone's throw from another Hilton, the **Homewood Suites**. Speaking of stones, check out the turquoise ones embedded in the lobby floor that give this otherwise typical, modern facility a touch of character. With a fitness room, 24-hour business center, and modem ports and two phones in each room, it is geared to business travelers, but given its proximity to kids' attractions, it draws a family clientele (kids under 17 stay free). There's an indoor swimming pool and whirlpool, and a fridge and microwave in each room. Within the hotel there's a bar and grill. ♦ 10 E Grand Ave (at N State St). 595.0000; fax 527.1989, 877/782.9444 ⟨

74 515 NORTH STATE STREET

The American Medical Association is headquartered in this 30-story building, designed in 1990 by famed Japanese architect **Kenzo Tange** with Chicago's **Shaw & Associates**. Tange's first major commission in the US, it is promoted as a "crisp, pure statement of assertive form, precise finish, and refined materials." It is also one of the few strong new statements of Modernism in a city whose architects have turned largely to historical allusion. The elegant two-story lobby contains a sculptured metal-and-glass stairway that provides an intriguing spatial experience. A **Chicago Atheneum** gallery in the lobby mounts interesting exhibitions of architecture and design. ♦ Between E Illinois St and E Grand Ave

75 HOMEWOOD SUITES

$$ Opened in 2000, this entry in the Hilton chain is in the heart of the new North Bridge zone. The good news for some visitors is that it's located in the same full-block complex as **ESPN Zone**; the bad news for others is that it's located in the same complex as ESPN Zone. Boasting 233 one-bedroom suites with separate sleeping areas and fully equipped kitchens with dishwasher, stovetop microwave, and refrigerator, it appears to be a place where you're expected to stay for a while. Each suite has two TVs, dual phone lines, voice mail, and data ports with high-speed Internet access. There's an indoor pool and fitness room with great views of the city, complimentary daily breakfast buffet and evening reception with beverages and a light meal Monday to Thursday. There is no restaurant in the hotel, but room service is available through two nearby restaurants. ♦ 40 E Grand Ave (between N Wabash Ave and N Rush St). 644.2222; 800.CALLHOME; fax 644.7777 ⟨ www.homewoodsuiteschicago.com

76 JOE'S SEAFOOD, PRIME STEAK & STONE CRAB

★★$$$ This is a joint effort between the owners of the famous **Joe's Stone Crab** in Miami and Rich Melman, the Lettuce Entertain You creator. One might well ask whether Chicago can stand yet another surf-and-turf emporium. Since Joe's opened in 2000, the long lines of hungry folks waiting outside for half of the 225 available seats that are not eligible for reservations has answered a definitive Yes! It's a dark, clubby atmosphere with vintage black-and-white photos on the walls. The fare ranges from Miami Joe's favorites (crab, creamed spinach, Key lime pie) to some Chicago spins (shrimp de jonghe, crab cakes). Portions are large for large guys. If you wish, you can forgo the wait for a table and eat at the bar, which has plenty of seats. ♦ Surf and turf ♦ Reservations recommended. M-Sa, lunch and dinner; Su, dinner. 60 E Grand Ave (at N Rush St). 379.5637 ⟨ www.leye.com

---

Restaurants/Clubs: **Red** | Hotels: **Purple** | Shops: **Orange** | Outdoors/Parks: **Green** | Sights/Culture: **Blue**

77 NORDSTROM

When the doors of this San Francisco–based department store finally opened in September 2000, people were lined up outside waiting to get in. Known both for its high-quality merchandise and knowledgeable, personable sales staff, **Nordstrom** has been a major retailing force in the Chicago area for nearly a decade, with several stores in high-end suburban shopping malls. But this is the first store to open in prime shopping turf within the city limits. With a glassed-in overhead pedestrian tunnel, Nordstrom is linked to the **Shops at North Bridge** mall on Michigan Avenue, connecting the Magnificent Mile with the increasingly bright and trendy River North neighborhood. Within the Nordstrom building are two shops, **Active Endeavors** sportswear and **Pistachio's** jewelry. For a bite to eat, there's the light fare at **Café Nordstrom** and **Cosi**, an Italian café. ♦ Daily. 55 E Grand Ave (at N Rush St). 464.1515; fax 379.4395 &
www.nordstrom.com

78 EAST BANK CLUB

Chicago's beautiful people come here to sweat. You need to know a member to gain admittance, but your hotel concierge might possibly be of assistance. It's worth a try just to see the 450,000-square-foot, four-floor health club, featuring indoor and outdoor swimming pools (the one outside has a 2-acre poolside deck with a café and bar), giant aerobics and exercise equipment areas, 21 racket-sports courts, two indoor running tracks, an indoor driving range, and, to top it all off, a white-linens restaurant. ♦ Daily. 500 N Kingsbury St (between W Kinzie St and W Grand Ave). 527.5800.
www.eastbankclub.com

79 CLUB GENE & GEORGETTI, LTD.

★$$$ Opened in 1941, this dark, clubby Italian steak house evokes another age. Diners, many of whom have been regular customers for years, are served in one of the four small dining rooms within an old three-story flat. Fare runs to prime aged steaks and especially good chicken Vesuvio. ♦ Steak house/Italian ♦ M-Sa, lunch and dinner. 500 N Franklin St (at W Illinois St). 527.3718 &
www.geneandgeorgetti.com

80 PIMLICO ANTIQUES LTD.

Here's a wonderland of 18th- and 19th-century furniture and accessories to discover, including china, porcelain, and exquisite mirrors. ♦ M-Sa. 500 N Wells St (at W Illinois St). 245.9199

Comedian Jack Benny was born in Chicago in 1894.

W A T E R W O R K S

81 WATERWORKS

This storefront shop offers an eye-popping selection of all things related to providing water in the home—faucets, sinks, and bathroom and kitchen furnishings. The sparkling options just may whet your appetite to do some remodeling. ♦ M-Sa. 503 N Wells St (between W Illinois and W Grand Sts). 527.4668; fax 527.1490.
www.waterworks.com

82 MAGGIANO'S

★$$ Another successful Lettuce Entertain You Enterprises venture, this airy *ristorante* serves good pastas, veal, and other regional Italian dishes. Spectacular sandwiches and fresh breads can be ordered from the attached bakery. ♦ Italian ♦ Daily, lunch and dinner. 516 N Clark St (between W Illinois St and W Grand Ave). 644.7700. Also at several suburban locations & www.leye.com

83 NAHA

★★★$$$ **Naha** is a highly praised family affair involving the partnership of chef Carrie Nahabedian, formerly at the Four Seasons in Beverly Hills, and her cousin **Michael**, who opened **Green Dolphin Street**. The 100-seat dining room, which features walnut floors and rich blues that evoke the Mediterranean coast, was designed by Michael's brother, Tom. When all 100 seats are taken, the place can be noisier than the dock at a Mediterranean port. But that is about its only drawback. The menu is California-meets-Armenia (Carrie's native land). For starters choose caramelized Belgian endive with candied lemons or broccoli and mascarpone ravioli. Move on to honey-roasted ranch squab with chickpeas, couscous, dried apricots, dates, and carrots or wood-grilled ribeye steak with oxtail red-wine sauce. Many good wines are available by the glass. Vanilla sorbet brings the meal to a smooth, satisfying conclusion. ♦ Contemporary ♦ M-F, lunch and dinner; Sa, dinner. Reservations recommended. 500 N Clark St (at W Illinois St) 321.6242 & www.naha-chicago.com

Chinese Restaurant & Satay Bar

84 BEN PAO

★$$ Yet another outpost in the Lettuce Entertain You empire, this time the theme is contemporary Chinese, with cuisine representing four regions and some traditional Asian dishes as well. Waterfalls, red pillars, and gold sculptured walls are part of the self-consciously picturesque décor. One very nice touch is a satay bar, at which diners can choose from a variety of skewered meats, Portobello mushrooms, sea scallops, and coconut shrimp, with a selection of dipping sauces. In warm weather, there's an outdoor patio. ♦ Chinese ♦ M-F, lunch and dinner; Sa, Su, dim sum brunch, dinner. 52 W Illinois St (at N Dearborn St). 222.1888 ♿ www.leye.com

85 STAR OF SIAM

★$ This airy storefront restaurant has been serving tasty Thai food since the days when most Chicagoans thought it was spelled t-i-e. Although its star has been eclipsed by the more upscale Asian eateries, it's still a great spot to loosen your tie and dig in. Some of its original patrons still insist that it's the best Thai restaurant in the city. ♦ Daily, lunch and dinner. 11 E Illinois St (at N State St). 670.0100

85 CHICAGO READER

Up the stairs from **Star of Siam** is the headquarters of *The Reader*, which has been Chicago's "alternative" weekly for much longer than its early readers (or its founder, Bob Roth) care to remember. The *Reader* model and format (a free publication paid for by advertising) has been adapted by hundreds of imitators across the country. Although it is mostly sought after for its listings of things to do every Thursday evening (the first copies are dropped right in the first-floor vestibule), it also has been known for showcasing some of the city's best journalists and critics, including regular contributors John Conroy, Michael Miner, Jonathan Rosenbaum, and the late Grant Pick. ♦ 11 E Illinois St (at N State St). 828.0350. www.chireader.com

86 JAZZ RECORD MART

Not just jazz, but blues and world music too. With 8,500 square feet of space, this store bills itself as the world's largest jazz and blues record store, and who's to say it's not? There are tens of thousands of new and used CDs, LPs, 45s, and 78s. Plus cassettes, videos, books, magazines, T-shirts, and posters. A special "killers rack" has what the store describes as the essential titles of jazz, blues, and world music. If you like jazz, plan to spend at least 3 hours here. If you're lucky, you might catch a live, in-store performance. ♦ M-Sa, 10AM-8PM; Su, noon-5PM. 444 N Wabash (at E Illinois St). 222.1467, 800/684.3480. www.jazzmart.com

86 AFTER-WORDS NEW & USED BOOKS

This large, bright store has a large selection of books and a comfortable lounge area on the lower level. If you're staying at a downtown hotel and need a good read, this is your place. ♦ M-Sa, 10:30AM-10PM; Su, noon-7PM. 23 E Illinois St (at N Wabash Ave). 464.1110

87 COCO PAZZO

★★★$$ This outstanding eatery boasts an airy, lofty setting, a friendly, knowledgeable waitstaff, and chef Tony Priolo's wonderful Tuscan-style creations. Start with the beets and greens salad or antipasto; consider the daily risotto, which might feature artichokes or wild mushrooms, and pasta such as rigatoni with sausage and peas in crème rosa; and savor one of the expertly prepared meat entrées such as leg of lamb roasted in the wood-burning oven. Be sure to save room for the ever-so-smooth *panna cotta* (a creamy vanilla gelatin). ♦ Italian ♦ M-F, lunch and dinner; Sa, Su, dinner. 300 W Hubbard St (at N Franklin St). 836.0900 ♿

88 BATON SHOW LOUNGE

Drawing a largely gay crowd and a throng of curious tourists, this club features drag shows that keep 'em coming back. ♦ Cover. W-Su, 8PM-2AM. 436 N Clark St (at W Hubbard St). 644.5269. www.thebatonshowlounge.com

89 FRONTERA GRILL

★★★$$ Since 1987, this colorful restaurant has served regional Mexican cuisine. Owners Deanna and Rick Bayless wrote a book, *Authentic Mexican Regional Cooking from the Heart of Mexico*, on the very topic. The ever-changing menu often includes the house specialty, *tacos al carbon*, chicken, duck, or skirt steak folded into a homemade tortilla. Mahimahi with two sauces and Yucatecan-style marinated venison in a spicy sauce of fresh tomatoes, *habañero* chilies, and sour orange juice are out of this world. Anything with a mole sauce is excellent. The adjoining **Topolobampo**, also owned by the Baylesses, shares a bar and waiting area. ♦ Mexican ♦ Tu-F, lunch and dinner; Sa, dinner. Reservations recommended. 445 N Clark St (between W

Hubbard and W Illinois Sts). 661.1434.
www.fronterakitchens.com

89 TOPOLOBAMPO

★★★$$$ Regional Mexican cooking gets even
more refined—and more expensive—than at the
wonderful **Frontera Grill** next door, both under
the stewardship of the acclaimed Baylesses.
Appetizers include extraordinary tamales
stuffed with smoked mussels, shredded game,
or other ingredients. Among the entrées is
Oaxacan-style chili-marinated capon breast
steamed in banana and avocado leaves. The
meals served here and next door come with
freshly made tortillas, cactus, chayote, and
regional renditions of beans and rice. ♦
Mexican ♦ Tu-F, lunch and dinner; Sa, dinner.
Reservations recommended. 445 N Clark St
(between W Hubbard and W Illinois Sts).
661.1434. www.fronterakitchens.com

90 GOLDEN TRIANGLE

This shop stocks a wonderful selection of
native crafts and art objects from the Golden
Triangle—Burma, Laos, and Northern
Thailand's Chiang Mai region. Carved objects
of teak and rainwood include charming spirit
houses. Thai legend has it that if you set one
on the corner of your property, making sure
that your house casts no shadow on it, the
spirits will peacefully live outside instead of
dropping in on you. ♦ M-Sa. 72 W Hubbard St
(at N Clark St). 755.1266.
www.goldentriangle.biz

91 BRASSERIE JO

★★$$$ When it opened a few years ago, when
Chicagoans just couldn't get enough bistro,
this was the hottest spot in town. It still cooks,
thanks to the presence of chef-owner Jean
Joho, whose attention to detail and flair for
creative touches is second to none. Entrées
range from such basics as coq au vin and
steak frites to the artful phyllo stuffed with
shrimp and mushrooms, served with lobster
sauce. The décor and ambiance are authentic,
from the zinc bar and French furniture to the
bustling big-room atmosphere. Plus the food is
good and the regional wine list has some tasty
bargains. ♦ French/bistro ♦ M-F, lunch and
dinner; Sa, dinner. 59 W Hubbard St (between
N Dearborn and N Clark Sts). 595.0800 &
www.brasseriejo.com

92 COURT HOUSE PLACE

The first Cook County courthouse was demolished soon after being built, having been
poorly designed and too small. This is the
second courthouse, built in 1892 by **Otto
Matz** and renovated into offices by **Solomon
Cordwell Buenz & Associates** in 1986. The
handsome Bedford limestone façade is
enhanced by the cast-iron and copper-coated
metalwork of the arched entrance. Beautiful
metalwork carries through to the lobby stair-
cases. As a courthouse, the building has a
colorful history. In 1897 sausage maker
Adolph Leutgert was tried, convicted, and
sentenced to life imprisonment for the murder
of his wife after her wedding ring and a small
fragment of bone were found in a vat at his
sausage factory. In 1924 Nathan Leopold and
Richard Loeb were tried and convicted here for
killing a 13-year-old boy for fun, as depicted in
Meyer Levin's novel *Compulsion*. Their defense
attorney was Clarence Darrow, whose impas-
sioned arguments against capital punishment
won them life sentences rather than the death
penalty. In the 1920s Carl Sandburg served as
an apprentice reporter here. Ben Hecht,
coauthor with Charles MacArthur of *The Front
Page*, honed his court-reporting skills here
during the same era. ♦ 54 W Hubbard St
(between N Dearborn and N Clark Sts)

93 RUTH'S CHRIS STEAK HOUSE

★★$$$ Part of a large chain operation, this
dark clubby joint serves up chops and steaks
as well as most local Chicago places do. Pass
on the appetizers to make room for the porter-
house, which can feed at least two. The potato
offering is au gratin, the dessert of choice is
chocolate mousse, the wine is red, and the
check will be steep. ♦ Steak house ♦ M-Sa,
dinner. Reservations recommended. 431 N
Dearborn St (at W Hubbard St). 321.2725 &
www.ruthschris.com

94 VONG'S THAI KITCHEN

★★ $$$ The reputation of New York chef Jean
Georges Vongerichten preceded him to
Chicago, setting up great expectations for this
successor to his highly regarded Thai-French
establishments in London, Hong Kong, and
the Big Apple. The 150 patrons who fill the
visually striking plaid- and gold-decorated
room at any one time do not go away disap-
pointed. Start with shrimp satay or tuna-wasabi
pizza and move on to a New York strip served
on a bed of pho noodles with green pepper-

CYCLING IN CHICAGO

When the weather is fine, there's no better way to enjoy the day than biking along the scenic lakefront path, with glittering high-rises and green parks on one side of you and windswept **Lake Michigan** on the other. This 20-mile-long blacktop trail runs parallel to **Lake Shore Drive**, stretching all the way from **Hollywood Avenue** in the north to **71st Street** in the south. Created and maintained by the parks department, the trail is a favorite place for Chicagoans to take in the great outdoors; in addition to cyclists, you'll find in-line skaters, dog walkers, joggers, and people out for an old-fashioned stroll. The trail's most interesting and widely used section is between **Belmont Avenue** and **16th Street**. (South of 16th Street, it's wise to ride with a companion for safety purposes.) This stretch of trail skirts the edges of the **Lincoln Park**, **Gold Coast**, and **Magnificent Mile** neighborhoods, offering the visitor a great way to see the sights. Many of Chicago's top attractions—including the **Adler Planetarium**, **Field Museum**, **Shedd Aquarium**, **Grant Park**, **Burnham Harbor**, **Buckingham Fountain**, **Lincoln Park Zoo**, and **Navy Pier**—are accessible from this section of the bike path. If that sounds too ambitious, pack a picnic and head for **Oak Street Beach** or **Fullerton Beach**.

corn sauce or sesame-tamarind duck with pineapple stir-fried rice. Finish with spiced pear cheesecake. ♦ Thai/French ♦ M-F lunch and dinner; Sa, Su, dinner. Reservations recommended. 6 W Hubbard St (at N State St). 644.8664 & www.vongsthaikitchen.com

95 KEVIN

★★★$$$ Kevin Shikami made such a name for himself at **Jimmy's Place Outpost** that he was able to open a restaurant where diners are grateful to get to know his Asian-French fusion cuisine on a first-name basis. In the warm, friendly space designed by Nancy Warren, a sumptuous meal begins with tuna tartare with green papaya salad. Move on to seared bluefin tuna and sea scallops in yuzu-wasabi dressing with banana tomato salad and soba noodles. If you're not in the mood for fish, try the rack of lamb in Chinese black-bean chili glaze. But be sure to save room for dessert. At **Kevin** the pastry chef is Cindy Schuman, who makes dramatic fashion statements with delights such as chocolate mousse–filled cornet with peanut butter ice cream in chocolate and caramel sauce. ♦ Contemporary ♦ M-F, lunch and dinner; Sa, dinner. Reservations recommended. 9 W Hubbard St (between N State and N Dearborn Sts). 595.0055 & www.kevinrestaurant.com

96 MUSEUM OF BROADCAST COMMUNICATIONS

Highlights of national radio and TV history, including an extensive library of rare tapes and kinescopes, are preserved at this lively museum. Exhibits showcase Chicago's significant role in early broadcasting and the evolution of TV advertising. Free. ♦ Daily. 400 N State St (at W Hubbard St). 245.8200. www.museum.tv

97 ANDY'S

★$$ One of the best and certainly the busiest of Chicago's jazz bars, for many years this was a grungy hangout where printers from the nearby daily newspapers convened at all hours. It retains an essence of crumminess with beat-up floors, dirty bathrooms, the scent of stale beer, and cigarette smoke. When Dick Goodman and Scott Chisholm bought it in the late 1970s, they started offering jazz—which is now played here about 80 hours a week. There are lunchtime sets Monday through Friday between noon and 2:30PM, music for the after-work crowd at 5PM, and a final set at 8:30PM. The huge roster of musicians is composed mostly of nationally known locals, among them the John Bany Trio with supreme sax player Brad Goode, the Mike Smith Quintet, and Dr. Bop and the Headliners. A menu of pretty good pizza, steaks, burgers, and ribs is offered between lunch and midnight. ♦ American ♦ No cover for lunch sets; cover during evening. M-F, 11AM-2AM; Sa, Su, 6PM-midnight. 11 E Hubbard St (between N Wabash Ave and N State St). 642.6805 &

98 SHAW'S CRAB HOUSE AND BLUE CRAB LOUNGE

★★$$$ The atmosphere is lively, sometimes almost frenetic, at this New England–style seafood house and lounge. The **Crab House** serves more than 40 fish entrées, plus chicken and pasta. Everything is absolutely fresh; in fact, a staff biologist inspects the seafood for purity. This place is so popular, however, that even with a reservation, you may get fed faster by opting for the adjacent **Blue Crab Lounge**. Here, seated on high stools, you'll find a limited but nevertheless

---

Restaurants/Clubs: Red | Hotels: Purple | Shops: Orange | Outdoors/Parks: Green | Sights/Culture: Blue

good list of raw-bar items and hot dishes, not to mention a fantastic thick chowder. The lounge also offers ethnic cuisine at such seasonal events as the Scandinavian crawfish feast. In October, there's an oyster-eating contest officiated by WXRT's Lin Brehmer. ♦ Seafood ♦ M-Sa, lunch and dinner; Su, dinner. Reservations recommended. 21 E Hubbard St (between N Wabash Ave and N State St). 527.2722 ᵴ www.shawscrabhouse.com

99 COURTYARD BY MARRIOTT

$$ A suburban hotel in the city is the best way to describe this establishment. King-size beds and large desks are offered in the 337 guest rooms. The **Courtyard Café** serves predictable breakfast and dinner. You'd do better to eat at one of the many alternatives nearby. ♦ 30 E Hubbard St (between N Wabash Ave and N State St). 329.2500, 800/321.2211; fax 329.0293 ᵴ

100 437 RUSH

★★$$$ Restaurateur Phil Stefani increased his standing with media and publishing folk when he reopened this shuttered space. For decades it was **Riccardo's**, a storied tavern where literati would gather at lunchtime, at happy hour, and into the wee hours, sometimes in the same day. In its new incarnation, Stefani has retained the signature curved bar in the front room and concentrated on upgrading the food, which previously had been nothing for even the most accomplished writer to write home about. He has definitely succeeded, elevating the room to an Italian steak house that arguably rivals any in the city. But the prices have gone through the ceiling as well, and only time will tell whether the city can support yet another steak house. Start with the crostini with garlic spinach and smoked prosciutto before moving on to any of

Chicago is the home of mail-order shopping. Aaron Montgomery Ward had just started up when the Great Fire hit in 1871, but he was back in business 6 months later. Ward's *Big Book* became the source of household goods for farmers across the Midwest. Richard W. Sears first sold watches, then expanded his stock. By 1895, the Sears catalog was 532 pages.

a dozen great steaks or chops. At lunchtime an upstairs café offers a nice selection of sandwiches and salads. ♦ Italian ♦ M-F, lunch and dinner; Sa, Su, dinner. 437 N Rush (at E Hubbard St). 222.0101 ᵴ www.stefanisrestaurants.com

101 KINZIE STREET BRIDGE

Until April 1992, this was just another bridge across the north branch of the Chicago River—then it took on a historical significance equal to that of Mrs. O'Leary's cow. It was at this site that newly installed but faulty pilings caused a freight tunnel to collapse, causing the flood that ranks alongside the Great Fire in the history of city disasters.

102 CHICAGO APPAREL CENTER

The **Merchandise Mart's** sister building, designed by **Skidmore, Owings & Merrill** in 1977, is connected to it by a bridge by **Helmut Jahn** that reflects the Mart's design. More than 8,000 lines of women's, children's, and men's clothing and accessories from around the world are represented here. Showrooms are closed to the public. If you act as if you know where you're going, however, you might be able to saunter upstairs. Once there, you may *discreetly* ask if they sell any samples. Some shops will, some won't. ♦ M-F. 350 N Orleans St (between the Chicago River and W Kinzie St). 527.7600 ᵴ

Within the Chicago Apparel Center:

HOLIDAY INN MART PLAZA

$$ Taking up the top floors (15 through 21), this hotel offers fantastic city views. The 525 rooms have modern décor, and amenities include an indoor swimming pool and exercise facilities. A couple of restaurants and bars are on the premises, but you'll do better to go out. ♦ 836.5000, 800/HOLIDAY; fax 222.9508 ᵴ

103 MERCHANDISE MART

Built by Marshall Field in 1931 to house wholesale offices and showrooms, this behemoth's total floor area of 4 million square feet makes up the second-largest building in the US (only the Pentagon is bigger). The **Mart's** thousands of showrooms display home and office furnishings, business products, and giftware, employing about 9,000 people and drawing 10,000 visitors every day (the showrooms are open only to the trade—architects and designers). It even has its own elevated train station on the **Brown Line**. Like many grandiose projects conceived in the Roaring Twenties, the building hit hard times soon after it opened, and Field sold it to Joseph P. Kennedy for a fraction of its worth; the Kennedys still own it today. The building underwent a 1986–1991 renovation by **Graham, Anderson, Probst & White,** and a 1991 project by **Beyer Blinder Belle** converted the first two floors into a retail mall with 85 shops and restaurants. These include mostly such chain stores as **Coconuts Records, The Limited, Crabtree & Evelyn, Coach,** and other specialty shops. ♦ M-Sa. W Kinzie St (between N Wells and N Orleans Sts). 527.4141, 800/677.MART ♿ www.merchandisemart.com

Within the Merchandise Mart:

LUXEHOME

Open to the public, as well as interior designers, architects, and custom builders, **LuxeHome** has more than 70,000 square feet of space in which it showcases some 25 boutiques that feature the high-end kitchen and bath products from domestic and international manufacturers. ♦ M-Sa. 527.7555, 800.677.MART. www.luxehome.com

104 KINZIE STREET CHOPHOUSE

★★$$ An unusual selection of Mediterranean-style entrées, including herb-crusted salmon, steaks, and smoked mozzarella and chicken ravioli, are on the menu at this bright, friendly bistro. ♦ Continental ♦ M-F, lunch and dinner; Sa, dinner. 400 N Wells St (at W Kinzie St). 822.0191. www.kinziechophouse.com

105 ASIAN HOUSE

The city's largest selection of Asian housewares is offered here, among them rosewood furniture, coromandel screens, hand-painted furniture, hand-crafted brass lamps, and porcelain vases from the People's Republic of China. ♦ M-Sa. 159 W Kinzie St (between N LaSalle and N Wells Sts). 527.4848

106 JAY ROBERTS ANTIQUE WAREHOUSE

Three floors and 54,000 square feet are filled with antique furniture, including armoires, sideboards, desks, and even marble and wooden fireplaces. Items come in every style and from every period—Chippendale to French Empire, country pine to Art Nouveau. And everything is in beautiful condition and reasonably priced. ♦ M-Sa. 149 W Kinzie St (between N LaSalle and N Wells Sts). 222.0167 ♿ www.jayroberts.com

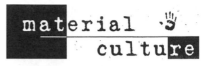

107 MATERIAL CULTURE

This large corner storefront of antiques and collectibles opened in 2000 and features a wide range of visually stunning Asian and African furniture and art. An area of specialization is handwoven rugs, and the store carries an extensive selection of handmade carpets, including Woven Legends, Black Mountain Looms, and the Tibetan carpets of Michaelian & Kohlberg. The emphasis here is on warmth and personal craftsmanship, and the store says that its prices are designed to "induce a pleasant feeling of culture shock." Still, expect to spend a few bucks, or just go to gape. ♦ M-Sa. 401 N La Salle St (at W Kinzie St). 467.1490; fax 467.1491. www.materialculture.com

108 MAMBO GRILL

★$$ North Shore native Roger Greenfield hasn't quite got the Lettuce Entertain You touch, but he is adventuresome. This place is an experience, from the attention-getting décor—spiky brass ornament, mauve marbleized walls, a ceiling emblazoned with names of foods in bold browns and maroons—to the pan-Latin menu. Try the Anaheim pepper stuffed with Portobello mushrooms, served over black-bean salsa and topped with three types of cheese and a roasted tomatillo sauce. ♦ Latin American ♦ M-Sa, lunch and dinner; Su, dinner. 412 N Clark St (between W Kinzie and W Hubbard Sts). 467.9797. www.mambogrill.com

109 KEEFER'S

★★★$$$ A latecomer to the steak-house revival, the clubby **Keefer's** quickly attracted devoted fans of the red-meat dining experience. Prime steaks are a cut above those at some other spots, but the thing that really sets apart the handiwork of chef John Hogan is the side dishes: Try the potato croquettes with cheese fondue or peas and pearl onions with bacon. The seafood entrées are also mouth-watering. Braised red snapper comes with basil-seasoned artichokes, olives, and leeks. Among appetizers, the seafood dumplings in lobster bisque are a standout. If you've got room, finish it off with poached pear with caramel sauce and a desert wine from the substantial wine list. ◆ Steak house ◆ M-F, lunch and dinner; Sa, dinner. Reservations recommended. 20 W Kinzie St (at N Dearborn St). 467.9525 ♿ www.keefersrestaurant.com

110 HARRY CARAY'S

★★$$$ The Flemish Gothic building, designed by **Henry Ives Cobb** in 1895, was originally owned by the Chicago Varnish Company, which made glosses for railroad equipment, coaches, carriages, pianos, and furniture. Now it's a restaurant filled with sports photos and memorabilia that was co-owned by legendary **Cubs** sportscaster Harry Caray until his death in 1998. The bar is 60.5 feet long—the distance between the pitcher's mound and home plate. Italian-American fare includes the big hit, chicken Vesuvio, as well as some of the best steaks in the city. When the **Cubs** are playing at **Wrigley Field**, the place stays open until midnight. ◆ Italian-American ◆ Daily, lunch and dinner. 33 W Kinzie St (at N Dearborn St). 828.0966 ♿ www.harrycarays.com

111 IBM BUILDING

IBM's regional headquarters are housed in an elegantly proportioned 52-story slab designed by the office of **Mies van der Rohe** and **C.F. Murphy Associates**. It was **Mies**'s last office building. The curtain wall of aluminum and bronze-colored glass is the ultimate refinement of this architectural form, which first appeared in **Mies**'s apartment buildings at 860-880 Lake Shore Drive. Modernists can pay homage to the master in the high-ceilinged lobby, which contains a small bust of the architect by sculptor Marino Marini. The granite plaza turns a cold shoulder to the river and is so windy that ropes are often set up to keep pedestrians from being blown away. ◆ 330 N Wabash Ave (between the Chicago River and E Kinzie St)

112 VERY TALL BUILDING

First the *Chicago Sun-Times* and Donald Trump announced plans to tear down the newspaper's longtime headquarters and build what could be the world's tallest building. Then the terrorist attack on the World Trade Center occurred, and it was decided that such a monolith could be a terrorist target, so the building's height was

At its height in 1965, enrollment in the nation's largest Catholic school system was 366,000. In 2005, it had dropped to 107,000.

scaled downward to 78 stories. Evidently, such security concerns are no longer an issue. In February 2005, with demolition already underway, Trump talk (with Mayor Daley's blessing) focused on the length of the building's spire and whether to make the building the tallest in North America or just one of the tallest in Chicago. The design firm for the hotel-condominium tower, which has reached new heights in advance publicity babble, is **Skidmore, Owings & Merrill**. Construction is expected to be completed in 2007, but if it follows the **Millennium Park** scheduling pattern, that date may go a few years higher.

113 REID-MURDOCH BUILDING

Until 1998, this was a building that most folks did not want to step into. It housed the city's traffic court, and the lucky ones exited with stern warnings about driving safely. Built in 1914 and designed by George C. Nimmons, the building is a fine example of industrial design. Originally a warehouse and office building for a wholesale grocery company, it was one of the first designs to respond to the 1909 Plan for Chicago's goal for riverfront redevelopment. The 320-foot-long façade rises 8 stories above the river (12 stories at the clock tower), combining the horizontal emphasis of the Prairie School with the large windows and expressed structure of the Chicago School. The brick and terra-cotta detailing merits a close look. It was restored in 2001 by Friedman Properties with **Daniel P. Coffey & Associates** as architect. Within the Reid-Murdoch Building, **Bob Chinn's Crab House** is the city edition of a popular suburban restaurant known for mai tais, seafood, and long lines. With **Shaw's** and other seafood alternatives nearby, it remains to be seen whether this place will be able to draw a crowd. ◆ 325 LaSalle St /320 N Clark St (between the Chicago River and W Kinzie St)

113 MARINA CITY

Chicago's first "city within a city" was designed in 1959 by **Bertrand Goldberg Associates** for 24-hour use, with residential, commercial, and recreational components. A base building housing a restaurant and marina provides a platform for a 10-story office building and twin towers with 40 stories of apartments above 20 levels of parking. The trapezoid-shaped apartments have walls that range from 8 feet long at the core to 21 feet at the balcony. They have maintained their popularity, even though the retail and entertainment businesses have failed miserably and the entire complex is badly in need of maintenance. Nevertheless, the buildings are a marvel of reinforced concrete construction and the finest example of Goldberg's organic

Marina City

architecture. ◆ 300 N State St (at the Chicago River)

114 SORRISO

$ Big with the after-work crowd, this friendly restaurant and bar is located a flight down from street level in the **Quaker Building**, yet offers a spectacular river view. The menu features Italian-style antipasti, soups, salads, and pizza. Complimentary appetizers come with cocktails. ◆ Italian ◆ M-F, lunch and dinner; Sa, dinner. 321 N Clark St (at the Chicago River). 644.0283 & www.sorrisoristorante.com

115 WESTIN RIVER NORTH

$$$ Formerly the **Hotel Nikko**, this addition to the Westin chain underwent a $9.4 million renovation. Now with 422 rooms and 17 suites (slightly fewer of each than before), the hotel still caters to the business traveler. Each room has three telephones with voice mail, data ports, and fax machine as well as TV, honor bar, hair dryer, and bathrobe. Most rooms have spectacular views of the river and city. Fitness and executive business centers are available, and the **Hana** lobby lounge serves sushi, with live jazz on the side. ◆ 320 N Dearborn St (at the Chicago River). 744.1900, 877/866.9216; fax 527.2664 & www.westinchicago.com

Within the Westin River North:

116 HOUSE OF BLUES

The Chicago branch of this national concert hall and entertainment emporium opened with great fanfare, thanks to a media promotion blitz that bordered on overkill. The music hall is noted for its excellent acoustics, and although few of the acts are known for playing authentic blues, it has come to be one of the top rock venues in the city. ◆ Cover after 10PM. Daily, with showtimes and hours varying. 329 N Dearborn St (between the Chicago River and W Kinzie St). 527.2583. www.hob.com

116 HOUSE OF BLUES HOTEL

$$ Capitalizing on the national popularity of the **House of Blues** and the local market demand for hotel rooms, Loews Hotels opened the **House of Blues Hotel**. With 367 guest rooms, including 22 luxury suites, this is a supercool place for the superhip to stay, with each room featuring "a concert of comforts": Internet access via TV, stereo with CD player, VCR, two phone lines, fax, and printer. Room service is available 24 hours a day, naturally. Attached to the hotel is a state-of-the-art health club and a 36-lane bowling alley. There's also an excellent restaurant, **Bin 36** (★★ $$), an American bistro and wine bar. ◆ 333 N Dearborn St (between the Chicago River and W Kinzie St). 245.0333, 800/23-LOEWS; fax 923.2444 & www.loews hotels.com

117 SMITH & WOLLENSKY

★★$$$$ Fans of the original acclaimed Big Apple steak house won't be surprised by the big bucks for beef at this Windy City spin-off. Although the meats are excellent cuts and expertly prepared, the prices are not quite so easy to swallow. The formal dining room and bar, with green-and-white-painted woodwork, are on the main entry level upstairs. Below, the more casual **Wollensky's Grill** offers many of the main menu selections, plus sandwiches, and leaves a little more in the pocket for some of the fine homemade desserts. Situated right on the river, both rooms offer good opportunities for people watching and Loop viewing. ◆ Steak house ◆ Daily, lunch and dinner. 318 N State St (between the Chicago River and W Kinzie St). 670.9900 & www.smithandwollensky.com

---

Restaurants/Clubs: Red | Hotels: Purple | Shops: Orange | Outdoors/Parks: Green | Sights/Culture: Blue

GOLD COAST

LINCOLN PARK

W North Ave.   W North Blvd.   E North Blvd.
1   2   3   4

■ Chess
Pavilion

OLD
TOWN

5

W Burton Pl.   W Burton Pl.   6   E Burton Pl.   7

8
9   10

11   12

N Wells St.   N LaSalle St.   N Clark St.   N Dearborn St.   N Dearborn Pkwy.   N State Pkwy.   N Astor St.

13
W Schiller St.   E Schiller St.   14
15
16

17   E Banks St.
18
19

Lake
Michigan

N Lake Shore Dr.   N Lake Shore Dr.   41

20   21   23   24   25   N Ritchie Ct.
22   E Goethe St.
26   Goudy   27
30   31   Square   28
                         Park

E Scott St.

32   33   34
            36 37 38   39
                40   E Division St.

35   N Astor St.   N Stone St.

29
Lakefront

Oak Street
Beach

W Goethe St.

W Division St.

W Elm St.   ←   41   E Elm St.
                         42

E Cedar St.
43
W Maple St.   →   44   45
                         47 48 49   E Bellevue Pl.   46
                              50

W Oak St.   51   E Oak St.   E Lake
                   52   Shore Dr.

53   N Bush St.   E Walton St.
W Walton St.
54
Washington
Square   55   E Delaware Pl.
                   56   57
W Delaware Pl.

N State St.   N Wabash Ave.   N Michigan Ave.

N

RIVER
NORTH

MAGNIFICENT MILE

km   1/8
mi   1/16   1/8   1/4

Century-old stone mansions rub shoulders with contemporary high-rises in the class-conscious Gold Coast community, bordered by **Lake Michigan, LaSalle Street, Delaware Place**, and **North Boulevard.** Chicago's power brokers live here: captains of commerce, the high-society set, even the city's Roman Catholic archbishop, not to mention ambitious up-and-comers who can toss off the steep rents. Highlights include the architecturally and historically significant **Astor Street District** and the striking swath of luxury apartments along **Lake Shore Drive.** A bit inland, first-class dining and famous Old World hotels, such as the **Omni Ambassador East,** cater to epicurean tastes, whereas the infamous **Rush Street** bar scene draws late-night throngs.

The Gold Coast was born in 1882, when entrepreneur Potter Palmer filled in a frog pond on Lake Shore Drive and put up a quarter-million-dollar "mansion to end all mansions," constructed under the direction of architects **Henry Ives Cobb** and **Charles Sumner Frost.** (In 1950, "Palmer's Castle," as it was called, was demolished and replaced by a high-rise apartment building at 1350 North Lake Shore Drive.) Other opulent homes followed. "On the shore the mansions of the millionaires form an uninterrupted line of sumptuous dwellings," wrote a visitor to the community in 1905. "They are of different sizes and styles . . . all are attempts to create something impressive." Among them was the Roman Catholic archbishop's residence, built in 1885 on a spacious plot of land on North Boulevard. Soon after, the archdiocese sold some of its nearby land holdings and neighboring houses were built, but the original residence continues to serve as home to Chicago's leading Catholic. Aristocratic dwellings, including town houses in Queen Anne, Romanesque Revival, and Georgian Revival styles, appeared along the side streets, most prominently on **Astor Street** and **Dearborn Parkway.**

Between 1895 and 1930, deluxe apartment buildings sprang up in the area, many of them elegant and ornate designs by architect **Benjamin Marshall.** During the Depression and World War II, construction slowed and the original housing began to deteriorate; many opulent homes were converted to apartments. Construction began anew in the 1960s and 1970s, but most of the more recent structures do not begin to approach the magnificence of their predecessors. Thankfully, many of the wonderful older buildings remain. The Astor Street District alone has about 300 buildings listed on the National Register of Historic Places. A walk along this or another of the quaint, tree-lined streets in the community is truly a pleasure.

Rush Street, in the neighborhood's midsection, is a different world altogether. In a tradition dating back to the 1920s, Rush Street is endowed with more restaurants and nightclubs per square foot than any other part of the city. For some time, it was an enclave of B-movie houses and adult bookstores. In the 1960s Chicago's raucous singles bar scene was born at Butch McGuire's on Division Street, just north of Rush Street. Hence, the term Rush Street today actually designates Rush and Division Streets combined, a nightly cacophony of merrymaking as local and out-of-town visitors descend to eat, drink, and dance the night away. It's such a mob scene on Friday and Saturday nights that the Chicago Police Department closes Division Street to automobile traffic to accommodate the hordes.

All area codes in this chapter are 312 unless otherwise noted.

1 LATIN SCHOOL OF CHICAGO

Housing one of the city's finest and most expensive progressive schools, with a high school student body of about 400, this five-story brick building has an Olympic-size swimming pool, a full-service cafeteria with an outdoor terrace, and art studios and a botanical garden soaking up sunlight on the top floor. Children in the lower grades are taught at a separate building at 1531 North Dearborn Parkway. There, nannies line the sidewalks every afternoon to pick up their young charges. ◆ 59 W North Blvd (between N Dearborn Pkwy and N Clark St)

2 1547 NORTH DEARBORN PARKWAY

Built in 1892, this Richardsonian town house (still a private residence) was originally the **Jacob Rehm House**. Rehm was a successful brewer who became Chicago's chief of police in the mid-1880s. He was instrumental in the creation of **Lincoln Park** and was one of the Chicago Park District's early commissioners. ◆ At W North Blvd

3 1550 NORTH STATE PARKWAY

When it was completed in 1912, this **Marshall & Fox** structure was the city's most luxurious apartment building. It's still one of the most gracious. The north side, overlooking the park, used to have a suite of public rooms 100 feet long that included a grand salon with a curving bay, a petit salon, a dining room, and an orangery. The apartments each had 15 rooms and occupied an entire floor. Bedrooms were arranged along the east side, with views of the lake, and the kitchen and service areas were tucked into the southwest corner. The building has since been subdivided into smaller apartments. ◆ At W North Blvd

4 1555 NORTH STATE PARKWAY

The private residence of the Roman Catholic Archbishop of Chicago is the oldest structure still standing in the Astor Street District. It was constructed in 1880 according to the design of **Alfred F. Pashley** on spacious grounds, before the surrounding area began to be developed. The 2.5-story Queen Anne–style building is constructed of redbrick with limestone trim and elaborate brick- and ironwork. Its steeply pitched roofs, numerous gables, and dormers are topped by 19 elaborate chimneys. The building, surrounded by beautifully landscaped grounds, is probably the largest and best preserved in the area. ◆ At E North Blvd

5 INTERNATIONAL MUSEUM OF SURGICAL SCIENCE

This 1918 building designed by **Howard Van Doren Shaw** and its neighbors at 1516 and 1530 North Lake Shore Drive are all Chicago landmarks. A sculpture on the front lawn by French artist Edouard Chaissing entitled *Hope and Help* portrays a heroic physician propping up his sickly patient. Inside, 32 rooms of displays depict the history of surgery in a degree of detail both gruesome and fascinating, including such early methods as trephination (drilling through the skull to release evil spirits), bloodletting by leech, wound-licking by serpent, cauterization with hot irons and boiling oil, bone-crushing orthopedic procedures, cesarean sections, amputations, gallstone operations, and plastic surgery. You name it, they've got it, in exhibits that incorporate vivid paintings, early medical textbooks, and actual pieces of surgical equipment. Thankfully for the queasy, exhibits also feature anesthesia, pharmaceuticals, X rays, laser surgery, and other modern techniques. ◆ Donation requested. Tu-Su. Tours available by advance reservation. 1524 N Lake Shore Dr (between E Burton Pl and LaSalle Dr). 642.6502

6 MADLENER HOUSE

Designed by **Richard E. Schmidt** and **Hugh M.G. Garden** in 1902 and renovated by **Brenner, Danforth & Rockwell** in 1963, this architectural landmark (pictured below) is a simple, almost severe, cubical building that shows influences of the Arts and Crafts and Prairie School movements. Garden designed the Sullivanesque ornament around the doorway. The Graham Foundation for Advanced Studies in the Fine Arts restored the house and uses it for offices, lectures, and a small display area. In the courtyard is a sculp-

ture garden of architectural fragments. ♦ M-Th, by appointment. 4 W Burton Pl (at N State Pkwy). 787.4071

7 PATTERSON-MCCORMICK MANSION

This 1892 Georgian Revival palazzo by **McKim, Mead & White** was commissioned by Joseph Medill, former Chicago mayor and editor and part owner of the *Chicago Tribune*, as a gift to his daughter, Mrs. Robert Patterson. The house was the setting for many lavish society gatherings and hosted kings and queens. It set new standards architecturally as well as socially: New York architect **Stanford White**'s meticulous Georgian design sounded the death knell for the picturesque Queen Anne and Romanesque Revival styles in favor of symmetrical, classical façades. When the industrialist Cyrus McCormick II bought the house in 1927, he commissioned an addition by **David Adler** that doubled its size. A rehabilitation and conversion was completed in 1979 by **Nagle Hartray & Associates** with restoration architect **Wilbert R. Hasbrouck**. It's now been divided into condominiums. ♦ 20 E Burton Pl (between N Astor St and N State Pkwy)

8 1451 NORTH ASTOR STREET

Built for Peter Fortune, who with his brothers ran the Fortune Brothers Brewing Company, this 1912 building is another by **Howard Van Doren Shaw**. Shaw designed several of the houses on Astor Street, including the Georgian Revival **Goodman House** at **No. 1355**. This is one of his most fanciful designs, an eclectic English Tudor brick-and-limestone house with elaborate carving above the front door. It was renovated in 1989 by **Marvin Herman & Associates** and remains a private residence. ♦ Between E Schiller St and E Burton Pl

8 1447 NORTH ASTOR STREET

Built for jeweler C.D. Peacock circa 1903, this is now the headquarters of the Junior League

of Chicago. The severe façade is enlivened by geometric brickwork at the top story. ♦ Between E Schiller St and E Burton Pl

9 1444 NORTH ASTOR STREET

A superb example of an Art Deco town house, this 1929 building was designed for Edward P. Russell by the firm **Holabird & Root**, architects of the **Board of Trade** and **919 North Michigan Avenue**. The sleek façade is of smooth limestone trimmed in highly polished black granite. A slightly projecting three-story curve of black iron creates a stylized bay for the upper floors. The house remains a private residence. ♦ Between E Schiller St and E Burton Pl

10 1443 NORTH ASTOR STREET

The **H.N. May House** is a good example of the Richardsonian Romanesque style that became popular in the late 1880s. The rock-faced granite façade has deep-set windows, a prominent gable, and an arched entrance. The rough wall contrasts wonderfully with the smooth carving of the third-floor window lintels and columns and the first-floor entry arch with carved panels. Completed in 1891, the design is by **Joseph Lyman Silsbee**, an early employer of **Frank Lloyd Wright**. The house is still a private residence. ♦ Between E Schiller St and E Burton Pl

11 ST. CHRYSOSTOM'S CHURCH

An English Gothic church built in 1894 by **Clinton J. Warren** for the neighborhood's elite Episcopal congregation, this structure underwent a major face-lift in 1923 and 1924, courtesy of consulting architects **Walcott, Bennett, Parsons & Frost**. An adjoining building was removed, and others were incorporated into the complex. In 1926 the American Institute of Architects awarded the church a gold medal for design. The altar and sanctuary were designed by **David Adler**. The resounding 43-bell carillon, manufactured in Croydon, England, was donated by steel manufacturer Charles R. Crane. ♦ 1424 N

THE BEST

Thomas Geoghegan

Labor Attorney/Playwright/Author of *Which Side Are You On?*

Standing at the corner of **Randolph** and **Des Plaines** and trying to imagine the Haymarket Massacre.

Driving by the steel mills on the **Far South Side**.

Browsing the shelves at the **Seminary Co-Op Bookstore**.

Riding the **Ravenswood El** and taking in the skyline.

The **Monadnock Building** and the **Merchandise Mart**.

Dinner at one of the restaurants on **Taylor Street**, followed by Italian ice at **Mario's**.

Restaurants/Clubs: Red | Hotels: Purple | Shops: Orange | Outdoors/Parks: Green | Sights/Culture: Blue

Dearborn St (between W Schiller St and W Burton Pl). 944.1083

12 1425 NORTH ASTOR STREET

Originally this was the home of William D. Kerfoot, a prominent realtor best remembered in Chicago as the man who, just 2 days after the Great Fire of 1871, erected the first business structure in the burned district. The Georgian Revival residence (pictured below) was built in 1895 and is plain except for the pair of small arched windows under an elaborate pediment on the second floor. In 1990 it was renovated by **Marvin Herman & Associates**; it's now a private residence. ♦ Between E Schiller St and E Burton Pl

12 1421 NORTH ASTOR STREET

This Romanesque Revival house of rusticated sandstone was built for lumber dealer George Farnsworth in 1889. (It's still privately owned.) Notice how the glass in the windows curves to fit the bay. The entrance is on the south through an elegant iron-and-glass porch. ♦ Between E Schiller St and E Burton Pl

13 1406 NORTH ASTOR STREET

Built in 1922 for Joseph T. Ryerson Jr. of the Ryerson Steel family and for many years chairman of the board of Inland Steel, this home was designed by the prominent society architect **David Adler** in the formal style of Parisian boulevard houses of the Second Empire. The elegant façade is symmetrical

1425 North Astor Street

(including chimneys at *both* ends of the house) and features rustication at the base and corners; tall, narrow windows on the second and third floors; a mansard roof with dormers; and delicate iron balconies. An interesting later addition to this private residence is visible only from a distance—a two-story rooftop pavilion capped by a steep slate roof. ♦ Between E Schiller St and E Burton Pl

14 36 EAST SCHILLER STREET

This 1894 house was built for Carter Henry Harrison Jr., who served five terms as Chicago's mayor (1897–1905, 1911–1915). His father had also served five terms as mayor, four of them consecutive, but was murdered by a crazed rival during the 1893 World's Columbian Exposition. William Wrigley Jr. was the second owner of this house; it remains a private residence. ♦ Between N Lake Shore Dr and N Astor St

14 38–50 EAST SCHILLER STREET

A series of seven row houses (all still privately owned) built in 1885 mixes Queen Anne, Romanesque Revival, and other influences. **No. 38** is faced with pale green stone and trimmed in red sandstone for an unusual polychrome effect. ♦ Between N Lake Shore Dr and N Astor St

15 CHARNLEY HOUSE

This three-story, seven-room house built for James Charnley was designed in 1892 by **Adler & Sullivan**, who apparently gave this commission to their 25-year-old chief draftsman, **Frank Lloyd Wright**. Although the house's blocky mass is unlike that of later Prairie School homes, it makes the most of the confining site. The client requested grand spaces, so more than half of the interior space is devoted to a central skylit stairwell. The intricate copper cornice and the balcony with its Sullivanesque design are the only significant ornamentation. Unlike the other houses on the street, this private home was not a re-creation of architecture from days past; it looked ahead to the 20th century. A restoration was completed in 1988 by **Skidmore, Owings & Merrill**. ♦ 1365 N Astor St (at E Schiller St)

16 1355 NORTH ASTOR STREET

This large-scale Georgian mansion (still privately owned) was designed in 1914 by **Howard Van Doren Shaw** for lumberman William C. Goodman, who lived in it only briefly. Shaw also designed the Loop's **Goodman Theatre**—donated by Goodman in honor of his deceased playwright son—and the family mausoleum at Graceland Cemetery. ♦ Between E Banks and E Schiller Sts

16 1349 NORTH ASTOR STREET

The façade of this circa-1880 building, which was remodeled by **Howard Van Doren Shaw** in 1920, makes an interesting contrast with his earlier work next door at **No. 1355**. This is a much less literal interpretation of the Georgian style, with elegant proportions but without applied ornament—an almost Modernist treatment. This private residence is often called the Court of the Golden Hands, after the detailing over the entrance. A 1990 renovation was drafted by **Michael Lustig & Associates**. ♦ Between E Banks and E Schiller Sts

17 1340 NORTH STATE STREET

Built in 1899 by **James Gamble Rogers** for prominent surgeon George Isham at a cost of $50,000, the residence gained notoriety in the 1960s as the **Playboy Mansion**, home to magazine publisher Hugh Hefner and his bunnies. Among other amenities, Hef installed a bowling alley, a firepole for getting from floor to floor, an indoor swimming pool, and a bar with an underwater view of the swimmers. After he moved to California, the house served as a dormitory for students of the **School of the Art Institute**; more recently, it's been divided into privately owned condominiums. ♦ Between W Goethe and W Schiller Sts

18 1316-22 NORTH ASTOR STREET

These Romanesque Revival town houses were built in 1889 by **Charles W. Palmer** for the entrepreneur Potter Palmer. It was a speculative venture—he didn't have any specific tenants in mind; he just believed the need was there—that turned out well for him. Note the unusual treatment of the rusticated stone on **Nos. 1316** and **1318**. They are private residences. ♦ Between E Goethe and E Banks Sts

19 1308–12 NORTH ASTOR STREET

The famous architect **John Wellborn Root** lived and died in the center town house of this series of three that he designed in sandstone and redbrick in 1887. After his death in 1891, his widow and his sister-in-law Harriet Monroe, founder of *Poetry* magazine, made their home here. The town houses are still private residences. ♦ Between E Goethe and E Banks Sts

20 CARL SANDBURG VILLAGE

This massive complex of high-rises, town houses, gardens, and shops was the product of urban renewal, constructed on land cleared of similarly grand houses fallen on hard times. Named after the Chicago poet and built from 1960 to 1972 by **Solomon Cordwell Buenz & Associates**, the village attracted thousands of young professionals to the neighborhood, stimulated the development of new retail businesses, and helped reinvigorate the whole area. ♦ Bounded by N Clark and N LaSalle Sts and W Division St and W North Ave

21 THREE ARTS CLUB

Designed in 1914 by **Holabird & Roche**, this club was founded by Gwetholyn Jones and friends—among them Jane Addams and Mrs. Ogden Armour (wife of the meatpacking giant)—to provide shelter in the "wicked city" to young women who were studying any of the three arts (painting, drama, or music) at such places as the **School of the Art Institute**. In today's more liberated climate, men are allowed in the summer, when tour groups often find shelter here, and the arts umbrella has been expanded to include fashion, interior design, and architecture. Similar clubs existed in London, Paris, and New York City, but only this one remains. The four-story building, which has been designated a Chicago landmark, resembles a formal Tuscan villa built around an open-air courtyard. On the first floor is a recital room with a marble fireplace and two grand pianos, a library, sitting room, drawing room, tearoom, and dining room, all with tall ceilings, decorative terra-cotta, and stenciling. Several of these rooms look out onto the central courtyard through tall, arched windows. Visitors are welcome to tour the first floor. Simply ring the doorbell, enter, and sign in at the front desk. ♦ Daily. 1300 N Dearborn St (at W Goethe St). 944.6250. www.threearts.org

22 3RD COAST

$ While away the hours at this artsy coffeehouse and wine bar, sipping delicious San Francisco spiced iced tea, cappuccino, or California wines, savoring salads and scones,

---

In 1886 British poet Robert Browning wrote that the most intelligent and thoughtful criticism of his work came from Chicago literary societies.

Chicago businessman Walter L. Newberry, founder of the Newberry Library, died at sea on his way to Paris in 1868. He was entombed in a rum barrel, which served as his coffin when he returned to Chicago.

Restaurants/Clubs: Red | Hotels: Purple | Shops: Orange | Outdoors/Parks: Green | Sights/Culture: Blue

reading trashy magazines, and gossiping with friends. ◆ American ◆ M-Th, Su, 11AM-2AM; F, Sa, 11AM-4AM. 1260 N Dearborn St (between W Division and W Goethe Sts). 649.0730

23 OMNI AMBASSADOR EAST

$$$ In 1926 **Robert S. De Golyer** designed this hotel as a mirror image of the **Ambassador West** across the street. The only Chicago member of the Historic Hotels of America, it boasts a gleaming green-and-white Italian marble lobby with German crystal chandeliers. Celebrity guests throughout the years have included Margaret O'Brien, Tallulah Bankhead, Frank Sinatra, Judy Garland, Cary Grant, Shirley MacLaine, David Bowie, Richard Pryor, and Alfred Hitchcock, who in 1958 shot scenes for *North by Northwest* here. Members of the British band Led Zeppelin had a memorable stay in 1977, when they destroyed their suite to the tune of $23,000, breaking lamps, tearing molding off the wall, and throwing a couch out their 11th-floor window. Those who stay in one of the 275 rooms and suites enjoy complimentary newspapers, temporary membership at nearby health clubs, limousine rides to downtown, and 24-hour room service from the **Pump Room**. ◆ 1301 N State St (at E Goethe St). 787.7200,

800/843.6664; fax 787.4760 ♿ www.omnihotels.com

Within the Omni Ambassador East:

PUMP ROOM

★★$$$$ Stop in, if only to say you've been here. The restaurant, named for an 18th-century spa in Bath, England, opened in 1938 and became popular almost immediately: Ronald Reagan and Jane Wyman held hands here; Humphrey Bogart and Lauren Bacall celebrated their marriage over breakfast in the highly coveted Booth One; and such notables as Marilyn Monroe, Paul Newman, Salvador Dalí, and Milton Berle all ate here. In those days the waiters were garbed in red swallow-tailed coats, the coffee-pourer sported a gold turban, and anything that could be impaled—from olives to flaming steaks—was served on swords. Celebrity dogs were treated royally in the nearby **Pup Room**, which served beef bones au naturel. Extensively renovated in 1998, the place still boasts glimmering chandeliers and stunning floral arrangements and still attracts an over-40 Chicago socialite crowd, coveting seats along the voyeuristic wall of windows overlooking State Street. And thankfully, at long last, the menu has been upgraded to a level worthy of the atmosphere and reputa-

VIBRANT VIEWS

Chicago can be a beautiful sight to behold, especially from these top 10 vantage points, many of which are described in greater detail throughout the book:

Lake Shore Drive is scenic by day and dramatic by night, especially from the three following lookouts: between **Wacker Drive** and **Grand Avenue**, heading south just past **Fullerton Drive**, and heading north from **Hyde Park**.

A rare close-up of the nighttime skyline is seen from **Grant Park** during such events as the Chicago Jazz Festival (unless a major event is taking place, the park is unsafe at night). Nearby **Buckingham Fountain** shows off with a multicolored light show.

The **Adler Planetarium/Meigs Field** peninsula and **Olive Park** provide wide-angle views of the city.

All of **Michigan Avenue**'s stunning architecture can be surveyed during the day from the steps of the **Art Institute**.

The **Michigan Avenue Bridge** presents a dazzling nighttime vista of buildings along the river plus the floodlit **Tribune Tower** and **Wrigley Building**. Continue north along the **Magnificent Mile**, which is particularly pretty when lighted for the Christmas holidays.

A drive along **Roosevelt Road** between Michigan Avenue and **Canal Street** presents a startling sneak-up-from-behind view of both the **South Loop** and the **Loop**.

The **CTA**'s **Brown** and **Orange** El routes encircle the Loop, providing surprises around every curve with almost-close-enough-to-touch passages beside buildings.

Picture-perfect views of **Lincoln Park**'s grassy meadows, trees, and lagoons with the skyline in the background can be found at the **Fullerton Drive Bridge** just west of Lake Shore Drive, the northern edge of **Diversey Harbor**, and from paddleboats in the **South Pond**.

Early-bird runners and bicyclists are privy to stunning sunrises over **Lake Michigan** from any place along the shore.

The observation decks atop the 1,454-foot-tall **Sears Tower** and the 1,123-foot-tall **John Hancock Center** offer fantastic bird's-eye views for miles around.

tion by chef Michael Gaspard. The accent is definitely French and changes come with the seasons. For openers, it's difficult to pass up sea scallops with truffles in asparagus vichyssoise. Main dishes can satisfy lovers of fish (seared ahi on lentil vinaigrette) or meat (rack of lamb with mini goat-cheese ravioli). Try the mixed berry surprise for dessert. ♦ French ♦ M-Sa, breakfast, lunch, dinner; Su, brunch; F, Sa, until midnight. Jacket required after 4:30PM. Reservations recommended. 266.0360

24 ASTOR TOWER

At 28 stories, one of the first skyscrapers to invade the Gold Coast is more than twice as tall as the earlier generation of apartment buildings. The units begin on the fourth floor, raised on thin concrete columns above the neighboring row houses. The columns run the full height of the building and are filled in with glass concealed by metal louvers that provide privacy and protection from the sun and wind. The louvers are adjustable from within, with difficulty; residents tend to leave them in a fixed position. **Bertrand Goldberg**, the architect of **Marina City**, designed this building in 1963, and although it lacks the characteristic curving shapes of his later work, it does show his fondness for exposed concrete and his willingness to experiment. ♦ 1300 N Astor St (at E Goethe St)

25 1301 NORTH ASTOR STREET

This high-rise apartment building with its understated Art Deco style was designed in 1928 by **Philip B. Maher**. Windows and recessed spandrels create a vertical rhythm. The second-generation Potter Palmer family originally occupied a three-story apartment at the top of the building. Just as the senior Palmers had made this neighborhood fashionable by building a mansion on uncharted territory, their offspring made it socially acceptable to live in cooperative apartments rather than houses. A similar building, designed 3 years later by the same architect, is located diagonally across the intersection at 1260 North Astor Street. ♦ At E Goethe St

26 GOUDY SQUARE PARK

This tree-shaded park is named after William C. Goudy, who was a prominent Chicago attorney. In 1990, neighborhood residents raised $350,000 to create a delightful children's play area. ♦ N Astor and E Goethe Sts

27 1260 NORTH LAKE SHORE DRIVE

This 1906 **Holabird & Roche** Georgian Revival residence on the corner was designed

a decade after the same architects had created its neighbor to the south, **No. 1258** (see below), but the difference in the two buildings' styles spans 4 centuries. The house is privately owned. ♦ At E Goethe St

27 1258 NORTH LAKE SHORE DRIVE

You can easily imagine Romeo courting Juliet from beneath the stone balcony of this three-story Venetian Gothic town house, designed in 1895 by **Holabird & Roche**. It's a private residence. ♦ Between E Scott and E Goethe Sts

28 1254 AND 1250 NORTH LAKE SHORE DRIVE

These two buildings, together with their neighbors, convey a sense of what bustling Lake Shore Drive must have been like in its heyday—an elegant promenade lined with mansions in a variety of historical styles, mostly Queen Anne, Romanesque, and Georgian. These two are wonderful examples of Richardsonian Romanesque, with rough-hewn blocks of stone, recessed entrances, arches, squat columns, and carved details (note especially the grinning face depicted on one of the column capitals of **No. 1254**). Both were designed by **Gustav Hallberg** and **Frank Abbott**. The house to the north was built for lawyer and businessman Mason Brayman Starring, the other for prominent realtor and developer Carl Constantine Heisen. After the original owners sold them, the houses fell into disrepair and subsequently were divided into tiny apartments that never quite took off. Later renovations by **Marvin Herman & Associates** joined the structures and turned them into four multimillion-dollar private residences. They are topped by a shared roof deck and have a live-in concierge. ♦ Between E Scott and E Goethe Sts

29 LAKEFRONT

Unlike other North Side neighborhoods, the Gold Coast possesses little in the way of a park along the lake, except for one tiny patch of green with a gazebo across from the Magnificent Mile's **Drake Hotel**. Otherwise, the lake here is fronted by concrete pathways and rocks—not all that bad, because it makes for a great place to walk, run, or ride a bicycle. And what the area lacks in grass, it makes up for in sand, with the glorious **Oak Street Beach**, which is the beach for Chicago's young and beautiful who want to see and be seen. Bronze-skinned volleyball players, perfect-10 models, all-American Frisbee-tossing frat brothers and sorority sisters, jet-setting flight attendants, plus lots of ordinary folks from the neighborhood and voyeurs from all over—they all blanket and roam these inviting sands weekend after steamy summer weekend. ♦ Pedestrian access via tunnel across from the Drake Hotel (N Michigan Ave and E Lake Shore Dr). Other tunnels are at the east end of E Division St and near the southern end of Lincoln Park. By car, take the LaSalle Dr exit from Lake Shore Dr, park in the lot near E North Blvd, then walk south.

On the Lakefront:

CHESS PAVILION

At the north end, this concrete structure with built-in chessboards attracts a mixed crowd of serious and not-so-serious chess players. If you're interested in playing, bring your own chess pieces and introduce yourself to an opponent. The view of the city is spectacular.

30 CLARIDGE HOTEL

$$ This small European-style hotel—quiet and quaint, with a cozy lobby (and lobby bar) and a personable staff—gets a thumbs-up for offering high quality at reasonable rates. Six of the 172 rooms are suites, 3 of them with wood-burning fireplaces. Perks include minibars, complimentary daily newspapers and continental breakfast, health club access, limousine service, and a multilingual concierge staff. Though owned by a Japanese firm, this hotel has a definite Chicago accent, with library shelves filled with books by home-grown writers, music composed by Chicago musicians in the lobby, and art by local artists on the walls. ♦ 1244 N Dearborn St (between W Division and W Goethe Sts). 787.4980, 800/245.1258; fax 266.0978 ♿ www.claridgehotel.com

31 1236–52 NORTH STATE STREET

These circa-1872 Italianate limestone row houses were the first residences built on the Gold Coast after the Great Fire of 1871. **Nos. 1240–44** were remodeled in 1916 by society architect **David Adler. No. 1240** later became the home of **Nathaniel Owings**, founding partner of the firm **Skidmore, Owings & Merrill**, and their renovation of **Nos. 1242–44** was one of the fledgling firm's first commissions. The houses are still privately owned. ♦ Between W Division and W Goethe Sts

32 LASALLE TOWERS

When viewed from the east, this 1920 building appears to have three-dimensional bay windows. The northern façade features **Adolf Loos**'s design for the **Tribune Tower** competition, whereas the south side copies the archway from the Transportation Building designed by **Louis Sullivan** for the 1893 World's Columbian Exposition. All of this is a masterpiece of trompe l'oeil by artist Richard Haas, who honors **Sullivan, Daniel Burnham, John Wellborn Root**, and **Frank Lloyd Wright** in portraits beneath the arch. Originally a hotel, this is now an apartment building, which was renovated in 1980-1981 by **Weese Seegers Hickey Weese**. ♦ 1211 N LaSalle St (between W Division and W Goethe Sts)

33 EDWARDO'S

★$$ There are several **Edwardo's** in the city offering tasty pizza with all-natural ingredients, including a whole-wheat crust. The spinach pizza is a tasty treat. ♦ Pizza ♦ Daily, lunch and dinner. 1212 N Dearborn St (between W Division and W Goethe Sts). 337.4490. Also at numerous locations throughout the city

THE BEST

Tony Judge
Radio Producer/Media Consultant

My favorite places in Chicago are where you see fossilized evidence of the city's great period of boom and bustle, approximately 1885 to the beginning of World War II. These include:

Cavernous **Union Station**, where in the '20s, when Chicago was America's great railroad hub, hundreds of passenger trains arrived and departed daily. Even after the renovation, it's full of echoes and pigeons.

The stunning vista from the top of the **Chicago Skyway** out over the oily **Little Calumet River**, lined with cold open-hearth furnaces, moribund ore docks, shuttered union halls, and slag heaps sprouting weeds—the skeletal remains of Chicago's steel industry.

The **Midway Plaisance** in **Hyde Park**, now a **University of Chicago** ditch, was once a grand canal where costumed gondoliers poled visitors to the wonders of the Columbian Exposition of 1893.

Shabby, broken-down **Garfield Park** was built on a grand European scale, with serpentine walkways, a bathing beach, an enormous conservatory with giant palm and banana trees. Exhausted factory workers spent their Sunday leisure time here, and entire families slept outdoors under the dark trees on hot summer nights.

34 ZEBRA LOUNGE

This tiny piano bar describes itself as a "civilized watering hole at the jungle's edge," and you half expect to see Tarzan or Jane swing by for a drink. Zebra stripes rule—on the wallpaper, in the light fixtures, in paintings, and on zebra artifacts. When the 20 or 30 people who cram into the room get loosened up, it's one big sing-along with the piano player. Casts from touring musicals sometimes drop in unexpectedly and do a number or two just for fun. ♦ M-F, Su, 4PM-2AM; Sa, until 3AM. 1220 N State St (between W Division and W Goethe Sts). 642.5140

35 McCONNELL APARTMENT BUILDING

When built in 1897 by **Holabird & Roche**, this elegant apartment building, with seven stories plus English basement, was considered a skyscraper. It's the oldest fireproof apartment building on the **North Side** and is closely related to the architects' Chicago School office buildings downtown. The simple, unornamented design expresses the structure within, and gracefully curving corner bays are similar to those of the firm's **Old Colony Building**. ♦ 1210 N Astor St (between E Division and E Scott Sts)

36 MOTHER'S

Best known for its giant basement dance floor jammed with people gyrating like maniacs, this club draws a crowd that tends to be younger and more suburban—not to mention more energetic—than those at other bars. Light shows, karaoke record-a-hit, lip-sync contests, and roaring rock music are overseen by hyperactive DJs. **Mother's Too** is two doors down. ♦ M-F, Su, 8PM-4AM; Sa, until 5AM. 26 W Division St (between N State and N Dearborn Sts). 642.7251

36 BUTCH McGUIRE'S

Chicago's original singles bar opened its doors in 1961. Proprietor McGuire estimates that his establishment has been instrumental in the meetings and marriages of more than 3,000 couples. The small menu features burgers and such in big portions. Your best bet for food here is the whopping weekend brunch, starting with one of the best Bloody Marys in

town. ♦ M-F, Su, 10AM-4AM; Sa, until 5AM. 20 W Division St (between N State and N Dearborn Sts). 337.9080

37 FIVE FACES

$ The famous five are James Dean, Marilyn Monroe, Elvis, Lucy, and Bogie, whose countenances are painted on the façade. Inside, the fare ranges from gyros and cheese fries to taffy apples. Frankly, the place is a dive, but in the middle of the night when you're done barhopping and are absolutely starving, you can always find something to order here—just eat it someplace else. ♦ Fast food ♦ Daily, 10:30AM-5AM. 10 W Division St (between N State and N Dearborn Sts). 642.7837

38 P. J. CLARKE'S

$ It has been called the "divorce bar"—it often seems as though most customers are either getting a divorce or getting over one. But what's important is that they're all enjoying themselves at this casual, ersatz old-fashioned tavern. The Caesar salad is great, and the beef barley soup is famous. The menu otherwise consists of burgers and Italian items. ♦ American ♦ Daily, lunch and late dinner. 1204 N State St (between W Division and W Goethe Sts). 664.1650. Also at 302 E. Illinois St (at Columbus Dr). 670.7500

39 1209 NORTH STATE STREET

A narrow wall of curving brick and glass conceals the **Frank Fisher Apartments**, an attractive example of Art Moderne forms executed in brick in 1938 by **Andrew N. Rebori**. Artist Edgar Miller designed the terracotta plaques on the façade, some of which, unfortunately, are missing. ♦ Between E Division and E Scott Sts

40 THE LODGE

Small and somewhat lodgelike with a dark wood décor, this neighborhood hangout is lively even when other bars on the street are dead. There's a great jukebox and complimentary chili bar. ♦ M-F, Su, 3PM-4AM; Sa, until 5AM. 21 W Division St (between N State and N Dearborn Sts). 642.4406

Restaurants/Clubs: Red | Hotels: Purple | Shops: Orange | Outdoors/Parks: Green | Sights/Culture: Blue

41 ALBERT'S CAFE

★$ The white-chocolate mousse cake will send you to heaven. This cozy European-style pastry and espresso shop also serves light meals such as Belgian waffles and salad niçoise. ◆ Café/patisserie ◆ Daily, lunch and dinner. 52 W Elm St (between N Dearborn and N Clark Sts). 751.0666

BISTROT ZINC

42 BISTROT ZINC

★★$$ If you're looking for a well-prepared meal at a moderate price, this lovely bistro is arguably the best value in the **Rush Street** neighborhood. It's the second installment of a restaurant by the same name west of **Wrigley Field** that has packed people in since it opened in the late '90s. The L-shaped bar seats only 15, but it's worth pausing and having a look at: Handcrafted in France, it is made of zinc. Turnip flan with wild mushroom ragout is a good start. Liver and onions is served with crème fraiche mashed potatoes and Madeira sauce. Finish with a chocolate crepe and you'll leave satisfied by an authentic bistro meal. ◆ French bistro ◆ M-F, lunch; Sa, Su, brunch; daily, dinner. Reservations recommended. 1131 N State St (at E Elm St). 337.1131

43 MELVIN B.'S

★$ This is the place to fraternize alfresco amid Chicago's youth culture. On hot afternoons there's hardly a table to be had. The food runs to burgers, ribs, and chicken salad; drinks, to margaritas and beer. ◆ American ◆ M-F, Su, until 2AM; Sa, until 3AM. 1114 N State St (between W Maple and W Elm Sts). 751.9897 &

44 BLUE AGAVE

★$$ A dozen Mexican beers and six kinds of margaritas (all with fresh-squeezed lemon juice) are served here, which tells you something about the crowd. A stuffed burro and wooden wagon dominate the entrance, and sombreros and serapes hang from the balconies. If you want to eat, head upstairs; all the standard Mexican fare is offered in abundance, plus a surf-and-turf dish called *monte-mar.* ◆ Mexican ◆ Daily, lunch and late dinner. 1050 N State St (at W Maple St). 335.8900

45 ORIGINAL PANCAKE HOUSE

$ It's an odd sight—a little whitewashed house right across the street from the gleaming glass and granite of the **Sutton Place Hotel**. Locals come here throughout the day for breakfast in a dining room that looks much like a sunny kitchen. ◆ American ◆ Daily, breakfast and lunch. 22 E Bellevue Pl (between N Lake Shore Dr and N Rush St). 642.7917. Also at 2020 N Lincoln Park West (at W Dickens Ave). 773/928.8130; 1517 E Hyde Park Blvd. 773/288.2322

45 TAVERN ON RUSH

★★$$$ On the lower level, it's your basic noisy, crowded bar, with a happening singles scene that some might call a meat market. Upstairs, it's your traditional steak house, a quiet dining room with wood, white tablecloths, and waitpersons poised to call 911. Ask to be seated near the French doors, and you'll have a choice balcony seat overlooking the action on Rush Street. The steak, which is grilled over charcoal, is top-notch. Stick with beef, and you'll do swell. With less traditional fare, you won't fare so well. Key lime pie is the dessert of choice. ◆ Steak house ◆ Daily, lunch and dinner. Reservations recommended. 1031 N Rush St (at E Bellevue Pl). 664.9600

46 FORTNIGHTLY OF CHICAGO

Originally the **Bryan Lathrop House**, this 1892 building was designed by his friend, noted New York architect **Charles McKim** of **McKim, Mead & White**. A guidebook published in 1933 called this "the most perfect piece of Georgian architecture in Chicago"—a judgment few would dispute. The symmetry of the graceful façade is gently broken by the off-center placement of the entrance. The only jarring note is struck by the longer central window of the third floor, which lacks its original balcony. In 1922 the building was remodeled by one of McKim's former pupils for **The Fortnightly**, the city's oldest women's club, which was described in the same guidebook as "the most truly highbrow of many women's organizations of this amazing city." In 1972 the building was again remodeled, this time by **Perkins & Will**. The ladies' literary society still inhabits the building and does not allow nonmembers to tour the building. ◆ 120 E Bellevue Pl (between N Lake Shore Dr and N Rush St). 944.1330

47 MORTON'S

★★$$$ The renowned steak-house chain began right here, and many think it's still the best steak in the city. The double filet mignons, 24-ounce porterhouses, 20-ounce strip steaks, and other generous cuts are perfectly prepared to order. Choose between steaming baked potatoes, crisp hash browns, or toasted potato skins, all extra on the à la carte menu. Gigantic lobster, whole chicken, and a good assortment of vegetables served in big portions round out the menu. Only entrée prices are listed on the menu, so you'll have to ask for the cost of appetizers, salads, and side dishes. ♦ Steak house ♦ Daily, dinner. Reservations recommended. Newberry Plaza, 1050 N State St (between W Oak and W Maple Sts), lower level. 266.4820 ♿ www.mortons.com

BAR • STEAKHOUSE
GIBSONS
ROXANNE LAUREN ATKINS

48 Gibsons Steakhouse

★★$$$ When talk turns to the often-debated subject of where to get the best steak in Chicago, this nominee—with its clubby dining room and crowded bar—is always in the running. In describing the size of the steaks, words like *humongous* and *gargantuan* come to mind. But quality is the real meat of the matter, and it would be hard to find better. Entrées come with soup or salad, but because you're throwing cholesterol cares to the wind, you may as well start with the chopped chicken livers. On the side, try a cheese-topped twice-baked potato and a mountain of fried onion rings. But try to save room for the strawberry shortcake—it's bigger than the steaks. ♦ Steak house ♦ Daily, dinner. Reservations recommended. 1028 N Rush St (at E Bellevue Pl). 467.9780 ♿ www.gibsonssteakhouse.com

FROG BAR™
For Fish™

48 Hugo's Frog Bar

★$$$ Following the success of his **Gibsons Steakhouse** next door, owner Hugo Ralli opened this establishment. The emphasis here is more on surf than turf, with a wide range of seafood specialties. But for those who must have their beef, the menu also includes great steaks from Gibsons. Live music adds to the festive atmosphere, with jazz and blues on some evenings, as well as a piano bar. ♦ American ♦ Daily, dinner to midnight. 1024 N Rush St (between E Oak St and E Bellevue Pl). 640.0999 ♿ www.hugosfrogbar.com

49 Sutton Place Hotel

$$$ In the late 1980s the sumptuous **Hotel 21** was built on this site, but it was sold after 2 years. Then it was **Le Meridien**, which retained its luxury from the striking glass and gray granite exterior to the Art Deco-inspired interior, the three-story atrium bar, and the state-of-the-art remote-controlled boardroom. Now **Sutton Place**, it has undergone some refurbishment, but it is still basically the same establishment. All 246 guest rooms and 41 suites have DVD and CD players, Internet access, and three phones with voice mail and a speakerphone. Six of the suites are duplex penthouses with spiral staircases. Weekend discounts and packages are available. Within the hotel, the eatery is a copy of the New York/L.A. **Whiskey Bar & Grill**, a wood-and-leather lounge that serves fair American fare and big drinks and is best known for being owned by supermodel Cindy Crawford's spouse, Rande Gerber. ♦ 21 E Bellevue Pl (at N Rush St). 266.2100, 866/378.8866; fax 266.2141 ♿ www.suttonplace.com

Jilly's

50 Jilly's Bistro

★★$$$ Formerly a Chinese restaurant and now an Italian steak house, **Jilly's** stands as proof that there's always room for one more steak joint here in Sinatra's kind of town. Red woodwork with black trim stakes out an atmosphere that evokes the good old days when nobody worried about cholesterol or high blood pressure. Stake out your turf in one of the clubby, curvy booths, sip a highball, and watch the meat sizzle on the grill in the open kitchen. It's all the standard fare, but Jilly's does a fair job of raising the standards. ♦ Italian steak house ♦ M-Sa, dinner, late dinner. 1009 N Rush St (between E Oak St and E Bellevue Pl). 664.2100; fax 664.0009

50 Backroom

This small, subterranean jazz club is housed in a former horse stable. The dozen or so tables are packed like sardines in front of the stage. Larger weekend crowds fill a balcony too. The audience ranges from music students to jazz fans, who come to hear Gahlib Ghallab, Bobby Lewis, and the Ken Chaney Xperience. ♦ Cover, two-drink minimum. Daily, from 8PM.

Nightly shows start at 9PM. 1007 N Rush St (between E Oak St and E Bellevue Pl). 751.2433. www.backroomchicago.com

51 G'BANI

A sign on the window of this funky fashion storefront says "Vote world peace, not world war." Inside the bright, pastel-colored rooms of the shop, you'll find extraordinary clothing and accessories for men and women that can make distinctive style statements in the best and worst of times. ♦ Daily. 949 N State St (at E Oak St). 440.1718 & www.gbani.com

51 PAPA MILANO

★$ Densely packed tables covered with old-fashioned red-and-white checkered cloths set the tone for generous portions of homemade spaghetti or lasagna with the now-departed Papa's famous tomato sauce. Local pols hang out here; it's been around forever. ♦ Italian ♦ Daily, lunch and dinner. 951 N State St (at E Oak St). 787.3710

52 TENDER BUTTONS

Button lovers Diana Epstein and Millicent Safro have enjoyed years of tremendous success with their flagship buttons-as-works-of-art emporium in Manhattan. Their Chicago shop carries a comparable inventory of thousands of buttons in every possible style and material from around the world, all displayed in a serene environment of antique furniture and display cases. You will find Art Deco celluloid buttons; playful children's buttons; buttons depicting Egyptian figures, animals, fruits, and vegetables; and 500 styles of men's blazer buttons. Many are antiques, such as those of English hand-carved horn or vintage Chinese enamel. ♦ M-Sa. 946 N Rush St (between E Walton and E Oak Sts). 337.7033

53 NEWBERRY LIBRARY

Designed in 1892 by **Henry Ives Cobb** in the Romanesque Revival style, this is more formal and less fortresslike than his Chicago Historical Society building (now the **Excalibur** nightclub). The carving around the first-floor arches is particularly beautiful. A 20-year renovation ended in 1982 with the opening of **Harry Weese**'s 10-story addition to the north, which provided climate-controlled storage facilities for some of the library's 1.4 million books, 5 million manuscript pages, and 75,000 maps. Subjects span Western Europe and the Americas from the Middle Ages to the 20th century. Among some 20 areas of special strength are the Italian Renaissance and the history of cartography. Anyone age 17 or older may make use of the library's noncirculating material. The Chicago Genealogical Society, founded here in 1967, houses one of the finest collections of genealogical data in the country and offers free monthly meetings

THE BEST

Lin Brehmer

Morning Host, WXRT—Chicago's Finest Rock

Best bar in which to eat and watch a ballgame: **Don Juan's** in Edison Park has a bar adjoining the dining room where you can enjoy venison fajitas with a Grand Gold Margarita and let your favorite baseball team break your heart on TV.

Best view of the city from your car: **Montrose Harbor** at dusk. In April you gaze over the twinkling lights of the smelt fishing nets. In August, you walk down to the water's edge. In February, you turn up the heat, stare at the storied skyline, and say with a sigh, "Like I could ever live anywhere else."

Best place to overeat after midnight: **Calo's** on North Clark. They usually have a cover band pumping out the unlikely hits of the '70s, '80s, and beyond. I once had a lamb-shank Vesuvio at 1AM.

Best sushi: Its modest exterior and far north location keep it from becoming overrun, but **Katsu** on Peterson is a charmer. Husband-and-wife owners make you feel at home on your first visit, and the monkfish foie gras will keep you coming back for more.

Best fine dining for the whole family: **Yoshi's Cafe** on Halsted has a kid's menu, crayons, and cuisine befitting its owner's stunning résumé. Watch out if your kids start drifting toward the risottos and raviolis on the main menu: You get what you pay for.

Best place to see the up-and-coming musical: It can get hot in the balcony in August and it's SRO on the floor, but the **Metro** on Clark is the granddaddy of them all. Local bands and touring recording artists who will soon be too famous to fit in there. Oh, if those walls could talk, don't let them talk about me.

Most comfortable concert experience: The **Old Town School of Folk Music** on Lincoln has a music room that holds a little over 300, and there isn't a bad seat in the house. It's so comfortable I'm always surprised when they say, "You can take that beer to your seat, you know." And if you're early for the show, slip into their music store and strum a 12-string acoustic. You'll feel better, much better.

on conducting family-tree searches. The library also sponsors classes, lectures, concerts, and art exhibits. One popular event is the annual mystery weekend in early spring, with a used-book sale as well as signings and readings by noted mystery authors. Within the **Newberry** is a branch of Hyde Park's excellent seminary co-op bookstore. ♦ M-Sa. Genealogical meetings first Sa of the month, except July and Aug. 60 W Walton St (between N Dearborn and N Clark Sts). 943.9090. www.newberry.org

54 WASHINGTON SQUARE

Directly in front of the **Newberry** is Chicago's first public park, the site of many a rousing public event in its early years. In 1855 Germans who owned and patronized Chicago's many beer gardens held a protest here over increases in liquor-license fees by the city council, as well as over the *Chicago Tribune*'s diatribes against the "Lager-beer-swilling and Sabbath-breaking Germans" who carried on a tradition of Sunday drinking. The Germans eventually prevailed. The site became known as **Bughouse Square** in the 1920s, when crowds gathered every Sunday evening to hear radical soapbox speakers. Today the park is a warm-weather gathering place for lunchtime strollers and assorted vagrants. ♦ Bounded by N Dearborn and N Clark Sts and W Delaware Pl and W Walton St

55 TALBOTT HOTEL

$$ Originally built in 1927, but now completely renovated with modern luxuries and amenities, this quaint European-style hotel bills itself as "a soothing oasis for the business traveler." However, with its hushed, elegant tone the **Talbott** is also a real pleasure for tourists in search of something tasteful and quiet. On cold days the fire in the lobby fireplace of this all-suites hotel crackles invitingly. There are 147 suites, each composed of living room, bedroom, and fully equipped kitchen. Their décor is decidedly modern, in contrast to the charming Old World lobby. Guests enjoy concierge service, nightly turndown, and complimentary continental breakfast and morning newspaper. **Basil's** is a pleasant café. Weekend packages and special rates for stays of a month or more are available. ♦ 20 E Delaware Pl (between N Rush and N State Sts). 943.0161, 800/825.2688; fax 944.7241 ও www.talbotthotel.com

56 CONTESSA BOTTEGA

Born and bred in Greece but laying claim to royal status via her father, a Roman count, designer Contessa Helena Kontos attracts a celebrated clientele with her glamorous collection of slinky, sensual eveningwear and showstopping daywear. Customers include Oprah Winfrey, Nancy Wilson, and Whitney Houston, who normally purchase made-to-order. The staff is friendly. ♦ M-Sa; Su, by appointment. 1 E Delaware Pl (at N State St). 944.0981. www.contessacosmetics.com

57 CRU CAFÉ AND WINE BAR

★$ Leather sofas, velvet banquettes, and vintage chandeliers add to the cool atmosphere of this European café done in brown and gold. There are 400 different wines to sip and a savory selection of cheeses to nibble. Sit outdoors when the weather is fine. In or out, the people watching is great entertainment. On Sunday there is a light brunch. ♦ Wine bar ♦ Daily, 11AM-2AM. 888 N Wabash Ave (at E Delaware Pl). 337.4078

OLD TOWN

This section of Chicago is home to an eclectic mix of people: longtime residents, offbeat artists, and briefcase-toting professionals. Anchored for a century by **St. Michael's Church**, the community is bounded by **LaSalle, Clark, Halsted, Division,** and **Wisconsin Streets** and **North Avenue**. Quaint shops, celebrated restaurants, and evening entertainment—from the audience-participatory *Tony n' Tina's Wedding* to the **Second City** comedy troupe—form a diverse commercial core on **Wells Street**. Also prominent is the **Old Town Triangle District**, with its fastidiously renovated 19th-century workers' cottages.

In the mid-1800s Old Town was known as the "Cabbage Patch," a patchwork of truck gardens and cow pastures near the city cemetery. The cemetery's 1868 conversion to **Lincoln Park** helped spawn Old Town's growth. Three years later, the Chicago Fire

prompted a massive influx of working-class Germans from the burned-out areas—the first in a series of immigrant groups who have lived here. The new arrivals earned their living in factories such as the Western Wheel Works bicycle company (now apartments on Wells Street) and the Oscar Mayer Sausage Company (now closed). Many of the small, solid homes they built stand today, most within the Old Town Triangle District.

By the end of the 19th century, the German population had become a dominant force in Old Town, and North Avenue, known as "German Broadway," developed into one long strip of shops, restaurants, and saloons catering to German tastes. St. Michael's Church, organized in 1852 by German Catholics, had become Chicago's largest German parish by 1892. As the 20th century dawned, however, the Germans began to depart for newer housing in northern neighborhoods, making way for new groups of immigrants. By 1920, North Avenue stores were owned by Russian Jews and frequented by Hungarians.

The end of World War II brought additional waves of ethnic groups to Old Town. The massive Cabrini-Green housing project, built just south of the neighborhood in the late 1950s, became home to lower-income residents. Relatively cheap housing in the area also attracted artists and urban pioneers, who began renovating and revitalizing older buildings. Thanks largely to their efforts, the Old Town Triangle District was declared a Chicago Landmark in 1977 and listed on the National Register of Historic Places in 1984— and housing was no longer inexpensive.

Old Town is perhaps best known for the Haight-Ashbury character taken on by Wells Street in the 1960s, when hippies and tourists descended to buy incense and psychedelic tie-dyes, listen to Pete Seeger and fellow folkies at the **Earl of Old Town**, a now-defunct club, and see the likes of Elaine May and Mike Nichols perform their special brand of social satire at Second City. The flower children and most of the businesses that served them are long gone, but some (such as Second City) have survived. The neighborhood still has an offbeat, creative atmosphere that supports such traditions as the immensely popular Old Town and Wells Street Art Fairs, which annually (on the second weekend of June) showcase work by local and other artists. For a peek at the local merchants, visit www.oldtownchicago.org.

All area codes in this chapter are 312 unless otherwise noted.

1 1826–34 North Lincoln Park West

These five brick row houses (pictured page 122), designed by **Adler & Sullivan** from 1884 to 1885, are rare examples of **Louis Sullivan**'s early residential work. Their Queen Anne design is enlivened considerably by his distinctive geometric ornamentation. Vertical bands decorated with terra-cotta distinguish the second and fourth houses. Those two have plain window openings to set off the ornament, whereas the other three have decorated arched window tops whose motif is repeated in the cornice. All are private homes. ◆ Between W Menomonee and W Wisconsin Sts

1 Charles Wacker House

Charles was the son of Frederick Wacker, and this circa-1870 home was originally the carriage house at the back of his father's property next door. One of the directors of the 1893 World's Columbian Exposition and chairman of the Chicago Plan Commission for 17 years, Charles was instrumental in implementing the 1909 Burnham Plan for the development of Chicago. Part of that legacy is the double-level **Wacker Drive**. The long front entrance stairway here—a trademark of Chicago houses of that era—was built high to accommodate a "modern" sewage system. The house remains a private residence. ◆ 1836 N Lincoln Park West (between W Menomonee and W Wisconsin Sts)

Restaurants/Clubs: Red | Hotels: Purple | Shops: Orange | Outdoors/Parks: Green | Sights/Culture: Blue

1826–34 North Lincoln Park West

1 FREDERICK WACKER HOUSE

A successful brewer and a leader in the city's German community, Wacker hired a Swiss architect to create this elaborate chalet in 1874. The basic form of the 2.5-story Chicago cottage—a gabled clapboard structure above a simple brick ground floor—proved well suited to this fanciful Alpine style. A wide, overhanging veranda is supported by large carved brackets, and smaller brackets are paired below the cornice. Elaborate wood carving decorates the window tops and the balustrades. Housepainter James F. Jereb gave the house a "Painted Lady" color scheme in 1987 and then signed and dated the lower left of the façade. This is a private residence. ♦ 1838 N Lincoln Park West (between W Menomonee and W Wisconsin Sts)

2 1802 NORTH LINCOLN PARK WEST

This 1872 structure (still a private residence) is one of the few wooden farmhouses remaining in Old Town. Note the contrast between the relatively plain long façade on Menomonee Street and the elaborate Italianate treatment of windows and cornice on the narrow end facing North Lincoln Park West. ♦ At W Menomonee St

3 FIRE RELIEF COTTAGE

Within a few days of the Chicago Fire in 1871, small cottages known as relief shanties sprang up. Built by the city at about $75 each for people who had been left homeless, some also served as distribution centers for food and clothing. This diminutive house is believed to have been one; today it's a private residence. ♦ 216 W Menomonee St (between N Wells St and N Lincoln Park West)

4 MIDWEST BUDDHIST TEMPLE

One of the largest immigrant groups to settle in Old Town in the 1940s and 1950s was the Japanese. In 1972 **Hideaki Areo** built this temple, which, despite its small size, dominates the area because it's raised on a one-story base and stands clear of surrounding buildings. The striated concrete base contains a large meeting room as well as classrooms and offices; its roof forms a terrace for ceremonial processions. The temple itself is of stucco and heavy timber with translucent clerestory windows and a traditional Japanese roof. The interior is simple: A small gold Buddha and an altar with candles and flowers are the primary embellishments in an airy room of white walls and ceilings. Visitors are welcome for meditation services. One weekend each summer, the temple sponsors the popular Ginza Festival, providing an introduction to Japanese food, dancing, and culture. ♦ 435 W Menomonee St (between N Fern Ct and N Cleveland Ave). 943.7801

5 NOOKIES

$ Somewhere between greasy spoon and restaurant, this place has been a neighborhood institution for years. On weekends people line up for omelettes, pancakes, burgers, and coffee. ♦ American ♦ Daily, breakfast, lunch, and dinner. 1746 N Wells St (between W St. Paul Ave and W Menomonee St). 337.2454. Also at 2114 N Halsted St (between W Dickens and W Webster Aves). 773/327.1400; 3334 N Halsted St (at W Buckingham Pl). 773/248.9888

6 GREEN, INC.

For nearly two decades, this shop has been luring plant lovers to its conservatory-like space. One room overflows with unusual houseplants; in another, exotic flowers grow in wild profusion. Its proprietor is full of good advice. ♦ Daily. 1718 N Wells St (at W St. Paul Ave). 266.2806

7 CRILLY COURT

This charming street is just a block away from busy Wells Street, but it seems a century apart. It was developed between 1885 and 1893 by Daniel F. Crilly, a South Side contractor who bought the block bounded by Wells and Eugenie Streets and North Park and St. Paul Avenues, cut a north–south street through the middle of it, and named it **Crilly Court**. On the west side, he built two-story Queen Anne–style row houses; on the east side, a four-story apartment building. Above the apartment doors are carved the names of his four children: Isabelle, Oliver, Erminie, and Edgar. Doors on the north and south sides are marked with the street names Eugenie and Florimond (the original name of St. Paul Avenue). Crilly then built another apartment building to the east; its Wells Street façade offers a wonderful example of late-19th-century storefronts with apartments above. In the 1940s Crilly's son Edgar renovated these buildings extensively, replacing the rear wooden porches with steel balconies and closing off the alleys to create private courtyards. His success led the way for others interested in reviving Old Town while preserving its architectural heritage. Over the years, the Crilly estate has leased units to many well-known Chicagoans, among them poet and journalist Eugene Field and Cyrus DeVry, director for many years of the **Lincoln Park Zoo**. Another resident was George K. Spoor, an early movie producer known for his films with Charlie Chaplin and the Keystone Cops; he sometimes preserved his films in his Crilly Court icebox. Commercial artist Haddon Sundblom, creator of the Quaker on the Quaker Oats cereal box and of Aunt Jemima, lived here, often using people in the neighborhood as his models. ♦ Between W Eugenie St and W St. Paul Ave

8 BREADSMITH

Looking for fresh bread or rolls to take home for dinner or to that picnic in the park? This shop has a nice selection of handmade, hearth-baked breads, and a few sweets to add to your pleasure. You can also get a quick cup of coffee instead of waiting on line down the street at Starbucks. ♦ Daily. 1710 N Wells St (between W Eugenie St and W St. Paul Ave) & www.breadsmith.com

8 HANDLE WITH CARE

One-of-a-kind creations by hot designers from Chicago or Paris hold center stage here. In addition to women's clothing, this boutique carries a stunning collection of jewelry. ♦ Daily. 1706 N Wells St (between W Eugenie St and W St. Paul Ave). 751.2929

8 HEARTWORKS

It's the place to go for a year's supply of birthday cards, plus memorable gift items such as a wooden comb and brush set, bird-houses made of twigs, rubber duckies for the bath, handmade vegetable-oil soaps, and gorgeous wrapping paper. They'll have the perfect little picture frame to take home to the neighbor who's been watering your plants while you've been traveling. ♦ Daily. 1704 N Wells St (between W Eugenie St and W St. Paul Ave). 943.1972

9 164–72 WEST EUGENIE STREET

Built in the 1880s, these row houses are elaborate examples of the Queen Anne style so popular in the late 19th century. These private residences feature a variety of window types and building materials—brick, stone, slate, terra-cotta—and a lively roofline punctuated by dormers, gables, and turrets. ♦ Between N LaSalle and N Wells Sts

10 TWIN ANCHORS

★$$ Opened in 1932, this may be the city's oldest rib joint. People from around the world show up at the lodgelike wood-paneled bar and restaurant after having heard about it over beers in Germany or during a snowstorm in Switzerland—or so say members of the Tuzi family, owners since 1978. Though the place is known for its baby-back pork ribs, the filet mignon and New York strip steak are also specialties. Arrive before 6PM to beat the crowd or have a drink and spin a few discs on the Jolson-to-Springsteen jukebox. ♦ American ♦ M-F, late dinner; Sa, Su, lunch and dinner. Reservations accepted for large groups only. 1655 N Sedgwick St (at W Eugenie St). 266.1616

11 SAVORIES

$ A simple neighborhood place for coffee, tea, sandwiches, pastries, and gift items. Locals come in to read their paper, buy coffee beans or a new mug, or pick up dessert to take home for dinner. ♦ Café ♦ Daily. 1651 N Wells St (between W North Ave and W Eugenie St). 951.7638

12 A NEW LEAF

There are many florists in Chicago, but this shop has an exceptional selection of fresh-cut flowers. Considering its high-rent location, the prices are especially reasonable. ♦ Daily. 1645 N Wells St (between W North Ave and W Eugenie St). 642.1576

12 MOODY CHURCH

This independent church devoted to evangelism and Bible education was designed in 1925 by **John R. Fugard**. The church was founded by Dwight L. Moody, a shoe salesman who came from Boston to Chicago to pursue a personal ministry serving poor street children. It now occupies one of the largest Protestant church buildings in the country and sends radio and television broadcasts of many of its services around the world. The immense Romanesque structure, redbrick trimmed in terra-cotta, is a 140-by-225-foot rectangle with a semicircle facing Clark Street. It seats 4,000 people on the main floor and the

---

Restaurants/Clubs: Red | **Hotels: Purple** | **Shops: Orange** | **Outdoors/Parks: Green** | **Sights/Culture: Blue**

cantilevered balcony. Everyone has an unob-
structed view of the pulpit and choir because
there are no interior columns. The vaulted
ceiling and supporting piers were suggested
by the design of the ancient Church of St.
Sophia in Istanbul. Interior stained-glass
windows were bestowed in memory of various
pastors and lay members of the church.
♦ 1630 N Clark St (between W North Ave and
W Eugenie St). 943.0466

13 St. Michael's Church

This landmark defines Old Town, because tradition decrees you are within the neighborhood's
boundaries if you can hear the church's bells.
The chiming carries farther than you might
think, with each of the five bells weighing
between 2,500 and 6,000 pounds. The growing
German community built a small church here in
1852 and replaced it with a larger one 17
years later, only to see it gutted by the 1871
Chicago Fire. (The *Daily Tribune* referred to the
remains of the tower and walls as "the most
impressive ruins on the North Side.") The determined parishioners rebuilt their church in only a
year and a decade later hired New York artist
Karl Labrecht to design the lavish interior. In
1888 an exterior renovation by **Herman T. Gaul**
was completed, and a steeple was added to
crown the tower. Circus acrobats thrilled crowds
at the dedication ceremony when they hung by
their heels from the cross at its summit. The
four-sided steeple clock was added the
following year. Parishioners have included prize-
fighter Nick Castiglione and actor Johnny
Weissmuller, who was an altar boy here before
learning to swing from the trees as Tarzan. ♦
1633 N Cleveland Ave (between W North Ave
and W Eugenie St). 642.2498

14 Tony n' Tina's Wedding

An interactive spoof of an Italian-American
wedding may seem an unlikely theatrical hit,
but that's exactly what this has become—and
a long-term hit at that. The audience of
"guests" mingles with the "bridal party" of
actors, dances to a band, eats an Italian
wedding supper, observes family spats, and
drinks champagne. The only difference
between this and a real wedding is that you
pay your way in rather than buying a gift.
♦ Shows Su, W-Sa. Reservations required.
230 W North Ave (between N Wells St and N
North Park Ave). 664.1456

15 Second City

A list of just a few of the people who have cut
their comedic teeth here makes an all-star roll

> Chicago's population grew tenfold between the year
> of the Chicago Fire, 1871, and the turn of the
> century.

call: Alan Arkin, Ed Asner, Elaine May, Jerry
Stiller, Anne Meara, John Belushi, Bill Murray,
and Shelley Long. The club was founded at
this location in 1959 by a small group of
theater lovers that included Mike Nichols and
Sheldon Patinkin. (They proudly snatched the
name **Second City** from essayist A.J. Liebling's
derisive profile of Chicago published in the
New Yorker in the early 1950s.) Their unique
brand of satirical comedy was an instant hit,
not only locally but also in the global theater
community. An official touring company was
formed in 1967 and continues to make
appearances worldwide. In the early 1970s,
another Second City opened in Toronto, where
John Candy, Gene Levy, Dan Aykroyd, and
Gilda Radner all honed their skills. The revue
has stuck to its original format: On an empty
stage, using few props, six or seven actors
lampoon contemporary life in a series of skits.
Then the actors ask the audience for ideas,
from which they improvise new sketches. (With
fine-tuning, these improvisations eventually
become parts of new shows, of which there
are two or three every year.) This theater has
blossomed into two cabaret-style settings next
door to each other and one suburban outpost
in Rolling Meadows—three different troupes
presenting three different revues at the same
time. Cocktails and hot beverages can be
purchased during the shows. Incidentally, the
original building's ornamental façade is from
the once-glorious **Garrick Theatre** downtown,
designed by **Adler & Sullivan** and demolished
in 1961. ♦ Credit cards accepted for drinks
only. Shows Tu-Su. Reservations
recommended; required F and Sa. 1608-16 N
Wells St (between W North Ave and W Eugenie
St). 337.3992. www.secondcity.com

15 Piper's Alley

What began as the Piper family bakery in the
1880s became the enclosed Piper's Alley in
the 1960s, a lively collection of shops
hawking love beads and Grateful Dead
albums to hippies and tourists. Those shops
have given way to a running-shoe store, a
Starbucks, and a movie theater. ♦ Daily. 1608
N Wells St (between W North Ave and W
Eugenie St). 337.0436

15 Adobo Grill

★★$$ Accessible through Piper's Alley or on
Wells Street, this bright, two-level restaurant
serves up traditional Mexican fare with alacrity
and some delightful twists. Paul LoDuca of
Vinci is the talented chef in charge. A front-
room bar is a popular spot to savor
margaritas, and the guacamole is prepared
tableside to your liking with a mortar and
pestle. ♦ Nuevo Latino. ♦ The restaurant has
become so deservedly popular that it has
opened a branch in Wicker Park. M-F, dinner;
Sa-Su, brunch and dinner. 1610 N Wells St
(at W North Ave). 266.7999. Also at 2005 W

Division St (at N Damen Ave). 252.9990. www.adobogrill.com

16 OLD TOWN ALE HOUSE

Dark, damp, dingy, and like home to its faithful, this bar serves construction workers elbow-to-elbow with **Second City** actors. A mural on the wall pays tribute to regulars over the years. The jukebox plays everything from Billie Holiday to Maria Callas. ◆ Daily, noon-4AM; Sa, to 5AM. 219 W North Ave (at N Wieland St). 944.7020

17 UP-DOWN TOBACCO SHOP

This shop has been on Wells Street since the 1960s, when many customers no doubt bought rolling papers here for uses other than tobacco. Owned by Diana Gits, the store takes you back to an even earlier era, when smoking was a sign of refinement: The air is rich with the scent of tobacco, and beautiful hand-carved pipes, gold cigarette cases, and a large selection of imported cigars and cigarettes are on display. ◆ M-Th, 10AM-11PM; F, Sa, 10AM-midnight; Su, 11AM-11PM. 1550 N Wells St (between W Schiller St and W North Ave). 337.8505

17 ZANIES

Chicago's premier stand-up comedy club is small, cramped, and very conducive to laughter. Featured performers range from national names like Larry Miller to less well-known local talents like Tim Walkoe and Mike Ostrowski. Comedian Emo Phillips got his start here. ◆ Cover and two-drink minimum. Shows Tu-Su. Reservations recommended. 1548 N Wells St (between W Schiller St and W North Ave). 337.4027. www.zanies.com

18 GALLERY OF VINTAGE POSTERS

With far more than posters, this is the Midwest's largest collection of European decorative items from the Belle Epoque: mirrors, frames, bowls, throws, plus distinctive posters of the era. ◆ Tu-Su. 1551 N Wells St (at W North Ave). 951.6681

19 OLD TOWN AQUARIUM

In addition to servicing home aquariums, this store carries the largest selection of saltwater fish in the city. A look in the spectacular aquarium in the front window reveals beautiful breeds of every color and stripe. The store specializes in locating rare species and will ship anywhere in the world. ◆ Daily. 1538 N Wells St (between W Schiller St and W North Ave). 642.8763. www.oldtownaquarium.com

19 FRESH CHOICE

$ This cheery yellow-and-white restaurant offers a choice of healthful meals, from the salad bar to the weekend omelette bar that gives you the option of an egg-white omelette. The true health fanatic can get an invigorating shot of wheat grass (a single 2-ounce shot equals 2 pounds of vegetables) or a glass of freshly squeezed carrot juice. Sandwiches are available, as are smoothies, yogurt, and Italian ices. ◆ Café ◆ Daily, breakfast, lunch, and dinner; open until midnight June-Aug. 1534 N Wells St (between W Schiller St and W North Ave). 664.7065

20 TRATTORIA ROMA

★$$ When it opened down the block in 1987 in a space the size of a postage stamp, this was arguably Chicago's first authentic trattoria. It has since spawned all sorts of imitators. This larger location is done in a vaguely surreal style, with plaster copies of Roman architectural fragments on the walls that give you the sense of dining amid the ruins. Good starters include crisp-crusted mini-pizzas or mussels marinara. Regular features include such standards as spaghetti scampi and rigatoni mozzarella. It's always busy, and reservations are not accepted, so line up early. ◆ Italian ◆ M-F, lunch and dinner; Sa, Su, dinner. 1535 N Wells St (between W Schiller St and W North Ave). 664.7907

21 FUDGE POT

Indulge yourself. The Dattalo family has perfected the art of homemade candy making over two generations. The chocolate-covered English butter toffee melts in your mouth, and fudge comes in ten flavors. It's hard to walk by too many times without having one of their taffy apples, made with fat Granny Smith or Delicious apples, depending on the season, and hand-dipped in homemade caramel. They're the best in the city! ◆ Daily. 1532 N Wells St (between W Schiller St and W North Ave). 943.1777

21 O'BRIEN'S RESTAURANT

★$$ With the atmosphere of a posh men's club—dark wood, deep green hues, and 2-ton chandeliers—this is truly a traditional steak house. The menu is heavy on substantial steaks and steaming baked potatoes. Try the famous thick cabbage soup. A piano bar deep within entertains until midnight. Free parking is a plus. ◆ Steak house ◆ M-Sa, lunch and dinner; Su, brunch and dinner. 1528 N Wells St (between W Schiller St and W North Ave). 787.3131

22 THE SPICE HOUSE

The aromas wafting out of this quaint storefront are hard to resist. The store is a cousin to

Restaurants/Clubs: Red | Hotels: Purple | Shops: Orange | Outdoors/Parks: Green | Sights/Culture: Blue

one in another Great Lakes city up the road, Milwaukee. You can get what you need to season practically any ethnic cuisine, and there are lectures and demonstrations for those who are serious about spicing up their cooking skills. Even if you're not a cook, it's worth stopping in for a sniff. ◆ Daily. 1512 N Wells St (between W Schiller St and W North Ave). 274.0378. Also in Evanston, 847/328.3711 & www.thespicehouse.com

22 TOPO GIGIO

★★$$ Named for the Italian equivalent of Mickey Mouse, this small *ristorante* nevertheless has an ambiance that is distinctly grown-up in appeal. Proprietors Frankie Neda and Lillo Tesdosi are very friendly, and the service is excellent. Homemade pasta is a crowd pleaser, as are herb-roasted chicken and a selection of veal dishes. This is a great spot for a romantic, leisurely dinner, so have an *aperitivo* and espresso too. ◆ Italian ◆ M-Sa, lunch and dinner; Su, dinner. 1516 N Wells St (between W Schiller St and W North Ave). 266.9355

23 HEAT

★★$$$ Sushi devotees and connoisseurs of Japanese food are getting along swimmingly at this pricey newcomer to the Old Town dining scene. You can actually choose your sushi while it's still swimming in the tank. The real draw, though, is the seasonally changing 11-course kaiseki dinner, which will set you back $95. Soft-shell crab with monkfish liver and grilled venison is a sight to behold and a treat to taste. And of course there's a large selection of sake to suit those who savor the drink. Reservations recommended. ◆ Japanese ◆ M-Sa, dinner. 1507 N Sedgwick St (between W North Ave and W Blackhawk St). 397.9818

24 WEST BURTON PLACE

There's a tiny park where **Burton Place** stops short of Wells Street, and it's worth a brief detour to walk along this quiet block to get to it (the street ends at LaSalle Street and starts again on the other side of Sandburg Village, in the Gold Coast). **No. 155** is a brick apartment building that was whimsically remodeled in 1927 by **Sol Kogen** and artist Edgar Miller. It's a sort of folk version of Art Deco, with a patchwork of glass block, mosaic, marble, terra-cotta, and old brick salvaged from demolished neighborhood buildings. Note too the interesting tile work on the sidewalk. ◆ West of N LaSalle St

In a remarkable engineering achievement, the flow of the Chicago River was reversed in 1900 to prevent sewage from flowing into Lake Michigan, the source of the city's drinking water.

25 BURTON PLACE

$ On a winter's night, go ahead and jockey with the regulars for a prime seat next to the crackling fire in this neighborhood bar. While you're here, try one of the great burgers. ◆ American ◆ Daily, until 4AM; Sa, until 5AM. 1447 N Wells St (between W Schiller St and W North Ave). 664.4699

25 BISTROT MARGOT

★★$$ This relatively new entry on the bistro circuit is proof that a city can never have too many bistros, provided the food is prepared well. Mosaic tiles and red leather chairs give this storefront space a bright atmosphere. The menu is equally bright, and the prices won't lighten your wallet too much. There's an excellent selection of pâtés to choose from to start with, before moving on to assorted entreés of grilled seafood and meats. The rack of lamb is top notch. During warm weather, an outdoor patio opens up. ◆ Bistro ◆ M-Sa, dinner; Su, brunch and dinner. 1437-39 N Wells St (between W Schiller St and W North Ave). 587.3660; 587.3668 & www.bistrotmargot.com

26 NOBLE HORSE EQUESTRIAN CENTER

Horses are indeed nobly stabled in this renovated 1917 building. In addition to supplying the steeds used for carriage rides along Michigan Avenue, in movies, and on TV, the stable offers horse owners complete boarding and training services. Riding lessons are available for all levels in English, hunt seat, and dressage. The public is welcome to drop in to admire the horses. ◆ Daily. 1410 N Orleans St (between W Schiller St and W North Ave). 266.7878. www.noblehorsechicago.com

27 OLD JERUSALEM

★$ The atmosphere is reminiscent of a lunchroom, but the Middle Eastern cuisine is delicious, from the freshest parsley-packed tabbouleh to the crisp, perfectly seasoned falafel. Share three or four different appetizers with companions for a very satisfying—and cheap—meal. ◆ Middle Eastern ◆ Daily, lunch and dinner. 1411 N Wells St (between W Schiller St and W North Ave). 944.0459

28 KAMEHACHI

★★$$ For years, a Nisei woman ran a popular sushi bar a few blocks up the street. Her granddaughter has taken over and expanded the place into this new space but retained the old commitment to fresh and consistently good food. For those unfamiliar with Japanese delicacies, the restaurant offers a "beginner's" meal that consists of all cooked items, as well as a wide variety of raw fish dishes for aficionados. An outdoor patio is available for summer dining. ◆ Japanese ◆ M-Sa, lunch and dinner; Su, dinner. 1400 N Wells St (at W Schiller St). 664.3663. Also at 240 E Ontario St (between N St. Clair and N Fairbanks Ct). 587.0600. www.kamehachi.com

29 ORSO'S

$$ Most restaurants come and go as the neighborhood changes. This one has staying power. Quaint, relaxed, and romantic, with a piano player, flickering candles on the tables, and a lovely patio and garden out back, it serves predictable pastas, eggplant parmigiana, roasted chicken, and such. ♦ Italian ♦ Daily, lunch and dinner. 1401 N Wells St (at W Schiller St). 787.6604

30 COBBLER SQUARE

Built in 1889, this former factory complex originally housed Western Wheel Works, the world's largest bicycle manufacturer. In 1911 the bikers moved out and a doctor with arthritic feet moved in, intending to make therapeutic foot products—and the rest, they say, is history. Dr. Scholl's footwear firm was one of Old Town's largest employers until 1981, when it left this location to seek cheaper labor. In 1985 the redbrick buildings, which encompass an entire square block, were renovated by **Kenneth Schroeder** into 295 loft apartments surrounding landscaped courtyards. What was probably the Evergreen Avenue entryway, flanked by pillars and topped with a little balcony, is now permanently closed by a cast-iron gate; the main level on the Wells Street side has a Pier One. ♦ 1350 N Wells St (between W Evergreen Ave and W Schiller St)

31 VILLAGE CYCLE CENTER

Here is one of the city's largest emporiums selling specialized and custom bikes. ♦ Daily. 1337 N Wells St (between W Goethe and W Schiller Sts). 751.2488. www.village cycle.com

32 SALPICON!

★★★$$ Aficionados of Mexican food shouldn't miss this place in a bright, casual storefront setting. Diners may savor a delightful variety of sophisticated regional offerings, starting with appetizers such as coarse guacamole, lobster seviche made with tequila, and jalapeño *chiles rellenos* with black-bean sauce. The mouthwatering entrées include grilled shrimp in sweet garlic sauce and breaded pork in roasted chili and tomato sauce. The flan is tasty and smooth as silk, but also consider poached oranges in cinnamon-orange syrup. Arrive before 6:30PM—there's a three-course, very reason-able prix-fixe menu. ♦ Mexican ♦ M-Sa, dinner; Su, brunch and dinner. 1252 N Wells St (between W Scott and W Goethe Sts). 988.7811. www.salpicon.com

32 FIRE ENGINE COMPANY NO. 27

The city had just purchased a fire engine from a manufacturer in Seneca Falls, New York, and needed a new building in the neighborhood to house it. In 1874 the Chicago Board of Public Works filled the order. The resulting two-story structure featured an Italianate design that was without precedent for a building of this type. It's now part of the North Wells Street Historic District, which includes the buildings from 1240 to 1260, and is on the National Register of Historic Landmarks. The tower that was used for drying the hoses and watching for fires has been shortened, and office workers now toil where firefighters used to sleep. ♦ 1244 N Wells St (between W Scott and W Goethe Sts)

33 HOUSE OF GLUNZ

Limousines double-park out front while the drivers run in to pick up a case of this rare vintage or that special champagne for their well-to-do employers. The store and the building—one of the first constructed after the Great Fire in 1871—don't look much different than they did when Louis Glunz started his wine and spirits business here in 1888. The exterior has a handsome dark green, gold-trimmed façade and an ornate cast-iron sign. Inside are stained-glass windows imported from Germany, all of the original wooden wine racks, rich-hued murals of wine-related scenes, and numerous antique wine bottles from the days when the company ordered wine by the barrel and decanted it into its own bottles. The shop specializes in rare vintage California Cabernets from smaller wineries, such as **Heitz**, **Grgich Hills**, and **Jordan**, and rare French wines, cognacs, and Armagnacs. They will prepare custom gift packages and ship anywhere. For a trip back in time, ask to visit the old wine-tasting room and the museum. The former, a dark, moody place, has bottles of significant wines arranged in racks and a wonderful collection of antique crystal wineglasses. The museum, which was the popular **Glunz Tavern** before Prohibition (when the shop switched to the legal sale of home-brewing ingredients), still has the original sandwich menu tacked to the wall, plus a number of well-worn cooperage tools. There's also a Schlitz memorabilia corner, the House of Glunz having been the first Chicago distributors of "the beer that made Milwaukee famous." Tours are available. ♦ Daily. 1206 N Wells St (at W Division St). 642.3000

Restaurants/Clubs: Red | Hotels: Purple | Shops: Orange | Outdoors/Parks: Green | Sights/Culture: Blue

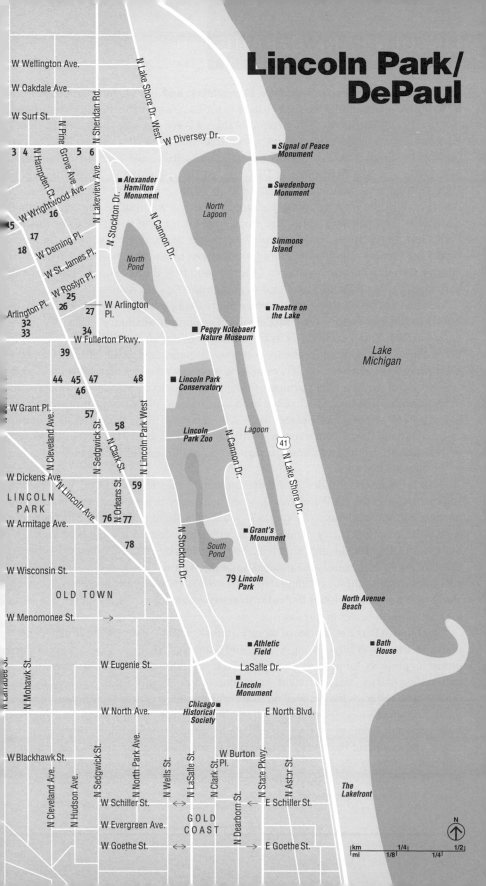

Lincoln Park/ DePaul

W Wellington Ave.

W Oakdale Ave.

W Surf St.

N Lake Shore Dr. West

N Sheridan Rd.

N Pine Grove Ave.

N Hampden Ct.

N Lakeview Ave.

N Stockton Dr.

N Cannon Dr.

W Diversey Dr.

3 4   5   6

■ *Signal of Peace Monument*

■ *Alexander Hamilton Monument*

■ *Swedenborg Monument*

North Lagoon

W Wrightwood Ave.   16

Simmons Island

15

17

North Pond

18   W Deming Pl.

W St. James Pl.

W Roslyn Pl.   25

Arlington Pl.   26   27   W Arlington Pl.

■ *Theatre on the Lake*

32
33

34
W Fullerton Pkwy.

■ *Peggy Notebaert Nature Museum*

Lake Michigan

39

44 45 47   48
46

■ *Lincoln Park Conservatory*

W Grant Pl.

N Cleveland Ave.

57

N Sedgwick St.

58

N Clark St.

N Lincoln Park West

Lincoln Park Zoo

N Cannon Dr.

Lagoon

N Lake Shore Dr.

41

W Dickens Ave.

N Lincoln Ave.

N Orleans St.

59

LINCOLN
PARK

W Armitage Ave.

76   77

N Stockton Dr.

■ *Grant's Monument*

78

South Pond

W Wisconsin St.

79 *Lincoln Park*

North Avenue Beach

OLD TOWN

W Menomonee St.   →

■ *Athletic Field*

■ *Bath House*

N Mohawk St.

W Eugenie St.

LaSalle Dr.

■ *Lincoln Monument*

W North Ave.

Chicago Historical Society ■

E North Blvd.

N Sedgwick St.

N North Park Ave.

N Wells St.

N LaSalle St.

N Clark St.

W Burton Pl.

N State Pkwy.

N Astor St.

The Lakefront

W Blackhawk St.

N Cleveland Ave.

N Hudson Ave.

N Dearborn St.

W Schiller St.   ↔

E Schiller St.

W Evergreen Ave.

GOLD
COAST

W Goethe St.   ↔

→   E Goethe St.

N

km   1/4   1/2
mi
1/8   1/4

LINCOLN PARK/DePAUL

A lakefront park, beaches with sky-blue waters, and the **Lincoln Park Zoo** draw affluent residents and envious visitors to the bustling Lincoln Park neighborhood, ringed by **Lake Michigan, Clybourn** and **Ashland Avenues, Old Town,** and **Diversey Parkway.** Local architecture provides more attractions, from **Mies van der Rohe** towers overlooking the park to 19th-century town houses on tree-lined streets in the landmark **Mid-North** and **Sheffield Historic Districts.** At the community's heart, the **DePaul University** campus spans many acres and lends its name to a gentrified neighborhood that combines the collegiate with the urbane. Award-winning restaurants, original boutiques, first-class bookstores, and much more vie for your attention along **Lincoln Park West, Clark Street,** and **Fullerton, Armitage,** and **Lincoln Avenues.** And then there's the famous nightlife, including productions by the **Steppenwolf Theatre** and **Victory Gardens Theater,** get-down Chicago sounds at **B.L.U.E.S.,** and billiards and barhopping along **Halsted Street** and Armitage and Lincoln Avenues.

Lincoln Park's evolution into something more than pastoral scenery began with the arrival in the mid-1850s of the **McCormick Theological Seminary** (which has since moved to Hyde Park), named after its industrialist benefactor Cyrus Hall McCormick. In the middle of farmlands, the seminary constructed chapels, academic buildings, and the **McCormick Row Houses,** an enclave of handsome town houses that still stand today. Another boost was the 1868 opening of the park from which the community draws its name. **Lincoln Park,** built on what had been a depressing city cemetery, quickly became one of the city's most popular places to visit. It remains so today; it boasts a fascinating zoo, a plant and flower conservatory, pretty lagoons, and grassy lawns. The Great Fire of 1871 also led to the area's construction boom, as burned-out Chicagoans moved in to the unpopulated area.

Quite the high-class residential district throughout the 1920s and 1930s, Lincoln Park suffered setbacks during World War II, when many homes were converted into poorly maintained rooming houses. By the 1950s suburban flight had left the community in such a sorry state that city administrators officially declared it a blighted area. The designation signaled the area's revival, however, as city funds became available for urban renewal. Dangerously dilapidated buildings were demolished, numerous vintage structures were beautifully rehabilitated, and new homes, apartment buildings, and retail stores were built. In the 1960s **DePaul University** embarked on a long-range expansion program that continues to this day.

Now **Lincoln Park** rates as one of the city's most desirable—not to mention expensive—places to live, especially among young professionals. Whereas urban pioneers once picked up property for peanuts, the price of a town house these days can hover near a half-million dollars—and apartment rentals don't come cheaply either. As a result, many middle-class residents have moved on to more affordable pastures. Some have relocated to the neighborhood's western edge, where the long-neglected **Clybourn Corridor** has undergone a dramatic conversion to upscale housing and retail stores. This part of the city is active around the clock; restaurants, theaters, and clubs are packed at night, especially on weekends. In warm weather, a steady stream of people wends its way to the park, zoo, and beach. So take along a good measure of patience: Wherever you're headed, you'll encounter crowds.

All area codes in this chapter are 773 unless otherwise noted.

1 BARNES & NOBLE

A large selection of books, a trendy coffee bar, visiting authors, talks on every imaginable subject, and great music in the background make this a fun place to shop any night of the week. It's also a popular hangout, especially among singles in the neighborhood. ♦ Daily, until 11PM. 659 W Diversey Pkwy (between N Clark and N Orchard Sts). 871.9004; fax 871.5893. Also at numerous locations throughout the city and suburbs. www.barnesandnoble.com

2 HANIG'S SLIPPER BOX

The city's largest collection of Birkenstock sandals, as well as classic shoe styles, can be found at this busy corner store. Keep an eye open for sidewalk sales with terrific buys on name-brand men's and women's shoes. ♦ Daily. 2754 N Clark St (at W Diversey Pkwy). 248.1977; fax 248.0793. www.hanigs.com

2 SHERWYN'S

Take one step backward into the 1960s and two steps forward into the New Age in Chicago's biggest and busiest health-food store. Friendly Birkenstock-shod clerks direct you through rows of organic produce; bulk nuts, grains, and herbs; 20 kinds of honey and olive oil; seaweeds; natural cosmetics; juicers; and self-help books and tapes. ♦ Daily. 645 W Diversey Pkwy (between N Clark and N Orchard Sts). 477.1934; fax 477.6632. www.sherwyns.com

3 INN AT LINCOLN PARK

$ Clean, friendly, and intimate. The real beauty of staying here is that you're within walking distance of the park, the lakefront, and the main thoroughfares of Diversey Parkway, Clark Street, and Lakeview's Broadway. There is no restaurant, but there is free parking—like manna from heaven in this part of town. ♦ 601 W Diversey Pkwy (at N Lehmann Ct). 348.2810, 866.744.PARK; fax 348.1912. www.innlp.com

4 VESPA OF CHICAGO

No matter how you got to town, if you want to leave on a scooter, this is the place to start your engine. ♦ M-Sa. 557 W Diversey Pkwy (between N Lehmann and N Hampden Cts). 929.8377. www.vespachicago.com

5 PARS COVE

★$$ The scene at this Persian restaurant is exotic and romantic, with its semisubterranean setting, stone floors, ceiling fans, and pianist playing smooth jazz. *Koubideh* (kabobs of ground lamb and beef) are traditional favorites. Don't miss melt-in-your-mouth *fesen jan* (chicken simmered in rich pomegranate-and-walnut sauce). ♦ Persian ♦ Daily, lunch and dinner. 435 W Diversey Pkwy (between N Lakeview and N Pine Grove Aves). 549.1515; fax 549.4148

6 ELKS NATIONAL MEMORIAL BUILDING

Built in 1926 by **Egerton Swartwout** in recognition of members of the Benevolent and Protective Order of Elks who died in World War I, and rededicated after subsequent wars, this is the city's most lavish memorial. The building is a massive circular structure with a flattened dome above an enormous colonnade. Beneath the colonnade is a frieze, 5 feet high and 16 feet long, with allegorical carvings of war and peace. Elks medals, photos, and memorabilia are available for viewing in the archives room. The adjacent **Elks Magazine Building** was designed in 1967 by **Holabird & Root**. ♦ Donation requested. M-F. 2750 N Lakeview Ave (at W Diversey Pkwy)

7 STEVE STARR STUDIO

Owner Steve is the undisputed Starr of Deco. Midnight-blue "Evening in Paris" perfume bottles, Art Deco lamps, chrome toasters, and eerie lighting make you feel like you're in a time warp. All of the aforementioned are for sale. What's not for sale, but is on view here, is Starr's personal collection of gorgeous Art Deco picture frames containing smiling photos of such famous customers as Diana Ross and Bette Midler. You can, however, take some of them home in *Picture Perfect*, the Rizzoli-published art book on movie stars that Starr wrote. Catch his column in *Windy City Times*. ♦ M-F, 2-6PM; Sa, Su, 1PM-5PM. 2779 N Lincoln Ave (at W Diversey Pkwy). 525.6530; fax 525.7520

7 DELILAH'S

The sign hanging outside this alternative music pub bears a portrait of Snow White on one side and the Evil Queen on the other—an apt reflection of the contrast between the staff

---

Restaurants/Clubs: Red | **Hotels: Purple** | **Shops: Orange** | **Outdoors/Parks: Green** | **Sights/Culture: Blue**

and clientele's pleasant demeanor and their occasionally menacing appearance. The goateed boys and black-clad punkettes who run the place are surprisingly friendly, even to guys in ties. DJs play tunes by unknown local bands when the well-stocked jukebox is idle. Upstairs is a small room with comfy chairs and a pool table. Sample one of the 26 kinds of whiskey available. ♦ Daily, until 2AM; Sa, until 3AM. 2771 N Lincoln Ave (between N Seminary Ave and W Diversey Pkwy). 472.2771. www.dclilahschicago.com

8 MAZA

★★$$ *Maza* means "appetizer" in Lebanese, and the signature dish at this attractive storefront restaurant (which replaced the once-funky, now-defunct Star Top Café) is (surprise!) the appetizer. There are 22 in all, an array of miniature samplings from spinach pie to tabbouleh, and they are so curious and tasty that *Chicago* magazine picked **Maza** as one of the best new restaurants in 2000. Other items include rack of lamb, grilled beef or chicken, and seafood. ♦ Lebanese ♦ Daily, dinner. 2748 N Lincoln Ave (between N Seminary Ave and W Diversey Pkwy). 929.9600 &

9 DESIGN SOURCE, INC.

Owned by an interior designer, Robert Turner, this shop offers an eclectic array of decorative home accessories, from 18th-century Chippendale chests to hammered-tin lamps from Mexico. ♦ Tu-Sa. 2661 N Lincoln Ave (between N Kenmore and N Seminary Aves). 472.1594

10 FATTOUSH

★$ This charming Lebanese café is a family affair—the Elakhaoui family, which includes the owner, his wife, and two daughters. They're all hard at work delivering some really delicious (and affordable) Middle Eastern treats. The hummus and falafels are top notch, and there are combinations that enable you to mix and match. For dessert, baklava of course. ♦ Lebanese ♦ Daily, lunch and dinner. 2652 N Halsted St (between W Wrightwood and W Diversey Aves). 327.2652

11 GRAMAPHONE LTD

Back when CDs came into being and music superstores threatened to knock independent retailers off the block, this friendly neighborhood shop cleverly positioned itself as the ultimate source for disco tunes on vinyl. Although it does carry CDs and different categories of music, **Gramaphone** has established an international reputation as perhaps the best store in the world for dance music—house, industrial, disco, you name it. Professional DJs swear by the place. Owner Carl Borowski, an accomplished blues harp

player who moonlights in the popular R&B band Cletus and the Sliders, will dazzle you with his knowledge of dance music. ♦ 2663 N Clark St (between W Drummond Pl and W Diversey Pkwy). 472.3683. www.gramaphonerecords.com

12 WIENER CIRCLE

$ Energetic staffers work elbow to elbow at a frantic pace to keep up the flow of condiment-laden "char dogs" and greasy fries. They stay open until the wee hours. ♦ Fast food ♦ Daily, lunch and dinner until 4AM; F, Sa, until 5AM. 2622 N Clark St (between W Wrightwood Ave and W Drummond Pl). 477.7444

13 ROSE ANGELIS

★$$ Tucked away in a residential corner of western **Lincoln Park** that's well off the beaten path, this fine Italian restaurant is wildly popular—and crowded to the rafters on weekends. Prime-time diners enjoy glasses of wine in the cozy, curtained storefront while they wait for tables. Go easy on the crusty, warm bread and save room for such yummy pasta entrées as ravioli Luigi (cheese-filled ravioli in sun-dried tomato sauce), *linguine frutta di mare* (with seafood), or *ravioli mezzalune al burro* (basil-pesto–filled spinach half-moon ravioli in a brown butter sauce). Just across the street, an annex named **Verona** serves coffee and dessert; notice the lovely murals covering its walls. ♦ Italian ♦ Tu-Su, dinner. No reservations accepted for parties of fewer than eight. 1314 W Wrightwood Ave (between N Lakewood and N Wayne Aves). 296.0081. www.roseangelis.com

14 ITTO SUSHI

★$$ Sushi and sashimi seem to be highly revered here, since *itto* refers to a spiritual gathering. You can watch the sushi chef prepare your selections and ceremoniously set them before you on the blond-wood counter at the sushi bar. Broiled fish and meat, teriyaki, and tempura are also served. The restaurant has its own parking lot, a rarity in this area. ♦ Japanese ♦ M-Sa, lunch and dinner. 2616 N Halsted St (between W Wrightwood Ave and W Diversey Pkwy). 871.1800

14 CORNER POCKET

The real hotshots shoot pool elsewhere, so customers here can enjoy a nice, quiet game at one of six tables. There's also a backyard beer garden. ♦ M-F, 4PM-2AM; Sa, Su, from noon. 2610 N Halsted St (between W Wrightwood Ave and W Diversey Pkwy). 281.0050

15 DAVE'S RECORDS

If you're looking for used CDs, don't come to this hooked-on-vinyl shop. "No CDs. Never had 'em, never will," says a sign in the window. But if you're looking for old LPs, come on in and start flipping through the stacks. ♦ Daily. 2604 N Clark St (at W Wrightwood Ave). 929.6325

16 Francis J. Dewes House

Designated a Chicago landmark in 1974, this house was built in 1896 for a wealthy German brewer in the Baroque Revival style by two European architects, **Adolph Cudell** and **Arthur Hercz**. The elaborate ornamentation of this privately owned home includes finely carved stonework and detailed cast-iron railings. Caryatids support a second-floor balcony at the Wrightwood Avenue entrance, and the western façade boasts a large stair-case window of stained and leaded glass. The house at the west side of the lot, a typical Chicago town house dressed in the Baroque finery of its neighbor, was built by Dewes for his brother. ♦ 503 W Wrightwood Ave (at N Hampden Ct)

17 Slithers

Women who seek solace in footwear can easily find it in this chic shoe boutique. Slither into this intimate but roomy double storefront and slither out feeling sleek. ♦ Daily. 2549-51 N Clark St (between W Wrightwood Ave and W Deming Pl). 871-2994; fax 871.4161. www.slithersshoes.com

18 Frances' Alley

$ This restaurant has been serving home-style meals to **Lincoln Park** folk since the 1930s. Some people swear by the mashed potatoes; others go for the potato  pancakes. No one seems to remember who Frances was, but her melt-in-your-mouth cheese blintzes are still a mainstay. Other offerings are largely cafeteria quality. ♦ Deli ♦ Tu-Su, breakfast, lunch, and dinner. 2552 N Clark St (between W Deming Pl and W Wright-wood Ave). 248.4580

19 Apollo Theater Center

A striking 350-seat space, this is one of the oldest commercial theaters outside the Loop. Producers often book it for big-budget produc-tions of off-Broadway hits such as *Lend Me a Tenor*, which attract suburbanites by the busload. The most popular long-running recent attraction was *The Vagina Monologues*. Seating is in five sections around a thrust stage. Try to avoid row F; it has less legroom. ♦ 2540 N Lincoln Ave (between W Altgeld St and N Sheffield Ave). Box office, 935.6100. www.apollochicago.com

20 Spacetime Tanks

Located in an unsightly 1970s condo/retail complex, this unique day spa specializes in isolation float tanks. These sealed pods (not for the claustrophobic) are filled with warm water laced with float-inducing minerals. Strip down, hop into a tank, and let your mind go free. Massages and sound-and-light experiences with earphones and goggles are also available. ♦ Daily, until 9PM. Appointment necessary. 2526 N Lincoln Ave (between W Altgeld St and N Sheffield Ave). 472.2700. www.spacetimetanks.com

21 Lilly's

Stuccoed caverns connected by archways, a long window overlooking Lincoln Avenue, a creaky wooden floor, and a little stage with a piano make for a neat, quirky place to come for live blues. Local talent predominates. ♦ Cover. Daily, 4PM-2AM. 2513 N Lincoln Ave (between W Altgeld St and W Lill Ave). 525.2422

22 Kingston Mines

When in town, movie stars and musicians inevitably show up in the audience at this blues club, which is creeping up on its third decade. Two stages feature live blues 7 days a week. Regular talent includes Lonnie Brooks, Valerie Wellington, Sam Lay, and Little Smokey Smothers. The place gets packed quickly, so arrive early or be prepared to stand all night. ♦ Cover. Daily; shows start at 9:30PM. 2548 N Halsted St (between W Lill and W Wrightwood Aves). 477.4646. www.kingstonmines.com

23 B.L.U.E.S.

For more than 2 decades, this dark, narrow nightclub with a little stage has been showcasing the big talents of such blues stars as Koko Taylor, Sunnyland Slim, Little Ed and the Imperials, Mark Naftalin, and many others. ♦ Cover. Daily; shows start at 9PM. 2519 N Halsted St (between W Fullerton and W Wrightwood Aves). 528.1012. Also at 1124 W Belmont Ave (between N Seminary and N Clifton Aves). 525.8989. www.chicagobluesbar.com

24 St. Clement's Catholic Church

George D. Barnett built this church in 1917-1918. The interior was restored in 1989 by **Holabird & Root** and is now one of the most beautiful spaces in the city. Every surface is embellished, from the painted dome to the marbleized columns, and the overall effect is sublime. Architect **Walker Johnson** of **Holabird & Root** designed the hanging light fixtures that provide computer-controlled illumination yet look as though they've been here forever. ♦ 642 W Deming Pl (at N Orchard St). 281.0371

25 ARLINGTON AND ROSLYN PLACE DISTRICT

If you'd like a respite from the 21st-century commercialism on this stretch of Clark Street, relief is literally just around the corner. Turn east at Roslyn or Arlington Place, tree-lined streets of century-old houses that together form a Chicago Landmark District. The wildly overgrown lot on Arlington just east of Clark Street is a small refuge for birds. St. James and Deming Places between Lakeview Avenue and Clark Street are lined with charming town houses. When you return to Clark Street and look south from the west side of the street at Deming Place, you're back in the 21st century, with a view of the **John Hancock Center** and **900 North Michigan Avenue**.

26 STEVE QUICK JEWELER

If the *Starship Enterprise* crew were into fine jewelry, they could find something here to accent their outfits. Futuristic earrings, bracelets, necklaces, and wedding bands combine diamonds and other precious and semiprecious stones (such as tourmaline and quartz), many cut at odd angles and mounted untraditionally. You can watch the staff designer at work inside the shop. ♦ Daily. 2471 N Clark St (at W Arlington Pl). 404.0034

27 THEURER/WRIGLEY HOUSE

Built in 1896 by **Richard E. Schmidt** and **Hugh M.G. Garden**, this is the only remaining mansion on Lakeview Avenue. Schmidt had apprenticed with **Adolph Cudell**, architect of the nearby **Francis J. Dewes House** (see page 133), and was well versed in German neoclassicism. The richness of materials used here is striking, with green copper and black iron trim set off against the orange façade. Terra-cotta is used for the long, narrow quoins, window frames, and the frieze and pediment above the entry porch. The conservatory at the southwest corner is original, but the sunroom above the entrance was added later. Schmidt

and Garden went on to design several Prairie School landmarks, including the **Madlener House** and the **Montgomery Ward Warehouse**. William Wrigley of chewing-gum fame bought the house in 1911; it remains a private residence. ♦ 2446 N Lakeview Ave (between W Fullerton Pkwy and W Arlington Pl)

28 CHICAGO COSTUME COMPANY

Owner Mary Hickey occasionally outfits local theatrical productions, including some at **Victory Gardens** and **Steppenwolf**. Here she rents and sells costumes of every sort, from nuns' habits to monster getups. ♦ M-Sa, 10AM-6PM. 1120 W Fullerton Ave (between N Seminary and N Racine Aves). 528.1264. www.chicagocostume.com

29 BLAKE

Fashion-forward European designs are featured in this uncluttered women's clothing store. Owners Marilyn and Dominic have pared the selection down to only the best of everything the upscale trendsetter *must* have. Labels include Ghost and Helmut Lang. ♦ Daily. 2448 N Lincoln Ave (between W Fullerton Ave and W Montana St). 477.3364

29 RED LION PUB

Anglophiles congregate at this authentic English pub that serves Sam Smith Nut Brown Ale and other imports. Posters of London line the walls. The triple-deck patio in back is great in warm weather. ♦ Daily, to 2AM. 2446 N Lincoln Ave (between W Fullerton Ave and W Montana St). 348.2695. www.theredlionpub.com

29 UNCLE DAN'S ARMY-NAVY CAMPING AND TRAVEL

This surplus-plus store stocks its shelves with everything from subzero-rated sleeping bags to French Foreign Legion kepis. The establishment caters to both serious campers and college students looking for funky winter hats. The staff is knowledgeable and friendly. Seasonal clothing is often on sale, so keep an eye peeled for bargains. ♦ Daily. 2440 N Lincoln Ave (between W Fullerton Ave and W Montana St). 477.1918

30 THREE PENNY THEATER

Although it's a little run-down, this cinema is a great place to catch double features of art and foreign films before they leave town. It also serves beer, wine, and cocktails. ♦ Daily. 2424 N Lincoln Ave (between W Fullerton Ave and W Montana St). 525.3449

31 BIOGRAPH THEATER

This storied movie house is most famous for being the place where gangster John Dillinger was ambushed and gunned down by federal agents in 1934 (trivia buffs know that the picture that night was *Manhattan Melodrama*). The landmark theater closed in 2002, but as this edition went to press, an ambitious renovation was underway to transform it into the home of the Victory Gardens Theater. Daniel P. Coffey is the architect. ♦ 2433 N Lincoln Ave (between W Fullerton Ave and W Altgeld St)

32 SALVATORE'S

★$$ Down a quiet side street, away from the hubbub on Clark, Northern Italian classics are served by candlelight. Choose from a dozen pasta dishes, scampi, scungilli, clams, beef, chicken, and veal. For dessert try chocolate cheesecake smothered in raspberry sauce or ice cream truffles in assorted flavors. ♦ Italian ♦ W-Su, dinner. 525 W Arlington Pl (between N Clark St and N Geneva Terr). 528.1200; fax 528.1272. www.salvatores.chicago.com

33 CHURCH OF OUR SAVIOR

When the Presbyterians left this site for their new church a block away in 1889, the Episcopalians bought it, razed the old building, and replaced it with a fashionable Romanesque church. Architect **Clinton J. Warren**, who designed the new churches for both denominations, later designed the **Congress Hotel** downtown. The church's main entrance is at the base of the turreted bell tower. Inside are five stained-glass windows by Louis Tiffany and walls of unusual unglazed terra-cotta. ♦ 530 W Fullerton Pkwy (between N Clark St and N Geneva Terr). 549.3832

34 2400 NORTH LAKEVIEW AVENUE

This 1963 high-rise was the last apartment building in Chicago designed by **Mies van der Rohe**, master of the elegant glass-and-aluminum curtain wall. Floor-to-ceiling windows provide residents with fabulous views of **Lincoln Park** and the lake. ♦ At W Fullerton Pkwy

35 FACETS MULTIMEDIA CENTER

The two screening rooms are dingy, cramped, and kind of depressing, but you forget all about that once the films start rolling. An eclectic schedule of foreign, art, and experimental films, plus revivals and retrospectives, provides Chicagoans with a welcome respite from the standard commercial fare. The center's programs of children's films are the nation's oldest and most extensive. Videos, film books, and film magazines are for sale in the lobby, and the basement offers video rentals of several thousand art and foreign films. ♦ Daily. 1517 W Fullerton Ave (between N Greenview and N Bosworth Aves). Recorded information 281.9075; fax 929.5437. www.facets.org

35 CHICAGO CENTER FOR THE PRINT

Representing more than 100 artists, primarily contemporary American printmakers, this quality art gallery is a great spot for browsing; etchings, lithographs, woodcuts, silkscreens, engravings, monoprints, and French and Swiss vintage posters can be found here. ♦ Tu-Su. 1509 W Fullerton Ave (between N Greenview and N Bosworth Aves). 477.1585; fax 477.1851. www.prints-posters.com

36 DEPAUL UNIVERSITY

This Catholic university was established in 1898 as **St. Vincent's College**. It was chartered as **DePaul University** in 1907, and for the next 50 years remained relatively small. In the 1960s it embarked on a major expansion program, and in 1973 it acquired the nearby campus of Presbyterian **McCormick Theological Seminary**. The purchase added considerable real estate to the university's holdings. **McCormick**, originally known as the **Indiana Theological Seminary**, had moved here in 1859 from New Albany, Indiana, thanks to a $100,000 gift from industrialist Cyrus McCormick. In subsequent decades, a Gothic chapel, many classroom halls, and a group of homes now known as the **McCormick Row House District** (see page 136) were built on the property. By 1892 the seminary was one of the largest landowners in the **Lincoln Park** area, with holdings valued at $1.3 million. In 1973 it moved to Hyde Park to affiliate with theology schools at the **University of Chicago**, providing DePaul with its own growth opportunity. DePaul now covers some 25 acres in the area and maintains a separate campus downtown. Its

---

Restaurants/Clubs: Red | Hotels: Purple | Shops: Orange | Outdoors/Parks: Green | Sights/Culture: Blue

student enrollment is nearly 15,000. ♦ W Fullerton Ave (between N Halsted St and N Clifton Ave). 312/362.8000. www.depaul.edu

On the DePaul University campus:

McCormick Row House District

One of the loveliest, most peaceful enclaves in the city lies just beyond wrought-iron gates on West Fullerton Avenue east of the elevated train stop. The 58 private residences here were designed by **A.M.F. Colton & Son** for the **McCormick Theological Seminary**, which built them (1882–1889) to generate rental income and leased the corner houses to professors. Chalmers Place is a private street surrounding a large grassy square, anchored by **DePaul University's Collegiate Gothic Commons Building** on the west and brick row houses to the north and south. It's like one of the private parks of London's residential squares but is accessible to anyone. DePaul owns the green space and the institutional buildings to the east and west, but the houses were sold to private owners when the McCormick moved to Hyde Park in 1973. Designed in a simple, almost severe version of the popular Queen Anne style, with alternating triangular and semicircular gables, the buildings have been beautifully restored, and their appearance is now monitored by a homeowners' association. The houses facing Fullerton and Belden Avenues were the first to be built, followed by those surrounding Chalmers Place.

St. Vincent de Paul Church

An enormous French Romanesque structure, the church was built by **James J. Egan** in 1895–1897, when the parish consisted of a mere 75 members. A century later, the church serves a densely populated community that

The Chicago Cubs have played in and lost the World Series a total of eight times. They won the World Series in 1907 and 1908.

Chicago's South Side was the training ground for many great jazzmen who then moved on to Hollywood and New York, among them Benny and Harry Goodman, Louis Armstrong, Louis Panico, Eddie Condon, Hoagy Carmichael, and Jess Stacy.

In 1980 a 1-mile stretch of 43rd Street on the Southwest Side was named Pope John Paul II Drive to commemorate the pontiff's visit to Chicago the previous year. In the first 6 months after the renaming, 23 street signs were stolen.

includes many university students. It's constructed of Bedford limestone, with ornate carving above the wide main entrance on Webster Avenue. The inside is notable too. The high altar of white Carrara marble is inlaid with mother-of-pearl and Venetian mosaic; marble and mosaic also grace the communion rail. Jewel-colored light streams through five German Baroque stained-glass windows, designed and produced in Munich, and a rose window in the west transept, which honors St. Vincent de Paul, founder of the Vincentian order in the 17th century. A 2,800-pipe organ installed in 1901 is still playing strong. ♦ 1010 W Webster Ave (at N Sheffield Ave). 327.1113

37 Children's Memorial Hospital

Established in 1892, this well-known hospital has a rooftop helipad for flying in patients from all over the country. The building was designed in 1961 by **Schmidt, Garden & Erickson**. ♦ 707 W Fullerton Ave (at N Orchard St). 880.4000

38 600 Block of West Fullerton Parkway

In the late 1800s, Fullerton Parkway was one of the most fashionable residential streets on the **North Side**. This tree-lined block is still among the prettiest in the city, with rows of three-story bay-fronted buildings of brick and stone. The block is anchored by **Lincoln Park Presbyterian Church**, a sturdy Romanesque structure designed by **Clinton J. Warren** in 1888. ♦ Between N Geneva Terr and N Orchard St

39 Neo

Despite its name, this club opened in 1980 and is now an elder of the city's dance club scene. Enter via an alleyway painted with bright geometric designs. Young urban professionals and die-hard clubsters dance to industrial and house music into the wee hours. The place doesn't get moving until midnight, at the earliest. ♦ Cover. Daily, 9PM-4AM; Sa, until 5AM. 2350 N Clark St (between W Belden Ave and W Fullerton Pkwy). 528.2622. www.neo-chicago.com

John Barleycorn
Memorial Pub Est. 1890

40 John Barleycorn Memorial Pub

$ In 1890 this sprawling neighborhood pub was built as a saloon. During Prohibition, it fronted as a Chinese laundry. Customers were

TERRIFIC TOURS

You can have a great time exploring Chicago on your own, but if you have special interests or limited time or want a little help getting acclimated, here are a few options:

The Chicago Architecture Foundation (224 S Michigan Ave, at E Jackson Blvd, 312/922.3432; John Hancock Center, 875 N Michigan Ave, between E Chestnut St and E Delaware Pl, 312/751.1380) offers more than 50 tours, providing a chance to visit and learn about different sections of the city. Guided by well-informed docents, some of the more popular tours include Loop Architecture Walking Tours and Frank Lloyd Wright in Oak Park. Inquire about special tours geared toward children. Tours are offered daily.

Art Encounter (927 Noyes St, between Noyes Ct and Ridge Ave, Evanston, 847/328.9222) offers two tours for art aficionados. One Saturday a month there's Gallery Walk—a walk through different art districts and art galleries conducted by local artists. On Wednesday afternoons the Expanded Visions tour provides an opportunity to visit artists' studios and collections in private homes. There are no tours during July and August.

The Chicago Historical Society (1601 N Clark St, at W North Blvd, 312/642.4600) offers periodic tours of Chicago churches. With its immense immigration from Ireland, Poland, Bavaria, and other predominantly Catholic areas—and the wealth generated around the turn of the 19th century—Chicago became home to an extraordinary number of magnificent church buildings. Though population shifts have caused hard times for many, the churches' windows and sculptures are still awe-inspiring. Call for tour schedules.

Chicago Horse and Carriage Ltd. (E Pearson St and N Michigan Ave, 312/94.HORSE) provides old-fashioned and romantic horse-drawn carriage rides through the **Magnificent Mile** and **River North** areas. Tours are offered year-round; call for departure times.

Chicago Motor Coach and London Motor Coach (750 S Clinton St, between W Polk and W Lexington Sts, 312/666.1000) provide double-decker buses with wacky tour guides to visit the usual tourist spots, from the **Hancock Building** to the **Field Museum**. Buses can be boarded at numerous places in the downtown area, and you can hop on and off as many times as you like for the price of one ticket. The buses run daily, year-round.

Chicago Supernatural Tours (708/499.0300) is a company for those who are interested in ghost stories and supernatural tales, offering day, night, and river tours of the Chicago area. Owner Richard Crowe even says that minor psychic occurrences have happened during the tours themselves. Call for information and departure points.

The Friends of the Chicago River (407 S Dearborn St, between W Congress Pkwy and W Van Buren St, 312/939.0490) is devoted to drawing interest to the often neglected river. The organization sponsors frequent walking tours and also provides maps for self-guided walks. Some of these river walks extend beyond the city into its environs. Call for tour schedules.

Graceland Cemetery (4001 N Clark St, at W Irving Park Rd, 773/525.1105) is the final resting place for any number of Chicago scions of industry and architecture, and few expenses were spared for their monuments. This elegantly landscaped cemetery is also home to **Louis Sullivan**'s **Getty Tomb**, representing the change in **Sullivan**'s style that in turn influenced a movement in modern American architecture. The **Chicago Architecture Foundation** offers guided walking tours of the cemetery each Sunday at 2PM between August and October; it also sells a book for self-guided tours. Cars are welcome to drive through the cemetery (no parking), and it is accessible by **CTA** bus 22 (**Clark**) or bus 80 (**Irving Park**).

Chicago from the Lake (River East Plaza, 435 E Illinois St at N McClure Ct, 312/527.2002) and *Chicago's First Lady* (Michigan Avenue Bridge, 312/358.1330) offer guided tours of the city's history and architecture from the lake and the river (the latter in conjunction with the **Chicago Architecture Foundation**). The 90-minute tours operate daily between April and November.

The Spirit of Chicago (Navy Pier, 700 E Grand Ave, at N Streeter Dr, 312/321.1241, 866/211.3804) lets you view Chicago from **Lake Michigan** while listening to Broadway show tunes performed by the waitstaff, dancing to live music, and indulging in a buffet. Cruises depart daily for brunch, lunch, and dinner. Sunset cocktail cruises and children's rates are available too.

Untouchable Tours (northwest corner of N Clark and W Ohio Sts, 773/881.1195) offers a two-hour bus tour of Prohibition-era gangster hangouts and hit spots, followed by an optional dinner-theater package. Tours are offered daily in summer, on weekends, and during some weekends in winter.

Restaurants/Clubs: Red | Hotels: Purple | Shops: Orange | Outdoors/Parks: Green | Sights/Culture: Blue

served by deliverymen who rolled in laundry carts loaded with bottles of bootleg liquor. The pub got its new name sometime in the 1960s. It serves 11 beers on tap and pretty good hamburgers, accompanied by classical music and a nonstop slide show of museum paintings and sculpture. Retire to the beer garden, weather permitting, or throw darts at the real bristle boards in the lounge. Weekday all-you-can-eat specials attract starving artists. ◆ American ◆ Daily, lunch and dinner to midnight. 658 W Belden Ave (at N Orchard St). 348.8899. Also at 3542 N Clark St (between W Eddy and W Addison Sts). 549.6000. www.johnbarleycorn.com

VICTORY GARDENS

41 VICTORY GARDENS THEATER

The company has presented nearly 200 productions since its founding in 1974, with an emphasis on the work of Chicago playwrights and world premieres. A number of productions, among them Beau Jeste by James Sherman, have gone on to popular acclaim in New York City. A Readers' Theater series features staged readings of new and not-yet-completed works. Recent popular productions have included Hello Dali, a folk-musical commentary on modern art, as well as Douglas Post's God and Country. The 195-seat main stage and a 60-seat studio, which is used for smaller productions, classes, auditions, and rehearsals, are on the first floor. In 2004, **Victory Gardens** acquired the historic **Biograph Theater** up the street, with plans to convert it to a live-performance space. ◆ Tu-Su. 2257 N Lincoln Ave (between N Geneva Terr and W Belden Ave). 871.3000. www.victorygardens.org

42 NATURAL SELECTION

Gifts of every variety are displayed in a tiny space redolent of scented candles and potpourri. Decorative ceramic items and jewelry are the specialty, with standouts such as Czechoslovakian glass earrings delicate in

The memorial service for celebrated newspaper columnist Mike Royko was held at Wrigley Field in 1998. At the service, eulogists recalled Royko's dry wit. One such example: Royko once gave books to all the researchers who had worked for him, inscribing each one: "You were the best. Don't tell the others."

design and color. ◆ M-Sa. 2260 N Lincoln Ave (between W Webster Ave and N Orchard St). 327.8886

42 POTBELLY SANDWICH WORKS

★$ The independent and far preferable alternative to Subway, this shop makes terrific submarine sandwiches and salads. Nothing fancy, but a good stop for a quick bite, especially if you're traveling solo. ◆ Café ◆ Daily, lunch and dinner. 2264 N Lincoln Ave (between W Webster and W Belden Aves). 528.1405. Also at 1442 W Webster Ave (between N Southport and N Greenview Aves). 755.1234; 190 N State St (at W Randolph St). 312/683.1234; and numerous other locations throughout the city. www.potbelly.com

43 STERCH'S

In the midst of the **Lincoln Avenue** rat race, this cozy neighborhood bar stands out for its simplicity. It's just a quiet place to meet a friend for a beer. ◆ Daily, until 2AM. 2238 N Lincoln Ave (between W Webster Ave and N Orchard St). 281.2653

44 ANN HALSTED HOUSE

Built in 1883, the oldest known residential commission of **Adler & Sullivan** was begun when the firm was still known as **D. Adler & Company**. The 27-year-old **Louis Sullivan** was integrating various influences—the Beaux Arts training he'd received in Paris (hence the façade's strict symmetry), the unusual Egyptoid ornamentation he'd seen in the Philadelphia office of architect **Frank Furness** (as in the rigid lotus flower in the gable pediment), and the picturesque use of materials that made the Queen Anne style so popular (as found on the elaborate chimneys). The house remains privately owned. ◆ 440 W Belden Ave (between N Clark St and N Cleveland Ave)

45 NONPAREIL

Look no further for that special gift: a full-size carved wood alligator head from Guatemala, ceramic coffee mugs decorated with Mexican Day of the Dead skulls, and purse-size plastic fez-capped Shriners, to name just a few of the choices at this eclectic shop. ◆ Daily. 2300 N Clark St (at W Belden Ave). 477.2933; fax 477.7849

46 PANACHE

Welcome to accessories heaven, a paradise of one-of-a-kind belts, earrings, necklaces, bracelets, scarves, and hair clips. The friendly sales staff is quick to assist. ◆ Daily. 2252 N Clark St (between W Grant Pl and W Belden Ave). 477.4537; fax 477.4538

47 TOWER RECORDS/ VIDEO/BOOKS

The famous West Hollywood record store opened its Chicago outlet in 1991. Boasting a huge inventory of CDs, tapes, and DVDs in every musical category, it also hosts signings by bands in town on tour. An attached video store with an impressive selection of rental tapes has challenged the local **Blockbuster** for neighborhood supremacy. The book section carries the latest in contemporary fiction, as well as music magazines from around the globe. Tower also serves as a **Hot Tix** counter for your discount theater tickets. ♦ Daily, until midnight. 2301 N Clark St (at W Belden Ave). 477.5994; fax 477.1915. Also at 214 S Wabash Ave (at E Jackson Blvd). 312/663.0660. www.towerrecords.com

48 AMBRIA

★★★★$$$$ Set in an elegant Art Nouveau dining room in the Belden-Stratford Building (formerly a luxury hotel), this restaurant's excellent French nouvelle cuisine places it among the city's top dining spots and makes it popular for business entertaining. Chef Gabino Sotelino's imaginative menu subtly blends East and West in such dishes as Japanese *mizuna* greens salad with warm, creamy, goat-cheese dressing. The dinner menu has wonderful seafood dishes, such as charcoal-grilled sea bass served on tomato *coulis* with sautéed thinly sliced potatoes. Desserts range from sorbets and unusual ice creams to the signature white chocolate mousse served with dark chocolate fudge. A five-course prix-fixe degustation dinner is available. ♦ French ♦ M-Sa, dinner. Jacket required. Reservations required. 2300 N Lincoln Park West (at W Belden Ave). 472.5959; fax 472.9077. www.leye.com

48 MON AMI GABI

★★$$ When Rich Melman and the folks at Lettuce Entertain You Enterprises (LEYE) aren't cutting deals with chefs and opening new restaurants with new concepts, they stay busy by changing the names of existing LEYE establishments. Case in point: **Un Grande Café**, a handsome, lively, and very early entry on the Chicago French bistro circuit, has been closed down and reopened as **Mon Ami Gabi**, a handsome, lively latecomer to the Chicago bistro circuit. It's the casual, less expensive sister of **Ambria** (see above) across the Belden-Stratford Building lobby. Service is friendly and excellent. Large windows afford a nice view across the street to **Lincoln Park** and the zoo, and there's an outdoor patio in front, which is a most pleasant spot during the nice weather. The satisfying entrées include steak frites (steak with french fries) and grilled chicken. Save room for some tasty desserts. ♦ Bistro ♦ Daily, dinner. Reservations recommended. 2300 N Lincoln Park West (at W Belden Ave). 348.8886. www.leye.com

49 CHARLIE'S ALE HOUSE

★$ The building, the stained-glass windows, and the massive mahogany bar date back to the 1930s. Owner Charlie Carlucci, one of the Carlucci restaurant clan, designed a room of old-fashioned wooden booths to match the bar. Pot roast dinners and other American mainstays anchor a small menu. The place is packed on weekends, doubly so when the beer garden is open. ♦ American ♦ M-F, dinner; Sa-Su, lunch and dinner; kitchen open until midnight. 1224 W Webster Ave (between N Racine and N Magnolia Aves). 871.1440

50 HAVANA GALLERY

This gallery features contemporary art by artists living in Cuba, including Pablo Perea, Sandra Dooley, and Eduardo Estrada. ♦ Th-Su. 1139 W Webster Ave (between N Clifton and N Racine Aves). 549.2492. www.havanagallery.com

50 SHEFFIELD HISTORIC DISTRICT

Less congested and more modest than the **Lincoln Park** neighborhood, the Sheffield district was built in the late 19th century as a working-class area. It now rivals its eastern neighbor in popularity and price. This is the archetypal gentrified neighborhood, where young couples and families have renovated decrepit housing and converted two or three flats into luxurious single-family homes. The Sheffield Neighborhood Association sponsors a garden walk every July, when residents show off their spectacular landscaping. Clifton Avenue, from Armitage to Webster Avenues, has the heaviest concentration of front gardens, which provide wonderful viewing all summer long. Architecturally, the area is full of small treasures that reward the careful viewer:

decorative brickwork, terra-cotta ornamentation, and carved stone lintels above doors and windows. ◆ Bounded by N Halsted St and N Racine Ave and W Armitage and W Belden Aves

50 KRIVOY

Owner Cynthia Hadesman gave the elegant boutique her grandmother's maiden name, which in Russian means "curve." Hadesman designs almost everything you see here, including sleek dresses and hand-painted silk scarves. There's an odd but interesting assortment of contemporary hats that incorporate antique Chinese tapestries. ◆ Daily. 1145 W Webster Ave (between N Clifton and N Racine Aves). 248.1466

50 MCSHANE'S EXCHANGE

Junk store junkie Denise McShane Caffrey was looking for a California-style upscale consignment shop in Chicago. When she couldn't find one to her liking, she opened her own. You'll find women's designer apparel at no more than one third of the original cost, including Ralph Lauren shirts and Maggie London silk dresses. ◆ Daily. 1141 W Webster Ave (between N Clifton and N Racine Aves). 525.0211. Also at 815 W Armitage Ave (between N Halsted and N Dayton Sts). 525.0282

51 KANGAROO CONNECTION

Owner Kathy Schubert, a frequent visitor Down Under, stocks her general store with items from Australia and New Zealand, including oilskin outback coats, Akubra hats, Aussie flags, Arnott's biscuits, boomerangs, kangaroo and koala aprons, and flyswatters in the shape of Australia. Stop by for a mail-order catalog. ◆ Tu-Sa. 1113 W Webster Ave (between N Seminary and N Clifton Aves). 248.5499. www.kangarooconnection.com

52 MCGEE'S TAVERN AND GRILL

$ On Friday and Saturday nights, the big bar inside and garden out back are hopping with yuppies. The fare emphasizes spilling-out-of-

In 1914 Chicago Police Chief Schuettler approved bloomer-style swimsuits for thin women but said they were "immoral, dangerous, and ridiculous on fat women." In 1916 a law was passed freeing women from the requirement to wear stockings under their bloomer bathing suits on Chicago beaches.

the-bun burgers and a variety of imported and domestic beers to wash them down. ◆ American ◆ Daily, until 2AM. 950 W Webster Ave (between N Bissell St and N Sheffield Ave). 549.8200

53 KELLY'S

$ This is the last of the neighborhood's old-fashioned taverns—dim, loaded with wood, and full of crazed spectators during TV broadcasts of **DePaul University** basketball games. Burgers, sandwiches, snacks, and salads are available throughout the day and late into the evening. On weekends, they dish up eggs, home fries, and other breakfast basics for the bleary-eyed. The bustling beer garden is just a train token's throw below the El tracks. ◆ American ◆ Daily, lunch and dinner. 949 W Webster Ave (between N Bissell St and N Sheffield Ave). 281.0656

54 2120–26 AND 2121–27 NORTH BISSELL STREET

Built in the 1880s, these private homes form the centerpiece of this symmetrical street, where three houses on each side share a cornice and pediment. Houses to the north and south are in pairs. Shallow rectangular bays create a continuous wall with a subtle rhythm. This street is typical of the Sheffield Historic District, although more cohesively designed than most. When the elevated train tracks were constructed in 1897, the neighborhood was already completely developed, so the houses on Bissell Street lost their backyards (and residents must have lost some of their hearing). ◆ Between W Dickens and W Webster Aves

55 ATHENIAN ROOM

*$ Families and college students line up early for dinner at this casual double storefront to partake of Greek-style chicken and skirt steak grilled up at reasonable prices. ◆ Daily. 807 W Webster Ave (at N Halsted St). 348.5155

55 GLASCOTT'S

Opened around the end of World War II, this Irish saloon boasts an ornately carved wooden bar from that era. Today it attracts mostly a yuppie crowd. Big windows offer views onto peaceful Webster Avenue and crowded North Halsted Street. ◆ Daily, until 2AM; Sa, until 3AM. 2158 N Halsted St (at W Webster Ave). 281.1205

55 SATURDAY'S CHILD

Interesting, durable toys from around the world are crammed into this shop. They're all chosen to actively engage a child's imagination. There are kits to build and erupt your own volcano, avant-garde doll clothes, and stained-glass-window coloring books, plus more traditional stuffed animals, puzzles, tops, and yo-yos. ♦ Daily. 2146 N Halsted St (between W Dickens and W Webster Aves). 525.8697

56 BACINO'S

$ They claim, here, to serve "America's first heart-healthy pizza," a stuffed spinach pizza that meets American Heart Association nutritional guidelines. But that's if you eat only one piece. Still, the pizzas are made with only natural ingredients. A no-reservations policy explains the long lines that form outside on weekends. ♦ Pizza ♦ Daily, lunch and dinner. 2204 N Lincoln Ave (at W Webster Ave). 472.7400, 472.8137. Also at 75 E. Wacker Dr (between N Wabash and N Michigan Ave). 312/263.2070

57 MID-NORTH DISTRICT

The sign at West Grant Place says that this area is significant for its concentration of 19th-century brick row houses. And it is. For a brief walking tour, head south and west to Hudson and Webster Avenues, walk south on Hudson to Dickens Avenue, then go west to Cleveland Avenue and walk north to Fullerton Parkway. You will see a wide range of building types, from early cottages that survived the 1871 fire to a stark Modernist dwelling, along with many beautiful renovations of late-19th-century architecture. ♦ Enter at W Grant Pl and N Clark St

Within the Mid-North District:

POLICEMAN BELLINGER'S COTTAGE

This 1869 house is one of the few wood structures to survive the Great Fire of 1871. Bellinger and his brother-in-law apparently kept the fire at bay by dousing individual sparks as they landed on the roof, rather than wasting precious water trying to keep the whole building wet. Coincidentally, it was designed by **W.W. Boyington**, the architect of the **Chicago Water Tower**, another famous survivor of the fire. The building, a private residence, is a typical Chicago cottage with a raised basement and high first floor. Charming details include decorative shingles, brackets, and a false front over the gable reminiscent of Wild West storefronts. ♦ 2121 N Hudson Ave (between W Dickens and W Webster Aves)

2100 BLOCK OF NORTH CLEVELAND AVENUE

An unfortunate example of what the *Old House Journal* calls "remuddling" is seen at **2125 North Cleveland Avenue.** The owners' desire to modernize their building (which probably seemed hopelessly outdated in the 1960s) resulted in a suburbanized façade that has no relationship to the original scale, forms, or materials. The two-story house at **No. 2147** (circa 1883) is sometimes attributed to a youthful **Louis Sullivan** because of the Egyptoid ornamentation and the unusual triangular bay. Alterations to the façade have made the composition awkward. A wonderful Art Deco façade gave **No. 2150** a face-lift early in the Depression. The spectacular two-story leaded-glass window is the highlight of a jazzy geometric composition. Irene Castle, of the dance team Vernon and Irene Castle, once lived here. These are all private residences.♦ Between W Dickens and W Webster Aves

2200 BLOCK OF NORTH CLEVELAND AVENUE

Some houses on this block were built in the last decade, whereas others have been here since the 1860s. None is more than four stories high, and the mix makes for a spectacular sight. The modernist fortress at **No. 2215** was the home of **Bruce Graham**, the retired **Skidmore, Owings & Merrill** partner who designed the **John Hancock Center** and **Sears Tower**, as well as this 1969 house. Working here on a considerably smaller scale, he created a very private residence of reinforced concrete with a black steel-bar gate. Italianate duplex town houses at **Nos. 2234–36** share an ornate cornice and columned porch. They were constructed around 1874, just before the fire zone (where wood construction was prohibited) was extended to this area. ♦ Between W Webster and W Belden Aves

2300 BLOCK OF NORTH CLEVELAND AVENUE

The blockiness and large scale of the freestanding residence at **456 West Belden Avenue** (circa 1890) set it apart from its neighbors. Although most architects advised the owner to tear it down and start over, he opted for renovation. The 1972 remodel by **Harry Weese & Associates** divided the basement into two apartments and left the top floors for the owner's home. Tour guides describe the house at **No. 2314** (circa 1880) as "riotously eclectic." The façade is a mixture of brick and stone, false-slate mansard, Gothic detailing, and a large gable with a finial and hooded dormer. The Georgian Revival porch was probably added later. The brick and sandstone residence at **No. 2325** (circa 1885) has an unusual corner rectangular bay in turret form. At **Nos. 2339** and **2343** stand two of the area's three wooden structures that predate the Great Fire of 1871 (**Policeman Bellinger's Cottage** is the other; see page 141). They probably escaped damage because the fire had almost died out by the time it got this far north. These are all private residences. ♦ Between W Belden Ave and W Fullerton Pkwy

58 Francis W. Parker School

Named for the 19th-century educator who successfully promoted the idea of schools to train teachers, **Parker** has long been known as Chicago's "progressive" private school, whereas the **Latin School of Chicago** is considered more traditional. Alumnus Abbott Pattison sculpted the figures of children at the main Clark Street entrance, which was designed by **Holabird & Root** in 1962. Parents of students include numerous Chicago celebs like the late Gene Siskel, who often volunteered for the school's extensive adult education classes. ♦ 330 W Webster Ave (between N Lincoln Park West and N Clark St). 549.0172

59 R.J. Grunts

$ The first of Chicago restaurateur Rich Melman's many hot spots is credited with introducing the salad bar to America. **Grunts** is an animated spot with checkered tablecloths and a menu covered with cartoon characters. Grub includes half-pound burgers. ♦ American ♦ Daily, lunch and dinner. 2056 N Lincoln Park West (at W Dickens Ave). 929.5363. www.leye.com

Bill Veeck, the maverick White Sox owner, actually got his baseball start working for the Cubs, where his father was general manager. In his teen years, Bill Jr. worked at Wrigley Field as a vendor and later helped plant the trademark ivy that still grows along the ballpark's outfield wall.

Tradition has it that after every Cubs game at Wrigley Field, a flag is flown atop the scoreboard. A white flag with a blue *W* indicates a win; a blue flag with a white *L* denotes a loss.

60 Vertel's

Many Chicago-area runners consider this *the* store for their sport, with its vast selection of shoes and gear and its well-versed staff. It's also big on racket sports and rents tennis rackets by the day. Meet fellow runners here for a fun run at 6:30PM Monday year-round. They'll also be glad to fill you in on race information by phone and will mail you entry forms. ♦ Daily. 2001 N Clybourn Ave (between N Racine and N Magnolia Aves). 248.7400, 248.7489

61 Big John's

★$ This homey tavern, with a stuffed moose that hangs above the fireplace, caters to quiet, sports-oriented folks. The kitchen serves burgers, bratwurst, sandwiches, and other bar fare. An ivy-covered wall frames the backyard beer garden, a calm, pleasant spot to sip a pint in the summer. ♦ American ♦ Daily, lunch and dinner until 11PM; bar open until 2AM. 1147 W Armitage Ave (between N Seminary and N Racine Aves). 477.4400

62 Dee's

★$$ If you have a craving for some good, basic Chinese food, owners Dee and Rocky Chang serve well-prepared renditions of familiar Mandarin and Szechuan fare, from moo shu pork to sweet-and-sour shrimp. Choose seating in the modern dining room, outdoor patio, or sunny gardenlike atrium. ♦ Chinese ♦ M, W-Su, dinner. Reservations recommended F and Sa. 1114 W Armitage Ave (between N Seminary and N Clifton Aves). 477.1500

63 Out of the West

Bright and airy as a Georgia O'Keeffe sky, this inviting boutique purveys all things Southwestern. Try on a pair of cowboy boots or admire the selection of sterling silver belt buckles and Native American jewelry, hand-carved fetishes, and colorful handwoven rugs. ♦ Daily. 1000 W Armitage Ave (at N Sheffield Ave). 404.9378

64 The Second Child

Among the ever-changing selection of upscale used children's clothing here, you may find fancy party shoes, velvet designer dresses,

Tony Lamas cowboy boots, or tiny mink coats for sizes between newborn and children's 14. Savings are generally about one-third below retail prices. They carry secondhand maternity clothes, cribs, and walkers too. ◆ Daily. 954 W Armitage Ave (between N Bissell St and N Sheffield Ave). 883.0880. www.2ndchild.com

65 ART EFFECT

This store carries contemporary women's clothing, often with a retro flair, and scads of wonderful jewelry by local and national designers. Robin Richman's hand-knit sweaters and Christopher Phelan's elegant sterling, copper, and glass jewelry are just a few of the wearable goodies. There also is a selection of artist-designed functional housewares, including welded steel end tables by Michael McClatchy and ceramics by Floyd Gomph. ◆ Daily. 934 W Armitage Ave (at N Bissel St). 929.3600. www.shoparteffect.com

66 ROTISSERIA METROPOLIS

★$ Spinning chicken is at the heart of affairs inside this neighborhood spot popular for its prices as well as its offerings. But the menu also has a good selection of sandwiches, thin-crust pizzas, soups, and salads. ◆ Daily, lunch and dinner. 924 W Armitage Ave (at N Bissel St). 868.9000

67 ACTIVE ENDEAVORS

Outfit yourself for such activities as camping, climbing, cycling, or running at this well-stocked sporting goods store. ◆ Daily. 935 W Armitage Ave (at N Bissell St). 281.8100. Also at 45 E Grand Ave (between N Wabash Ave and N Rush St). 312/822.0600. www.activeendeavors.com

68 OLD TOWN SCHOOL OF FOLK MUSIC CHILDREN'S CENTER

The venerated folk concert venue and music shop moved to new, larger quarters (4544 N Lincoln Ave), but the school maintains a presence here, providing programs for children. ◆ M-Sa. 909 W Armitage Ave (between N Fremont and N Bissell Sts). 525.7793. www.oldtownschool.org

69 CELESTE TURNER

This popular fashion boutique, staffed by friendly and knowledgeable salespeople, recently expanded to double-storefront size, to be able to carry a larger inventory and to provide a more pleasant shopping experience to its customers. A wide range of designer fashions and accessories for women supplied by an interesting assortment of New York and Los Angeles designers keeps the regulars coming

back for more. ◆ Daily. 859 W Armitage Ave (at N Fremont St). 549.3390; fax 549.3396. www.celesteturner.com

70 CHARLIE TROTTER'S

★★★★$$$$ Dubbed a "mecca of fine dining" by *Chicago* magazine, this chic restaurant in a renovated town house consistently garners rave reviews. Chef Trotter himself presides over the ever-evolving menu, which may include an appetizer of marrow-soft sea scallops stuffed with caviar; a full-flavored, but not too sweet, minted watermelon sorbet; and such entrées as sea bass fillets served with roasted garlic noodles, and smoked lobster subtly coated with apricot-infused olive oil. For a truly memorable evening, have the daily degustation or vegetable degustation, typically eight or nine small tasting courses, each of which is more wonderful than the last. Parties of two to four may reserve a table in the kitchen and dine while observing the staff at work, although the scene is really too noisy and bustling to be entirely enjoyable. ◆ International ◆ Tu-Sa, dinner. Jacket and tie required. Reservations required. 816 W Armitage Ave (between N Halsted and N Dayton Sts). 248.6228; fax 248.6228

the sole of chicago

70 LORI'S DESIGNER SHOES

Great women's shoes and accessories at great prices are the point here, not fancy displays. Lori Brian lines up designer shoes, boots, and bags in tidy rows and marks 10% to 50% off the regular retail prices. ◆ Daily. 824 W Armitage Ave (between N Halsted and N Dayton Sts). 281.5655. Also in Northfield and Highland Park. www.lorisshoes.com

71 BEDSIDE MANOR, LTD.

This little store is like a cozy bedroom filled with antique-style brass and iron beds, handmade Amish quilts, imported linens, and down comforters. They will ship anywhere in the US. ◆ Daily. 2056 N Halsted St (between W Armitage and W Dickens Aves). 404.2020

72 B. LEADER & SONS, INC.

Owner Mike Leader's grandfather started the business in 1909. Today it's the city's oldest family-owned jeweler. Glass cases mounted

---

on old-fashioned workbenches display rings, brooches, earrings, and necklaces hand-crafted in 14- and 18-karat gold and platinum inset with diamonds and precious stones. The shop sells diamonds at near wholesale prices. Don't miss the collection of vintage time-pieces from Grandpa's day. ♦ Tu-Sa. 2042 N Halsted St (between W Armitage and W Dickens Aves). 549.2224. www.leaderjewelers.com

73 Cafe Ba-Ba-Reeba!

★★$$$ Crowds of beautiful people sip Spanish wines and sherries while grazing their way through ever-changing varieties of tapas, such as marinated octopus, potato-and-egg tortillas, and *pisto manchego*, a Span-ish ratatouille. Entrées include a delicious seafood paella. The Iberian atmosphere carries through to the garden patio. ♦ Spanish ♦ M, Su, dinner; Tu-Sa, lunch and dinner. 2024 N Halsted St (between W Armitage and W Dickens Aves). 935.5000. www.leye.com

74 Lincoln Park Farmer's Market

On Saturday mornings in warm weather, this parking lot for Lincoln Park High School is quite the scene. Professionals in SUVs idle away their dollars jockeying for parking spaces, then idle away their time doing due diligence on 5-cent ears of corn. ♦ Sa, May–October. 700 W Armitage Ave (at N Orchard St)

75 Robinson's No. 1 Ribs

$$ Charlie Robinson's old family recipe took top honors in Chicago's 1982 First Annual Royko Ribfest, a half-goofy, half-serious competition that came into being when *Chicago Tribune* columnist Mike Royko (now deceased) and his neighbors started squabbling over who among them made the

The late Mayor Richard J. Daley, noted for his public malapropisms, said the following at a press confer-ence during the infamous 1968 Democratic National Convention in Chicago: "Gentlemen, get the thing straight, once and for all—the policeman isn't there to create disorder, the policeman is there to pre-serve disorder."

best barbecued ribs. This place barbecues ribs, chicken, hot links, pork, and beef to eat in or take out. ♦ Barbecue ♦ Tu-F, lunch and dinner; Sa, Su, dinner. 655 W Armitage Ave (between N Howe and N Orchard Sts). 312/337.1399; fax 337.1403

76 Geja's Cafe

★$$$ Fondue lives on at this romantic hideaway, with subdued lighting, intimate booths, and live flamenco and classical guitar music. Dinners include abundant portions of meat or seafood and fresh vegetables, ready to cook at your table. Save room for dessert, perhaps fruit and cake dipped in chocolate. One warning: The air here grows thick with the smells of Sterno and cigarette smoke. (There is a nonsmoking section, which is a little better.) ♦ Fondue ♦ Daily, dinner. 340 W Armitage Ave (between N Orleans and N Sedgwick Sts). 281.9101; fax 281.0849

77 Park West

First it was a concert hall, then a dance hall, then a concert hall again. Now it's both. Concerts have included performers from David Grisman to Yoko Ono to Asleep at the Wheel; the music ranges from reggae to rock to clas-sical. Sometimes dancing follows; other times dancing is the main event, with a band or recorded music. Flexible seating accommo-dates hundreds. ♦ Tickets or cover charge. Hours vary. 322 W Armitage Ave (between N Clark and N Orleans Sts). Box office and events schedule, 929.5959

78 Ranalli's on Lincoln

$ Although the pizza is just average in quality and above average in price, on summer evenings patrons fill the 75 or so outdoor tables while crowds gather on the sidewalk to wait for their names to be bellowed through a megaphone. If your wallet is full, this is a good place to relax and sample some unusual brews—the menu features more than a hundred brands of beer. ♦ Pizza ♦ Daily, lunch and dinner. 1925 N Lincoln Ave (between N Lincoln Park West and W Armitage Ave). 312/642.4700. Also at 24 W Elm St (between N State and N Dearborn Sts). 312/440.7000

79 Lincoln Park

The park's thousand acres of lakefront land sweep north of North Boulevard along Lake Michigan with broad, grassy meadows, mature shade trees, two lagoons, and paths that wind around and through it all. Chicago's parks are meant to be used, and this one certainly is:

running, bicycling, strolling, barbecuing, playing badminton—if it's fun, it's done. (See the "Lakeview/Wrigleyville" chapter for information about **Lincoln Park**'s northern sector.)

Within Lincoln Park:

CHICAGO HISTORICAL SOCIETY

Designed in 1932 by **Graham, Anderson, Probst & White,** this is the society's fourth location since its founding in 1857. One of its earlier homes went up in flames, and another now serves as the **Excalibur** nightclub in **River North.** Its current home, with the park as its backyard, was erected with much pride and fanfare. The original building is a Georgian Revival structure of redbrick with limestone. It's oriented to the east, with a columned portico and broad stairway stretching down to sloping lawns and a statue of Abraham Lincoln by Augustus Saint-Gaudens. The 1972 annex, designed by **Alfred Shaw,** shifted the entrance to Clark Street and allowed the museum to expand, but to many it resembled a mausoleum. In 1988 a second addition, designed by **Holabird & Root,** concealed the first in a modern wrapping of brick and limestone accented with white-painted steel. The inviting entrance incorporates large areas of gridded glass that visually open the museum to the street. Among the museum's numerous holdings are one of the nation's largest 19th-century women's costume collections, extensive artifacts from the Civil War and the Chicago Fire, and Chicago architectural records and drawings. A historical library is available to the public and is frequently used by students and scholars. The museum hosts special programs throughout the year, including tours of many city neighborhoods. One new program of special note that soon will be available to the public is a fascinating audio program featuring the remarkable recordings of more than a quarter century of radio interviews on WFMT by Studs Terkel, the legendary oral historian and Pulitzer Prize–winning author. In 2005, the museum is embarking on an ambitious redesign and renovation that will, among other things, reposition its displays. Pardon their dust. ♦ Admission; free Monday. Daily. 1601 N Clark St (at W North Blvd). 312/642.4600; fax 312/266.2077. www.chicagohs.org

Within the Chicago Historical Society:

BIG SHOULDERS CAFÉ

★$ A sunny, pleasant, two-story café is dominated by **Daniel Burnham**'s impressive terra-cotta arch, which originally served as the main entrance to the Union Stock Yard National Bank. The café serves refreshing salads and sandwiches, luscious soups, vegetarian dishes, and irresistible desserts such as warm brownies topped with ice cream, then drizzled with caramel sauce and sprinkled with toasted coconut. ♦ American ♦ M-Sa, lunch; Su, breakfast and brunch. 312/587.7766

GIFT SHOP

Yes, Chicago souvenirs are available here, but better still are the beautifully illustrated books on local history, architecture, and culture. There's a large section on Chicago's ethnic groups, and another on Abraham Lincoln and the Civil War. ♦ Daily. 312/642.4600

COUCH MAUSOLEUM

Opened in 1868, **Lincoln Park** sits on land that was once a cemetery. Mass exhumations relocated almost all the remains to private cemeteries. The Couch family, however, won a lawsuit against the city to keep the tomb of Ira Couch exactly where it was—which is now in a clump of trees behind the **Chicago Historical Society**. Couch was a tailor who later owned the **Tremont House Hotel** at its original location downtown. (It's now in the **Michigan Avenue** area.) One other grave remains in the park, near the **Farm-in-the-Zoo.** Dating from 1852, it marks the remains of David

Chicago Historical Society

Restaurants/Clubs: Red | Hotels: Purple | Shops: Orange | Outdoors/Parks: Green | Sights/Culture: Blue

CELLULOID HEROES

Chicago is a deservedly popular location for movie production. Flicks filmed or set in the city include:

Adventures in Babysitting (1988): Elizabeth Shue plays a babysitter who takes her two charges to downtown Chicago, where various mishaps ensue.

All the Rage (1999): Steppenwolf Theatre Company member Joan Allen joins another local talent, Andre Braugher, a story about handguns moving through people's lives.

The Babe (1992): John Goodman plays Babe Ruth in a sentimental biography of the Yankee slugger.

Backdraft (1991): Robert De Niro and Kurt Russell star in Ron Howard's story about two firefighting brothers at odds with each other. You can count on spectacular fire scenes in this flick.

Barbershop (2002): A day in the life of a South Side barbershop with Ice Cube and Cedric the Entertainer.

Barbershop 2: Back in Business (2004): Another day, same barbershop.

Blink (1993): Madeline Stowe plays a blind woman caught up in a murder investigation.

Blues Brothers (1980): John Belushi and Dan Ackroyd star in the comedy classic with a famous police chase scene on Lower Wacker Drive.

The Breakfast Club (1985): Judd Nelson, Molly Ringwald, and Ally Sheedy star in this teen movie about five students sitting out a school detention, coining the name the Brat Pack in the process.

Child's Play (1989) and *Child's Play II* (1991): Chucky, the murderous doll, comes to life in this sometimes tongue-in-cheek horror thriller and its sequel.

Dennis the Menace (1993): The comic strip character's adventures, starring Nick Castle and Walter Matthau.

Eight Men Out (1988): Director John Sayles retells the story of baseball's most corrupt incident, when the 1919 Chicago **White Sox** accepted bribes and threw the World Series. Watch for legendary Chicagoan Studs Terkel.

Flatliners (1990): Medical students Kiefer Sutherland, Julia Roberts, Kevin Bacon, and William Baldwin experiment with life after death.

The Fugitive (1993): Harrison Ford stars as Dr. Richard Kimble in this runaway hit based on the television series. Best Chicago moment—the St. Patrick's Day Parade.

Groundhog Day (1992): Bill Murray and Andie McDowell relive the day over and over and over again.

Henry: Portrait of a Serial Killer (1986): Before *Wild Things*, John McNaughton's disturbing story of the life of a Texas mass murderer, with Michael Rooker and Tracy Arnold.

High Fidelity (2000): Hometown favorite John Cusack gets support from sister Joan in a comedy about a record store owner who is charting his top five breakups.

Home Alone (1991) and *Home Alone 2* (1992): Macaulay Culkin fends off two bumbling burglars after his parents accidentally leave him behind.

Kennison, a participant in the Boston Tea Party who lived to be 115.

NORTH AVENUE BEACH

Unlike the Gold Coast's trendy Oak Street Beach, the sands of North Avenue are everyone's. Fit or fat, hip or hopelessly outdated, well heeled or waiting to win the lottery—all are welcome. The beach curls out into Lake Michigan just above North Boulevard and stretches a long, lazy mile north. From May to September, volleyball nets sprout like mushrooms—bring your own gear or reserve a court at the beach house (it's actually a ship onshore), which contains changing rooms, rest rooms, and a small concession stand. There's also a restaurant where you can eat rather well, by beach standards. By car, exit Lake Shore Drive at LaSalle Drive. Look for parking in the lot just south of the beach, or head west and check for spaces along the streets through **Lincoln**

22 January 1930 marked Chicago's coldest day on record—32 degrees below zero. The hottest day was 117 degrees, on 14 July 1954.

Just Visiting (2001): Christina Applegate time-travels from 12th-century France to the 21st century, stopping at the **Field Museum**.

Mad Dog and Glory (1992): Robert De Niro, Uma Thurman, and Bill Murray star in another John McNaughton crime story.

Malcolm X (1992): Spike Lee's retelling of the life of the Black Muslim leader, who spent his early years in and around the Chicago area.

North by Northwest (1959): Alfred Hitchcock's suspense masterpiece may be best remembered for its Mount Rushmore conclusion, but many of the interior shots were filmed in the **Omni Ambassador East.**

Only the Lonely (1991): Cop John Candy's Irish mother, played by Maureen O'Hara, resists his romance with Italian girlfriend Ally Sheedy.

The Package (1990): Gene Hackman plays an army sergeant rooked into a Russian–American conspiracy plot.

Primal Fear (1996): A tale of corruption in the Catholic Church and Chicago politics, starring Richard Gere as an arrogant attorney who defends an altar boy accused of murdering the archbishop.

Pushing Tin (1999): Homegrown star John Cusack and Billy Bob Thornton compete for screen space in a flight of fancy involving two cocky air traffic controllers.

Risky Business (1984): Shy teenager Tom Cruise lets loose when his parents leave him home alone.

Road to Perdition (2002): Sam Mendes directs Tom Hanks and Paul Newman in this adaptation of Max Allan Collins's dark-themed graphic novel.

Sixteen Candles (1984): Molly Ringwald turns 16 in John Hughes's comic coming-of-age story.

Sleepless in Seattle (1992): Long-distance romance between Baltimore resident Meg Ryan and Chicago transplant Tom Hanks reaches its high point in New York City.

Surviving Christmas (2004): Ben Affleck is a lonely millionaire who pays a family, headed by James Gandolfini, to let him spend Christmas with them.

Uncle Buck (1990): In this John Hughes comedy, actor John Candy's character is left to take care of his brother's kids for a few days.

The Untouchables (1987): Brian DePalma and David Mamet teamed up to bring the popular TV series to the big screen, with help from Kevin Costner, Sean Connery, and Robert De Niro. The banquet (or baseball bat) scene was filmed in the **Blackstone Hotel.**

When Harry Met Sally (1990): Meg Ryan and Billy Crystal play friends who could never, ever be lovers—or could they? They begin their journey to New York from the **University of Chicago** campus in **Hyde Park.**

While You Were Sleeping (1994): **CTA** token clerk Sandra Bullock poses as the fiancée of one brother while falling in love with the other.

Park. You can also bus or cab it to North Avenue, then take the pedestrian bridge over Lake Shore Drive.

SOUTH POND

Don't just stand on the shoreline looking at the water—get onto it! Paddleboats are for rent from the boathouse near **Café Brauer** (see page 148) by the hour May through October. In winter, however, heed the signs: Stay off the ice.

LincolnPark Zoo

LINCOLN PARK ZOO

A gift of two swans from New York's Central Park to Chicago in 1868 gave rise to a booming population of more than 2,000 of these graceful birds a century later. As for other zoo highlights, head for the **Great Ape**

Restaurants/Clubs: Red | Hotels: Purple | Shops: Orange | Outdoors/Parks: Green | Sights/Culture: Blue

House, where primate families cavort only a thick pane of glass away from your face. Then escape the world in the **Rookery**, a serene habitat filled with winged creatures cavorting amid ponds and waterfalls. And on a hot day, there's nothing as refreshing—or mesmerizing—as watching the sea lions make waves in their little blue pond. The zoo adds a touch of the wild to the city: On warm summer nights, high-rise neighbors can hear the wolves howling. ♦ Free. Daily. 2200 N Cannon Dr (south of W Fullerton Dr). 312/742.2000. www.lpz.com

Within Lincoln Park Zoo:

FARM-IN-THE-ZOO

The sign over the cattle barn used to read "Beef Animals" until somebody realized that it wasn't a respectful way to refer to Bossy. Cows, horses, sheep, pigs, and other creatures some city dwellers have never before seen in the flesh reside in a 5-acre replica of a Midwestern farm. Goat milking, butter churning, and meet-the-animals pet fests are scheduled throughout the day. ♦ 312/935.6700

CAFÉ BRAUER

A superb example of Prairie School architecture, this two-story building overlooking the South Pond was built in 1908 by **Dwight H. Perkins** of **Burnham & Root** as the **Lincoln Park Refectory**. Chicago businesspeople frequented the café for lunch in the early part of the 20th century, when a complete meal cost 65 cents. Over the years, however, business declined, largely as a result of a state law prohibiting the sale of liquor in public parks. In 1941 the café closed and sat neglected for 50 years until the Chicago Park District, the Lincoln Park Zoological Society, the Levy Organization, and a group of architects and historians teamed up to restore it to its original state. The building is now on the National Register of Historic Places. Partners in the restoration were **Harry J. Hunderman** of **Wiss, Janney, Elstner Associates**; **Meisel & Associates**; and **Lawrence B. Berkeley & Associates**.

Fastidious attention was paid to detail: The company that manufactured the original French pan roof tiles was contracted to produce replacements, which required the reinvention of a glaze to match the originals. The walls were peeled down to the original salt-glazed bricks. Designs for new light fixtures were based on old lighting found during renovations. The second-floor Great Hall, which is rented out for gala events, boasts polished hardwood floors, decorative stained glass, Rookwood-style tile murals, a dramatic skylight, and stained-glass and bronze chandeliers. On the first floor is a cafeteria decorated with handsome tile, oak paneling, and brass rails. Unfortunately, the food—hot dogs, hamburgers, little pizzas—isn't

up to the setting. ♦ Daily; until 3PM, Nov-Mar. 2021 N Stockton Dr (between LaSalle and W Fullerton Drs). 312/281.2565

LINCOLN PARK CONSERVATORY

Three acres of greenhouses built here in 1891 provide a lush home to plant life from all corners of the earth. In the dead of winter, you can walk into a warm tropical garden of banana palms and spider plants. Four seasonal flower shows, including Christmas poinsettias and Easter lilies, draw busloads of rapt observers. A stately garden of some 20,000 flowers, most started from seed in the greenhouses, is planted each spring in the promenade out front. The fountain sculpture *Storks at Play*, by Augustus Saint-Gaudens and Frederick MacMonnies, serves as the outdoor backdrop to a million wish-you-were-here snapshots. ♦ Free. Daily. N Stockton Dr (just south of W Fullerton Dr). 312/742.7736. www.chicagoparkdistrict.com

THE NOTEBAERT NATURE MUSEUM

Named for a donor who provided $5 million of the total $31.2 million construction cost, this is the new location for the Chicago Academy of Sciences. Opened in the autumn of 1999, this eye-catching building was designed by **Ralph Johnson** of **Perkins & Will**. Composed of a set of interconnected pavilions topped by dramatically sloping roofs, the structure does not rise above tree line, and it reflects the sandy beaches along the lakeshore to the east. Inside, the lobby is a towering space, with limestone walls and floor giving the building a comfortable feeling closer to an old lodge than to a traditional formal museum. The interior of the building is spacious and airy, with hands-on exhibits designed by New York firm **Lee H. Skolnick**. This is a most welcome contrast to its predecessor, a dusty, old-fashioned objects-in-boxes museum first opened in 1893. The major attraction of the museum is the *Butterfly Haven*, a two-story-high, 4,000-square-foot glass-enclosed exhibit in which thousands of butterflies and moths are displayed against the backdrop of Chicago's skyline. In the *City Science* exhibit, visitors walk through a two-story "home," which shows how the elements of nature are used by human beings to live—it includes a wall that lights up to reveal a shadow of a mouse running through the walls. The building's location, though pleasant, unfortunately adds to the traffic congestion nightmare along Fullerton Avenue during the summertime. ♦ Daily. 2430 N Cannon Drive (at W Fullerton Ave). www.chias.org

ROCKS AT FULLERTON DRIVE

These immense stone steps that lead to the lake are a veritable outdoor theater on summer weekends. The beautiful people walk their beautiful dogs; cool dudes swerve on in-line skates, balancing blaring boom boxes on their shoulders; and teenagers in love stroll arm in arm dressed in matching skin-tight studded black-leather swimsuits. ♦ Fullerton Dr (just east of N Lake Shore Dr)

THEATRE ON THE LAKE

At this community theater owned and managed by the Chicago Park District, amateur actors strut their stuff in a summer series that has them belting out tunes from *The Music Man, Evita,* and other Broadway hits. A show at the screened-in theater can be fun when the weather is right; otherwise, the absence of air-conditioning makes it stifling. The low ticket prices help compensate. ♦ Box office: Tu-F, 3-9PM; Sa, 4-9PM. Shows: Tu-Sa, 8PM. Reservations recommended. N Lake Shore Dr (just north of Fullerton Dr). 312/742.7771

NORTH POND

Tool around in a paddleboat (the boathouse is on the northeast side of the pond). Practice angling (bring your own pole—there are no rentals here) at the south end in the casting pond, or just rest on a grassy hill and enjoy the great view of the city to the south.

NORTH POND CAFÉ

★★ $$ The view of the park is lovely from this charming restaurant located in the field house at the north edge of **North Pond.** Drawing inspiration from both the Arts and Crafts movement and the Prairie School, the décor features lots of oak and an intimate atmosphere. Chef Bruce Sherman has picked up right where Mary Ellen Diaz left off, using locally grown ingredients to craft imaginative regional dishes for an ever-changing menu. The Wisconsin butternut squash soup is a true taste treat. Herbed lamb and sheep's milk cheese with lavender honey is also top-notch. ♦ American ♦ Tu-Sa, dinner; Su, brunch and dinner. Reservations recommended. 2610 N Cannon Dr (between W Fullerton Dr and W Diversey Pkwy). 477.5845. www.northpondrestaurant.com

80 THE HIDEOUT

★ This bar really is hidden away, bringing back memories of the Weed Street district before it became so self-consciously aimed at tourists. If you can find it, you'll find a nice place to relax and have a beer—and also to hear live music peformed by the likes of Sally Timms, Robbie Fulks, and Jon Langford and lesser-knowns such as Susanna & the Hollywoods and Miss Mia & Ratso. The owners of this place always

seem willing to open up their doors for a bene-fit event. ♦ Daily. Sometimes a cover. 1354 W Wabansia Ave (at N Throop St). 227.4433. www.hideoutchicago.com

81 KARYN'S FRESH CORNER

Not just a health-food market and restaurant, it's a lifestyle. A wide range of healthy delica-cies are available for takeout, or you can dine in and order from a changing vegan menu. If you're alone, there's no need to bring some-thing to read. There are about a thousand fly-ers describing programs and events that involve aromatherapys, colon cleansing, spiri-tual retreats, and exercise programs to put your mind and body into a state of constant perfection. ♦ Daily, breakfast, lunch, and din-ner. 1901 N Halsted (at W Wisconsin Ave). 312/255.1590. www.karynraw.com

82 VINCI

★★$$ This casual, attractive storefront restau-rant is owned by chef Paul LoDuca, who also operates **Adobo Grill**. A gluten-free menu is available on request. The changing specialties here are homemade pastas and fish, including a seafood mixed grill. Some say their Portobello mushrooms are the best in the city. ♦ Italian ♦ Daily, dinner; Su, brunch. 1732 N Halsted St (between W North Ave and W Willow St). 312/266.1199. www.vincichicago.com

83 TRATTORIA GIANNI

★★$$$ Chef Giovanni De Lisi serves regional Italian cuisine in a cramped little dining room with crisp linens and black-and-white photos of Italy. The menu is small but ever-changing. An excellent possibility is *saltimbocca sorrentino,* veal topped with mozzarella and prosciutto. The tiramisù is out of this world. ♦ Italian ♦ Tu-Sa, dinner; Su, lunch and dinner. 1711 N Halsted St (between W Concord Pl and W Willow St). 312/266.1976. www.trattoriagianni.com

Steppenwolf

84 STEPPENWOLF THEATRE

Founded in a church basement in 1976, this company has gone on to present more than 100 productions and win national renown—for itself as well as for a number of its actors. (Then-unknown founding members included actor-director Gary Sinise and actors John Malkovich and Laurie Metcalf.) They have been honored with numerous Jefferson Awards for Chicago Theater Excellence. Since 1982, many of the company's productions have gone on to New York, including *True West, Balm in Gilead, Orphans,* and *The Grapes of Wrath;* the latter received several Tony Awards as well as the Outer Critics Circle Award for Outstanding Broadway Play. This state-of-the-art theater complex, containing a 500-seat main stage and a 200-seat studio, opened in the spring of 1991. In 2000, Steppenwolf opened The Garage, a 60-seat space for smaller productions; one of the early ones was *House of Lily,* by Lydia Stryk. Recent main stage productions of note have included Terry Johnson's *Lost Land and The Bluest Eye,* an adaptation of a Toni Morrison novel. ♦ 1650 N Halsted St (between W North Ave and W Willow St). Box office, 335.1650. www.steppenwolf.org

85 ROYAL-GEORGE THEATRE CENTRE

Two theaters, a cabaret, a restaurant, a piano lounge, and a wine cellar make up this entertainment complex. A number of Chicago companies rent the theaters to stage their performances. The auditorium, with balcony and box seating, seats 457 and tends to offer mainstream productions. A 60-seat gallery theater hosts experimental shows. Recent popular productions have included *Verbatim Verboten,* a dark, hilarious interpretation of scripts of actual conversations not intended to be overheard. ♦ 1641 N Halsted St (between W Concord Pl and W Willow St). Box office, 312/988.9000

86 BLUEBIRD LOUNGE

Located on a bleak block of the Clybourn Corridor, this dark booth-lined bar attracts a mellow, artsy crowd. The kitschy 1950s lamps and objets d'art give the lounge a *Blue Velvet–*meets–*Leave It to Beaver* feel. The bartenders play CDs of artists ranging from Jimi Hendrix to the Meat Puppets. Several imported beers are available on tap. ♦ Daily. 1637 N Clybourn Ave (between N Dayton St and N Sheffield Ave). 312/642.3449

87 CRATE & BARREL OUTLET STORE

The same cool kitchenware and home accessories available at the store's other locations are here, but at amazing discounts because they're either out of season or mail-order returns. A regular **Crate & Barrel** is one block west. ♦ Daily. 800 W North Ave (at N Halsted St). 312/787.4775. www.crateandbarrel.com

88 TRANSITIONS BOOKPLACE

Budding New Age philosophers will find plenty here to excite their interest. At this store, the shelves are stocked with books on more than 250 topics, from addiction to crystals to Zen. The shop also hosts special events that often feature appearances by well-known authors such as Deepak Chopra, Whitney Streiber, and Richard Bach. There is also a café on the premises that serves light fare. ♦ Daily, until 9PM. 1000 W North Ave (at N Sheffield Ave). 312/951.READ. www.transitionsbookplace.com

89 NORTH BEACH

Sand volleyball courts inside a bar? Yes, Virginia, it's a viable club concept in Chicago. In fact it was so popular that the owners have added four bowling lanes and a miniature golf course. At night, this place is a club for adults who never grew up; on weekends during the daytime, it's a place for kids, with opportunities to reserve it for birthday parties. ♦ M-F, 4:30PM-2AM; Sa, Su, from 9AM. 1551 N Sheffield Ave (between W Weed St and W North Ave). 312/266.7842. www.northbeachclub.com

90 CROBAR

At this huge alternative dance club, leather-clad bikers rub epaulets with the silk-covered shoulders of aspiring models. Bondage-à-go-go dancers perform their provocative routines atop platforms that soar over the sprawling wooden dance floor, while the elite mingle upstairs in the velvet-tufted booths of the **Fellini Room**. A windowed skydeck overlooking the dance floor provides respite for those with throbbing eardrums. There's live music Thursday; DJs spin dance tracks Friday and Saturday; on Sunday the G.L.E.E. (Gays, Lesbians—Everyone's Equal) Club convenes for dancing into the wee hours. Dress code: no running shoes, T-shirts, or hats. ♦ Cover. W-Su, until 4AM. 1543 N Kingsbury St (at W Weed St). 312/266.1900. www.crobar.com

90 ZENTRA

According to its owners, this is a "transglobal nightclub." We think that means there's a fusion of Western and Eastern themes. And certainly, confusion reigns in this 10,000-square-foot, four-room club. There's a set of swings, a copper island bar, roomy booths, and vividly painted "hookah girls" offering hits from hookah pipes, water pipes with fruit-flavored tobacco. ◆ Cover. W-Sa, 10PM-4AM. 923 W Weed St (at N Kingsbury St). 312/787.0400 ぜ www.zentranightclub.com

91 TRACKSIDE

This offtrack betting parlor features Southern-style décor and a remarkably clean and cheery ambiance, a far cry from the smoke-filled OTBs of yesteryear. The spacious facility features races from local (**Maywood Park**, **Balmoral Park**, **Sportsman's Park**, **Hawthorne**, and **Arlington**) and national racetracks. Burgers, barbecue, and sandwiches are served at the bar and in the restaurant. ◆ Daily, 10AM-11PM. 901 W Weed St (at N Fremont St). 312/787.9600. www.tracksideotb.com

91 CIRCUS

Adding to locals' perception of this neighborhood as a tourist and dance club ghetto, the gimmick at this club is tightrope walkers, fireeaters, and men on stilts. The overhead sign dangling from a 10-foot clown puppet reads "Good luck getting a drink!" Which means that the joke just might be on you. ◆ Club. ◆ Cover. Tu-Sa, 10PM-4AM. 901 W Weed St (at

N Fremont St). 312/266.1200. www.circus-nightclub.com

92 NEW CITY YMCA

The **North Side's** most modern **Y** swarms with young professionals who sign up as fast as they can say, "Good-bye, price-gouging health clubs!" The running tracks, pool, exercise classes, weight rooms, and more are open to out-of-town Y members for free, and to other visitors for a nominal daily fee. ◆ M-F, 5:30AM-10:30PM; Sa, Su, 7AM-6PM. 1515 N Halsted St (between W Evergreen and N Clybourn Aves). 312/440.7272. www.ymcachgo.org

Illinois has 13 nuclear power plants and ranks first in the US in number of nuclear power plants and capacity to create nuclear energy.

Chicago's Century of Progress World's Fair opened in 1933, in the midst of the Great Depression. Fair organizers hoped that the emphasis on jobs through technology would give fairgoers a sense of optimism during that bleak time.

Restaurants/Clubs: Red | **Hotels: Purple** | **Shops: Orange** | **Outdoors/Parks: Green** | **Sights/Culture: Blue**

151

BUCKTOWN/WICKER PARK

What is now Chicago's hottest new neighborhood used to be one of its scruffiest. In the 1950s, **Bucktown** was known primarily as the setting for Nelson Algren's novels about tough guys and losers and those who fell through the cracks of respectable society. Even the name reflects its humble history: At the turn of the 19th century, so

DEPAUL

Holstein Park

BUCKTOWN

Wicker Park

Clemente Park

RIVER WEST

Eckhart Park

UKRAINIAN VILLAGE

W Wrightwood Ave.
W Fullerton Ave.
W Belden Ave.
W Lyndale St.
W Webster Ave.
W Shakespeare Ave.
W Charleston St.
W Dickens Ave.
W Armitage Ave.
W Homer St.
W Cortland St.
W Cortland St.
W Churchill St.
W Bloomingdale Ave.
W Bloomingdale Ave.
W Wabansia Ave.
W Caton St.
W North Ave.
W Pierce Ave.
W Le Moyne St.
W Le Moyne St.
W Schiller St.
W Hirsch St.
W Evergreen Ave.
W Blackhawk St.
W Ellen St.
W Division St.
W Haddon Ave.
W Thomas St.
W Augusta Blvd.
W Chicago Ave.

N Western Ave.
N Elston Ave.
N Damen Ave.
N Clybourn Ave.
N Hoyne Ave.
N Oakley Ave.
N Milwaukee Ave.
N Wilmot Ave.
N Winnebago Ave.
N Winchester Ave.
N Wolcott Ave.
N Honore St.
N Hermitage Ave.
N Paulina St.
N Wood St.
North Branch Chicago River
N Southport Ave.
N Racine Ave.
John F. Kennedy Expwy.
W Cortland St.
N Campbell Ave.
N Western Ave.
N Oakley Blvd.
N Leavitt St.
N Hoyne Ave.
N Damen Ave.
N Winchester Ave.
N Wolcott Ave.
N Wood St.
N Paulina St.
N Ashland Ave.
N Noble St.
N Elston Ave.
N Honore St.

62
90
94

km
mi
1/8
1/4
1/4
1/2

many immigrant families kept goats in their front yards that the neighborhood was nicknamed Bucktown. The name hasn't changed, but almost everything else has. Over the last 20 years, this area bordered by the **John F. Kennedy Expressway** and **Western, Chicago,** and **Fullerton Avenues** has transformed itself into a hip, artsy bohemia.

In the late 1800s, many of Chicago's solid German middle-class citizens moved into the area around Wicker Park, near the intersection of **North** and **Damen Avenues.** As they rose in fortune and social status, prominent neighborhood residents (like retailer W.A. Wieboldt, O.W. Potter, the president of Illinois Steel, and the Uihlein family of the Schlitz brewery) built mansions in Italianate, Second Empire, and Queen Anne styles along Damen, **Hoyne,** and **Pierce Avenues** and **Oakley Boulevard.** The architecture in the area reflects the wide variety of housing built in Chicago between the Great Fire of 1871 and the turn of the 19th century: from the small, wooden structures built by newly arrived immigrants to the stately homes erected by second and third generations of prosperous burghers. By 1905, factories moved in, and the neighborhood underwent another significant change, as many stately homes became boarding houses for immigrant Polish workers. Soon, the three-way intersection of **Milwaukee Avenue, Ashland Avenue,** and **Division Street** formed the beginning of Chicago's "Polish Downtown." Through the years, as Chicago's Polish population grew to become the largest in the US, these businesses worked their way up Milwaukee Avenue (see the "Additional Highlights" chapter).

In the 1980s, the yuppies—daunted by sky-high real-estate prices in neighborhoods like **Lincoln Park/DePaul**—headed west across the Kennedy Expressway, bringing gentrification in their wake. Today most of the old mansions of **Wicker Park** have been restored to their former elegance, and the population is a culturally diverse hodgepodge of older people who've lived here for decades, young business commuters, struggling artists, and entrepreneurs. Trendy boutiques abut old-fashioned bakeries, cool coffeehouses collide with auto parts stores, and new art galleries, jazz and rock clubs, and restaurants and cafés seem to open (and close) every month. To the casual observer, many parts of the area still seem rough around the edges, but to the in-crowd, this is the place to be.

All area codes in this chapter are 773 unless otherwise noted.

---

1 CAFE BOLERO

$ Run by a husband-and-wife team, this restaurant combines the owners' different ethnic backgrounds (he's Cuban, she's Serbian), producing an eclectic menu that offers Cuban sandwiches of grilled pork and cheese with fried plantains, and homemade grilled sausage with feta cheese and peppers. Whatever you order, expect hearty portions and cheap prices. ♦ International ♦ Daily, lunch and dinner. 2252 N Western Ave (at W Belden Ave). 227.9000

2 ST. HEDWIG'S

Originally built to serve the Polish community in the area, this Roman Catholic church was the last building designed by German architect **Adolphus Druiding.** The cornerstone was laid in 1899 and the church was completed in 1901 at a cost of $160,000. At that time, there were 4,000 registered parishioners, with 800 children enrolled in the school. Today the small congregation consists of Polish and Spanish immigrant families and a growing number of young professionals who have moved into the

---

Restaurants/Clubs: Red | Hotels: Purple | Shops: Orange | Outdoors/Parks: Green | Sights/Culture: Blue

THE BEST

Judy Markey

Syndicated Columnist, *Chicago Sun-Times*;
Talk Show Host, WGN Radio

Best hotel lobbies for late-afternoon drinks—the **Four Seasons** and **Inter-Continental**, both located on Michigan Avenue. The first one is drop-dead gorgeous; the second has bunches of free food and a lovely yesteryear feeling.

Best lunch place when spring is almost here and you have to be at the lake—**Rocky's Fish Shack**, slightly south of **Navy Pier**.

Best ladies' room in the city—the **Drake Hotel**. Makes you feel as if you belong to a country club. Posh, private, relaxing.

Best secret windswept place for winter kissing—the dock for **Wendella** boat rides during the off-season. Located down the stairs from the **Wrigley Building**. Desolate, great view, romantic, but I have first dibs.

Most real mix-it-up place with fabulous Greek lamb chops and no shortage of Damon Runyon types—**Miller's Pub**, on **Wabash Avenue**, right next to the **Palmer House**.

A good hidden, romantic restaurant that's jammed for lunch but not for dinner—**Trattoria No. 10** on **North Dearborn Street**. Great lighting for women over 40; fabulous food; not an annoying people-watching sideshow spot.

Best crab cakes, Caesar salad, and seafood in general—**Blue Crab Lounge** at **Shaw's Crab House**, on **Hubbard**. It never misses.

neighborhood since the 1990s. ◆ 2226 N Hoyne Ave (between W Webster Ave and W Lyndale St). 486.1660; fax 486.1684

3 JEAN ALAN

The designers at this home furnishings boutique give stylish new life to vintage furniture. A pink Murano glass lamp with a trumpet-shaped base has been topped with a gorgeous new lampshade of silk flowers. A voluptuous mohair sofa on cabriole legs has been reupholstered in a grayish purple fabric, then accented with chartreuse cushions. The selection of hand-crafted pillows is excellent and fun. ◆ Tu-Su. 2134 N Damen Ave (at W Shakespeare Ave). 278.2345; fax 278.2389

3 BIG CAT PRESS

It's been 20 years since young artist-bartender Tony Fitzpatrick, unable to get anyone in the Chicago art establishment to look at his unconventional drawings on slate, went door to door at galleries in Greenwich Village until he found someone to hang his work. That was the first of dozens of openings around the world, including a recent exhibit at the Museum of Contemporary Art. Fitzpatrick has come to be regarded as Chicago's modern-day Renaissance man, garnering acclaim as a poet and actor, as well as attention for causes such

as abolishing the death penalty. But his primary role is as an artist, and Fitzpatrick has carved out a niche producing remarkably detailed etchings on a wide range of themes. The aim of **Big Cat Press,** the storefront studio that he opened here in 1995, is "to bring strange new visual language to a 500-year-old medium." In addition to Fiztpatrick's work, **Big Cat** produces etchings by Teresa S. Mucha and a pair of artists better known for their other creative pursuits: actor and humorist Martin Mull and musician Jon Langford, founding member of the Mekons and the Waco Brothers. Visitors are encouraged to stop by and buy or to see a demonstration of the etching process. ◆ M-F. 2124 N Damen Ave (between W Charleston St and W Shakespeare Ave). 342.5381. www.tonyfitzpatrick.com

3 MERITAGE CAFE AND WINE BAR

★★★$$$ A variety of more than 20 boutique West Coast wines by the glass is only the first of the pleasant surprises at this designer storefront with blond wood and shiny, metallic décor. Another is that there is dining on the pleasant, enclosed veranda year-round. Most striking, though, is the sumptuous Pacific Northwest–inspired menu from chef Jonathan Harootunian. The adventurous might try the daily wild game special; another interesting choice is pan-roasted scallops with marinated black beans, asparagus, orange-saffron oil, and sweet-potato purée. It's no surprise that

Chicago magazine named this place one of the best new restaurants. ♦ Eclectic American ♦ Daily, dinner. 2118 N Damen Ave (at W Charleston St). 235.6434; fax 235.6434

4 G BOUTIQUE

If sex is the subject on your mind, **G** is a good place to be. Opened late 2002, the bright storefront carries a wide and curious range of accessories, from sexy clothing to naughty novelties. ♦ 2131 N Damen Ave (between W Dickens and W Webster Aves). 235.1234. www.boutiqueg.com

4 VIVE LA FEMME

Without the fanfare of Marina Rinaldi, this charming boutique operated by Stephanie Francis Sack sets out to prove that when it comes to designer fashions for plus-size women, style goes beyond size. If you thought you had to be supermodel-thin to look dazzling, this shop will make you think again. ♦ M-Sa. 2115 N Damen Ave (between W Dickens and W Webster Aves). 772.7429. www.vivelafemme.com

5 ROBIN RICHMAN

Beautiful hand-knit sweaters are just the beginning of what this talented women's fashion designer has to offer. In addition to carrying a stunning collection of clothing and accessories in this cozy storefront, Richman is something of a neighborhood pioneer. Hers was one of the first boutiques to open in the area and one of the few that has been able to withstand the test of time and vicissitudes of trendiness. ♦ M-Sa. 2108 N Damen Ave (between W Dickens Ave and W Charleston St). 278.6150

6 SAFFRON

Bucktown boutiques tend to open and close at the drop of a designer hat, but this charming shop has been going strong for more than 5 years. Offering an imaginative array of ready-to-wear and custom-made clothing, **Saffron** also carries an interesting selection of accessories and gifts. ♦ Tu-Su. 2064 N Damen Ave (between W Armitage and W Dickens Aves). 486.7753. www.saffronchicago.com

6 THE RED BALLOON

If you're looking for an alternative to the big chains to buy stuff for your little ones, this busy storefront is a good one. It carries a smart selection of gifts, books, toys, and clothing for kids from infants through pre-schoolers. ♦ M-Sa. 2060 N Damen Ave (between W Armitage and W Dickens Aves).

489.9800; fax 489.9801. www.theredballoon.com

7 LE BOUCHON

★★★$$ A dozen tables in a single room decorated with French travel posters and a pressed-tin ceiling make up this intimate, stylish, authentically French restaurant. Sophisticated diners come here to try the simple yet exquisite cooking of chef Jean-Claude Poilevey and the attentive ministrations of his wife, Susanne, who serves as hostess and manager. Anything-but-typical entrées include steak with shallots and sautéed rabbit, hunter's style. ♦ French ♦ M-Sa, dinner. Reservations recommended. 1958 N Damen Ave (between W Homer St and W Armitage Ave). 862.6600. www.lebouchonofchicago.com

7 GLORY

★★$$ Sharon Cohen, former culinary manager of **Eli's**, brings hearty New England fare to the belly of the Heartland. The food is the thing here. It's good and there's plenty of it. Yankee pot roast with lobster mashed potatoes is guaranteed to stick to your ribs. On the lighter side, try cheddar baked eggs. If you're never had a "cabinet" (Rhode Island milk shake), you're in for a sweet treat. If you've got any room to spare, you can top it all off with—what else—Boston cream pie. And on your way out, pick up some maple syrup to take home. ♦ American ♦ M-W, lunch and dinner; Th-Su, breakfast, lunch, and dinner. 1952 N Damen Ave (between W Homer St and W Armitage Ave). 235.7400

8 ST. MARY OF THE ANGELS

Dedicated in 1920 after almost nine years of construction and a cost of $400,000, this Catholic church is modeled after St. Peter's Basilica in Rome. The massive structure, which was designed by architect **Henry J. Schlacks**, takes up an entire city block. It was scheduled to shut down in the early 1990s but concerned parishioners protested and raised enough money to keep it open. ♦ 1825 N Wood St (between W Bloomingdale Ave and W Cortland St). 278.2644

9 CAFFE DE LUCA

★$ At first glance, it looks like just another coffee bar, but this casual café is a great place to relax and nibble on muffins, and many people do. Shelves inside the door are stacked with brochures and flyers on upcoming events and things to do in the neighborhood. If you're exploring the Bucktown/Wicker Park area, this is as good a place as you'll find to take a break or plan

Restaurants/Clubs: Red | Hotels: Purple | Shops: Orange | Outdoors/Parks: Green | Sights/Culture: Blue

your expedition. ◆ Daily. 1721 N Damen Ave (between W Wabansia Ave and W Churchill St). 342.6000. www.cafedeluca.com

9 Cans

A pool table, backgammon boards, and a laserdisc jukebox are some of the props for this hot spot, quirkily decorated with a mix of exposed brick walls, 1950s living-room furniture, 1920s wall sconces, and a molded plywood bar that serves coffee drinks, beer on tap, and numerous champagnes and single-malt scotches to an artsy, young clientele. ◆ Daily, 8AM-2AM. 1640 N Damen Ave (between W Concord Pl and W Wabansia Ave). 278.7176

10 Pagoda Red

In this 8,000-square-foot loft, you'll find unusual 18th- and 19th-century Chinese furniture and artifacts, handwoven Tibetan carpets, carved stone posts, vintage silk clothing, and other Asian treasures. ◆ Tu-Sa. 1714 N Damen (at W Wabansia Ave). 235.1188; fax 235.5858. www.pagodared.com

11 Club Lucky

★$$ One of the most popular hangouts in Bucktown is a Deco-style restaurant outfitted with Formica-topped tables and bar and ceiling fixtures that are exact replicas of the original fixtures in the Empire State Building. The menu features plentiful portions of real Italian home cooking. Try *pasta e fagioli* (macaroni-and-bean soup) or rigatoni with veal meatballs. It's a popular place for lunch, when hearty and huge sandwiches cost only about $5 each. ◆ Italian ◆ M-F, lunch and dinner; Sa, Su, dinner. 1824 W Wabansia Ave (at N Honore St). 227.2300. www.clublucky.com

12 Ole A. Thorp House

Built in 1891 by Ole Thorp, who was the proprietor of an import–export business and a real-estate developer as well, this privately owned mansion is a good example of the Romanesque architecture popular in this neighborhood at the turn of the 19th century. Distinctive features include a rounded-corner turret, an expansive front gable, and a façade of rusticated gray stone. ◆ 2156 W Caton St (at N Leavitt St)

13 Red Hen Bread

★$ This bright storefront bakery serves up some tasty sweets and treats (including tradi-

New heights: In 1955, the Prudential Building was the city's tallest, at 601 feet. As of 2005, there are four buildings over 1,000 feet.

tional Italian pizza), but its reputation is built on bread. Some people, including the restaurateurs whom it supplies, think it's the best in Chicago, but they'd get an argument from fans of **D'Amato's** (1124 W Grand Ave, at N May St). ◆ Daily. 1623 N Milwaukee Ave (between W North Ave and W Caton St). 342.6823. Also at 500 W Diversey Pkwy (at N Pine Grove St). 248.6025

14 Latino Chicago Theater Company/The Firehouse

Operating out of this old firehouse since 1987, the company promotes theater with Latino themes by Latino playwrights. Works are performed in English. ◆ 1625 N Damen Ave (between W North and W Wabansia Aves). 486.5120

15 Feast

★ ★ ★ $$ A feast is what you're in for at this funky spot featuring the dazzling creations of owner Debbie Sharpe, caterer to such visiting celebs as Madonna and the Rolling Stones. Sharpe's creations—a mouthwatering blend of flavors from around the world—are best expressed in dishes such as artichoke gnocchi in butter-sage sauce, braised lamb shanks served over cannellini beans with red-wine reduction, and black-bean–and–jalapeño ravioli in *poblano* cream sauce, sprinkled with roasted corn. A nice wine selection, good desserts, and reasonable prices for food of such quality make this one sweet spot. ◆ International ◆ Daily, lunch and dinner; Sa, Su, brunch. 1616 N Damen Ave (beween W North Ave and W Wabansia Ave). 772.7100. www.feastrestaurant.com

16 Cafe Absinthe

★★$$$ Don't be deceived by the looks of this place: The scruffy alley entrance leads to one of Chicago's most elegant and hippest restaurants. The kitchen prepares only a short menu, with dishes rotated regularly. Typical appetizers might include wild-boar salad and grilled octopus, with entrées such as quail with polenta and grilled venison loin. Upstairs is a small dance club called **Red Dog**, which has developed a reputation as one of the hippest places to see or be seen. Step out to house music until you catch Saturday-night fever. ◆ International ◆ Daily, lunch and dinner. Reservations recommended. 1954 W North Ave (between N Winchester and N Damen Aves). 278.4488

17 IGGY'S

★$ More than just a restaurant, Iggy's is a hip hangout for people in the know. Industrial metal and neon lighting accent the red and black interior. A better-than-it-needs-to-be menu features fried calamari, artichoke heart fritters, and lemon-butter bowtie pasta. But **Iggy's** is more than just a place to eat and drink. There's a Sunday-night cult or horror movie, a Sunday brunch with a build-your-own Bloody Mary, sometimes a strolling mariachi band. In the summer, there are two outdoor dining options— a sidewalk café and a rooftop garden with a nice view of downtown. ♦ American/bar ♦ M-F, dinner; Sa-Su, lunch and dinner. 1840 W North Ave (at N Honore St). 773-227-IGGY

18 HANS D. RUNGE HOUSE

Covered with intricately wrought lathe and scrollwork, this privately owned house was constructed in 1884 by the president of the Wolf Brothers Wood Milling Company. It is, however, best known as the **Paderewski House**, because of a concert given on the wide porch by the famous Polish pianist and statesman in 1930. Between World Wars I and II the house served as the Polish consulate. ♦ 2138 W Pierce Ave (between N Hoyne Ave and N Leavitt St)

19 SPRING

★ ★ ★$$$ On the site of a former Russian bathhouse, **Spring** has been remodeled with rock gardens to achieve a sense of Zen-like satisfaction that fuses harmoniously with the mostly seafood creations of chef Shawn McClain. The service is attentive, which is essential, because you'll need a translator to explain some of the offerings. For example, the seasonal oysters come topped with ponzu (citrus soy sauce), and the roasted wild sea bass and wild mushrooms are served on a succotash of edamame (green soy beans). It all translates to a refreshing dining experience. Even if you're not up for surfing selections such as braised baby monkfish with roasted eggplant in smoked tomato bouillon, there's plenty of good turf to stake out, like Korean-spiced beef tenderloin with short-rib pot stickers. For a concluding sweet treat, try the coconut mochi brûlée with warm pineapple. ♦ Contemporary ♦ Tu-Su, dinner. Reservations recommended. 2039 W North Ave (between N Damen and N Hoyne Aves) 395.7100 & www.springrestaurant.net

20 FLATIRON BUILDING

Designed in 1929 by **Holabird & Root**, today this old office building houses about 25

different art galleries and artists' studios. ♦ Tu-Sa, noon-5PM or by appointment. 1569-79 N Milwaukee Ave (at W North Ave). 278.7677

Within the Flatiron Building:

TRE VIA

★★$$ This sleek ristorante has been drawing crowds since it opened in 2004. Separate dining rooms on different levels intersected by a long bar make one wonder why it wasn't called Due Via. Chef Matt Carlson cut his chops at **Blackbird**, so you know you'll be getting something good. While the menu doesn't contain any surprises, everything is executed well. There are fine sendups of traditional dishes such as spaghetti carbonara and nice treatments of entrées such as veal skirt steak. The pizzas make for good openers. ♦ Dinner, Tu-Su. 227.7990. www.treviachicago.com

OCCULT BOOKSTORE

This offbeat bookstore originally opened in 1915 and has moved several times since. But wherever it goes, its customers follow for books on magic, astrology, ancient Egyptian religion, psychic development, and other phenomena, as well as candles, incense, and oils. Get your palm or tarot cards read by the in-store practitioner or arrange to have your astrology chart done. ♦ Daily, noon-6PM. 1579 N Milwaukee Ave, Third floor. 292.0995. www.occultbookstore.com

20 FILTER

★★$ In a cool triangular corner space with great views of the street, this bohemian café offers a comfortable challenge to the Starbucks across the street. Smokers and nonsmokers relax at tables and old couches, nibbling scones and sipping coffee, working on their laptops or reading newspapers, whiling away the hours. The menu features tasty breakfast fare and a great selection of sandwiches. If you're looking to spend a day exploring Wicker Park, **Filter** is a great starting-off point. ♦ Daily, breakfast, lunch, and dinner. 1585 N Milwaukee Ave (at North Ave). 227.4850 &

21 DOUBLE DOOR

This rock club features a range of acts, from local bands to major alt-country and rock. Watch for the occasional surprise appearance by the Rolling Stones. ♦ Cover. Daily, until 2 AM. 1572 N Milwaukee Ave (between W North Ave and N Honore St). 489.3160. www.doubledoor.com

Restaurants/Clubs: Red | **Hotels: Purple** | **Shops: Orange** | **Outdoors/Parks: Green** | **Sights/Culture: Blue**

157

21 MYOPIC BOOKS

With three floors of used books to browse, this shop is a bookworm's delight. The staff is friendly and knowledgeable. Pour yourself a cup of coffee and relax at one of the tables on the second floor. The store hosts readings and experimental-music performances during the evenings on a regular basis and is open late. ◆ M-Sa, 11AM-1AM; Su, until 10PM. 1564 N Milwaukee Ave (between N Honore St and N Damen Ave). 862.4882. www.myopicbooks.com

22 HERMANN WEINHARDT HOUSE

In 1888 this mansion was built for Hermann Weinhardt, a Wicker Park politician and furniture company president. Still privately owned, the structure has a mixture of traditional Victorian and Bavarian styles. Reminiscent of a mountain chalet, the house abounds with decorative elements of gingerbread and pressed metal bargeboard. ◆ 2135 W Pierce Ave (between N Hoyne Ave and N Leavitt St)

23 ADOLPH BORGMEIER HOUSE

Built in 1890 by the treasurer of the Johnson Chair Company, this privately owned home is a good example of Romanesque architecture. The façade is brick with polished granite columns and features elaborately carved stone and terra-cotta details. ◆ 1521 N Hoyne Ave (between W Le Moyne St and W Pierce Ave)

24 MOD

★★$$$ Just as the notion of mod went out of style with the *Man from U.N.C.L.E.*, one wonders if this superhip retro eatery will expire before the fourth adventure of Austin Powers. In the meantime, the multicolored boxy décor will serve as a pleasant if trendy backdrop to some very good eating. Chef Kelly Courtney prepares traditional American dishes accented with upscale herbs and spices and relying on organic ingredients. The menu changes as frequently as costumes at a Cher concert, because it is designed to utilize seasonal ingredients. ◆ American contemporary ◆ Daily, dinner. Reservations recommended. 1520 N Damen Ave (between W Le Moyne St and W Pierce Ave). 252.1500. www.modrestaurant.net

25 THYME CAFÉ

★★$$ Following up on the success of his River West restaurant, **Thyme**, chef-owner John Bubala found the time (and place) to open a sister operation in a 120-year-old building. The notion is to evoke a Parisian café. Exposed brick, pine floors, and counter seating give the storefront space a casual feel. The menu is simple French/American. You can't go wrong with the steak frites, and there are delicious crepes for dessert. ◆ Contemporary ◆ Daily, dinner. 1540 N Milwaukee Ave (between Honore St and N Damen Ave). 227.1400 ᕒ www.thymechicago.com

26 EARWAX CAFÉ

★$ Old circus banners line the walls of this neighborhood hangout, which serves hearty breakfast burritos and an assortment of vegetarian dishes, teas, and coffees. ◆ Vegetarian ◆ Daily, lunch and dinner. 1561 N Milwaukee Ave (between W North Ave and N Honore St). 772.4019

27 NICK'S

The young, hip crowd that frequents this place drinks and shoots pool until the wee hours of the morning. ◆ Daily, 4PM-4AM. 1516 N Milwaukee Ave (at N Honore St). 252.1155

28 BONGO ROOM

★$ This is a pleasant café where early birds listen to opera, sip cappuccino, and nibble on muffins or tasty egg dishes before heading off to work. Later, those without such regular lifestyles move in and occupy the space. ◆ Café ◆ Daily, breakfast and lunch. 1470 N Milwaukee Ave (between W Evergreen and W Wolcott Aves). 489.0690

29 ORANGE SKIN

Looking for supercool items to decorate your living space? **Orange Skin** has a few notions to offer. From ashtrays to bookcases to high-tech objects with no readily apparent function, this storefront shop carries an intriguing collection of home furnishings and unique gifts. ◆ 1429 N Milwaukee Ave (between N Wood and N Honore Sts). 394.4500; fax 394.4588. www.orangeskin.com

30 LOUIS AND LENA HANSEN HOUSE

This privately owned house is situated on one of the few remaining large lots that were once de rigueur for the ornate mansions that lined this stretch of Hoyne Avenue. Built in 1879, the redbrick-and-stone building is an excellent example of Italianate design; of particular note are the elaborately decorated door frames, window lintels, and woodwork. ◆ 1417 N Hoyne Ave (between W Schiller and W Le Moyne Sts)

31 HARRIS COHEN HOUSE

Built in 1890 for a clothing company executive, this Romanesque mansion is distinguished by its tall, conical roof and ornate detailing that is more typical of Italianate and Second Empire designs. Framing a huge stone porch, the façade features polished granite columns and elaborate stone carvings. This is still a private residence. ◆ 1941 W Schiller St (between W Evergreen and N Damen Aves)

32 MIRAI SUSHI

★★★$$ If one restaurant epitomizes the comeback of sushi, it is this sleek two-story restaurant and lounge, with a façade made almost entirely of glass. The stretch of Division Street that it overlooks has not yet caught up to the gentrification of other blocks, but odds are that it soon will. The upper-level lounge has a futuristic atmosphere, enhanced by the presence of a DJ spinning vinyl. You can dine graciously on the lower level or take advantage of the late-night sushi bar upstairs. A satisfying selection of maki rolls includes shiitake mushrooms, spicy tuna, and yellowtail-scallion. For dessert, how about tempura banana with wasabi ice cream? ◆ Sushi ◆ Daily, dinner, late dinner. 2020 W Division St (between N Damen and N Hoyne Aves). 862.8500

33 RAINBO CLUB

An authentic neighborhood bar that was a hangout for writers Nelson Algren and Simone de Beauvoir, it's now the domain of neighborhood regulars. ◆ M-F, Su, 4PM-2AM; Sa, 4PM-3AM. 1150 N Damen Ave (between W Haddon Ave and W Division St). 489.5999

34 PHYLLIS' MUSICAL INN

This club opened years ago as a Polish-American bar with polka music and dancing. Today the music is contemporary—jazz, blues, progressive rock—and the crowd young and energetic. There's live music of one sort or another every night. ◆ Cover. Daily, 2PM-2AM. 1800 W Division St (at N Wood St). 486.9862

34 THE SMOKE DADDY

★★$ The concept here is rhythm & barbecue. The ribs are as tasty as any you'll find in the city. Or maybe it just seems that way because you're eating them while some legendary blues musician such as Mark Naftalin or Smokey Smothers is tickling the ivories or picking the strings. If you're looking for an evening that combines good honest eating with authentic blues listening, you'd be hard pressed to find a better spot. ◆ Daily, dinner, late dinner. Cover for music. 1804 W Division St (between N Wood and N Honore Sts). 772.MOJO. www.thesmokedaddy.com

35 LEO'S LUNCHROOM

★$ This grungy, tiny diner looks as if it hasn't changed since the 1930s, but it offers some of the best and cheapest food in the area, making it popular with impoverished artists. Everything is tasty and the portions are generous. ◆ American ◆ Tu-Su, breakfast, lunch, and dinner. 1809 W Division St (between N Wood and N Honore Sts). 276.6509

36 LEONA'S

★$ A link in a popular family-run pizza chain, this restaurant provides a homey atmosphere along with hearty Italian meals, and thin-crust, deep-dish, or stuffed pizzas with a choice of 26 toppings. ◆ Italian ◆ Daily, lunch and dinner. 1936 W Augusta Blvd (between N Winchester and N Damen Aves). 292.4300; fax 292.4391. www.leonas.com

37 POLISH MUSEUM OF AMERICA

Nicolaus Copernicus, Marie Curie, Lech Walesa, and Pope John Paul II are among the notables of Polish descent honored at this museum. Pianist and statesman Ignacy Paderewski rates an entire room. The complete Polish-culture exhibition from the 1939 World's Fair was moved here from New York City. ◆ Donation requested. Daily, 11AM-4PM. 984 N Milwaukee Ave (at W Augusta Blvd). 384.3352; fax 278.4595. www.pma.prcua.org

38 GREEN ZEBRA

★★★$$ Can a primarily vegetarian restaurant survive in the city of big shoulders? It can when the chef-owner is Shawn McClain. Since it opened in 2004, this cozy room that seats 40 has been packed practically every night. The small-plate offerings are imaginative vegetable dishes with Asian accents. Don't miss the avocado panna cotta layered with tomato gelee and topped with crème fraîche foam. For folks who don't believe in veggie-only dinners, there are a few poultry and fish items. Desserts include ginger baba cake with banana sorbet. ◆ Tu-Su, dinner. Reservations recommended. 1460 W Chicago Ave (at N Greenview Ave). 312.243.7100

39 WEST TOWN TAVERN

★★$$ As the settlement of Wicker Park extends into the West Town/Ukrainian Village neighborhood, new restaurants are popping up to meet the demand. This is a reasonably priced exposed-brick storefront that serves up such eclectic comfort foods as brown sugar–cured pork chop with roasted garlic mascarpone cheese grits and herbed succotash. ◆ M-Sa, dinner. 1329 W Chicago Ave (at N Throop St). 312.666.6175. www.westtowntavern.com

LAKEVIEW/WRIGLEYVILLE

In Lakeview there's something going on every day of the week. Within the 3-square-mile neighborhood, bordered by **Lake Michigan, Ashland Avenue, Diversey Parkway,** and **Irving Park Road,** you can sail, sunbathe, bike, or run at **Belmont Harbor**; dance the night away at one of the many dance clubs along **Belmont** and **Sheffield Avenues**; admire old mansions on **Hawthorne Place**; view historic gravestones at **Graceland Cemetery**; catch a play by the **Live Bait Theater** or another nearby company; congregate at **Roscoc's** café; browse for antiques and vintage clothing at one of a dozen offbeat shops along **Halsted Street**; enjoy a cocktail while you wash your clothes at **Saga's Launder-Bar and Cafe**; catch a classic flick at the **Music Box**; chow down on Japanese sashimi, Ethiopian stews, French crepes, Spanish tapas, and other ethnic eats on **Clark Street**; or root for the **Cubs** at **Wrigley Field**.

Lakeview began as a peaceful settlement where farmers grew celery and greenhouse flowers. Between the 1830s and 1850s, while Chicago proper was becoming citified, immigrants from Germany and Luxembourg, attracted by the high ground and fertile fields, began moving to Lakeview. By 1854 the rapidly growing community boasted its own overnight inn, **Lakeview House,** which enjoyed a panoramic view of the lake from the corner of what is now **Grace Street.** In 1857 Lakeview was incorporated as a township, and plans were made to improve access to Chicago's northernmost boundary, less than a mile south at **Fullerton Avenue.** Residents pitched in to finance the paving-over of mud flats with **Lakeview Plank Road.** Today **Broadway** follows the road's original route.

Wealthy Chicagoans saw an opportunity to build spacious homes and apartment buildings along the lakefront. Meanwhile working-class immigrants continued to settle farther inland where factories proliferated. Tool-and-die plants prospered using workers who had brought their skills from Western Europe, and a brickmaking industry supplied

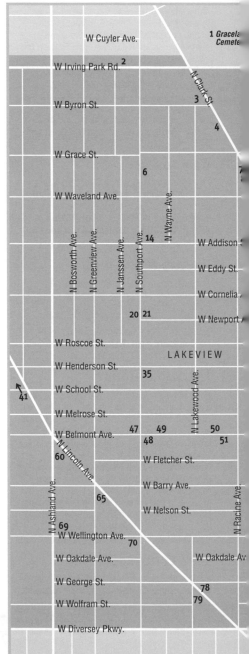

most of the city's bricks during the 1870s and 1880s. Row after row of affordable balloon-frame houses was built for workers. Next came German saloons and beer gardens, among them Schlitz Brewing Company taverns, where the specialty was the company's beer. Many of the houses and saloons from that era still stand, as do some of the original opulent gray stone dwellings near the lake. In 1889 Lakeview was annexed to the city of Chicago.

During the 1920s the expanding population sparked an apartment-house building boom, especially along **Lake Shore Drive**, where elegant structures rose to take

advantage of the view. Since the 1950s, steel-and-glass high-rises have joined these gracious elders. In the 1970s an influx of baby boomers in search of affordable housing led to construction of new buildings and the much-needed renovation of thousands of sturdy but dilapidated Victorian homes. Restoration continues to work its way westward, particularly in the vicinity of **Wrigley Field**, an area that real-estate agents dubbed Wrigleyville. Today a diverse population of nearly a half-million people resides in Lakeview, including single young professionals, working-class families, affluent retirees, and the city's largest gay population.

All area codes in this chapter are 773 unless otherwise noted.

1 GRACELAND CEMETERY

Chicago's 19th-century movers and shakers, as well as famous architects **Louis Sullivan, Daniel Burnham, John Wellborn Root**, and **Ludwig Mies van der Rohe**, are buried here. Established in 1860, this is Chicago's most significant burial ground, architecturally and otherwise. Landscape architect H.W.S. Cleveland created early designs for the cemetery, with paths and plots sodded to produce a uniform surface. Park designer and landscape architect Ossian Simonds, consulting designer for **Lincoln Park**, created a naturalistic landscape of native plants. The cemetery's buildings were all designed by **Holabird & Roche**. In death, as in life, waterfront property has cachet. Look for some of Chicago's most prominent names at lakeside. **Bertha** and **Potter Palmer** lie here in a tomb suggestive of a Greek temple. **Marshall Field** is nearby, beneath the stone memorial *Memory* by sculptor Daniel Chester French. One of the more interesting monuments is that of **George Pullman**, inventor of the Pullman sleeping car and founder of the company town of **Pullman** on the city's **South Side**. A tall Corinthian column marks his grave. But beneath that, Pullman's coffin is sunk in a room-size concrete block, the top overlaid with railroad ties and more concrete, precautions taken by Pullman's family to protect the body from railroad workers angry over the bitter Pullman strike of 1894. Next to the **Pinkerton** family's plot are plots for the original Pinkerton employees. **Kate Warn**, the first female detective, is buried here. The most famous monument architecturally is the **Carrie Eliza Getty Tomb**, built in 1890. The delicately carved blocks of gray Bedford limestone and the bronze gates are some of architect Louis Sullivan's finest decorative work. Sullivan, who died in poverty, lies not far away under a simple marker designed by his former employee George Grant Elmslie. ◆ Daily. 4001 N Clark St (at W Irving Park Rd)

2 GONE TO POT

Potter Marcy Glick works in a dusty studio in the back of her store, in which she features her own handmade colored inlaid clay as well as a changing gallery of works by about 60 other craftspeople. The selection may include blown glass, masks, weavings, watercolors, wood carvings, candlesticks, and clothing (even hand-painted bicycle shorts). Ask her to show you around the studio; she might craft a piece while you watch. The newly opened "seconds outlet" offers handmade crafts by more than 100 artists. ◆ Tu-F, noon-6PM; Sa, 11AM-5PM. 1432 W Irving Park Rd (between N Southport and N Greenview Aves). 472.2274

3 LIVE BAIT THEATER

The theater is the home of the **Live Bait Theatrical Company**, founded in 1987 by actor, artist, and playwright Sharon Evans and her husband, playwright John Ragir. The company produces work by emerging Chicago playwrights and solo artists. Over 16 years, **Live Bait** has launched more than 115 original productions. ◆ 3914 N Clark St (between W Byron St and W Irving Park Rd). 871.1212. www.livebaittheater.org

4 NORTH ALTA VISTA TERRACE

Forty row houses built in various styles between 1900 and 1904 line this blocklong street, developed by S.E. Gross. The detailed façades of these private residences, many in Georgian or Classic Revival style, are more reminiscent of London or Edinburgh than of the surrounding Chicago streets. The architect is unknown. ◆ Between W Grace and W Byron Sts

On 25 May 1981, "Spider" Dan Goodwin scaled the Sears Tower while hundreds of astonished spectators looked on. Later the same year, when Goodman attempted to climb the John Hancock Center, Chicago firefighters doused him with water, forcing him to turn back.

5 "NUTS ON CLARK"

This 30,000-square-foot warehouse is chock-full of bags, boxes, and barrels of chocolates, licorice, party mints, dried fruit, cognac cordials, macadamia nuts, and cinnamon drops, plus pastas, gourmet coffees, and wine. Most candies and nuts are already weighed and packaged in clear plastic with price labels slapped on. Coffee beans are weighed and ground for you. The company ships everywhere. ♦ M-Sa. 3830 N Clark St (between W Grace and W Byron Sts). 549.6622. Also at several other locations. www.nutsonclark.com

6 MUSIC BOX THEATER

Built in 1929, this movie palace showed some of the early talkies, then closed down, opening intermittently over the years to show porno, Spanish, and Arabic films. After a major renovation in 1983, it reopened as Chicago's only locally owned first-run movie house and now shows art, foreign, and vintage films. It boasts great period details: the lobby's multicolored tile floor, squishy old chairs, and a ceiling that twinkles with tiny lights set amid painted clouds. The sign out front is the last working neon and incandescent marquee in the city. In 1992 the theater added a tiny multiplex-style screening room next to the main room. Phone ahead to make sure that the movie you want to see is playing on the big screen. ♦ 3733 N Southport Ave (between W Waveland Ave and W Grace St). 871.6604. www.musicboxtheater.com

7 GINGERMAN TAVERN

The same customers have been hanging out at this worn-around-the-edges tavern for 15 years—drinking beer, listening to classic music tapes, and shooting pool. Those aging hippies have now been joined by younger compatriots who appreciate an unpretentious neighborhood bar. ♦ Daily, until 2AM. 3740 N Clark St (between W Waveland and N Racine Aves). 549.2050

8 METRO/SMART BAR/ CLUBHOUSE

Arguably the best concert hall in the city—and possibly the whole Midwest—in which to see live rock music, **Metro** hosts such national and international bands as the Meat Puppets, the Pogues, and the Mekons, as well as top local acts. It served as the stage for the Smashing Pumpkins' final show. There's plenty of room to dance or watch from seats behind the stage or in the balcony. For post-concert dancing and people watching, head downstairs to the jam-packed **Smart Bar**. The décor and dress are black; the crowd is punk and artsy. **Clubhouse**, the adjacent coffeehouse, serves java, tea, and alcohol-free drinks in a cramped space filled with alternative-rock memorabilia. ♦ Cover. Daily. 3730 N Clark St (between W Waveland and N Racine Aves). Metro: 549.0203; Smart Bar: 549.4140; Clubhouse: 549.2325. www.metrochicago.com

9 RAW BAR

★$ The bar is black lacquer; the barstools, tables, and chairs are black; the bartender has slicked-back black hair; and the menu includes a variety of raw shellfish, plus papaya and blueberry daiquiris. The result is a strange sort of chic. ♦ Seafood ♦ Daily, dinner until 2AM. 3720 N Clark St (between W Waveland and N Racine Aves). 348.7291; fax 348.9282. www.rawbarandgrill.com

10 WRIGLEY FIELD

Built in 1914, this field (see the seating chart page 164) was originally named **Weeghman Park**, after Charles Henry Weeghman, owner of the Federal League's **Chicago Whales**. When the league folded after two years, Weeghman purchased the **Cubs** and moved them to his new ball field. A live bear cub was present at the park when the team played its first game here on 20 April 1916. The park was given its current name in 1926, after William Wrigley Jr. purchased the **Cubs**. It was designed by **Zachary Taylor Davis**, who also built the original **Comiskey Park**, home of the **White Sox** on the **South Side**. (That field was torn down in 1992 and replaced by a modern stadium near the original site.) Street parking is restricted during day games, and even more so during night games, when cars must display official resident stickers. Some neighborhood entrepreneurs set up makeshift lots in their yards. The **CTA** also has designated parking lots in outlying areas, from which you can catch a shuttle bus to the park. Taking the El is really a better bet than driving; the stadium was placed at this site because of its proximity to the **Red Line** Addison Street stop. ♦ 1060 W Addison St (between N Sheffield and N Seminary Aves). 404.2827; CTA information, 836.7000

Restaurants/Clubs: **Red** | Hotels: **Purple** | Shops: **Orange** | Outdoors/Parks: **Green** | Sights/Culture: **Blue**

11 KIT KAT LOUNGE AND SUPPER CLUB

★$$ Folks who have been on vacation to Puerto Vallarta may already have experienced the offbeat pleasures of the **Kit Kat**, a Mexican cabaret and restaurant that features a food menu with an Asian accent and a drink menu with 25 variations on the martini. Cushy booths are lined with leopard- and snakeskin vinyl. To set the retro mood, performers dressed up as Hollywood icons lip-sync standards from the '40s. ◆ Cabaret ◆ Tu-Su, dinner until 1AM. 3700 N Halsted St (at W Waveland Ave). 525.1111 &
www.kitkatchicago.com

12 BROWN ELEPHANT

This veritable warehouse of a resale shop carries housewares, books, records, and clothing. Most clothes are in good condition and even fashionable—and they're cheap: Men's dress shirts go for $1.50, and women's sweaters start at $3. Some of the shoppers trying on women's clothes, by the way, are men. All profits go to Chicago's Howard Brown Memorial Clinic, a treatment center for patients with AIDS. ◆Daily, 11AM-6PM. 3651 N Halsted St (between W Addison St and W Waveland Ave). 549.5943. Also at 5228 N Clark St. 271.9382

13 CIRCUIT NIGHTCLUB

Opened in 1996, this has become one of the most popular gay dance clubs in the city. It started in the back of a run-down coffee shop, but popularity led to an extensive renovation. Remnants of the coffee shop remain at the front bar, called **Rehab**. In the back room, guest DJs spin a variety of dance tunes, and the fun is hosted by such personalities on the Chicago club circuit as Miss Kitty and Miss Foozy. ◆ Cover. No credit cards. M-Th, Sun, to 2AM; Fr, to 4AM; Sa, to 5AM. 3641 N Halsted St (between W Addison St and W Waveland Ave). 325.2233 & www.circuitclub.com

14 JULIUS MEINL COFFEE SHOP

Tired of the same old Starbucks formula for getting your caffeine buzz? The Meinl coffee empire of Vienna has chosen Chicago as the place to strike its first claim to the American coffee bar market. Opened late in 2002, this Old World café serves coffee the way the Viennese think it was meant to be served: on a silver platter with a glass of water. You can get that with a *topfenstrudel* (farmer's cheese strudel with orange zest and raisins), or you can do what most locals have been doing — forgoing Old World traditions and grabbing a paper cup on the run to the El to face the daily grind. ◆ M-F, 5:30 AM-1PM; Sa, Su, 6AM-11PM. 3601 N Southport Ave (at W Addison St). 868.1857. www.meinl.com

15 CUBBY BEAR LOUNGE

Stretching around the corner directly across the street from **Wrigley Field**, the lounge is a sports bar by day and an eclectic music club by night. Acts have included Queen Ida's Cajun zydeco band and the Mekons. There are four pool tables on the upper deck and a beer garden. ◆ Cover W-Sa nights. Daily. 1059 W Addison St (at N Clark St). 327.1662. www.cubbybear.com

16 WILD HARE & SINGING ARMADILLO FROG SANCTUARY

An award-winning renovation transformed this once dingy and broken-down bar into a clean, comfortable bilevel nightclub that bills itself as "the reggae capital of America." Reggae bands perform every night, attracting folks from all walks of life. Despite the spacious layout, the club gets crowded on weekends, so arrive early and stake out a spot before the band starts. ◆ Cover. M-F, Su, 8:30PM-2AM; Sa, to 3AM; from 4PM for Cubs day games. 3530 N Clark St (between W Cornelia Ave and W Eddy St). 327.4273. www.wildharereggae.com

17 ADDIS ABEBA

★$$ Ethiopian food is the specialty, including good kabobs and meat and seafood stews, both mild and spicy. Accompany your meal with the traditional *tej*, a sweet honey wine. ◆ Ethiopian ◆ Daily, dinner. 3521 N Clark St (between N Sheffield Ave and W Addison St). 929.9383

17 IMPROV OLYMPIC

Second City may have started the improv movement, but it doesn't have a corner on the market. **Improv Olympic** got its start with the assistance of the late Del Close of Second City fame. The specialty here is long improvisation, and there are two rooms where some

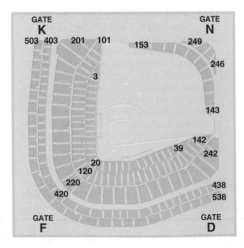

CHILD'S PLAY

After taking the children on the requisite trip to the top of the **Sears Tower** and for a ride on the **Ferris wheel** at **Navy Pier**, what's a parent to do? Not to worry—Chicago offers plenty of activities to please the most curious and fidgety kids. Here are ten of the best:

1. Museum of Holography: This small museum is filled with astonishing holographic images of such varied beings as *Tyrannosaurus rex*, Dracula, and Michael Jordan. For the really curious kid, there are tours that explain the physics of light and the laser process.

2. Old Town School of Folk Music: Offering music classes for 6-month-old children and concerts for kids between the ages of 2 and 10 years, this school is a music-loving parent's dream come true. On Sundays in autumn the school hosts the Music Maze, where children can build cardboard instruments and participate in sing-alongs and rhythm and drawing classes. There's always something swinging here.

3. Museum of Broadcast Communications: The public archives here contain 6,000 TV programs, 8,000 commercials, and 49,000 hours of radio programs—pick your kid's favorite and plug in. For a unique souvenir of your visit, head over to the Kraft Television Center: Up to four family members can don gold blazers and read from news TelePrompTers while museum staffers videotape a 20-minute segment that you can take home for a cost of $20.

4. Chicago Children's Museum: Now in a 57,000-square-foot space in the **Navy Pier's Family Pavilion**, the museum offers something for every personality; there's a three-story *Climbing Schooner*, the Inventing Laboratory, a *Waterways* exhibit where children can experiment with the wet stuff without getting in trouble, and even a replica of a landfill, among other attractions.

5. John G. Shedd Aquarium: Children and their adult companions love the *Coral Reef* exhibit, a 90,000-gallon re-creation of a Caribbean coral reef complete with divers who talk to visitors through a microphone while they feed sharks, sea turtles, eels, and hundreds of tropical fish.

6. Museum of Science and Industry: *Curiosity Place* is an interactive exhibit where kids (it's most suited for those under 6) and their parents can move freely between areas filled with water, sound, blocks, sand, machines, and light to experiment with action and reaction in a fun and educational way.

7. Farm-in-the-Zoo: Cows, horses, sheep, pigs, and other creatures some city dwellers have never before seen in the flesh reside in a 5-acre replica of a Midwestern farm. Goat milking, butter churning, and meet-the-animals pet fests are scheduled throughout the day.

8. Lincoln Park Zoo: More than 2,000 swans, a **Great Ape House**, and the **Rookery**, a serene habitat filled with winged creatures cavorting amid ponds and waterfalls, are just some of the delights at this zoo within the city.

9. Field Museum: Natural history comes alive in this wonderful building. Kids will marvel at Sue the dinosaur and the giant elephant towering in the grand main floor lobby, and you'll have trouble keeping them away from the wishing fountains at either end.

10. Rock 'n' Roll McDonald's: This neon-flickering Micky D's is packed with 1950s memorabilia, from a flaming-red 1963 Corvette to Archie and Veronica dolls and arcade games. While your kids devour their Big Macs, you'll enjoy listening to the sounds of Buddy Holly, Connie Francis, and Elvis.

very clever people strut their stuff: a cabaret and a theater named for Close. There are as many as a dozen shows running at a time, so there always seems to be a new one to see. With the **Cubs** up the street no longer putting on a comedy act, Chicago needed another club to take up the laugh slack near **Wrigley Field**. ♦ Admission. Daily, 7PM-1AM. 3541 N Clark St (at W Addison St). 880.0199. www.improvolympic.com

18 ANGELINA RISTORANTE

★★$$ Sylvester Stallone look-alike Nunzio Fresta named this trattoria after his Sicilian grandmother. He and partners Callin Fortis and Ken Smith serve tender veal marsala, pasta carbonara, and other Italian favorites in a room made romantic with gauzy curtains, old wine bottles, candles, and flowers. The restaurant has become a neighborhood institution and even offers special discounts to locals. ♦ Italian ♦ M-Sa, dinner; Su, brunch and dinner. 3561 N Broadway (between W Brompton Ave and W Addison St). 935.5933

19 TEMPLE SHOLOM

Loebl, Schlossman, & Demuth were students at the **Armour Institute** (later the **Illinois Institute of Technology**) in 1921 when they teamed up with **Coolidge & Hodgdon** to

Restaurants/Clubs: Red | Hotels: Purple | Shops: Orange | Outdoors/Parks: Green | Sights/Culture: Blue

THE BEST

Kenan Heise
Author-Historian

The dust of Chicago's greatness can be found in **Graceland Cemetery**. It is very tourable. The front office has a brochure and guide booklet to help you. A young architecture student I took there stood with his feet a foot off the ground in front of the grave marker for **Louis Sullivan**, the architect who helped free his art from the slavery of foreign entanglements.

Also there is the grave of another inspirer, **John Peter Altgeld**, former governor of Illinois, whom poet Vachel Lindsay described as "the eagle forgotten." He did brave things for prisoners, immigrants, the poor, and the politically disenfranchised. He was hero to both Clarence Darrow and President John F. Kennedy.

Be sure to see the grave of **George F. Pullman**, who gave his name to the sleeper car and the company town, now part of Chicago's far **South Side**. You will wish you had X-ray vision so you could see the mass of rails and cement used to protect his coffin from a paranoid fear that his former employees would desecrate his remains.

Chicago society queen **Bertha Palmer** and her husband, **Potter**, upstage almost everyone else in the place with their elegant Greek-pillared monument.

The founder of the National Baseball League, **William A. Hurlbert**, and former heavyweight boxing champion **Jack Johnson** both, to use a euphemism, rest here.

I recommend the island in **Lake Willomere** for the grave of **Daniel Burnham**, the Lorado Taft sculpture for the Graves family grave marker, the pyramid mausoleum, and, most of all, the **Getty Tomb**, designed by **Louis Sullivan** and called a "requiem in architecture."

Enjoy the place.

---

design this handsome structure for the North Side's oldest Jewish Reform congregation. Construction took place between 1928 and 1930. The dome and octagonal plan are reminiscent of Byzantine architecture, as are the decorative motifs on the exterior, which is faced with Wisconsin Lannon stone and trimmed with Indiana limestone. The octagonal dome rises 90 feet above the 90-by-90-foot sanctuary, which normally seats 1,350, although it can be reconfigured to seat 2,500 for High Holy Day services. ♦ 3480 N Lake Shore Dr (at W Stratford Pl). 276.1990 &

20 FOURTH WORLD ARTISANS

This small shop features unique hand-crafted decorative accessories, art, and clothing from artists and craftspeople around the world. ♦ Tu-F, noon-7PM; Sa, 11AM-6PM; Su, noon-5PM. 3440 N Southport Ave (between W Roscoe St and W Cornelia Ave). 404.5200

21 SAGA'S LAUNDER-BAR & CAFÉ

$ It's "loads of fun" at this unique operation, which is a combo Laundromat, restaurant, and bar. The 66-washer, 48-dryer self-service laundry is decorated with old washboards, soap ads, and other antique laundry gear. Customers (most of them in their 20s and 30s) load their clothes into washers, then head through a doorway to the bar and restaurant for such straightforward fare as chicken soup and turkey-salad sandwiches. The bar serves drinks with names like the Triple-Loader and Polyester Blend. A lightboard hooked up to each of the washers blinks to let diners know when it's time to move clothes to the dryer. ♦ American ♦ Daily, lunch, and dinner; Sa, Su, breakfast. 3435 N Southport Ave (at W Newport Ave). 929.WASH

22 MATSUYA

★★$$ One of the best choices for sushi on Clark Street, this establishment offers two well-lit rooms with blond wood tables and booths and a long sushi bar where you can see your food being prepared. Seaweed-rolled *makimono*, molded *oshi-sushi*, and other raw-fish dishes are available individually or in combinations—all at remarkably reasonable prices. Also recommended are the noodle soups and top-notch appetizers such as grilled squid in ginger sauce and *sunomono* (marinated cucumbers and crabmeat). They prepare cooked fish well too, offering delicately broiled red snapper, butterfish, and others each day. ♦ Japanese ♦ M-F, dinner; Sa, Su, lunch and dinner. Reservations recommended F and Sa. 3469 N Clark St (between N Sheffield Ave and W Addison St). 248.2677

23 STRANGE CARGO

Palm trees and leather trunks in the front window suggest a tropical theme. True, you'll find lots of Hawaiian shirts, muumuus, even grass skirts, but it's really a vintage general store carrying all sorts of items from the 1940s through 1970s. Everything is arranged by type—hats, shoes, shirts, dresses—in two rooms. Impulse purchases are encouraged at the cash register with a tempting display of tacky and cheap plastic earrings. ♦ Daily, from noon. 3448 N Clark St (between W Newport and W Cornelia Aves). 327.8090

The Outpost

24 THE OUTPOST

★★$$ "Life's short, eat well" is the motto of this Australian-themed eatery and bar. The food is consistently good. Entrées include stone crab–filled red pepper ravioli with lobster cream–tomato sauce; grilled venison with sweet-potato hash and juniper berry wine sauce; and grilled filet mignon with mushroom, pecan, and double-bacon compote. ♦ International ♦ Tu-Sa, dinner; Su, brunch and dinner. 3438 N Clark St (at W Newport Ave). 244.1166

25 ARCO DE CUCHILLEROS

★$$ This small storefront tapas bar serves traditional dishes such as paella, *patatas*, and *bravas* along with innovative ones such as a sautéed spinach, raisin, and pine-nut tart. ♦ Spanish ♦ Tu-Su, brunch and dinner. 3445 N Halsted St (between W Roscoe St and W Cornelia Ave). 296.6046; fax 296.6091 ♿

26 PENNY'S NOODLE SHOP

★$ This bright, corner storefront gets crowded most evenings, as well it should. It has to rank as one of the best dining bargains in the city. The cuisine is Asian and includes practically anything that calls for noodles. Appetizers such as spring rolls and satay are well prepared. The entrées, a range of noodle soups, bowls, and curries, are all priced at less than $6. You can avoid the long wait at tables by opting to eat at the counter, where you also get a view of the kitchen. The restaurant serves nonalcoholic beverages only, but you're welcome to bring in your own beer and wine. ♦ Asian ♦ Tu-Su, lunch and dinner. 3400 N Sheffield Ave (at W Roscoe St). 281.8222. Also at 950 W Diversey Pkwy (between N Sheffield and N Mildred Aves). 281.8448; and 1542 N Damen Ave (at W Pierce Ave). 394.0100

27 EL JARDIN CAFE

★$ Operated by Gus Quinones of the family that owns the nearby restaurant of the same name (see page 169), this airy, informal café serves simple, tasty Mexican fare. The collegiate crowd that lines up on the sidewalk on weekends is not there for the food. They come for Gus's deadly margaritas. Beware. ♦ Mexican ♦ Daily, breakfast, lunch, and dinner. 3401 N Clark St (at W Roscoe St). 935.8133

28 99TH FLOOR

Shoppers virtually crawl over one another in the tight aisles here to get at the fashions on the racks. It's hard to see exactly what's there until your eyes adjust to the dark: Almost everything is black, with an occasional white skull or gold crucifix accent, including crushed-velvet baby-doll dresses, men's topcoats, studded leather collars, and motorcycle caps. The shoes are stunning, from pointy-toed purple velvet cowboy boots to Doc Martens lace-up boots and women's thigh-high red vinyl boots. ♦ Daily. 3406 N Halsted St (between W Roscoe St and W Newport Ave). 348.7781

29 HAWTHORNE PLACE DISTRICT

This quiet district (which includes Stratford Place, one block north) is one of the few remnants of residential neighborhoods dominated by single-family homes that once stretched from the Gold Coast northward to Rogers Park. The area was subdivided in 1883 and developed by the brothers Benjamin, George, and John McConnell. Benjamin lived in the oldest house (1884), **568 West Hawthorne Place**; John lived at **546 West Hawthorne Place**. Many famous Chicago design firms had commissions here, including **Burnham & Root**, who designed a home for George Marshall in 1884 at **574 West Hawthorne Place**; **Mayo & Mayo**, who designed the house at **580 West Hawthorne Place** for Dr. Alphons Bacon; **Adler & Sullivan**, whose house for George Harvey, president of his own insurance firm, was built in 1888 at **600 West Stratford Place**; and **Huehl & Schmid**, who designed **606 West Stratford Place**. It remains a residential area. ♦529-93 W Hawthorne Pl and 600–06 W Stratford Pl (between N Lake Shore Dr and N Broadway)

30 BEST WESTERN HAWTHORNE TERRACE

$ This comfortable, newly remodeled facility has 59 rooms and junior suites with two-line phones, data ports, and satellite TV. There's also a fitness center with sauna and whirlpool. The reasonable price and great North Side location (you can walk to **Wrigley Field**) make it a nice, affordable alternative for people who want to set up shop away from the business and tourist bustle of downtown. ♦ 3434 N Broadway (at Hawthorne Terr). 244.3434, 888/675.2378; fax 244.3435. www.bestwestern.com

THE BEST

Kevin J. Bell

Director, Lincoln Park Zoological Gardens

Dining:

The variety of restaurants is one of the greatest things about Chicago. Fast for at least a week before you get here (!) to make room for

Sausage or spinach/mushroom-stuffed pizza at **Pizzeria Due**. Don't plan on being too active after you eat; you'll need all your energy just for digesting.

Steaks and, of course, cheesecake, at **Eli's**.

Sunday brunch buffet at the **Ritz-Carlton**—especially the desserts.

Out and about, any one of these will make your day:

A bike ride along the lakefront on the bike path from **Foster Avenue** to **LaSalle Drive**.

The **Art Institute of Chicago** on Tuesday evenings, when it's open late.

The picture-perfect view from **Lincoln Park**'s Café Brauer of Chicago's famous skyline framed by the café's 1912-era loggias.

A **Cubs** game at **Wrigley Field** any day.

A walk along the waterfront behind the **Northwestern University** campus in **Evanston**.

A day at the **Kane County Flea Market** in **St. Charles**, held only the first weekend of every month. It's an antiques hunter's delight.

Lincoln Park Zoo when the gates open first thing in the morning at 7.

The view at dusk, looking north down **Michigan Avenue** from the **Michigan Avenue Bridge**. On your left, the **Wrigley Building** looks like a giant wedding cake; on your right, the **Tribune Tower** appears to be a sand castle.

31 3400 NORTH LAKE SHORE DRIVE

A fine example of the first generation of luxury high-rises along Chicago's lakefront, this vintage ten-story building designed by **Peter J. Weber** commanded monthly rents of $1,200 when it opened in 1922. Each 6,000-square-foot apartment featured a salon; living room; dining room; breakfast room; solarium (some of them survive); five bedrooms, each with a private bath; kitchen, service, and laundry rooms; three maid's rooms with baths; and a servants' hall. A 1989 renovation by **Himmel/Bonner** divided the original 24 apartments into 51 units, which still feature high ceilings, polished oak floors, and marble fireplaces; many have French balconies and fabulous lake views. Today's tenants pay close to $4,000 per month. ♦ At W Roscoe St

32 ROSCOE'S

The bar and the adjacent café once were an old-fashioned corner grocery store, vestiges of which remain visible in the tin ceiling and mahogany woodwork. Though the bar—its crowd primarily gay men—appears small from the front, it actually stretches back to two additional bars and a dance floor located in what used to be a coach house. The whole shebang has come a long way from its staid origins. ♦ M-F, Su, to 2AM; Sa, to 3AM. 3356 N Halsted St (at W Roscoe St). 281.3355; fax 281.1013

33 P.S. BANGKOK

★★$$ Owner Suradet Yongsawaii prepared take-out food in a Bangkok market before

emigrating to the US. Although always busy, his storefront restaurant maintains a calm atmosphere, with linen tablecloths and dinner candles. The extensive menu starts with 33 appetizers. Curry entrées prepared with coconut milk are special standouts. The noodle dishes are unlike those at other Thai restaurants; the sauce on *pad thai*, for example, is almost caramelized. ♦ Thai ♦ Tu-Su, lunch and dinner. Reservations recommended F and Sa. 3345 N Clark St (between W Buckingham Pl and W Roscoe St). 871.7777; fax 871.9997

34 SILVER MOON

Would-be Fred Astaires and Ginger Rogerses will find all the right vintage clothes here, including tailcoats, top hats, 1920s silk dresses with long trains, and red velvet capes. The inventory also includes vintage housewares, bridal dresses, and some furniture. Do some serious digging in the racks to make sure you've spotted all the good stuff. ♦ Tu-Su. 3337 N Halsted St (between W Buckingham Pl and W Roscoe St). 883.0222. www.silvermoonvintage.com

35 SPARE TIME

Like **Schubas Tavern** down the street (see page 173), this bowling alley/pool hall is housed in an old Schlitz tavern, and the old-fashioned charm still comes through. Formerly called **Southport Lanes**, it's the only bowling alley in the city that still employs pin-boys to manually reset the pins. There are just four lanes and they fill up fast; call first to make sure someone hasn't rented them out for a private party. The bar has beautiful wood and stained glass, and a spacious back room boasts six pool tables. In warm weather, the sidewalk café makes for great people watching. Food includes burgers, salads, wings, nachos, and the like. ◆ Daily, to 2AM. 3325 N Southport Ave (between W School and W Henderson Sts). 472.1601; fax 472.1978

36 EL JARDIN

$$ Once a quaint Mexican restaurant with terrific food, this place's quality slipped when it expanded to accommodate demand, and you can still expect a wait. It's always packed with young professionals downing fizzy margaritas and platters of *bistec à la Mexicana* (steak) and *enchiladas verdes* (with spicy green sauce). Brunch features fruit, soups, tamales, and meat and fish entrées. The main dining room resembles a plaza, with redbrick floors, whitewashed walls, and big windows. In warm weather, sit out on the peaceful patio, which is shielded from the busy street by tall stucco walls. ◆ Mexican ◆ M-Sa, lunch and dinner; Su, brunch and dinner. 3335 N Clark St (between W Buckingham Pl and W Roscoe St). 528.6775; fax 528.0857

37 THAI CLASSIC

★$ They serve tasty chicken with basil leaves and coconut-milk curries, along with other customary dishes, but the standouts are seafood specials such as shrimp with garlic, basil leaves, and peppers. The seasoning is milder than at other Thai restaurants. Seating is either American style or Asian style on pillows at low tables with sunken wells for your legs. ◆ Thai ◆ Daily, lunch and dinner. 3332 N Clark St (between W School and W Roscoe Sts). 404.2000 ﾐ www.thaiclassicrestaurant.com

38 PLATIYO

★★★$$ Ten years after opening **Mia Francesca**, the popular Italian restaurant next door, Scott Harris has teamed with superchefs Patrick Concannon from **Don Juan** and Kevin Karales from **Frontera** and **Topolobampo** to create a wonderful Mexican restaurant. Paintings of desert scenes adorn the brick walls to create an airy, cheerful setting, but the real artistry in this intimate storefront is the food, which combines traditional dishes and more adventurous offerings. Tasty openers include tortilla soup with shredded chicken and cubes of fresh cheese and a meatless *queso fundido*. Among entrées, choose from wood-grilled pork chop with mashed sweet potatoes and mango mole, braised lamb shank with stewed white beans and bacon, and *carne asada* with garlic-flavored mushrooms. Desserts come from Bomb Pon, a Pilsen bakery, and include a delicious pistachio flan

with thin chocolate base. The place only seats 65, so reservations are definitely recommended. ◆ Mexican ◆ Daily, dinner. 3313 North Clark St (between W Aldine Ave and W Buckingham Pl). 477.6700 ﾐ

38 MIA FRANCESCA

★★★$ Chef-owner Scott Harris puts together an interesting, ever-changing menu that features six daily pastas, three fresh fish choices, and an occasional beef or veal dish. All of the desserts are made in-house; they include tiramisù and lemon mascarpone mousse. Expect a crowd, even on weeknights; good food and reasonable prices make this one of the neighborhood's most popular eateries. The wine bar is a great spot to enjoy an appetizer and a drink while waiting for a table. ◆ Italian ◆ Daily, dinner. 3311 N Clark St (between W Aldine Ave and W Buckingham Pl). 281.3310. www.miafrancesca.com

38 HUBBA-HUBBA

For more than a decade, mother and daughter Ellen Freedman and Julie Schneider have offered moderately priced women's romantic and classic-style clothing and accessories. In the process, their store became a neighbor-hood institution at a location across Clark Street. Success has enabled them to expand and move to this larger location. In addition to carrying the lines of emerging, unknown designers, they also carry vintage costume jewelry and vintage clothing. Everything is well displayed and in excellent condition. Look for their colorful crinoline skirts and flouncy party dresses. ◆ Daily. 3309 N Clark St (between W Aldine Ave and W Buckingham Pl). 477.1414; fax 477.1412 ﾐ www.hubbahubba.com

39 THE CLOSET

The name refers not only to the size of the room but also to the process of coming out of the closet. The motorcycles out front belong to the predominantly lesbian crowd that hangs out at the bar or dances to music videos on the postage stamp–size dance floor. ◆ M-F, Su, to 4AM; Sa, to 5AM. 3325 N Broadway (between W Aldine Ave and W Roscoe St). 477.8533

40 WINDY CITY SWEETS

Glass cases brim with chocolates; gummy worms, bears, and fish; chunky caramels; red licorice whips; roasted and raw nuts; and dried fruits. The shop's staff will create a nice gift package from your hand-picked selections. ◆ Daily. 3308 N Broadway (between W Aldine Ave and W Buckingham Pl). 477.6100; fax 477.6225. www.windycitysweets.com

Restaurants/Clubs: Red | Hotels: Purple | Shops: Orange | Outdoors/Parks: Green | Sights/Culture: Blue

MUSICAL CHAIRS

Always famous for its blues and jazz, and a superb symphony orchestra, Chicago's musical repertoire continues to grow. Today the city is becoming increasingly known as home to rock artists like Nicholas Tremulus, Poi Dog Pondering, and the Waco Brothers; whether you're into opera or reggae, folk or gospel, you can probably hear it in Chicago. Below is a sampling of some of the city's best listening posts. For information on specific acts or schedules, call the individual location or consult weekly entertainment listings in the *Reader, New City, Tribune,* or *Sun-Times.* Online check out www.chireader.com.

Blues

Bill's Blues ◆ 1029 Davis St, Evanston. 847/424.9800

Blue Chicago ◆ 736 N Clark St (between W Superior St and W Chicago Ave). 312/642.6261

B.L.U.E.S. ◆ 2519 N Halsted St (between W Fullerton and W Wrightwood Aves). 773/528.1012

Buddy Guy's Legends ◆ 754 S Wabash Ave (at E Eighth St). 312/427.0333

Kingston Mines ◆ 2548 N Halsted St (between W Lill and W Wrightwood Aves). 773/477.4646

Rosa's ◆ 3420 W Armitage Ave (between N Kimball and N St. Louis Aves). 773/342.0452

The Smoke Daddy ◆ 1804 W Division St (between N Wood and N Honore Sts). 773/772.6656

Classical and Opera

Civic Opera House ◆ 20 N Wacker Dr (between W Madison and W Washington Sts). 312/332.2244. www.lyricopera.com

Orchestra Hall/Symphony Center ◆ 220 S Michigan Ave (between E Jackson Blvd and E Adams St). 312/294.3333. www.cso.org

Country and Folk

Carol's Pub ◆ 4659 N Clark St (at W Leland Ave). 773/334.2402

Martyrs' ◆ 3855 N Lincoln Ave (between W Grace and W Byron Sts). 773/404.9494

Old Town School of Folk Music ◆ 4544 N Lincoln Ave (between W Montrose and W Wilson Aves). 773/728.6000

Eclectic Offerings

Cubby Bear Lounge ◆ 1059 W Addison St (at N Clark St). 773/327.1662

Double Door ◆ 1572 N Milwaukee Ave (at N Damen Ave). 773/489.3160

Elbo Room ◆ 2871 N Lincoln Ave (at W George St). 773/549.5549

FitzGeralds ◆ 6615 Roosevelt Rd (between East and Clarence Aves), Berwyn. 708/788.2118

The Hideout ◆ 1354 W Wabansia Ave (at N Throop St). 773/227.4433

Schubas Tavern ◆ 3159 N Southport Ave (at W Belmont Ave). 773/525.2508

Irish

Abbey Pub ◆ 3420 W Grace St (at N Elston Ave). 773/478.4408

41 WISHBONE

★★$ When the first **Wishbone** opened more than ten years ago in a remote location on West Grand Avenue near Damen, reports about the mouthwatering food spread quickly by word of mouth. Pretty soon there were long lines of people waiting outside in a neighborhood most of them had never set foot in. That small storefront has since closed, but a much larger installment in the West Loop and this location

are packing people in. The attraction is Southern-style home cooking, in generous portions. Beans and rice with ham or chicken, shrimp and sautéed spinach, blackened catfish, crab and black-eyed peas—these are just a few of the pickings, which are anything but slim. Breakfast is a feast; cornbread fans will be in heaven. And the prices are so affordable, you might call them dirt cheap. In addition, the folk-art décor makes for a pleasant setting, and there's an outdoor seating option in warm

Fado Irish Pub ♦ 100 W Grand Ave (at N Clark St). 312/836.0066

Chief O'Neill's Pub ♦ 3471 N Elston Ave (between W Belmont Ave and W Addison St). 773/583.3066

Jazz

Andy's ♦ 11 E Hubbard St (between N Wabash Ave and N State St). 312/642.6805

Backroom ♦ 1007 N Rush St (at E Elm St). 312/751.2433

Cotton Club ♦ 1710 S Michigan Ave (between E 18th and E 16th Sts). 312/341.9787

Green Dolphin Street ♦ 2200 N Ashland Ave (at W Webster Ave). 773/395.0066

The Green Mill ♦ 4802 N Broadway (at W Lawrence Ave). 773/878.5552

Jazz Showcase ♦ 59 W Grand Ave (between N Dearborn and N Clark Sts). 312/670.2473

Pops for Champagne ♦ 2934 N Sheffield Ave (at W Oakdale Ave). 773/472.1000

Velvet Lounge ♦ 2128 S Indiana Ave (between E 21st and E 22nd Sts). 312/791.9050

Latin

Coobah ♦ 3423 N Southport Ave (at W Newport Ave). 773/528.2220

Mambo ♦ 3336 N Milwaukee Ave (at N Keystone Ave). 733/481.2050

Reggae

Wild Hare & Singing Armadillo Frog Sanctuary ♦ 3530 N Clark St (between W Cornelia Ave and W Eddy St). 773/327.4273

Rock, Pop, and Dance Clubs

Beat Kitchen ♦ 2100 W Belmont Ave (at N Hoyne Ave). 773/281.4444

Bottom Lounge ♦ 3206 N Wilton Ave (at W Belmont Ave). 773/975.0505

Circus ♦ 901 W Weed St (at N Fremont St). 773/266.1200

Crobar ♦ 1543 N Kingsbury St (at W Weed St). 312/337.5001

Empty Bottle ♦ 1035 N Western Ave (at W Cortez St). 773/267.3600

Funky Buddha Lounge ♦ 728 W Grand Ave (between N Union and N Halsted Sts). 773/666.1695

Metro ♦ 3730 N Clark St (between W Waveland and N Racine Aves). 773/549.0203

Phyllis' Musical Inn ♦ 1800 W Division St (at N Wood St). 773/486.9862

Red Dog ♦ 1958 W North Ave (between N Winchester and N Damen Aves). 773/278.1009

Subterranean ♦ 2011 W North Ave (at N Milwaukee Ave). 733/278.6600

Thurston's ♦ 1248 W George St (between N Racine and N Lakewood Aves). 773/472.6900

Transit ♦ 1431 W Lake St (at N Ogden Ave). 312/491.9729

The Vic ♦ 3145 N Sheffield Ave (at Belmont Ave). 733/742.0449

weather. If you want to take a break from fancy dining, this is one great place to do it. Bring your own spirits. ♦ Cajun/American ♦ Daily, breakfast, lunch, and dinner. 3300 N Lincoln Ave (at W Melrose St). 549.4105; fax 549.4154 ♦. Also at 1001 W Washington Blvd (at N Morgan St). 850.2663. www.wishbonechicago.com

42 SHEFFIELD'S WINE AND BEER GARDEN

Once a quiet corner tavern where actors and their hangers-on hung out, the club has gentrified along with the neighborhood but hasn't lost too much of its artsy charm. Jeremy Turner's disturbing artwork still holds pride of

Restaurants/Clubs: Red | Hotels: Purple | Shops: Orange | Outdoors/Parks: Green | Sights/Culture: Blue

THE BEST

Roberta Lieberman
Art Dealer, Zolla/Lieberman Gallery

If you don't mind the wind that sweeps in from **Lake Michigan,** my Chicago neighborhood—**Streeterville**—is a great place for walking.

If you are a jogger or cyclist, you can run or ride for uninterrupted miles along the lake from the **Museum of Science and Industry** on the **South Side** to **Hollywood Avenue** on the north. If you're not, walk along **Lake Shore Drive** from **Oak Street** to **Lincoln Park** and admire the magnificent late-

19th-century and early-20th-century apartment buildings.

If you're a shopper, head south on **Michigan Avenue** (aka the **Magnificent Mile**), taking a detour down **Oak Street** for the boutiques, and don't stop till you reach **Ohio Street**. In the meantime you will have passed three formidable vertical malls—**900 Michigan Avenue**, **Water Tower Place**, and **Chicago Place**—not to mention almost every major department store of the Western world.

But should your fancy be culture, you can also walk to the **Museum of Contemporary Art**, the **Art Institute of Chicago**, the **Chicago Symphony Orchestra**, the **Lyric Opera**, and (best of all) the multitude of galleries located in the **River North** district.

place in the front room, and a cat is still curled up by the fireplace in the back. The bar is well stocked with microbrews from around the country and several decent wines. Pamphlets with thorough descriptions of potable selections are available for serious beer-heads. In summertime, the adjacent beer garden (complete with shaded pool table) is packed to the fences. ◆ M-F, Su, to 2AM; Sa, to 3AM. 3258 N Sheffield Ave (at W School St). 281.4989. www.sheffieldschicago.com

43 CHICAGO COMICS

The guys behind the counter look as if they're playing hooky from high school—or could it be that sitting around reading comic books keeps a person forever young? They stock all the usual superheroes—Superman, Batman, Wonder Woman—plus Dick Tracy, Teenage Mutant Ninja Turtles, animated videos, posters, T-shirts, and a messload of toys and oddities. You can also pick up hard-to-find Marvel and DC editions from the "Silver Age" (early 1960s), as well as black-and-white alternative comics and Japanese Manga. ◆ Daily. 3244 N Clark St (between W Belmont Ave and W School St). 528.1983. www.chicagocomics.com

44 YOSHI'S CAFÉ

★★★$$$ Japanese-born chef Yoshi Katsumara ingeniously and deliciously pairs classical French technique with Japanese and American accents. The menu changes regularly, but look for a starter of California goat cheese and bell pepper in melt-away pastry swathed in red bell pepper–cream sauce, and an entrée of veal medallions with candied ginger and lemon zest. Fresh seafood selections may include tuna prepared in a light oil infused with basil, garlic, and tomato, or strips of salmon and Dover sole. The wine list is adequate. Tables for a total of 50 diners are tucked closely together and graced with fresh flowers. ◆ French ◆ Tu-Sa, dinner; Su, brunch

and dinner. Reservations recommended. 3257 N Halsted St (at W Aldine Ave). 248.6160

45 UNABRIDGED BOOKSTORE

Enter a rich library of polished wood shelves packed with books. Contemporary literature, gay and lesbian subjects, travel, and cooking are all well represented, and the store frequently hosts readings by authors. A yellow card next to a book means someone on the staff really loves it and wants you to read it too. ◆ M-F, 10AM-10PM; Sa, Su, 10AM-8PM. 3251 N Broadway (between W Melrose St and W Aldine Ave). 883.9119 ⑃

45 HE WHO EATS MUD

Don't be surprised if you step in for one greeting card and walk out with five. The stock includes beautiful reproductions of art masterpieces and all kinds of cards—ranging from those that amuse to one-of-a-kinds made by artists. ◆ Daily. 3247 N Broadway (between W Melrose St and W Aldine Ave). 525.0616 ⑃

46 THE MELROSE

★★$ The food is unremarkable coffee-shop fare—cheeseburgers, omelettes, salads—but it's available around the clock, and the sidewalk patio is fun in decent weather. ◆ Coffee shop ◆ Daily, 24 hours. 3233 N Broadway (at W Melrose St). 327.2060

47 ZOU ZOU

★★$ It's just a hole-in-the-wall storefront with a few tables and a take-out counter, but this Mediterranean delicatessen serves up delicious regional delicacies fast and at great prices. The falafel sandwich is a great change of pace from a burger, and it comes with tangy potato salad. All entrées are under $10, and you can't go wrong with the couscous. If you're in the neighborhood and in the market for cheap eats, this is the place. It's also a great stop before going to catch some music at **Schubas** across the street. ◆ M-Sa, lunch and dinner. 1406 W Belmont Ave (at N Southport Ave). 755.4020

48 SCHUBAS TAVERN/ HARMONY GRILL

$ This neo-Gothic building was constructed in the early 1900s by the Schlitz Brewing Company, one of several taverns the company built in Chicago to serve its beer. (The façade still sports the Schlitz logo in terra-cotta.) In the late 1980s brothers Chris and Michael Schuba purchased and revived the tavern, with its green tin ceiling, 30-foot-long mahogany bar, and great jukebox loaded with oldies. The back room is a great spot for live music, attracting such national folk acts as Loudon Wainwright III, Steve Earle, and the Lost Nation String Band. In an adjacent storefront, the **Harmony Grill** serves well-prepared and reasonably priced American cuisine—burgers, sandwiches, soups, and salads. There are no real surprises, but it's all done pretty well. ◆ American ◆ Cover for music. M-F, lunch and dinner; Sa-Su, brunch and dinner. 3159 N Southport Ave (at W Belmont Ave). 525.2508; fax 525.4573. www.schubas.com

49 UNCLE FUN

Rubber hot dogs, statuettes of *Star Trek* characters, Dr. Seuss T-shirts, and various odds and ends abound in this cramped toy store. Artists flock to the shop to pick through the dozens of drawers full of junk—lighters, tiny plastic baby heads, and other seemingly useless raw material. Collectors snap up vintage valentines or Beatles dolls, and slackers spend hours browsing for weird toys from the 1950s. ◆ W-Sa, noon-7PM; Su, noon-5PM. 1338 W Belmont Ave (between N Lakewood and N Southport Aves). 477.8223. www.unclefunchicago.com

50 HOWARD'S WINE CELLAR

Those in the know say that Howard Silverman is a rare vintage when it comes to helping you find the perfect Barolo to go with that leg of lamb you're roasting. Although he carries a wide range of domestics, his specialty is European wines and great bargains from Australia. Browse through his impressive collection and you'll be able to host, and toast to, any occasion. ◆ Tu-Sa and by appointment. 1244 W Belmont Ave (between N Racine and N Lakewood Aves). 248.3766

51 THEATRE BUILDING

Over the years, the two stages here have been home to hundreds of productions by non-Equity theater companies, including the **Northlight Theatre Co.**'s *Bubbe Meises* and

Hartzell Production's *Vampire Lesbians of Sodom*. ◆ 1225 W Belmont Ave (between N Racine and N Southport Aves). 327.5252

52 JEANNY'S

★★$ It may look like a standard Chinese restaurant, but the food transcends the décor. Dishes are uniformly good and reasonably priced, and the service is pleasant. Some of the more popular dishes are Mandarin chicken (crunchy chicken pieces sautéed with minced hot peppers in a sweet-hot sauce with fresh broccoli) and Mongolian beef (sliced beef sautéed with green onions and bamboo shoots, topped with crispy rice noodles). Eat in or order to go. ◆ Chinese ◆ M-Sa, lunch and dinner; Su, dinner. 1053 W Belmont Ave (between N Kenmore and N Seminary Aves). 248.1133

53 LEONA'S ORIGINAL PIZZA

★$ The late Leona Szemla opened her first restaurant in 1950. Today the Toya family—Leona's grandchildren—runs five of them. The dinner line starts forming on the sidewalk by 6PM, but a free glass of wine helps you wait patiently. There are two bustling floors plus a deck filled with checkered-cloth–covered tables. Peruse the long Italian menu but don't miss the flaky thin-crust whole-wheat pizza with a choice of 28 toppings, from artichokes to zucchini. ◆ Italian/pizza ◆ Daily, lunch and dinner. 3215 N Sheffield Ave (between W Belmont Ave and W School St). 327.8861. Also at 1936 W Augusta Blvd (between N Winchester and N Damen Aves). 292.4300; 6935 N Sheridan Rd (between W Farwell and W Morse Aves). 764.5757; 1419 W Taylor St (between S Loomis and S Laflin Sts). 850.2222; 7443 W Irving Park Rd (between N Osceola and N Olcott Aves). 625.3636. www.leonas.com

54 BERLIN

The crowd, largely gay and lesbian, gyrates to DJ tapes, music videos, and occasional live acts. The exhibitionistic do their dancing atop go-go platforms. The décor's theme changes monthly, and special events include a pet costume contest (that's people dressed as pets), "drag" races, and a monthly 1970s disco night. ◆ Cover. Daily, to 4AM. 954 W Belmont Ave (between N Wilton and N Sheffield Aves). 348.4975. www.berlinchicago.com

55 ANN SATHER

★$ In 1946 the owner for whom this eatery is named spent her life savings to buy the **Swedish Diner**; ten years later she moved down the block to this larger location.

Restaurants/Clubs: Red | Hotels: Purple | Shops: Orange | Outdoors/Parks: Green | Sights/Culture: Blue

Although Ann is no longer around, the menu—course after course of such Swedish mainstays as meatballs, dumplings, and over-cooked vegetables—remains the same. On weekends, crowds line up for breakfasts of Swedish pancakes with lingonberries, Swedish potato sausage, cinnamon rolls, and limpa bread. The upstairs banquet room is a frequent meeting place for community groups. ♦ Swedish/American ♦ Daily, breakfast, lunch, and dinner. 929 W Belmont Ave (between N Clark St and N Sheffield Ave). 348.2378. Also at 3411 N Broadway (at W Hawthorne Pl). 305.0018; 3416 N Southport Ave (at W Roscoe St). 404.4475; 2665 N Clark St (at W Drummond Pl). 327.9522; 5207 N Clark St (at W Foster Ave). 271.6677. www.annsather.com

55 STANDARD INDIA

★$ The dim lighting and worn furnishings are a bit depressing, but the food compensates. Try *saag paneer* (spicy spinach with chunks of Indian cheese) and the delicate chicken *makhani* (with tomato and parsley). A good way to sample many entrées is the inexpensive prix-fixe buffet Monday through Thursday evening. ♦ Indian ♦ Daily, lunch and dinner. 917 W Belmont Ave (between N Clark St and N Sheffield Ave). 929.1123; fax 929.1876

56 J. TOGURI MERCANTILE CO.

This Japanese department store carries a full range of kimonos, china, and various imports from Asia. The long aisles are lined with ceramic soup bowls and spoons, bamboo bird cages, paper lanterns, and Japanese-language books, magazines, and cassette tapes. ♦ M-Sa. 851 W Belmont Ave (between N Clark St and N Sheffield Ave). 929.3500; fax 929.0779

57 JACK'S AMERICAN BLEND

★★$$ Art Deco meets high-tech décor at this trendy eatery owned by brothers Michael and Jack Daniel Jones. It was named one of the best new restaurants for 1998 by *Chicago* magazine. Imaginative dishes include appetizers such as Thai fettuccine, polenta with wild mushrooms, and Southwestern quesadillas stuffed with smoked chicken. Entrée highlights are seared tuna with wasabi mashed potatoes in sake-ginger-lime sauce, braised lamb shank with couscous in rosemary-mint sauce, and honey-soy pork tenderloin with garlic-lemon spinach and apple-mango chutney. A bonus: The windows of this corner storefront permit people watching on Halsted and Belmont. ♦ Contemporary ♦ M-Sa, dinner; Su, brunch and dinner. Reservations recommended. 3201 N Halsted St (at W Belmont Ave). 244.2112; fax 244.3777

58 RECKLESS RECORDS

Alternative rock, a huge collection of obscure imports, plus a good supply of used records make for an inventory that runs the gamut from *Religious Industrial Sludge* to *The Best of the Lovin' Spoonful*. Bands play live in the store on Saturday, twice a month. ♦ M-Sa, until 10PM; Su, until 8PM. 3157 N Broadway (between W Briar Pl and W Belmont Ave). 404.5080. Also at 1532 N Milwaukee Ave (at W North Ave). 235.3727. www.recklessrecords.com

58 PLEASURE CHEST

It used to be almost frightening to venture into this black cavern of erotica. Although a studded leather belt or two remain, the hard-core items have otherwise given way to sexy lingerie, greeting cards, board games, condoms, and anatomically correct candles. ♦ Daily, 10AM-midnight. 3155 N Broadway (between W Briar Pl and W Belmont Ave). 525.7151; fax 525.6395. www.lovetoyexpress.com

59 THE BELMONT

This fine, solid, vintage brick building with limestone trim was designed by **A.L. Himmelblau** in 1923. It has something of an elegant dowager look to it—aged but brimming with character. For years it operated as a hotel, but in 1993 its 334 units were converted to private apartments. ♦ 3170 N Sheridan Rd (at W Belmont Ave)

60 HEALING EARTH RESOURCES

With the air thick with incense and New Age music in the background, it's a cinch you'll find crystals here. You will, along with Indian weavings, silver jewelry, self-help books, air cleaners, and ionizers. The adjacent **Earth Cafe** sells organic juices, fresh wheatgrass, and light vegetarian meals (such as avocado sandwiches) to eat in or take out. ♦ Daily. 3111 N Ashland Ave (between W Barry and W Belmont Aves). 327.8459; fax 327.8616 ᴴ www.healingearthresources.com

61 THE VIC/BREW & VIEW

This faded theater has a split personality. **The Vic**, one of the city's most popular live concert venues, hosts performers across the pop-rock spectrum: Jackson Browne, Diamanda Galas, Skinny Puppy, and the Pogues have all appeared here. When no concerts are scheduled, it becomes a second-run movie theater known as the **Brew & View**, which sells beer during the flicks and permits smoking. The crowds can get boisterous. (Weeknight screenings are tamer.) The theater's screen is one of the largest in the city, and the price is right—$2.50 for a double feature. ♦ Daily. 3145 N Sheffield Ave (between W Fletcher St and W

Belmont Ave). 472.0366; Ticketmaster 312/559.1212

62 BRIAR STREET THEATRE

Built in 1901 as a stable for Marshall Field and Company's delivery horses and carriages, the building was purchased in 1930 by Martin H. Kennelly (who later became mayor) and turned into a warehouse for his moving-and-storage company. In the 1970s Swell Pictures, a video and film production company, converted it into a soundstage. Since 1985 it has served as a rental space for theater, dance, and music. Thanks to the building's origins as a stable, there are no columns—and hence there are excellent sightlines. Recent productions have included *Blue Man Group* and the road company of *Having Our Say*. ◆ 3133 N Halsted St (between W California Terr and W Briar Pl). Box office, 348.4000, fax 348.4172 க்

63 MURPHY'S ROSE GARDEN

If you're strolling down Broadway, take a moment to detour east on Briar Place. In front of a three-flat residence on an otherwise nondescript block is a lovely rose garden. Although small, it is one of the nicest and best-maintained private rose gardens in the city. ◆ 458 W Briar Pl (between N Sheridan Rd and N Cambridge Ave)

64 LINCOLN PARK/
℗ BELMONT HARBOR

The park's lower boundary starts a couple of miles south in the community of the same name and stretches northward just beyond Hollywood Avenue, hugging the lakefront the whole way. With each neighborhood, the character shifts—adjacent communities boast beaches, but Lakeview possesses nary a grain of sand, just plenty of concrete slabs that front the shoreline as a deterrent to erosion. Determined locals spread beach towels and picnic gear across flat-topped rocks and in nearby grassy meadows on warm summer days; more active parkgoers make the most of a soft gravel path and parallel asphalt path that traverse the park for miles. The paths attract a steady flow of runners, bicyclists, roller skaters, and—when the snowfall is right—cross-country skiers. Early birds hit the trails at dawn, starting their day with the astounding sight of the bright red sun coming up over the lake. Look south from Diversey Harbor to one of the most dramatic views of Chicago's skyline, day or night—it's a scene that professional photographers are forever snapping. Another great view is found about a half mile north, at the tip of the long finger of the parkway stretching around Belmont Harbor (access is by foot from the northern edge of the harbor). Both harbors

are home to hundreds of boats between April and October. The **Belmont Yacht Club** is private but welcomes members of yacht clubs from other cities. Anyone can use the free boat-launching ramp at Diversey Harbor. (Sailboats are not recommended on Diversey Harbor, as boats must pass beneath a low bridge to reach the lake.) The **Chicago Sailing Club** (871.SAIL) at the north end of Belmont Harbor rents boats and also provides instruction. ◆ The park is accessible by car from several exits along N Lake Shore Dr. By foot, enter anywhere between W Diversey Dr and W Belmont Ave; north of Belmont, use the two underpasses at the ends of W Roscoe and W Addison Sts, or the auto/pedestrian underpass at W Irving Park Rd.

Within Lincoln Park:

DIVERSEY DRIVING RANGE

℗ Golfers of all ages and skill levels line up to practice their swing at 35 tees at this Chicago Park District facility bounded by Diversey Harbor, Lake Shore Drive, and several highrises. For those who prefer to putter around, there's also a miniature golf course. ◆ Fee. Daily, Apr-Nov. W Diversey Dr (just east of N Lake Shore Dr West)

BRIAR PLAYLOT

℗ A sturdy setup of swings, slides, monkey bars, a sandbox, and more, all shaded by trees, provides the best recreation around for many a neighborhood high-rise kid.

TOTEM POLE

Also known as "Kwa-Ma-Rolas," this pole is a reproduction of an original, carved at the turn of the 19th century by the Kwakiutl Indians of British Columbia. Shaped from a single 4-foot-long cedar log, the pole starts at the base with the head of a sea monster, continues with an upside-down baleen whale with a man on its back, and is topped by a *kulos*, a member of the thunderbird family, with its wings spread. The original was acquired in 1926 by James L. Kraft, founder of the Kraft cheese company, during a collecting trip to the Pacific Northwest. Kraft donated the pole to the Chicago Park District and dedicated it to the city's schoolchildren. In the 1970s two Pacific Northwest carvers who came to Chicago to work on a project for the **Field Museum of Natural History** were shown the original totem and immediately recognized its historic value to the Kwakiutl. At their urging, the Canadian government requested the pole's return. It is now on display at the **Museum of the University of British Columbia**. This replica, carved by descendants of the original artisans, was installed in the park in 1986.

Restaurants/Clubs: Red | Hotels: Purple | Shops: Orange | Outdoors/Parks: Green | Sights/Culture: Blue

TENNIS COURTS

Ten outdoor tennis courts are available on a first-come, first-served basis. Good luck—locals seem to always get there first. ◆ Daily; closed Nov-Mar

MAROVITZ/WAVELAND
GOLF COURSE

The only North Side lakefront site for golf was recently renamed in honor of octogenarian judge Abraham Lincoln Marovitz, but locals still call it **Waveland**. The nine-hole course is dramatically set between Lake Michigan and the Lakeview skyline, which you can gaze at during the long hours waiting to tee off. You may get onto the greens quicker by joining the determined crowd that lines up at about 5:30AM or by reserving a tee-off time in advance through **Ticketmaster**—which will almost double the otherwise low greens fee. Each player must have a golf bag and five clubs to gain access to the course; all are available for rent. Caddies are not permitted. ◆ Daily, Apr-Nov. 312/245.0909

65 CHICAGO ANTIQUE MALL

This warehouse of an antiques store comprises some 25 different dealers' stalls, all overseen by proprietor Sue Kress. The selection is strong on Art Deco pieces and Victorian furniture. **Cavalier Antiques** has a striking display of 19th-century chandeliers, which are dripping with crystals and completely wired for the 21st century, and there's an impressive collection of maps and globes dating back to the 16th century. Most of the dealers here will pack and ship your purchases. ◆ Daily, 11AM-6PM. 3036 N Lincoln Ave (between W Wellington and N Greenview Aves). 929.0200; fax 929.0842 ♿

66 POMPEI BAKERY

★★ $ This lively corner pizza emporium is the North Side branch of a popular eatery that has prospered in a South Side Italian neighborhood since 1909. Do not confuse the pizza here with Chicago-style deep-dish. It's Old World Italian—thick, hearty baked bread topped with an assortment of delicious, fresh ingredients. The service is a smart variation on cafeteria style—place and pay for your order, then stake out a table while your mouth waters with anticipation. The menu also offers a variety of above-average pasta options and great soups. You can lounge for a while or drop in for a quick score, making this a great place when you're on the go or when you've got kids in tow. ◆ Daily, lunch and dinner. 2955 N Sheffield Ave (at W Wellington Ave). 325.1900; fax 325.1942. Also at 1531 W Taylor St (at S Ashland Avenue). 312/421.5179. www.pompeipizza.com

67 HOUSE OF FINE CHOCOLATES

Willie Rahmig opened his candy shop in 1945 and, two generations later, his family still makes chocolates and fillings from scratch in the kitchen in back. Try a hand-dipped chocolate filled with amaretto or nibble a white-chocolate swan. There are baked goods too. ◆ Tu-Su. 3109 N Broadway (between W Barry Ave and W Briar Pl). 525.8338; fax 525.6160. www.houseoffinechocolates.com

68 LEATHER ON LEATHER

There are many creative uses for leather. One of the more unusual ones is making leather animals (a refreshing alternative to stuffed furry ones). And that's just one of many notions that leather craftsman David, who has had a shop at another location since 1973, has come up with. Come up with your own idea, and he might be able to make it for you. Or he'll repair that treasure you're not ready to part with. Other, more practical items include belts, pants, skirts, and jackets. About 60% of the great stuff in this two-level storefront is made on the premises. If you like the smell of leather, it's well worth a stop just to sniff around. ◆ Tu-Su. 3011 N Broadway (between W Wellington and W Barry Aves). 868.4200

69 LITTLE BUCHAREST

★$ Reds and browns dominate both the décor and the food in one of the few Romanian restaurants in the city. The veal paprikash, chicken à la Bucharest with liver and white-wine stuffing, and other dishes are terrific, but their low prices are even more notable. Rich homemade chocolate tortes will do you in if dinner doesn't. Watch for summertime outdoor feasts, when the restaurant takes over a block of Wellington Avenue for a festive pig and lamb roast. ◆ Romanian ◆ Daily, lunch and dinner. Reservations recommended F and Sa. 3001 N Ashland Ave (at W Wellington Ave). 929.8640; fax 929.1910

70 ST. ALPHONSUS CHURCH

A monumental Gothic church built for a German congregation, this is a neighborhood landmark not only because it juts out above all the surrounding structures but also because of its imposing siting at this six-cornered intersection. It was built between 1889 and 1897 by **Adam Boos** and **Josef Bettinghofer**, then **Schrader & Conradi**. ◆ 2950 N Southport Ave (at W Wellington Ave)

71 TERRACOTTA ROW

Five buildings were constructed on Oakdale Avenue in the 1880s by the Northwestern Terra Cotta Company, which became a national leader in the terra-cotta industry. Three still stand in good condition: **1059**, **1057**, and **1048 West Oakdale Avenue**. The last (and most elaborate) was the home of Henry Rokham, the company's president. It features gables with prominent corner pieces, an Italianate sunburst and flower finial, a gabled roof, a corbelled chimney, and extensive trim. On the building's west side is a terra-cotta relief of a woman in a skirt and bonnet seated at a spinning wheel. The houses are all private residences. ♦ W Oakdale Ave (between N Sheffield and N Seminary Aves)

72 POPS FOR CHAMPAGNE

One of the city's most elegant jazz clubs, it features well-known local combos. Plush booths, Art Deco sconces, a semicircular bar, and a gleaming black grand piano atop an elevated stage set the scene. Taittinger Blanc de Blanc 1981, Dom Pérignon 1982, and more than 100 other champagnes are available, many by the glass, along with some 20 other sparkling wines. Light appetizers and desserts are served too. The brick outdoor patio is lovely in the summer, although the music can't be heard there. ♦ Cover and minimum. Daily. 2934 N Sheffield Ave (at W Oakdale Ave). 472.1000. www.popschampagne.com

73 BINNY'S BEVERAGE DEPOT

Shopping for wine and liquor is as pleasurable as drinking it, thanks to the imagination of Michael Binstein, for whom this store is named. Recently, he expanded his popular store to build into the adjacent **Ivanhoe Theater**, preserving a neighborhood landmark that had fallen into disuse. The effect is like entering a medieval castle through a modern looking-glass. Inside there's plenty to look at. **Binny's** carries a wide variety of beer and liquor at some of the best prices in the city. The selection of wine is excellent and the salespeople are knowledgeable and helpful. But perhaps the nicest touch is the baby grand piano, usually played to dazzling effect on Friday and Saturday afternoons by Jeff Manuel, one of Chicago's premier lounge talents. ♦ Daily. 3000 N Clark St (at W Wellington Ave). 935.9400. Also at 213 W Grand Ave (between N Wells and N Franklin Sts). 312/332.0012

74 ERWIN

★★$$ This cozy storefront restaurant offers interesting variations on heartland fare. From white-bean pâté served with bread to delicious apple pie, everything is well prepared, and service is first-rate. Entrées include wood-grilled pork chops, steaks, and fresh fish, but look for some surprises too, such as noodles with roasted rabbit and wild mushrooms. ♦ American ♦ Tu-Sa, dinner; Su, brunch and dinner. 2925 N Halsted St (between W Diversey Pkwy and W Oakdale Ave). 528.7200 & www.erwincafe.com

75 BUCA DI BEPPO

★$$ Flocked wallpaper plastered with Italian-themed pictures in gaudy frames sets the lively mood and atmosphere in this frenetic family restaurant. Traditional Italian fare is much better than it has to be, and portions are huge! The space is broken up into many small rooms, each one seemingly decorated more brightly than the last. This is a great casual spot to bring *la famìglia* or another large group for a Sunday feed. Chances are good that you'll almost get your own private room. Relax and feel free to spill some sauce on your shirt. Be sure to check out the decorations in the rest rooms. *Buon appetito.* ♦ Daily, dinner. 2941 N Clark St (at W Oakdale Ave). 348.POPE; fax 348.1458. www.bucadibeppo.com

76 NANCY'S ORIGINAL STUFFED PIZZA

$ Deep-dish pizza is a Chicago original, and several pizza joints compete ferociously for tourist bucks by claiming to be the best, first, or healthiest. This pizzeria offers an excellent pie (deep-dish, heaped with ingredients, then topped with a crust and an extra layer of tomato sauce) without all the hype. The dimly lit restaurant is decorated like a 1970s basement rec room, but given the quality of pizza and the lack of crowds, the ambiance is tolerable. There's takeout too. ♦ Pizza ♦ Daily, lunch and dinner. 2930 N Broadway (between W Oakdale and W Wellington Aves). 883.1977

76 BROADWAY JOES

Redolent of incense, this bright corner store-front tobacco shop recalls a time when head shops were common (and cigarettes were cheaper). Pipes and inexpensive gift items stand alongside serious smoker's supplies. ♦ Daily. 2900 N Broadway (at W Oakdale Ave). 665.2085

77 SPARE PARTS

Striking fashion accessories for men and women are imported from around the world. The soft leather briefcases, handbags, wallets, and daily business planners from South America, Italy, and Spain are real beauties. ♦ Daily. 2947 N Broadway (between W Oakdale and W Wellington Aves). 525.4242 & www.shopspareparts.com

---

Restaurants/Clubs: Red | Hotels: Purple | Shops: Orange | Outdoors/Parks: Green | Sights/Culture: Blue

77 BOBTAIL SODA FOUNTAIN

★★$ Could an ice cream parlor really be one of the hottest places in town? So far, so cool for this old-fashioned shop that opened in 2004 and smartly didn't resort to ye or olde or shoppe in its name. Instead the place took its name from the handle on an old-fashioned soda fountain. When it opens—at six in the morning!—it serves up the best Belgian waffles this side of Brussels and steaming hot coffee. For lunch and dinner, there's grilled cheese. And there are ice cream creations all the time. You can watch the ice cream being made through a glass window that overlooks the on-site "factory." The counter help won't mind if you call them jerks, just as long as you leave a tip.
◆ M-Th, 6AM-11PM; F-Sa, 7AM-midnight; Su, 8AM-11PM. 2951 N Broadway (at Wellington Ave). 773/880.7372.
◆ www.bobtailsodafountain.com

78 ELBO ROOM

Once a factory, this two-story space is now a performance venue for jazz orchestras, poets, rock and country bands, and comedy troupes. Barrett Deems and his band play every Tuesday night. The stage is downstairs, cozily surrounded by tables, but the coolest seats in the house are the booths recessed off the main room and located directly below the sidewalks. The club takes its name from the building's triangular shape. ◆ Cover. M-F, Su, 8PM-2PM; Sa, to 3AM. 2871 N Lincoln Ave (at W George St). 549.5549. www.elboroom-chicago.com

79 POWELL'S BOOKSTORE

Arguably the best used-book store in the city, this shop stocks about 100,000 books spread out through three rooms in a neat, organized fashion. The subject range is vast: The large literature collection ranges from yellowing leather-bound volumes of classics to contemporary paperbacks; there's a good selection of children's books; and you will find beautiful art books on everything from Renaissance painters to photography. Best of all, the prices are consistently lower than at similar stores—there's even a bin of free books for true literary scavengers! ◆ Daily. 2850 N Lincoln Ave (between W Diversey Pkwy and N Lakewood Ave). 248.1444. Also at 1501 E 57th St (at Lake Park Ave). 955.7780; 828 S Wabash Ave (between E Ninth and E Eighth Sts). 312.341.0748. www.powellschicago.com

80 COMEDYSPORTZ

Are you ready for fast-paced improvisation with a competitive edge? That's the theme behind **ComedySportz**, a growing national network of local affiliates that presents live improv performances and provides training for aspiring standup comedians. Comedy-Sportz claims to be "dedicated to enriching lives and transcending all boundaries by celebrating the creative imagination of the human spirit . . . in four minutes or less." They've chosen to set up their Chicago headquarters at a venue that formerly served as home for a promising theater company. Sign up for classes and workshops or stop by to watch the performances of other trainees. ◆ 2851 N Halsted St (between W Diversey Pkwy and W Oakdale Ave). 549.8080. www.comedysportzchicago.com

81 LA CREPERIE

★$ Chicago's only creperie resembles a French bistro out of a 1960s movie. Create your own entrée, starting with buckwheat crepes and adding your choices of fillings such as broccoli, cheese, chicken, and mushrooms. Dessert crepes with butter and sugar are delectable—and it's all quite inexpensive. ◆ Crepes ◆ Tu-Su, lunch and dinner. 2845 N Clark St (between N Broadway and W Surf St) 528.9050 & www.lacreperieusa.com

82 CENTURY MALL

This six-story mall rose from the innards of a former movie palace dating from the 1930s. The façade, much of it preserved from the original structure, is a study in grandiose terra-cotta detailing. Inside, many of the original features remain, and recently the mall was upgraded with the addition of—a movie theater! All the stores are accessible by elevator or by a curving concrete ramp that lends the mall a distinct nautical look. A small food court downstairs serves burgers, pizza, and sushi. ◆ Daily. 2828 N Clark St (between W Diversey Pkwy and N Orchard St). 929.8100 &

Within Century Mall:

GAMERS PARADISE

Parcheesi, Monopoly, playing cards—you name the game, they've got it. Don't miss the extensive collection of chess sets, from ancient marble to high-tech steel. ◆ Third floor. 549.1833; fax 549.0221 & www.gamers.com

83 BORDERS

In addition to selling books, this megachain bookstore often features free music, poetry readings, and interesting speakers. The environment is both pleasant and stimulating, with the requisite in-store café. ◆ M-Th, Su, until 11PM; F, Sa, until midnight. 2817 N Clark St (between N Broadway and W Surf St). 935.3909; fax 935.4184 & www.borders.com

84 LAWRY'S TAVERN

★$ This tavern (not to be confused with the prime rib restaurant downtown) was a neighborhood institution decades before jazz clubs and fern bars moved in. Back then it was owned by the father of the current owner, Lawrence Price. It looks like any other saloon, but three nights a week tables are covered with checkered tablecloths and families line up for a fried-chicken feast (Wednesday and Saturday) and an all-you-can-eat fish fry (Friday). The bargain prices are one of the city's best-kept secrets; regulars would like it to stay that way. ◆ American ◆ W-F, Sa, dinner. 1028 W Diversey Pkwy (between N Sheffield and N Seminary Aves). 348.9711. www.lawrystavern.com

85 SELECT CUT STEAK HOUSE

★$$ This bustling corner neighborhood spot is a restaurant that gets right to the meat of the matter: steak at prices you can afford. An 18-ounce T-bone goes for $18.95 and is served with sourdough bread and choice potato or rice. At lunchtime, $7.50 will fetch you a 7-ounce steak sandwich. On weekends, the breakfast special is eggs and—you guessed it—steak. ◆ Steak house ◆ M-F, lunch and dinner; Sa, Su, breakfast, lunch, and dinner. 2808 N Halsted St (at W Diversey Pkwy). 244.1500. www.selectcut.com

86 BREWSTER APARTMENTS

Originally known as the **Lincoln Park Palace**, this eight-story structure was commissioned in 1893 by B. Edwards, publisher of *American Contractor* magazine, who wanted a building of small, elegant apartments. Designed by **E.H. Turnoch** and renovated in 1972 by **Mieki Hayano**, it has been designated a Chicago landmark for its excellent early application to a residential building of the principles of metal-frame construction, in which the use of an iron or steel frame made it possible to erect higher buildings. The exterior is faced in rusticated stone; the upper stories are banded by a large terra-cotta frieze with details in the style of **Louis Sullivan**, and the terra-cotta cornice features lion heads. The entryway on North Pine Grove Avenue, originally the ladies' entrance, is flanked by four polished jasper colonettes inset with windows. Make a friend in the building so that you can see the interior, which boasts one of the most fabulous remaining 19th-century atriums in the city. Patterns of intertwined tendrils and oak leaves adorn the lobby moldings, and open-case elevators, staircases, and bridges are all woven in extraordinary cast-iron lattice-work. ◆ 2800 N Pine Grove Ave (at W Diversey Pkwy)

87 330 AND 340 WEST DIVERSEY PARKWAY

Designed as the **Commonwealth Promenade** by **Mies van der Rohe** in 1957, these residential high-rises are refined and well detailed, especially at the corners. The precise placement of the towers on their lot and their glassy curtain walls create units that are lit brightly and naturally and have fabulous views. ◆ Between N Commonwealth Ave and N Sheridan Rd

KENWOOD/HYDE PARK

Middle-class, liberal-minded, and more racially integrated than any other part of the city, Hyde Park/Kenwood is an urban oasis of smarts and savvy. Bordered by **Lake Michigan**, **Cottage Grove Avenue**, and **61st** and **47th Streets**, it is home to the 175-acre **University of Chicago**. Vast parklands provide public recreation as well as homes for the beloved **Museum of Science and Industry** in **Jackson Park** and the distinguished **DuSable Museum of African-American History** in **Washington Park**. Popular restaurants, alluring shops, and some of the city's best bookstores make up the main shopping districts along **53rd**, **55th**, and **57th Streets**. The imposing architecture

ranges from I.M. Pei's University Apartments on 55th Street to rows of 19th-century mansions along Kenwood and Kimbark Avenues between 48th and 49th Streets, from Frank Lloyd Wright's Prairie School–style Robie House to the Gothic Rockefeller Chapel, both on the University of Chicago campus.

Hyde Park was created in 1852 when Chicago lawyer Paul Cornell purchased 300 acres of lakefront property and promoted it among affluent Chicagoans as a suburb and summer-home site, giving it a name with appropriately upper-class connotations. Success was ensured when he deeded property to the Illinois Central Railroad in return for regular commuter train service to the Loop; prosperous Chicagoans began to build their homes here. Adding to the attraction was the development of bordering parks designed by famous landscape architect Frederick Law Olmsted.

Kenwood, north of Hyde Park Boulevard, was founded in 1856 when Chicago dentist John A. Kennicott built an estate there and named the community after his mother's ancestral home in Scotland. Close to both the commuter train and the bustling Union Stockyards, about 3 miles northwest, Kenwood attracted meatpacking king Augustus Swift, as well as Sears, Roebuck & Company mogul Julius Rosenwald, and numerous others whose mansions matched their status as business giants. The construction of nearby workers' cottages to house their servants simultaneously created a large Irish community. Both areas escaped the 1871 Chicago Fire, leaving them with some of the city's oldest homes and spurring a housing boom. Rapid growth prompted annexation to Chicago in 1889, despite protests by middle-class residents who preferred suburban status. Four years later, the World's Columbian Exposition, commemorating the 400th anniversary of Columbus's arrival in America, was held here in Jackson Park, causing a further boom of hotels, apartment buildings, and stores. The exposition's legacy also lives on throughout Jackson Park; the Museum of Science and Industry, for example, is situated in what had been the fair's Palace of Fine Arts.

In 1892, just a year before the fair, the University of Chicago was founded by John D. Rockefeller on Hyde Park land donated by retailer Marshall Field. Faculty, staff, and students moved in and transformed what had been a largely conservative, commerce-minded community into a liberal and intellectual one. By the 1920s, Hyde Park had become something of a resort community, with luxurious lakefront hotels attracting visitors from throughout the city and beyond. After World War I and again after World War II, increasing numbers of African Americans began to settle here. To diminish racial conflict, neighbors formed block clubs that encouraged integration.

Throughout the 1940s and 1950s, however, both Kenwood and Hyde Park faced serious downturns. Affluent residents left Kenwood in droves, and the neighborhood declined in socioeconomic status, spurred by odoriferous downwind drafts from the stockyards. Though Hyde Park supported a bohemian community of artists, writers, and a satirical group called the Compass Players, founded by Mike Nichols and Elaine May and later to become Second City, it was turning into a run-down and crime-ridden community. In the late 1950s a long and controversial process of urban renewal commenced. Although some buildings were preserved and restored, whole blocks were torn down to make way for new construction. Hyde Park has since stabilized, portions of Kenwood have undergone restoration, and gentrification is now on a steady course toward the community's western border and farther north in Bronzeville. A proper visit to Hyde Park and Kenwood is best as a daylong event, perhaps concluded by an evening concert or play at the university or dinner at one of the area restaurants.

All area codes in this chapter are 773 unless otherwise noted.

KENWOOD

1 4855 SOUTH WOODLAWN AVENUE

The late Black Muslim leader Elijah Muhammad lived in this Moorish home. It is now privately owned by minister Louis Farrakhan, controversial head of the Nation of Islam. ♦ Between E 49th and E 48th Sts

2 GEORGE BLOSSOM HOUSE

In this 1892 **Frank Lloyd Wright** project, the round-headed Palladian windows and Ionic capitals give no hint that the 25-year-old designer would develop into a revolutionary American architect. But the Roman brick foundation and deep eaves of this private residence anticipate his later Prairie School designs. ♦ 4858 S Kenwood Ave (between E 49th and E 48th Sts)

2 WARREN MCARTHUR HOUSE

Like the **Blossom House** next door, this house was a bootlegged commission, a job done on the side by **Frank Lloyd Wright** in 1892 while he was still employed by **Louis Sullivan**. The large gambrel roof that dominates this privately owned house sits atop symmetrical octagonal bays with leaded windows. ♦ 4852 S Kenwood Ave (between E 49th and E 48th Sts)

3 RAMADA INN LAKESHORE

$$ There are panoramas of Lake Michigan and the city skyline from many of the 184 rooms, so be sure to ask for a room with a view. The tone here is comfortably low key. Amenities include an outdoor swimming pool, access to a nearby health club, business/conference facilities, and a free shuttle bus to downtown and local restaurants and sights. ♦ 4900 S Lake Shore Dr (at E 49th St). 288.5800, 800/237.4933; fax 288.5819 ♿

4 JULIUS ROSENWALD HOUSE

Rosenwald was head of Sears, Roebuck & Company and a famous philanthropist. His 42-room mansion was designed in 1903 by **Nimmons & Fellows**, the architects of many Sears facilities. The Roman-brick house with Prairie School elements is oriented to the south and originally looked out over elaborate gardens. Unfortunately, this private residence is run down, but it's still an interesting piece of Chicago history. ♦ 4901 S Ellis Ave (at E 49th St)

5 ERNEST J. MAGERSTADT HOUSE

Characteristic of Prairie School architect **George W. Maher**'s work is the use of Roman brick, elaborately detailed column capitals, and a light color palette. Maher's "rhythm-motif" theory of architecture called for the repeated application of a single decorative element throughout. In this 1908 house (still a private residence), the decorative element is the poppy, rendered especially well in the leaded glass windows. ♦ 4930 S Greenwood Ave (between E 50th and E 49th Sts)

6 4944 SOUTH WOODLAWN AVENUE

Heavyweight boxing champion Muhammad Ali used to punch around in this place, his massive brick mansion of a home, built in 1916 for $40,000. It now belongs to the Islamic Foundation and is not open to the public. ♦ Between E 50th and E 49th Sts

7 K.A.M. ISAIAH ISRAEL TEMPLE

The oldest Jewish congregation in the Midwest, **Kahilath Anshe Ma'ariv**, founded in 1847, merged with the **Isaiah Israel** congregation and made their home in one of Chicago's most magnificent houses of worship. The brick-and-limestone temple, designed in 1924 by **Alfred S. Alschuler**, uses Byzantine style in its octagonal form and arch-and-dome construction. A minaret rising behind the dome is actually a smokestack. The ornamentation is derived from that of a second-century synagogue in Tiberias in Palestine. The temple houses the **Morton B. Weiss Museum of Judaica**, which has a small but valuable collection of Jewish artifacts. ♦ 1100 E Hyde Park Blvd (at S Greenwood Ave). 924.1234 ♿ www.kamii.org

8 REGENTS PARK

Between the twin towers of this luxury apartment building complex is the 1.3-acre **Bergen Garden**. Designed by landscape architect Phil Shipley, it sports a small waterfall, fountains, and lagoons and is home to numerous species of birds, plants, and trees. It may be toured only by prearrangement. Shipley also designed the **Regents Club** health club, open to members only. Gourmet groceries and take-out meals are available at the **Market in the Park**, open daily. ♦ 5050 S Lake Shore Dr (at E Hyde Park Blvd). Tour reservations 288.5050; market 734.3687

HYDE PARK

9 ISIDORE H. HELLER HOUSE

Frank Lloyd Wright was working his way toward the Prairie School–style in this 1897 project, which features the exaggeratedly horizontal Roman brick, widely projecting eaves, and geometric forms of that slightly later style. This is a city house—narrow but deep, just like the lot, with a more closed façade at ground level. A beautiful third-floor frieze of molded plaster is by sculptor Richard Bock, a frequent collaborator. It's a private residence. ♦ 5132 S Woodlawn Ave (between E 52nd St and E Hyde Park Blvd)

10 CORNELL VILLAGE

Gospel singer Mahalia Jackson lived in this middle-income, mixed-race housing development until the end of her life. ♦ 5201 S Cornell Ave (between E 53rd St and E Hyde Park Blvd)

11 CEDARS OF LEBANON

★$ Restaurants in Hyde Park generally cater to either of two kinds of patrons: pairs of students, usually on a date, or crowds that mix faculty and students and visitors—often all engaged in one discussion. This place attracts both with spinach pie, made while you wait, fresh hummus, and tasty lamb. ♦ Middle Eastern. ♦ Daily, lunch and dinner. 1206 E 53rd St (at S Woodlawn Ave). 324.6227

12 HARPER COURT

When artists elsewhere in Hyde Park were displaced by urban renewal, this two-story structure was built by supporters of the arts as cheap gallery space. These days, the tenants are commercial—it's a shopping center, spread over four buildings, smack dab in the middle of a parking lot. Surprisingly, an artsy air persists. ♦ Daily. 5225 S Harper Ave (between E 53rd and E 52nd Sts)

Within Harper Court:

SUNFLOWER SEED

Hyde Park appears to be the only neighborhood in the city able to support two health-food stores within a stone's throw of each other. This one is well stocked with vitamins, teas, and other necessities of healthful living. ♦ M-Sa. 363.1600

DR. WAX

If you can't peddle those old Bee Gees albums around the corner at **2nd Hand Tunes**, try here before using them as Frisbees. ♦ Daily. 493.8696; fax 493.8494. Also at 1121 W Berwyn Ave (at N Broadway). 784.3333. www.usedcds.com

ARTISANS 21 GALLERY

Among the members' work showcased at this cooperative gallery are unusual hand-painted pottery and woven garments in rich hues. ♦ Tu-Su. 288.7450

WINDOW TO AFRICA

Owner Patrick Woodtor brings authentic fabrics, baskets, jewelry, and other crafts and art back from trips to his native West Africa. ♦ Daily. 955.7742. www.africaninternationalhouse.org

DIXIE KITCHEN & BAIT SHOP

★$ Decorated with fishing gear, old phonograph albums, and other items that lend it the ambiance of a Southern flea market, this place offers well-prepared food at rates that even students can afford—well, most students. The menu ranges from traditional Southern dishes to spicy down-home soul food, and it's all skillfully executed. Fried green tomatoes make a good starter, followed by such entrées as gumbo, country-fried steak, and blackened catfish. For dessert—pecan pie and peach cobbler, of course. The wine list isn't exceptional, but the beer choices will have you whistlin' "Dixie." ♦ Southern ♦ Daily, lunch and dinner. 363.4943 ♿ www.dixiekitchenchicago.com

13 MELLOW YELLOW

★$ The prizewinning chili is served five ways, from the usual bowlful to over spaghetti and topped with cheese, onions, and sour cream. Some prefer the fresh croissants and good coffee at breakfast at this bright, friendly spot with a big yellow awning out front. ♦ American ♦ Daily, breakfast, lunch, and dinner. 1508 E 53rd St (between S Lake Park and S Harper Aves). 667.2000

13 BONNE SANTÉ

University communities are usually full of health-food shops; this one mainly carries healthful, organic groceries, but it also has a wonderful juice bar that makes fabulous protein shakes. ♦ Daily. 1512 E 53rd St (between S Lake Park and S Harper Aves). 667.5700

THE BEST

Steve Crescenzo
Writer

Drinking margaritas at **El Jardin**'s outdoor patio all day, then stumbling over to the **Wild Hare** for live reggae music and Red Stripe beer that night.

The view looking south from **North Pond Café**. It takes in the lagoon, most of **Lincoln Park's** trees, and the Chicago skyline.

The Boodles gin martinis at **Club Lucky**. Close your eyes and you can almost see Sinatra walk in the door.

The **Kingston Mines** on a Sunday night. The music is just as good, but the crowds aren't as intense.

Taking a day off work and boating up the **Chicago River** at sunrise. The city is just waking up, everyone else is going to work . . . and you're going to spend the day on the water.

The Portobello mushroom lasagna at **Cucina Bella** . . . even people who hate mushrooms get addicted to it.

13 VALOIS

★$ Named in a *Chicago Tribune* list of "top greasy spoons," this spot with the slogan "See your food" has been dishing out wholesome and cheap cafeteria fare for nearly 70 years. At lunchtime four or five guys behind the little counter hustle to deliver corn on the cob, hot beef sandwiches, roasted pork, overcooked vegetables, and cheap sides of coleslaw. The biscuits and gravy are tops, and the breakfasts are good. Customers cover the socioeconomic gamut. In 1991, its patrons were the subject of the highly lauded book *Slim's Table*, by **U of C** grad student Michael Dunier. ♦ Cafeteria ♦ Daily, breakfast, lunch, and dinner. 1518 E 53rd St (between S Lake Park and S Harper Aves). 667.0647

14 5300 BLOCK OF UNIVERSITY AVENUE

This street is the perfect spot for a spring or summer stroll. Home to many university professors, the block has a neighborhoodwide reputation for its resplendent flower gardens. ♦ Between E 54th and E 53rd Sts

15 BOYAJIAN'S BAZAAR

Handicrafts and gifts from the Near East, Asia, and Africa cram this tiny storefront. Best of all are the boxes and boxes of beads in myriad colors, patterns, and materials: Freshwater pearls, Baltic amber, old Bohemian crystals, African trade beads, hand-glazed Chinese porcelain, Indian camel bone, and Jamaican wood are just a few. ♦ Daily. 1305 E 53rd St (between S Dorchester and S Kimbark Aves). 324.2020

16 FREEHLING POT & PAN CO.

Everything for the kitchen is here, all of very high quality—from long-lasting All-Clad and

University of Chicago professor Mortimer Adler collaborated with university president Robert Maynard Hutchins to start the Great Books program in 1952.

Scanpan cookware, shimmering baking tins for muffins and scones, and 19-quart boiling pots to ceramic Thanksgiving turkey platters. ♦ M-Sa. 1365 E 53rd St (between S Dorchester and S Kimbark Aves). 643.8080

16 2ND HAND TUNES

Lincoln Park's excellent used-record empire has an outlet here, as well as locations in Evanston and Oak Park. ♦ Daily. 1377 E 53rd St (between S Dorchester and S Kimbark Aves). 684.3375. Also at 2604 N Clark St (between W Wrightwood Ave and W Drummond Pl). 281.8813. www.2ndhandtunes.com

16 RIBS 'N' BIBS

$ Smell that hickory smoke? Here's where die-hard Hyde Park rib fans come for yummy full and half slabs and rib tips. ♦ Barbecue ♦ Daily, lunch and dinner until midnight. 5300 Dorchester Ave (at E 53rd St). 493.0400

17 HYDE PARK ART CENTER

A community art school and the **Ruth Horwich Gallery**, set in the ballroom of the former **Del Prado Hotel** (now an apartment building), carry on the legacy of what used to be the **57th Street Artists Colony**. The gallery has played an important part in the careers of emerging artists, debuting the work of Ed Paschke, among others. On your way in, note the painted terra-cotta Indians in headdresses decorating the lobby ceiling. ♦ M-Sa, 10AM-5PM. 5307 S Hyde Park Blvd (between E 54th and E 53rd Sts). 324.5520; fax 324.6641 &

18 EASTVIEW PARK

Yes, those really are green, squawking parrots flapping around in this tiny park with a view of the lake. Native to the South American Andes, the Adam and Eve of the flock were probably pet store escapees. Today their 50-or-so offspring live a liberated lifestyle year-round in giant stick nests they've constructed in an ash tree. The tree is just across the street from the entrance to the **Hampton House**

Condominiums, where, by the way, Chicago's late mayor Harold Washington lived.
♦ Bounded by S Lake Shore and S Shore Drs, S Everett Ave, and E 55th and E 53rd Sts

19 WOODLAWN TAP

Chicago Bears fans cheering football games on the TV, debating academicians, and literary and dramatic types all feel at home at this sallow-walled, sagging-floored, longtime **University of Chicago** hangout. Live jazz on Sunday nights. ♦ Daily, until 2AM. 1172 E 55th St (between S Woodlawn and S University Aves). 643.5516

20 UNIVERSITY APARTMENTS

In 1955 buildings along this entire stretch of 55th Street were demolished as part of a grand plan of urban renewal for Hyde Park. These "traffic island apartments," built between 1959 and 1962 by **I.M. Pei**, **Harry Weese & Associates**, and **Loewenberg & Loewenberg**, were a cornerstone of the plan. A little swimming pool is hidden at their western edge. ♦ 1400-1450 E 55th St (between S Harper and S Kenwood Aves)

21 HYDE PARK CO-OP

No longer recognizable as an **I.M. Pei** design, this urban renewal project sprang up in 1959 to replace demolished structures. It has undergone some renewal itself and contains new shops selling shoes, sporting goods, children's clothes, and the like. Among the old-time businesses is the **Hyde Park Cooperative Society Grocery Store**, the oldest single-store cooperative in the country, founded in 1932. (You need not be a co-op member to shop here.) A post office and credit union are in its basement. ♦ Daily, 7 AM-11PM. E 55th St and S Lake Park Ave. 667.1444

22 MORRY'S DELI

★$ Kosher hot dogs, corned beef, pastrami, and the like are available at this New York-style deli. For breakfast, there's Morry's special—a bagel with cheese, egg, salami, and pastrami. ♦ Deli ♦ Daily, breakfast, lunch, and dinner. 5500 S Cornell Ave (at E 55th St). 363.3800

22 NILE

$ A clean spot with Middle Eastern cuisine at prices students can afford. In addition to falafel and hummus, there's chicken *shawarma* (boneless chicken that is marinated, then rotisseried and sliced thin), and shish kebabs of lamb, beef, or chicken. ♦ Middle Eastern ♦ Daily, lunch and dinner. 1611 E 55th St (between S Cornell and S

Lake Park Aves). 324.9499. www.campusfood.com

22 THAI 55TH

$ One of three Thai joints in a one-block stretch, this one also caters to student appetites and budgets. Bangkok chicken is again a favorite, but here it's served with almonds, bell peppers, onions, and scallions. ♦ Thai ♦ Daily, lunch and dinner. 1607 E 55th St (between S Cornell and S Lake Park Aves). 363.7119

23 SNAIL

$ A light and cozy place that college students love because the food is so very reasonably priced. The Thai curry sauce can be ordered on seafood, chicken, beef, or pork and is one of the most popular dishes here, along with Bangkok chicken, which is marinated, breaded, deep-fried, and then stir-fried. ♦ Thai ♦ Daily, lunch and dinner. 1649 E 55th St (between S Hyde Park Blvd and S Cornell Ave). 667.5423. www.snailthai.com

23 SIAM

$ This storefront café offers traditional Thai cuisine at reasonable prices. The most popular dishes here include Bangkok chicken, which is breaded and stir-fried with bell peppers and cashews, and *pad ped talay* (shrimp, scallops, and squid stir-fried with vegetables in a red curry sauce). Delivery is available. ♦ Thai ♦ Daily, lunch and dinner. 1641 E 55th St (between S Hyde Park Blvd and S Cornell Ave). 324.9296

24 PROMONTORY POINT

A pretty, landscaped park jutting out into Lake Michigan at 55th Street was created from landfill in the 1920s. "The Point" is a pleasant place for a warm-weather picnic or Frisbee toss, not to mention a perfect vantage point for a dramatic view of the city skyline to the north and the hazy shores of Indiana southward. Swimming is forbidden because the waters are quite deep and dangerous, but a bit farther south is the **57th Street Beach**, a spacious and safe place to swim or catch a few rays. ♦ E 55th St (just east of S Shore Dr)

25 COURT THEATRE

Designed in 1981 by **Harry Weese**, this is one of the city's premier professional theaters, presenting innovative renditions of classics with an occasional foray into more modern works. Typical offerings have included Oscar Wilde's sparkling *The Importance of Being Earnest* and Donna Blue Lachman's *Frida: The Last Portrait*, about Frida Kahlo. The well-designed proscenium stage and theater provide good sightlines from every one of the 250 seats. ◆ M, Tu, Th-Su. 5535 S Ellis Ave (between E 56th and E 55th Sts). 753.4472 ё www.courttheatre.org

26 DAVID AND ALFRED SMART MUSEUM OF ART

Founded by the University of Chicago in 1974 to house its substantial art holdings, the museum has a large permanent collection ranging from Christian and Byzantine artifacts to furniture by **Frank Lloyd Wright** and contemporary paintings by Mark Rothko. The adjacent courtyard holds four sculptures: *Reclining Figure* by Henry Moore; *Grande Radar* by Arnaldo Pomodoro; *Why?* by Richard Hunt; and *Truncated Pyramid* by Jene Highstein, a memorial to a university student who was brutally murdered in 1990. Adjoining the museum is the **Cochrane-Woods Art Center**, which houses the art history department. Both buildings were designed by New Yorker **Edward Larrabee Barnes**, who also designed the Walker Art Center in Minneapolis. ◆ Free. Tu-Su. 5550 S Greenwood Ave (between E 56th and E 55th Sts). 702.0200 ё www.uchicago.edu

27 5551 SOUTH UNIVERSITY AVENUE

George Fred Keck designed the startlingly modern **House of Tomorrow** at the 1933 Century of Progress World's Fair, but he had few commissions during the Depression. This one, designed with his brother, **William Keck**, was built in 1937. Decades ahead of its time, the three-unit cooperative apartment building is a study in simplicity, practicality, and fine detailing. The metal louvers act as blinds, providing privacy and regulating heat gain through the windows. Both architects occupied units in the building at one time. ◆ Between E 56th and E 55th Sts

28 HYDE PARK HISTORICAL SOCIETY

Housed in a restored 1893 cable-car station, the museum documents Hyde Park history, culture, art, and architecture. ◆ Free. Sa, Su, 2-4PM. Lectures and tours of the neighborhood available by prearrangement. 5529 S

The Manhattan Project's first controlled nuclear reaction occurred in 1942 in a squash-court laboratory under the football field at the University of Chicago.

Lake Park Ave (between E 56th and E 55th Sts). 493.1893

29 WINDERMERE HOUSE

Designed by **Rapp & Rapp** in 1924, this was once one of Hyde Park's grandest hotels, playing host to such celebrated guests as John D. Rockefeller and Edna Ferber. Thomas Mann started writing *Dr. Faustus* here while visiting his daughter, a student at the university. It has since been converted to rental apartments. ◆ 1642 E 56th St (between S Hyde Park Blvd and S Cornell Ave)

Within Windermere House:

PICCOLO MONDO

★$ Authentic Italian food is served at this gourmet grocery store and simply appointed restaurant, a good choice for lunch during a visit to the **Museum of Science and Industry**. In fair weather you may dine alfresco on the terrace overlooking **Jackson Park**. Salads, sauces, and pastas such as *rotolo*—layered dough, Italian cheeses, ham, and spinach topped with *besciamella* (cream) sauce—are all made on the premises. ◆ Italian ◆ M-Sa, lunch and dinner; Su, dinner. 643.1106

30 PROMONTORY APARTMENTS

The continuing shortage of steel after World War II dictated that **Mies van der Rohe** use reinforced concrete to build this 1949 high-rise apartment building, his first such structure. The visible expression of underlying structure for which **Mies** is famous is seen here, as the columns are stepped back at the 6th, 11th, and 16th stories, emphasizing that the load lightens as the building rises. ◆ 5530 S Shore Dr (between E 56th and E 55th Sts)

31 DUSABLE MUSEUM OF AFRICAN-AMERICAN HISTORY

Named in honor of Chicago's first permanent settler, Jean Baptiste-Pointe DuSable, a Haitian of mixed African and European parentage, the museum's extensive artifacts, photos, and paintings trace the black experience in America. There are permanent exhibits such as *Up From Slavery*, which vividly depicts the life of African-Americans from pre–Civil War days to the civil rights movement, and *Illinois Black History Makers*. The Works Progress Administration period and the 1960s black arts movement are particularly well represented. The gift shop carries jewelry, fabrics, and other arts and crafts by African-American, Egyptian, Haitian, and African artists. The museum building has an unusually institutional look because it was previously a park administration building and then a police lockup. The front steps descend to the beautiful lawns of **Washington Park**, designed by famed landscape architect **Frederick Law**

Olmsted. Beyond the brick terrace, imagine the race course that filled the park a century ago with city swells. ♦ Admission. Sundays free. Children under 6 free. Daily. 740 E 56th Pl (just east of S Payne Dr). 947.0600 ♿ www.dusablemuseum.org

University of Chicago

Founded in 1892 by John D. Rockefeller, with an initial enrollment of 594, the prestigious private university today has more than 10,000 students attending undergraduate programs and graduate schools of law, medicine, business, and theology, among others. More than 60 Nobel Prize winners have been associated with the university as students or faculty. The campus, spanning 175 acres, is composed of stately Gothic architecture laid out by **Henry Ives Cobb**. Some 70 other architects have since contributed buildings; the best way to see the architecture and sculpture is to take a guided tour. ♦ Free tours M-Sa, 10AM; tours leave from the Visitors' Center (Ida Noyes Hall, 1212 E 59th St, between S Dorchester and S Woodlawn Aves), where metered parking is also available. 702.1234; tours, 702.8370. www.uchicago.edu

32 *Nuclear Energy* Sculpture

A dramatic bronze by Henry Moore commemorates the site of the world's first self-sustained nuclear chain reaction, carried out during World War II by Enrico Fermi and his scientific team under the stands of the now-demolished **Stagg Field**. Moore described the piece as evoking the human skull, a mushroom cloud, and cathedral architecture. ♦ S Ellis Ave (between E 57th and E 56th Sts)

33 Joseph Regenstein Library

It looks like concrete, but the building's facing is actually a roughly textured, grooved limestone that was chosen to blend with the cladding of the surrounding buildings. Built in 1970, the seven-story "Reg" was designed as the **Graduate Research Library**. Each floor is dedicated to a particular discipline—business, geography, military science, film, and music, to name a few—and is divided into stacks, offices, reading areas, and faculty studies. **Walter A. Netsch Jr.** of **Skidmore, Owings & Merrill** also designed the libraries at **Northwestern University** and the **University of Illinois at Chicago**. Of special interest are the **Center for Children's Books** (fourth floor) and the **Map Collection** (sub-basement level), which includes atlases, gazetteers, travel guides, and 350,000 maps and aerial-view photos for most regions of the world. An exhibit area on the first floor is open to the general public; access to the rest of the library is restricted. ♦ M-F, until 4:30PM; Sa, until noon. 1100 E 57th St (between S University and S Ellis Aves). 702.8740 ♿

34 57th Street Books

Before the birth of the superstore, the Midwest's greatest concentration of books lay on this block and the next. The shops here still boast the greatest selection. At this one, help yourself to a cup of coffee brewing in the reading area and linger in front of the fireplace for as long as you like, working your way through the wide-ranging general-interest titles. A separate kids' reading area with toys supplements the substantial children's book collection. The store's complete collection of Penguin Classics titles is a standout. ♦ M-Sa, until 10PM; Su, until 8PM. 1301 E 57th St (at S Kimbark Ave). 684.1300. www.semcoop.com

35 Edwardo's of Hyde Park

★$$ This restaurant makes some of the city's tastiest deep-dish pizzas, using natural ingredients and herbs grown on the premises. ♦ Pizza ♦ Daily, lunch and dinner. 1321 E 57th St (between S Kenwood and S Kimbark Aves). 241.7960. Also at numerous locations throughout the city

35 Medici on 57th

★$$ Deep-dish pizza, burgers, and many varieties of rich, strong coffee are specialties at this neighborhood hangout. Dim lighting and rough wooden booths covered with graffiti qualify it as a true collegiate coffeehouse. ♦ Pizza/coffeehouse ♦ Daily, breakfast, lunch, and dinner until midnight. 1327 E 57th St (between S Kenwood and S Kimbark Aves). 667.7394. www.medici57.com

36 O'Gara & Wilson, Ltd.

Chicago's oldest bookstore, which was established in 1882 and has operated under other names, is furnished with old-fashioned ladders on tracks. The store's 40,000 used and out-of-print titles include a comprehensive art section and what may be the city's best array of British and American literary criticism. Newly acquired books are put out every Friday night. ♦ M-Th, 10AM-9PM; F, Sa, 10AM-10PM; Su, noon-8PM. 1448 E 57th St

Museum of Science and Industry

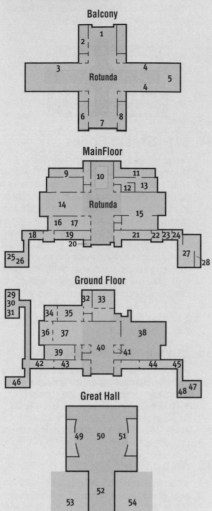

Balcony

1
2
3 Rotunda
4
4 5
6 8
7

MainFloor

9
10
11
12 13
14 Rotunda
15
16 17
18 19
20
21 22 23 24
27
25 26
28

Ground Floor

29
30
31
32 33
34 35
36 37
38
39
40 41
42 43
44 45
46
48 47

Great Hall

49 50 51
52
53 54

1 Regenstein Hall of Chemistry
2 Reusable City
3 Take Flight
4 Grainger Hall of Basic Science
5 Prenatal Development
6 The Heart
7 The Brain
8 AIDS: The War Within
9 Yesterday's Main Street
10 Coal Mine
11 Petroleum Planet
12 Enterprise
13 Toymakers 3000 Enterprise
14 The Great Train Story
15 Temporary Exhibits
16 Baby Chick Hatchery
17 Genetics
18 Out of the Vault
19 Robots Like Us
20 Members' Lounge
21 Networld
22 World Live Theater
23 Whispering Gallery
24 Imaging
25 Navy: Technology at Sea
26 Flight Simulators
27 Virtual Reality
28 Auditorium
29 Omnimax Theater
30 Henry Crown Space Center
31 Galaxy Shop
32 Yesterday's Firefighters
33 Colleen Moore's Fairy Castle
34 Plumbing
35 Energy Lab
36 Volunteer office
37 The Farm
38 Brain Food Court
39 Idea Factory
40 Jollyball
41 Foucault Pendulum
42 Eye Spy
43 Circus
44 Ships Through the Ages
45 Racing Cars
46 U-505 Submarine
47 Group Center
48 Kid's Stop Shop
49 Big Idea Store
50 Main Entrance
51 Ticketing
52 Pioneer Zephyr
53 Parking Garage
54 Parking Garage

(between S Harper and S Blackstone Aves). 363.0993 &

37 POWELL'S BOOKSTORE

Used books on all topics fill the store from floor to ceiling. Although the store specializes in academic remainders, it also stocks antiquarian books and has a substantial selection of rare used children's books. There are cheap paperbacks galore and—better yet—occasional freebies. ♦ Daily, until 11PM. 1501 E 57th St (at S Harper Ave). 955.7780. Also at 828 S Wabash Ave (between E Ninth and E Eighth Sts). 312/341.0748; 2850 N Lincoln Ave (between W Diversey Pkwy and N Lakewood Ave). 248.1444. www.powellschicago.com

38 JACKSON PARK

This park was originally developed as the site of the World's Columbian Exposition of 1893, which celebrated the 400th anniversary of Columbus's arrival in the New World and attracted more than 27 million visitors. The exposition's designer-in-chief was famed visionary **Daniel Burnham**. **Frederick Law Olmsted**, who created New York City's Central Park, designed the landscaping; artists Augustus Saint-Gaudens, Daniel Chester French, and Lorado Taft contributed statues. The major buildings were designed by a dozen architects from around the country, among them **Louis Sullivan**, who created the **Transportation Building**. The result was a "White City" of gleaming temporary buildings housing exhibits from around the world that ranged from a demonstration of gold mining in South Africa to a miniature replica of Des Moines, Iowa. The South Pond contained a reproduction of Christopher Columbus's *Santa Maria*. Gondoliers in 15th-century costume plied the lagoons. Today **Jackson Park** retains some features of the exposition, but tennis courts, baseball diamonds, and an 18-hole golf course have been added. The ponds have become harbors, home to the **Jackson Park Yacht Club** (a private club, but open to members of yacht clubs elsewhere in the country). The **Wooded Island** is a kind of nature retreat with many varieties of trees, wildlife, and 300 species of birds. At its northern end is the **Japanese Garden**, a re-creation of the exposition's Japanese Pavilion tea garden. The only building remaining from the fair is the **Palace of Fine Arts**, now home to the **Museum of Science and Industry**. ♦ Bounded by Lake Michigan and S Stony Island Ave and E 67th and E 56th Sts &

Within Jackson Park:

MUSEUM OF SCIENCE AND INDUSTRY

The building most often visited by tourists in Chicago was originally the **Palace of Fine Arts**, which was designed by **Charles B. Atwood** and built for the 1893 World's Columbian Exposition. Most of the exposition's buildings were little more than set decorations of timber and plaster and did not survive long, but the **Palace of Fine Arts**, designed to safeguard important artwork, was made of brick. It was the most overtly classical of the expositions buildings. **Atwood** was inspired by two cultures: The colonnaded porches and caryatids (the 13-foot-tall maidens supporting the porch pediments) are of Greek origin; the dome is Roman. The Greek elements are derived from many of the buildings on the Acropolis in Athens, including the Parthenon and the Erechtheum. After the exposition closed, the building was used by the **Field Museum** (now at Burnham Harbor) until 1920 and then was renovated to house the new science and technology museum funded largely by philanthropist and Sears mogul Julius Rosenwald. The renovation took place between 1929 and 1940. The exterior was designed by **Graham, Anderson, Probst & White**; **Shaw, Naess & Murphy** were responsible for the interior. Until 1991, when it began charging admission, the museum was the second most visited in the country (after the Air and Space Museum in Washington, DC), hosting 4.5 million visitors each year. The traffic took its toll on the physical plant, and the museum has embarked on an ambitious capital improvement and exhibit redesign program called MSI 2000 to modernize the facility for the next century. The museum's 14 acres (see floor plan page 188) are a whirlwind of sound, light, and activity as visitors push buttons, operate computers, turn cranks, watch videos, hear recordings, and otherwise engage in the more than 2,000 wide-ranging interactive exhibits. Special attractions include a captured World War II German submarine; a high-tech exhibit unlocking the mysteries of the human brain; a replica of a

Southern Illinois coal mine, complete with a coal train and a hoist down a mine shaft; cross-sections of a human cadaver (employees call him "Deli-Man"); a simulated space-shuttle ride; a walk along a turn-of-the-19th-century cobblestone street; *Colleen Moore's Fairy Castle*, an enchanting dwelling furnished with more than 1,000 miniature treasures; and "The Great Train Story," a must-see for railroad lovers young and old. Also displayed are a fully restored "silver streak" San Francisco *Zephyr* train and a full-size United Airlines Boeing 727, modified so that visitors may see the interior engine and controls and equipped to demonstrate a simulated takeoff. The museum also holds an annual Christmas Around the World festival. In 1986 an addition designed by **Hammel, Green & Abrahamson** was built to accommodate the futuristic **Henry Crown Space Center**, which houses the *Apollo 8* and *Aurora 7 Mercury* spacecrafts and chronicles our galactic adventures. Within the center, the domed **Omnimax Theater**, with a five-story, 76-foot-wide screen and 72-speaker sound system, presents outstanding films several times a day. In late 1998, a major renovation project was completed that involved the construction of a multilevel parking garage and restoration of an old parking lot to a grassy campus. Although this beautification project is a welcome addition, it has one drawback: Parking is no longer free. Numerous gift shops throughout the museum carry a wide variety of science toys, books, postcards, and other souvenirs. Food services sell sandwiches, pizza, salads, and so forth. A better bet is to get your fill of museum sights, then venture into the neighborhood to satiate your appetite. ♦ Admission. Additional charge for Omnimax. Daily. E 57th and S Cornell Drs. 684.1414. www.msichicago.org

39 JOHN CRERAR LIBRARY

Built in 1984 by **Stubbins Associates** and **Loebl Schlossman & Hackl**, this is just one of the university's seven libraries, which have combined holdings of some five million books, seven million manuscripts and archival

For 3 years in a row, the Nobel Prize for economics was won by University of Chicago professors—1990: business professor Merton Miller; 1991: law professor Ronald Coase; 1992: economics professor Gary Becker.

Two famous alumni of Chicago's Hyde Park High School are singer Mel Tormé and comedian Steve Allen.

Restaurants/Clubs: Red | Hotels: Purple | Shops: Orange | Outdoors/Parks: Green | Sights/Culture: Blue

THE BEST

Hank Seifert

Professor of Immunology
Northwestern University

Best hangover breakfast: **Sarkis** on Gross Point Road in Evanston where Wilmette/Evanston/Skokie meet. Omelettes are king, but a Disaster Loretta (sausage with cheese, onions, green peppers, and tomatoes on French bread) is a close second.

Best funky breakfast: The **Lucky Platter** on Main Street in Evanston. The 1960s meet the South.

Best business lunch value: **Wolfgang Puck's** at the Museum of Contemporary Art (MCA).

Best artery-clogging lunch: The **Chuckwagon** on Central Street in Wilmette. The Nikkie, with gyros meat topping a cheeseburger (or double cheeseburger, if you dare), is truly a heart attack on a bun.

Northshore sushi value: **Haki Hanna** on Lake Street just off the Edens in Wilmette. No-nonsense, quality sushi with reasonable prices and fast service.

Old-time tavern: **Meier's** on Lake Street, just west of the Edens in Wilmette. Home of the tater tot.

Best hidden Streeterville bar: **Fitzer's Pub** in the **Fitzpatrick Hotel** on Superior Street.

Northshore Mexican food: **Little Mexican Café** on Church Street in Evanston.

Most underappreciated winter activity: Big 10 basketball at **Northwestern**.

---

pieces, and 350,000 maps. The **Crerar** has one of the most extensive science collections in the world—a million volumes in pure and applied sciences, from agriculture to zoology. Nonstudents are welcome to browse the first of its three floors, where they may read periodicals and use reference materials and computer search services. On request, the circulation desk will page materials from elsewhere in the library, but nonstudents may not check books out. Don't miss the *Crystara*, a sculpture in aluminum and Waterford crystal by John Mooney, that is suspended from the central skylit atrium. ◆ M-Sa. 5730 S Ellis Ave (between E 59th and E 57th Sts). 702.7715

40 UNIVERSITY OF CHICAGO BOOKSTORE

More than a bookstore—an experience. Academic and general-interest titles range from medical texts to children's books. The second floor is your source for **University of Chicago** T-shirts, sweatsuits, baby booties, and other memorabilia. ◆ M-Sa. 970 E 58th St (east of S Drexel Ave). General books, 702.7712; textbooks, 702.7116 &

41 UNIVERSITY OF CHICAGO MAIN QUADRANGLE

In 1891 architect **Henry Ives Cobb** chose Late English Gothic as the predominant style for the campus to establish a tone resembling that of Oxford and Cambridge. It also gave an air of instant permanence to the university, which had sprung up almost overnight from swampy property next to the site of the World's Columbian Exposition. The **Main Quad** covers four blocks and contains 35 buildings that break down into six smaller courtyards. Gray Bedford limestone is used throughout. The choice of Gothic, a style with much variety, has proven wise, as it blends well with modern

motifs. Most of the rest of the campus shows how architects of the past 50 years have reinterpreted it. **Cobb Hall**, in the middle of the western edge of the **Quad**, **Cobb Gate**, and **Hull Court** were all designed by **Cobb**. Over the years other buildings were designed by **Shepley, Rutan & Coolidge**; **Holabird & Roche**; **Dwight H. Perkins**; and others. Explore the quadrangle by entering through **Cobb Gate** across from the **Regenstein Library** (see page 187) on 57th Street. Look up on the tunnel-like entranceway to see the most incredible profusion of gargoyles since Notre Dame Cathedral. ◆ Bounded by S University and S Ellis Aves and E 59th and E 57th Sts

On the Main Quadrangle:

JONES LABORATORY

The human-made element plutonium was first isolated and weighed in room 405 in 1942. The building, designed by **Coolidge & Hodgdon** in 1929, is now a National Historic Landmark. ◆ 5747 S Ellis Ave

RENAISSANCE SOCIETY

In addition to classrooms, **Cobb Hall** contains an art gallery with an illustrious history. Founded in 1915, the society quickly developed a reputation for providing a forum for art's avant-garde, hosting groundbreaking exhibits of works by Picasso, Braque, Miró, Matisse, and Klee, among others. Exhibits have also examined time and the concept of time, for example. ◆ Free. Daily, until 4PM. Cobb Hall, 5811 S Ellis Ave, fourth floor. 702.8670

TOWER GROUP

Wandering among this group of classroom buildings in the northeast corner of the main quad, you'd think you were in England. These buildings were constructed in the late 1890s; the Gothic Revival architecture here is stunning.

Within the Tower Group:

MANDEL HALL

In 1904 the **Chicago Symphony Orchestra** gave its premier performance here, in the university's assembly hall. In 1976, under the direction of **Skidmore, Owings & Merrill**, the hall's proscenium stage and guts were modernized and the Victorian-era detailing was restored. Plays, lectures, and concerts are presented here, among them performances by the **Chamber Orchestra of Lincoln Center**, the university's **Contemporary Chamber Players**, and the annual University of Chicago Folk Festival. ♦ 702.8511 ♿

REYNOLDS CLUB

Some surprisingly good performances are mounted here by the school's **University Theater**, especially considering that pre-med students and English grads are putting on the show (the university has no drama major). The bill is mostly classics such as *Romeo and Juliet* and *The Glass Menagerie*. ♦ 702.8787; box office, 702.7300

HUTCHINSON COMMONS

A formal men's club atmosphere—dark wood paneling, with portraits of university presidents and trustees watching from the walls—is the setting for casual self-serve fare. Sandwiches and such are offered in the **Deli**, and the adjacent **C Shop** sells ice cream and sweets. ♦ Cafeteria ♦ Daily. 493.2808

42 SEMINARY CO-OP BOOKSTORE

Ensconced within the university's **Chicago Theological Seminary**, which was built in 1923 by **Herbert Riddle**, this semi-subterranean bookstore carries roughly 100,000 titles in academic and general subjects, from *Neurobiology of Cognition* to the complete works of Charles Dickens. The store is especially strong in social sciences, religion, philosophy, and fiction and also provides mail-order service. A second location with more general offerings is **57th Street Books** (see page 187). ♦ Daily. 5757 S University Ave (at E 58th St). 752.4381. www.semcoop.com

43 FREDERICK C. ROBIE HOUSE

Robie, a bicycle and automobile parts manufacturer, hired **Frank Lloyd Wright** to build him a house with lots of sunlight, no curtains, and rooms that flowed into one another. He got all that in this bold Prairie School house (pictured on page 235) that made his name famous when it was finished in 1909. The interlocking masses are complex, yet the house is full of repose, with strong horizontal lines in the sweeping eaves, the bands of beautifully leaded casement windows, and the limestone sills. **Wright** had for some years been designing homes where the entrance was not immediately apparent; here it's at the back of the house and very private. **Wright** also designed the furniture, lamps, and rugs. The magnificent dining-room set is part of the collection of the nearby **Smart Museum of Art** (see page 186). Refuting **Wright**'s reputation as an arrogant architect with little concern for client needs or budget, Robie late in his life lauded **Wright** for sticking to the original budget of $60,000 and called the commission "the cleanest business deal I ever made." The house has been renovated and restored several times; a National Historic Landmark, it is currently owned by the **University of Chicago**. ♦ Fee. Tours M-F, 11AM, 1PM, 3PM; Sa, Su, every half hour, 11AM-3:30PM; or for groups by prior arrangement. 5757 S Woodlawn Ave (at E 58th St). 834.1361. www.wrightplus.org

44 ORIENTAL INSTITUTE

This university organization has supported research and archaeological excavations in the Near East since 1919. It found a permanent home in 1931 in a building designed by **Mayers, Murray & Phillips**. Most of the artifacts in its world-class collection—only a fraction of which are actually displayed in the expansive museum—are treasures from digs in Iraq, Iran, Turkey, Syria, and Palestine. The

Damen Avenue was named after the Reverend Arnold Damen (1815–1890), the Jesuit priest who founded Loyola University, Holy Family Church, and St. Ignatius High School. During the Chicago Fire of 1871 Damen vowed that if his church was spared, a candle would burn forever at Holy Family Church. Even though the fire started just blocks from the church, winds blew it in the other direction. A light has burned perpetually at the church for over 100 years.

Restaurants/Clubs: Red | **Hotels: Purple** | Shops: Orange | **Outdoors/Parks: Green** | **Sights/Culture: Blue**

Rockefeller Memorial

pieces date from 9000 BC to AD 900. A number of other museums refer to this collection to date their own pieces. Ancient life from the everyday to the otherworldly is represented in clay tablets, papyrus scrolls, well-preserved mummies, a gargantuan statue of King Tut, a monumental winged bull from Iraq, and literally tons of other fascinating objects. Free films on topics related to the Near East are shown Sundays at 2PM. The **Suq** (Arabic for "market") museum store carries authentic reproduction jewelry, gifts, and crafts sought out in Near East *suqs*, along with postcards and books such as *How to Write Your Name in Hieroglyphics*. ♦ Free. Tu-Su; W, until 8:30PM. Guided group tours available with advance reservations. 1155 E 58th St (between S Woodlawn and S University Aves). 702.9514. www.uchicago.edu

45 5855 SOUTH UNIVERSITY AVENUE

This 1894 **Henry Ives Cobb** building is the private home of the university's president (now Michael Randel). Until 1993 the house was inhabited by Hanna Holborn Gray, the first woman to be president of any major private American university. ♦ At E 59th St

Legendary blues harmonica player Paul Butterfield grew up in Hyde Park and, as a teenager, would hang out near South Side blues clubs to meet musicians such as Muddy Waters and learn music. Paul's older brother, Peter, a Chicago artist, recalls that Paul taught himself to play harmonica at the Promontory Point.

45 ROCKEFELLER MEMORIAL CHAPEL

University of Chicago founder John D. Rockefeller donated the **University Chapel**, which was built by **Bertram G. Goodhue** in 1928. It was renamed in Rockefeller's honor in 1937 after his death; by the terms of his bequest, it is always to be the tallest building on campus. Perhaps the grandest Gothic house of worship in Chicago, the chapel is 265 feet long and 207 feet high, with masonry walls up to 8 feet thick; steel is used only in the beams supporting the roof, which weighs 800 tons. The interior is richly decorated but delicately colored. Be sure to look up at the tiled vaulted ceiling. Also noteworthy are the sculptures of saints and Old Testament prophets, and the magnificent organ. Concerts on the chapel's 72-bell carillon, named after Laura Spellman Rockefeller (JDR's mother), are performed throughout the year; call for the schedule. For a tour of the carillon, meet 30 minutes before a concert at the chapel door. The chapel also hosts three orchestral concerts each year, including Handel's *Messiah*. ♦ 5850 S Woodlawn Ave (at E 59th St). 702.2100 &

46 MIDWAY PLAISANCE

This blockwide, mile-long strip of land just west of the main fairgrounds of the World's Columbian Exposition of 1893 (now Jackson Park) was home to the exposition's **Bazaar of Nations**. Among the exhibits were replicas of a German village, an Irish market town, a Chinese teahouse, a Hawaiian volcano, the Swiss Alps, and the streets of Cairo, where the undulations of a belly dancer named Little Egypt scandalized visitors. The world's first Ferris wheel took compartments the size of streetcars up for a bird's-eye view at 250 feet. The **Midway**'s festive atmosphere has had a lasting legacy: To this day, fairs and carnivals everywhere have their own "midways," avenues of concessions and amusements. Fronted by the Gothic structures of the university, the Midway has become a recreational site where students and neighbors play football and soccer, toss Frisbees, jog, and, during the winter, ice-skate or go cross-country skiing. Two sculptures mark its western and eastern ends.

On the west, the monumental *Fountain of Time*, created by Lorado Taft in 1922, depicts humanity passing before the figure of Time. On the eastern end is a statue of Thomas Masaryk, president and liberator of Czechoslovakia, sculpted by Albin Polasek in 1949. ♦ Bounded by S Stony Island and S Cottage Grove Aves and E 60th and E 59th Sts

47 MIDWAY STUDIOS

The former studios of sculptor Lorado Taft are now a National Historic Landmark and house the university's art and design department. Visitors are welcome. ♦ Free. M-F. 6016 S Ingleside Ave (between E 61st and E 60th Sts). 753.4821. www.cova-uchicago.edu

48 SCHOOL OF SOCIAL SERVICE ADMINISTRATION BUILDING

This 1965 **Mies van der Rohe** building includes most of his favorite design elements—a steel frame, large expanses of glass, and an open plan. The lobby is one of his best. ♦ 969 E 60th St (between S Ellis and S Ingleside Aves)

49 LAIRD BELL LAW QUADRANGLE

This quad is one of Chicago's few projects by **Eero Saarinen**, the famous architect of the TWA Terminal at John F. Kennedy Airport in New York and the St. Louis Gateway Arch. The library, built in 1960, is sheathed in angled panels of dark glass that appear pleated; to the east is the auditorium. In 1987 **Cooper-Lecky** built an addition to the back of the building. The sculpture outside, *Construction in Space in Third and Fourth Dimensions*, is by Antoine Pevsner. ♦ 1111 E 60th St (between S University and S Ellis Aves)

To honor their best players through the years, sports teams retire their uniform jerseys. Chicago sports franchises have retired the jerseys of 33 players.

Bears: 13; White Sox: 8; Cubs: 4; Blackhawks: 5; Bulls: 3

Handling the press was not one of the strong points of the original Mayor Daley (Richard J.), christened "Boss" by Mike Royko. Nor has it been for his son, the current mayor (Richard M.), known to some as "Boss Lite." Richard J: "We have had a lot of dishonest newspapermen in this town. I could spit on some of them from here." Richard M: "Go scrutinize yourself! I get scrootened every day . . . from each and every one of you."

GAY CHICAGO

America's third largest city (2.8 million people) has always been a town of two spirits, and it still is. Chicago has enough style, culture, and architecture to impress even the most sophisticated (or jaded) of city dwellers and, at the same time, enough Nelson Algren grit to energize those looking for something a little on the wild side. Other cities have tried to spit-and-polish their images, but Chicago remains true to its blue-collar roots. It will always be a bit of a frontier town—and proud of it. The factory workers and waitresses, police officers and hustlers, teachers and street cleaners that Carl Sandburg and Studs Terkel wrote about are still a major presence, and Chicago's gay and lesbian population has become an emerging and vocal part of Chicago's rich cast of characters.

Most Chicagoans are firmly anchored in their no-nonsense, Midwestern sensibility. They're no more impressed with the **University of Chicago**, which has produced more Nobel Prizes and imprint scientists than any other university in the world, than with the **Chicago Bulls**, arguably the best basketball team in the sport's history. But they're equally proud of both. Chicagoans don't wear their pride on their sleeves—they pin it to their chests. In fact, the nickname Windy City has nothing to do with the breeze off **Lake Michigan** and everything to do with the city's history of boasting journalists and long-

For nos. 50-59, see pg. 206

For nos. 5-49, see pg. 197

winded politicians. With the country's seventh-largest gay and lesbian population, the city by the lake is the queer capital of the Midwest. Folks come from Indiana, Michigan, Wisconsin, and Ohio—and as far away as Iowa, Missouri, and Kansas—to indulge in Chicago's open gay and lesbian life. The community here is highly visible—very involved in the local theater and arts scene and supporting no less than four weekly gay publications. The only thing missing is a true community center. The gay community's pull, however, reaches well beyond the confines of the **Lakeview** neighborhood and its gay hub, **North Halsted Street**. Democratic mayor Richard Daley's office has a high-profile liaison to the gay and lesbian community; the annual Gay and Lesbian Pride Parade is a must event for important local and state leaders; and the city even sponsors a Gay and Lesbian Hall of Fame. There have been substantive political victories as well: In 1997 the city extended same-sex domestic partner benefits to its employees, and it has had a gay-inclusive antidiscrimination ordinance since 1988. (Cook County, of which Chicago is the county seat, followed suit shortly thereafter.)

Settled in the 1830s and annexed to the city of Chicago in 1889, the **North Side** neighborhood of **Lakeview** (also known as Boys Town or New Town) is ground zero for gay life. Here, dozens of bars, shops, and restaurants happily cater to gay and lesbian clientele and the sight of two men or two women holding hands doesn't merit so much as a raised eyebrow. Lesbians are a part of life in Boys Town, but many more seem to cluster in **Andersonville**, an up-and-coming neighborhood to the north where new cafés, restaurants, and shops attract women (and some men who prefer to be removed from the overheated Halsted scene).

Plenty of gays and lesbians number among Chicago's 22 million annual visitors, and the reception they find among the local tribe is usually friendly, if not familiar. As a rule, Chicagoans are polite, and there's definitely less attitude in the bars than you might find in Los Angeles or Miami Beach. But locals also tend to stick to their own and don't always welcome outsiders with open arms.

Chicago, like every other city in the world, has its quirks. You might never know whether you are on, say, West Sheridan Street or North Sheridan Avenue, because no one uses full names when giving addresses; "Sheridan" is plenty. Hot dogs come with pickles and tomatoes, but you'll be hard-pressed to find sauerkraut. And everyone you meet will swear they know exactly where Oprah lives, but no two people will take you to the same place. Chicago's quirks and rough edges are smoother than they were when Sandburg called it "coarse and strong and cunning." But even though the rat-tat-tat of the tommy gun and the hard-boiled world of the stockyards and machine politics are gone, most would agree that Chicago still plows ahead "with lifted head singing so proud to be alive." Today he might add that the natives are proud to be gay as well.

Symbols

♂ predominantly/exclusively gay male-oriented

♀ predominantly/exclusively lesbian-oriented

♂♀ predominantly/exclusively gay-oriented, with a male and female clientele

1 MANHANDLER

♂ Guys come here for one reason: to handle men. The notoriously dark (and active) rear patio is open year-round, but no need to worry about frostbite in embarrassing places: In the winter, the boys gather 'round portable heaters. Naturally, weekends and summer are peak times. If manhandling is not your scene,

Restaurants/Clubs: Red | Hotels: Purple | Shops: Orange | Outdoors/Parks: Green | Sights/Culture: Blue

One, the first stage play to deal with the subject of AIDS, debuted in the Windy City in 1982. The production, by Lionheart Gay Theatre on North Halsted Street, was well received and moved on to other cities. The play's author and lead both succumbed to the disease in 1994.

don't bother: This hole-in-the-wall is nearly two miles from the Halsted bar strip and, frankly, a bit of a dump. ♦ M-F, Su, noon-4AM; Sa, noon-5AM. 1948 N Halsted St (between W Wisconsin St and W Armitage Ave). 773/871.3339

2 MUSEUM OF CONTEMPORARY ART (MCA)

The country's largest contemporary art museum boasts a whopping 45,000 square feet of exhibition space. Opened in 1996, the boxy, modernist $46 million building, designed in limestone and aluminum by **Josef Paul Kleihues**, offers bright and airy galleries that show off an ambitious parade of revolving exhibitions. The permanent collection tours most of the great talents of 20th-century art, including such gay artists as Francis Bacon, Andy Warhol, and Jasper Johns. There's also a restaurant, a 300-seat theater, and a beautiful sculpture garden. ♦ Admission; free first Tu of the month. Tu, 10AM-8PM; W-Su, 10AM-5PM. 220 E Chicago Ave (at Mies van der Rohe Way). 312/280.2660 ♿ www.mcachicago.com

3 BATON SHOW LOUNGE

♂ Much more than the usual drag shows, these girls put on extravaganzas—and none more extravagant than the annual "Miss Continental" pageant. Reserve on weekends, 'cause this place is packed with local gays—and the inevitable straight tourists looking for something more exciting than **The Hard Rock Cafe**. ♦ Cover, two-drink minimum. W-Su, 8PM-2AM. Shows: 8:30PM, 10:30PM, 12:30AM. 436 N Clark St (at W Hubbard St). 312/644.5269

4 ART INSTITUTE OF CHICAGO

Completed in 1892, this classical-Renaissance grande dame covers mostly Western art and photography and features a renowned Impressionist collection. The queer contingent includes Nan Goldin and Kathleen Blackshear, among others. Plenty of other famous pictures are in residence too, including Edward Hopper's *Nighthawks*, Grant Wood's *American Gothic*, Matisse's *Bathers by a River*, and Seurat's pointillist *Sunday Afternoon on the Island of La Grande Jatte*. Round out the experience with a meal in the cafeteria (or at one of the museum's two good restaurants), blow some cash in the shop, or rest your tired feet in the spectacular gardens. ♦ Admission; free Tu. M, W-F, 10:30AM-4:30PM; Th, 10:30AM-8PM; Sa, Su, 10AM-5PM. S Michigan Ave (between E Jackson and E Monroe Drs). 312/443.3600 ♿ www.artic.com

5 CHARLIE'S CHICAGO

♂ What can you say about a place with a mirrored disco ball shaped like a cowboy boot? Well, on weekends it's packed with a fun herdful of cowpokes in tight jeans and ten-gallon hats. Can't do the touch-dance thing? Get here early, and they'll teach ya how. ♦ M-Tu, 3PM-2AM; W-F, 3PM-4AM; Sa, 3PM-5AM; Su, 3PM-4AM. 3726 N Broadway (between W Waveland Ave and N Halsted St). 773/871.8887 & www.charliesonline.com

5 GENESEE DEPOT

★★$$ This homey spot is a Lakeview fave with gay gourmands who fancy something a tad fancier than a burger. The rustic dining room and traditional American comfort fare (hearty soups, veal chops, and mashed potatoes) make it especially appealing on cold Chicago days—even if you do have to bring your own liquor. ♦ American ♦ Tu-Sa, dinner. 3736 N Broadway (between W Waveland Ave and N Halsted St). 773/528.6990 &

5 THE NORTH END

♂ _Underrated_ is the word for this friendly,
♀ "regular guys" kinda place that offers something for everyone: music videos, pool tables, dancing boys, comedy acts, sexy contests—and, of course, plenty of cruising. It's just the right mix of casual and fun that every city needs, and it makes a great starter to (or escape from) a night at **Cell Block** across the

street. ♦ M-F, 3PM-2AM; Sa, 2PM-3AM; Su, 2PM-2AM. 3733 N Halsted St (between W Waveland Ave and N Broadway). 773/477.7999

5 BOBBY LOVE'S

♂ This cozy saloon, formerly **Dandy's**, is a great pickup spot—if you're hoping to pick up on great conversation, neighborhood news, and good vibes. Drop lighting, purple walls, and a golden wood bar add to the charm. A predominantly gay clientele populates this convivial spot, where people come to relax and unwind; some of them play darts (the bar has a league team). Stop in for a quick one, and you're liable to stay all evening. ♦ Daily, noon-2AM. 3729 N Halsted St (between W Waveland Ave and N Broadway). 773/525.1200

6 CELL BLOCK

♂ Yes, Virginia, there *are* friendly leather bars—and this is one of them. It's equally popular with macho studs, leather wannabes, and the just plain curious, all of whom mix comfortably around the front bar and the pool table. Despite good dance music from DJs on the weekend, the dance floor sees little use; the real action is at the back bar, with hard-core videos, a mazelike back room, and a strictly enforced leather dress code. Oh, and on Friday there are live demonstrations of proper hot wax, shaving, vacuum pump, and other arcane techniques. Afterward, get your accoutrements at the **Leather Cell**, a tiny shop that feels more like a souvenir stand. ♦ M-F, 4PM-2AM; Sa, 2PM-3AM; Su, 2PM-2AM. 3702 N Halsted St (between W Waveland Ave and W Bradley Pl). 773/665.8064. www.cellblockchicago.com

7 THE BROWN ELEPHANT

Lakeview's old T-shirts, mismatched dishes, books, and record albums (from *Oklahoma!* to Gloria Gaynor) come to find new homes at this enormous secondhand shop. All proceeds go to the **Howard Brown Health Center**, the largest AIDS services facility in the Midwest—and a favorite charity with local guppies. This can be a gold mine for bargain hunters. ♦ Daily, 11AM-6PM. 3651 N Halsted St (between W Addison St and W Waveland Ave).

On 1 January 1962 homosexuality became legal in Chicago, as a revision of Illinois criminal statutes eliminated the prosecution of sodomy.

In December 2002, Tom Tunney, owner of Ann Sather restaurant, became the first openly gay member of the City Council, when he was appointed by Mayor Daley to replace Bernard Hansen, who retired because of health problems.

773/549.5943. Also at 5228 N Clark St (at W Farragut Ave). 773/271.9382. ♿ www.howardbrown.org

8 CIRCUIT NIGHTCLUB

♂ This dance club first came to life in 1996 in the back of a run-down coffee shop. Since remodeled, the front-room bar has been renamed **Rehab** and serves up frozen drinks. A rotating lineup of DJs spins dance tunes at the requisite volume for a mostly young clientele, and the proceedings are hosted by local personalities such as Miss Kitty and Miss Foozy. ♦ Admission: no cover Tu and Su. Su-Th, 4PM-2AM; F to 4AM; Sa, to 5AM. 3641 N Halsted St (between W Addison St and W Waveland Ave). 773/325.2233. www.circuit-club.com

9 NORTH COAST CAFE

★★$ Often forgotten by the brunch bunch who flock to the **Melrose** and **Nookies Tree**, this cozy spot is friendlier and usually less crowded than those more popular neighborhood eateries. The food is better too, with tried-and-true chicken entrées, burgers, and eggs. Such Greek specialties as "flaming cheese" are also worth writing home about—it's a tasty appetizer brought ablaze to the table and served with pita bread. ♦ Greek/American ♦ Daily, dinner; brunch Sa, Su. 3613 N Broadway (between W Addison St and W Patterson Ave). 773/549.7606

10 THE MAJESTIC HOTEL

$$ On a quiet, tree-lined street, this recently remodeled vintage hotel is within easy striking distance of the Halsted scene. The 52 rooms are on the small side, but it's comfy, romantic, and popular enough to make early room (and restaurant) reservations a good idea. ♦ 528 W Brompton Ave (between N Sheridan Rd and N Pine Grove Ave). 773/404.3499, 800/727.5108; fax 773/404.3495. www.cityinns.com

11 ANGELINA RISTORANTE

★★$$ This Italian bistro's two dining rooms are as sweetly ornate as a jewelry box, with candles and flowers, gauzy curtains, and softly painted walls. It's a favorite spot for good *fettuccine norte* (with prosciutto and chicken in a Parmesan cream sauce) or veal marsala at good prices. Rumor has it that this is Madonna's favorite Italian in Chicago (with the possible exception of a guy named Vic). ♦ Italian ♦ M-Sa, dinner; Su, brunch and dinner. 3561 N Broadway (between W Brompton Ave and W Addison St). 773/935.5933 ♿

12 LEATHER SPORT

Affiliated with the folks who own **Cupid's Treasures** up the block, this shop claims to

aim to please "big bad boys . . . & girls."
♦ Daily, 11 AM–midnight. 3505 N Halsted St (between W Cornelia and W Brompton Aves). 773/868.0914

12 LAS MAÑANITAS

★★★$$ Come for the great mix-and-match combo platters, but stay for the out-of-this-world margaritas (or is it the other way around?). Don't mind the clichéd serape wall hangings—this is a great place to hang out with friends, and one of Chicago's very best cantinas. ♦ Mexican ♦ Daily, lunch and dinner. 3523 N Halsted St (at W Brompton Ave). 773/528.2109 &

12 CUPID'S TREASURES

The sweet array of leather, lingerie, and love toys never fails to shock the straight **Cubs** fans who wander in from **Wrigley Field** after the game. Fortunately, everyone's laid back and keeps a sense of humor. For the nonstraight, there's lots of fun stuff to browse, poke, and squeeze (though the plastic-sealed porn mags are a drag). ♦ M-Th; Su, 11AM–midnight; F-Sa, 11AM–1AM. 3519 N Halsted St (between W Cornelia and W Brompton Aves). 773/348.3884

12 LITTLE JIM'S

♂ The original Halsted Street gay bar (since 1975), this locale has evolved into one of the most notoriously cruisy spots on the strip. With porn on the video, patrons propped against the wall like eighth-grade girls at a school dance, and a space too narrow to avoid brushing up against passersby, it's very conducive to making new "friends"—especially after 2AM, when other bars close, and the place suddenly becomes very popular. Maybe it's because the booze flows until 4AM and there's no cover charge. ♦ M-F, 9AM–4AM; Sa, 11AM–5AM; Su, 11AM–4AM. 3501 N Halsted St (at W Cornelia Ave). 773/871.6116

13 CORNELIA'S

★★★$$ The New England farmhouse décor (barn-board siding, antiques), warm, inviting atmosphere, and innovative menu make this a hit with a gay-heavy following. Menu highlights include lobster and scallops flambéed with brandy and tossed with spinach linguine, and T-bone steak prepared with rosemary, sage, and thyme and served with horseradish and mashed potatoes. The pork chops, marinated in Dijon mustard and then grilled, may be the best in the city. Vegetarians will delight in the mixed vegetable grill with risotto. A variety of other steak, chops, and chicken dishes is available for those looking for good ol' American fare. Standout desserts include tiramisù and

flourless chocolate cake. The menu and most of the wine list, featuring selections from the world over, change every 6 months.
♦ Italian/American ♦ Tu-Su, dinner. 748 W Cornelia Ave (between N Broadway and N Halsted St). 773/248.8333 & www.ilovecornelias.com

14 RAM BOOKSTORE

♂ The relatively paltry assortment of male mags and videos in the front is little more than an excuse for this joint's true raison d'être: a large, well-populated back room. The large, rambling maze of booths offer a fine selection of films—and well-placed holes in the wall that let you check out your neighbor (and then some). If this is your speed, the price of admission is still less than you'd spend on some guy from Tulsa at a bar—and scoring here is practically ensured. Always busy, this place is at its peak when the bars close. ♦ Shop: daily, 24 hours. Back room: daily, 11:30AM–6AM. 3511 N Halsted St (between W Cornelia and W Brompton Aves). 773/525.9528

14 HYDRATE

♂ Formerly the Manhole, this watering hole is a hot place to get dehydrated during wee hours on weekends when the sweat really starts to fly. But overhead misters are strategically situated to keep dancing patrons cool at all times. There are two rooms in this storefront space—one blue and one red. As the night wears on, a garage-type door rolls down over the red-room window to seal in the sound and fun. There are also two moods to every evening—the early hours, when activities range from lube wrestling to lotto to karaoke, and late night, when guest DJs spin pulsating tunes and the action heats up. ♦ Cover. M-F, Su 8PM–4AM; Sa, 8PM–5AM. 3458 N Halsted St (at W Cornelia Ave). 773/975.9244. www.hydratechicago.com

15 GAY MART

♂♀ Big and cluttered, this mini–department store is crammed with the usual gay-positive everything, from cards and rainbow wind chimes to kitschy-campy T-shirts and other assorted nonessentials. (How about a set of *Wizard of Oz* cookie jars?) Their slogan: *If it's queer it's here!* ♦ M-Th, 11AM–8PM; F, Sa, 11AM–9PM; Su, 11AM–7PM. 3457 N Halsted St (at W Cornelia Ave). 773/929.4272

15 VILLA TOSCANA

$ Strategically located but still charming and low key, this 1891 house set back a bit from the street offers seven rooms furnished with period antiques (only one has a private bath).

Restaurants/Clubs: Red | Hotels: Purple | Shops: Orange | Outdoors/Parks: Green | Sights/Culture: Blue

You may take the sun (or shiver) in the lovely garden or soak in the outdoor hot tub (open year-round) after a long day of seeing the sights. Breakfast is included in the room rate. Book ahead for weekend stays. ♦ 3447 N Halsted St (between W Roscoe St and W Cornelia Ave). 773/404.2643; 800/404.2643; fax 773/404.2643; rochus1@ibm.net; www.villa-toscana.com

16 VOLTAIRE

★★★ $$$ In the spot formerly occupied by **Madam B**, crowds of boys line up three deep at the polished wood bar or grab a table in the cabaret room to hear resident diva Amy Armstrong croon show tunes. It's a pretty mellow scene, but those seeking an even quieter evening opt for the **Derby Room**, where chef Daniel Blejski's contemporary American menu offers a wide range of choices: from salads, sandwiches, and burgers to more daring fare such as seared ahi tuna and grilled vegetable-and-goat-cheese napoleons. ♦ Contemporary. ♦ Su-F, 5PM-1:30AM; Sa, 5PM-2:30AM. 3441-43 N Halsted St (between W Roscoe St and W Cornelia Ave). 773/281-9320

16 BUCK'S SALOON

♂ There's no dance floor, no atmosphere, and no décor except for the moose heads—fetchingly adorned with leather collars—and swordfish mounted on the reddish walls at this well-situated bar. The one source of music is a jukebox (okay, with a good selection), and the old-fashioned regulars in this old-fashioned saloon are here for serious drinking and (maybe) a bit of conversation. Which is fine, if that's your speed—but guys in search of cute boys and a hot scene will usually pass right by. Still, the best picture window on the strip and a surprisingly nice back patio give this no-nonsense bar a certain *je ne sais quoi*. ♦ M-F; Sa, 10AM-3AM; Su, 10AM-2AM. 3439 N Halsted St (between W Roscoe St and W Cornelia Ave). 773/525.1125

17 THE OUTPOST

★★$$ An eclectic new menu each month draws on influences from around the globe. From blackberry-stuffed New Zealand venison to wild Alaskan salmon with caramelized shiitake mushrooms, there is always something new and exciting to try. Complementing the menu are more than 200 wines by the bottle and 40 by the glass. A favorite of gays and straights alike, this eatery is the choice of folks who love good food and wine but prefer a casual atmosphere and reasonable prices. ♦ American ♦ M-Sa, dinner; Su, brunch and dinner. 3438 N Clark St (at W Newport Ave). 773/244.1166 &

18 PENNY'S NOODLE SHOP

★$ Tasty noodles and saucy entrées draw gays and lesbians to this cool little triangular fast-food joint. Don't miss the chicken satay and *lad nar*. Bring your own alcoholic beverage. ♦ Asian ♦ Tu-Su, lunch and dinner. 3400 N Sheffield Ave (at W Roscoe St). 773/281.8222

19 CHICAGO DINER

★★$$ For the organic enthusiast/vegetarian crowd, this well-regarded spot with its funky-yet-casual décor is a real winner. The tequila-marinated seitan fajitas are a treat, and the lentil loaf is just like Mom would have made if she'd been a vegetarian. Tempting vegan desserts include rich cocoa-mousse cake and dense carrot cake with creamy frosting. There's no bar as such, but an assortment of beers, wines, and standard cocktails are available. ♦ Vegetarian ♦ M-F, lunch and dinner; Sa, Su, brunch and dinner. 3411 N Halsted St (between W Roscoe St and W Cornelia Ave). 773/935.6696. www.veggiediner.com

19 7-ELEVEN

Not just any old **7-Eleven**—the "gay 7-Eleven" is a Chicago landmark for everything it contributes to local queerdom: the only cash machines near the bars, cheaper cigarettes, and pay phones that actually work. Not much a bar type? Buy a Slurpee and cruise from the parking lot. ♦ Daily, 24 hours. 3407 N Halsted St (at W Roscoe St). 773/348.6581 ♿

20 BEST WESTERN HAWTHORNE TERRACE

$ This comfortable, newly remodeled facility has 59 rooms and junior suites with two-line phones, data ports, and satellite TV. There's also a fitness center with sauna and whirlpool in case you're not up for a night at **Steamworks**. The reasonable price and great location (you can crawl home from Halsted Street) make it a nice, affordable alternative for folks who want to dodge the business and tourist bustle of downtown. ♦ 3434 N Broadway (at Hawthorne Terr). 244.3434, 888/675.2378; fax 244.3435

21 ROSCOE'S

♂ Hints of its past life as a mom-and-pop grocery still linger in the tin molding and original woodwork, but Ma and Pa would flip if they got an eyeful of today's cruisy front bar, well hung with video screens and modern art on multicolored walls. Practically a mandatory stop on the Boys Town homo tour, this place is packed—especially on the weekends—with a crew that as a rule is younger, more ethnically mixed, and a bit more rambunctious than the folks across the street at **SideTrack**. There's more action in the back, with a cozy tête-à-tête nook (complete with gas fireplace), a billiards room, and a dance floor where live game shows are held on Wednesday evenings. ♦ M-Th, 2PM-2AM; F, Su, 1PM-2AM; Sa, 1PM-3AM. 3354-56 N Halsted St (at W Roscoe St). 773/281.3355

21 BAD BOYS

♂ Skintight Shirt Central for gym queens, this is also the perfect place to shop for new skivvies. ♦ M-Th, noon-9PM; F, Sa, 11AM-9PM; Su, noon-6PM. 3352 N Halsted St (between W Buckingham Pl and W Roscoe St). 773/549.7701. Also at 1500 W Balmoral Ave (at N Clark St). www.badboyschicago.com

22 COCKTAIL

♂♀ This popular, polished cruise bar is making a name for itself by picking up the runover from **SideTrack** and **Roscoe's**—while also attracting a diverse, often young, and cute following of its own. Come here early for a prime spot by the huge picture window if you want to see—and be seen by—la crème. ♦ M-F, 4PM-2AM; Sa, 2PM-3AM; Su, 2PM-2AM. 3359 N Halsted St (at W Roscoe St). 773/477.1420

22 SIDETRACK

♂ This sleek and popular spot is yet another place to nurse a drink while watching old comedy skits, scenes from campy movie classics, and music videos. Cruising is a popular feature here too. In fact, there aren't many slow nights—Monday might be devoted to show tunes and Thursday to comedy, and on weekends it's shoulder-to-shoulder. Fans of fresh air will love the roof deck, dancing queens will love the dance floor, and the all-chrome rest room offers multiple ways to check your 'do. ♦ M-F, 3PM-2AM; Sa, 2PM-3AM; Su, 2PM-2AM. 3349 N Halsted St (between W Buckingham Pl and W Roscoe St). 773/477.9189 ♿

23 P. S. BANGKOK

★★$$ The food at this hyperactive Thai storefront is as good as the décor is ugly, and that's saying a lot. Owner and chef Suradet Yongsawaii learned the trade in a Bangkok market, and his mastery shows in the huge menu, which starts with no less than 33 appetizers. The curries and noodle dishes are delightful; the sauce on the *pad thai* is almost caramelized. The gay quotient fluctuates, but with food this good (and portions this big) at reasonable prices, who cares? ♦ Thai ♦ Daily, lunch and dinner. Reservations recommended F and Sa. 3345 N Clark St (between W Buckingham Pl and W Roscoe St). 773/871.7777 ♿

24 NOOKIES TREE

$ A step above diner level—but at diner prices—this homo hangout isn't a bad choice for eggs, burgers, soups, and sandwiches (and they make a mean Monte Cristo). It's popular for Saturday and Sunday brunch too. ♦ American ♦ M-Th, Su, breakfast, lunch, and dinner; F, Sa, 24 hours. No credit cards accepted. 3334 N Halsted St (at W Buckingham Pl). 773/248.9888

25 GENTRY ON HALSTED

♂♀ Show-tune queens and some lesbians flock to this small, dark, and cozy spot to catch various cabaret shows or to sing along with a piano player who knows 'em all. In summer, the glass doors open the bar right out onto Halsted. ♦ M-F, Su, 4PM-2AM; Sa, 4PM-3AM. 3320 N Halsted St (between W Aldine Ave and W Buckingham Pl). 773/348.1053 ♿ Also at 440 N State St (at W Hubbard St). 312/836.0933. www.gentryofchicago.com

---

Restaurants/Clubs: Red | Hotels: Purple | Shops: Orange | Outdoors/Parks: Green | Sights/Culture: Blue

26 THE CLOSET

♂ Who wants to go back into the closet? A lot of
♀ women, just about every night of the week.
Plenty of guys squeeze in here too
(sometimes they outnumber the gals), despite
the wee dance space, and just about everyone
has a rollicking good time under the ubiqui-
tous video screens. ♦ M-F, 2PM-4AM; Sa,
noon-5AM; Su, noon-4AM. 3325 N Broadway
(between W Aldine Ave and W Roscoe St).
773/477.8533 ♿

27 PLATIYO

★★★ $$ Gays and straights flock to this spot
with a common singular purpose: loading up
on great food. Ten years after opening **Mia
Francesca**, the popular Italian restaurant next
door, Scott Harris has teamed with superchefs
Patrick Concannon from **Don Juan** and Kevin
Karales from **Frontera** and **Topolobampo** to
create a wonderful Mexican restaurant. Paint-
ings of desert scenes adorn the brick walls to
create an airy, cheerful setting, but the real
artistry in this intimate storefront is the food,
which combines traditional dishes and more
adventurous offerings. Tasty openers include
tortilla soup with shredded chicken and cubes
of fresh cheese and a meatless *queso
fundido*. Among entrées, choose from wood-
grilled pork chop with mashed sweet potatoes
and mango mole, braised lamb shank with
stewed white beans and bacon, and *carne
asada* with garlic-flavored mushrooms.
Desserts come from Bomb Pon, a Pilsen
bakery, and include a delicious pistachio flan
with thin chocolate base. The place seats only
65, so reservations are definitely
recommended. ♦ Mexican ♦ Daily, dinner.
3313 Clark St (between W Aldine Ave and W
Buckingham Pl). 477.6700 ♿

27 BUDDIES' RESTAURANT AND BAR

★$ A place for eating rather than getting plas-
tered, the small, nondescript dining room
serves good basic grub like burgers,
sandwiches, and soups; it's particularly
popular with weekend brunchers. The adjacent
bar is about as nondescript but lively and
friendly, with a funkier mix of ethnicities than
usually found in Halsted hangouts.
♦ American ♦ Restaurant: Tu-F, lunch and
dinner; Sa, Su, brunch and dinner. Bar: M-F;

The nation's first transsexual political candidate,
Joan Jett-Blakk, ran for mayor of Chicago against
Richard Daley in 1990, and in 1992 ran for presi-
dent of the US as the candidate of the Blakk
Pantsuit Party. S/he came up with that election's
most memorable slogan: "Lick Bush in '92."

Sa, 9AM-3AM; Su, 9AM-2AM. 3301 N Clark
St (at W Aldine Ave). 773/477.4066; fax
549.6679

27 MIA FRANCESCA

♂ ★★★$ If longer is better, then the lines of
♀ people waiting to get into this casual trattoria
must mean fabu food. Yes, it's crowded and
noisy and they don't take reservations, but
chef-owner Scott Harris offers a seasonal menu
that changes daily and is worth every minute of
the wait (which can be 2 hours or more unless
you come early or after 10PM). If your tummy
won't hold out, head for the patio or wine bar,
order drinks and appetizers, and accept your
bitter fate. Typical starters include bruschetta
topped with tomato, fresh mozzarella, and
arugula; carpaccio of sirloin with tomato, basil,
capers, Parmesan, mushrooms, and avocados;
linguine arlecchino (shrimp, scallops, and
clams sautéed with cherry tomatoes, garlic,
and olive oil and served over pasta); and
rigatoni impazzite (pasta with a cream,
spinach, ham, and red pepper sauce). Continue
with *pesce saltimbocca* (roasted monkfish
wrapped in prosciutto with sage and white
wine) or *pollo arrosto alla romana* (chicken
roasted with garlic, shallots, rosemary, and
lemon, and served with potatoes). ♦ Italian ♦
Daily, dinner. 3311 N Clark St (between W
Aldine Ave and W Buckingham Pl).
773/281.3310. www.miafrancesca.com

28 STEAMWORKS

♂ The former **Unicorn Club** and **BodyShop
Fitness Center** have merged to form **Steam-
works**. Same hot place, same hot stuff,
different name. There's a complete gym for gay
men who really want to pump iron and buff up
and lay claim to their share of Sandburg's
"city of big shoulders." The two-story state-of-
the-art bathhouse offers a different kind of
workout and attracts mostly a young, good-
looking crowd (and the men who love them).
The "water area," with its sauna, steam, and
huge whirlpool, is a great place to make a
splash, and the rooftop deck is a popular spot
in summer (sorry, no nudity). It's wildly
popular on weekends and on Tuesday and
Thursday nights, when admission is reduced
(a membership fee is required). Get there by
7PM if you want your own room. Food and
drinks are available. ♦ Admission. Daily, 24
hours. 3246 N Halsted St (between W
Belmont and W Aldine Aves). 773/929.6081
www.steamworksonline.com

29 YOSHI'S CAFE

★★★$$$ In a town known for fine
restaurants, this eatery is consistently ranked
among the best. A nudge toward more casual
dining only enhanced the excellent Asian-
inspired French menu, which changes
regularly but does especially well with

seafood, grilled meat, and duck. You might start your meal with California goat cheese and bell pepper in pastry swathed in red bell pepper cream sauce, then proceed to the grilled fresh tuna with a red-wine glaze and wasabi mashed potatoes. Served at tables closely tucked together and graced with fresh flowers, it's definitely the finest fare in Lakeview. ◆ Asian/French ◆ Tu-Sa, dinner; Su, brunch and dinner. Reservations recommended. 3257 N Halsted St (at W Aldine Ave). 773/248.6160 ♿

30 HE WHO EATS MUD

♂
♀ It is a card store—but we're not talking Hallmark here. The walls of this shop are lined with a prime selection of hilarious, artistic, and/or erotic cards. Before you buy your queer Uncle Walt some tired old T-shirt, check out the campy assortment here. It may not be heaven, but as souvenir shops go, it's pretty close to perfect. ◆ Daily, noon-6PM. 3247 N Broadway (between W Melrose St and W Aldine Ave). 773/525.0616

30 UNABRIDGED BOOKSTORE

A refreshing alternative to the "mega" trend, this is what great bookstores used to be like: intimate and personal, with an excellent lineup of subjects and titles and a friendly sales staff who will bend over backward for you—even calling the competition if the store doesn't have what you're looking for. But unlike the stores of yesteryear, there's also a meaty gay and lesbian section. ◆ M-F, 10AM-10PM; Sa, Su, 10AM-8PM. 3251 N Broadway (between W Melrose St and W Aldine Ave). 773/883.9119 ♿

31 CHICAGO SWEAT SHOP

♂
♀ For those who like an audience, this is *the* gym: With its huge picture windows, you might as well be on stage. Clean and pleasant, it offers a good assortment of equipment and free weights, along with aerobics classes for every level. The staff is knowledgeable too—if you can break through the attitude. At peak hours the joint gets packed with a gayer-than-not crowd—though it's not especially cruisy. Maybe everyone's too busy posing for the windows. ◆ M-Th, 5:30AM-11PM; F, 5:30AM-10PM; Sa, 7AM-9PM; Su, 8AM-9PM. 3215 N Broadway (between W Belmont Ave and W Melrose St). 773/871.2789. www.chicagosweatshop.com

31 THE MELROSE

★★$ The main reason to come here for Sunday brunch is to try to figure out who among your fellow patrons are the couples, who are just friends, and who are tricks from the night before. It's an around-the-clock scene with breakfast anytime, huge helpings of decent diner fare, saucy servers, and an outdoor dining area that rivals any bar for cruisiness. Some complain about the food, saying it's mediocre, others about the over-the-top scene, but it's still one of the gayest spots in Lakeview. ◆ Coffee shop ◆ Daily, 24 hours. 3233 N Broadway (at W Melrose St). 773/327.2060

32 BELMONT ROCKS, LINCOLN PARK

♂
♀ Some of summertime's hottest tanning and cruising (in the flirting sense) take place at this legendary spot, roughly where West Belmont Avenue would meet Lake Michigan if it ran through the park. Neighborhood gay boys of all ages and races (and the occasional lesbian) perch on the smooth slate slabs by the water; some even take a dip, though there's no beach. It's a real zoo during the Gay and Lesbian Pride weekend in June, when a number of parties are held here, including a post-parade bash sponsored by African-American groups. Don't miss the colorful graffiti, poetry, and touching tributes to friends lost to AIDS that are painted on some of the rocks. ◆ At Belmont Harbor

33 HOWARD'S WINE CELLAR

Those in the know say that Howard Silverman is a rare vintage when it comes to helping you find the perfect Barolo to go with that leg of lamb you're roasting. Although he carries a wide range of domestics, his specialty is European wines and great bargains from Australia. Browse through his impressive collection and you'll be able to host and toast to any occasion. ◆ Tu-Sa and by appointment. 1244 W Belmont Ave (between N Racine and N Lakewood Aves). 248.3766

34 BAILIWICK REPERTORY THEATER

Well regarded in theatrical circles around the country, this company has staged some of America's best and most popular gay and lesbian works since 1981—including the hit play *Party*, which got its start here. New playwrights are the specialty, so if you relish discovering the next Terence McNally or Tony Kushner, get your tickets now. ◆ 1229 W Belmont Ave (between N Racine and N Southport Aves). 733/883.1090 ♿

35 LEONA'S ORIGINAL PIZZA

★$ It all started right here at the first (and still the best) location of this Italian restaurant

---

chain. For superb pizza (try the thin-crust with sausage and artichoke) and huge portions of pasta at fair prices, you can't do much better. Sure, there's a crowd and there's a wait, but the waiting crowd is kept happy with free pizza snacks and small glasses of wine. ♦ Italian ♦ Daily, lunch and dinner. 3215 N Sheffield Ave (between W Belmont Ave and W Melrose St). 773/327.8861 ♿ Also at numerous locations throughout the city. www.leonas.com

36 BERLIN

♂ Some say its day has passed, but for those who want to get away from Halsted (even if
♀ it's only two blocks), this sleek, hardy perennial is worth a look. Here hard-core club kids meet Boys Townies, and everybody hits the dance floor together. Wednesday brings both "Disco Night" and the popular "Women's Obsessions Night" (guys are welcome with a female chaperone). ♦ Cover. M-F, 6PM-4AM; Sa, 8PM-5AM; Su, 8PM-4AM. 954 W Belmont Ave (between N Wilton and N Sheffield Aves). 773/348.4975. www.berlinchicago.com

37 ANN SATHER

♂ ★$ Ann founded the **Swedish Diner** with her life savings in 1946, and more than a half
♀ century (and a new name) later, this eatery is beloved by local queers—not so much for the food as for its support of the gay and lesbian community (and yes, those famous cinnamon rolls). Numerous gay and lesbian organizations meet in the upstairs banquet rooms (a former funeral parlor), and the restaurant is the location of choice for many community events. On the weekend, the breakfast crowds line up for Swedish pancakes with lingonberries, potato sausage, and limpa bread. The location near the **City Suites Hôtel** (see below) makes it more or less the hotel's unofficial dining room. ♦ Swedish/American ♦ Daily, breakfast, lunch, and dinner. 929 W Belmont Ave (between N Clark St and N Sheffield Ave). 773/348.2378 ♿

37 CITY SUITES HÔTEL

$ Don't let the dull façade and the noisy traffic outside turn you off—this charmer with a pleasant lobby and 45 cozy rooms is arguably the most popular small hotel in Lakeview. Gay and lesbian travelers in partic-

Chicago is the only major American city to have a Gay and Lesbian Hall of Fame sponsored by the office of the mayor. Each year since 1992, the public nominates Chicagoans who have made significant contributions to the gay and lesbian community, and new members are inducted in a ceremony presided over by the mayor.

ular flock here, so reserve early for big events like Gay and Lesbian Pride. There's no restaurant, but **Ann Sather** (see opposite) is where the guests head. ♦ 933 W Belmont Ave (between N Clark St and N Sheffield Ave). 773/404. 3400, 800/248.9108; fax 773/404.3405. www.cityinns.com

38 SPIN

♂ Thought of by some as a downmarket **Roscoe's**, this dance and video club with a
♀ small dance floor nonetheless draws a youngish crowd, particularly for its "Dollar Drinks" on Wednesday nights. There are live bands every Tuesday, and the back bar hosts a drag show every Saturday. ♦ Cover charge W, Sa. M-Tu, Th-F, Su, 4PM-2AM; W, 8PM-2AM; Sa, 4PM-3AM. 800 W Belmont Ave (at N Halsted St). 773/327.7711. www.spin-nightclub.com

39 ANNEX THREE

If you don't have the energy to get down to the **Baton**, you can get an appetizer-size serving of female impersonators right near Boys Town on the last Saturday night of every month. Otherwise this place, owned by the owner of Baton, is just a big renovated space with two full bars that draws straights as well as gays for high-volume conversation, an eclectic jukebox, and darts. ♦ 3160 N Clark St (between W Belmont Ave and W Fletcher St). Daily, until 2AM. 327.5969

40 LUCKY HORSESHOE

♂ Don't mind the ugly exterior: This is actually a very handsome bar. But who notices fancy woodwork when there are seminaked boy-babes bumping and grinding on three stages while (mostly) older fans stuff their G-strings full of crumpled dollar bills? The dancing delights take center stage ten times a week (every night and afternoons on the weekend). Everyone in Chicago makes fun of this place, but it draws a crowd well beyond the over-50 man-in-the-raincoat set. ♦ M-F, 2PM-2AM; Sa, noon-3AM; Su, noon-2AM. 3169 N Halsted St (at W Belmont Ave). 773/404.3169

41 PLEASURE CHEST

This branch of the national purveyor of perversion for the masses is way too bright, but it still carries a good assortment of condoms and lubes. On the whole it's a place for the type of tourists who giggle at (but won't admit using) vibrators and other "marital aids." ♦ Daily, noon-midnight. 3155 N Broadway (between W Briar Pl and W Belmont Ave). 773/525.7151 ♿

42 THE BAGEL

★★★$ This is the only place in Lakeview for "just like Grandma's" matzoh-ball soup and excellent corned beef on rye. No wonder it's a popular stop for gay guys and gals. Weekend brunch is especially crowded, so expect a wait. ♦ Deli ♦ Daily, breakfast, lunch, and dinner. 3107 N Broadway (between W Barry Ave and W Briar Pl). 773/477.0300 ♿

43 LEATHER ON LEATHER

There are many creative uses for leather. One of the more unusual ones is making leather animals (a refreshing alternative to stuffed furry ones). And that's just one of many notions that leather craftsman David, who has had a shop at another location since 1973, has come up with. Come up with your own idea, and he might be able to make it for you. Or he'll repair that treasure you're not ready to part with. Other, more practical items include belts, pants, skirts, and jackets. About 60% of the great stuff in this two-level storefront is made on the premises. If you like the smell of leather, it's well worth a stop just to sniff around. ♦ M-Sa. 3011 N Broadway (between W Wellington and W Barry Aves). 868.4200

44 BOBTAIL SODA FOUNTAIN

♂ ★★$ Boys and girls of all stripes are flocking to this old-fashioned shop that opened in 2004 ♀ and defied convention by not using the words ye, olde, or shoppe in its name. Instead it's named for the handle on an old-fashioned soda fountain. When it opens—at 6 in the morning!—it serves up the best Belgian waffles this side of Brussels and steaming hot coffee. For lunch and dinner, there's grilled cheese. And there are ice cream creations all the time (for a lift, try the cream espresso). You can watch the ice cream being made through a glass window that overlooks the on-site "factory." The counter help won't mind if you call them jerks, just as long as you leave a tip. ♦ M-Th, 6AM-11PM; F-Sa, 7AM-Midnight; Su, 8AM-11PM. 2951 N Broadway (at W Wellington Ave). 773/880.7372. www.bobtailsodafountain.com

45 WILLOWS HOTEL

$ Set in a lovely renovated 1920s building on a quiet street, this hostelry usually has more than a handful of heterosexuals among its guests. Happily, everyone gets along just fine. Enjoy the elegance of the lobby, with its pillars, statues, and fireplace—your room is likely to be more modest. There's no restaurant. ♦ 555 W Surf St (between N Cambridge Ave and N Broadway). 773/528.8400, 800/787.3108; fax 773/528.8483. www.cityinns.com

46 MALE HIDE

♂ The best leather shop in the city offers a fine selection of merchandise—both polite and naughty, including prêt-à-porter jackets, vests, chaps, and pants. If you don't buy off-the-rack, custom tailoring is available. If your needs are more on the order of toys, check out the downstairs showroom. ♦ Tu-Sa, noon-8PM; Su, 1-5PM. 2816 N Lincoln Ave (at W Diversey Pkwy). 773/929.0069

47 STEVE STARR STUDIO

Owner Steve is the undisputed Starr of Deco. Midnight-blue "Evening in Paris" perfume bottles, Art Deco lamps, chrome toasters, and eerie lighting make you feel like you're in a time warp. All of the aforementioned are for sale. What's not for sale but is on view here is Starr's personal collection of gorgeous Art Deco picture frames containing smiling photos of such famous customers as Diana Ross and Bette Midler. You can, however, take some of them home in *Picture Perfect,* the Rizzoli-published art book on movie stars that Starr wrote. Be sure to catch his column in the *Windy City Times.* ♦ M-F, 2-6PM; Sa, Su, 1PM-5PM. 2779 N Lincoln Ave (at W Diversey Pkwy). 525.6530; fax 525.7520

48 CENTURY MALL

What becomes of old Chicago theaters? They turn into shopping centers. Its interior now high-tech in look but low-end merchants, this ornate 1930s movie palace–turned–six-story mall in Lakeview is definitely more RadioShack than Hammacher Schlemmer. Fortunately, it does offer some hipper shopping such as **Cignal** for clothes and **Gamers Paradise** for (what else?) games. And given its location, it's something of a gay promenade. The **Bally Total Fitness** (929.6900) on the top floor, in fact, is as known for its cruisy showers as its workout equipment. A recent renovation added a movie theater! ♦ Shopping center: M-F, 10:30AM-9PM; Sa, 10:30AM-6PM; Su, noon-6PM. Health club: M-F, 6AM-11PM; Sa, Su, 8AM-8PM. 2828 N Clark St (at W Diversey Pkwy). 773/929.8100 ♿

48 DAYS INN AT LINCOLN PARK

$ On the border between Lakeview and Lincoln Park—a bastion of straight yuppiedom to the south—this chain hotel with 119 clean, functional rooms has a certain following among gay and lesbian visitors. Reserve well ahead, because it also happens to be popular with touring rock bands whose record labels won't spring for tonier digs downtown—sellout nights (especially on weekends) aren't unusual. There's no restaurant. ♦ 646 W Diversey Pkwy (between N Clark and N Orchard Sts). 773/525.7010, 888/LPN.DAYS ♿ www.lpndaysinn.com

49 INN AT LINCOLN PARK

$ Formerly the Comfort Inn, this is a clean, friendly 75-room motel. The rooms are

---

Restaurants/Clubs: Red | Hotels: Purple | Shops: Orange | Outdoors/Parks: Green | Sights/Culture: Blue

smallish, but the real beauty of staying here is that you're within walking distance of most of the scene; the Halsted strip, the lakefront park, and other main thoroughfares. And the hotel provides parking—like manna from heaven in this part of town. It's best to reserve ahead. There's no restaurant or coffee shop. ◆ 601 W Diversey Pkwy (between N Lehmann Ct and N Clark St). 773/348.2810, 800/228.5150; fax 773/348.1912 &

50 GERBER/HART LIBRARY

♂ ♀ Named after Henry Gerber, the postal worker who started Chicago's first gay rights organization back in 1924, and lesbian attorney Pearl M. Hart, this is the Midwest's largest gay and lesbian circulating library and archives. Since 1981 it has amassed more than 10,000 books and scores of archival items, such as video recordings of the **Chicago Gay Men's Chorus** and a collection of campy 1960s pulp novels dealing with homosexuality. Though much of the material would be of interest only to scholars, visitors might appreciate the center's big September book sale, as well as the regular art exhibits, performances, talks, and film and video presentations. ◆ M, Th, 6-9PM; F-Su, noon-4PM. 1127 W Granville (at N Broadway St). 773/381.8030. www.gerberhart.org

51 HOLLYWOOD BEACH

♂ ⓟ For a certain set of younger, gym-toned, tan-and-model types, this stretch of beachfront under the Chicago skyline is *the* place to strut. It's about a 10-minute drive north of the **Belmont Rocks** and draws big crowds for the summer weekend volleyball games (both pick-up and organized). ◆ At the eastern end of W Bryn Mawr Ave

52 TOM BOY

$$$ Lesbian owned but very popular with the entire community, this eclectic restaurant gets a lot of press—and for good reason. The entrées range from a simple grilled chicken breast to New Zealand lamb chops accompanied by sautéed spinach and twice-baked potatoes topped with Gorgonzola cheese. The wonderfully whacked-out porcupine shrimp (surrounded by phyllo dough on a bed of

Well before O.J. Simpson's "trial of the century," the nation was riveted by one of the most sensational criminal trials of the Roaring Twenties. Law students Richard Leopold and Nathan Loeb were found guilty of kidnapping and murdering 14-year-old Bobbie Franks. The 1924 thrill killing and trial (which resulted in life in prison for both) riveted the nation and inspired several films, including Alfred Hitchcock's *Rope*, Richard Fleischer's *Compulsion*, and, most recently, *Swoon*, by gay filmmaker Tom Kalin.

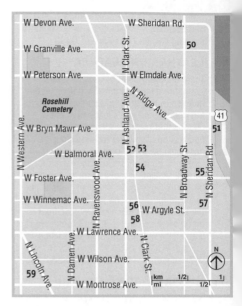

blueberry-mango sauce) is an absolute must. ◆ International ◆ M-Sa, dinner. Reservations required. 5402 N Clark St (at W Balmoral Ave), Andersonville. 773/907.0636. www.tomboyrestaurant.com

53 STAR GAZE

♂ ♀ ★$ Open since 1999, this community-minded storefront restaurant has two spacious rooms—one a sports bar with casual dining, the other a more formal dining room that turns into a dance bar. During summer, a beer garden in back is a popular spot. While the menu offers many standard bar-food items, the specialties have a decidedly Puerto Rican influence: *jibarito de bistek con arroz* is a tasty steak sandwich with plaintains and spicy rice. **Star Gaze** prides itself on hosting fundraising events and does not charge rent for nonprofit organizations. ◆ Daily, lunch and dinner. 5419 N Clark St (between W Balmoral and W Rascher Aves). 773/561.7363. www.stargazechicago.com

54 WOMEN & CHILDREN FIRST

A popular Andersonville landmark, this bookstore carries a broad assortment of lesbian and other women's titles, videos, and music. (As the name suggests, it carries kids' books too.) It's a big favorite with local ladies, and a common book-tour stop for big-name female authors (Alice Walker, Gloria Steinem, and Patricia Ireland, to name a few). A recent expansion meant more shelf space as well as the addition of comfortable reading chairs, a playpen, and a bottomless pot of complimentary coffee. Free parking in back.

♦ M-F, 11AM-9PM; Sa, 10AM-7PM; Su, 11AM-6PM. 5233 N Clark St (at W Farragut Ave). 773/769.9299. www.womenandchildrenfirst.com

54 Reza's

★★$$ Doggie bags are popular here, thanks to the enormous portions of excellent Middle Eastern food at great prices. The sprawling brick-walled dining room is a fun place to try tender lamb with dill-infused rice—or your choice of any number of savory kebabs, stews, game hens, and other (mostly) Persian delights. Another plus: *Chicago* magazine voted the waiters here the best-looking in the city. ♦ Middle Eastern ♦ Daily, lunch and dinner. 5255 N Clark St (at W Berwyn Ave). 773/561.1898 & www.rebasrestaurant.com.

55 Early to Bed

♂♀ Believing that many women are uncomfortable in traditional sex shops, owner Searah Deysach opened this alternative store in the fall of 2001, with the purpose of creating a place where women (as well as men) can shop for sex toys in a clean, welcoming space. Judging by the steady stream of customers, her theory is proving to be true. ♦ Tu-Su. 5232 N Sheridan Rd (between W Foster and W Berwyn Aves). 773.271.1219. www.early2bed.com./pages/home.html

56 Chicago Eagle

♂ Some consider this joint Chicago's "serious" leather bar—dark, no dance floor, X-rated flicks on the video screen, and **The Pit**, a sinister-looking basement with a strict leather dress code. It's got the look down cold, but these days it feels somewhat more like a relic than a hot spot. Still, it appeals to members of the old guard and to those trying to get a feel for the golden days of leather of the 1970s. It's also a short cab ride north from the **Cell Block** if you're not ready to call it a night down on Halsted. On Fridays a women's leather club called Sluts meets here. ♦ M-F, Su, 8PM-4AM; Sa, 8PM-5AM. 5015 N Clark St (between W Argyle St and W Winnemac Ave). 773/728.0050. www.chicagoeagle.com

56 Man's Country

♂ Like the **Chicago Eagle** (which is located in the same building), this bathhouse harks back to a lost era. The most ethnically diverse in town (and especially popular with African-American guys), it is a large, somewhat run-down "adult entertainment complex" that claims to have 100,000 members, as well as the Midwest's largest steam room (there's also a whirlpool and even a dance floor). Most weekends feature gay

porn stars strutting their stuff for the crowd; Monday, Wednesday, and Thursday are discount nights. ♦ Daily, 24 hours. Membership required. 5015 N Clark St (between W Argyle St and W Winnemac Ave). 773/878.2069. www.manscountrychicago.com

57 Big Chicks

♂♀ This place may look like an ordinary neighborhood bar, but it's actually one of the city's most happening nightspots. On the dance floor artsy types groove with gym boys, some gals, and heavy-duty club kids to an eclectic sound that flows from old Donna Summer to the latest club jams to Nirvana. When DJs aren't spinning, the jukebox here may well be the best in the city—and it's always free. It's fun every night, but on Sunday afternoon free pizza, a barbecue (in the summertime), and a crowd of friendly folks make this the place to be. ♦ M-F, Su, 3PM-2AM; Sa, 3PM-3AM. 5024 N Sheridan Rd (between W Argyle and W Winona Sts). 773/728.5511. www.bigchicks.com

58 Man's World

♂ The least well known of the city's bathhouses attracts an older—and less gym-toned—group of guys than the **Unicorn**. With a steam room, a sauna, and a whirlpool, it's small, clean, and moderately crowded after work and on weekends. For those into real daddies, this is the place. A modest one-time membership fee is required to get into this private club. ♦ M-Th, Su, 10AM-2AM; F, Sa, 24 hours. 4862 N Clark St (between W Lawrence Ave and W Ainslie St). 773/728.0400

59 The Rainbow Room

♀ Different musical themes (salsa, oldies, alternative, and dance) are highlighted throughout the week at this lesbo bar and café. It's a bit out of the way, and the dance floor is tiny, but the crowd, heavy on baby dykes, is well worth the trip. ♦ Tu-F, 6PM-2AM; Sa, 7PM-3AM; Su, noon-2AM. 4530 N Lincoln Ave (between W Sunnyside and W Wilson Aves). 773/271.4378 &

At the request of Cardinal Joseph Bernardin, the Windy City Gay Chorus sang at his November 1996 funeral.

In contrast to the yearly Celtic snits in Boston and New York, gays and lesbians have marched proudly—and without incident—in Chicago's annual St. Patrick's Day Parade since 1994.

Restaurants/Clubs: Red | Hotels: Purple | Shops: Orange | Outdoors/Parks: Green | Sights/Culture: Blue

Highlighted route shows the Boulevards (see pg. 214)

W Foster Ave.

41

1

2

W Lawrence Ave.

3 Argyle St.

Foster Avenue Beach

Lincoln Park

41

North Branch Chicago River

W Montrose Ave.

4

19

5

W Irving Park Rd.

7

W Addison St.

8

9

W Belmont Ave.

N Lincoln Ave.

N Western Ave.

N Kedzie Ave.

N Elston Ave.

6

N Ashland Ave.

N Broadway

N Clark St.

N Halsted St.

N Lake Shore Dr.

Montrose Harbor

Belmont Harbor

Lake Michigan

W Diversey Pkwy.

10

W Logan Blvd.

11

N Milwaukee Ave.

John F. Kennedy Expwy.

W Fullerton Ave.

12

N Lincoln Ave.

N Stockton Dr.

W Armitage Ave.

13

64

W North Ave.

Humboldt Park

W Augusta Blvd.

W Chicago Ave.

N Oakley Blvd.

N Wood St.

W Grand Ave.

15

N Ogden Ave.

90

94

E Ontario St.
E Ohio St.

Wacker Dr.

Sacramento Blvd.

Hamlin Blvd.

Garfield Park

W Washington Blvd.

17

18

16

W Randolph St.

W Washington Blvd.

W Warren Blvd.

19

W Jackson Blvd.

20

21

22

Union Station (Amtrak)

290

Eisenhower Expwy.

Rush-Presbyterian-
St. Luke's Medical Center

23

Greyhound Bus Station

Grant Park

Chicago Harbor

S Clark St.

S Michigan Ave.

S Independence Blvd.

W Taylor St.

W Roosevelt Rd.

24

25

26

Meigs Field

Douglas Park

W Ogden Ave.

27

Blue Island Ave.

28

S Canal St.

S Indiana Ave.

W Cermak Rd. (W 22nd St.)

Blue Island Ave.

South Branch Chicago River

41

S Lake Shore Dr.

Cook County Jail

Adlai E. Stevenson Expwy.

55

S Western Blvd.

S Archer Ave.

W 31st St.

29

W 35th St.

31

30

Dan Ryan Expwy.

S Dr. Martin Luther King Jr. Dr.

Burnham Park

32

W Pershing Rd.

S Ashland Ave.

S Halsted St.

33

34

90

94

S Michigan Ave.

E Oakwood Blvd.

S Drexel Blvd.

W 47th St.

E Hyde Park Blvd.

N

km
mi

1
1

2
2

W Garfield Blvd.

35

University of Chicago

There's more to Chicago than the bustling Loop, the elegant Gold Coast, and the affluent North Side. If you wander off the beaten tourist trails, you will find areas of rich ethnic diversity that offer plenty of interesting eats, good shopping, and enjoyable entertainment.

In the southern half of the city are the historic town of **Pullman** (built for his workers by the infamous railroad magnate of the same name) and the Hispanic neighborhoods of **Pilsen** and Little Village, as well as **Chinatown, Greektown,** and **Little Italy.** North of downtown is teeming **Argyle Street,** where you can still buy live fish in the custom of Southeast Asian shoppers, and **Lincoln Square,** where Mayor Daley can occasionally be seen dining on hearty German fare with his friends.

All area codes in this chapter are 312 unless otherwise noted.

1 PASTEUR

★★$$ This popular Vietnamese restaurant, which was included by *Chicago* magazine in a list of the city's best restaurants and is located in a former greasy spoon, offers an array of delicious dishes. Some tend toward the unusual and decidedly upscale, such as marinated clams with ginger sauce. ◆ Vietnamese ◆ Daily, lunch and dinner. 5525 N Broadway (between W Catalpa and W Bryn Mawr Aves). 773/878.1061. www.pasteur-restaurant.com

1 ROGERS PARK

Rogers Park was originally a north suburban community of single-family homes. In the 1920s apartment buildings went up and the area began to attract a diversity of ethnic groups, including large numbers of Irish Catholics and Jews. Though they no longer predominate, their influence is still seen in such institutions as **Loyola University,** numerous synagogues, and kosher delis along Devon Avenue. A visit to Rogers Park offers a glimpse of handsome houses, exposure to bits of curious culture, and the opportunity to go to the beach, because the community's eastern edge runs right along Lake Michigan. It also can be quite dicey in sections, so stay alert. ◆ Bounded by Lake Michigan and N Kedzie Ave and by W Devon Ave and W Howard St. www.luc.edu

A few sights not to miss:

LOYOLA UNIVERSITY

Founded as **St. Ignatius** in 1870, the school received its charter as **Loyola Academy for Boys** in 1909. It became a coeducational university in 1914. The tiny lakefront campus is a surprisingly peaceful oasis of densely packed classroom buildings and residence halls. The main building of **Mundelein** (6363 N Sheridan Rd), a Catholic women's college now part of **Loyola,** is a dramatic limestone Art Deco skyscraper on Devon Avenue. ◆ 6525 N Sheridan Rd (at W Loyola Ave). 773/274.3000. www.luc.edu

LAKEFRONT

A broad, sandy beach starts at North Shore Avenue and stretches several blocks northward. Backed by grassy parkland, it's perfect for a picnic. Along with the usual suntan set are neighborhood families, many of them recent émigrés chatting away in anything from Spanish to Russian. There are other beaches along the city shoreline, including **Foster Avenue Beach.** Beyond that, the next closest beach is in Evanston, but that suburb charges a fee to swim off its sands. ◆ Between W North Shore and W Touhy Aves

HEARTLAND CAFÉ

$ This lively restaurant with a broad wooden deck out front has been serving hearty but bland health food such as gigantic salads brimming with sprouts and thick sandwiches to ex-hippies and other left-leaning types for a long time. And now live jazz can sometimes be heard here. The **Heartland** is one of the last businesses along Glenwood Avenue north of Pratt Boulevard that hark back to the age of Aquarius, along with the No Exit Cafe. ◆ Health food ◆ Daily, breakfast, lunch, and dinner. 7000 N Glenwood Ave (at W Lunt Ave). 773/465.8005. www.heartlandcafe.com

Restaurants/Clubs: Red | Hotels: Purple | Shops: Orange | Outdoors/Parks: Green | Sights/Culture: Blue

DEVON AVENUE

Russian and Urdu are the languages you'll most likely hear on Devon between Western and Sacramento Avenues. A mainly Jewish community until the 1970s, it's now heavily Indian and Pakistani, with a more recent influx of Russian immigrants. Today Russian delis, Greek fruit markets, and Indian jewelers mix in profusion.

Highlights of this vibrant neighborhood include **Chicago Hebrew Bookstore** (2942 W Devon Ave, between N Richmond St and N Sacramento Ave; 773/973.6636) and **Russia Books** (2746 W Devon Ave, at N California Ave; 773/761.3233). **Jai Hind Foods and Video** (2658 W Devon Ave, at N Washtenaw Ave; 773/973.3400) has a marvelous, neatly arranged array of both food and videos, plus a restaurant and a jewelry store. **Sari Niketan** (2611 W Devon Ave, between N Rockwell St and N Talman Ave; 773/338.9399) and some 15 other stores sell exquisite fabrics in 6-yard lengths for traditional wraparound saris. If you have an appetite for a spicy meal, you'll find plenty of opportunities to satisfy it. Among the choices are the upscale **Viceroy of India** (2520 W Devon Ave, between N Campbell and N Maplewood Aves; 773/743.4100), the less fancy Gandhi India (2601 W Devon Ave, at N Rockwell St; 773/761.8714), **Udupi Palace** (2543 W Devon, at N Maplewood Ave; 773/338.2152), **Usmania** (2253 W Devon, at Oakley Ave; 773/262.1900), and **Sonargaon** (2306 W Devon, at N Oakley Ave; 773/262.8003).

2 RAVENSWOOD/LINCOLN SQUARE

Once a predominantly German neighborhood, Ravenswood is now home to Greeks, Koreans, Thais, and a burgeoning group of professional people seeking moderately priced housing. An intriguing mix of Old World–style European shops, delicatessens, pastry shops, and all sorts of ethnic restaurants line the mall.
♦ Bounded by N Ashland and N Kedzie Aves and W Montrose and W Foster Aves

Highlights of the neighborhood include

LUTZ CONTINENTAL CAFE AND PASTRY SHOP

★$ For some, this German pastry shop is the ideal place to take Grandma. It offers napoleons, Linzer tortes, coffee cakes bursting with almonds, homemade ice cream, and weak coffee served on pretty china in a

America's movie industry started in 1907 at Essanay Studios, which was on Chicago's North Side, on Argyle Street near Broadway. Charlie Chaplin made his only Chicago film, *His New Job*, here before California's milder climate lured the industry westward.

dining room with pink tablecloths or on a plant-filled outdoor patio. Soups, crepes, and sandwiches are also served. ♦ Bakery/café ♦ Tu-F, 7AM-8PM; Sa, Su, 7AM-10PM; café from 11AM. 2458 W Montrose Ave (between N Artesian and N Campbell Aves). 773/478.7785

GRECIAN TAVERNA

★$$ Charming and casual, this tavern combines Mediterranean style with a sense of solid American neighborhood comfort. Try the flaming cheese appetizer followed by roast leg of lamb. The thick Greek coffee is an excellent way to end the meal. ♦ Greek ♦ Daily, lunch and dinner. 4761 N Lincoln Ave (between W Sunnyside and W Lawrence Aves). 773/878.6400

OLD TOWN SCHOOL OF FOLK MUSIC

Founded in 1957, and at this location since 1999, the school is a local and national resource for the teaching, performance, and appreciation of folk music. It offers dozens of classes in beginning guitar, harmonica, Irish ballad singing, barn dancing, African drumming, and more. A large library/museum carries an extensive collection of recordings and vintage instruments. The well-stocked retail store sells instruments ranging from guitars to Latin percussion *afuche cabasas* and Polish *pokaleles* (ukuleles); its books and tapes cover folk music from Africa to Peru and from Pete Seeger to Chicagoan David Bromberg. Several nights a week, boisterous sing-alongs and workshops are open to the public. The school also presents a regular series of concerts by a wide range of noted national artists and hosts the annual Festival of Latin Music. In this new location, the auditorium has great acoustics, and with a flexible definition of folk music in its booking policy, the **Old Town School** has become one of the city's great venues to see a variety of music. Be sure to check out the murals by Tony Fitzpatrick on your way into the show. Call for a complete schedule of forthcoming events.
♦ 4536 N Lincoln Ave (between W Sunnyside and W Wilson Aves). 773/728.6000. www.oldtownschool.org

QUAKE COLLECTIBLES

Is your G.I. Joe missing pants? This shop is the place to get the guy some new duds and perhaps replace a tire on that Hot Wheels dragster or expand your *Star Wars* lunchbox collection. ♦ Tu-Su. 4628 N Lincoln Ave (between W Wilson and W Eastwood Aves). 773/878.4288

KELMSCOTT GALLERY

This spectacular building with the Art Nouveau façade was built in 1920 as the **Krause**

UNDER FIRE: CHICAGO'S 1871 INFERNO

No one knows for certain how Chicago's Great Fire of 1871 started. Legend long held that the first flames crackled in a haystack when Mrs. O'Leary's cow knocked over a lantern in the barn behind her cottage west of the **Loop**. However, in 1997 lawyer and historian Dick Bales reviewed the evidence and concluded the following: Although the fire probably did start in the barn, the likely culprit was human, not bovine. His research points to Daniel "Peg Leg" Sullivan, who he believes was in the barn and started the fire when a spark fell from his pipe.

He notes that Sullivan could not have seen the O'Leary barn from where he said he was standing, nor, given his wooden leg, could he have run fast enough to do what he said he did—save a calf and alert Mrs. O'Leary. Whatever the origin, the outcome was the same.

It was 8 October 1871, a Sunday evening, and the weather was unusually dry. The fire department, exhausted from battling a big blaze in another neighborhood, didn't arrive quickly enough, and the fire was soon out of control. Strong winds swept it through the **West Side**, where the fire destroyed ramshackle wooden houses along with lumberyards and factories. The voracious flames spread to the downtown area, consuming financial buildings on **LaSalle Street** and stores along **State Street**, including all the supposedly fireproof structures.

Most of the city's 300,000 residents fled for safety to the edge of the **Chicago River**, where they were treated to a horrific panoramic view of the fire's 4-mile course. The Great Chicago Fire burned steadily for 3 solid days.

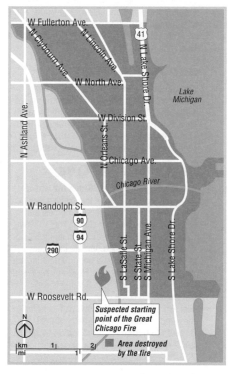

Losses topped $200 million, and 1,688 acres were leveled between the lake, the river, **Fullerton Avenue** on the **North Side**, and **12th Street** on the **South Side**. Downtown Chicago had practically disappeared. Gone too were the homes of nearly one-third of the city's population. The roaring inferno bent streetcar rails, burned down telegraph poles, melted 15,000 water-service pipes, and scorched 28.5 miles of wooden sidewalks. In the aftermath, the bodies of 250 people were found, and many more may have died but gone uncounted.

Yet Chicago was quick to bounce back. Within a week after the last flame flickered, more than 5,000 temporary structures had been built and the construction of 200 permanent buildings had begun. The City Council wisely passed an ordinance that required new buildings in the downtown area to be constructed of brick and iron. Architects had a field day designing buildings that were taller and more elaborate than those they replaced. The homeless moved into wooden cottages built a short distance from the center of town and soon were creating new neighborhoods in the city's outskirts. Chicago was almost entirely rebuilt within 3 years.

Ironically, one survivor of the fire was the O'Leary cottage (although no one's quite sure what happened to the cow). Today the **Chicago Fire Department Academy** stands on the site. Fascinating remnants of the blaze are on view at the **Chicago Historical Society**.

Music Store; it was the last commissioned work of architect **Louis Sullivan**. Restored by **Michael J. Pado**, it now houses a gallery that specializes in **Frank Lloyd Wright** artifacts, drawings, and furniture. ♦ Tu-Sa. 4611 N Lincoln Ave (between W Wilson and W Eastwood Aves). 773/784.2559

MERZ APOTHECARY

The pharmacists here fill regular prescriptions, but they'll also advise you about homeopathic remedies. The turn of the 19th-century interior is packed with pure plant extracts, herbs, aromatherapy oils, and European toiletries.

Restaurants/Clubs: Red | Hotels: Purple | Shops: Orange | Outdoors/Parks: Green | Sights/Culture: Blue

♦ M-Sa. 4716 N Lincoln Ave (between W Leland and W Lawrence Aves). 773/989.0900. www.smallflower.com

CHICAGO BRAUHAUS

★★$$ A traditional Austrian band holds forth in this old-fashioned German restaurant. Robust fare such as sauerbraten and sausage are offered; more unusual dishes like roasted rabbit are also on the menu. Whatever you order, be sure to accompany your meal with a frosty mug of German beer. ♦ German ♦ M, W-Su, lunch and dinner. 4732 N Lincoln Ave (between W Leland and W Lawrence Aves). 773/784.4444. www.chicagobrauhaus.com

TIMELESS TOYS

This small shop offers a grand stock of wooden dollhouses and castles imported from Europe, puppets from all over the world, and a nice sampling of children's books. ♦ Daily. 4740 N Lincoln Ave (between W Leland and W Lawrence Aves). 773/334.4445

ANNOYANCE THEATER

Annoyance Productions has been kicking around the city in one form or another since 1987. In 2004, the company signed a lease for a new home and production facility. It should be open sometime in 2005. ♦ 4840 N Broadway (at W Gunnison St). 773-929.6200

GREEN MILL JAZZ CLUB

Dating back to 1907, the **Green Mll** was a famous speakeasy during the Roaring Twenties and roared through the Thirties, Forties, and Fifties as a top-shelf jazz club. In the 1980s, Dave Jemillo restored the club to its Prohibition-era décor and breathed new life into a city landmark. The artists who perform here include Von Freeman, Brad Goode, Howard Levy, Wilbur Campbell, and Kurt Elling. Seating is first come, first served, so come early if you want to get a seat. On Sunday evenings, the club is home to the world-famous Uptown Poetry Slam. Daily, 5 PM-2 AM (music starts around 8 PM). ♦ 4802 N Broadway (at W Lawrence Ave). 773/878.5552. www.greenmilljazz.com

RIVIERA THEATRE

Built in 1917 by George and C.W. Rapp (Rapp & Rapp), this funky old movie house from the days of Balaban & Katz is now one of the city's most popular rock music venues. ♦ 4746 N Racine Ave (at N Broadway and W Lawrence Ave). 773/275.6800. www.rivieratheatre.com

3 ARGYLE STREET

Although smaller than the older Chinatown, this Asian enclave is worth a visit for delicious Vietnamese food and a stroll through interesting shops. ♦ East of N Broadway

In and around Argyle Street:

TRUNG-VIET

This grocery store doubles as a pharmacy. Proprietor Quoc Tran and his colleague Van Troung, who ran a medicine shop in Saigon for more than 35 years, will concoct a special medicine for whatever ails you from such traditional ingredients as powdered tiger bones and Chinese tree bark. ♦ Daily. 4938 N Sheridan Rd (between W Ainslie and W Argyle Sts). 773/561.0042

NHU HOA CAFE

★$ A bright pink awning signals the entrance to this Laotian/Vietnamese restaurant. The expansive menu has Polaroid photos of the more popular dishes. Try Laotian *keng phet kay*, delicately yet devilishly spiced curried chicken with peas, bamboo shoots, and coconut milk, served with a steaming pot of rice. ♦ Vietnamese/Laotian ♦ Tu-Su, lunch and dinner. 1020 W Argyle St (between N Sheridan Rd and N Kenmore Ave). 773/ 878.0618

VIET HOA MARKET

The scent of pungent spices hits you as you walk through the door of this Vietnamese grocery store, which has an especially nice selection of unusual teas and produce. ♦ Daily. 773/334.1028

HUA GIANG

★★$ An amazing variety of delicious Vietnamese food is offered at very low prices. Try the do-it-yourself appetizer: grilled shrimp or beef, rice noodles, and vegetables, which you tuck and roll into rounds of rice paper. As a main course, the traditional catfish in caramelized sauce cooked in a clay pot is superb. Finish with refreshing Vietnamese iced coffee. ♦ Vietnamese ♦ M-W, F-Su, lunch and dinner. 1104-06 W Argyle St (between N Winthrop Ave and N Broadway). 773/ 275.8691

4 ARUN'S

★★★$$$ This is a palace for Thai connoisseurs who come prepared to empty their wallets. Openers include crab spring rolls and diced grilled pork with lemongrass, chilies, and mint. Among the mainstays are prawns in garlic-lime sauce, and *panang* beef curry with roasted spices. The Singha beer has never tasted so good or cost so much. Save room for an interesting variety of Thai custards. ♦ Thai ♦ Tu-Sa, dinner; Su, brunch and dinner. 4156 N Kedzie Ave (at W Berteau Ave). 773/539.1909. www.arunsthai.com

5 LASCHET'S INN

★★$ You don't have to go to a microbrewery or sit among pretentious beer snobs to find the really good stuff. This authentic German tavern, run by your host and hostess Franz and Ursula, serves the best beer you can find anywhere in the city—and some excellent homemade German food as well. ♦ Daily, dinner. 2119 W Irving Park Rd (between N Lincoln and N Western Aves). 773/478.7915

6 ABBEY PUB

No longer just a sprawling Irish bar on the Northwest Side, the **Abbey** has become one of the best live-music venues in the city, using one of its large rooms to book an eclectic mix of well-known and up-and-coming acts ranging from the Proclaimers to the Drive-By Truckers to local faves J-200. Large crowds still gather at odd hours to watch international soccer matches on large-screen TVs. Food is just average, but the beer selection will quench all thirsts. Daily until 2 AM. 3420 W Grace St (at N Elston Ave). 773/463.5808. www.abbeypub.com

7 MARTYRS'

Featuring rockabilly every Monday night and attracting talents such as James McMurtry and Loudon Wainwright III, this friendly bar has become one of the best rooms in the city for music. And there's a good selection of imported beers as well. ♦ Cover. 3855 N Lincoln Ave (between W Grace and W Byron Sts). 773/404.9494. www.martyrslive.com

8 PAULINA MARKET

A real meat emporium, this sprawling family-owned butcher's shop sells specialty cuts of beef, lamb, pork, and veal, as well as an array of smoked meats. A zillion varieties of homemade sausages line one wall, forming an eye-popping display. Hot oven-roasted chicken, turkey breast, loin of pork, and fresh ham are also available. Friendly counter help will provide advice and recipes if asked. ♦ M-Sa. 3501 N Lincoln Ave (at N Hermitage Ave). 773/248.6272 ♿ www.paulinamarket.com

9 BEAT KITCHEN

Opened in 1991 by Alan Baer, who for years operated **Orphans** in Lincoln Park, this rock 'n' roll bar quickly earned a reputation as one of the best small venues in the city. It generally draws good bands, including local faves like the New Duncan Imperials and Alluring Strangers. The kitchen's fare—pizza, gumbo, blackened chicken—is a pleasant surprise. ♦ Cover for shows. Daily to 2AM; music from about 9:30PM. 2100 W Belmont Ave (at N Hoyne Ave). 773/281.4444. www.beatkitchen.com

10 IXCAPUZALCO

★★$$ This charming little storefront restaurant has an open kitchen behind the bar, from which you can watch chef Geno Bahena, formerly at **Frontera Grill**, mixing up moles and cooking up Mexican delicacies. ♦ Daily, lunch and dinner; closed Tu. 2919 N Milwaukee Ave (at N Drake Ave). 773/486.7340

10 MILWAUKEE AVENUE

Chicago's Polish population is the largest in the world outside of Warsaw. The full length of this avenue and the neighboring streets were predominantly Polish from about 1867 until the middle of the 20th century. A drive along this strip reveals plenty of Polish delicatessens, restaurants, and stores labeled with signs in that language, but they are increasingly interspersed with enterprises of different ethnic origins. ♦ Between John F. Kennedy Expwy and N Harlem Ave

Make sure you don't miss the following:

ABRIL

★$ This bright, friendly Mexican restaurant offers a great vantage point for watching the hustle and bustle on the square. It also serves good margaritas and enchiladas. ♦ Mexican ♦ Daily, lunch and dinner. 2607 N Milwaukee Ave (at N Kedzie Ave). 773/227.7252

ANDY'S DELI

Some 65 kinds of sausages and meats, plus cheeses, pierogi, and other Polish delicacies fill the glass cases and shelves in this delicatessen. ♦ Daily. 3055 N Milwaukee Ave (at N Lawndale Ave). 486.8160. Also at 1737 W Division St (between N Hermitage Ave and N Wood St). 486.8870; 5438 N Milwaukee Ave (between N Manila and W Catalpa Aves). 631.7304. www.andysdeli.com

CZERWONE JABLUSZKO/RED APPLE RESTAURANT

$ The all-you-can-eat buffet—a mere $5.50 for lunch and $6.50 for dinner on weekdays, $6.95 on Saturday and Sunday—draws crowds to this bright room with a basket of apples on every table. Load up on roast chicken or turkey, pierogi, pig's trotters, and boiled potatoes. Finish with cheese-filled crepes, fresh fruits, or a torte. ♦ Polish ♦ Daily, lunch and dinner. 3123 N Milwaukee Ave (between N Ridgeway and N Hamlin Aves). 773/588.5781. Also at 6474 N Milwaukee Ave (at W Imlay Ave). 773/763.3407

POLONIA BOOK STORE

One of the largest Polish bookstores in the country, this shop carries books (in English and in Polish) by Polish authors as well as Polish translations of American potboilers. ♦ M-Sa. 4738 N Milwaukee Ave (at W Giddings St). 773/481.6968

Restaurants/Clubs: Red | Hotels: Purple | Shops: Orange | Outdoors/Parks: Green | Sights/Culture: Blue

11 THE BOULEVARDS

For a comprehensive view of residential Chicago in all its social and architectural grandeur and grimness, nothing beats an afternoon drive along the city's boulevard system. Conceived by landscape architect Frederick Law Olmsted in 1869, the boulevards were intended to create a network of parks linked by grassy thoroughfares that would encircle the city. Olmsted himself created much of the design, along with architects **William Le Baron Jenney** and **Jens Jensen**. Starting at Logan Boulevard and Diversey Parkway on the North Side and concluding on Oakwood Boulevard on the South Side, the system is 28 miles long and links six squares and seven parks. Along the way, you'll see stunning mansions and churches—some in mint condition, others completely dilapidated—and, of course, people of all ethnic and socioeconomic persuasions. You'll pass **Logan Square**, **Humboldt Park**, **Garfield Park** (while you're here, consider a stop at the **Garfield Conservatory**, which dwarfs the one in Lincoln Park), **Douglas Park**, Cook County Jail, and the **University of Chicago**. A word of caution: Unless you are *very* streetwise, you'd be smart not to get out of your car and wander in any section of the boulevards south of Chicago Avenue until you reach Hyde Park.

Along the Boulevards:

LOGAN SQUARE

In the center of Logan Square stands the **Illinois Centennial Monument**, designed by **Henry Bacon** in 1918 to commemorate Illinois's first hundred years of statehood. Teens who hang out here call this monument "the turkey," even though it's actually an eagle. Named after Civil War general John A. Logan, the area of the boulevards between Bloomingdale and Diversey Avenues is slowly but steadily rebuilding from a period of neglect; it has been known for decades for its ethnic diversity. ♦ N Milwaukee Ave and N Kedzie Blvd

12 GREEN DOLPHIN STREET

★★$$$ In one of the more intriguing rehabs in the gentrification scheme, what was once an auto glass repair shop and junkyard has been transformed into a sleek glass-walled riverside eatery that boasts elegant dining in one room and features live jazz in an adjacent one. The menu is strong on seafood and game, with such entrées as sautéed Chilean sea bass and grilled antelope medallions with rosemary broth. The service is surprisingly knowledgeable and efficient for a place noted for its hipness. Dinner guests do not have to pay the cover charge to stay for the music. ♦ Continental ♦ Cover for club. Daily, dinner. Reservations recommended Sa and Su. 2200

N Ashland Ave (at W Webster Ave). 773/395.0066 & www.jazzitup.com

13 ROSA'S

This club bills itself as "Chicago's friendliest blues lounge"—and it must be the truth when people come this far off the beaten track. All blues, no tourists. Free parking is available at the gas station next door. ♦ Cover. Daily, 8PM-2AM; music starts around 9:30PM. 3420 W Armitage Ave (between N Kimball and N St. Louis Aves). 773/342.0452. www.rosaslounge.com

14 UKRAINIAN VILLAGE

For more than a century, this neighborhood and similar enclaves to the north have been destinations for immigrants from Germany, Poland, and other Eastern European countries. These communities have also recently attracted urban pioneers from elsewhere in the city in search of sturdy housing in relatively stable neighborhoods, but the European flavor still lingers. This may be the city's quietest and cleanest neighborhood. ♦ Bounded by N Damen and by N Western Aves and W Grand and W Chicago Aves

Among the Village's highlights:

UKRAINIAN NATIONAL MUSEUM

Ukrainian pottery, weaving, intricately decorated Easter eggs, and photos from the old country are among the exhibits in this small museum set in an old house. Tours that include talks on Ukrainian culture and history are given spontaneously by enthusiastic guides. © Nominal admission. Th-Su, 11AM-4PM, or by appointment. 2249 W Superior St (at N Oakley Blvd). 312/421.8020

15 DAMATO'S BAKERY

Coal-fired ovens may be the key factor in making the Italian bread made here in this corner shop the best in Chicago. Next door, at the deli counter in the back of **Bari Foods**, a neighborhood grocery, you can get an Italian cold-cuts sub sandwich on **Damato's** bread. It may turn out to be the thing you remember most about your trip to Chicago. ♦ 1124 W Grand Ave (at N May St). 312/733.5456

16 RANDOLPH STREET MARKET DISTRICT

It was only a matter of time before developers set their sights on the funky old warehouses in the West Loop as prime candidates for renovation; visitors already had good reasons for coming to the area. Oprah opened her television studio here (Harpo Productions, 1058 W Washington Blvd) several years ago. Michael Jordan and the Bulls drew people west to the United Center (1901 W Madison St) after the old Chicago Stadium was torn down. And

THE BEST

Wilbert R. Hasbrouck, FAIA

Architect, Hasbrouck Peterson Zimoch Sirirattumrong

An architect in Chicago is like a kid in a candy store. Downtown Chicago is literally a three-dimensional encyclopedia of modern architecture. Even with limited time, one can still enjoy Chicago's buildings.

The best starting point is the **Chicago River** at **Dearborn Street**. The panorama to the south is simply breathtaking, but the walk down Dearborn Street is even more so.

Just north of the river are the **Marina City Towers**, **Bertram Goldberg**'s monument to modernity. As one

walks south, other modern structures by **Cesar Pelli**, **Jack Brownson**, **Mies van der Rohe**, and **Skidmore, Owings & Merrill**, as well as a host of others, quickly become apparent. The **Loop**'s oldest office building, the **Delaware** (1871–1872), still stands, beautifully restored at Dearborn and **Randolph**. Further on, one passes the **Marquette**, **Monadnock**, **Fisher**, **Manhattan**, and **Pontiac** Buildings, all giving eloquent testimony to the 19th-century Chicago School of Architecture.

Dearborn Street ends, dramatically, at **Dearborn Street Station** (1882), now restored and adapted for shopping. A half block north is the **Prairie Avenue Bookshop**, an architect's paradise, where virtually every current book on architecture can be found in splendid surroundings.

the city polished up, if superficially, some of the territory between the Loop and the United Center for the 1996 Democratic National Convention. One major benefit of this overhaul has been the emergence of Randolph Street near Halsted Street as a diners' paradise. During the day, especially in the early-morning hours, the Randolph and Fulton markets still teem with activity as trucks deliver produce and restaurateurs come to shop for ingredients for their day's menu. In the evening, you can easily find a fine restaurant merely by having a cab drop you at the intersection of Randolph and Halsted and wandering down the block. For those who prefer to have a plan in place, a better bet would be to pick up a copy of *Chicago* magazine. You'll find vital info about these and other excellent restaurants: **Avec** (615 W Randolph St; 312/337.2002), **Blackbird** (619 W Randolph St; 312/715.0708), **Bluepoint Oyster Bar** (741 W Randolph St; 312/207.1222), **Dragonfly** (832 W Randolph St; 312/787.7600), **Marche** (833 W Randolph St; 312/226.8399), **Moro** (945 W Fulton Market Ave; 312/491.0058), **Red Light** (820 W Randolph St; 312/733.8880), and **Vivo** (838 W Randolph St; 312/733.3379). ♦ W Randolph St (between N Jefferson and N Peoria Sts)

17 ONE SIXTYBLUE

★★★ $$ Painted cobalt blue on the outside and designed by Adam Tihany (who did Cirque 2000 and Jean Georges in New York and **Spago** in Chicago), this fine-dining outpost well west of the Loop is a real eye-catcher. High ceilings and an open kitchen lend a sense of space. Because there's even a private dining room to accommodate investor Michael Jordan, whose basketball exploits brought people out to the **United Center** a

few blocks away, legroom was a consideration in the design. As for the food, there's a definite French accent to Martial Noguier's cuisine, but he leans more toward vegetable reductions than cream sauces. Gnocchi with rock shrimp and asparagus in lobster-tarragon sauce is a great way to warm up. Once the game is underway, Delmonico steak with Portobello mushroom, Yukon Gold potato purée, and ginger-balsamic vinegar broth makes a great play. Close things out with baked Alaska with roasted almonds. Because you're a cab ride away from your next stop, you may want to stay after dinner in the comfy lounge with the zinc-topped bar to enjoy a drink and sample some cheeses. ♦ Contemporary. ♦ M-Sa, dinner. Reservations recommended. 160 N Loomis St (between W Washington Blvd, W Randolph St, and N Ogden Ave). 312/850.0303; fax 312/829.3046. www.onesixtyblue.com

18 MUSEUM OF HOLOGRAPHY

This small museum is filled with astonishing holographic images—an enormous *Tyrannosaurus rex*, Dracula, and Michael Jordan, to name three of the most popular. There's a medical exhibit, where you can experience the interior of a heart. While you're walking through other rooms, a pitchfork may lunge at you out of the darkness or you may see a prisoner pacing behind bars, but it's all an illusion. Holographic jewelry, watches, and bookmarks are for sale in the gift shop. ♦ Admission. W-Su, 12:30-4:30PM. 1134 W Washington Blvd (at N May St). 312/226.1007

19 WEST LOOP GALLERY DISTRICT

As the West Loop gains more standing as a neighborhood for tourists to venture into, numerous gallery owners are relocating from

River North and River West or setting up new shops in the many loft spaces in the area. Among the better known galleries are the **Jan Cicero** (312/733.9551), **Fassbender Stevens** (312/666.4302), and **Thomas McCormick** (312/226.6800) Galleries, all at 835 W Washington Blvd; and **Julia Friedman** (312/455.0755), **Rhona Hoffman** (312/455.1990), and **Aron Packer** (312/226.8984) Galleries, all at 118 N Peoria St. Pick up a copy of *Chicago Gallery News* or visit the web site (www.chicagogallerynews.com) to compile a list of galleries to visit.

20 UNITED CENTER

Named for its corporate sponsor, United Airlines, and lacking the charm and grit of the original **Chicago Stadium**, which was torn down to make way for skyboxes, this is the arena where the **Blackhawks** play hockey and the **Bulls** play basketball and, on occasion, where concerts, circuses, ice shows, and political conventions are held. ♦ 1901 W Madison St (between S Wood St and S Damen Ave). 312/455.7000

21 HUBBARD STREET DANCE COMPANY

Founded in 1978, this popular troupe is considered by many to be Chicago's premier dance company, staging performances here and around the world. Artistic director Lou Conte leads his talented dancers through a uniquely American blend of styles, from ballet to jazz. More than 300 students a year take classes at Conte's studio, also located here. You might catch a glimpse of classes or rehearsals through the windows overlooking Wabash Avenue. ♦ 1147 W Jackson Blvd (between S Halsted St and S Ashland Ave). 312.850.9766. www.hubbardstreetdance.com

22 GREEKTOWN

Greek immigrants began to settle in Chicago's Near West Side in the late 1800s. At one time, so many resided in one triangle-shaped community that it became known as the Delta, after the triangular Greek letter. A number of Greek restaurants still do a brisk lunchtime and dinner business in the neigh-

borhood, which is a quick cab ride from the Loop. ♦ S Halsted St (between W Van Buren and W Monroe Sts)

Highlights of Greektown include

SANTORINI

★★$$ Seafood stars at this romantic stucco-walled villa complete with a crackling fireplace. As a starter, try the charcoal-grilled octopus. Fresh fish entrées range from Norwegian salmon with dill sauce to terrific crisp-fried *baccalo* (cod filet), which comes with a potent potato-garlic purée. There's a nice list of Greek wines and beers. ♦ Greek ♦ Daily, lunch and dinner. Reservations recommended weekends. 800 W Adams St (at S Halsted St). 312/829.8820 ↧ www.santorinichicago.com

GREEK ISLANDS

$ The crowd is boisterous, the waitstaff bustles, and the muraled, polished-wood environs are bright and airy. Though the food can sometimes be disappointing, portions are large and Greek wines are available. ♦ Greek ♦ Daily, lunch and dinner. Reservations recommended for parties of five or more. 200 S Halsted St (at W Adams St). 312/782.9855 ↧ www.greekislands.com

ARTOPOLIS BAKERY & CAFÉ

★★$ This is just the eatery that this neighborhood has sorely needed for a long time. It's a roomy, quiet spot—everything that most Greektown restaurants are not. This is a most pleasant location for a quick replenishing bite or a long leisurely marathon of sampling fine, fresh traditional Greek offerings. ♦ Greek ♦ Daily, lunch and dinner. 306 S Halsted St (between W Jackson Blvd and W Van Buren St). 312/559.9000. www.artopoliscafé.com

PARTHENON

★$$ Not to be confused with the real place by the same name in the old country, this multiroom opah den is a cut above most in the neighborhood, especially if your tastes run toward squid. ♦ Greek ♦ 314 S. Halsted St (between W Jackson Blvd and W Van Buren St). 312/726.2407

23 NATIONAL ITALIAN AMERICAN SPORTS HALL OF FAME

The names of some of the greatest athletes whose names end in vowels will roll off your tongue as you read them in the Tommy and Jo Lasorda Exhibits Gallery. This sparkling new facility includes an interactive area for kids, a museum store, and rooftop café, and soon will have a 225-seat theater in the basement called the Frank Sinatra Performing Arts Center. ♦ M-F. 9:30AM-4:30PM. 1431 W Taylor St (at S Bishop St). 312/226.5566. www.niashf.org

23 UNIVERSITY OF ILLINOIS AT CHICAGO (UIC)

Architect **Walter A. Netsch Jr.** of **Skidmore, Owings & Merrill** was the chief designer for the campus, which also features buildings by **C.F. Murphy Associates, A. Epstein & Sons, Harry Weese & Associates**, and **Solomon Cordwell Buenz & Associates**, among others. The majority of the buildings were constructed between 1965 and 1971. **Netsch** had a vision of bold architectural geometry that he described as "field theory," in which squares were overlaid and rotated. His buildings are easy to pick out on campus. The **Art and Architecture Laboratories** (845 W Harrison St) is geometrically logical in plan but difficult to navigate internally. The **Behavioral Sciences Building** (1007 W Harrison St) is even more complex in plan and was designed with offices along the many-faceted exterior walls and laboratories in the large, windowless interior section. **University Hall** (601 S Morgan St), the 28-story administration building, was of great interest at the time of its construction because it is 20 feet wider at the top than at the bottom. A new era of building was ushered in with the 1988 construction of the **Student Residence and Commons**, designed by **Solomon Cordwell Buenz & Associates**. UIC's first student residence, the three-building complex forms a defined campus boundary at the corner of Halsted and Harrison Streets and offers pleasant common areas. Change continues with the ongoing reconstruction of the central campus. Though **Netsch's** original plans had intellectual purity (the sound of one hand clapping, a critic has said), they had little aesthetic appeal for students or faculty. Nor did they work very well for their intended purpose. The bilevel walkways, the top levels of which were never used and the bottoms of which soon began to leak, are being done away with in a refreshing alteration by **Daniel P. Coffey & Associates**. ♦ Bounded by S Des Plaines and S Morgan Sts, S Racine Ave, W Maxwell St, W Vernon Park Pl, and W Van Buren St. www.uic.edu

Within the UIC campus:

JANE ADDAMS' HULL-HOUSE MUSEUM

In 1889 Jane Addams and Ellen Gates Starr opened the doors of America's first settlement house. Here thousands of needy neighbors—mostly immigrants from the surrounding slums—received education, political support, and cultural edification. Addams and her compatriots—mostly college-educated women—proved instrumental in abolishing child labor, establishing labor unions, and improving public health, among numerous other accomplishments. Programs continued to grow to meet varied needs of the community, which necessitated a remodeling of the house and the addition of several new structures; in its heyday, **Hull-House** occupied a 13-building complex. It continued to play a significant part in the neighborhood's life until the 1950s. Several social service organizations under the organization's umbrella are now scattered throughout the city, but this original location has been converted to a museum owned by the **University of Illinois**. In 1963 the additions were demolished and the house restored to resemble the country estate it was when it was built in 1856 by an unknown architect. It contains fascinating exhibits that document the history of the neighborhood. ♦ Free. M-F, Su. 800 S Halsted St (between W Taylor and W Harrison Sts). 312/413.5353. www.uic.edu/jaddams/Hull

24 AL'S ITALIAN BEEF

★ $ Forget the deep-dish pizza, and try another of Chicago's signature foods: an Italian beef sandwich. Dedicated chowhounds say that the best is at **Johnnie's** (7500 W North Ave; 708/452.6000), all the way out in Elmwood Park, but **Al's** is a good place to try one. ♦ M-Sa. 1079 W Taylor St (between S Carpenter and S Aberdeen Sts). 312/226.4017.

24 LITTLE ITALY

This neighborhood stretches primarily along Taylor Street west from Morgan Street. Access is a bit tricky because of some nonthrough streets. To get here, take a cab or drive west from the Loop on Harrison Street, turn south on Halsted Street, proceed two blocks to Taylor Street, and head west. Between Racine Avenue and Loomis Street, just east of Ashland Avenue, is a relatively well-maintained low-rise public housing project; north of it is **Arrigo Park**, which includes a statue of Christopher Columbus. Across the park along Lexington Street are a few blocks of restored Victorian houses; now home both to neighborhood Italian families and **University of Illinois** faculty, these were originally built as the city's Irish Gold Coast. (It's quite safe to wander through here during the day.)

A few places to see in Little Italy:

TUSCANY

★★$$$ From the splashy neon sign over the entrance to the dining room with glass doors that open in the summer to create a garden-like atmosphere, this place is stylish. The kitchen's rotisseries produce superb whole chicken, among them *paillard di pollo al palio* (grilled chicken breast marinated in herbs and topped with fresh mozzarella and tomatoes). The daily specials are often the best choice. ♦ Italian ♦ M-F, lunch and dinner; Sa, Su, dinner. Reservations required. 1014 W Taylor St (between S Morgan and S Miller Sts). 312/829.1990 ♿ Also at 3700 N. Clark St (at W Waveland Ave). 773/404.7700

MARIO'S ITALIAN LEMONADE

This little wooden sidewalk stand, brightly painted green, white, and red, is famous for the old-fashioned Italian treat it serves. Choose from more than a dozen syrup flavors, poured over cones of shaved ice. ♦ Daily, May-Oct. 1070 W Taylor St (between S Carpenter and S Aberdeen Sts). No phone

CONTE DI SAVOIA

This international gourmet grocery store is stocked with homemade Italian pastas, sauces, and sausages; mozzarella made fresh daily; imported olive oils and tomatoes; and Italian chocolates and baked goods. There's also an espresso and cappuccino bar. They will ship your purchases anywhere in the world. ♦ Daily. 1438 W Taylor St (between S Bishop and S Laflin Sts). 312/666.3471

BAR & GRILL

HAWKEYE'S BAR & GRILL

$$ An authentic Chicago experience, this place attracts rowdy fans attending **Bulls** and **Blackhawk** games at the nearby **United Center**. Many come here first for lunch or dinner, then board a bus to the game, leaving their car in the restaurant's parking lot. Diehards return afterward to celebrate or mourn. The food tends to things that go well with beer, like the build-your-own burger, double-baked chili (served in a bowl of bread with lots of cheese), and chicken in various presentations. ♦ American ♦ Daily, lunch and dinner. Reservations recommended. 1458 W Taylor St (at S Laflin St). 312/226.3951

ROSEBUD

★★$$$ Even with reservations, you'll stand in line to get seated at this enormously popular place. The food is sometimes worth the wait. For starters, try the fried zucchini or the delightful escarole soup with Italian sausage. Though pastas tend to be overcooked, the portions are big enough for two (there's a surcharge if you split them). Chicken Vesuvio, hard to do right, is good and garlicky here. Spumoni is a must for dessert. ♦ Italian ♦ M-F, lunch and dinner; Sa, Su, dinner. Reservations recommended. 1500 W Taylor St (at S Laflin St). 312/942.1117. Also at 55 E Superior St (at N Rush St). 312/266.6444

25 CHICAGO FIRE DEPARTMENT ACADEMY

Standing on the very spot where the Great Fire of 1871 is believed to have begun, this academy trains today's firefighters. Visitors are welcome to drop by for an impromptu tour, but call in advance to be sure that you'll arrive when recruits are actually going through their paces—running through drills on three-story fire escapes, rappelling along ropes down brick walls, jumping into nets, or chopping up cars to extricate imaginary auto-accident victims. ♦ M-F. 558 W DeKoven St (between S Clinton and S Jefferson Sts). 312/747.7239 ♿

26 ROOSEVELT ROAD

A bustling wholesale district before World War II, especially for clothing jobbers, Roosevelt Road east of the Dan Ryan Expressway is a mere shadow of its former self. (West of the Dan Ryan Expressway, Roosevelt Road steadily deteriorates and becomes one of the city's grimiest, and most dangerous, thoroughfares.) The infamous **Maxwell Street Market** has been removed to accommodate expansion of the **University of Illinois at Chicago**. ♦ Between S Canal St and Dan Ryan Expwy

A sampling of stops along Roosevelt Road follows:

EPPEL'S

$ Start your day with breakfast before the sun comes up with folks from the neighborhood. Omelettes are immense, the hash browns are crispy, and the coffee is good and hot. Best of all, the prices can't be beat. ♦ Coffee shop ♦ Daily, 4:30AM-4:30PM. 554 W Roosevelt Rd (between S Clinton and S Jefferson Sts). 922.2206

MANNY'S

★$ This large two-room cafeteria doling out huge helpings of comfort food from steam tables boasts that it has been serving "Chicago's best corned beef since 1942." According to a June 1994 article in *Gourmet*, "if Damon Runyon had written about Chicago, **Manny's** would have been his favorite setting." ♦ American ♦ M-Sa, breakfast and lunch, 5AM-4PM. 1141 S Jefferson St (at W Roosevelt Rd). 312/939.2855

27 PILSEN AND LITTLE VILLAGE

These neighborhoods on the West Side were the port of entry for European immigrants from the 1870s through 1950s. Today they are home primarily to Mexican immigrants. The main streets—18th, 26th, and Halsted Streets and Ashland and Blue Island Avenues—are a jumble of brightly colored stores, bakeries, and restaurants. In fact, 26th Street is also known as Avenida Mexico. Regular events celebrate the community's Mexican heritage, including the annual Fiesta Del Sol held in late July; also in summer, Mexican rodeos, or *charreadas*, are held. Both take place at **Plaza Garibaldi** (W 26th St and California Blvd; 312/847.0990). A fascinating spectacle takes place every Good Friday, when residents reenact the Passion of Christ, staged over an eight-block stretch of 18th Street, culminating in a simulated crucifixion at Plaza Garibaldi. An artists' community has sprung up on the eastern border of Pilsen, along Halsted and 18th Streets, attracting residents ranging from computer artists from the **University of Illinois** to hair stylists from Oak Street. Wander around on a Saturday afternoon and follow those who appear to be in the know into the often hidden shops and galleries. Among the highlights is **Prospectus Gallery** (1210 W 18th St, between S Racine Ave and S Allport St; 312/733.6132), which features contemporary North American and Latin American art. Another local find is the **Blue Rider Theater**, where buoyant personality Donna Blue Lachman performs one-woman shows, including portrayals of Frida Kahlo and Rosa Luxemburg (1822 S Halsted St, between W 19th and W 18th Sts; 312/733.4668). The best time to visit the area is Saturday afternoon, when the streets teem with locals out shopping. **CTA** service to the area is slow and not the safest; take a cab or drive. As the area can be a bit seedy—especially at night—stick to main thoroughfares. ♦ Bounded by S Halsted St, S Kostner and S Western Aves, the Chicago River, Chicago Sanitary and Ship Canal, and W 16th St

A sampling of sights in Pilsen and Little Village:

CHICAGO ARTS DISTRICT

When the rents go up, where do the artists go? To this gentrifying neighborhood on the Near Southwest Side. The **Chicago Arts District** is a 12-square-block area centered near South Halsted and 18th Streets with more than a dozen galleries. ♦ 312.923.1010; fax 312/923.1090. www.chicagoartsdistrict.com

CASA AZTLAN

The murals on the front of this social services center were contributed by numerous artists from the area. They depict Benito Juárez and other Mexican heroes, as well as the evolution of the neighborhood. ♦ 1831 S Racine Ave (between W 19th and W 18th Sts). 312/666.5508

NUEVO LEON

★★$ Authentic Mexican dishes draw locals and visitors alike. For something different, order the breaded fried brains. ♦ Mexican ♦ M-Th, Su, breakfast, lunch, and dinner until midnight; F, Sa, until 3AM. 1515 W 18th St (between S Laflin St and S Ashland Ave). 312/421.1517. Also at 3657 W 26th St (at S Lawndale Ave). 773/522.1515

SABAS VEGA CARNICERIA

The glass cases are laden with Mexican *chorizo* (sausage), steaks, and a variety of delicious freshly made specialties such as cactus salad to take out. ♦ Daily. 1808 S Ashland Ave (between W 18th Pl and W 18th St). 312/666.5180

NUEVO LEON BAKERY

An authentic Mexican *panaderia* tempts you with warm *bobolillos* (a type of bread) and an assortment of sugar-laden deep-fried or baked pastries. Hand-pick your selections with a pair of tongs and a paper plate. ♦ Daily, 6AM-9PM. 1634 W 18th St (between S Ashland Ave and S Paulina St). 312/243.5977

Charles A. Dana, a newspaper editor from New York, nicknamed Chicago the Windy City in 1893. He was referring to the city residents' bragging during the Columbian Exposition, but the nickname soon became associated with the winds blowing from Lake Michigan. In fact, Chicago ranks only 16th in windiest US cities. (Great Falls, Montana, is first.)

Restaurants/Clubs: Red | **Hotels: Purple** | **Shops: Orange** | **Outdoors/Parks: Green** | **Sights/Culture: Blue**

THE BEST

Patrick McGuire

School Administrator

Best budget day in the Loop:

1. Take in free exhibits at the **Chicago Cultural Center** and **Harold Washington Library**.

2. Lunch on juicy Amish-raised chicken and tasty side dishes in the *Jetsons*-like atmosphere of **Taza** (Arabic for *fresh*) on Wabash.

3. In hot weather, walk around **Buckingham Fountain** and let the spray cool you and the international

tourists posing for pictures; then walk to the **Museum Campus**, sit on the sloping lawn in front of the **Field Museum**, and enjoy a superb view of **Monroe Harbor** and **Navy Pier**.

4. In cold weather, visit the stores in DePaul University's **Chicago Music Mart**, at State and Jackson, including the comprehensive **Crow's Nest Records**, the peaceful **Afrocentric Books**, and the legendary sheet-music emporium **Carl Fisher Music** in the basement.

5. Spend the money you have left on treats for the family at **Garrett's Popcorn**, at Wabash and Jackson, where the wait is worth it at this portal to South Side working Chicago.

MEXICAN FINE ARTS CENTER

Opened in 1987, the first Mexican cultural center in the Midwest remains the largest and busiest, with regularly changing exhibitions. Live multilingual shows are presented in the theater. The **Tzintzuntzan** gift shop sells outstanding Mexican arts and crafts. ◆ Free. Tu-Su. 1852 W 19th St (between S Wood St and S Damen Ave). 312/738.1503 & www.mfacm.org

28 CHINATOWN

Chicago's first Chinese immigrants, who began to arrive in the 1870s, originally settled in the South Loop. At the turn of the 20th century, those connected with the On Leong fraternal organization founded an official Chinatown on the city's South Side near Cermak Road. Only a few blocks square, the community is densely populated, with about 10,000 residents. The main streets—whose names appear on street signs in Chinese characters as well as in English— are Wentworth Avenue, Cermak Road (22nd Street), and Archer Avenue. These boundaries have extended farther north to 18th Street with **Chinatown Square**, a shopping mall and 600-unit apartment complex built on former railroad yards in 1993. In the 1970s a smaller Chinatown sprang up on the North Side along Argyle Street, but the neighborhood has evolved into Little Saigon, with more of a Southeast Asian than a Chinese community between Sheridan Road and Broadway. Although Chicago's Chinese populace is spread throughout the city and suburbs, these neighborhoods are wonderful microcosms of Asian culture, from the exotic grocery stores to the Chinese New Year parades held in both communities each February, complete with fire-breathing dragons and dancing, firecracker-tossing lions. ◆ Bounded by S Wentworth Ave, S Canal St, the Chicago River, Adlai E. Stevenson Expwy, and W 18th St

Among the finds to be found in Chinatown:

THREE HAPPINESS

★$$ Skip the regular menu, which pales in comparison with the dim sum, a seemingly endless array of steamed dumplings, deep-fried pastries, and other exotica. ◆ Chinese ◆ Daily. 2130 S Wentworth Ave (at W Cermak Rd). 312/791.1228

ON LEONG MERCHANTS ASSOCIATION

Constructed in the 1920s, the ornamental building with its twin-pagoda roof long served as a kind of Chinese city hall, with a courtroom where disputes among community members were settled. Today, except for a couple of retail stores on the ground level, the building is vacant, having been seized by the federal government in 1988 after a raid on a gambling operation inside. The fraternal organization now meets at 218 West 22nd Place (312/842.0807); it has become much more circumspect about its activities. ◆ 2214 S Wentworth Ave (at W Cermak Rd)

CHIU QUON BAKERY

Steamed buns stuffed with pork or lotus-seed paste, sesame balls, watermelon cake, and almond cookies are just a few of the fresh-baked treats here. You can order to take out or sit down and eat in the little tearoom in back. ◆ Daily, 7AM-9PM. 2242 S Wentworth Ave (between W 23rd St and W Cermak Rd). 312/225.6608

Frida's

FRIDA'S BAKERY

Right across the street from **Chiu Quon**, this cross-cultural bakery offers a good selection of American and French specialties as well as the familiar Chinese baked goods. This and several other Western-style bakeries along the street are reminders that there's still a significant Italian population in the residential area west of Wentworth. ♦ Daily, 7AM-9PM. 2228 S Wentworth Ave (between W Alexander St and W 22nd Pl). 312/808.1113

WOKS 'N' THINGS

You'll be able to open your own Chinese restaurant after a visit here. The small but well-stocked shop carries woks in a dozen sizes, the largest fit for an emperor at 30 inches across. ♦ Daily. 2234 S Wentworth Ave (between W Alexander St and W 22nd Pl). 312/842.0701

EMPEROR'S CHOICE

★★$$ Chef Ron Moy's distinctive cuisine is showcased in this contemporary and bright restaurant. Seafood shines, especially plump oysters or fresh sole lightly seasoned with ginger, cilantro, and black beans. Order the outstanding Peking duck a day in advance. ♦ Chinese ♦ Daily, lunch and dinner, late kitchen. 2238 S Wentworth Ave (between W Alexander St and W 22nd Pl). 312/225.8800

TEN REN TEA

A tea lover's delight, featuring about 50 varieties of teas—loose, boxed, and tinned—including ordinary black tea, Oriental Beauty tea, Iron Goddess of Mercy tea, and $118-per-pound Ten Wu tea grown on the highest-altitude tea plantation in Taipei expressly for this Taiwanese tea conglomerate. The red-clay teapots are one of a kind. ♦ Daily. 2247 S Wentworth Ave (between W 23rd St and W Cermak Rd). 312/842.1171

DONG KEE COMPANY

A one-stop shop for china, woks, kitchen gadgets, gifts, teas, and even fresh-made almond cookies. ♦ Daily, 9AM-7PM. 2252 S Wentworth Ave (at W Alexander St). 312/225.6340

29 BRIDGEPORT

The 11th Ward is historically the center of Chicago politics, and Bridgeport serves as its county seat. Until the current mayor, Richard M. Daley, moved to Dearborn Park in the South Loop in 1993, he lived here, as did his father, the late Richard J. Daley. This ward also produced the legendary Ed Kelly, who served from 1933 to 1947, when his overt corruption prompted Democratic machine leaders to install a figurehead reformer, Martin Kenelly, also from Bridgeport, in his place. Known for its corner churches and corner bars, Bridgeport is a quiet Irish Catholic neighborhood

mostly of tidy little bungalows with perfectly manicured lawns. ♦ Bounded by S Normal Ave, the Chicago River, and W Pershing Rd

Among the Bridgeport sights to be seen:

SCHALLER'S PUMP

Directly across the street from the 11th Ward Regular Democratic Organization headquarters, this is a neighborhood tavern where beer and politics mix famously, as long as you've got the right point of view. Don't speak kindly of the late Harold Washington, Jane Byrne, or the Republican Party. ♦ M-F, 11AM-2AM; Sa, 5:30PM-3AM; Su, 3:30PM-9PM. 3714 S Halsted St (between W 37th Pl and W 37th St). No phone

BUBBLY CREEK

The south fork of the south branch of the Chicago River runs along the west side of Bridgeport four blocks west of Halsted Street. Used as a sewer by meatpacking houses, Bubbly Creek got its name from the natural fermentation of animal carcasses that took place in it. Yes, it still bubbles.

30 ILLINOIS INSTITUTE OF TECHNOLOGY (IIT)

In 1938 German architect **Ludwig Mies van der Rohe** was recruited by Chicago architect **John A. Holabird** to head the architecture department at the **Armour Institute of Technology**. When Armour merged with the **Lewis Institute** in 1940 to become **IIT**, Mies was asked to design a campus for the new school, a task that occupied him until his retirement from the faculty in 1958. His goal was a visually unified campus, with a rational master plan and a repetitive module on which each building's design would be based. The Chicago grid street plan inspired the uncompromisingly rectilinear campus layout (see the campus map on page 222), arranged to define but not enclose the open spaces between buildings. The most famous aphorism attributed to Mies is "less is more," an apt description of his clean, uncluttered designs. Another of his sayings, equally applicable to his work, is "God is in the details." The progression of Mies's design is revealed in subtle developments from one building to the next, and the campus provides an unusual opportunity to see his philosophy develop. In 1976 the American Institute of Architects recognized the IIT campus as one of the 200 most significant works of architecture in the US. Although IIT itself is safe, the housing projects to the south can be very dangerous, especially at night. Use your judgment on whether to drive, take a cab, or ride on the **Englewood** or **Dan**

Restaurants/Clubs: Red | Hotels: Purple | Shops: Orange | Outdoors/Parks: Green | Sights/Culture: Blue

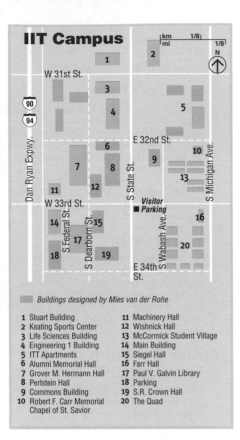

IIT Campus

Buildings designed by Mies van der Rohe

1 Stuart Building
2 Keating Sports Center
3 Life Sciences Building
4 Engineering 1 Building
5 ITT Apartments
6 Alumni Memorial Hall
7 Grover M. Hermann Hall
8 Perlstein Hall
9 Commons Building
10 Robert F. Carr Memorial Chapel of St. Savior
11 Machinery Hall
12 Wishnick Hall
13 McCormick Student Village
14 Main Building
15 Siegel Hall
16 Farr Hall
17 Paul V. Galvin Library
18 Parking
19 S.R. Crown Hall
20 The Quad

Ryan Els (both stop at **35th Street**). Free visitor parking is available in a lot at the southeast corner of 33rd and State Streets. Group tours are available on request. ♦ Bounded by S Michigan Ave and Dan Ryan Expwy and by 35th and 30th Sts

Among the campus's most notable buildings are the following:

MAIN BUILDING

The only remaining structure from the institutions that preceded IIT provides the sharpest possible contrast with Mies's vision. Designed in 1891 by **Patton & Fisher**, this brick and terra-cotta structure was the main classroom building for the old **Armour Institute**, founded by Philip Armour, one of Chicago's most prominent meatpackers. Characteristic of Romanesque designs of this time, it features rusticated masonry at the first level, with smooth brick above and two series of roundheaded windows. ♦ 3300 S Federal St (at W 33rd St)

ALUMNI MEMORIAL HALL

With **Perlstein** and **Wishnick Halls**, this 1946 building forms Mies's first completed open quadrangle. The skin consists of buff-colored brick panels, steel, and panes of glass, which for the first time in the architect's work fill the entire bay. Mies devoted much thought to how a building turns a corner; here, the corners are gracefully serrated. **Holabird & Root** served as associate architects on the project. ♦ 3201 S Dearborn St (at W 32nd St)

PERLSTEIN HALL

Also designed by Mies in 1946 in association with Holabird & Root, this steel-framed building has a light court that was designed by **Walter A. Netsch Jr.** of **Skidmore, Owings & Merrill**. ♦ 10 W 33rd St (at S State St)

S.R. CROWN HALL

The most famous building on campus and a world-renowned masterpiece of structural Expressionism, this hall consists of an elegant and spare skin of steel and glass stretched over a column-free space 220 feet by 120 feet. No fireproofing materials obscure the view of the structure, which features a roof hung from four steel-plate girders. The 18-foot interior height and minimal partitions create an unusual spatial experience. Students in architecture, planning, and urban design work in a space that sharply contrasts with the typical design-school studio, which is often carved into small cubbyholes. Here, the openness promotes interaction and learning from other students, as well as from the faculty. In keeping with students' long hours, the building is usually open early and late Monday through Saturday during the school year. ♦ 3360 S State St (between W 35th and W 33rd Sts)

ROBERT F. CARR MEMORIAL ST. SAVIOR CHAPEL

Known as the "God box," the chapel was designed by Mies in 1952 with the same stark vocabulary as **Crown Hall** and the campus boiler plant. Mies originally intended the entire building to be of steel construction; because of the cost, however, only the roof was made of steel. The brick walls create a private enclosed space—unlike the typical college chapel, but well suited to contemplation. ♦ 65 E 32nd St (between S Michigan and S Wabash Aves)

PAUL V. GALVIN LIBRARY

Architects after Mies continued to be inspired by his vision for the campus. Walter A. Netsch Jr. at Skidmore, Owings & Merrill carefully studied Crown Hall before designing this library in 1962; from the front, you can compare and contrast the two buildings. ♦ 35 W 33rd St (at S Dearborn St)

31 U.S. CELLULAR FIELD

Home of the **Chicago White Sox**, this stadium opened in 1991. It was built with public funds after ball club president Jerry M. Reins-

U.S. Cellular Field-Comiskey Park

dorf threatened to move the team out of town. It is generally regarded as a badly designed stadium—because of the multiple levels of skyboxes installed, sitting in the concrete upper deck has been likened to watching a ball game from an airplane. The "new" park is located on 35th Street, across from the site of the original **Comiskey Park**. Built in 1910 and demolished in 1992, it was the nation's oldest ballpark. Now it's a parking lot; there's a plaque where home plate once stood. Street parking around the stadium is virtually nonexistent, so you'll have to park in one of the official lots, which are a nightmare to get in and out of, or in a private lot to the west. The **CTA**'s **Red Line** from the Loop runs along the Dan Ryan Expressway two blocks east. East and south of the park are Stateway Gardens and Robert Taylor Homes, two of the city's most decaying, crime-ridden public housing complexes. ♦ W 35th St (between S Wentworth and S Normal Aves). 674.1000

32 CITY CENTER

When you stand at this intersection, 12 blocks west of the house at 3602 South Lowe Avenue where Mayor Richard M. Daley grew up, you are at the exact geographical center of the city. ♦ W 37th and S Honore Sts

33 INTERNATIONAL AMPHITHEATRE

Once one of the largest and busiest convention and exhibit halls in the country (and the site of the infamous Democratic Convention of 1968), this huge building has been used infrequently since **McCormick Place** was built. Today it hosts the occasional rodeo, boxing match, and bargain clothing sale. ♦ 4220 S Halsted St (between W 45th St and W Exchange Ave)

33 OLD STONE GATE

This triple-arched gate, most likely designed by **John Wellborn Root**, marked the entrance to the **Union Stock Yards**. A wooden gate built in 1875 stood on this spot but was replaced circa 1879 by the stone one, now a national landmark. It marks the entrance to an industrial park once filled with acres and acres of animal pens. ♦ W Exchange Ave and S Peoria St

34 ST. GABRIEL'S CHURCH

Constructed between 1887 and 1888, this is the only Catholic church in Chicago built by **Burnham & Root**. **Daniel Burnham** was the son-in-law of John Sherman, president of the Union Stock Yard & Transit Company. **John Wellborn Root** designed the church, which, with its massive brick structure and spacious interior, is reminiscent of the firm's **Rookery Building** and evokes Carl Sandburg's metaphor of big shoulders. Although a section of the 160-foot-tall tower was removed, the church still looms over the neighborhood, serving as a tribute to the Reverend Maurice J. Dorney, the founder of the parish, who was known as "The King of the Yards." ♦ 4501 S Lowe Ave (at W 45th St)

estaurants/Clubs: Red | Hotels: Purple | Shops: Orange | Outdoors/Parks: Green | Sights/Culture: Blue

St. Gabriel's Churc

35 PULLMAN

Chicago industrialist George M. Pullman, manufacturer of the Pullman Sleeping Car, built this quaint "model town" on the city's Far South Side for his factory workers. Designed in the 1880s by architect **Solon S. Beman** and landscape architect Nathan F. Barrett, the 1,800-building community was intended not so much to make workers happy as to increase overall productivity by providing clean and pleasant surroundings. The town was said to be patterned after Saltaire in Northern England, built by textile manufacturer Sir Titus Salt. Pullman's workers, whom he called his "children," were required to live here, paying rent and utilities at rates that earned him a 6% annual profit. In 1893 the company fired thousands of employees and cut the wages of remaining workers by an average of 25%. Pullman did not, however, reduce their rent, leading to the near starvation of many of these hard-pressed employees and their families during the winter of 1893–1894. That spring, the workers went on strike, and in the summer, member unions of the American Railway Union, led by Eugene V. Debs—who later founded the

Social Democratic Party—staged sympathy strikes. When violence erupted, President Grover Cleveland sent in federal troops. Debs was sentenced to 6 months in prison. Although the workers lost the strike, Pullman drew little sympathy. Upon his death in 1897, he was buried beneath several protective tons of steel rails and concrete in **Graceland Cemetery**, as his family feared enemies would rob his grave. In 1907 the town was sold to its residents, who still form a very tightly knit community. Pullman was declared a national landmark in 1971, and since then many efforts have been made to restore and revitalize the area. More than 80% of the original buildings still stand. A walk through the area is a visit to a small 19th-century town of handsome brick row houses and common buildings. The structures are Victorian in style, with plain Italianate town houses, lavish Queen Anne residences, and many examples of Romanesque arches, one of the architect's signature design elements. Note that in December 1998, the landmark Pullman Administration Building and Clock Tower, which had previously housed company offices, was tragically destroyed in a fire. ♦ Exit I-94 at E 111th St. Go west just a few blocks and turn left on Forrestville Avenue, and you'll be right in front of the Hotel Florence.

Highlights of the town include the following:

HOTEL FLORENCE

In 1881 **Solon S. Beman** made this turreted and gabled fantasy in the Queen Anne style. Named after Pullman's daughter, the hotel was the grandest structure in the town. It contained

---

The original nicknames for the Bridgeport neighborhood were Hardscrabble and Cabbage Patch.

In 1915 only 10 families owned more than one-twelfth of Chicago's land. The Marshall Field family alone owned land worth $100 million.

CHICAGO THEATER: SECOND TO NONE

The **Steppenwolf Theatre Company** may have put Chicago on the international theater map, but the award-winning ensemble is hardly the only show in town. Other stellar theaters in the Windy City include the **Goodman**, **Victory Gardens**, and **Court**, where new works and refreshing new interpretations of old works are often premiered. **Second City** invented improvisational theater almost 40 years ago, and the craft continues there today, as well as at the **Improv Olympic** and the **Players Workshop**.

Unlike any other theater community in the country, Chicago is known for developing risk-taking new works. There is a thriving off-Loop theater scene, where more than a dozen Equity companies and scores of non-Equity troupes tread the boards. Small theater companies like **Roadworks** and **Organic/Touchstone** have established their own reputations, and even more alternative fare is being produced by such daring young groups as the **Annoyance Theater** and **Live Bait Theater**.

The Joseph Jefferson Awards Committee honors excellence in local professional theater. The 40-member panel judges more than a hundred productions each year, bestowing "Jeff" Awards for superior work in Equity shows and noncompetitive citations for outstanding work in non-Equity productions.

In the recent past, however, some of Chicago's nonprofit and experimental theaters have fallen by the wayside, unable to compete with the big commercial productions coming out of London and New York. But with **Lookingglass Theatre Company**'s move to N Michigan Ave and **Victory Gardens**' move to the historic Biograph, the Chicago theater scene is looking strong.

For up-to-the-minute information, consult publications such as the *Reader, New City, Chicago Tribune,* and *Chicago* magazine. To charge theater tickets by phone, call the **Ticketmaster Arts Line** (312/902.1500). **Hot Tix** booths, which are owned and operated by the League of Chicago Theatres, offer half-price and discounted day-of-performance tickets, as well as full-price tickets to **Ticketmaster** events. All **Hot Tix** sales must be made in person; booths are found at the following locations:

The Loop: 78 W Randolph St (between N Clark and N Dearborn Sts); M, noon-6PM; Tu-F, 10AM-6PM; Sa, 10AM-5PM

Magnificent Mile: 163 E Pearson St (at Michigan Ave); M-Sa, 10AM-6PM; Su, noon-5PM

Tower Records: 2301 N Clark St (at W Belden Ave); 214 S Wabash Ave (at E Jackson Blvd); Tu-Sa, 10AM-6PM; Sun, noon-5PM

the only bar in Pullman, which was open only to guests. This National Historic Landmark is no longer renting rooms. The hotel in recent years has been a museum operated by the **Historic Pullman Foundation**. In 2000, it was closed for extensive renovation, and it is still uncertain when it will reopen.

PULLMAN UNITED METHODIST CHURCH

Built in 1882 as **Greenstone Church**, this was the only religious structure in the original company town. Pullman had intended all workers to worship together in a community church, but in the end each religious group chose its own minister. Even the church had to pay rent to the Pullman Company, although none of the separate congregations could afford to on its own. The Methodists bought the church in 1907 and changed its name. **Solon S. Beman**'s green serpentine limestone walls contrast sharply with the brick buildings in the rest of the town. ♦ 11211 S St. Lawrence Ave (at E 112th St)

PULLMAN STABLES

The carved horses' heads above the entrance mark the only place in Pullman where the residents could keep their horses. Carriages were also available for rent here. ♦ 11201 S Cottage Grove Ave (at E 112th St)

HISTORIC PULLMAN FOUNDATION VISITOR CENTER

Across the street from the stables is a non-descript building that now houses the foundation's visitors' center. A video presentation introduces visitors to the area, and guided tours are available from the center on selected Sundays between spring and fall. ♦ Daily. 11141 S Cottage Grove Ave (at E 112th St). 773/785.8181 or 773/785.9801

Baggage for O'Hare International Airport is marked ORD because the original name for the field was Orchard.

Restaurants/Clubs: Red | Hotels: Purple | Shops: Orange | Outdoors/Parks: Green | Sights/Culture: Blue

ENVIRONS

Some of Chicago's finest attractions aren't in Chicago at all. The surrounding suburbs are home to a variety of fascinating sites: There's the wealth of **Frank Lloyd Wright** buildings in **Oak Park**, the **Baha'i House of Worship** in Wilmette, and the **Chicago Botanic Garden** in Glencoe, to name a few. You'll even find what many consider Chicago's best restaurant, **Le Français**, in the suburb of **Wheeling**. For more information on Chicago's environs, call the **Illinois Tourist Information Office** at 800/226.6632. www.enjoyillinois.com.

1 LE FRANÇAIS

★★★$$$$ The suburb of Wheeling is home to what some still say is the best restaurant in Chicago. In 2004, Roland Licconi took over as chef. Expect not only meticulously prepared French food but also an impressive 80-page wine list. ◆ French ◆ M-Sa, dinner. Reservations required. 269 S Milwaukee Ave (between Palatine and Dundee Rds), Wheeling. 847/541.7470 ♿ www.lefrancais.com

2 ARLINGTON HEIGHTS

Flower-filled **Le Titi de Paris** serves French classics and more daring specials (Tu-F, lunch and dinner; Sa, dinner; reservations recommended; 1015 W Dundee Rd/Rte 68, at Kennicott Ave; 847/506.0222). This is also the town for **Arlington International Racecourse** (Euclid Ave, between N Wilke Rd and Rte 53; 847/255.4300), which has thoroughbred racing between May and September, including the Arlington Million in August.

3 GENEVA/ST. CHARLES/BATAVIA

Drive the roaring Eisenhower Expressway (Interstate 290) and Interstate 88 westward from the Loop for about an hour, and you end up in these three lovely towns along the Fox River. Antiques-lovers' heaven, they boast hundreds of dealers, as well as numerous shops selling arts and crafts. On the first weekend of every month, the **Kane County Flea Market** (Randall Rd and Rte 64, St. Charles) shows the wares of up to a thousand dealers. Many 19th-century Victorian homes and other landmark buildings throughout all three towns have been preserved and are open to the public. Special museums include the **Garfield Farm Museum** west of Geneva (admission; open W and Su, 1-4PM, June-Sept; Garfield Rd, north of Rte 38; 630/584.8485 www.garfieldfarms.org &), which spans 212 acres and depicts farm life in the mid-19th century. Recreational opportunities include bicycling along riverfront trails, canoeing, fishing, golfing at nearby courses, and cross-country skiing. Geneva's Third Street is one of the Chicago area's most charming places to shop; dozens of antiques and gift stores line this street of 19th-century brick and wooden houses. Restaurants abound, particularly in Geneva, which was established in the same year as Chicago: The **Mill Race Inn** (4 E State St, at the Fox River; 630/232.2030 &) is a special treat for dinner, as is **302 West** (302 W State St, at S Third St; 630/232.9302). ♦ For more information, call the St. Charles Visitors' Bureau, 800/777.4373; the St. Charles Chamber of Commerce, 630/584.8384; the Geneva Chamber of Commerce, 630/232.6060; or the Batavia Chamber of Commerce, 630/879.7141.

4 BROOKFIELD ZOO

ⓟ A sprawling suburban zoo (see the map on page 228) 17 miles west of the Loop spans 204 acres of naturalistic habitats and gardens that are home to more than 2,000 animals

representing 425 different species. Among the highlights are **Tropic World of Apes and Monkeys**, the world's largest indoor zoo exhibit, which simulates rain forest regions of Asia, Africa, and South America. The **Seven Seas Panorama** includes an arena for viewing dolphins (there's a nominal ticket charge in addition to general admission) as they perform acrobatics and demonstrate echolocation, their form of sonar communication. The **Children's Zoo**, open to visitors of all ages, presents baby animals and goats, lambs, and horses to pet. **Backstage at the Zoo** offers, for an extra charge, in-depth tours of selected animal exhibits for kids aged 7 and older. The **Zoo Shop** is well stocked with attractive animal-theme gifts and souvenirs, plus more than 4,500 books on animals and nature. Several fast-food restaurants are on the premises. ♦ Admission and parking fees; half-price admission on Tu and Th. Daily. First Ave and 31st St, Brookfield. By commuter train from **Union Station**, take the **Burlington Northern, Santa Fe** line to the **Hollywood Metra Station**. 708/485.0263. www.brookfieldzoo.org

5 MORTON ARBORETUM

ⓟ The 1,500-acre refuge for woody plants from around the world was created in 1922 by Joy Morton, founder of the Morton Salt Company, on the grounds of his estate in what is now the western suburb of Lisle. (Apparently the whole family was fond of trees; Morton's father was J. Sterling Morton, a Nebraska statesman who originated Arbor Day.) This peaceful spot is a walker's delight, with grassy slopes in every direction, trees and shrubs both familiar and unusual, and six lakes. The numerous display gardens include the **Hedge Gardens**, with more than 100 formally laid out hedges, and the **Fragrance Garden**, abloom with fragrant flowers and foliage. There's an indoor visitors' center, but the big attractions are outdoors, so dress for the weather. An introductory program, including a tour by foot or open-air bus, will show you around. You can tour the grounds in your own car along an 8-mile route or set off on hiking trails. The arboretum is packed on weekends during April and May, when magnolias and other flowering trees go into bloom, and in mid- to late October, when fall colors reach their peak. Visit on a weekday instead if you can. Eats are available at a fast-food restaurant, as well as in the full-menu **Gingko** (630/719.2467) restaurant overlooking Meadow Lake. ♦ Admission. Daily. 4100 Illinois Rte 53 (just north of I-88), Lisle. Group tour reservations, 630/719.2465 & www.mortonarb.org

---

Restaurants/Clubs: Red | **Hotels: Purple** | Shops: Orange | **Outdoors/Parks: Green** | Sights/Culture: Blue

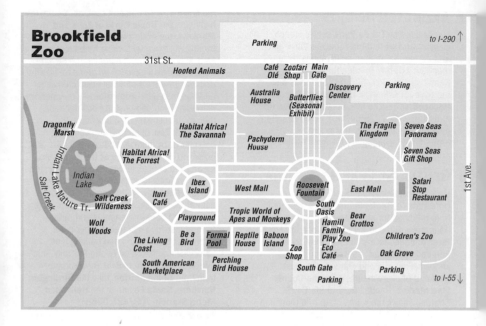

Brookfield Zoo

NORTH SHORE

A journey northward along **Lake Michigan** through **Evanston**, **Wilmette**, **Kenilworth**, **Winnetka**, **Glencoe**, and **Highland Park**—some of the city's most affluent suburbs—makes a pleasant day trip, whether it's nature scenes, gigantic mansions, or other sights you're interested in. **Sheridan Road** meanders through the entire area. ◆ You may reach a number of these areas by **CTA**'s **Evanston Express**, also called the **Purple Line**; **Metra** trains go there too. For information on public transportation, call 773/836.7000.

6 HIGHLAND PARK

Continuing your drive along Sheridan Road, you will pass the **Ward W. Willits House** (1445 Sheridan Rd, between Beech St and Forest Ave), a Prairie School house built in 1902 by **Frank Lloyd Wright** that is still a private residence. Also while in town, don't miss **Carlos,** for exquisitely prepared nouvelle cuisine (daily, dinner; reservations required; 429 Temple Ave, between Lauretta Pl and Waukegan Ave; 847/432.0770). Another Highland Park highlight is the **Ravinia Festival**, which hosts evening performances in a parklike setting from June through September (enter the park from Sheridan, Green Bay, or Lake Cook Rds; 847/266.5100; www.ravinia.org). The high-powered performers range from Bonnie Raitt to the **Chicago Symphony Orchestra**, as well as dance companies and chamber orchestras. You can reserve seats in the roofed arena, but most concertgoers bring a blanket, a bottle of wine,

and a picnic and settle on the grassy lawns beneath the stars. In the town of Highwood just to the north, chef Gabriel Viti has two eateries of note: the elegant **Gabriel's** (310 Green Bay Rd; 847/433.0031; Tu-Sa, dinner) and the more casual **Miramar** (301 Waukegan Ave; 847/433.1078; M-F, lunch and dinner; Sa-Su, dinner).

7 GLENCOE

The **Chicago Botanic Garden**, where plants, trees, and flowers from around the world are cultivated on 300 acres of landscaped hills and islands, makes its home here. The park is interspersed with lakes, naturalistic wooded areas, and nature and prairie trails (free; parking fee; daily, 8AM-sunset; 1000 Lake Cook Rd, between Green Bay Rd and Hwy 41; 847/835.5440; www.chicago botanic.org). Spring and autumn, of course, are particularly beautiful times. The garden's **Education Center** houses the **Museum of Floral Arts**, the **Plant Information Service**, a gift shop, and the **Food for Thought Café**. You may also bring along a picnic lunch and eat at one of several designated areas in the garden. Two architecturally notable buildings in Glencoe are the **Glasner House** (850 Sheridan Rd, between Beach and Maplehill Rds), a private residence built in 1904 by **Frank Lloyd Wright**, and the reinforced-concrete **Temple of North Shore Congregation Israel** (1185 Sheridan Rd, between Aspen La and County Line Rd), which was designed in 1963 by **Minoru Yamasaki** and completed in 1983 by **Hammond, Beeby & Babka**.

8 WILMETTE

Sheridan Road takes you right by the breath-taking **Baha'i House of Worship** (100 Linden Ave, at Sheridan Rd; 847/853.2300). On the National Register of Historic Places, this is the first house of worship erected in the United States for the Baha'i faith, which originated in Iran and has followers throughout the world. It was constructed under the direction of architect **Louis J. Bourgeois** from 1920 to 1953. Farther north along Sheridan Road you will come to **Plaza del Lago**, an upscale shopping center that includes a **Crate & Barrel** furniture store. Wilmette is also home to the **Kohl Children's Museum**, which features numerous hands-on displays, plus puppet shows, sing-alongs, and other special events (admission; daily; 165 Green Bay Rd, between Isabella St and Oakwood Ave; 847/256.6056). It also has the area's nicest beach, **Great Gillson Beach**, where sailboats can be rented as well; for beach and boat-rental information, call 847/256.9662.

9 EVANSTON

Home to the 160-building campus of **Northwestern University**, Evanston has a small-town yet cultured feeling. Numerous art galleries, interesting shopping (primarily along Chicago, Sherman, and Orrington Avenues), fine restaurants, and a pretty lakefront make it a pleasant place to visit. One highlight is the 113-foot-tall 19th-century **Grosse Point Lighthouse** (admission; tours Sa, Su, 2PM, 3PM, 4PM, June-Sept; no children under age 5; 2535 Sheridan Rd, between Milburn and Central Sts; 847/328.6961). On the grounds of **Northwestern University**'s Evanston campus is the **Mary & Leigh Block Gallery**. This fine arts museum contains an outdoor sculpture garden and a permanent collection of works by 20th-century artists (free; Tu-Su; 1967 Sheridan Rd, between Emerson and Foster Sts; 847/491.4000). The **Evanston Historical Society/Dawes House** is a national landmark mansion (admission; M-W, Su, 1-5PM; 225 Greenwood St, between Sheridan Rd and Forest Ave; 847/475.3410 www.evanstonhistorical.org). Among the eateries, **Trio** (1625 Hinman Ave; 847/733.8746) and **Va Pensiero** (1566 Oak Ave, between Grove and Davis Sts; 847/475.7779) are the most elegant, and **Lucky Platter** (514 Main St, between Hinman and Chicago Aves; 847/869.4064) is the most whimsical in décor and healthful in menu (it's vegetarian). The Evanston Lakefront is a beautiful spot, and you can walk its entire length from Main Street to the **Northwestern** campus.

OAK PARK/RIVER FOREST

The village of Oak Park richly deserves its reputation as a mecca for architecture buffs, for it was here that **Frank Lloyd Wright** created what is now known as the Prairie School of Architecture. **Wright** lived in Oak Park between 1889 and 1909. Twenty-five of his buildings still stand in the village, and another six survive in the adjoining suburb of River Forest. Prairie School designs are characterized by sweeping horizontal lines, wide eaves, and decorative details. Significant works in the two villages by such other noted Prairie School architects as **William Drummond**, **Tallmadge & Watson**, **George W. Maher**, **John Van Bergen**, **Purcell & Elmslie**, **E.E. Roberts**, and **Robert Spencer** number in the hundreds.

As if the architectural heritage were not enough, Oak Park is also the birthplace of Ernest Hemingway. His boyhood homes still stand, as does **Oak Park and River Forest High School**, where young Ernest edited the school newspaper, *Trapeze*, and was memorialized in the yearbook with the tagline "There are none so clever as Ernie." A leisurely visit might include a stop at one of Oak Park's many eating establishments. If you come by car, stop in at the **Oak Park Bakery** just south of the **Eisenhower Expressway** (904 S Oak Park Ave; 708/383.1712) for world-class *kolachkes* (sweet yeast buns), cinnamon crisps, almond crescents, and other baked goods. **Philander's** (Carleton Hotel; 1120 Pleasant St, at S Maple Ave; 708/848.4250), named after turn-of-the-20th-century photographer Philander Barclay, serves delicious seafood and boasts a gallery of photos

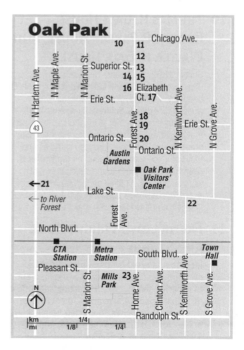

Oak Park

of old Oak Park. **Petersen Ice Cream** (1100 Chicago Ave, at N Marion St; 708/386.6131), two blocks west of the **Frank Lloyd Wright Home and Studio** (below), is perfect for a simple meal of sandwiches, salads, and delicious baked goods after a tour. The place is famous throughout the Chicago area for its own terrifically rich ice cream. Downtown Oak Park along **Lake Street** has several other restaurants.

Guided tours of Oak Park are available almost every day of the week (for information, call the **Oak Park Visitors' Center**; 708.1500 www.visitoakpark.com). A highlight, though, is the annual **Wright Plus** tour on the third Saturday of May; it offers rare viewings of the interiors of privately owned homes designed by Wright and several other local architects. ◆ Oak Park is easily reached by the **Metra West Line** train from **Ogilvie Transportation Center** or the **Green Line CTA**. The **23 Washington** express bus is another option.

10 THOMAS H. GALE HOUSE, ROBERT P. PARKER HOUSE, AND WALTER H. GALE HOUSE

Built in 1892, 1892, and 1893, respectively, these are three of **Frank Lloyd Wright**'s so-called bootlegged houses, designed while he was working for **Adler & Sullivan**. These large Victorian cottages barely hint at the radical departure that Wright was soon to make from this vertical, turreted style. The closely spaced spindles and band of leaded glass windows on the **Walter H. Gale House** are clues to the direction Wright's work would take. All three are private residences. ◆ 1027, 1019, and 1031 Chicago Ave (between Forest Ave and N Marion St), Oak Park

11 FRANK LLOYD WRIGHT HOME AND STUDIO

More than any of his other works, **Wright**'s own home and studio show the development of his style, serving as "architectural laboratories." This small cottage facing Forest Avenue was the first home Wright created for himself, and he worked on it between 1889 and 1911. It began as a shingled cottage, built low to the ground and graced with diamond-paned leaded windows. A spectacular barrel-vaulted playroom was added in 1895 to accommodate his family of four sons and

two daughters. In 1897 he added the attached studio, which he remodeled almost continuously during the years he lived here. Inside are Wright's office, a library, and a double-height drafting room featuring a balcony suspended by a complex and graceful system of chains. Wright separated from his wife and left Oak Park in 1909, but his family remained in the house. He remodeled the complex in 1911, adding living space in the studio and rental units to the home to provide some income. The house has been restored by the **Frank Lloyd Wright Home and Studio Foundation** to appear as it did in 1909. ◆ Admission. Tours: M-F, 11AM, 1PM, and 3PM; Sa, Su, every 15 minutes between 11AM and 3:30PM. 951 Chicago Ave (at Forest Ave), Oak Park. 708/848.1976 ♿

12 A.J. REDMOND HOUSE

Oak Park resident **E.E. Roberts** was a popular architect for houses, stores, schools, and churches in Chicago and the western suburbs. This solid brick and stone house, built in 1901, is a more expensive version of the classic Oak Park house—rectilinear, 2.5 stories, hip-roofed, with a broad front porch and wide eaves. Roberts was extremely talented with decorative details, a gift visible here in the leaded, colored-glass windows. It's a private residence. ◆ 422 Forest Ave (between Elizabeth Ct and Chicago Ave), Oak Park

13 W.M. HARMAN HOUSE

Originally a grandly scaled, low-roofed Italianate house by an unknown architect, this home had already received a hipped roof when **Frank Lloyd Wright** was commissioned to remodel it in 1908. Most of Wright's work is inside; the geometric wood mullions in the windows are about the only exterior evidence of his involvement. The house remains a private home. ◆ 400 Forest Ave (between Elizabeth Ct and Chicago Ave), Oak Park

14 E.E. ROBERTS HOUSE

E.E. Roberts opened his own office in Oak Park in 1893 and was working in the Queen Anne style when this house was built in 1896.

An extensive remodeling courtesy of the architect in 1911 changed the home to incorporate more of the Prairie School details—wide eaves and leaded glass windows in particular—that Roberts was using at the time. It's a private residence. ♦ 1019 Superior St (between Forest Ave and N Marion St), Oak Park

14 NATHAN MOORE HOUSE

Frank Lloyd Wright experimented with many styles in the 1890s and mastered more than a few. The first house he built on this site in 1895 was a Tudor mansion, with decorative half-timbering at the upper levels. The coach house at the west end of the lot gives some idea of the style of the original commission. Moore's house burned in 1922, and Wright rebuilt it in an eclectic style with Tudor overtones. Terra-cotta embellishments include rows of balls with Sullivanesque "organic" ornament and window detailing. Orienting the house toward the yard rather than the street increased the light and privacy; it also faced a house later remodeled for Moore's daughter Mary (see **Edward R. Hills/ DeCaro House** below). This is a private residence. ♦ 333 Forest Ave (at Superior St), Oak Park

15 ARTHUR B. HEURTLEY HOUSE

Designed by **Frank Lloyd Wright** in 1902, this is a classic example of his Prairie School house—low, solid, with exaggeratedly wide eaves and a delightfully mysterious entry behind a half-hidden round brick arch. The main living area is on the second floor, providing lovely treetop views of Forest Avenue from the living and dining rooms. The roof visually floats above the bands of leaded casement windows, especially in the evening when the lights are on. This house remains a private home. ♦ 318 Forest Ave (between Elizabeth Ct and Chicago Ave), Oak Park

16 EDWARD R. HILLS/ DeCARO HOUSE

Nathan Moore hired **Frank Lloyd Wright** in 1905 to remodel an 1886 Stick-style home for his daughter Mary and her husband. He turned it 90 degrees on the lot and practically rebuilt it, inside and out. During an extensive restoration in 1976, the house was virtually destroyed by fire and then rebuilt by the DeCaro family, who had it designed as closely as possible to Wright's original plan. Note the carefully detailed roof, which shows the layering of shingles to emphasize the horizontal line, a detail common to many Prairie School homes at the time of construction but rarely retained

in subsequent reroofings. This is a private residence. ♦ 313 Forest Ave (between Erie and Superior Sts), Oak Park

17 MRS. THOMAS H. GALE HOUSE

The widow of **Frank Lloyd Wright**'s client for his "bootlegged" house on Chicago Avenue (see page 230) commissioned Wright for this residence in 1909. It was one of the last houses he built in Oak Park. The dramatically cantilevered balconies show the beginning of the design direction Wright would take in the 1930s, particularly in works such as Fallingwater, the great house he designed for Edgar Kaufman in Pennsylvania. Strongly horizontal, even to the flat roof, the house is more starkly modern than the neighboring Wright houses on Forest Avenue. It remains a private residence. ♦ 6 Elizabeth Ct (between N Kenilworth and Forest Aves), Oak Park

18 PETER A. BEACHY HOUSE

It is thought that **Frank Lloyd Wright**'s talented employee **Walter Burley Griffin** influenced the look of this brick and stucco house, designed by Wright in 1906. Compared with most of his works from this era, the house is more massive and blocky. Wright was originally commissioned to remodel and add to a small wooden Gothic cottage on the site; no trace of this original structure is visible. The house is built to the scale of the site, deep and with a room-size side porch that takes advantage of the width of the lot. Wood mullions rather than lead cames define the windows. The great gable across the front is echoed by three smaller gables that roll down the sides of this immense home. The house is still a private residence. ♦ 238 Forest Ave (between Ontario St and Elizabeth Ct), Oak Park

19 J.D. EVERETT HOUSE

This 1888 home by **Wilson, Marble & Lamson** is a fine example of an exuberant Queen Anne house executed in wood, characteristic of the style popular in Oak Park homes when the young **Frank Lloyd Wright** arrived in the village. Variety of form, especially in window shapes and gables, and a many-angled roof were important attributes of this style. The architects practiced together only briefly but as individuals and in other partnerships designed many homes and public buildings throughout the 1880s. This is a private residence. ♦ 228 Forest Ave (between Ontario St and Elizabeth Ct), Oak Park

20 FRANK W. THOMAS HOUSE

Built in 1901, this is **Frank Lloyd Wright**'s first true Prairie School house in Oak Park. The

WEB SITES

Surfing Chicago? Here are a few suggestions.

www.ci.chi.il.us (official city of Chicago web site)
www.artic.edu (Art Institute)
www.metromix.com (*Chicago Tribune*'s guide to the city)
www.chireader.com (the *Reader* has the most and best listings)
www.citysearch.com (listings for shopping, dining, and events)
www.chicagogallerynews.com (the inside scoop on the gallery scene)
www.chicagotribune.com (daily news and free archives for previous 2 weeks)
www.chicagohs.org (Chicago Historical Society has interesting facts and tales)

ground level contains only utility rooms. A mysterious yet compelling roundheaded doorway leads to stairs, hidden from the street view, that take the visitor up to the full-length leaded-glass front door. The living rooms are elevated, providing some privacy from pedestrians and motorists on Ontario Street and lovely views over Forest Avenue to **Austin Gardens**, formerly the Henry Austin estate. The leaded glass is perhaps the most spectacular element of the house and is best appreciated in the early evening. It's a private residence. ♦ 210 Forest Ave (between Ontario St and Elizabeth Ct), Oak Park

21 WILLIAM DRUMMOND HOUSE

Architect **William Drummond** went to work for **Frank Lloyd Wright** in his Oak Park studio in 1899 and remained on his staff until the studio closed in 1909. This home, built in 1910, especially reflects the influence of an unbuilt project Wright designed for the *Ladies' Home Journal* in 1905, "A Fireproof House for $5,000." Drummond's work typically has less decorative embellishment than that of his Prairie School colleagues but is noteworthy for his mastery of proportion and warm, livable interiors. The porch of this private residence was originally open and had several large trees growing through it. ♦ 559 Edgewood Pl (between Lake and Oak Sts), River Forest

Oak Park resident Edgar Rice Burroughs created the literary figure Tarzan.

Chicago has 131 forest preserves, 572 parks, and 31 beaches. Its public lakefront is 27 miles long.

In 1918 Illinois, Wisconsin, and Michigan became the first states to give women the right to vote in national elections.

21 ISABEL ROBERTS HOUSE

Frank Lloyd Wright designed this house in 1908 for his secretary and bookkeeper. The plan is cruciform and the interior is spacious, with a two-story living room in front. Originally built in stucco, the house was later covered with brick. It's another private residence. ♦ 603 Edgewood Pl (between Lake and Oak Sts), River Forest

21 WILLIAM H. WINSLOW HOUSE

Frank Lloyd Wright's first great commission after leaving **Adler & Sullivan** was a groundbreaking design. The **Winslow House** is strikingly simple and modern for 1893. Set low to the ground with no visible basement, the house is firmly anchored visually by its foundation and by the low hipped roof with its extremely deep eaves. The color palette is fresh and warm, and the broad band of geometric ornament at the second-floor level enriches the simplicity of the forms. Look through the porte cochere on the north to see the stables, also designed by Wright. This is a private residence. ♦ 515 Auvergne Pl (just north of Lake St), River Forest

22 UNITY TEMPLE

A National Historic Landmark, built between 1905 and 1908, **Unity Temple** is deservedly one of **Frank Lloyd Wright**'s most famous buildings. Economic concerns and the architect's interest in the material led to the choice of reinforced concrete, a sharp contrast with the stone and brick churches that began to line Lake Street in the 19th century. The choice of material dictated simple forms, which in Wright's hands became a complex set of interlocking rectangles embellished with simple geometric decoration on the piers between the high windows. Although the building can appear gloomy from outside, a skylight and clerestory windows beautifully

The Best

Marc Schulman
President, Eli's

Experience the magic of the **Michigan Avenue** lights during the holiday season. Don't miss the lighting of the trees sponsored by the Greater North Michigan Avenue Association on the Saturday evening before Thanksgiving.

Take a walking tour of **Graceland Cemetery** to learn who built Chicago and how. Also take any of the other tours offered by the Chicago Architectural Foundation.

Take your children to the **Eli M. Schulman Playground** at **Seneca Park** (just east of the historic **Water Tower**).

Also walk into **Engine Company 98** of the Chicago Fire Department next door.

Take a ride through Chicago's boulevard system. Favorite stops—the **Garfield Park Conservatory**, the *Statue of the Republic* in **Jackson Park** commemorating the 1893 World's Fair, and Lorado Taft's *Fountain of Time* on the **Midway**.

Spend an afternoon at **Lincoln Park Zoo** (one of the only free zoos in the country), then walk along the park's lagoon and through the **Gold Coast** back to Michigan Avenue.

On a hot summer night, Italian ice at **Mario's Italian Lemonade** on **Taylor Street**.

A visit to the **Chicago Children's Museum** (at **Navy Pier**).

---

illuminate the inside. The golden glass of the skylight panes ensures a pleasing quality of light even on overcast days. ♦ Admission. Self-guided tours Mar-Nov, M-F, 10:30AM-4:30PM; Dec-Feb, daily, 1PM-4PM. 875 Lake St (at N Kenilworth Ave), Oak Park. 708/383.8873

23 Pleasant Home

Investment banker John Farson commissioned architect **George W. Maher** to design this home in 1899, and named it for the intersection where it stands. It is one of Maher's great early designs and shows a debt to **Frank Lloyd Wright**'s Winslow House in River Forest (see page 232). The house exhibits Maher's preferred palette, which was lighter than that of his Prairie School colleagues; vanilla Roman brick and cream-colored trim were favored here. Maher used several motifs that are repeated throughout the house and on some of the furnishings. The "Roman tray," a

rectangle with an extra dollop on each end resembling the bottom of a shallow triangle, appears in the fence, in the medallions on either side of the front porch, in the magnificent windows by the front door, and on many of the door plates and drawer pulls. A lion's head can be seen on the third-floor dormer, on the front of the house near the foundations, and on some of the furniture. The interior has elements of Victorian as well as Prairie styles and offers a fascinating example of a house at the turning point of the designer's developing style. Much of the interior detailing and some of the furniture remain. The home is open for tours and also houses the **Historical Society of Oak Park and River Forest**, a museum with a small Hemingway display as well as other mementos of early Oak Park. ♦ Admission. Th-Su, 1PM-4PM; tours at 1PM, 2PM, and 3PM. 217 Home Ave (at Pleasant St), Oak Park. 708/383.2654

Restaurants/Clubs: Red | Hotels: Purple | Shops: Orange | Outdoors/Parks: Green | Sights/Culture: Blue

ARCHITECTURAL HIGHLIGHTS

Chicago is the world's largest outdoor museum of modern architecture. Turn almost any corner in the Loop, and you'll discover a building that marks a structural, technical, or aesthetic achievement. This is the birthplace of the skyscraper and home to three of the world's tallest buildings, including the record-holding Sears Tower. Not all of the landmarks are 100 stories tall, however. Chicago's architectural heritage encompasses many styles and movements; some are world famous and some are only now gaining the appreciation they deserve. But all have contributed to a vibrant cityscape that continues to inspire visitors and residents alike.

After Chicago's Great Fire of 1871 destroyed 4 square miles of the central city, architects, engineers, and artisans arrived in great numbers to take part in the massive rebuilding effort. The rapidly increasing land values in the central business district motivated developers to build as high as they possibly could. The invention of the elevator, along with technological advances in foundation laying and wind-bracing metal framing, made it possible to construct buildings taller than five stories. Most important was the discovery of how to protect the metal structure from fire by cladding it in terra-cotta. (The cast-iron columns and beams of Chicago's supposedly fireproof earlier buildings had melted in the intense heat of the blaze.) With this knowledge, the only remaining limitation was the weight of the building itself.

William Le Baron Jenney is frequently called the father of the skyscraper, as much for his role in training a new generation of Chicago architects as for his own considerable achievements. Jenney's structural innovations included designing the first buildings that were supported entirely by their metal frameworks, such as the Manhattan Building in the Loop. Even the exterior walls did not support their own weight; they were hung on the steel structure like drapery (today they are known as curtain walls). Many architects believed that the new structural technology should be reflected in equally innovative exterior forms. The powerful designs of these early buildings led historians to refer to them collectively as the Chicago School of Architecture, the first truly modern architecture. The chief characteristic of this style is the straightforward expression of structure, with a masonry grid overlaying the steel framework and the spaces between them filled with large panes of glass. Ornamentation became subordinate to expression of the framework; ornamentation was most often used on the bottom and top floors to create a three-part façade composition resembling the base-shaft-capital design of classical columns. Projecting bay windows created a lively rhythm while admitting abundant daylight, increasing rentable square footage and improving cross-ventilation. A key feature is the Chicago window, a three-part window with a large fixed pane flanked by a pair of smaller sash windows.

The three outstanding Chicago School firms were Adler & Sullivan, Holabird & Roche, and Burnham & Root. And architect Louis Sullivan is revered today not only for his buildings but for the unique style of ornamentation he developed, of which the Carson Pirie Scott store in the Loop is the most spectacular example. Holabird & Roche is the firm most closely associated with the Chicago School, having established a style of solid, straightforward structures with the Pontiac and Marquette Buildings (in the South Loop and Loop, respectively). Burnham & Root created the masterpieces of the Rookery and Monadnock Buildings in the Loop; after the early death of John Wellborn Root in 1891, the firm's work became increasingly

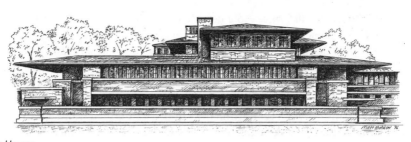

Robie House

classical. Root's successor as chief designer, **Charles B. Atwood**, completed work on the **Reliance Building** in the Loop, a tour de force that combines lush ornamentation with a clear display of structure, proving that the two were not incompatible.

Daniel Burnham became increasingly influential as a city planner. His 1909 Plan of Chicago was the country's first all-encompassing urban plan. He is also known as the design chief for the 1893 World's Columbian Exposition. However, much to the consternation of his fellow Chicago architects (particularly **Louis Sullivan**), he let East Coast architects dominate the fair stylistically. The resulting neoclassical "White City" helped shift local taste away from buildings that displayed their structure to those that disguised it in historical garb. The formal Beaux Arts style was deemed especially suitable for the city's growing cultural institutions; prominent examples include the **Art Institute** and the **Cultural Center**, which were designed in the 1890s by the Boston firm **Shepley, Rutan & Coolidge**.

In the early 1900s **Frank Lloyd Wright** and his contemporaries were developing a modern style now known as the Prairie School. The houses designed in this style generally have low, ground-hugging forms, hovering roofs with deep eaves, and bands of casement windows. The interiors feature broad, centrally located hearths, natural woodwork, earth colors, and rooms tied together by open floor plans and uniform wall treatments. The break from the historically inspired Victorian styles began in the 1890s with designs such as the **Charnley House** in the Gold Coast and the **Winslow House** in River Forest, both by Wright. The largest groups of Prairie Houses are in the suburbs, especially in Oak Park, where Forest Avenue and surrounding streets are lined with houses by Wright and members of his Oak Park studio. The **Madlener House** in the Gold Coast, by **Hugh M.G. Garden** and **Richard E. Schmidt**, and the houses on Hutchinson Street by **George W. Maher** exemplify the rectilinear, horizontal, and beautiful detailing characteristics of this style. Wright's **Robie House** (pictured above) at the University of Chicago is the most famous Prairie School house, a National Historic Landmark, and an American masterpiece. The prosperity of the 1920s created a building boom, and the 1920 construction of the **Michigan Avenue Bridge** pushed development north of the river. Three of the four buildings at this prominent river crossing are wonderful examples of the fanciful borrowings from European sources that characterized architecture at the time: the **Wrigley Building**, the **Tribune Tower**, and **360 North Michigan Avenue**.

The Tribune Tower was the result of a 1922 design competition—a competition that is famous for the lasting influence of its many losing entries. For example, **Eliel Saarinen's** second-place design was adapted by **Holabird & Root** in 1928 for the building just across the river at **333 North Michigan Avenue**, Chicago's first Art Deco skyscraper. This successor firm to Holabird & Roche, whose name changed in 1927 when **John Root Jr.** became a partner, designed most of Chicago's Art Deco masterpieces, including the **Board of Trade**. The decade's other prolific firm was **Graham, Anderson, Probst & White**, which carried on Daniel Burnham's practice.

The Depression brought an abrupt halt to construction, and in the next two decades the city's architects received few commissions. In the late 1930s Nazi persecution spurred the immigration of several German architects; many of them settled in Chicago, including **Ludwig Mies van der Rohe.**

In the 1940s Mies designed the campus of the **Illinois Institute of Technology**, where he taught architecture. When the postwar economic recovery arrived, Mies began to receive commissions for apartment buildings, and the steel-and-glass towers he designed at **860-880 North Lake Shore Drive** in 1952 ushered in a new era of skyscraper design.

Mies was as concerned with structural expression and exploitation of new technology as the architects of the 1880s had been, and the "glass box" era that he began is often called the Second Chicago

NBC Tower

School. The firm of **Skidmore, Owings & Merrill (SOM)** furthered the global dominance of Modernism between the 1950s and the 1970s. SOM architect **Bruce Graham** and engineer Fazlur Khan together designed some of the tallest buildings in the world. The **John Hancock Center** of 1969 flaunts its unusual structure, with giant wind-bracing X's marching up its four sides. The **Sears Tower** is much less demonstrative, using a "bundled tube" structural system that is far from obvious to the casual observer.

Just when this style seemed to have become formulaic, the inevitable rebellion began with *postmodernism*, a catchall term for anything outside the strict canon of the Modernist style. It landed in the heart of the city with such buildings as **Kohn Pedersen Fox's 333 West Wacker Drive**, a wedge of green glass bowed to follow the river, and **A. Epstein & Sons' 150 North Michigan Avenue**, with its bisected triangular towers and sloping glass roof. SOM itself has now officially abandoned Modernism, creating such period pieces as **Adrian Smith's** Art Deco **NBC Tower** (pictured left). And **Thomas Beeby's** award-winning design for the **Harold Washington Library Center**, the most recent great building in Chicago, is a fusion of historical references that pays tribute to the city's classical architecture.

The pluralism of the 1980s has inspired greater scrutiny of the orthodox Modernist view of Chicago's architectural history and caused critics to take a second look at works previously dismissed as eclectic. Much credit for this revisionism goes to early rebels such as **Ben** and **Harry Weese, Stanley Tigerman, Larry Booth**, and **Jack Hartray**. Perhaps the most important development is that architects and a growing number of concerned citizens now rigorously fight the destruction of the city's historical buildings to ensure that Chicago's rich architectural heritage will remain one of its chief glories.

HISTORY

The land that today is Chicago lay below the ocean 400 million years ago. A series of gigantic glaciers created the lakes, rivers, and trails used by the native Potawatomi, Wea, Miami, and Illinois tribes, and later traveled by European explorers.

1682 French explorer René-Robert Cavelier Sieur de La Salle first refers to the area as *Che-cau-gou*, an Indian name with several possible meanings, including "wild onion" and "strong and great."

1763 The French, having claimed the land, bequeath it to the English as part of their settlement in the Seven Years' War.

1783 The British hand over the land to the newly independent United States of America.

1784 Jean Baptiste Point du Sable becomes the area's first non-Indian settler when he builds a house and trading post where the **Chicago River** enters **Lake Michigan**, the Chicago portage.

1795 Native Americans surrender a 6-square-mile piece of land at the mouth of the Chicago River, clearing the way for the establishment of what is now downtown Chicago.

1803 To protect the growing European community from Native Americans and to provide a strategic United States military site, **Fort Dearborn** is built just south of the Chicago River, where **Michigan Avenue** is today.

1812 When the British declare war on the United States, **Fort Dearborn** occupants evacuate their haven and are massacred by the Indians.

1816 A second **Fort Dearborn** is constructed. It stands until 1856.

1827 The federal government issues a land grant for the building of a canal between Lake Michigan and the Mississippi River. Construction begins in 1836, and the first boats travel it in 1846.

1829 The city's first meatpacking plant is constructed by Archibald Clybourne, one of Chicago's earliest butchers.

1833 The **Village of Chicago**, covering an area of 1 square mile, is officially chartered with a population of 340. A group of 76 Indian chiefs signs a treaty surrendering more land, and they begin moving their tribes to reservations.

1836 Shopkeepers Caroline and Henry Clarke build a two-story white frame house in what is now the suburbs. More than a century and a half later, the **Clarke House** is Chicago's oldest surviving building, located in the **Prairie Avenue Historic District**.

1837 Chicago is incorporated as a city and has a population of 4,170.

1839 William Stuart founds the *Daily American*, the city's first daily newspaper.

1847 The *Chicago Tribune* newspaper is founded.

1848 The Chicago Board of Trade is created.

1849 Chicago's first beer is brewed by German immigrant Adolph Mueller.

1850 Chicago's population reaches 29,963.

1851 The **Illinois Central Railroad**, the country's first land-grant railroad, is chartered. Allan Pinkerton is hired as Chicago's first detective.

1853 The city's population tops 60,000. Chicago now has seven daily newspapers.

1854 A paid city fire department is established. (Four years later, it is discovered that a blaze that destroyed a lumberyard was set by firefighter "Beast" Brown after the lumberyard owner refused to buy tickets to the Fireman's Ball.)

1855 A riot breaks out when police try to stop Germans from drinking beer, as ordered by Mayor Levi Boone, who considers the practice "foreign and anti-American."

1857 The **State Street** area becomes a retail center when the 32-stall **Market Hall** is constructed. The city's first steel-rolling mill, the **North Chicago Rolling Mill**, opens.

1858 Illinois adopted son Abraham Lincoln makes his first Senate campaign speech. Later in the year, he debates the subject of slavery with rival Stephen A. Douglas on the balcony of the **Tremont House Hotel**. Chicago has become the country's chief railroad shipper, with 20 million bushels of produce transported each year.

1859 Chicago's first horse-drawn railways go into operation. The **University of Chicago** opens; in 1886 it closes due to a lack of funds and internal problems. A second, unrelated **University of Chicago** opens successfully in 1892.

1860 The Republican National Convention, held downtown, nominates Abraham Lincoln for president. The city's population approaches 110,000; half of the inhabitants are foreign-born.

1863 Chicago overtakes Cincinnati as the country's pork-packing center.

1864 George Pullman builds the *Pioneer*, the first specially constructed railway sleeping car.

1865 The **Union Stock Yards**, the largest in the world, begin operation on Christmas Day.

1866 Construction of **Lincoln Park** begins on land that had previously served as the city cemetery.

1867 Real-estate mogul Potter Palmer becomes the city's first millionaire. Philip D. Armour opens a meatpacking plant.

1869 Burlesque makes its United States debut at **Crosby's Opera House** with Lydia Thompson and her British Blondes.

1871 The Great Chicago Fire, which presumably started in Mrs. Kate O'Leary's barn, rages through the city for 3 days, destroys millions of dollars in property, and leaves one-third of the population homeless.

1872 The City Council passes an ordinance outlawing wooden buildings downtown.

1873 The Bread Riot starts when starving workers marching to the Relief and Aid Society are driven into the **LaSalle Street Tunnel** at **Randolph Street** by Chicago police and clubbed to death.

1874 The *Chicago Daily News* is founded and quickly becomes the city's largest newspaper.

1877 Federal troops are called in to end the railroad workers' strike.

1879 Carter H. Harrison is elected mayor for the first of five straight terms.

1880 The city's population reaches a half million.

1882 The **Chicago Stock Exchange** is established. Charles T. Yerkes builds the city's first cable car line.

1886 The Haymarket Massacre occurs when a bomb explodes in the midst of a group of police officers who had been sent in to control the crowd assembled for a labor rally at **Haymarket Square**. In retaliation, the police fire upon the crowd. A monument to the dead police officers is built; in the 1960s it is blown up, and in 1972 it is relocated to police headquarters.

1887 **Fort Sheridan** is constructed on the lakefront north of the city and is run by US Army troops to protect Chicagoans from anarchists. Although there is no evidence that any of the seven anarchists being held by the police made or threw the bomb that killed seven police officers during the Haymarket rally, four labor leaders—George Engel, Adolph Fischer, A.R. Parsons, and August Spies—are convicted and executed by hanging. A fifth, Louis Lingg, is found in his cell with his head blown off.

1892 Telephone communications are established between Chicago, New York, and Boston.

1893 The World's Columbian Exposition opens in **Hyde Park**. Mayor Carter H. Harrison is assassinated on the last day of the fair. Governor John Peter Altgeld pardons three Haymarket rioters, an action that will prevent his reelection.

1896 The Municipal Voters' League accuses 26 of the city's 34 aldermen of being crooks.

1897 The $2 million **Chicago Public Library** opens on the lakefront. The **Loop** rapid transit system, which encircles the downtown area, is constructed.

1900 Chicago's booming population approaches 1.7 million. Ada and Minna Everleigh open the **Everleigh Club**, proclaimed the Midwest's most elegant and expensive brothel.

1903 A fire at the **Iroquois Theater** kills 603 people. **Essanay Studio**, one of the country's first movie studios, opens. It later moves to California.

1905 **Orchestra Hall** opens. The Industrial Workers of the World (IWW) labor union is organized.

1906 Upton Sinclair's novel *The Jungle* is published, exposing inhumane and dangerously unsanitary working conditions in the Chicago stockyards.

1912 Prostitution is made illegal, and all the bordellos that had lined Michigan Avenue are closed.

1914 Tens of thousands of African-Americans migrate from the South in search of industrial work. William Hale "Big Bill" Thompson, future pal of gangster Al Capone, is elected mayor.

1915 The excursion steamer *Eastland* capsizes in the Chicago River, killing 835 people.

1919 Race riots break out when a black man enters a segregated **South Side** beach; 15 whites and 25 blacks die.

1920 Chicago's population reaches 2.7 million, a third of which is Catholic. Prohibition begins, and bloody gang wars erupt over the control of bootlegging.

1922 Chicago sends a letter to other American cities urging a constitutional amendment that would legalize the sale of wine and beer.

1929 Seven of Al Capone's rivals are machine-gunned to death in a **North Side** garage in the St. Valentine's Day Massacre.

1931 Al Capone is found guilty of tax evasion and sentenced to ten years in prison.

1933 Mayor Anton J. Cermak, the first Czechoslovakian ever elected to such an office in the US, is shot to death in Miami by an assassin who was trying to kill President Franklin D. Roosevelt.

1942 The first atomic chain reaction is set off in a nuclear reactor at the University of Chicago under the direction of Enrico Fermi.

1949 The **Midwest Stock Exchange** is formed as a result of a merger between the Chicago Stock Exchange and exchanges in Cleveland, St. Louis, and Minneapolis/St. Paul.

1950 Chicago's population reaches 3,621,000.

1955 Richard J. Daley is elected mayor, a post he continues to hold for six terms, spanning 21 years.

1957 *Life* magazine reports that the Chicago police department is the most corrupt law enforcement agency in the nation.

1959 The **Chicago White Sox** win the **American League** pennant. Air raid sirens, turned on in celebration, set off a citywide panic.

1960 Investigations reveal that corrupt Chicago cops are working with a gang of burglars. Orlando Wilson, chair of the criminology department at the University of California, is appointed police commissioner.

1968 Riots break out in the city's African-American neighborhoods in reaction to the assassination of Martin Luther King Jr. Mayor Daley issues police a shoot-on-sight order to try to bring a halt to the violence, in which seven people are killed and 500 injured. During the Democratic National Convention, fighting ensues between police and anti-Vietnam War demonstrators.

1969 The Chicago Eight, including Abbie Hoffman, go on trial, accused of inciting riots during the convention. Black Panthers Fred Hampton and Mark Clark are slain when Chicago police, working with a floor plan provided by the FBI, raid Hampton's apartment at dawn, firing a hundred shots.

1971 The **Union Stock Yards** close. The Reverend Jesse Jackson founds Operation PUSH (People United to Save Humanity) to serve the city's poor.

1975 The **Water Tower Place** high-rise shopping mall opens on **North Michigan Avenue**. Chicago Mob chieftain Sam "Momo" Giancana is shot seven times in the head while cooking sausages in his **Oak Park** basement. He dies.

1978 Chicago alderpersons vote themselves a 60% pay hike soon after President Jimmy Carter asks Americans to limit wage increases to 7%. **State Street** is turned into a pedestrians-only mall.

1979 Jane Byrne replaces ex-mayor Michael Bilandic, whose failure to get the city back on its feet after a 4-foot snowstorm infuriated Chicagoans. She hires her husband, Jay McMullen, as her $52,000-a-year political advisor.

1980 The population, though decreasing, still stands at an impressive 2,969,570.

1981 The Chicago Mob puts out a $100,000 contract on Mayor Byrne when she fails to support casino gambling in the city. No one takes up the offer.

1983 Chicago elects its first African-American mayor, Harold Washington, setting off council wars as the old guard fights to maintain control of the city.

1984   The **Chicago Cubs** win the Eastern Division title but lose the national pennant to the San Diego Padres.

1986   The **Chicago Bears** win the Super Bowl, making coach Mike Ditka the city's newest hero and restaurateur. When he is fired in 1992, his restaurant, no longer trading on his celebrity, closes.

1987   Mayor Washington dies of a heart attack. Chaos ensues as aldes and alderpersons vie for control.

1989   Richard M. Daley, son of the late Richard J., is elected mayor.

1990   The United States Census Bureau counts 2,725,979 people living in Chicago; it becomes the third-largest city (rather than second-largest), after New York and Los Angeles. The metropolitan area numbers over seven million. After long controversy, lights are installed in **Wrigley Field**, and the Chicago Cubs begin playing night games.

1992   A section of the freight tunnel under the Chicago River caves in, causing flooding that paralyzes the **Loop** for two weeks.

1993   The **Bulls** win the National Basketball Association championship for the third consecutive year. The team's star guard, Michael Jordan, Chicago's most famous resident, retires.

1994   Chicago lawyer Dawn Clark Netsch wins the Democratic nomination for governor; her running mate is also a woman, making this the nation's first all-female gubernatorial ticket. For the first time in history, the president of the Cook County Board is not a white, male Democrat. African-American John Stroger, the Democratic Party's nominee, defeats Joe Morris, a white Republican.

1995   Mayor Richard M. Daley is reelected for a third term. Michael Jordan comes out of retirement to rejoin the Bulls.

1996   With 72 victories, the Bulls set an NBA record for the most wins ever in a single season. They go on to win the NBA championship.

1997   *Chicago Tribune* columnist Mike Royko dies.

1998   Harry Caray, Chicago Cubs broadcaster, raconteur, and restaurateur, dies.

1999   The *Chicago Tribune* publishes an investigative story about Mayor Daley's ties to the Duffs, a Mob-connected family with a janitorial service firm that receives millions of dollars in contracts to clean up at city events. A series of power outages, including a massive one in the Loop, provokes Mayor Daley and others to outrage at Commonwealth Edison.

2000   Chicago 2000, an exhibit in which 100 photographers capture a year in the life of the city, draws thousands of visitors to the **Cultural Center**. Following its Chicago run, the acclaimed exhibit travels to cities throughout the world.

2001   Following the terrorist attack on the World Trade Center, the city announces new security plans for its prominent skyscrapers: the Sears Tower, the **AON Building,** and the **John Hancock Center**.

2002   **United Airlines,** Chicago's "hometown" airline, declares bankruptcy. Rod Blagojevich, son-in-law of alderman Dick Mell, is elected the first Democratic governor in Illinois since 1972. Lisa Madigan, daughter of Southwest Side politician Mike Madigan, becomes the state's first female attorney general.

2003:   Twenty-one people are killed and 50 injured in a stampede to the exit at the **E-2** South Side dance club after a security guard sets off pepper spray. Questions loom about how the club, which had been ordered shut down, managed to stay open.

Thirteen people are killed and 57 injured when a third-story wooden porch collapses during a summer party in the **Lincoln Park** neighborhood. The porch appears to be in violation of the city's building code.

2004:   Another scandal hits the Daley administration when an investigation reveals that the city has been paying $40 million a year to politically connected trucking companies—some with Mob ties, some posing as minority-owned—to do little or no work while city trucks stand idle. As of March 2005, 27 people have been indicted.

An independent commission established to investigate the 2003 Cook County Administration building fire, in which six people were trapped in a stairwell and died, finds fault with the fire department and the building's evacuation plan.

2005:   The husband and mother of U.S. District Court judge Joan Lefkow are murdered in what appears to be a contract killing. Suspicions turn to followers of white supremacist Matthew Hale, in prison after being convicted of soliciting Judge Lefkow's murder the previous year.

INDEX

INDEX

RESTAURANTS

Only restaurants with star ratings are listed below. All restaurants are listed alphabetically in the main (preceding) index. Always call in advance to ensure a restaurant has not closed, changed its hours, or booked its tables for a private party. The restaurant price ratings are based on the average cost of an entrée for one person, excluding tax and tip.

★★★★ An Extraordinary Experience
★★★ Excellent
★★ Very Good
★ Good

$$$$ Big Bucks ($40 and up)
$$$ Expensive ($25–$40)
$$ Reasonable ($16–$24)
$ The Price Is Right (less than $15)

Cafe Ba-Ba-Reeba! $$$ **144**
Café Spiaggia $$ **59**
Chicago Brauhaus $$ **212**
Chicago Chop House $$$ **92**
Chicago Diner $$ **200**
Cyrano's Bistrot & Wine Bar $ **96**
Emperor's Choice $$ **221**
Erwin $$ **177**
Filter $ **157**
437 Rush $$$$ **102**
Genesee Depot $$ **197**
Gibson's Steakhouse $$$ **117**
Glory $$ **155**
Green Dolphin Street $$$ **214**
Harry Caray's $$$ **104**
Heat $$$ **126**
Hua Giang $ **212**
Ixcapuzalco $$ **213**
Jack's American Blend $$ **174**
Jeanny's $ **173**
Jilly's Bistro $$$ **117**
Joe's Seafood, Prime Steak &
    Stone Crab $$$ **97**
Kamehachi $$ **126**
Kiki's Bistro $$$ **83**
Kinzie Street Chophouse $$ **103**
Laschet's Inn $ **212**
Matsuya $$ **166**
Maza $$ **132**
The Melrose $ **172, 203**
MOD $$$ **158**
Mon Ami Gabi $$ **139**
Morton's $$$ **116**
Nine $$$ **18**
North Coast Cafe $ **198**
North Pond Café $$ **149**
Nuevo Leon $ **219**
The Outpost $$ **167, 200**
Pasteur $$ **209**
Pompei Bakery $ **176**
P.S. Bangkok $$ **168, 201**
Pump Room $$$$ **112**
Reza's $$ **207**
Reza's (River North/River West) $
    91
Rosebud $$$ **218**
Russian Tea Cafe $$ **30**
Ruth's Chris Steak House $$$
    100
The Saloon $$$ **65**
Santorini $$ **216**
Scoozi! $$ **88**
Shaw's Crab House and Blue
    Crab Lounge $$$ **101**
Signature Room $$$ **64**
Smith & Wollensky $$$$ **105**
The Smoke Daddy $ **159**

Szechwan $$ **75**
Tavern on Rush $$$ **116**
Thyme Café $$ **158**
Topo Gigio $$ **126**
Trattoria Gianni $$$ **149**
Trattoria No. 10 $$ **25**
Tre Viva $$ **157**
Tuscany $$$ **218**
Vinci $$ **149**
Vong's Thai Kitchen $$$ **100**
West Town Tavern $$ **159**
Wishbone $ **170**
Zou Zou $ **172**

───────────────

★

Abril $ **213**
Addis Abeba $$ **164**
Albert's Cafe $ **116**
Al's Italian Beef $ **217**
Andy's $$ **101**
Ann Sather $ **173, 204**
Arco de Cuchilleros $$ **167**
Athenian Room $ **140**
Ben Pao $$ **98**
Bice $$$ **73**
Big Bowl Asian Kitchen $ **95**
Big John's $ **142**
Blue Agave $$ **116**
Bongo Room $ **158**
Buca di Beppo $$ **177**
Buddies' Restaurant and Bar $
    202
Caffé Baci $ **32**
Caffe de Luca $ **155**
Cape Cod Room $$$ **61**
Carson's—the Place for Ribs $$
    91
Cedars of Lebanon $ **183**
Chalfins' Deli $ **65**
Charlie's Ale House, $ **139**
Cielo $$$ **72**
Club Gene & Georgetti, Ltd. $$$
    98
Club Lago $ **85**
Club Lucky $$ **156**
Coq D'Or $ **61**
The Corner Bakery $ **32**
Cosi $ **29**
Cru Café and Wine Bar $ **119**
Dee's $$ **142**
Dixie Kitchen & Bait Shop $ **183**
Earwax Café $ **158**
Edwardo's (Gold Coast) $$ **114**
Edwardo's (South Loop) $ **44**

Edwardo's of Hyde P
El Jardin Cafe $ **167**
Fattoush $ **132**
Fogo de Chao $$$ **90**
Garden Restaurant $ **38**
Geja's Cafe $$$ **144**
Giordano's $$ **88**
Grecian Taverna $$ **210**
Green Door Tavern $ **88**
Hard Rock Cafe $$ **92**
Heaven on Seven $ **24**
The Hideout **149**
Houston's $$ **93**
Hugo's Frog Bar $$$ **117**
Iggy's $ **157**
Italian Village $$ **28**
Itto Sushi $$ **132**
Joe O'Neil's Bar & Grill $ **73**
Kit Kat Lounge and Supper Club
    $$ **164**
La Creperie $ **178**
Lawry's Tavern $ **178**
Lawry's—The Prime Rib $$$ **93**
Leona's (Bucktown/Wicker Park)
    $ **159**
Leona's Original Pizza (Lake View)
    $ **173, 203**
Leo's Lunchroom $ **159**
Little Bucharest $ **176**
Lou Mitchell's $ **33**
Lutz Continental Cafe and Pastry
    Shop $ **210**
Maggiano's $$ **98**
Mallers Coffee Shop & Deli $ **27**
Mambo Grill $$ **103**
Manny's $ **219**
Medici on 57th $$ **187**
Mellow Yellow $ **183**
Melvin B.'s $ **116**
Miller's Pub $$ **30**
Morry's Deli $ **185**
Mr. Beef $ **90**
Nacional 27 $$ **89**
Nhu Hoa Cafe $ **212**
Nick's Fishmarket $$$ **27**
Old Jerusalem $ **126**
Pane Caldo $ **59**
Papa Milano $ **118**
Pars Cove $$ **131**
Parthenon $$ **216**
Penny's Noodle Shop $ **167, 200**
Piccolo Mondo $ **186**
Potbelly Sandwich Works $ **138**
Raw Bar $ **163**
Red Hen Bread $ **156**
Rock Bottom Brewery $ **97**
Rose Angelis $$ **132**

HOTELS

The hotels listed below are grouped according to their price ratings; they are also listed in the main index. The hotel price ratings reflect the base price of a standard room for two people for one night during the peak season.

$$$$ Big Bucks ($300 and up)
$$$ Expensive ($200–$300)
$$ Reasonable ($130–$200)
$ The Price Is Right (less than $130)

$$$$

$$$

$$

$

FEATURES

BESTS

CREDITS

*Writer and Researcher
for the Eighth Edition*
Paul Engleman

Research Assistants
Dan Salemme
Phoebe Judge

Gay Chicago Writers
David Appell
Paul Balido
Roy DeLaMar

Editorial Supervisors
Edwin Tan and Lyndee Stalter

Design Director
Leah Carlson-Stanisic

Jacket Design
Chin-Yee Lai

Map Designer
Patricia Keelin

Associate Director of Production
Dianne Pinkowitz

Senior Production Editor
Rita Madrigal

ACCESS® PRESS does not solicit individuals, organizations, or businesses for inclusion in our books, nor do we accept payment for inclusion. We welcome, however, information from our readers, including comments, criticisms, and suggestions for new listings. Send all correspondence to: ACCESS® PRESS, 10 East 53rd Street, New York, NY 10022.

PRINTED IN HONG KONG

Look for these other Access Guides at your local bookstore:

ACCESS Boston

ACCESS California Wine Country

ACCESS Florence & Venice

ACCESS London

ACCESS Los Angeles

ACCESS Montreal & Quebec City

ACCESS New Orleans

ACCESS New York City

ACCESS Paris

ACCESS Philadelphia

ACCESS Rome

ACCESS San Diego

ACCESS San Francisco

ACCESS Seattle

ACCESS Sydney

ACCESS Washington, DC